European Commission

General Report
on the Activities of
the European Union

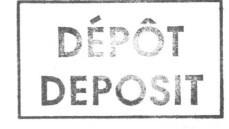

1998

Brussels • Luxembourg, 1999

A great deal of additional information on the European Union is available on the Internet. It can be accessed through the Europa server (http://europa.eu.int).

Cataloguing data can be found at the end of this publication.
Luxembourg: Office for Official Publications of the European Communities, 1999

ISBN 92-828-4924-4

Printed in Belgium

The President and the Members of the European Commission to the President of the European Parliament

Sir,

We have the honour to present the General Report on the Activities of the European Union for 1998, which the Commission is required to publish by Article 156 of the EC Treaty, Article 17 of the ECSC Treaty and Article 125 of the EAEC Treaty.

In accordance with the procedure described in the declaration on the system for fixing Community farm prices contained in the Accession Documents of 22 January 1972, the Commission will shortly be sending Parliament the 1998 Report on the Agricultural Situation in the European Union.

And, in accordance with an undertaking given to Parliament on 7 June 1971, the Commission is preparing its Twenty-eighth Annual Report on Competition Policy.

Please accept, Sir, the expression of our highest consideration.

Brussels, 9 February 1999

Jacques SANTER President		Édith CRESSON	
Leon BRITTAN Vice-president		Ritt BJERREGAARD	
Manuel MARÍN Vice-president		Monika WULF-MATHIES	
Martin BANGEMANN		Neil KINNOCK	
Karel VAN MIERT		Mario MONTI	
Hans VAN DEN BROEK		Franz FISCHLER	
João de Deus PINHEIRO		Emma BONINO	
Pádraig FLYNN		Yves-Thibault de SILGUY	
Marcelino OREJA		Erkki LIIKANEN	
Anita GRADIN		Christos PAPOUTSIS	

NOTE

Legislative instruments under the co-decision procedure are mentioned in the Report followed by '(Table I)'. Instruments under the consultation and cooperation procedures are followed by '(Table II)'. International agreements are followed by '(Table III)'. No footnotes are given for these instruments, which are listed in three separate tables annexed to the Report. The relevant references (OJ, COM, Bull.) for all the stages of the legislative procedure concerning each instrument, together with the appropriate point numbers in text, are given in the tables.

As a rule, no references are given in text for intermediate stages of procedures which started before 1 January 1998 and were not completed at 31 December 1998. These references also appear in the tables.

Standardised abbreviations for the designation of certain monetary units:

ATS   Austrian schilling
BEF   Belgian franc
DEM   German mark
DKK   Danish crown (krone)
ESP   Spanish peseta
FIM   Finnish markka
FRF   French franc
GBP   pound sterling
GRD   Greek drachma
IEP   Irish pound (punt)
ITL   Italian lira
LUF   Luxembourg franc
NLG   Dutch guilder
PTE   Portuguese escudo
SEK   Swedish crown (krona)
USD   United States dollar

Contents

The European Union in 1998

The historic decision to change over to the euro, implementation of the European Union's new strategy for employment, the legislative proposals for Agenda 2000 and the launch of the process of enlarging the European Union were the highlights of 1998. The Union has assumed a new role on the international stage. The year was also marked by the efforts of the institutions to bring the Union closer to the people.

The Council, meeting at Heads of State or Government level, decided on 3 May that 11 Member States satisfied the conditions for adopting the single currency on 1 January 1999. This decision marks the changeover to the third stage of economic and monetary union in accordance with the schedule laid down in the Treaty. The European Central Bank came into being on 1 June, and the legal framework needed to introduce the euro was completed, the high point coming on 31 December when the Council set the fixed and irrevocable conversion rates between the national currencies of the 11 Member States participating in the euro.

Supported by the constant progress achieved by the Member States in economic convergence (sound public finances, very low inflation, exchange rate stability) and the mechanisms for closer coordination of economic policies put in place as part of the preparation for the euro, economic and monetary union has made the European Union a centre of stability and largely spared it the effects of the financial crises which affected several regions of the world in 1998.

By strengthening Europe's capacity to promote growth and employment, the single currency increases the need to go even further in the coordination of economic policies and to implement a genuine European employment strategy. Appreciable progress was made on this front in 1998, with the Member States drawing up for the first time national action plans to implement the guidelines for employment adopted in 1997, while the Commission presented a number of important policy documents in this area. When approving the guidelines for employment for 1999, the Vienna European Council stressed the need to strengthen this process still further, setting verifiable target figures and deadlines and putting in place common indicators and a coherent statistical basis, *with a view to drawing up a European pact for employment with increased involvement of the social partners.*

The various Community policies were also harnessed to help create an environment favourable to growth, competitiveness and employment.

Initiatives taken in social policy, particularly on the free movement of workers, modernising the organisation of work, promoting the social dialogue, and working time, are important elements in this European strategy.

Investment is a key element in job creation. Measures adopted by the Council and the Commission to provide financial assistance to innovative, job-creating small and medium-sized businesses and to promote risk capital, the implementation of the trans-European networks and the granting of loans by the European Investment Bank for job-creating investment projects and in fields such as education, health and the urban environment made an important contribution. The Commission suggested that the Member States should increase the share of their budgets devoted to public investment.

The raft of measures drawn up in 1997 to combat harmful tax competition and make tax structures more employment-friendly were put into effect. Significant progress was made in implementing other aspects of the action plan for the single market, relating in particular to the elimination of barriers to trade, intellectual property and financial services. Liberalisation of the internal energy market continued, with the adoption by Parliament and the Council of the directive on the internal market in natural gas. 1998 was also the first year that the telecommunications market was fully opened up to competition.

The adoption by Parliament and the Council of the fifth framework programme for research and technological development, which will cover all the Union's research activities until 2002, and which will mark a real break with the previous programmes, both in its more concentrated and more integrated approach and in its operation, makes an important contribution to the development of the knowledge society and is a response to the challenges that face European society today. In the fields of education, vocational training and youth, essential factors for the promotion of innovation, competitiveness, employment and social integration, the Commission adopted its proposals for new Community programmes (2000-04).

Translating into legislative form the broad lines of its 'Agenda 2000' communication, which is intended to give the Union more effective policies and to put in place an appropriate financial framework to imple-

*ment them, particularly with a view to the future enlargement, the Com-
mission presented a series of detailed proposals concerning agriculture,
the Structural Funds and the Cohesion Fund, trans-European networks,
pre-accession instruments and the financial perspective for the period
2000-06, and a report on the operation of the own resources system
and the possible options in this field. At its Cardiff and Vienna meetings, the European Council, while stressing that Agenda 2000 formed a
whole which could be subject only to overall agreement, stated its determination to reach such agreement in March 1999, so that the formal
adoption of the texts could go through before June 1999. It stated its
wish that the reform of the Union's policies should be accompanied by
a reform of its institutions, welcoming the 'Tomorrow's Commission' initiative launched by the Commission. While agreeing that ratification of
the Amsterdam Treaty by the Member States should be completed as a
matter of priority (10 Member States ratified it in 1998), it stressed the
need to deal quickly with the institutional questions that had been left
pending by this Treaty, but which needed to be resolved before enlargement.*

*Following the decisions taken in December 1997 by the Luxembourg
European Council, the process of enlarging the European Union was
launched in March. The European Conference, bringing together the
Member States of the Union and the European countries which are eligible to join and share its values and objectives, held its first meeting at
Heads of State or Government level, while the process of accession to
the European Union by the central European applicant countries and
Cyprus was opened by a ministerial meeting, and accession partnerships
with the countries of central Europe were established. The opening of
accession negotiations with Cyprus, Hungary, Poland, Estonia, the Czech
Republic and Slovenia was the subject of six separate bilateral ministerial meetings, the negotiations on substance which started in November
already leading to the first concrete results. The Commission produced
the first regular reports on progress towards accession achieved by the
10 applicant countries of central Europe, Cyprus and Turkey. The European Union welcomed the reactivation of Malta's application to join.*

*The launch of the enlargement process gives European integration a new
dimension, extending it across the whole continent. The European Union
also took on a new role on the international stage. By creating one of
the largest currency areas in the world, the introduction of the euro
gives it worldwide responsibilities. The European Council stressed the
need for Europe to speak with one voice, with appropriate representation for the euro area in bodies such as the G7 and the International
Monetary Fund, and to play a decisive role in strengthening the inter-*

national financial system. The Union's role in the world will also be strengthened when the provisions of the Treaty of Amsterdam on the common foreign and security policy enter into force. The Vienna European Council accordingly called on the Council to draw up common strategies for Russia first of all, then for Ukraine, the Mediterranean region and the western Balkans, and stressed the need to strengthen cooperation with the Western European Union and to appoint someone with sufficient political standing as the CFSP High Representative as soon as possible.

In 1998, the European Union and Switzerland successfully concluded negotiations on a comprehensive, balanced set of sectoral agreements. The European Union consolidated its partnership with the Mediterranean countries and strengthened its links with the independent States of the former Soviet Union, seeking to help Russia overcome its current economic and financial difficulties. It launched a transatlantic economic partnership with the United States, aimed at removing trade barriers and pursuing multilateral liberalisation, and tightened its links with the countries of Latin America and Asia. The success of the second Asia-Europe Summit, while the Union's Asian partners were facing economic and financial difficulties, demonstrated the solidity of the partnership created with these countries. The Union opened negotiations with the ACP countries with a view to drawing up a new partnership for development agreement, which will replace the Lomé Convention from the year 2000. It continued its endeavours to promote peace, notably in south-eastern Europe, the Middle East and the Great Lakes region of Africa, human rights and development. The Union offered improved trading conditions to countries which respect international social and environmental standards and to the least advanced countries, adopted a common position on human rights, democratic principles, the rule of law and good governance in Africa, and took measures against a number of countries for their failure to respect human rights. It continues to be the leading humanitarian aid donor in the world.

To enhance the safety of Union citizens, the Vienna European Council approved an action plan for implementing the provisions of the Treaty of Amsterdam on an area of freedom, security and justice once it enters into force. In this field, 1998 was marked by the entry into force of the Europol Convention, by progress made in implementing the action programme on the fight against organised crime approved in 1997 and by the conclusion of a pre-accession agreement on organised crime between the Member States and the applicant countries.

The quality of life of its citizens was a thread common to various strands of Union activities in 1998. In the field of environmental protection and the promotion of sustainable development, significant progress was made in combating greenhouse gas emissions, atmospheric pollution caused by motor vehicles, acidification and substances that deplete the ozone layer. The continuation of efforts to achieve a more environment-friendly distribution of traffic between the different modes of transport, the emphasis placed on environmental objectives, such as the reduction of carbon dioxide emissions, in the new framework programme for the energy sector, the place given to environmental protection in the agriculture section of Agenda 2000 and the new progress achieved in fishery resource conservation, with the adoption of a regulation prohibiting the use of drift nets, illustrate the ever greater extent to which the environment is being incorporated into all the Community's policies. The Union's activity in favour of consumers also saw important legislative advances in 1998 with the adoption of directives on the indication of the prices of products, injunctions and consumer credit. In the field of public health, the creation of a network for monitoring communicable diseases and the ban on advertising and sponsorship for tobacco products were significant achievements.

Bringing the Union closer to the people means both achieving greater openness and ensuring that decisions are taken at a level as close as possible to the citizen. With this in mind the institutions of the Union improved access to their documents and stepped up their information activities, and also specified the conditions of implementation of the subsidiarity and proportionality principles, which are legally binding and must be fully respected.

In 1998, European integration acquired a new impetus. The single currency was launched. The coordination of the efforts made to promote employment produced encouraging results. The enlargement process is well under way. The Union must continue its efforts to serve its citizens. It is in this spirit that the European Council designed a strategy for the Union, the 'Vienna strategy for Europe', and it is in the same spirit that the Union is approaching 1999.

Chapter I

Agenda 2000

1.   On 18 March, in parallel with the enlargement process (→ *points 795 et seq.*), the Commission adopted detailed proposals translating into legislation the guidelines presented in July 1997 in its communication 'Agenda 2000 — For a stronger and wider Union' ([1]). These proposals, which are intended to implement the policy reforms proposed in Agenda 2000, fall into four main groups: agriculture; the Structural Funds and the Cohesion Fund; pre-accession instruments; and the financial perspective for the period 2000-06, together with the interinstitutional agreement on budgetary discipline. One of the proposals is also intended to amend the financial regulation on trans-European networks. Together with the proposals the Commission also presented a communication setting out an overall view ([2]).

Agriculture ([3])

2.   The proposals adopted by the Commission on 18 March include amended regulations on the common organisation of the market in cereals and other arable crops (Table II), beef and veal (Table II), milk (Table II) and olive oil (Table II), a horizontal regulation laying down common rules for direct support schemes (linking support to compliance with environmental criteria, modulating aid relative to employment and introducing a degressive formula for the highest aid payments) (Table II), and changes to the EAGGF financing regulation (Table II). The Commission also proposed a new regulation on rural development aid, the financing of which would be split between the Guarantee Section of the EAGGF for Objective 1 regions, and the Guidance Section for other regions (Table II). On 16 July the Commission added a further proposal,

---

[1]   COM(97) 2000; 1997 General Report, points 29 to 44; Supplement 5/97 — Bull.
[2]   COM(1998) 182; Bull. 3-1998, point I.2.
[3]   Detailed information on the various proposals is to be found in Section 20 ('Agricultural policy') of Chapter IV (→ *points 547 to 555*).

for a regulation on the common organisation of the market in wine (Table II).

3.   In their broad outlines these proposals, most of which are to take effect in 2000, follow the prescription for further reform of the common agricultural policy set out in Agenda 2000, with adjustments to take account of the extensive consultations held by the Commission. In line with Agenda 2000, the proposals provide for further reductions in market support prices and an increase in direct aid for farmers in order to make the EU's agriculture more competitive on domestic and world markets, thereby reducing the risk of a recurrence of expensive and unsaleable surpluses while avoiding over-compensation. Lower prices will benefit consumers and leave more room for price differentiation in favour of quality products, while a more market-orientated approach will prepare the way for integration of new Member States and strengthen the EU's position in the coming WTO negotiating round. The Commission also proposes that greater emphasis be placed on food safety and environmental concerns; this is the principle of 'eco-conditionality' (introduced by the proposal for a horizontal regulation). The proposed regulation on rural development aid will bring together for the first time in a single text all the provisions connected with the financing of rural development measures by the EAGGF.

Structural Funds and Cohesion Fund ([1])

4.   The proposals for new regulations on the Structural Funds and the Cohesion Fund will provide the legal framework for support from these funds in the next programming period (2000-06). They are based on the three principles set out in Agenda 2000, namely concentration, simplification and clarification of responsibilities. As well as a new framework regulation embodying the general provisions applicable to all the funds and reducing the number of objectives and Community initiatives to three each (Table II), the Commission is proposing new 'vertical' regulations for each of the four Funds (European Regional Development Fund (Table II), European Social Fund (Table II), EAGGF-financed rural development aid *(→ points 2 and 3)* and the Financial Instrument for Fisheries Guidance (Table II)), and two amendments to the regulation on the Cohesion Fund (Table II).

([1])   Detailed information on the various proposals is to be found in Section 11 ('Economic and social cohesion') of Chapter IV *(→ points 348 to 354).*

5.   The key elements of these proposals appear in the Agenda 2000 communication. The Commission is proposing that the total budget for the structural and cohesion policies be held at 0.46 % of GNP during the period 2000-06, i.e. EUR 287 billion (at 1999 prices). Of this amount, about EUR 240 billion, including EUR 21 billion for the Cohesion Fund, will be available in the present Member States (compared with EUR 208 billion for 1993-99 on the same price basis). The remaining EUR 47 billion will be for structural aid to new member countries and applicant countries. This substantial commitment to the cohesion policy will be further reinforced by concentrating resources on the poorest regions and those with the worst structural problems, particularly unemployment. The aim is also to simplify the current procedures and decentralise the decision-making process, which will be devolved wherever possible to the authorities of the Member States and regions concerned. This more decentralised approach entails increased responsibility for monitoring and supervision of programmes at national and regional level and actual implementation of financial adjustments where necessary. In framing its proposals the Commission has drawn on the experience gained in recent years in improving financial management and control under the SEM 2000 initiative (→ points 1141 to 1144).

Trans-European networks (TENs)

6.   The proposed amendment of the regulation on general rules for the granting of Community financial aid in the sphere of trans-European networks (Table II) is intended primarily to improve the financing of TEN projects, making more use of multiannual programming in order to facilitate public-private partnerships by making funding available for the lifetime of a project and introducing risk-capital participation as a new form of financing. It also raises the maximum rate of Community aid to 20 % in exceptional cases and gives an indication of the spending needed, estimated at EUR 5.5 billion for the period 2000-06, including some EUR 5 billion for transport networks.

Pre-accession instruments

7.   The Commission adopted three proposals for regulations on pre-accession aid, one setting up an instrument for structural policies for pre-accession (ISPA) (Table II), a second establishing an agricultural pre-accession instrument financed by the EAGGF (Table II) and a third coordinating the three pre-accession aid instruments (the above two instruments, plus the existing PHARE programme) (→ points 812 to

815), in order to avoid any duplication of effort (Table II). The measures to be taken under the three pre-accession aid instruments will be incorporated, for the sake of consistency, in the accession partnerships (→ *point 806)* with each of the applicant countries. The total amount of the pre-accession aid will be about EUR 3 billion a year for the period 2000-06 (i.e. over twice the amount available in 1999). The PHARE programme will focus on accession by setting two priority aims endorsed by the Luxembourg European Council (¹): the strengthening of administrative and legal capacity (some 30 % of the total amount), and investment linked with the adoption and application of EU rules (about 70 %). The agricultural instrument will help modernise agriculture and the food industries by improving processing, marketing and quality control and by providing aid for rural development; ISPA will provide support for the transport networks and environmental conservation.

Financial perspective and interinstitutional agreement

8.   On 18 March the Commission presented a communication on the establishment of a new financial perspective for the period 2000-06 (²), a report on the implementation of the interinstitutional agreement on budgetary discipline and proposals for renewal (³) and a report, accompanied by a proposal for a regulation (Table II), on the Guarantee Fund for external actions (⁴).

9.   The proposals for the financial perspective closely follow those in Agenda 2000: the figures have changed only because they are presented at 1999 prices rather than 1997 prices (⁵). As requested by the Luxembourg European Council, the financial perspective is presented on the basis of the current 15 Member States, leaving a sufficient margin to finance enlargement, and is accompanied by a table showing an estimate of the costs linked with enlargement and details of how they are to be financed (⁶). The Commission considers that the amounts which should be released in order to cope with the initial costs of enlargement during the period 2000-06 still leave room for an ample contingency reserve under the own resources ceiling (1.27 % of gross national product), taking into account the increase in the ceiling as a result of enlargement.

(¹)   Bull. 12-1997, point I.5 *18*.
(²)   COM(1998) 164; Bull. 3-1998, point I.23.
(³)   COM(1998) 165; Bull. 3-1998, point I.24.
(⁴)   COM(1998) 168; Bull. 3-1998, point I.25.
(⁵)   The tables attached to the financial perspective proposals are to be found in Section 2 ('Budgets') of Chapter VII (→ *point 982)*.
(⁶)   1997 General Report, point 44; Bull. 12-1997, point I.7 *39*.

10. The report on implementation of the interinstitutional agreement on budgetary discipline and improvement of the budgetary procedure analyses the way in which the agreement has worked in practice since 1993 and suggests improvements which could be incorporated in a new agreement, in particular the consolidation of all the interinstitutional agreements on budgetary matters, which cover matters such as the classification of expenditure, respect for financial ceilings in legislation, the need for a legal basis for items in the budget and the conciliation process in the budgetary procedure ([1]). On 29 April the Commission formalised its proposals in a draft agreement which it presented to the Council and Parliament ([2]).

11. On the basis of a report on the operation of the regulation establishing the Guarantee Fund for external actions, the Commission also proposed that the 'provisioning rate' for new loans be cut to 6 % and the reserve reduced to EUR 150 million from the year 2000 in order to maintain present lending capacity.

12. On 7 October the Commission added to these texts a report on the operation of the own resources system, which puts forward various options for financing the Community budget *(→ point 984).*

The other institutions' reactions

13. The Council conducted an initial examination of the proposals on agriculture in May ([3]). In June the Cardiff European Council called on the Council to intensify its work in order for agreement to be reached on the package as a whole no later than March 1999.

14. In June and again in November, Parliament adopted resolutions on the parts of Agenda 2000 concerning economic and social cohesion ([4]) and agriculture ([5]). On cohesion, it approved the main options adopted by the Commission. On agriculture, it called for the pricing and market policy to be readjusted in favour of Mediterranean products (although it considered the price reductions suggested by the Commission for cereals, beef and veal and milk to be excessive) and pressed for downward

---

([1])   OJ C 331, 7.12.1993; Twenty-seventh General Report, points 1078 to 1080.
([2])   Bull. 3-1998, point I.1.
([3])   Bull. 5-1998, point I.1.
([4])   OJ C 210, 6.7.1998; Bull. 6-1998, point II.5; OJ C 379, 7.12.1998; Bull. 11-98, points I.3 and I.7.
([5])   OJ C 210, 6.7.1998; Bull. 6-1998, point II.3; OJ C 379, 7.12.1998; Bull. 11-1998, point I.2.

modulation of direct aid. Parliament also stressed the importance of rural development policy and food policy.

15.   The regulations on the organisation of the market in olive oil were adopted by the Council on 20 July. The Economic and Social Committee (in July and September) and the Committee of the Regions (in September and November) delivered their legislative opinions, while Parliament delivered its opinion on first reading of the proposals concerning general provisions on the Structural Funds, the ERDF, the ESF and the trans-European networks in November. On 21 December the Council adopted a common position on the TEN proposal ([1]).

16.   The Vienna European Council noted the progress made in the negotiations ([2]). Pointing out that Agenda 2000 was a package on which there had to be overall agreement, it reaffirmed its determination to reach such an agreement at the European Council meeting scheduled to take place in Brussels in March 1999, and hoped that the legislative texts would be definitively adopted by June 1999.

([1])   For the exact situation regarding each procedure, see Table II ('Legislation under the consultation and cooperation procedure') at the end of this Report.
([2])   Bull. 12-1998.

Chapter II

European Union citizenship

17. On 2 July the European Parliament adopted a resolution (¹) on the second report from the Commission on citizenship of the Union (²). Parliament stressed that Union citizenship was a key factor in European integration and, *inter alia,* called on Member States to ensure that the free movement of persons was fully implemented and to improve the information available on voting rights, the right to stand for election, the right of petition and access to the European Ombudsman.

Section 1

The right to free movement and residence

18. In a communication adopted on 1 July (³), the Commission set out the initiatives it had taken or was intending to take to ensure follow-up of the recommendations of the high-level panel on the free movement of persons (⁴). The Commission also published, on 3 April (⁵), a third (⁶) communication concerning the information provided by Member States on the visa regimes applicable to citizens of non-Member countries not featured on the common list annexed to Council Regulation (EC) No 2317/95 (⁷).

(¹) OJ C 226, 20.7.1998; Bull. 7/8-1998, point 1.1.1.
(²) COM(97) 230; 1997 General Report, point 45.
(³) COM(1998) 403; Bull. 7/8-1998, point 1.1.2.
(⁴) 1997 General Report, point 46.
(⁵) OJ C 101, 3.4.1998.
(⁶) Previous communications: OJ C 379, 14.12.1996; OJ C 180, 14.6.1997.
(⁷) OJ L 234, 3.10.1995; 1995 General Report, point 3; 1997 General Report, point 47.

Section 2

The right to vote and to stand for election

19. On 7 January the Commission adopted a report(¹) on the application of Council Directive 93/109/EC on the right to vote and to stand for election to the European Parliament(²). The report concerns the 1994 elections for the then 12 Member States, the September 1995 elections in Sweden and the October 1996 elections in Austria and Finland. The Commission found that the directive had on the whole been satisfactorily transposed by Member States and did not itself require amendment, but that the citizens in question had made little use of their rights under the directive and that the information given to citizens and the exchange of information between Member States needed improvement. The Commission also considered that, in view of the latest population figures, Luxembourg should continue to be granted an exemption enabling it to apply a minimum residence requirement to the next elections to the European Parliament in June 1999.

20. The transposition of Council Directive 94/80/EC of 19 December 1994, laying down detailed arrangements for the exercise of the right to vote and to stand as a candidate in municipal elections by citizens of the Union residing in a Member State of which they are not nationals(³), had been completed for all Member States except Belgium. In a judgment delivered on 9 July, the Court of Justice censured this Member State for its failure to fulfil its obligations under Article 14 of the directive(⁴).

(¹)   COM(97) 731; Bull. 1/2-1998, point 1.1.1.
(²)   OJ L 329, 30.12.1993; Twenty-seventh General Report, point 15.
(³)   OJ L 368, 31.12.1994; 1994 General Report, point 4.
(⁴)   Case C-323/97, [1998] ECR.

Section 3

Right of petition and right of access to the Ombudsman

21. On 16 July Parliament adopted a resolution on the deliberations of its Committee on Petitions during the parliamentary year 1997/98 ([1]). The Committee dealt with around 450 petitions, mainly relating to social security, the environment, taxation, the free movement of persons and the recognition of qualifications. The petitions with the highest number of signatures (around 30 000 each) were concerned with genetically-modified foods and the construction of high-speed train lines in Italy. The Commission was asked for an opinion on most of the petitions examined, and it sent communications to Parliament on the various cases concerned. In a number of cases petitioners' wishes were met as a result of action taken by the Commission and Parliament. The Committee also modified its working procedures to speed up the process of examining the petitions submitted to it.

22. Also on 16 July Parliament adopted a resolution ([2]) on the third annual report (1997) ([3]) by the European Ombudsman, Mr Söderman. Of the 1 412 complaints received and examined by the Ombudsman in 1997, some 75 % fell outside the scope of his mandate. However, 196 complaints were deemed admissible and investigated further, including 163 cases concerning the Commission. The most frequent subjects of complaint were the Commission's recruitment policy, its policy on contracts and its action on the environment, questions of openness and access to documents, fraud and procurement procedures. The Ombudsman also launched an inquiry into the transparency of recruitment procedures, exercising his own power of initiative.

23. Likewise on 16 July Parliament passed a resolution ([4]) on the special report presented to it by the Ombudsman in December 1997 and published in February 1998 ([5]) following his own-initiative inquiry into public access to documents held by the Community institutions and bodies.

---

[1]   OJ C 292, 21.9.1998; Bull. 7/8-1998, point 1.1.3.
[2]   OJ C 292, 21.9.1998; Bull. 7/8-1998, point 1.1.4.
[3]   Report available on the Internet at the following address: http://www.euro-ombudsman.eu.int.
[4]   OJ C 292, 21.9.1998; Bull. 7/8-1998, point 1.1.5.
[5]   OJ C 44, 10.2.1998; Bull. 1/2-1998, point 1.1.2.

Chapter III

Human rights and fundamental freedoms

Section 1

General

24.   On 10 December, to mark the 50th anniversary of the Universal Declaration of Human Rights, the European Union adopted a declaration in which it underlined the need to strengthen its capacity to achieve its objectives on the protection and promotion of human rights through concrete measures [1]. The declaration was later endorsed by the Vienna European Council [1]. The Commission supported the creation of a Master's degree in human rights and democratisation, and the drafting of an EU human rights agenda for the new millennium.

25.   Parliament adopted a resolution on respect for human rights in the European Union in the year 1996 on 17 February [2]. A similar resolution for 1997 was adopted on 17 December [1]. Among the issues addressed were immigration and the right of asylum, racism and xenophobia, economic, social, trade-union and cultural rights, equality between women and men, the rights of people belonging to national minorities, and children's rights. Reaffirming every person's right to the freedom of expression, Parliament called on Member States to ratify the European Charter for Regional and Minority Languages. On 17 September [3] it also called on the Member States to abolish discrimination against homosexuals and lesbians and, on 17 December [1], to improve prison conditions and make more use of alternative penalties.

---

[1]   Bull. 12-1998.
[2]   OJ C 80, 16.3.1998; Bull. 1/2-1998, point 1.2.3.
[3]   OJ C 313, 12.10.1998; Bull. 9-1998, point 1.1.3.

Section 2

Racism and xenophobia

26.   The management board of the European Monitoring Centre for Racism and Xenophobia, set up in June 1997 ([1]), held its inaugural meeting in Vienna in January and met twice again during the year, appointing a director of the Centre and adopting its programme of activities. The prime objective of the Centre, whose importance was underlined by the Vienna European Council in December ([2]), is to provide the Community and its Member States with objective, reliable and comparable data at European level on racism, xenophobia and anti-Semitism with a view to improving the exchange of information and experience. On 21 December the Council concluded a cooperation agreement between the Centre and the Council of Europe (Table III).

27.   On 25 March the Commission adopted a communication on an action plan against racism ([3]) designed to pave the way for future initiatives to tackle racism at European level in the light of the entry into force of the Treaty of Amsterdam, which contains new provisions on non-discrimination ([4]). The plan has four main strands: adopting legislative initiatives on the basis of Article 13 of the Amsterdam Treaty, integrating action against racism into Community policies and programmes, developing and exchanging new models to combat racism and improving information and communication. It follows a request by Parliament, which called on 29 January ([5]) for the results of the European Year against Racism (1997) ([6]) and related initiatives to be consolidated in an action programme. It was endorsed by the Cardiff European Council in June ([7]), the Economic and Social Committee on 10 September ([8]) and Parliament on 18 December ([2]).

([1])   1997 General Report, point 57.
([2])   Bull. 12-1998.
([3])   COM(1998) 183; Bull. 3-1998, point 1.1.2.
([4])   1997 General Report, point 7.
([5])   OJ C 56, 23.2.1998; Bull. 1/2-1998, point 1.2.4.
([6])   1997 General Report, point 56.
([7])   Bull. 6-1998, point I.12, 43.
([8])   OJ C 407, 28.12.1998; Bull. 9-1998, point 1.1.1.

Section 3

Trafficking in human beings

28. In a communication adopted on 20 May the Commission set out a package of measures to combat violence against children, young people and women (¹). These included proposals on the gathering and exchange of relevant data, working with Europol *(→ point 967)* on registers of missing children and running information and awareness campaigns as part of the European Year against Violence Towards Women (1999). Building on the Daphne initiative (²), it also proposed a five-year Community action programme (covering the years 2000 to 2004) which would be open to the 11 countries applying for EU membership and would provide a legal basis for activities in this area (Table II).

29. On 9 December the Commission adopted a communication on further actions in the fight against trafficking in women (³), which follows on from the 1996 communication on the subject (⁴). On 5 October the Council adopted conclusions on the fight against child pornography (⁵). Further information on the steps taken in this field can be found in Section 3 ('Police and customs cooperation') of Chapter VI.

30. On 11 March Parliament adopted a resolution on International Women's Day and the violation of women's rights (⁶) in which it stressed the need to improve information for women on their fundamental human rights, in particular on the occasion of the European Year against Violence Towards Women. It also rejected all forms of discrimination against women on the basis of religious doctrines or perceptions and called on all Member States to prohibit the practice of sexual mutilation.

(¹)   COM(1998) 335; Bull. 5-1998, point 1.1.1.
(²)   1997 General Report, point 60.
(³)   COM(1998) 726; Bull. 12-1998.
(⁴)   COM(96) 567; 1996 General Report, point 965.
(⁵)   Bull. 10-1998, point 1.1.1.
(⁶)   OJ C 104, 6.4.1998; Bull. 3-1998, point 1.1.1.

Section 4

Ethics in science and new technologies

31. The European Group on Ethics in Science and New Technologies (EGE) set up by the Commission on 16 December 1997 (¹), has replaced the Group of Advisers on the Ethical Implications of Biotechnology (1991-97). It has more members (12 instead of 9) and broader responsibilities ('science and new technologies' instead of 'biotechnology'), and will examine all issues that it considers appropriate to address on its own initiative. It can also be called upon to give an opinion not only by the Commission, but also, and this is an innovation, by the Council or the European Parliament.

32. The inaugural meeting of the EGE was held on 19 February in the presence of Commission President Santer. After adopting its rules of procedure on 20 July, the EGE then delivered two opinions to the Commission — on 21 July concerning the ethical aspects of human tissue banks and on 23 November on the ethical implications of human embryo research.

33. In a resolution adopted on 15 January (²), the European Parliament advocated a universal and legally binding ban on the cloning of human beings.

(¹) 1997 General Report, point 64.
(²) OJ C 34, 2.2.1998; Bull. 1/2-1998, point 1.2.1.

Section 5

Outside the European Union

34. The European Union continued its policy of promoting the development and consolidation of democracy and the rule of law and universal respect for human rights and fundamental freedoms. On 25 May the Council adopted a common position on human rights, democratic principles, the rule of law and good governance in Africa *(→ point 931)* and on 29 June it approved a document setting out the preconditions to be met before the European Union would send observers to elections *(→ point 668).* Electoral observers were dispatched to a number of countries that requested them, including Bosnia and Herzegovina, Cambodia and Togo.

35. In the face of sustained serious violations of democratic principles and human rights in many countries, the EU kept up its pressure on the countries concerned through behind-the-scenes representations and statements condemning such practices *(→ points 676 to 687).* During its monthly debates on human rights Parliament also commented on the human rights situation in many countries(¹).

(¹) Afghanistan: OJ C 313, 12.10.1998; Bull. 9-1998, point 1.1.5; Algeria: OJ C 379, 7.12.1998; Bull. 11-1998, point 1.1.2; Australia: OJ C 34, 2.2.1998; Bull. 1/2-1998, point 1.2.7; Belarus: OJ C 80, 16.3.1998; Bull. 1/2-1998, point 1.2.8; Cambodia: OJ C 313, 12.10.1998; Bull. 9-1998, point 1.1.6; Cameroon: OJ C 138, 4.5.1998; Bull. 3-1998, point 1.1.1; Chad: OJ C 210, 6.7.1998; Bull. 6-1998, point 1.2.5; Chile: OJ C 80, 16.3.1998; Bull. 1/2-1998, point 1.2.9; China: OJ C 34, 2.2.1998; Bull. 1/2-1998, point 1.2.19; OJ C 167, 1.6.1998; Bull. 5-1998, points 1.1.5 and 1.1.6; Colombia: OJ C 104, 6.4.1998; Bull. 3-1998, point 1.1.3; OJ C 167, 1.6.1998; Bull. 5-1998, point 1.1.7; Congo (Brazzaville): OJ C 104, 6.4.1998; Bull. 3-1998, point 1.1.4; Congo (Democratic Republic): OJ C 34, 2.2.1998; Bull. 1/2-1998, point 1.2.17; OJ C 80, 16.3.1998; Bull. 1/2-1998, point 1.2.18; El Salvador: OJ C 313, 12.10.1998; Bull. 9-1998, point 1.1.9; Equatorial Guinea: OJ C 210, 6.7.1998; Bull. 6-1998, point 1.2.2; Former Yugoslav Republic of Macedonia: Bull. 12-1998; Georgia: OJ C 292, 21.9.1998; Bull. 7/8-1998, point 1.2.1; Guatemala: OJ C 167, 1.6.1998; Bull. 5-1998, point 1.1.8; Guinea-Bissau: OJ C 210, 16.7.1998; Bull. 6-1998, point 1.2.1; OJ C 292, 21.9.1998; Bull. 7/8-1998, point 1.2.2; Indonesia: OJ C 210, 6.7.1998; Bull. 6-1998, point 1.2.3; Iran: OJ C 80, 16.3.1998; Bull. 1/2-1998, point 1.2.11; Bull. 12-1998; Jamaica: OJ C 104, 6.4.1998; Bull. 3-1998, point 1.1.5; Kenya: OJ C 34, 2.2.1998; Bull. 1/2-1998, point 1.2.12; Mauritania: OJ C 80, 16.3.1998; Bull. 1/2-1998, point 1.2.13; Myanmar: OJ C 80, 16.3.1998; Bull. 1/2-1998, point 1.2.14; OJ C 167, 1.6.1998; Bull. 5-1998, point 1.1.9; OJ C 292, 21.9.1998; Bull. 7/8-1998, point 1.2.3; OJ C 313, 12.10.1998; Bull. 9-1998, point 1.1.7; Nicaragua: OJ C 104, 6.4.1998; Bull. 1/2-1998, point 1.1.6; Nigeria: OJ C 80, 16.3.1998; Bull. 1/2-1998, point 1.2.15; North Korea: OJ C 104, 6.4.1998; Bull. 3-1998, point 1.1.8; Pakistan: OJ C 210, 6.7.1998; Bull. 6-1998, point 1.2.4; Bull. 12-1998; Palestinian Territories: OJ C 313, 12.10.1998; Bull. 9-1998, point 1.1.4; Philippines: OJ C 313, 12.10.1998; Bull. 9-1998, point 1.1.8; Russia: OJ C 34, 2.2.1998; Bull. 1/2-1998, point 1.2.20; OJ C 379, 7.12.1998; Bull. 11-1998, point 1.1.4; South-east Asia: OJ C 167, 1.6.1998; Bull. 5-1998, point 1.1.4; South Korea: OJ C 34, 2.2.1998; Bull. 1/2-1998, point 1.2.16; Sudan: OJ C 292, 21.9.1998; Bull. 7/8-1998, point 1.2.5; OJ C 313, 12.10.1998; Bull. 9-1998, point 1.1.10; Bull. 12-1998; Syria:

36. The importance attached by the European Union to democratic principles and human rights was also reflected in its contribution to the deliberations of various international organisations and forums, including the United Nations General Assembly, the UN Commission on Human Rights, the conference on the human dimension of the Organisation for Security and Cooperation in Europe, the Council of Europe and the Rome diplomatic conference on the setting-up of an International Criminal Court.

37. Intensifying its international campaign against the death penalty, an integral part of its human rights policy, the EU issued a statement on 29 June outlining a concerted programme of démarches on the subject of capital punishment it intended to make in international forums and to non-member countries [1].

38. On 17 December [2] Parliament adopted resolutions on human rights in the world in 1997 and 1998 and European Union human rights policy and on the Commission's 1995 communication on the external dimension of human rights policy [3]. Other Parliament resolutions concerned the abolition of the death penalty [4], the International Criminal Court [5], the work of the UN Commission on Human Rights [6], the return of the property of holocaust victims [7] and child soldiers.

The Sakharov prize for freedom of the spirit was awarded by the President of Parliament on 16 December to the Kosovo Albanian leader, Mr Ibrahim Rugova [2].

39. The Commission committed ECU 86.1 million in 1998 under Chapter B7-70 of the Community budget (European initiative for democracy and the protection of human rights). Financing under this chapter, suspended following a ruling of the Court of Justice on 12 May

---

OJ C 104, 6.4.1998; Bull. 3-1998, point 1.1.9; Togo: OJ C 292, 21.9.1998; Bull. 7/8-1998, point 1.2.6; Turkey: OJ C 138, 4.5.1998; Bull. 4-1998, point 1.1.3; OJ C 167, 1.6.1998; Bull. 5-1998, point 1.1.11; OJ C 379, 7.12.1998; Bull. 11-1998, points 1.1.5 and 1.1.6; United States: OJ C 34, 2.2.1998; Bull. 1/2-1998, point 1.2.10; OJ C 138, 4.5.1998; Bull. 4-1998, point 1.1.2; Vietnam: OJ C 292, 21.9.1998; Bull. 7/8-1998, point 1.2.7; Yugoslavia (Federal Republic) OJ C 379, 7.12.1998; Bull. 11-1998, point 1.1.3.
[1] Bull. 6-1998, point 1.4.30.
[2] Bull. 12-1998.
[3] COM(95) 567; 1995 General Report, point 76; Supplement 3/95 — Bull.
[4] OJ C 210, 6.7.1998; Bull. 6-1998, point 1.2.6; Bull. 12-1998.
[5] OJ C 104, 6.4.1998; Bull. 3-1998, point 1.1.10; OJ C 210, 6.7.1998; Bull. 6-1998, point 1.2.8; OJ C 379, 7.12.1998; Bull. 11-1998, point 1.1.7.
[6] OJ C 80, 16.3.1998; Bull. 1/2-1998, point 1.2.21.
[7] OJ C 292, 21.9.1998; Bull. 7/8-1998, point 1.2.8.

(→ point 1062), resumed after the interinstitutional agreement on the legal bases *(→ point 1033)*. On 3 December Parliament adopted a resolution on the management and funding of the initiative ([1]).

([1])   OJ C 398, 21.12.1998; Bull. 12-1998.

Chapter IV

The Community economic and social area

Section 1

Economic and monetary policy

Priority activities and objectives

40.   *The Council, meeting at the level of Heads of State or Government, decided on 3 May that 11 Member States fulfilled the necessary conditions for the adoption of the single currency on 1 January 1999. Hailed as a historic step by all the Heads of State or Government, this decision marks the accomplishment of economic and monetary union in accordance with the timetable set out in the Treaty. The European Central Bank thus came into being on 1 June 1998, when the decisions appointing the members of its Executive Board took effect. The legislative environment necessary for the introduction of the euro was also supplemented with the adoption of various instruments relating, among other things, to the legal framework for the euro, the denominations and technical specifications of euro coins, and the powers of the European Central Bank. The adoption by the Council of the fixed and irrevocable conversion rates between the national currencies of the 11 participating Member States and the euro on 31 December was the last major piece of legislation prior to the actual launch of the single currency.*

The year was also marked by the economic and financial crises which affected several regions of the world, in particular south-east Asia and Russia. These upheavals did not prevent the European Union from enjoying economic growth and stability. In this regard, the stabilising effect of the euro was evident even before its introduction.

Economic situation

41. The year saw both a strengthening and a rebalancing of economic activity in the European Union. According to the Commission's autumn economic forecasts, GDP growth for the European Union stood at 2.9 % in 1998 (2.7 % in 1997). Following the Asian crisis, which spread to most emerging economies, the international environment was much less buoyant than in recent years. However, the recovery of internal demand (consumption and investment) within the European Union largely offset the weakness of external demand. This non-inflationary growth benefited from the particularly favourable monetary conditions afforded by low interest rates and stable European exchange rates. In this respect, the forthcoming introduction of the euro bolstered Europe against international financial turmoil. Inflation fell from 2.1 % in 1997 to 1.6 %, largely as a result of falling oil and raw material prices. Economic growth again enabled the average public deficit to be reduced, from 2.3 % of GDP in 1997 to 1.8 %, and public debt to fall, from 71.9 % of GDP in 1997 to 70.3 %. Unemployment also declined to 10 % of the working population (against 10.7 % in 1997).

Economic policy coordination

Broad economic policy guidelines

42. The broad guidelines of the economic polices of the Member States and the Community for 1998 were formally adopted by the Council on 6 July (¹). In accordance with Article 103(2) of the EC Treaty, they had previously been the subject of a Commission recommendation of 13 May (²), a draft Council recommendation of 5 June (³) and a conclusion adopted by the European Council at its meeting in Cardiff (⁴), which stressed the need to strengthen this instrument for ensuring surveillance, coordination of economic policies and promotion of sustained convergence. For its part, Parliament approved the Commission's approach in a resolution adopted on 28 May (⁵). In December the Vienna European Council stressed the need to deepen and strengthen economic policy coordination (⁶).

(¹) OJ L 200, 16.7.1998; Bull. 7/8-1998, points 1.3.2 and 2.3.1.
(²) COM(1998) 279; Bull. 5-1998, point 1.2.1.
(³) Bull. 6 1998, point 1.3.2.
(⁴) Bull. 6-1998, points I.5 and 1.3.2.
(⁵) OJ C 195, 22.6.1998; Bull. 5-1998, point 1.2.1.
(⁶) Bull. 12-1998.

43. The success of economic and monetary union, prosperity and employment are the main priorities of these broad guidelines, which advocate the pursuit of a macroeconomic strategy centred on growth and stability and backed by a monetary policy geared towards price stability, sound budgetary policies pursued in accordance with the stability and growth pact (¹) and wage developments compatible with price stability and a strengthening of investment, and the implementation of structural reforms on the goods, services and capital markets and on the labour market (based in the latter case on the employment guidelines) (→ point 111).

44. The ground for the debate on the broad economic policy guidelines was prepared by the adoption on 25 February, of a Commission communication on growth and employment in the stability-oriented framework of EMU (²). In this communication, which this year replaced the traditional annual economic report, the Commission analysed the economic situation, the main challenges in the years to come and the main economic policy priorities. Its approach was backed by the Economic and Social Committee on 29 April (³), by Parliament on 30 April (⁴) and by the Committee of the Regions on 19 November (⁵).

Stability and convergence programmes

45. In accordance with Regulation (EC) No 1466/97 (⁶), adopted as part of the stability and growth pact, the Council examined the stability programmes of Finland and the Netherlands and the convergence programmes of Greece and Denmark and, on the Commission's recommendation (⁷), adopted opinions on these programmes on 12 October (⁸) and 1 December (⁹). On 19 January, it adopted conclusions on the implementation of Italy's convergence programme (¹⁰).

(¹)   1997 General Report, point 95.
(²)   COM(1998) 103; Bull. 1/2-1998, point 1.3.1.
(³)   OJ C 214, 10.7.1998; Bull. 4-1998, point 1.2.2.
(⁴)   OJ C 152, 18.5.1998; Bull. 4-1998, point 1.2.1.
(⁵)   Bull. 11-1998, point 1.2.1.
(⁶)   OJ L 209, 2.8.1997; 1997 General Report, point 95.
(⁷)   Bull. 9-1998, points 1.2.1 (Greece) and 1.2.2 (Finland); Bull. 11-1998, points 1.2.2 (Denmark) and 1.2.3 (Netherlands).
(⁸)   OJ C 372, 2.12.1998; Bull. 10-1998, points 1.2.1 (Greece) and 1.2.2 (Finland).
(⁹)   OJ C 3, 6.1.1999; Bull. 12-1998 (Denmark and the Netherlands).
(¹⁰) Bull. 1/2-1998, point 1.3.2.

Excessive deficits

46.   On 1 May, in the context of the excessive deficit procedure laid down by Article 104c of the EC Treaty, the Council, acting on the Commission's recommendation ([1]), abrogated the decisions on the existence of an excessive deficit for Belgium, Germany, Spain, France, Italy, Austria, Portugal, Sweden and the United Kingdom ([2]). On 29 June it adopted, again on the Commission's recommendation ([3]), a recommendation ([4]) on bringing to an end the excessive government deficit in Greece, the only Member State which was still in that position.

Aspects relating to economic coordination

47.   On 2 December the Commission adopted a communication on government investment in the framework of economic strategy ([5]), in which it suggested that Member States increase the relative share of investment in their budgets without compromising the objective of fiscal balance required by the growth and stability pact. This matter, which was examined by the Vienna European Council in December ([6]), was also the subject, on 2 July, of an own-initiative Economic and Social Committee opinion ([7]). The Economic and Social Committee also took the view, in an own-initiative opinion of 9 September ([8]), that a convergence of Member States' wage policies was necessary and examined, in an own-initiative opinion of 10 September ([9]), the potential influence of social policy on economic performance. For its part, on 16 December, Parliament stressed the need, in the context of monetary union, for an adjustment mechanism in cases of asymmetric shocks ([6]).

---

[1]   Bull. 3-1998, point 1.2.3.
[2]   Decisions 98/307/EC to 98/315/EC (OJ L 139, 11.5.1998; Bull. 5-1998, point 1.2.2).
[3]   Bull. 5-1998, point 1.2.3.
[4]   Bull. 6-1998, point 1.3.3.
[5]   COM(1998) 682; Bull. 12-1998.
[6]   Bull.12-1998.
[7]   OJ C 284, 14.9.1998; Bull. 7/8-1998, point 1.3.1.
[8]   OJ C 407, 28.12.1998; Bull. 9-1998, point 1.2.3.
[9]   OJ C 407, 28.12.1998; Bull. 9-1998, point 1.2.8.

Preparations for the third stage of EMU

Decision on the participating Member States

48.   The Council, meeting at the level of Heads of State or Government, decided on 3 May that 11 Member States (Belgium, Germany, Spain, France, Ireland, Italy, Luxembourg, the Netherlands, Austria, Portugal and Finland) fulfilled the necessary conditions for the adoption of the single currency on 1 January 1999 ([1]). It also found that Greece and Sweden did not at this stage fulfil the necessary conditions, with the United Kingdom having given notification that it did not intend to move to the third stage of EMU on 1 January 1999 and Denmark having notified its intention not to participate in the third stage.

49.   This decision completed the procedure laid down in Article 109j of the EC Treaty, which had begun on 24 and 25 March with the adoption by the European Monetary Institute (EMI) ([2]) and the Commission ([3]) of their respective reports on progress towards convergence. On that basis, the Commission recommended on 25 March that the Council ([4]) recommend that the Heads of State or Government confirm that the 11 Member States referred to above met the necessary conditions for adopting the single currency on 1 January 1999. On 1 May the Council adopted to that end Recommendation 98/316/EC ([5]), which was endorsed by Parliament on 2 May ([6]).

50.   On 30 April, Parliament also adopted a resolution ([7]) on the reports of the EMI and the Commission and on the Commission's recommendation. For its part, the Council accompanied its recommendation with a statement welcoming the Greek Government's determination to pursue its policies of fiscal consolidation and structural adjustment with a view to joining the third stage of EMU by 1 January 2001 ([8]), as well as with a declaration which stressed the need for closer coordination of economic policies in order to realise the full benefits of the changeover to the single currency and in which Member States agreed to start

---

([1])   Decision 98/317/EC (OJ L 139, 11.5.1998; Bull. 5-1998, point 1.2.5).
([2])   Bull. 3-1998, point 1.2.2.
([3])   COM(1998) 1999; Bull. 3-1998, point 1.2.1.
([4])   Bull. 3-1998, point 1.2.4.
([5])   OJ L 139, 11.5.1998; Bull. 5-1998, point 1.2.5.
([6])   OJ C 167, 1.6.1998; Bull. 5-1998, point 1.2.5.
([7])   OJ C 152, 18.5.1998; Bull. 4-1998, point 1.2.4.
([8])   Bull. 5-1998, point 1.2.7.

implementing Regulation (EC) No 1466/97 *(→ point 45)* from 1 July 1998.

51. Following the decision on the participating Member States, the Council adopted a series of measures concerning the legal framework for the introduction of the euro, conversion rates, denominations and technical specifications of euro coins, and the establishment of the European Central Bank *(→ points 52 to 59)*.

Legal framework for the introduction of the euro

52. On 3 May the Council adopted Regulation (EC) No 974/98 on the introduction of the euro (Table II). Together with Regulation (EC) No 1103/97 ([1]), this regulation forms the legal framework for the introduction of the euro and lays down in particular the conditions for replacing the currencies of the participating Member States with the euro and the rules on legal tender as regards euro notes and coins.

Fixing of conversion rates

53. On 31 December the Council adopted the fixed and irrevocable conversion rates between the currencies of the 11 Member States participating in the euro with effect from 1 January 1999 ([2]). These rates are indicated in Table 1. On 3 May, in order to give markets some idea of these rates as the third stage of EMU approached, the ministers and Central Bank governors of the Member States adopting the euro on 1 January 1999, the Commission and the European Monetary Institute adopted a joint communiqué ([3]) specifying the method to be applied to determine the irrevocable conversion rates for the euro and, in particular, laying down the bilateral central rates to be used.

Technical preparations for and practical aspects of the introduction of the euro

54. On 3 May, the Council adopted Regulation (EC) No 975/98 (Table II), which provides that the euro coins to be put into circulation will comprise eight denominations (1 cent, 2 cent, 5 cent, 10 cent, 20 cent,

---

([1])   OJ L 162, 19.6.1997; 1997 General Report, point 92.
([2])   Regulation (EC) No 2866/98 (OJ L 359, 31.12.1998; Bull. 12-1998).
([3])   OJ C 160, 27.5.1998; Bull. 5-1998, point 1.2.11.

TABLE 1

Conversion rates
(Equivalent in national currency of EUR 1)

Currency	= EUR 1
ATS	13.7603
BEF	40.3399
DEM	1.95583
ESP	166.386
FIM	5.94573
FRF	6.55957
IEP	0.787564
ITL	1 936.27
LUF	40.3399
NLG	2.20371
PTE	200.482

50 cent, 1 euro and 2 euro) and lays down their technical specifications. On 29 July, the Commission proposed that this regulation be amended with regard to the 10 and 50 cent coins in order to make them easier to handle for blind and partially sighted people and more precisely identifiable by vending machines (Table II). On 21 December, the Council adopted a common position on this proposal. On 23 November, it reached agreement on the arrangements applicable to collector coins and commemorative coins intended for circulation [1]. On 22 July, the Commission adopted a communication on measures to combat counterfeiting of euro notes and coins (→ point 1014).

55. In a communication adopted on 11 February [2], the Commission presented the conclusions of the expert group set up in 1997 [3] to examine various practical aspects of the introduction of the euro (bank charges for conversion operations, dual pricing, impact on SMEs, role of education and training). Further to a round table on these matters held on 26 February, it adopted on 23 April three recommendations [4] on banking charges for conversion to the euro, on dual display of prices and other monetary amounts, and on dialogue, monitoring and information, the aim being to facilitate the changeover to the euro. These were endorsed by Parliament on 10 March [5] and by the Council on 3

[1]   Bull. 11-1998, point 1.2.9.
[2]   COM(1998) 61; Bull. 1/2-1998, point 1.3.6.
[3]   1997 General Report, point 93.
[4]   Recommendations 98/286/EC to 98/288/EC (OJ L 130, 1.5.1998; Bull. 4-1998, point 1.2.3).
[5]   OJ C 104, 6.4.1998; Bull. 3-1998, point 1.2.5.

May ([1]). Parliament also adopted resolutions on the impact of the introduction of the euro on capital markets, electronic money and the consumer (13 January) ([2]), on tourism (10 March) ([3]), on Community policies, institutions and legislation (6 October) ([4]), and on the role of the euro as a parallel currency in those Member States not adopting it on 1 January 1999 (15 December) ([5]), while the Economic and Social Committee issued opinions on the consequences of the single currency for the internal market on 9 September ([6]) and on the euro and employment on 2 December ([5]).

56.   Further to the communication plan it launched in 1996 ([7]), the Commission set out, in a communication adopted on 6 February ([8]), its information strategy for the euro, which the Committee of the Regions endorsed on 13 May ([9]) and Parliament on 16 December ([5]).

Establishment of the European Central Bank (ECB)

57.   On 26 May, by Decision 98/345/EC taken by common accord at the level of Heads of State or Government ([10]), the governments of the Member States adopting the single currency appointed the President (Mr Duisenberg), the Vice-President (Mr Noyer) and the other members of the Executive Board (Mr Issing, Mr Padoa-Schioppa, Mr Domingo Solans and Mrs Hämäläinen) of the ECB. These appointments took effect on 1 June, when the European System of Central Banks (ESCB) and the European Central Bank were established ([11]). In accordance with Article 50 of the ESCB Statute, this decision followed on from a Council recommendation adopted on 3 May ([12]) and endorsed by the European Monetary Institute on 5 May ([13]) and by Parliament on 13 May ([14]). The Council, meeting at the level of Heads of State or Government, had previously reached a political agreement on these appointments on 3 May ([15]).

---

[1]   Bull. 5-1998, point 1.2.10.
[2]   OJ C 34, 2.2.1998; Bull. 1/2-1998, points 1.3.8, 1.3.10 and 1.3.11.
[3]   OJ C 104, 6.4.1998; Bull. 3-1998, point 1.2.6.
[4]   OJ C 328, 26.10.1998; Bull. 10-1998, point 1.2.4.
[5]   Bull. 12-1998.
[6]   OJ C 407, 28.12.1998; Bull. 9-1998, point 1.2.15.
[7]   1996 General Report, point 74.
[8]   COM(1998) 39; Bull. 1/2-1998, point 1.3.7.
[9]   OJ C 251, 10.8.1998; Bull. 5-1998, point 1.2.14.
[10]   OJ L 154, 28.5.1998; Bull. 5-1998, point 1.2.12.
[11]   Bull. 6-1998, point 1.3.4.
[12]   OJ L 139, 11.5.1998; Bull. 5-1998, point 1.2.12.
[13]   OJ C 169, 4.6.1998; Bull. 5-1998, point 1.2.12.
[14]   OJ C 167, 1.6.1998; Bull. 5-1998, point 1.2.12.
[15]   Bull. 5-1998, point 1.2.12.

58. In June the Council adopted two regulations and two decisions designed to establish the legal framework which the ECB requires in order to operate. Decision 98/382/EC (Table II) defines the statistical data to be used for determining the key for subscription of the capital of the ECB. Decision 98/415/EC (Table II) lays down the scope and conditions for consultation of the ECB by national authorities regarding draft legislation within its field of competence. Lastly, Regulations (EC, ECSC, Euratom) Nos 1197/98 (Table II) and 1198/98 (Table II) extend the privileges and immunities of the Communities to the members of the Governing Council and of the General Council of the ECB and to its staff.

59. On the ECB's recommendation, the Council adopted on 23 November regulations laying down the ECB's powers to apply minimum reserves (Table II), impose sanctions on firms (Table II) and collect statistical information (Table II).

Preparatory work of the European Monetary Institute (EMI) and the European Central Bank (ECB)

60. The establishment on 1 June of the ESCB and the ECB gave rise to the winding-up of the EMI. During its final year of existence, the Institute had completed its task of strengthening the coordination of monetary policies and preparing for the third stage of EMU. In addition to its convergence report *(→ point 49)*, the EMI published in May its last annual report([1]), in which it examined the economic, monetary and financial situation in the Union and reported on its preparations for the third stage of EMU. On 16 July this report was the subject of a Parliament resolution([2]). Parliament had expressed its view on the EMI's interim report on legal convergence in the Member States on 10 March([3]).

61. The first meetings of the Governing Council and the General Council of the ECB were held on 9 June([4]). After having determined its structure and organisation, the ECB acted swiftly to carry out the preparatory work necessary for it to be fully operational from 1 January 1999. In addition to the recommendations for regulations which it transmitted to the Council *(→ point 59)*, it adopted several decisions con-

---

([1])   Bull. 5-1998, point 1.2.15.
([2])   OJ C 292, 21.9.1998; Bull. 7/8-1998, point 1.3.6.
([3])   OJ C 104, 6.4.1998; Bull. 3-1998, point 1.2.7.
([4])   Bull. 6-1998, points 1.3.5 and 1.3.6.

cerning, among other things, the conditions for subscribing to its capital ([1]), euro notes ([2]), the terms of employment of its staff, and access to its documents, as well as regulations on the minimum reserves and the consolidated balance sheet of financial institutions ([3]). The ECB also adopted guidelines on the collection of statistical information and, in September, published a report entitled 'The single monetary policy in Stage III: General documentation on ESCB monetary policy instruments and procedures', which contains a detailed description of the monetary policy instruments and procedures to be applied in the third stage of EMU. Also in September it signed an agreement with the central banks of the Member States outside the euro zone laying down the operating procedures for an exchange-rate mechanism in the third stage. For its part, Parliament, in a resolution adopted on 2 April, stressed that the independence of the ECB called for a correspondingly high level of democratic accountability ([4]).

Economic and Financial Committee

62. In accordance with Article 109c of the EC Treaty, the Commission adopted on 25 February, a proposal for a decision on detailed provisions concerning the composition of the Economic and Financial Committee ([5]), which is to replace the Monetary Committee from the beginning of the third stage of EMU. It proposed that the Member States, the Commission and the ECB should each appoint two members to the Committee, which would therefore have a total of 34 members. The members appointed by the Member States would be selected from among senior officials from their administrations and national central banks. The Council adopted this decision on 21 December ([6]). In a resolution adopted on 14 July, Parliament expressed its regret at not being consulted about these detailed provisions ([7]).

63. On 31 December the Council adopted a decision on the statutes of the Economic and Financial Committee ([8]), about which the Commission had given its opinion on 18 December ([9]).

([1])   Decisions 1999/31/EC and 1999/32/EC (OJ L 8, 14.1.1999).
([2])   Decision 1999/33/EC (OJ L 8, 14.1.1999).
([3])   Regulations (EC) Nos 2818/98 and 2819/98 (OJ L 356, 30.12.1998).
([4])   OJ C 138, 4.5.1998; Bull. 4-1998, point 1.2.5.
([5])   OJ C 125, 23.4.1998; COM(1998) 110; Bull. 1/2-1998, point 1.3.4.
([6])   Decision 98/743/EC (OJ L 358, 31.12.1998; Bull. 12 1998).
([7])   OJ C 292, 21.9.1998; Bull. 7/8-1998, point 1.3.5.
([8])   Decision 1999/8/EC (OJ L 5, 9.1.1999; Bull. 12-1998).
([9])   COM(1998) 783; Bull. 12-1998.

External aspects

64. On 4 November the Commission adopted a proposal for a Council decision on the representation of the euro zone at international level ([1]). In December the Vienna European Council, stressing that the changeover to the euro would entail global responsibilities for the European Union which would require it to speak with one voice and to be effectively represented within institutions such as the G7 (→ *points 881 and 882*) and the International Monetary Fund (→ *points 70 and 71*), reached agreement on the arrangements for such representation ([2]). The external aspects of the transition to the third stage of EMU were the subject of Parliament resolutions on 13 January and 3 December ([3]) and of an Economic and Social Committee opinion on 26 March ([4]).

65. At the Commission's recommendation ([5]), the Council adopted on 23 November and 21 December two decisions enabling France ([6]) and Portugal ([7]) to maintain their exchange-rate agreements with the West African Economic and Monetary Union, the Economic Community of Central African States, the Comoros (France) and Cape Verde (Portugal).

66. On 31 December the Council adopted, at the Commission's recommendation ([8]), three decisions ([2]) defining the position to be adopted by the Community in negotiations with Monaco, San Marino and the Vatican on bilateral agreements on monetary matters and, on a proposal from the Commission ([9]), a decision ([2]) authorising France to introduce the euro from 1 January 1999 in Saint-Pierre-et-Miquelon and Mayotte, which do not form part of the Community.

Operation of the European Monetary System (EMS)

67. The EMS functioned smoothly in 1998, with most member currencies trading at exchange rates close to their central parities. The Greek drachma joined the exchange-rate mechanism on 16 March ([10]) and

---

[1]   COM(1998) 637; Bull. 11-1998, point 1.2.6.
[2]   Bull. 12-1998.
[3]   OJ C 34, 2.2.1998; Bull. 1/2-1998, point 1.3.9; OJ C 398, 21.12.1998; Bull. 12-1998.
[4]   OJ C 157, 25.5.1998; Bull. 3-1998, point 1.2.8.
[5]   COM(1998) 412; Bull. 7/8-1998, point 1.3.3 (France); COM(1998) 663; Bull. 11-1998, point 1.2.4 (Portugal).
[6]   Decision 98/683/EC (OJ L 320, 28.11.1998; Bull. 11-1998, point 1.2.5).
[7]   Decision 98/774/EC (OJ L 358, 31.12.1998; Bull. 12-1998).
[8]   COM(1998) 789; Bull; 12-1998.
[9]   COM(1998) 801, Bull. 12-1998.
[10] Bull. 3-1998, point 1.2.9.

remained slightly above its central rate for the rest of the year. On 16 March the central rate of the Irish pound was revalued by 3 % ([1]).

68. This stability within the exchange-rate mechanism was accompanied by very weak inflationary pressures within the Member States, a fact which made for convergence of long-term interest rates at historically low levels. On 31 December the short-term interest rates of Member States adopting the euro on 1 January converged to form a single rate within the euro zone.

69. On 31 December the central rates of the new exchange-rate mechanism (EMS Mark Two), applicable from 1 January 1999, were fixed. The Greek drachma will be subject to a standard fluctuation margin (15 % in either direction), while that of the Danish crown will be more limited (2.25 % in either direction).

International economic, monetary and financial matters

70. The 50th meeting of the Interim Committee of the International Monetary Fund, chaired by Mr Maystadt and attended by Mr Brown for the Council Presidency and Mr de Silguy for the Commission, was held on 16 April. While cautiously optimistic about global growth prospects, the Committee stressed a number of downside risks which called for resolute action by countries to support global non-inflationary economic growth and, in particular, called on the Asian countries most affected by the crisis to employ firm monetary policies to underpin the recovery in exchange rates, fiscal discipline and the implementation of structural reforms. It welcomed progress towards EMU but stressed the need to make further headway with fiscal consolidation and structural reforms, particularly with regard to the labour market. The Committee reaffirmed its view that the Fund's sphere of activity should be extended in the area of capital movements.

71. On 6 October the Interim Committee held its 51st meeting in Washington under the new chairmanship of Mr Ciampi, with Mr Edlinger and Mr de Silguy attending for the Council Presidency and the Commission respectively. Concerned about recent developments in Russia, the severity of the crisis in Asia and their negative effects on the economic outlook, the Committee felt that recovery depended on the authorities' willingness to introduce economic, financial and institutional

---

([1]) Bull. 3-1998, point 1.2.10.

reforms and that the globalisation of the world economy had reinforced the need for building sound financial systems, an objective to which the Fund could contribute by intensifying its surveillance of financial sector issues and capital flows and by communicating its recommendations more effectively. The Committee called on the private sector to play an increased role in forestalling and resolving financial crises and stressed the need to finalise the new arrangements to borrow.

72.   In December the Vienna European Council called on Europe to play a decisive role in devising a new international monetary and financial system. In a resolution adopted on 17 September ([1]), Parliament stressed the need, in the face of the globalisation of financial markets, for effective international regulatory and supervisory bodies. On 3 December it repeated its call for the international financial system to be strengthened ([2]).

73.   Economic dialogue with the associated countries of central and eastern Europe continued in 1998 within the context of the accession partnerships (→ point 806), with the Commission examining the economic progress made by each country. A seminar bringing together the Council, the Commission, the Member States and the countries of central Europe was held in Vienna in October on the subject of the world economic situation. The economic dialogue with the associated Mediterranean countries also continued.

Financial activities

74.   On 3 July the Commission adopted its annual report on the borrowing and lending activities of the Community in 1997 ([3]). The volume of borrowing by the Community institutions in 1997 amounted to ECU 23.7 billion, 31.7 % up on 1996 (ECU 18 billion), while lending totalled ECU 26.9 billion, 13.5 % up on 1996 (ECU 23.7 billion). The detailed table of lending activities during the period 1996-98 and the total amount of borrowings in 1998 can be found in Section 5 of Chapter VII ('Borrowing and lending operations') (→ point 1016).

75.   Activities relating to the general budget guarantee for borrowing and lending operations are dealt with in Section 6 ('General budget

---

([1])   OJ C 313, 12.10.1998; Bull. 9-1998, point 1.2.4.
([2])   OJ C 398, 21.12.1998; Bull. 12-1998.
([3])   COM(1998) 409; Bull. 7/8-1998, point 1.6.9.

guarantee for borrowing and lending operations') of Chapter VII
(→ points 1017 et seq.).

Macrofinancial assistance

76. The first tranche (ECU 125 million) of the ECU 250 million loan
which the Council decided in July 1997 ([1]) to grant to Bulgaria was
disbursed in February. The second tranche (ECU 125 million) was disbursed in December. The second tranche (ECU 15 million) of the ECU
40 million loan which the Council decided, also in July 1997, to grant
to the Former Yugoslav Republic of Macedonia ([2]) was disbursed in February. The ECU 110 million loan to Georgia signed in December
1997 ([3]) was disbursed in July, and the first tranche (ECU 10 million) of
outright grants to that country was disbursed in August. Under the same
Council decision ([3]), an ECU 28 million loan to Armenia was signed and
disbursed in December.

77. Given the difficult balance-of-payments situation confronting
Ukraine, the Council decided in October to grant additional macrofinancial assistance to that country of up to ECU 150 million on condition
that economic reforms were continued and agreements with international
financial institutions complied with (Table II).

78. On 3 April the Commission proposed that exceptional aid of up to
ECU 30 million be awarded in the form of outright grants to Azerbaijan
(Table II), among other things in order to alleviate the social hardship of
the adjustment measures being implemented in that country. On 29 June
the Council requested that the grants in question be made by way of
clearly defined programmes using existing legal bases ([4]). The Commission proposed on 3 September (Table II) and 13 November (Table II)
respectively that macrofinancial aid be granted to Albania (up to ECU
20 million) and Bosnia-Herzegovina (up to ECU 30 million).

79. The annual Commission report on the implementation of macrofinancial assistance to third countries (1996) was adopted on 13
January ([5]).

([1]) 1997 General Report, point 107.
([2]) 1997 General Report, point 109.
([3]) 1997 General Report, point 111.
([4]) Bull. 6-1998, point 1.4.108.
([5]) COM(1998) 3; Bull. 1/2-1998, point 1.3.12.

Development of financing techniques

80. With the participation of 15 specialised financial institutions, the Commission continued to develop the 'Eurotech capital' scheme, the purpose of which is to stimulate investment in high technology. It also developed further the JOP programme (joint venture programme PHARE-TACIS), which has been extended until 1999. Since the 1991 launch of this programme, in which 86 financial intermediaries are participating, 1 695 projects have received Community support totalling ECU 124 million.

81. The proposal for an amendment of the TENs (trans-European networks) financial regulation *(→ point 6)* presented by the Commission as part of the implementation of Agenda 2000 provides for the Commission to put up risk capital for network projects via investment funds and the like.

82. Other support measures for SMEs and capital investment are dealt with in Section 7 ('Enterprise policy') of this chapter *(→ points 262 et seq.).*

Operations concerning the New Community Instrument (NCI)

83. There were no NCI borrowing or lending operations during the year (1).

Financing ECSC and Euratom activities

84. In accordance with the Commission's 1994 decision (2), the ECSC did not conclude any new loans in 1998 and, consequently, ceased obtaining resources in the form of borrowings. It completed its low-cost housing loan activities (Article 54, second paragraph, of the ECSC Treaty), paying a total of ECU 20 444 795 from its own funds under decisions taken before 31 December 1997. The financial report of the ECSC for 1997 was adopted by the Commission on 14 July.

---

(1) Commission reports on the rate of utilisation of the NCI: COM(1998) 409; Bull. 7/8-1998, point 1.6.9 (second half of 1997); COM(1998) 661; Bull. 11-1998, point 1.5.7 (first half of 1998).
(2) 1994 General Report, point 1160.

85.   As regards Euratom, no lending operations were undertaken this year.

European Investment Bank (EIB)

86.   The European Investment Bank (¹) granted loans totalling ECU 29 526 million in 1998 (ECU 26 203 million in 1997) in support of Community policies, including ECU 4 410 million within the framework of financial cooperation with non-member countries (see Table 2).

87.   Within the European Union, the EIB stepped up implementation of its special Amsterdam action programme (²). In this context, SME special window operations amounted to ECU 218 million and health and education operations to ECU 1 386 million while, in accordance with the request of the Amsterdam European Council, loans for environmental protection and trans-European networks continued to increase (→ point 88).

88.   Loans signed in 1998 in the European Union countries, in a macroeconomic context characterised by some degree of recovery of economic activity, totalled ECU 25 116 million (ECU 22 958 million in 1997). In accordance with the task assigned to it, the EIB attempted to give priority to channelling the funds it borrowed on the financial markets to investment projects contributing to the development of the less-favoured regions. This assistance accounted for some 72 % of its financing operations in the European Union. Loans for trans-European transport and energy infrastructure amounted to ECU 8 993 million. Financing for environmental protection totalled ECU 6 165 million and for the supply and efficient use of energy ECU 2 248 million. In the industrial and service sectors, assistance totalled ECU 4 588 million: ECU 1 844 million in the form of individual loans and ECU 2 745 million in the form of global loans concluded with a number of partner banks and financial institutions..

89.   Operations outside the Union amounted to ECU 4 410 million (compared with ECU 3 245 million in 1997). In the central European countries assistance totalled ECU 2 317 million, including ECU 1 320

(¹)   Copies of the EIB's annual report and of other publications relating to the Bank's work and its operations can be obtained from the main office (Information and Communications Department, 100, boulevard Konrad Adenauer, L-2950 Luxembourg; fax (352) 4379-3189) or from its external offices.
(²)   1997 General Report, point 121.

TABLE 2

Contracts signed in 1998 and from 1994 to 1998

(million ECU)

	1998		1994–98	
	Amount	%	Amount	%
Belgium	858	3.4	3 935	3.7
Denmark	745	3.0	3 846	3.7
Germany	5 168	20.6	16 831	16.0
Greece	736	2.9	3 246	3.1
Spain	3 152	12.6	14 252	13.5
France	2 837	11.3	12 750	12.1
Ireland	263	1.0	1 278	1.2
Italy	4 387	17.5	18 559	17.6
Luxembourg	109	0.4	289	0.3
Netherlands	426	1.7	2 309	2.2
Austria	358	1.4	1 645	1.6
Portugal	1 505	6.0	6 490	6.2
Finland	551	2.2	1 434	1.4
Sweden	664	2.6	2 709	2.6
United Kingdom	3 074	12.2	13 924	13.2
Other ([1])	282	1.1	1 812	1.7
Union total	25 116	100	105 309	100
ACP and OCTs	695	15.8	2 345	15.6
Mediterranean	966	21.9	4 413	29.4
Central and eastern Europe	2 387	54.1	6 951	46.3
Latin America and Asia	362	8.2	1 292	8.6
Non-Union total ([2])	4 410	100	15 002	100
Overall total	29 526		120 310	

([1]) Projects of Community interest located outside the territory of the Member States.
([2]) Includes risk capital from budgetary resources:
   (i) ACP and OCTs: ECU 272 million in 1998 and ECU 856 million from 1994 to 1998;
   (ii) Mediterranean: ECU 86 million in 1998 and ECU 177 million from 1994 to 1998.

million under the pre-accession facility. This went mainly to communications infrastructures intended to strengthen links with Union countries and to extend the trans-European networks. An amount of ECU 70 million was granted to the Former Yugoslav Republic of Macedonia to finance road infrastructures. In the Mediterranean area financing totalled ECU 966 million, including ECU 86.1 million in risk capital. In the ACP countries and the OCTs financing totalled ECU 560 million, including ECU 271.9 million in risk capital and ECU 135 million for South Africa. Lastly, the EIB continued its operations in various Latin American countries (ECU 212 million) and Asia (ECU 150 million).

90.   The EIB obtained the funds needed for its lending activities by borrowing a total of ECU 30.1 billion on capital markets; 39 % of this amount was raised in Community currencies and in euro. It also developed its euro-denominated issues, thereby intensifying its strategy in favour of the introduction of the single currency.

91.   In order to allow the EIB (the outstanding loans and guarantees of which may not exceed 250 % of its subscribed capital) to pursue its activities normally, the Board of Governors decided in June to increase the Bank's subscribed capital, with effect from 1 January 1999, from ECU 62 013 million to ECU 100 000 million.

European Investment Fund (EIF)

92.   The volume of EIF activities ([1]) increased again in 1998. At the end of the year, its outstanding guarantee operations totalled ECU 2 599 million (ECU 2 172 million in 1997), of which 67 % concerned guarantees for infrastructure projects connected with trans-European networks and 33 % guarantees for operations involving SMEs. The latter included ECU 653 million for the 'Growth and environment' programme ([2]) and ECU 31 million granted under the new SME guarantee mechanism established by Decision 98/347/EC (→ point 262). The EIF's investment operations were also stepped up. At the end of the year signed amounts relating to the special window created by the EIB for high-technology SMEs (→ point 87) totalled ECU 62 million (ECU 6.4 million in 1997) and those relating to the risk-capital window for SMEs created by Decision 98/347/EC ECU 8 million. The EIF's acquisitions of equity participations totalled ECU 59 million. Overall, its commitments were spread over 15 different investment funds during the year.

93.   The number of EIF shareholders was 78 at the end of 1998, comprising 76 banks and financial institutions as well as the European Community and the EIB, the latter two holding 30 and 40 % of the authorised capital respectively. In 1998 the EIF paid its first dividends (ECU 3.6 million) to shareholders.

---

[1]   Copies of the EIF's annual report can be obtained from its office (43, avenue J. F. Kennedy, L-2968 Luxembourg).
[2]   1997 General Report, point 114.

European Bank for Reconstruction and Development (EBRD)

94.   The seventh annual meeting of the EBRD, held in Kiev (Ukraine) on 11 and 12 May, approved the Bank's accounts for 1997. At the meeting, the Community's representative stressed the positive consequences of the enhanced partnership between the Commission and the EBRD in the enlargement process and of the launch of the euro for all the countries benefiting from the EBRD's operations, and more particularly those which had applied for accession. Following a unanimous vote by the Board of Governors, Mr Köhler succeeded Mr de Larosière as President, taking up his duties with effect from 1 September.

95.   According to an initial evaluation of the 1998 results, the EBRD concluded 96 new operations costing a total of ECU 2 373, of which ECU 773 million was in the form of participations, ECU 1 567 in the form of loans and ECU 33 in the form of guarantees.

96.   In 1998 the Commission disbursed ECU 4 387 500 following the European Community's decision to subscribe for extra shares in the capital of the EBRD [1].

---

[1]   Decision 97/135/EC (OJ L 52, 22.2.1997; Bull. 1/2-1997, point 1.3.21).

Section 2

Statistical system

Priority activities and objectives

97. On 22 December the Council adopted a decision on the Community statistical programme 1998-2002 (Table II) which, in accordance with the framework regulation on Community statistics (¹), sets out the principles, key domains and objectives of the action planned and identifies the strategies and work schedules for each planning period. While pinpointing three top priorities (economic and monetary union; competitiveness, growth and employment; the enlargement of the European Union), it also provides for the maintenance of the current statistical support to decision-making under the existing policies.

Framework and guidelines

98. In the economic statistics domain, the Council adopted on 16 February, a regulation establishing the principles for allocating financial intermediation services indirectly measured (FISIM) within the European system of national and regional accounts (ESA) (Table II). On 20 July it adopted two regulations (²), the first extending the coverage of goods and services of the harmonised index of consumer prices and the second basing the calculation of the index on the total household final monetary consumption expenditure incurred on the economic territory of each Member State, the Commission having examined, in its report of 27 February (³), the arrangements for Member States to draw up the indices under the terms of Council Regulation (EC) No 2494/95 (⁴) and the comparability of the indices. The Council further adopted, on 19 May, a regulation establishing a Community framework for the production of short-term economic statistics (Table II) and, on 16 February, a regulation concerning structural statistics on insurance services (Table II).

99. In the field of trade in goods, the Council amended on 12 February Regulation (EC) No 1172/95 on the statistics relating to the trading

---

(¹) OJ L 52, 22.2.1997; 1997 General Report, point 131.
(²) Council Regulations (EC) No 1687/98 and (EC) No 1688/98 (OJ L 214, 31.7.1998; Bull. 7/8-1998, point 1.7.2).
(³) COM(1998) 104; Bull. 1/2-1998, point 1.7.4.
(⁴) OJ L 257, 27.10.1995; 1995 General Report, point 85.

of goods by the Community and its Member States with non-member countries so as to provide for Member States to use a single nomenclature of non-member countries ([1]). Under the SLIM initiative *(→ point 151)* it adopted, on 20 July, a common position on a proposal for an amendment to Regulation (EEC) No 3330/91 on the statistics relating to the trading of goods between Member States (Table I).

100. On 2 December the Commission adopted a report on ways of improving the comparability of statistics to monitor and evaluate progress under the European employment strategy *(→ point 112)*. In the social domain the Council also adopted, on 9 March ([2]), Regulation (EC) No 577/98 providing for the organisation by each Member State of a continuous labour force sample survey intended to provide the Commission with comparable statistics on the level and structure of employment and unemployment and on trends in these factors, and the Commission proposed on 3 September to produce regular and comparable statistics on earnings and labour costs ([3]).

101. Under the agriculture heading, the Council decided, on 22 October, to put forward a more flexible system of statistical surveys of areas under vines (Table II), and on 18 May, the Commission set out the characteristics of the 1999/2000 basic Community survey of the structure of agricultural holdings ([4]). On 11 November it proposed to reorganise the use of aerial-survey and remote-sensing techniques for 1999-2003 (Table II).

102. The Council also adopted, on 25 May, a regulation replacing Directive 78/546/EEC and introducing a more modern system of collecting statistics on the carriage of goods by road (Table II). The Commission proposed on 27 July to establish a Community statistical information infrastructure relating to the industry and markets of the audiovisual and related sectors ([5]).

103. Concerning external relations, there were several meetings during the year with the countries of central and eastern Europe which are applicants for accession, the purpose being to clarify the Community statistical patrimony, particularly in the fields of economics, agriculture and fisheries.

---

[1]   OJ C 48, 19.2.1998; Bull. 1/2-1998, point 1.7.2.
[2]   OJ L 77, 14.3.1998; Bull. 3-1998, point 1.6.2.
[3]   COM(1998) 491; Bull. 9-1998, point 1.6.1.
[4]   Decision 98/377/EC (OJ L 168, 13.6.1998).
[5]   SEC(1998) 1325; Bull. 7/8-1998, point 1.7.3.

Publications

104. Eurostat's leading publications in 1998 included the *Eurostat Yearbook 1997,* also available on CD-ROM, *A social portrait of Europe, Sustainable development indicators, The economic accounts of the European Union* and a volume on Portugal in the *Portrait of the regions* series. The statistical information available free of charge at the Eurostat site on the Europa Internet server *(→ point 1153)* was expanded and improved, particularly by the regular updating of some 100 macroeconomic indicators on the European Union and the euro zone. Eurostat also extended its network of data shops, in collaboration with the national statistical institutes concerned, by opening data and publications sales offices in the Netherlands, Portugal and Switzerland.

Section 3

Employment and social policy

Priority activities and objectives

105. The process of implementing without delay the employment-related provisions of the Amsterdam Treaty continued in 1998, in line with the decisions taken by the Amsterdam and Luxembourg European Councils. The Member States produced the first series of national action plans for implementing the employment policy guidelines, which were further revised with a view to application in 1999. The Commission meanwhile presented communications on Community policies in support of employment, on employment rates, on ways of improving the comparability of statistics to monitor and evaluate the European employment strategy, on the modernisation of employment services, on job opportunities in the information society and on undeclared work. The Vienna European Council pointed to the need to reinforce the process of multilateral surveillance in connection with implementation of the employment guidelines, with a view to developing a European employment pact.

In the social policy field, new directives adopted under the Protocol on social policy were extended to the United Kingdom, while a directive on safeguarding supplementary pension rights was adopted by the Council. Various measures initiated by the Commission had a significant impact on workers' freedom of movement, modernisation of work organisation, promotion of the social dialogue, working time and employee information and consultation. A new social action programme covering the years 1998 to 2000 was also adopted.

Social action programme

106. On 29 April, the Commission adopted a new social action programme for the period 1998-2000 ([1]). This programme, placing the employment strategy at the heart of social policy, is designed to build on the impetus created by the Amsterdam Treaty ([2]), and to carry forward the achievements of the previous programme (1995-97) ([3]). The key

---

([1])   COM(1998) 259; Bull. 4-1998, point 1.2.7.
([2])   1997 General Report, points 142 and 168.
([3])   COM(95) 134; 1995 General Report, point 595.

elements underpinning the programme are: jobs, skills and mobility; the changing world of work; and creation of a more inclusive society. This programme was welcomed by the Economic and Social Committee on 9 September ([1]), and by Parliament on 18 November ([2]).

Employment

107.   The annual report on employment in Europe (1998) ([3]), adopted by the Commission on 20 November, provides an overview of the changing employment situation in Europe, with close analysis of the impact of SME development, globalisation, enlargement and public finance restructuring.

108.   Following on from the conclusions of the extraordinary Luxembourg European Council on employment ([4]), and in the wake of the Council's adoption of the first guidelines for employment (1998) ([5]), all the Member States prepared, and submitted to the Commission by mid-April, their national action plans for employment. With a communication adopted on 13 May ([6]), the Commission presented a preliminary analysis of these plans to the Cardiff European Council which, in June, welcomed the plans and called on the Member States to implement them speedily ([7]).

109.   Having regard in particular to the reports on the implementation of the national employment plans submitted by the Member States in the summer, the Commission presented, on 14 October, the draft joint annual report on employment for 1998 ([8]), taking stock of the process launched in Luxembourg, describing the labour market situation in the Member States, assessing the progress made in implementing the 1998 guidelines, and highlighting ten examples of good practice in employment policy. The joint annual report was adopted by the Council on 1 December ([9]).

([1])   OJ C 407, 28.12.1998; Bull. 9-1998, point 1.2.6.
([2])   OJ C 379, 7.12.1998; Bull. 11-1998, point 1.2.11.
([3])   COM(1998) 666; Bull. 11-1998, point 1.2.13.
([4])   1997 General Report, point 148.
([5])   OJ C 30, 28.1.1998; 1997 General Report, point 149.
([6])   COM(1998) 316; Bull. 5-1998, point 1.2.16.
([7])   Bull. 6-1998, point I.6.
([8])   Bull. 10-1998, point 1.2.11.
([9])   Bull. 12-1998.

110. The national employment plans were also examined by the Committee of the Regions on 19 November ([1]). In an own-initiative opinion adopted on 9 September ([2]), the Economic and Social Committee advocated various measures geared to making territorial employment pacts more effective ([3]).

111. In tandem with the draft joint report, the Commission adopted, on 14 October, its proposed employment policy guidelines for 1999 ([4]), with Parliament's opinion being delivered on 18 November ([5]). On the basis of this proposal, the Council reached agreement, on 1 December, on draft guidelines for 1999, which were approved by the Vienna European Council ([6]). The Commission went on to adopt, on 16 December, a proposal for a Council resolution formalising the guidelines ([6]). While retaining the key elements of the 1998 guidelines (employability, entrepreneurship, adaptability and equal opportunities), the 1999 guidelines focus on certain horizontal principles to be observed by the Member States when implementing the guidelines generally, with greater efforts being made to promote equal opportunities and lifelong learning, exploit the job-creating potential of the services sector, create a climate more conducive to SMEs, boost employment through tax-benefit systems and allowances, and integrate older workers and disadvantaged groups.

112. The Vienna European Council ([6]) welcomed the progress achieved in respect of employment indicators as shown in the 1998 joint report. It pointed to the need to reinforce the process of multilateral surveillance for implementation of the guidelines through additional verifiable objectives and deadlines at both European and national level, common performance and policy indicators, and a consistent statistical basis. In this context, the European Council was pleased with the report on ways of improving the comparability of statistics to monitor and evaluate progress under the European employment strategy ([7]), which the Commission adopted on 2 December in response to a request from the Cardiff European Council ([8]). From the point of view of a European employment pact, the need for increased involvement and responsibility on the part of the social partners was also acknowledged.

([1])   Bull. 11-1998, point 1.2.15.
([2])   OJ C 407, 28.12.1998; Bull. 9-1998, point 1.2.7.
([3])   1997 General Report, point 72.
([4])   COM(1998) 574; Bull. 10-1998, point 1.2.12.
([5])   OJ C 379, 7.12.1998; Bull. 11-1998, point 1.2.14.
([6])   Bull. 12-1998.
([7])   COM(1998) 698; Bull. 12-1998.
([8])   Bull. 6-1998, point I.6. *14.*

113. In line with the wishes of the Luxembourg European Council on employment (¹), the Commission adopted, on 14 October, its first report (1998) on employment rates; in this report, the Commission emphasises the Member States' commitment to raising employment rates as an objective of economic policy and considers how each Member State could help to achieve this goal (²). The report shows, in particular, that there is considerable scope for increasing employment rates among women and in the services sector.

114. Following on from its November 1997 communication on Community policies in support of employment (³), the Commission adopted, on 3 June, a further communication on the same subject (⁴), in which it identifies the main challenges facing the Community, looks at how Community policies can contribute to devising and implementing a coordinated strategy for employment, with particular emphasis on greater economic integration as a means of boosting growth and jobs, and points to measures which may help to get Community policies in support of employment up and running.

115. On 13 November, the Commission adopted a communication on 'modernising the public employment services to support the European employment strategy', calling for concerted action by the main parties involved with a view to improving the services and optimising their contribution to the common employment strategy (⁵).

116. On 25 November, the Commission adopted a communication on job opportunities in the information society (⁶), in response to a request from the Luxembourg European Council on employment (⁷). The Commission believes that prospects for employment in the information society are bright, so long as the European Union is resolved to make the most of this rapidly developing and expanding sector.

117. In a communication on undeclared work, adopted on 7 April (⁸), the Commission drew attention to the extent of the problem (estimated to be between 7 and 16 % of the European Union's gross domestic product) and called on the other institutions and the Member States to

---

(¹) Bull. 11-1997, point I.4. 22.
(²) COM(1998) 572; Bull. 10-1998, point 1.2.10.
(³) COM(97) 611; 1997 General Report, point 147.
(⁴) COM(1998) 354; Bull. 6-1998, point 1.3.13.
(⁵) COM(1998) 641; Bull. 11-1998, point 1.2.12.
(⁶) COM(1998) 590; Bull. 11-1998, point 1.2.17.
(⁷) Bull. 11-1997, point I.5. 35.
(⁸) COM(1998) 219; Bull. 4-1998, point 1.2.8.

identify the causes of undeclared work and to take action to combat it within the overall employment strategy.

118. By means of Decision 98/171/EC, adopted on 23 February, the Council provided a legal basis for Commission activities forming part of the European employment strategy, concerning analysis, research, co-operation and action in the field of employment (Table II).

Social protection and social security

119. On 23 April, the Commission adopted its 1997 report on social protection in Europe([1]). This report highlights the changing demographic, social and economic context affecting the Member States' social protection systems in comparison with the previous report([2]), and describes the corresponding adjustments made. It is designed also to contribute to the debate on the future of social protection in the European Union, with a clear link being established between social protection systems and the European employment strategy.

120. On 29 June, the Council adopted Directive 98/49/EC on safeguarding the supplementary pension rights of employed and self-employed persons moving within the Community (Table II). This directive, paving the way for action to overcome obstacles to the free movement of workers in relation to supplementary pensions, provides for: preservation of acquired rights; cross-border payment of benefits; continuation of contributions to a supplementary pension scheme in the country of origin during periods of posting to another Member State; fuller information to be given to scheme members as to their pension rights and the choices available to them when they move to another Member State.

121. The Council also updated, on 4 June, Regulations (EEC) No 1408/71 and No 574/72 on the application of social security schemes to employed persons, to self-employed persons and to members of their families moving within the Community (Table II); on 29 June, the scope of these regulations was extended to special schemes for civil servants (Table II). The Commission proposed, on 30 September, that these regulations be further updated (Table II) and, on 21 December, that Regulation (EC) No 1408/71 be simplified (Table II).

([1])   COM(1998) 243; Bull. 4-1998, point 1.2.11.
([2])   COM(95) 457; 1995 General Report, point 613.

122. In conjunction with the Council Presidency, the Commission organised a conference on the social protection of elderly dependent people in the European Union and Norway, which took place in London in June; a symposium on the theme 'A society for all ages: employment, health, pensions and solidarity between generations in the light of demographic change' was held in Vienna in October. The Commission report on the demographic situation in the European Union was, moreover, the subject of a Parliament resolution in March (¹) and of a Committee of the Regions opinion in May (²).

Freedom of movement for workers

123. Following up its action plan in respect of freedom of movement for workers (³), which was the subject of an Economic and Social Committee opinion delivered on 28 May (⁴) and of a Parliament resolution adopted on 16 July (⁵), the Commission proposed, on 22 July, that the core instruments of legislation governing workers' freedom of movement, namely Regulation (EEC) No 1612/68 and Directive 68/360/EEC, be updated in order to boost the European employment strategy by creating conditions more conducive to labour-market mobility, extend individual rights and improve transparency by incorporating the relevant case-law of the Court of Justice (Table I). The Commission proposed also that the advisory committees on freedom of movement and on coordination of social security schemes be merged (Table I).

124. On 3 July, the Commission adopted its report on the activities of the EURES (European employment services) network for the 1996-97 period (⁶), showing that the provision of EURES services increased markedly, both quantitatively and qualitatively, in this period. The EURES Internet site on the Europa server (⁷), officially inaugurated at the Cardiff European Council with the launch of the 'Europe direct' service *(→ point 1152)*, is a key source of information for job-seekers and employers as regards living and working conditions in the different Member States, providing access to the EURES database of job vacancies and links to all the Internet sites of the participating public employment services.

(¹)   OJ C 104, 6.4.1998; Bull. 3-1998, point 1.2.11.
(²)   OJ C 251, 10.8.1998; Bull. 5-1998, point 1.2.19.
(³)   COM(97) 586; 1997 General Report, point 155.
(⁴)   OJ C 235, 27.7.1998; Bull. 5-1998, point 1.2.22.
(⁵)   OJ C 292, 21.9.1998; Bull. 7/8-1998, point 1.3.14.
(⁶)   COM(1998) 413; Bull. 7/8-1998, point 1.3.11.
(⁷)   http://europa.eu.int/jobs/eures.

125. In a resolution adopted on 28 May, Parliament stressed the need to improve the situation of frontier workers, in particular to avoid any form of double taxation (¹).

Labour law and industrial relations

126. In the wake of its Green Paper entitled 'Partnership for a new organisation of work' (²), the Commission adopted, on 25 November, a communication urging the social partners, especially at Community level, to become involved in the creation of a new framework for the modernisation of work (³).

127. On 29 June, the Council updated Directive 77/187/EEC on the approximation of the laws of the Member States relating to the safeguarding of employees' rights in the event of transfers of undertakings, businesses or parts of businesses (Table II). On 20 July, moreover, the Council consolidated the Community legislation governing collective redundancies (Table II).

128. Parliament, for its part, called on the Member States, on 15 January, to proceed with the exchange of information on employee participation in profits and enterprise results (⁴); on 2 July, it called for transnational trade union rights to be enshrined in the EU Treaty (⁵). In a resolution adopted on 8 October, concerning the restructuring of Levi Strauss, Parliament called on the Commission to link the granting of European business subsidies to certain economic and social conditions (⁶).

129. In line with the wishes of the Luxembourg European Council (⁷), at the beginning of the year the Commission instructed a high-level group of experts, chaired by Mr Gyllenhammar, to evaluate the economic and social impact of industrial change. In its final report, forwarded to the Commission on 29 October, the group advocated a concerted approach towards anticipating and preparing for change. It believes in particular that: the social dialogue is a vital tool in this process; large companies should publish a report on 'managing change',

(¹)   OJ C 195, 22.6.1998; Bull. 5-1998, point 1.2.21.
(²)   COM(97) 128; 1997 General Report, point 150; Supplement 4/97 — Bull.
(³)   COM(1998) 592; Bull. 11-1998, point 1.2.16.
(⁴)   OJ C 34, 2.2.1998; Bull. 1/2-1998, point 1.3.16.
(⁵)   OJ C 292, 21.9.1998; Bull. 7/8-1998, point 1.3.16.
(⁶)   OJ C 328, 26.10.1998; Bull. 10-1998, point 1.2.14.
(⁷)   Bull. 11-1997, point I.5. 28.

setting out their policies for dialogue and training; and companies which fail to make suitable provision for employee training should not receive public aid. The group recommended also that greater emphasis be placed on the development of information technologies, the promotion of job-creating sectors, the involvement of local participants in the development of regions affected by business closures, and the creation by the Commission of an observatory to address these issues.

Health and safety at work

130.   On 7 April, the Council adopted Directive 98/24/EC on the protection of the health and safety of workers from the risks related to chemical agents (Table II), together with conclusions on the protection of workers for whom the risk of exposure to asbestos is highest [1]. Moreover, on 22 December, the Council adopted a common position on a proposal for a directive aimed at protecting workers who may be at risk from explosive atmospheres (Table II).

131.   The Commission meanwhile proposed, on 18 March, an update to Directive 90/394/EEC on the protection of workers from the risks related to exposure to carcinogens (Table II), and the Council reached a common position on the proposal on 22 December; on 3 September [2], technical adjustments were made to Directive 82/130/EEC [3] concerning electrical equipment for use in potentially explosive atmospheres in mines susceptible to firedamp. The Commission also proposed, on 27 November, making adjustments to Directive 89/655/EEC concerning the minimum safety and health requirements for the use of work equipment by workers, so as to provide better coverage of problems connected with falls (Table II).

132.   The Advisory Committee on Safety, Hygiene and Health Protection at Work published its 22nd annual report [4] and delivered opinions in the fields of standardisation, training and socioeconomic appraisal. The Safety and Health Commission for the Mining and Other Extractive Industries organised two workshops, one focusing on safety and health in quarries and the other dealing with safety and health in the extractive industries. The activities of the Senior Labour Inspectors Committee

---

[1]   OJ C 142, 7.5.1998; Bull. 4-1998, point 1.2.15.
[2]   Directive 98/65/EC (OJ L 257, 19.9.1998).
[3]   OJ L 59, 2.3.1982; Sixteenth General Report, point 328.
[4]   COM(1998) 522.

included the organisation of topic sessions devoted to inspection practices, priorities and methods, and risk assessment.

133.   On 3 September, the Commission adopted a mid-term report ([1]) on the Community programme concerning safety, hygiene and health at work (1996-2000) ([2]).

Social dialogue

134.   On 20 May, the Commission adopted a communication on adapting and promoting the social dialogue at Community level ([3]). With the aim of strengthening the social dialogue at European level, making it more flexible and involving the social partners more closely in the development and implementation of Community policies, the Commission envisages a series of measures entailing information, consultation, employment partnership and negotiation. This approach was endorsed by Parliament on 18 November ([4]). In the same vein, the Commission put forward a proposal, on 20 May, for amending Decision 70/532/EEC setting up the Standing Committee on Employment (Table II).

135.   At cross-industry level, the Social Dialogue Committee met on five occasions in 1998, with the social partners' contribution to the European employment strategy being its main preoccupation. It also examined the Commission communication on the social dialogue *(→ point 134)*, the 1998-2000 social action programme *(→ point 106)*, and the issues of demography and competitiveness. As announced at the 1997 Social Dialogue Summit ([5]), the social partners entered into negotiations for a new agreement on fixed-term contracts. They also organised a seminar on working time, in July, and submitted a contribution to the Vienna European Council dealing mainly with the economic situation and the guidelines for employment, and incorporating a code of good practice for the integration of people with disabilities into the labour market. At the Social Dialogue Summit in Vienna on 4 December ([6]), the social partners discussed their contribution to the 'adaptability' pillar of the employment strategy in the light of the Commission communication on work organisation *(→ point 126)*.

([1])   COM(1998) 511.
([2])   COM(95) 282; 1995 General Report, point 619.
([3])   COM(1998) 322; Bull. 5-1998, point 1.2.23.
([4])   OJ C 379, 7.12.1998; Bull. 11-1998, point 1.2.21.
([5])   1997 General Report, point 164.
([6])   Bull. 12-1998.

136. At sectoral level, the charter on the employment of children in the footwear sector ([1]) was extended to the distributive trade sector, and the social partners in the textile and clothing sector carried out an initial appraisal of the code of conduct adopted in 1997 ([1]).

Implementation of the protocol on social policy

137. In line with the United Kingdom's decision, taken at the Amsterdam European Council ([2]), to accept directives based on the protocol on social policy, Directive 97/81/EC on part-time work and Directive 97/80/EC on the burden of proof in cases of discrimination based on sex were extended to the UK on 7 April and 13 July respectively (Table II). Welcoming the framework agreement which forms the basis of the directive on part-time work, the Committee of the Regions, in an opinion delivered on 12 March, called on the social partners to extend the agreement to other forms of atypical work ([3]).

138. Following the first round of social partner consultation resulting from the White Paper on sectors and activities excluded from the working time directive ([4]), which was, moreover, the subject of an Economic and Social Committee opinion delivered on 26 March ([5]) and of a Parliament resolution adopted on 2 July ([6]), the Commission decided, on 31 March, to initiate the second stage of consultation ([7]). Negotiations were opened in most of the sectors concerned and the social partners reached agreement, in June, in the railway sector and, in September, in the maritime sector, but failed to reach agreement in the road sector. On 18 November, the Commission adopted a communication ([8]), four proposals for directives (Table II), and a recommendation ([9]), focusing on the working time of all workers in the excluded sectors.

139. With UNICE having declined, at the end of the consultation process launched in 1997 ([10]), to negotiate on employee information and consultation, the Commission adopted, on 11 November, a proposal for

---

([1]) 1997 General Report, point 166.
([2]) 1997 General Report, point 168.
([3]) OJ C 180, 11.6.1998; Bull. 3-1998, point 1.2.20.
([4]) COM(97) 334; 1997 General Report, point 159.
([5]) OJ C 157, 25.5.1998; Bull. 3-1998, point 1.2.19.
([6]) OJ C 292, 21.9.1998; Bull. 7/8-1998, point 1.3.17.
([7]) Bull. 3-1998, point 1.2.18.
([8]) COM(1998) 662; Bull. 11-1998, point 1.2.19.
([9]) Bull. 11-1998, point 1.2.19.
([10]) 1997 General Report, point 170.

a directive aimed at establishing a general framework for such information and consultation within the Community (Table II).

Measures to promote social integration

140. The second European forum on social policy ([1]) took place in Brussels from 24 to 26 June, bringing together more than 1 300 representatives of non-governmental, national and international organisations, trade unions, employers' associations, governments and EU institutions. In this connection, an 'open forum' for dialogue and exchanges of information and good practice was organised by the platform of social non-governmental organisations and the European Trade Union Confederation.

141. On 20 January, the Commission adopted a report ([2]) on the evaluation of the third Community action programme to assist people with disabilities ([3]), which was endorsed by Parliament on 15 December ([4]). Moreover, on 18 November, Parliament adopted a resolution on sign language ([5]). The Council meanwhile adopted, on 4 June, Recommendation 98/376/EC ([6]) aimed at introducing a standardised model of parking card for people with disabilities, recognised in all the Member States. The Economic and Social Committee, for its part, in an opinion delivered on 1 July, drew attention to the costs of poverty and social exclusion ([7]).

142. On 16 December, the Commission proposed that a Community action programme be implemented with the aim of fostering the integration of refugees in the Member States (Table II).

Structural operations

143. On 22 June, the Commission presented its 1996/97 activity report concerning readaptation aid for workers in the coal and steel industries (Article 56 of the ECSC Treaty). The distribution by Member State and

---

([1])   First forum: 1996 General Report, point 559.
([2])   COM(1998) 15; Bull. 1/2-1998, point 1.3.21.
([3])   Decision 93/136/EEC (OJ L 56, 9.3.1993; Twenty-seventh General Report, point 602).
([4])   Bull. 12-1998.
([5])   OJ C 379, 7.12.1998; Bull. 11-1998, point 1.2.23.
([6])   OJ L 167, 12.6.1998; Bull. 6-1998, point 1.3.19.
([7])   OJ C 284, 14.9.1998; Bull. 7/8-1998, point 1.3.20.

by sector of funds granted in 1998 in terms of such aid is set out in Table 3.

TABLE 3

Readaptation aid — Appropriations committed (1998 programmes)

| Member State | Steelmaking and iron-ore mining | | Coalmining | | | |
| | Traditional aid | | Traditional aid | | Social measures | |
	Number of workers	Amount (ECU)	Number of workers	Amount (ECU)	Number of workers	Amount (ECU)
Belgium	991	2 973 000				
Denmark						
Germany	2 113	6 339 000	6 019	16 207 345	2 770	11 080 000
Greece	1	3 000				
Spain	847	1 967 610	2 655	7 965 000	2 655	10 552 000
France			1 248	3 744 000	1 162	3 962 000
Ireland						
Italy	390	1 170 000				
Luxembourg	260	780 000				
Netherlands						
Austria						
Portugal	245	735 000				
Finland						
Sweden						
United Kingdom	5	15 000	500	1 250 000	500	1 250 000
Total	4 852	13 982 610	10 422	29 166 345	7 087	26 844 000

European Foundation for the Improvement of Living and Working Conditions

144. In 1998, the Foundation coordinated research in the six priority areas (employment, equal opportunities, health and well-being, sustainable development, social cohesion, participation) identified in its four-year programme (1997-2000) [1], organised conferences, seminars and workshops in support of the research programme, published various reports and participated in several international conferences.

---

[1]   1996 General Report, point 586.

International cooperation

145.   As part of the pre-accession strategy, the Commission organised, from 14 to 16 September in Riga (Latvia), a conference on the coordination of social security systems, with the aim of making the authorities of the applicant central European countries more aware of the realities of applying Community law in the social security field.

146.   Various events were organised in connection with the declaration of intent signed in May 1996 with the United States (¹) (symposiums on codes of conduct and international labour standards, held in Brussels in February, and in Washington in December; workshop on work organisation, held in Brussels in June; conference on health and safety at work, held in Luxembourg in October; conference on the role of the information society in the employment of people with disabilities, held in Madrid in October); also, as part of the action plan launched with Canada in December 1996 (²), a conference on the 'transition towards a society of knowledge' was held in Vancouver in November. The annual tripartite conference with Japan took place in Brussels on 15 and 16 January, on the theme of 'equal opportunities for women and men'.

147.   Cooperation with international organisations was also continued. From 2 to 18 June, the Commission participated in the International Labour Organisation's conference, which resulted in the adoption of a declaration on fundamental principles and rights at work; a draft convention on the worst forms of child labour was also examined during the conference.

(¹)   1996 General Report, point 587.
(²)   1996 General Report, point 895.

Section 4

Internal market

Priority activities and objectives

148.   Considerable progress has been achieved in 1998 in relation to the four strategic objectives set out in the action plan for the single market: making the legislation more effective, removing key market distortions, removing sectoral obstacles to market integration, and delivering a single market for the benefit of all citizens. The most striking developments took place in the fields of taxation, where all the measures laid down in 1997 to combat harmful tax competition were implemented, intellectual property, with the adoption by the European Parliament and the Council of directives on the legal protection of biotechnological inventions and designs and the adoption by the Commission of a Green Paper on combating counterfeiting and piracy, and financial services, with the presentation by the Commission of an overall framework of measures and a number of legislative initiatives.

Implementation of the action plan for the single market

149.   Under the action plan for the single market adopted in 1997 ([1]), the Commission published, in May and November, a single market scoreboard, which seeks to provide an overall view of progress on the implementation of the action plan, the transposition of directives into national law, the application of the legislation, the economic integration of the single market, and the problems encountered. In December the European Parliament ([2]) and the European Council ([2]) welcomed this initiative and urged the Member States to make further efforts to transpose Community legislation into national law. On 9 September ([3]) the Economic and Social Committee welcomed the May edition and asked the Commission to continue issuing this publication beyond 1999. On 25 March it had also adopted an additional opinion ([4]) on the Commission's action plan.

---

[1]   ESC(97) 1; 1997 General Report, point 180.
[2]   Bull. 12-1998.
[3]   OJ C 407, 28.12.1998; Bull. 9-1998, point 1.2.13.
[4]   OJ C 157, 25.5.1998; Bull. 3-1998, point 1.2.25.

150.   On 24 September (¹), following a Commission communication of 13 May entitled 'Making single market rules more effective' (²), the Council asked the Member States to attach the highest priority to the effective and complete transposition of single market legislation within the deadlines set.

151.   Following the Commission report on the second phase of the SLIM initiative for simplifying legislation for the internal market (³), the European Parliament, in February (⁴), and the Cardiff European Council, in June (⁵), urged the Commission to extend the scope of this initiative.

152.   As part of the new service 'Europe direct' *(→ point 1152)* a new programme entitled 'Dialogue with citizens and business' was launched in June at the Cardiff European Council, in order to increase awareness of the opportunities offered by the single market and at the same time to identify any gaps in it.

153.   In a communication adopted on 30 March (⁶), the Commission presented a pilot project for setting up a business test panel. By directly consulting the firms on the panel on certain legislative proposals, the Commission wishes to improve its information about the administrative charges and adjustment costs which may be incurred as a result of these proposals. The first consultation of the business test panel concerned the proposal on tax representatives *(→ point 188).*

154.   On 7 April the European Parliament and the Council decided to extend until 31 December 1999 the action plan for the exchange between Member States' administrations of national civil servants responsible for applying the Community legislation necessary for achieving the internal market (Karolus programme), and to open this programme to the associated countries of central Europe, the EFTA countries belonging to the EEA, and Cyprus (Table I). On 22 June they also set up a three-year action programme which seeks, by encouraging training and information projects for the legal professions, to improve the application of the rules of Community law (Robert Schuman project) (Table I).

(¹)   Bull. 9-1998, point 1.2.14.
(²)   COM(1998) 296; Bull. 5-1998, point 1.2.28.
(³)   1996 General Report, point 106; 1997 General Report, point 183.
(⁴)   OJ C 80, 16.3.1998; Bull. 1/2-1998, point 1.3.22.
(⁵)   Bull. 6-1998, point I.8. 24.
(⁶)   COM(1998) 197; Bull. 3-1998, point 1.2.23.

155.   On 23 September the Commission adopted a communication on the 'Euro-Mediterranean partnership and the single market' (¹), which was approved by the Council on 7 December (²) and contains an action programme for the European Union's Mediterranean partners, concerning training, technical assistance, consultancy and cooperation and covering the various aspects of the single market (customs and taxation, elimination of technical barriers to trade, intellectual property, financial services, data protection, accounting and auditing, and competition).

Free movement of goods

156.   On 7 December the Council adopted a resolution on the free movement of goods (²) and a regulation establishing a Commission intervention mechanism, based on an early-warning system, for eliminating certain barriers to trade (Table II). In an own-initiative opinion of 25 March, the Economic and Social Committee had drawn attention to the risks of new barriers to trade resulting from the adoption by the Member States of new regulations in fields already harmonised (³).

Application of Articles 30 to 36 of the EC Treaty

157.   The Commission continued to monitor compliance with Articles 30, 34 and 36 of the EC Treaty, which concern the elimination of restrictions on imports between Member States. At 31 December there were 313 outstanding cases of infringement, and 167 new complaints were lodged in 1998.

Technical aspects

158.   On 22 June the European Parliament and the Council adopted Directive 98/34/EC (⁴), which provides for an information procedure in the field of technical standards and regulations (Table I) and codifies Directive 83/189/EEC and its successive amendments. Later, on 20 July, they adopted Directive 98/48/EC, which extends the field of application of Directive 98/34/EC to the rules on information society services

---

(¹)   COM(1998) 538; Bull. 9-1998, point 1.2.35.
(²)   Bull. 12-1998.
(³)   OJ C 157, 25.5.1998; Bull. 3-1998, point 1.2.24.
(⁴)   The Commission has published in all the Community languages an explanatory leaflet on this procedure (Luxembourg, Office for Official Publications of the European Communities, ISBN 92-828-2786-0).

(Table I). On 30 March the Council had stressed the need to improve the application of the principle of mutual recognition by taking account, in particular, of experience of the operation of Directive 83/189/EEC ([1]).

159. In application of Directive 83/189/EEC and subsequently of Directive 98/34/EC, the Commission received in 1998 604 notifications of draft technical regulations, bringing the total number of notifications received since the entry into force of Directive 83/189/EEC to 5 455. It sent detailed opinions in 54 cases ([2]) on account of infringements of Community law which the drafts under consideration were likely to cause. The Member States sent such opinions in 89 cases ([2]). Furthermore, the number of notifications under the information procedure on technical regulations provided for by the Agreement on the European Economic Area (EEA) rose from 12 in 1997 to 37 in 1998. For its part, the Commission sent, on behalf of the Community, a total of 10 observations ([3]) to EFTA countries which are signatories to the EEA Agreement. This same procedure also applies informally to Switzerland. The number of notifications from that country fell from 20 in 1997 to 13 in 1998. The Commission sent it, on behalf of the Community, 5 observations. Further information on Community activities on standardisation can be found in Section 6 ('Industrial policy') of this chapter *(→ points 235 and 236).*

160. In the chemicals sector, the European Parliament and the Council adopted on 16 February, a directive on the marketing of biocidal products (Table I), and on 22 December, an extension until 31 December 2001 of the exemption granted to Austria, Finland and Sweden regarding the marketing of fertiliser containing cadmium (Table I). The Council adopted common positions on 13 October on this latter proposal, on 24 September on a proposal to recast the legislation on the classification, packaging and labelling of dangerous preparations (Table I) and on 14 December on a proposal to amend Directive 76/769/EEC relating to restrictions on the marketing and use of certain dangerous substances and preparations (Table I). On 23 January, the Commission proposed a more stringent surveillance system for the manufacture and marketing of drug precursors (Table I).

---

[1]   Bull. 3-1998, point 1.2.26.
[2]   Figure at 1 January 1999. The time limit for issuing detailed opinions on projects notified in 1998 is 31 March 1999.
[3]   Figure at 1 January 1999. The time limit for issuing observations on projects notified in 1998 is 31 March 1999.

161.   In the medicinal products sector, the Commission published on 22 July an interpretative communication (¹) concerning Community marketing authorisation procedures (²) and adopted on 25 November a communication on the single market in medicinal products (³). On 27 July it also adopted a proposal for a regulation on orphan drugs (medicinal products for treating rare diseases) (Table I). On 14 December the Council adopted a regulation laying down the structure and the amounts of the fees payable to the European Agency for the Evaluation of Medicinal Products (Table II). In conclusions adopted on 18 May, it also laid down general guidelines for Community policy on pharmaceutical products (⁴). On 5 November, the European Parliament adopted a resolution (⁵) on the report (⁶) presented in 1997 by the Commission on homeopathic medicines.

162.   On 27 October the European Parliament and the Council adopted Directive 98/79/EC on *in vitro* diagnostic medical devices (Table I).

163.   In the cosmetics sector, the Commission amended, on 5 March, the Annex to Directive 76/768/EEC (⁷) in order to prohibit the incorporation into these products of materials likely to involve risks of transmissible spongiform encephalopathies.

164.   In the foodstuffs sector, the European Parliament and the Council adopted on 15 October, Directive 98/72/EC amending Directive 95/2/EC concerning food additives other than colorants and sweeteners (Table I). On 8 December they also arrived at an agreement on proposals for directives on foodstuffs treated by ionisation (Table I) and on coffee and chicory extracts (Table I). On 10 March the European Parliament also adopted a resolution (⁸) on the Commission's Green Paper on the general principles of food law in the European Union (⁹). The Council adopted, on 26 May, Regulation (EC) No 1139/98, which lays down Community rules for the labelling and presentation of foodstuffs produced from genetically modified organisms (Table II) and, on 17 December, a common position on a proposal for a directive to extend the

---

(¹)   OJ C 229, 22.7.1998.
(²)   Regulation (EEC) No 2309/93 and Council Directives 93/39/EEC, 93/40/EEC and 93/41/EEC (OJ L 214, 24.8.1993; Twenty-seventh General Report, point 77).
(³)   COM(1998) 588; Bull. 11-1998, point 1.2.31.
(⁴)   Bull. 5-1998, point 1.2.38.
(⁵)   OJ C 359, 23.11.1998; Bull. 11-1998, point 1.2.30.
(⁶)   COM(97) 362.
(⁷)   OJ L 77, 14.3.1998.
(⁸)   OJ C 104, 6.4.1998; Bull. 3-1998, point 1.2.27.
(⁹)   COM(97) 176; 1997 General Report, point 191.

coverage of Directive 85/374/EEC on *de facto* liability for defective products to agricultural raw materials and hunting products (Table II).

165. In the motor vehicle sector, the European Parliament and the Council adopted on 14 December a directive harmonising the type-approval of vehicles intended for the transport of dangerous goods by road (Table I). The Commission adopted proposals for directives on the following: on 2 April, the interior fittings of motor vehicles (Table I); on 23 April, liquid fuel tanks and rear protective devices for motor vehicles (Table I); on 20 May, speedometers for two- or three-wheel motor vehicles (Table I); and, on 28 September, heating systems for the passenger compartment of motor vehicles (Table I).

166. On 22 June the European Parliament and the Council adopted a codified version of the directive on machinery (Table I).

Veterinary and plant-health fields

167. Activities in the veterinary and plant-protection fields are dealt with in Section 20 ('Agricultural policy') of this chapter *(→ points 563 to 569)*.

Customs

168. Activities relating to the operation of the customs union are dealt with in Section 3 ('Common commercial policy') of Chapter V *(→ points 715 to 718)*.

Free movement of persons

Abolition of controls at internal frontiers, right of entry and right of residence

169. Activities relating to the abolition of controls at internal frontiers and to rights of entry and rights of residence are dealt with in Section 1 ('Rights of free movement and residence') of Chapter II *(→ point 18)*.

Right of establishment, mutual recognition of qualifications

170. In order to facilitate the permanent exercise of the profession of lawyer in a Member State other than that in which the qualification was acquired, the European Parliament and the Council adopted on 16 February Directive 98/5/EC, which provides in particular for establishment under the original professional title and the replacement of the aptitude test by a more flexible verification of professional qualifications (Table I). On 29 June the Council also adopted a common position on the proposal for a directive, presented by the Commission in 1996, on the recognition of diplomas in the craft, distributive trade and services sectors (Table I). On 13 March ([1]) the European Parliament stated its position on the review of Directive 85/384/EEC on the mutual recognition of qualifications in architecture ([2]). On 27 May the Economic and Social Committee adopted an own-initiative opinion on freedom to set up a business in the single market ([3]).

Free movement of workers

171. Activities relating to the free movement of workers are dealt with in Section 3 ('Employment and social policy') of this chapter *(→ points 123 to 125)*.

Freedom to provide services

Financial services

172. Further to the request of the Cardiff European Council ([4]), the Commission adopted on 28 October a communication ([5]) setting out an overall framework for action in the field of financial services to enable this sector to fully realise its potential in the context of the introduction of the euro. In December the Vienna European Council welcomed this initiative ([6]).

([1])   OJ C 104, 6.4.1998; Bull. 3-1998, point 1.2.33.
([2])   OJ L 223, 21.8.1985; Nineteenth General Report, point 285.
([3])   OJ C 235, 27.7.1998; Bull. 5-1998, point 1.2.29.
([4])   Bull. 6-1998, point I.7.
([5])   COM(1998) 625; Bull. 10-1998, point 1.2.27.
([6])   Bull. 12-1998.

173. As part of the follow-up to its communication 'Financial services: Enhancing consumer confidence' ([1]), the Commission adopted on 21 September two proposals for directives (Table I) to define a regulatory framework for electronic money, in particular by harmonising the conditions for authorising establishments issuing such money and the prudential requirements applicable to them. On 1 July it also adopted a framework for action, which included a proposal for common action to combat fraud and counterfeiting concerning means of payment other than cash *(→ point 973).* Its 1997 communication on electronic means of payment ([2]) was also the subject of an opinion of the Economic and Social Committee on 28 January ([3]), and of a European Parliament resolution on 20 February ([4]).

174. On 14 October the Commission adopted a proposal for a directive establishing a regulatory framework for the distance selling of financial services within the single market (Table I). The purpose of this proposal is to guarantee the consumer a high level of protection regarding retail financial services sold by telephone, by electronic mail or by courier while offering suppliers of financial services a clear legal framework in this field. On 17 July the Commission also adopted two proposals for directives on institutions for collective investment in transferable securities (Table I), which are intended to remove the existing barriers to the activities of such bodies while guaranteeing a high level of protection for investors.

175. On 19 May, the European Parliament and the Council adopted Directive 98/26/EC (Table I), which aims to reduce the systemic risks inherent in payment and securities settlement systems and to limit the perturbations caused by the insolvency of a participant in such a system. On 22 June they also adopted Directives 98/31/EC, 98/32/EC and 98/33/EC (Table I), which provide, respectively, for: incorporating into Directive 93/6/EEC on the capital adequacy of investment companies and credit institutions more precise capital requirements for the market risks to which such bodies are exposed; enabling all the Member States to apply a risk weighting of 50 % instead of 100 % under Directive 89/647/EEC on a solvency ratio for credit institutions; and introducing more precise and more realistic prudential requirements with regard, in particular, to over-the-counter derivatives.

---

[1]   COM(97) 309; 1997 General Report, point 201.
[2]   COM(97) 353; 1997 General Report, point 204.
[3]   OJ C 95, 30.3.1998; Bull. 1/2-1998, point 1.3.43.
[4]   OJ C 80, 16.3.1998; Bull. 1/2-1998, point 1.3.42.

176.   The application of Directive 91/308/EEC on prevention of the use of the financial system for money laundering was the subject of a Commission report on 1 July([1]). In its resolution of 12 May([2]), the European Parliament examined the Commission's interpretative communication on freedom to provide services and the interest of the general good in the second banking directive([3]).

177.   On 22 October([4]) and 9 September([5]) respectively, the European Parliament and the Economic and Social Committee delivered their opinions on the Commission's draft interpretative communication([6]) on freedom to provide services and interest of the general good in the insurance sector. On 29 October the European Parliament and the Council adopted Directive 98/78/EC on the supplementary supervision of insurance undertakings in an insurance group (Table I), with the main aim of preventing insurance groups from evading the solvency requirements imposed by the existing directives. Furthermore, on 3 December the Commission's White Paper on supplementary pensions in the single market([7]) was the subject of a European Parliament resolution([8]) On 29 January, the Economic and Social Committee adopted an own-initiative opinion entitled 'Consumers in the insurance market'([9]).

Other services

178.   In a communication adopted on 4 March([10]), the Commission presented a set of follow-up measures to its Green Paper on commercial communications in the internal market([11]), the purpose of which is to facilitate the cross-border provision of such services while appropriately protecting the public-interest objectives pursued. This communication was adopted by the Council on 18 May([12]).

179.   On 20 November the European Parliament and the Council adopted Directive 98/84/EC on the legal protection of conditional-access services (Table I). This directive requires the Member States to prohibit,

---

([1])   COM(1998) 401; Bull. 7/8-1998, point 1.3.28.
([2])   OJ C 167, 1.6.1998; Bull. 5-1998, point 1.2.45.
([3])   OJ C 209, 10.7.1997; Bull. 6-1997, point 1.3.53.
([4])   OJ C 341, 9.11.1998; Bull. 10-1998, point 1.2.30.
([5])   OJ C 407, 28.12.1998; Bull. 9-1998, point 1.2.24.
([6])   1997 General Report, point 206.
([7])   COM(97) 283; 1997 General Report, point 207.
([8])   OJ C 398, 21.12.1998; Bull. 12-1998.
([9])   OJ C 95, 30.3.1998; Bull. 1/2-1998, point 1.3.47.
([10]) COM(1998) 121; Bull. 3-1998, point 1.2.39.
([11]) COM(96) 192; 1996 General Report, point 133.
([12]) Bull. 5-1998, point 1.2.46.

and apply appropriate sanctions to, all commercial activities involving unauthorised access to a protected service, such as the sale of decoders, smart cards or pirate software, without, however, invoking the fight against piracy to restrict the free movement of services and legitimate conditional-access devices originating in another Member State.

180. Information on electronic commerce can be found in Section 16 ('Information society and telecommunications') of this chapter *(→ point 461).*

Free movement of capital and financial integration

181. The free movement of capital and payments has for the most part already been achieved, and the Commission ensures that the few restrictions which continue to appear are rapidly removed. Most of the small number of complaints received in this connection from economic operators concern barriers to the acquisition of real estate in other Member States. The Commission sent the Member States a questionnaire on the legal aspects of the intra-Community investment referred to in its communication of July 1997 (¹), as a result of which full information was collected on the legal provisions on such investments and on the privatisation of companies previously under State control. In addition, a gradual reduction in the obstacles to capital movements and payments was noted in the countries which have applied for accession to the European Union.

Taxation

182. On the basis of a communication (²) setting out a strategy for the better functioning of mutual assistance on recovery of taxes, the Commission put forward a proposal on 25 June (Table I) to amend Directive 76/308/EEC on such mutual assistance in order to (a) extend its field of application to direct taxes and (b) to combat fraud.

Direct taxation

183. The three components of the range of measures presented by the Commission and approved by the Council in 1997 to tackle harmful tax

---

(¹)   OJ C 220, 19.7.1997; 1997 General Report, point 210.
(²)   COM(1998) 364; Bull. 6-1998, point 1.3.32.

competition (¹) were implemented in 1998. On 9 March (²) the Council decided to set up a group of representatives of the Member States and the Commission to assess the tax measures likely to fall within the field of application of the code of conduct for business taxation (³), while on 4 March the Commission adopted a proposal for a directive (Table II) on a common tax system applicable to payments of interest and duties between associated companies in different Member States, in order to abolish taxes deducted at source on payments of interest and duties between associated companies in different Member States, and, on 20 May, a proposal for a directive (Table II) for guaranteeing minimum effective taxation of savings income in the form of interest within the Community, by allowing the Member States to opt either for applying a deduction at source of at least 20 % in the case of natural persons residing in other countries of the Union or for communicating the information on such payments to the Member States in which the beneficiaries are resident for tax purposes.

184. The European Council reaffirmed in June in Cardiff (⁴) and in December in Vienna (⁵) its determination to put an end to harmful tax competition (⁴). At the Vienna meeting it also came out in favour of reinforced cooperation on tax matters. On 18 June the European Parliament recommended that the measures for tackling harmful tax competition be extended to cover new areas (⁶). On 25 November the Commission adopted a first annual report on the implementation of the measures for tackling such competition (⁷).

185. On 1 December the Council adopted conclusions on the external dimension of taxation of savings (⁵).

Indirect taxation

186. On 30 March the European Parliament and the Council adopted an action programme ('Fiscalis') to improve, by exchanging information and coordinating the training of the civil servants concerned, the practical application of the systems of indirect taxation in the internal market (Table I).

(¹) 1997 General Report, point 211.
(²) Bull. 3-1998, point 1.2.46.
(³) OJ C 2, 6.1.1998; 1997 General Report, point 211.
(⁴) Bull. 6-1998, point I.7.
(⁵) Bull. 12-1998.
(⁶) OJ C 210, 6.7.1998; Bull. 6-1998, point 1.3.31.
(⁷) COM(1998) 595; Bull. 11-1998, point 1.2.36.

187.   In the context of the SLIM initiative *(→ point 151),* the Commission put forward a proposal on 17 June to simplify the VAT system by replacing the Community reimbursement procedures by the possibility for taxable persons to deduct from their periodical declarations the tax they have paid in a Member State other than that in which they are established (Table II). This proposal for a directive, which also provides for restrictions on the right to deduct tax in order to reduce the disparities in the rules applicable in the Community, particularly with regard to private cars, is accompanied by a proposal for a regulation (Table II) to set up a system of bilateral compensation of claims between Member States and to introduce appropriate supervisory measures.

188.   On 27 November, also as part of the implementation of the SLIM recommendations, the Commission proposed an amendment to the rules applicable to tax representation with regard to VAT, so as to cut down the number of cases in which the Member States can oblige a taxpayer to appoint a tax representative (Table II).

189.   On 12 October the Council adopted a directive supplementing the Community VAT system with regard to the special system applicable to investment gold (Table II). On 30 November the Commission proposed that limits be set on the range of the normal VAT rate (Table II). Following the Commission's 1997 report [1], the European Parliament had, on 17 September, stated its position on the structure of reduced VAT rates [2].

190.   On 17 June the Commission adopted a communication entitled 'Electronic commerce and indirect taxation' [3], which contains guidelines for ensuring the certainty, simplicity and neutrality of the Community VAT system with regard to electronic commerce, with a view to promoting its growth. This communication was endorsed by the Council on 6 July [4] and by the Economic and Social Committee on 9 September [5].

191.   The Commission also put forward the following proposals: on 10 February, to simplify the tax treatment of private motor vehicles transferred definitively to or used temporarily in a Member State other than that in which they are registered (Table II); on 15 May, to make tech-

---

[1]   COM(97) 559; 1997 General Report, point 214.
[2]   OJ C 313, 12.10.1998; Bull. 9-1998, point 1.2.28.
[3]   COM(1998) 374; Bull. 6-1998, point 1.3.30.
[4]   Bull. 7/8-1998, point 1.3.32.
[5]   OJ C 377, 2.12.1998; Bull. 9-1998, point 1.2.31.

nical adjustments to the tax system for tobacco products (Table II); and, on 16 December, to extend certain exemptions regarding reductions in the excise rates on mineral oils (Table II). On 29 April it also presented a communication on measures to combat excise duty fraud (→ *point 1014*).

192.   The abolition of duty-free sales with effect from 1 January 1999 was the subject of two European Parliament resolutions, on 3 April [1] and 12 July [2], of an own-initiative opinion of the Committee of the Regions, on 16 September [3], and of conclusions by the Vienna European Council in December [4]. In addition, on 14 December the Council adopted a directive and a regulation granting Germany and Austria exemptions until 31 December 2002 regarding the flat-rate amounts of the customs franchises (Table II).

Company law

193.   Following its Green Paper on the role, the position and the liability of the statutory auditor within the European Union [5], which was the subject of a European Parliament resolution [6] on 15 January, the Commission set out, in a communication adopted on 7 May, the broad lines of a work programme in this area, the main areas of which concern reviews of auditing standards, audit quality control systems and rules on the independence of statutory auditors [7]. On 7 January, the Commission also adopted an interpretative communication concerning certain articles of the fourth and seventh Council directives on annual and consolidated accounts [8].

Intellectual and industrial property

194.   On 15 October the Commission adopted a Green Paper on combating counterfeiting and piracy in the single market, with the aim of launching a consultation to assess the impact of counterfeiting and piracy on the European economy, the effectiveness of existing legislation

---

[1]   OJ C 138, 4.5.1998; Bull. 4-1998, point 1.2.37.
[2]   OJ C 226, 20.7.1998; Bull. 7/8-1998, point 1.3.35.
[3]   OJ C 375, 2.12.1998; Bull. 9-1998, point 1.2.32.
[4]   Bull. 12-1998.
[5]   COM(96) 338; 1996 General Report, point 141.
[6]   OJ C 34, 2.2.1998; Bull. 1/2-1998, point 1.3.48.
[7]   Bull. 4-1998, point 1.2.35.
[8]   OJ C 16, 20.1.1998; Bull. 1/2-1998, point 1.3.49.

and the need for additional measures (^{1}). The Green Paper on the Community patent and the patent system in Europe (^{2}) was the subject of an opinion of the Economic and Social Committee (^{3}) on 25 February, of a Commission information note (^{4}) on 29 July, and of a European Parliament resolution on 19 November (^{5}).

195. On 6 July the European Parliament and the Council adopted a directive on the legal protection of biotechnological inventions (Table I), with the aim of providing a stable legislative framework allowing the use of research results while taking account of the ethical aspects relating, in particular, to the protection of the human body. On 13 October they also adopted a directive on the alignment of national provisions on the legal protection of designs (Table I). On 24 April the Commission proposed that the Council approve, on behalf of the Community, the World Intellectual Property Organisation's treaties on copyright, performances and phonograms (Table III).

Data protection

196. Directive 95/46/EC on the protection of personal data (^{6}) entered into force on 25 October. Furthermore, the Council authorised the Commission to negotiate a draft recommendation of the Council of Europe on the protection of personal data collected and processed for insurance purposes (Table III), in July, and draft guidelines for the protection of persons with regard to the collection and processing of personal data on information highways (Table III), in March.

Public procurement

197. Following its 1996 Green Paper (^{7}), the Commission adopted, on 11 March, a communication entitled 'Public procurement in the European Union' (^{8}), in which it lays down the priority measures for simplifying the present system, improving implementation of the rules and developing a favourable environment for suppliers. The Council, on 18

(^{1})   COM(1998) 569; Bull. 10-1998, point 1.2.16.
(^{2})   COM(97) 314; 1997 General Report, point 220.
(^{3})   OJ C 129, 27.4.1998; Bull. 1/2-1998, point 1.3.54.
(^{4})   Bull. 7/8-1998, point 1.3.37.
(^{5})   OJ C 379, 7.12.1998; Bull. 11-1998, point 1.2.39.
(^{6})   OJ L 281, 23.11.1995; 1995 General Report, point 135.
(^{7})   COM(96) 583; 1996 General Report, point 224.
(^{8})   COM(1998) 143; Bull. 3-1998, point 1.2.42.

May (^{1}), and the Committee of the Regions, on 16 September (^{2}), endorsed this approach.

198. On 16 February, the European Parliament and the Council formally adopted Directive 98/4/EC on procedures for awarding contracts in the water, energy, transport and telecommunications sectors (Table I). On 23 April the Commission also adopted a report on access to third country public procurement in these sectors (^{3}).

(^{1}) Bull. 5-1998, point 1.2.47.
(^{2}) OJ C 373, 2.12.1998; Bull. 9-1998, point 1.2.26.
(^{3}) COM(1998) 203; Bull. 4-1998, point 1.2.36.

Section 5

Competition (¹)

Priority activities and objectives

199.   The Commission continued its drive to modernise Community competition law in 1998 with the aim of ensuring that it more closely reflected economic realities and administrative requirements. In particular, it proposed an overall review of the Community policy on vertical restraints and new procedural rules in the field of State aid. It also adopted a framework for State aid for training. With a view to ensuring that markets functioned smoothly, it continued to enforce strictly the competition rules with regard to restrictive agreements between enterprises, abuses of dominant positions and merger operations. For its part, the Council adopted a regulation empowering the Commission to adopt regulations exempting certain categories of aid and a regulation establishing new rules on aid to shipbuilding. The Community's international activity was marked by the signing of a new agreement with the United States of America.

On 15 April the Commission adopted the Twenty-seventh Report on Competition Policy (²).

Competition rules applying to businesses

200.   New cases under Articles 85 and 86 of the EC Treaty totalled 509, comprising 216 notifications, 192 complaints and 101 cases where the Commission acted on its own initiative. New cases under Articles 65 and 66 of the ECSC Treaty totalled 12. The Commission received 225 notifications and took 238 decisions under the merger regulation (Regulation (EEC) No 4064/89). Lastly, it took 10 decisions under Article 66 of the ECSC Treaty.

(¹)   Only the most significant cases are dealt with in this section. For further details, see the Twenty-eighth Report on Competition Policy (1998), to be published by the Office for Official Publications of the European Communities in mid-1999 in conjunction with this General Report. A report on the application of the competition rules in the European Union in 1998, prepared under the sole responsibility of the Directorate-General for Competition in conjunction with the Twenty-eighth Report on Competition Policy, is also available.

(²)   Bull. 4-1998, point 1.2.40.

General rules

201. Further to its Green Paper on vertical restraints in EC competition policy (¹), the Commission adopted on 30 September a communication (²) accompanied by proposals for amendments to Regulation No 17 (Table II) and Regulation 19/65/EEC (Table II) with the aim of creating conditions for the adoption of a single block exemption covering all vertical restraints between producers and distributors in respect of intermediate and final goods and in respect of services, except for a limited number of hard-core restraints. The principal objective of this block exemption is to grant companies which lack market power a safe harbour within which it is no longer necessary for them to assess the validity of their agreements in the light of the EC competition rules. The Commission advocates inclusion in the block exemption of market-share thresholds beyond which companies cannot avail themselves of this safe harbour.

202. After consulting the parties concerned by its notice of May 1997 (³), the Commission adopted on 7 January, a notice concerning the status of voice communications on the Internet viewed from the angle of competition law (⁴) in which it takes the view that these communications do not at present constitute voice telephony since they do not yet satisfy all the criteria laid down in the definition of this service in the Community directives. With a view to enhancing transparency, it also adopted on 31 March a notice on the application of the competition rules to access agreements in the telecommunications sector which spells out the principles underlying these agreements, the relationship between competition law and sector-specific legislation, and the way in which competition law is applied across the sectors involved in the provision of new telecommunications services (⁵).

Prohibited restrictive agreements

203. On 28 January, the Commission fined the car manufacturer Volkswagen ECU 102 million for prohibiting its Italian dealers from selling Volkswagen and Audi cars to foreign buyers, mainly from Germany and Austria, thereby restricting intra-Community trade (⁶).

(¹)   COM(96) 721; 1997 General Report, point 232.
(²)   COM(1998) 544; Bull. 9-1998, point 1.2.36.
(³)   1997 General Report, point 236.
(⁴)   OJ C 6, 10.1.1998; Bull. 1/2-1998, point 1.3.55.
(⁵)   Bull. 3-1998, point 1.2.50.
(⁶)   OJ L 124, 25.4.1998; Bull. 1/2-1998, point 1.3.57.

204. On 21 January, acting under Article 65 of the ECSC Treaty, the Commission prohibited a price cartel in the stainless steel sector. The six companies concerned had agreed on a concerted change in the method for calculating a price supplement known as the 'alloy surcharge', thereby contributing to a substantial increase in prices for stainless steel ([1]).

205. On 14 October, the Commission imposed fines of ECU 50.2 million on British Sugar, Tate & Lyle, Napier Brown and James Budgett for concluding pricing agreements on the white granulated sugar market. Between 1986 and 1990, the four companies, which held 90 % of the UK market, pursued a concerted strategy of higher pricing on both the industrial and retail markets. Tate & Lyle benefited from a reduced fine to take account of the fact that it had cooperated with the Commission in providing evidence ([2]).

206. On 21 October, the Commission decided to condemn a district heating pipe cartel and to fine the participants ECU 92.21 million for market sharing, price fixing and bid rigging. The cartel began in Denmark and soon extended to all the Member States ([3]).

207. On 11 March, the Commission condemned the exclusivity condition imposed by Unilever as part of its terms for supplying freezer cabinets on the Irish ice-cream market. Unilever supplied freezer cabinets to its retailers solely on the understanding that they were used exclusively for the storage of Unilever products ([4]).

208. On 16 September, the Commission condemned a number of agreements entered into under the Trans-Atlantic Conference Agreement (TACA). It found that several of these agreements, which essentially concerned price fixing, constituted restrictions on competition which were incompatible with Article 85(1) of the Treaty and that they did not qualify either for the group exemption for shipping conferences or for an individual exemption pursuant to Article 85(3). The Commission also decided to impose a fine of ECU 273 million on TACA members for abusing a dominant position ([5]).

---

[1] OJ L 100, 1.4.1998; Bull. 1/2-1998, point 1.3.58.
[2] Bull. 10-1998, point 1.2.43.
[3] Bull. 10-1998, point 1.2.45.
[4] OJ L 246, 4.9.1998; Bull. 3-1998, point 1.2.51.
[5] Bull. 9-1998, point 1.2.38.

Permissible forms of cooperation

209.   On 27 May, on completion of the first case dealt with under new Article 2(4) of Regulation (EEC) No 4064/89 (→ points 214 et seq.), the Commission authorised the creation of a joint venture between Telia, Telenor Nextel, and Schibsted Multimedia which will offer Internet services to Swedish users [1]. On 23 June it authorised the creation of a joint venture between Deutsche Telekom, France Télécom and the Enel Group which will provide a full range of telecommunications services in Italy [2]. On 8 July the Commission authorised the acquisition by British Telecom, Air Touch and Grupo Acciona of joint control over Airtel, a company active in mobile telephony in Spain [3]. These three operations will not create or strengthen a dominant position or lead to anti-competitive cooperation on the part of the parent companies.

210.   In the context of transatlantic alliances between airlines, the Commission published on 30 July a communication [4] which proposed remedies pursuant to Article 89(1) of the EC Treaty with a view to exempting the alliances agreed between British Airways and American Airlines and between Lufthansa, SAS and United Airlines. The Commission's proposals are designed to open up the routes operated by these alliances to new entrants.

Dominant positions

211.   By decision of 14 January, the Commission noted that the company operating Frankfurt airport, which has a monopoly in ramp-handling services at the airport, had abused its dominant position by prohibiting both self-handling (by airline companies themselves) and third-party handling (by denying other companies access to the ramp). It therefore ordered the company to end its monopoly [5].

212.   On 12 June, the Commission found that Aéroports de Paris had also abused its dominant position by imposing discriminatory commercial fees on service providers or airlines providing groundhandling or self-handling services such as catering, cleaning and freight handling. It therefore ordered the company to discontinue this practice [6].

---

[1]   Bull. 5-1998, point 1.2.54.
[2]   Bull. 6-1998, point 1.3.37.
[3]   Bull. 7/8-1998, point 1.3.45.
[4]   OJ C 239, 30.7.1998; Bull. 7/8-1998, point 1.3.40.
[5]   OJ L 72, 11.3.1998; Bull. 1/2-1998, point 1.3.64.
[6]   OJ L 252, 12.9.1998; Bull. 6-1998, point 1.3.38.

213.   By decision of 17 June, the Commission imposed a fine of ECU 6 million on AAMS (Amministrazione autonoma dei monopoli dello Stato) for abusing its dominant position on the Italian market for the wholesale distribution of cigarettes and ordered it to discontinue its discriminatory arrangements. AAMS protected its own cigarette production by its long-standing practice of imposing on foreign manufacturers wholesale distribution contracts containing numerous restrictive clauses which limited access to the Italian market [1].

Mergers

214.   In 1998 the Commission received 225 notifications and adopted 238 final decisions under the merger regulation (Council Regulation (EEC) No 4064/89 of 21 December 1989 on the control of concentrations between undertakings) [2]. Most of the cases were cleared at the end of the first stage of examination, lasting one month, but the Commission found it necessary to initiate the second stage of examination, lasting a further four months, in respect of 10 planned operations. In most of these cases, the Commission made its authorisation subject to conditions.

215.   Regulation (EC) No 1310/97 [3], which amends Regulation (EEC) No 4064/89, entered into force on 1 March (Table II). Fourteen cases were notified on the basis of the new thresholds provided for by this regulation. Fourteen notified cases concerned joint ventures and required the simultaneous application of the merger regulation and Article 85 of the EC Treaty.

216.   On 4 February, the Commission authorised Hoffmann-La Roche to acquire Boehringer Mannheim subject to compliance by Hoffmann-La Roche with its undertaking to divest most of its clinical chemistry *in vitro* diagnostics business and to license Roche's PCR technology [4].

217.   On 11 February, the Commission authorised the acquisition by Agfa Gevaert AG of DuPont's graphic arts business on the basis of an undertaking by Agfa to end exclusive arrangements which would have

---

[1]   Bull. 6-1998, point 1.3.39.
[2]   OJ L 395, 30.12.1989; Twenty-third General Report, point 376.
[3]   1997 General Report, point 242.
[4]   Bull. 1/2-1998, point 1.3.87.

bound the new company to equipment suppliers and distributors, notably as regards negative offset printing plates ([1]).

218. On 20 May, the Commission authorised the merger between Price Waterhouse and Coopers & Lybrand, two of the 'Big Six' auditing and accounting firms. After an investigation, it concluded that the merger would not create or strengthen a position of dominance on any of the national large company markets for audit and accounting services; large companies are dependent for such services on the Big Six since only they can provide them. The Commission carried out a two-pronged investigation from the viewpoint of both single and collective dominance ([2]).

219. By two decisions adopted on 27 May, the Commission prohibited the Bertelsmann/Kirch/Première and Deutsche Telekom/BetaResearch mergers. The purpose of these projects is the acquisition by CLT-UFA (linked to the Bertelsmann Group) and Kirch of joint control of the pay-television channel Première and of BetaDigital, which was under the sole control of Kirch, and the acquisition by CLT-UFA, Kirch and Deutsche Telekom of BetaResearch, also under the sole control of Kirch. Both operations would have created the framework for digital pay-television in Germany. Première would have achieved a monopoly position as a programme platform and as a marketing platform. At the same time, a dominant position would have been achieved by BetaDigital for technical services for pay-television and by Deutsche Telekom as regards cable transmission; Deutsche Telekom would also have strengthened its dominant position for cable networks. The commitments proposed by the parties were deemed insufficient to resolve the numerous competition problems identified ([3]).

220. On 8 July, the Commission authorised the merger between Worldcom and MCI, subject to the fulfilment of certain undertakings. The merger would have given these two telecommunications companies a combined market share of some 50 % of the market for 'top-level' or universal Internet connectivity. They agreed to divest MCI's Internet assets to an independent third party. This case was the subject of close cooperation with the US authorities ([4]).

221. On 11 November, the Commission authorised, subject to conditions, the acquisition by Skanska of Scancem, both companies being

---

([1])   Bull. 1/2-1998, point 1.3.94.
([2])   Bull. 5-1998, point 1.2.61.
([3])   Bull. 5-1998, point 1.2.64.
([4])   Bull. 7/8-1998, point 1.3.44.

active in the building materials business in Scandinavia. It concluded that the operation would reinforce the dominant position of the new company on the Swedish cement market and would create a dominant position on the markets for ready-mix concrete, dry-packed concrete and precast concrete. Skanska has undertaken to sell its stake in Scancem and to divest Scancem's cement business to an independent buyer ([1]).

State aid

General policy

222.   During the year ([2]) the Commission received 714 ([3]) notifications of new aid schemes or amendments to existing aid schemes and registered 135 ([4]) cases of unnotified aid schemes. In 568 ([5]) cases it decided not to raise any objection; in 100 ([6]) cases it decided to initiate proceedings under Article 93(2) of the EC Treaty or Article 6(4) of Decision No 3855/91/ECSC ([7]), as a result of which it took 26 ([8]) positive final decisions, 40 ([9]) negative final decisions and 11 ([10]) conditional final decisions. It decided to propose appropriate measures under Article 93(1) of the EC Treaty in respect of 5 ([11]) existing aid schemes.

223.   On 1 July, the Commission adopted its sixth survey on State aid in the European Union in manufacturing and certain other sectors ([12]). The survey covers the years from 1994 to 1996 and includes for the first time Austria, Finland and Sweden. On 18 February, the Commission adopted a proposal for a Council regulation (Table II) laying down detailed rules for the application of Article 93 of the EC Treaty which are designed to codify and clarify the procedural rules applicable to the processing of State aid. On 16 November, the Council endorsed this proposal pending a Parliament opinion. On 7 May, it adopted Regulation (EC) No 994/98 (Table II), which empowers the Commission to adopt

---

([1])　Bull. 11-1998, point 1.2.42.
([2])　For a discussion of the most significant cases, see the Twenty-eighth Report on Competition Policy.
([3])　Of which 6 in the coal industry, 44 in transport, 276 in agriculture and 46 in fisheries.
([4])　Of which 0 in the coal industry, 0 in transport, 32 in agriculture and 6 in fisheries.
([5])　Of which 3 in the coal industry, 15 in transport, 204 in agriculture and 38 in fisheries.
([6])　Of which 0 in the coal industry, 9 in transport, 25 in agriculture and 0 in fisheries.
([7])　OJ L 362, 31.12.1991; Twenty-fifth General Report, point 254.
([8])　Of which 2 in the coal industry, 3 in transport, 5 in agriculture and 0 in fisheries.
([9])　Of which 1 in the coal industry, 2 in transport, 6 in agriculture and 0 in fisheries.
([10])　Of which 0 in the coal industry, 1 in transport, 2 in agriculture and 0 in fisheries.
([11])　Of which 0 in the coal industry, 0 in transport, 2 in agriculture and 0 in fisheries.
([12])　COM(1998) 417; Bull. 7/8-1997, point 1.3.68.

block exemption regulations for certain categories of horizontal aid and for aid below a given threshold.

Horizontal aid

224. On 22 July, the Commission adopted a framework for State aid for training ([1]). The framework clarifies the circumstances in which public funding for training may be caught by the competition rules on State aid. It also sets out the criteria which the Commission will apply in ascertaining whether aid is compatible with the common market.

225. On 11 November, the Commission adopted a notice on the application of the State aid rules to measures relating to direct business taxation ([2]), in which it sets out the criteria it will apply when examining or reviewing Member States' tax arrangements.

Industry schemes

226. On 29 June, the Council adopted Regulation (EC) No 1540/98, which establishes new rules on aid to shipbuilding (Table II). This regulation, which replaces Directive 90/684/EEC ([3]) with effect from 1 January 1999, is designed to make shipbuilding subject to arrangements similar to those for other industries, among other things by prohibiting contract-related operating aid with effect from 31 December 2000. On 21 January, the Commission adopted an initial report on the monitoring of restructuring programmes for shipyards in Germany and Spain ([4]).

227. On 8 May, the Commission adopted a mid-term report (1994-97) ([5]) on the application of Community rules for State aid of the Member States to the coal industry ([6]). On 24 March, it also adopted a report on the application of those rules in France, Germany, Portugal, Spain and the United Kingdom in 1995 ([7]).

([1]) Bull. 7/8-1998, point 1.3.70.
([2]) Bull. 11-1998, point 1.2.49.
([3]) OJ L 380, 31.12.1990; Twenty-fourth General Report, point 205.
([4]) SEC(1998) 71.
([5]) COM(1998) 288; Bull. 5-1998, point 1.2.123.
([6]) Decision No 3632/93/ECSC (OJ L 329, 31.12.1993; Twenty-seventh General Report, point 288).
([7]) Bull. 3-1998, point 1.2.109.

228.   In response to a request from the Amsterdam European Council ([1]), the Commission adopted on 17 June a report on services of general economic interest in the banking sector ([2]) pursuant to which it will in future apply Article 90(2) of the EC Treaty to the sector on a case-by-case basis.

Regional schemes

229.   The new multisectoral framework adopted in 1997 ([3]) came into force on 1 September. In addition, as part of the implementation of the guidelines on national regional aid ([4]), the Commission updated the national ceilings for aid coverage in December using the latest figures ([5]). In February, it had proposed appropriate measures to the Member States in order to set an expiry date of 31 December 1999 for the current maps of regions eligible for regional aid with a view to harmonising that date and aligning it on that for the Structural Funds and in order to amend, where appropriate, the existing schemes expiring after 31 December 1999 so as to bring them into line with the new rules. These measures were accepted by all the Member States.

International cooperation

230.   The agreement with the United States of America regarding the consolidated application of positive comity principles ([6]) was signed on 3 and 4 June and entered into force on 4 June (Table III). The Commission proposed, also on 4 June, that a draft agreement be concluded with Canada concerning the application of competition law (Table III). This draft agreement lays down arrangements for cooperation in the field between the two partners and contains provisions on positive comity.

---

[1]   Bull. 6-1997, point I.3.
[2]   SEC(1998) 835.
[3]   1997 General Report, point 264.
[4]   1997 General Report, point 265.
[5]   Bull. 12-1998.
[6]   1997 General Report, point 266.

Section 6

Industrial policy

Priority activities and objectives

231.   In 1998 the Commission continued to analyse the key factors in the competitiveness of European industry and implement the measures announced in its communications on the benchmarking of competitive performance. It also launched an initiative designed to enable business services to make a greater contribution to industrial efficiency. Last but not least, it attached particular importance to taking the environment into account in industrial policy and, in this connection, adopted a communication on the competitiveness of the recycling industries.

Industrial competitiveness

General

232.   To follow up its communication on the benchmarking of competitive performance (¹), the Commission worked jointly with Member States on four pilot projects on the benchmarking of framework conditions in the areas of financing innovation (lead country: Denmark), new technologies and organisational change (lead country: Finland), logistics (lead country: Ireland) and skills (lead country: Spain). On 16 November, the Council approved the results of these projects and called on the Commission to submit proposals for wider use of benchmarking (²). In preparation for the Council's discussions on competitiveness on 16 November, the Commission presented a report on the competitiveness of European industry in 1998 (³).

233.   On 14 May, the European Parliament adopted a resolution on the competitiveness of European industry calling, in particular, for measures to improve the underlying conditions for companies, for the creation of European structures capable of bringing industrial partners together in

---

(¹)   COM(97) 153; 1997 General Report, point 268.
(²)   Bull. 11-1998, point 1.2.66.
(³)   Document available from the Office for Official Publications of the European Communities.

major research cooperation projects and for adoption of the European
company statute (¹).

International industrial cooperation

234. The Commission continued to promote international industrial
cooperation in accordance with the principles set out in its 1994 communication on industrial competitiveness (²). The measures to promote
cooperation between companies from the European Union and from the
central European countries focused on helping the latter to adjust to the
existing Community legislation and to the conditions of competition prevailing on the internal market. In particular, the Commission supported
an event organised by the Federation of Austrian Industry with a view
to closer cooperation between industrial federations to help industries in
central European countries to gear up for joining the European Union.
The industrial development programme in Bosnia-Herzegovina, which
relies heavily on cooperation with the private sector in the European
Union, became operational in January. To follow up the declaration
adopted at the Euro-Mediterranean Conference of Industry Ministers in
1996 (³), two projects were started — one on industrial zones, and the
other on specialised service centres — and a report was produced on the
legal aspects of promotion of foreign investment in the Mediterranean
countries. Meetings between industrialists were organised in Turkey and
Lebanon. The second round table (⁴) for industrialists from Russia and
the European Union, held in May, set up working parties. In Asia, the
Commission concentrated on closer cooperation on high-tech activities
(software in India and joint development of subcontracting products
using information technologies in China). In Latin America, the Commission continued to encourage partnerships between the private sector
in Europe and Latin America in branches of industry undergoing rapid
changes and forced to adapt to fiercer competition, for example motor
industry suppliers (growing strongly in the Mercosur countries, largely as
a result of investment in these countries by European manufacturers)
and environmental industries.

(¹) OJ C 167, 1.6.1998; Bull. 5-1998, point 1.2.82.
(²) COM(94) 319; 1994 General Report, point 203; Supplement 3/94 — Bull.
(³) 1996 General Report, point 188.
(⁴) First round table: 1997 General Report, point 269.

Standardisation

235. On 13 May, the Commission adopted a report([1]) on efficiency and accountability in European standardisation under the new approach([2]), examining to what extent a balance has been struck between the voluntary nature of standardisation, the independence of the standardisation organisations and the need for accountability in order to draw on standards in regulatory policy, and drawing practical conclusions. To follow up this report, on which the Council adopted conclusions on 18 May([3]), various measures were started, notably the setting-up of a global information system on the Internet by the European standardisation bodies. Last but not least, the cooperation agreement between the Commission and the European standardisation bodies([4]) was updated and several initiatives were taken with the cooperation of these bodies in the field of information and communication technologies, notably on electronic commerce to follow up the Commission communication on the subject([5]).

236. A meeting was held in Geneva in September to follow up the Global Standards Conference([6]) and examine the progress made worldwide on electronic commerce, services to the public, use of information and communication technologies by individuals, and interoperability of communications infrastructure. Projects were started under the PHARE programme *(→ points 812 et seq.)* to encourage central European countries to participate in European standardisation.

Quality policy

237. The Commission continued to implement the quality policy outlined in its communications on benchmarking and competitive performance([7]). Information and awareness campaigns on quality were targeted on industrial undertakings, aimed, in particular, at promoting tools such as self-assessment and benchmarking. The fourth European Quality Week was held in November with the theme 'Quality in Europe: sharing

---

[1] COM(1998) 291; Bull. 5-1998, point 1.2.30.
[2] Nineteenth General Report, point 210.
[3] Bull. 5-1998, point 1.2.31.
[4] Eighteenth General Report, point 139.
[5] COM(97) 157; 1997 General Report, point 499.
[6] 1997 General Report, point 270.
[7] COM(96) 463; COM(97) 153; 1996 General Report, point 186; 1997 General Report, point 268.

benefits, sharing responsibilities'. The European quality prizes for SMEs and big businesses were awarded in October.

Business services

238. On 21 September, the Commission adopted a communication (¹) on the contribution of business services to industrial performance proposing a common policy framework to improve the information available on business services and remove the barriers to access to this market in the Member States in order to create a single market in business services. This approach was endorsed by the Council on 16 November (²).

Industry and environment

239. In June the Cardiff European Council restated the need to integrate environmental concerns in all Community policies, as called for by the Amsterdam Treaty (³). As part of its industrial policy, the Commission continued to implement the concept of sustainable industrial development by promoting eco-efficiency strategies and developing tools and indicators for environmental performance and management in industry. It also encouraged the use of environmental instruments based on market mechanisms, risk assessment, and economic analysis of environmental regulations, particularly as regards climate change, water and waste management. Special attention was also paid to the negotiation of environmental agreements with industry (particularly the motor industry). More detailed information about taking environmental considerations into account in industry is given in Section 17 ('Environment') of this chapter (→ points 487 et seq.).

(¹) COM(1998) 534; Bull. 9-1998, point 1.2.56.
(²) Bull. 11-1998, point 1.2.65.
(³) Bull. 6-1998, point I.11.

Individual sectors

Steel industry

240. On 26 January([1]) and 20 July([2]) respectively, the Commission adopted the forward programmes for steel for the first and second halves of 1998. On 15 December it adopted the draft forward programme for steel for the first half of 1999 and for 1999 as a whole([3]). As part of the pre-accession strategy, it also adopted a communication entitled 'A global approach to promote regional and social conversion and to facilitate industrial restructuring in the central and east European countries: the case of steel' *(→ point 807)* on 7 April and organised a multilateral forum on steel in these countries on 22 and 23 October. On the basis of the results of the studies begun in 1996 and 1997 on the steel industry in Russia and Ukraine([4]), assistance was provided to steel undertakings in these two countries, particularly on management and control.

241. The restructuring of the steel industry and imports of steel into the Community were the subject of conclusions adopted by the Council on 16 November([5]), and a resolution adopted by the ECSC Consultative Committee on 23 October([6]).

Raw materials industry

242. In accordance with the guidelines set out in its 1996 report on the non-energy extractive industry([7]), the Commission focused in particular on the environmental performance of the sector and on certain external aspects. For example, the dialogue with Russia on the mining and raw materials industries was put on an institutional footing by setting up a subcommittee under the partnership and cooperation agreement.

([1])   OJ C 31, 29.1.1998; Bull. 1/2-1998, point 1.3.137.
([2])   OJ C 233, 25.7.1998; Bull. 7/8-1998, point 1.3.110.
([3])   Bull. 12-1998.
([4])   1997 General Report, point 275.
([5])   Bull. 11-1998, point 1.2.67.
([6])   Bull. 10-1998, point 1.2.63.
([7])   1996 General Report, point 193.

Chemical industry

243. To follow up its communication on an industrial competitiveness policy for the European chemical industry ([1]), the Commission organised two seminars in conjunction with the German Chemical Industry Federation — one in September on the promotion of environmental agreements, and the other in October on the comparative analysis of competitiveness.

Wood and paper industry

244. The Commission published a reference document on best available techniques in the pulp and paper industries ([2]), launched studies, in conjunction with the industry, on the competitiveness of the European wood-processing and publishing industries and on renewable energy sources and energy from biomass, and carried out an analysis of the structure and operation of the construction timber market in preparation for a review of Directive 68/89/EEC concerning the classification of wood in the rough ([3]). The Advisory Committee on Community Policy regarding Forestry and Forestry-based Industries ([4]), which was reorganised in 1997 ([5]), held two plenary sessions. At international level, the European Union took part in the second session of the Intergovernmental Forum on Forests ([2]) in August and September.

Mechanical engineering industry

245. The Commission updated the programme to monitor developments in the competitiveness of the European mechanical engineering industry established to follow up its 1994 communication ([6]). It also continued to organise regular dialogue meetings with the industry. As part of the enlargement process, negotiations started on protocols with Hungary and the Czech Republic on mutual recognition of conciliation procedures for medical devices, pressure equipment, gas appliances and machinery. A start was made on the implementation of the mutual recognition agreements with Australia, Canada, New Zealand and the United States *(→ point 729)* concerning medical devices.

([1])   COM(96) 187; 1996 General Report, point 193.
([2])   1997 General Report, point 278.
([3])   OJ L 32, 6.2.1968.
([4])   Seventeenth General Report, point 194.
([5])   Decision 97/837/EC (OJ L 346, 17.12.1997).
([6])   COM(94) 380; 1994 General Report, point 223.

Electrotechnical industry

246. The Commission published the study started in 1997 ([1]) on the competitiveness of the electrotechnical industry in the European Union.

Motor industry

247. The high-level dialogue group set up in 1997 ([2]) met twice in 1998. The Commission also continued to promote industrial cooperation activities to assist small suppliers of motor vehicle components. The accession of the European Union to the revised 1958 UN-ECE agreement on the approval of motor vehicle equipment and parts became effective on 24 March (Table III).

Maritime industries

248. On 6 February ([3]), the Economic and Social Committee approved the Commission communication on a new shipbuilding policy ([4]). Representatives of all branches of the industry, the Member States and the Commission met in Lisbon on 2 and 3 June at the ninth plenary session of the Maritime Industries Forum. Also in Lisbon, the results of the G7 maritime information society initiative (MARIS) were presented at a conference on 8 September.

Aerospace industry

249. The communication entitled 'The European aerospace industry: meeting the global challenge' ([5]) was welcomed by the Economic and Social Committee on 28 January ([6]), by the European Parliament on 19 November ([7]) and by the European industry and the Member States. Most of the players concerned recognised the need to restructure this industry and to create an integrated European grouping in the aerospace and defence sectors.

([1])   1997 General Report, point 280.
([2])   1997 General Report, point 282.
([3])   OJ C 129, 27.4.1998; Bull. 1/2-1998, point 1.3.140.
([4])   COM(97) 470; 1997 General Report, point 284.
([5])   COM(97) 466; 1997 General Report, point 286.
([6])   OJ C 95, 30.3.1998; Bull. 1/2-1998, point 1.3.139.
([7])   OJ C 379, 7.12.1998; Bull. 11-1998, point 1.2.68.

Space industry

250. The European Parliament, on 13 January(¹), and the Economic and Social Committee, on 28 January(²), both endorsed the strategy outlined in the communication on the European Union and space(³). The Commission strengthened its ties with the space industry and service providers, who approved its proposal to set up a European space industry forum.

Defence-related industries

251. The Commission communication on implementing European Union strategy on the defence-related industries(⁴) and the action plan it contained were welcomed by the Economic and Social Committee on 2 July(⁵). The Commission proposed a revision of the Community arrangements for monitoring exports of dual-use goods *(→ point 727)* and launched consultations on other topics included in the action plan. Matters relating to the restructuring of the defence industries were discussed at a high-level meeting bringing together for the first time the Commission, the Member States' ministries concerned, the Western European Union and the Western European Armaments Group.

Railway industry

252. The Commission continued to examine, in conjunction with the industry, the structural problems of the railway industry and the work involved in drawing up technical specifications for interoperability to implement Directive 96/48/EC on the interoperability of the trans-European high-speed rail system(⁶). It also launched the mass transit rail initiative for Europe (MARIE) designed to establish regular dialogue between industrialists, operators and local authorities with regard to urban and regional railways.

(¹)   OJ C 34, 2.2.1998; Bull. 1/2-1998, point 1.3.138.
(²)   OJ C 95, 30.3.1998; Bull. 1/2-1998, point 1.3.139.
(³)   COM(96) 617; 1996 General Report, point 202.
(⁴)   COM(97) 583; 1997 General Report, point 288.
(⁵)   OJ C 284, 14.9.1998; Bull. 7/8-1998, point 1.3.113.
(⁶)   OJ L 235, 17.9.1996; 1996 General Report, point 327.

Textiles and clothing

253. The Economic and Social Committee, on 29 April (¹), the European Parliament, on 30 April (²) and 14 July (³), and the Council, on 7 May (⁴), all welcomed the action plan for the competitiveness of the European textile and clothing industry submitted by the Commission (⁵) and called for it to be implemented.

Biotechnology

254. In conjunction with the UK Presidency, the Commission organised a conference on the prospects for modern biotechnology in Brussels on 25 June. It also stepped up the dialogue with the leading players on the international stage, namely the USA and Japan, particularly in the context of transatlantic business dialogue.

Information and communication technologies industry

255. To implement the action plan set out in its 1997 communication on the information and communication technologies industries (⁶), the Commission started activities to promote standardisation, raise awareness of technologies and technological development and improve skills. The European Parliament considered skills vital to the industry's competitiveness in a resolution adopted on this communication on 30 April (⁷). Action was taken to define and disseminate job and general training profiles for the main activities in the information and communications technologies industries in order to develop education programmes tailored more closely to the needs of the industry.

Construction industry

256. The Economic and Social Committee, the European Parliament and the Council welcomed, on 29 April (⁸), 30 April (⁹) and 7 May (¹⁰)

(¹)   OJ C 214, 10.7.1998; Bull. 4-1998, point 1.2.63.
(²)   OJ C 152, 18.5.1998; Bull. 4-1998, point 1.2.63.
(³)   OJ C 292, 21.9.1998; Bull. 7/8-1998, point 1.3.112.
(⁴)   Bull. 5-1998, point 1.2.84.
(⁵)   COM(97) 454; 1997 General Report, point 290.
(⁶)   COM(97) 152; 1997 General Report, point 293.
(⁷)   OJ C 152, 18.5.1998; Bull. 4-1998, point 1.2.61.
(⁸)   OJ C 214, 10.7.1998; Bull. 4-1998, point 1.2.64.
(⁹)   OJ C 152, 18.5.1998; Bull. 4-1998, point 1.2.64.
(¹⁰) Bull. 5-1998, point 1.2.85.

respectively, the communication from the Commission on the competitiveness of the construction industry (¹) and called on the Commission to
implement an action plan for this industry. The Commission started
broad consultations with the Member States and the industry to this
end. It also virtually completed its programme of standardisation mandates for the construction products sector (²) with the adoption of 19
decisions (³) establishing the procedures for attesting the conformity of
given families of products and defining the corresponding standardisation mandates for the European standardisation bodies.

Recycling industries

257. On 22 July, the Commission adopted a communication on the
competitiveness of the recycling industries (⁴). Noting that recycling is an
important component of waste management strategy and an industrial
activity with promising growth potential but constrained by imperfect
markets and structural weaknesses, the Commission proposed action on
four main fronts: standardisation, enhancing market transparency, innovation, and changes in the regulatory framework. It also set up a recycling forum bringing together all concerned, from both the private and
public sectors, to identify the action to be taken. The Council endorsed
the Commission's approach in conclusions adopted on 16 November (⁵).

(¹)   COM(97) 539; 1997 General Report, point 295.
(²)   1996 General Report, point 213; 1997 General Report, point 295.
(³)   OJ L 42, 14.2.1998; OJ L 80, 18.3.1998; OJ L 127, 29.4.1998; OJ L 194, 10.7.1998; OJ
      L 201, 17.7.1998.
(⁴)   COM(1998) 463; Bull. 7/8-1998, point 1.3.111.
(⁵)   Bull. 11-1998, point 1.2.69.

Section 7

Enterprise policy, distributive trades, tourism and cooperatives

Priority activities and objectives

258. During 1998, the second year of operation of the third multi-annual programme for small and medium-sized enterprises (SMEs) ([1]), the European institutions took initiatives aimed at promoting entrepreneurship and improving access to finance for innovative, job-creating SMEs.

Policy to assist SMEs and the craft sector

Enterprise policy and entrepreneurship

259. In a communication adopted on 7 April ([2]), the Commission presented a set of priority measures to be implemented at national and European levels in order to promote entrepreneurship in Europe. These comprise on the one hand measures targeted at individuals to encourage them to start up businesses and equip them with the necessary skills to make their businesses successful and on the other proposals for establishing a favourable environment for the creation, growth and longevity of businesses. This communication was the subject of a favourable opinion adopted by the Economic and Social Committee on 27 May ([3]).

Improving the business environment and access to finance

260. On 30 April, the BEST task force, which was set up in 1997 ([4]) to further the simplification of the administrative environment for businesses, submitted a report to the Commission containing recommendations for improving the quality of legislation and reducing the constraints on the development of businesses, particularly SMEs. As

---

([1]) OJ L 6, 10.1.1997; 1996 General Report, point 215. This programme has been opened up to seven countries of central Europe (→ *point 809*).
([2]) COM(1998) 222; Bull. 4-1998, point 1.2.66.
([3]) OJ C 235, 27.7.1998; Bull. 5-1998, point 1.2.88.
([4]) 1997 General Report, point 297.

requested by the Cardiff European Council [1], on 30 September the Commission adopted a communication [2] on an action plan for implementing these recommendations at Community, national and regional levels.

261.   Further to its 1997 communication [3], on 25 March the Commission adopted a proposal for a directive on combating late payment in commercial transactions (Table I). It also adopted, on 24 March [4], an assessment of the results of the 1994 recommendation on the transfer of small and medium-sized businesses [5]. For its part, in a resolution adopted on 14 July [6] the European Parliament expressed support for the guidelines set out in the Commission's communication on the participation of European Economic Interest Groupings (EEIGs) in public contracts and programmes financed by public funds [7].

262.   On 19 May, the Council adopted Decision 98/347/EC on measures of financial assistance for innovative and job-creating SMEs (Table II). This decision, which follows from a proposal presented by the Commission on 21 January, fits into the initiative for employment launched by the European Parliament and approved by the Luxembourg European Council on employment [8]. Its aim is to support the investment activity of SMEs by providing them with easier access to funding and thereby to stimulate their growth and the creation of jobs. The decision provides for the establishment of three complementary facilities: a risk-capital window, administered by the European Investment Fund (EIF), which is aimed at SMEs in the start-up phase, a system of financial contributions, under the responsibility of the Commission, to SMEs for the setting-up of new transnational joint ventures within the European Union ('joint European ventures'), and a system of guarantees, administered by the EIF, to increase the volume of loans accessible to small or newly founded SMEs. By the end of the year there were already 80 financial intermediaries taking part in the 'Joint European venture' programme.

263.   The Commission also, in a communication adopted on 31 March [9], put forward an action plan for promoting the development of

---

[1]   Bull. 6-1998, point I.8. 20.
[2]   COM(1998) 550; Bull. 9-1998, point 1.2.57.
[3]   OJ C 216, 17.7.1997; 1997 General Report, point 298.
[4]   OJ C 93, 28.3.1998; Bull. 3-1998, point 1.2.80.
[5]   OJ L 385, 31.12.1994; 1994 General Report, point 192; 1997 General Report, point 300.
[6]   OJ C 292, 21.9.1998; Bull. 7/8-1998, point 1.3.114.
[7]   OJ C 285, 20.9.1997; COM(97) 434; 1997 General Report, point 299.
[8]   1997 General Report, points 148 and 302; Bull. 11-1997, points I.2. 8 and I.6. 47.
[9]   Bull. 3-1998, point 1.2.79.

capital investment markets in Europe, and the Cardiff European Council in June welcomed this plan ([1]). The Commission's communication on capital markets for SMEs ([2]) was examined by the Economic and Social Committee on 27 May ([3]) and by the European Parliament on 17 September ([4]). A third banks/SMEs round table was set up in October ([5]).

264. On 5 November ([6]), the Commission launched a new initiative on seed capital aimed at stimulating the supply of proprietorial or quasi-proprietorial financing for the founding and transfer of small businesses.

265. As a contribution to getting SMEs ready for the introduction of the euro, the Group of Experts on Small Enterprises and the Euro and the Working Party on Acceptance of New Prices and Values in Euro submitted their reports to the Commission, which incorporated them into its communication of 11 February on the practical aspects of the introduction of the euro (→ point 55).

266. The fifth report of the European Observatory for SMEs was the subject of a European Parliament resolution adopted on 17 September ([7]).

Support measures for businesses

267. Following the call for applications issued in December 1997 ([8]), there are now 233 Euro Info Centres (EICs), which are the first stop for businesses seeking European information, and 17 of these are 'network heads'. In 1998, 44 national or European professional organisations also became associate members of the EIC network. The network further includes 20 correspondent EICs in non-member countries (central Europe and the Mediterranean basin). Two Europartenariat meetings, in Apeldoorn (Netherlands) in June and in Valencia (Spain) in November, provided an opportunity for contacts between businesses from more than 60 countries.

---

[1]　Bull. 6-1998, point I-8.
[2]　COM(97) 187; 1997 General Report, point 301.
[3]　OJ C 235, 27.7.1998; Bull. 5-1998, point 1.2.87.
[4]　OJ C 313, 12.10.1998; Bull. 9-1998, point 1.2.58.
[5]　1994 General Report, point 193; 1997 General Report, point 301.
[6]　Bull. 11-1998, point 1.2.70.
[7]　OJ C 313, 12.10.1998; Bull. 9-1998, point 1.2.59.
[8]　1997 General Report, point 304.

268. The Commission started its evaluation of the 'Euro management — Research and technological development' pilot scheme. It also launched a European technology transfer network, one of the aims of which will be to identify 15 regional SME platforms and coordinate them with research centres, and a study of European-level networking of SME clusters. It also continued to support the activities of Normapme, the European standardisation bureau for craft industries and SMEs.

269. The second European Forum on Subcontracting [1] was held in Graz (Austria) on 5 and 6 October, bringing together some 180 experts in the field. Two IBEX (International Buyers' Exhibition) 'reverse fairs' were also organised in 1998, the first in Sweden on the car industry and the second in France, on aeronautics. The Commission also published a practical guide on legal aspects of industrial subcontracting and a guide to alliances, and conducted studies aimed at better definitions and measurements of subcontracting.

Concerted action and coordination with related Community policies

270. Under the heading of concerted action between the Member States and the Commission, five seminars on best practice for improving the business environment, a forum on the problems associated with the various phases in the life cycle of businesses and a forum on services to growing businesses (with participants from the applicant countries of central Europe) were held in 1998.

271. In a resolution of 5 November [2], Parliament welcomed the Commission report on the coordination of activities in support of SMEs and the craft sector in 1997 [3] and advocated enhanced coordination.

272. The definition of SMEs set out in Recommendation 96/280/EC [4] was used in several legislative acts adopted in 1998, such as Decision 98/347/EC on measures of financial assistance for innovative and job-creating small and medium-sized enterprises (→ point 262) and the decision concerning the rules for participation in the fifth framework programme for research (→ point 287).

---

[1] First forum (Madrid): Twenty-sixth General Report, point 238.
[2] OJ C 355, 23.11.1998; Bull. 11-1998, point 1.2.71.
[3] COM(97) 610; 1997 General Report, point 307.
[4] OJ L 107, 30.4.1996; General Report 1996, point 216.

Cooperatives, mutual societies, associations and foundations

273. The Commission communication on promoting the role of voluntary organisations and foundations ([1]), which was the subject of a number of conferences in the Member States, also received favourable opinions from the Economic and Social Committee on 28 January ([2]), from the Committee of the Regions on 13 March ([3]) and from the European Parliament on 2 July ([4]). All three opinions stressed the importance of the non-profit-making sector and the need to involve it more in Community programmes. On 13 March, the Commission adopted the decision setting up a consultative committee for cooperatives, mutual societies, associations and foundations ([5]).

Distributive trades

274. In Brussels, in March, the Commission organised the first of a series of seminars to be held each year on the situation of trade in Europe and the broad prospects for its development. It also launched an operation to identify good practice in the field of distributive trades in less favoured rural areas. On 30 June, consumers' and retailers' representatives signed an agreement on a voluntary code of practice for the transition to the euro.

275. Information about electronic commerce will be found in Section 16 ('Information society, telecommunications') of this chapter *(→ point 461)*.

Tourism

276. Following the Court of Auditors' special report 3/96 ([6]), which was the subject of a resolution adopted by the European Parliament on 17 February ([7]), the Commission carried out a special audit of its operations in the tourism sector from 1990 to 1995, which it presented to the European Parliament in July. In a resolution of 7 October ([8]), the Euro-

---

([1]) COM(97) 241; 1997 General Report, point 309.
([2]) OJ C 95, 30.3.1998; Bull. 1/2-1998, point 1.3.144.
([3]) OJ C 180, 11.6.1998; Bull. 3-1998, point 1.2.84.
([4]) OJ C 226, 20.7.1998; Bull. 7/8-1998, point 1.3.116.
([5]) Decision 98/215/EC (OJ L 80, 18.3.1998).
([6]) OJ C 17, 16.1.1997; 1996 General Report, point 1072.
([7]) OJ C 80, 16.3.1998; Bull. 1/2-1998, point 1.3.143.
([8]) OJ C 328, 26.10.1998; Bull. 10-1998, point 1.2.65.

pean Parliament stressed the need for rapid adoption of a multiannual framework programme for tourism [1].

277. On 31 March, the European Parliament adopted a resolution on improving safety, consumers' rights and trading standards in the tourism sector [2]. Quality in this sector was also the subject of a conference held in Mayrhofen (Austria) in July. There were also conferences on SMEs in the tourism sector in Llandudno (United Kingdom) in May and on the introduction of the euro in this sector in Brussels in October. The high-level working party responsible for identifying opportunities for the tourism sector to step up its contribution to employment submitted its report to the Commission in October.

278. In an own-initiative opinion adopted on 13 May [3], the Committee of the Regions highlighted the role of urban tourism in developing the local economy. The fight against child sex tourism was the subject of an own-initiative opinion adopted by the Economic and Social Committee on 2 July [4], and also of a conference held in Brussels in November.

---

[1]   1996 General Report, point 227.
[2]   OJ C 138, 4.5.1998; Bull. 4-1998, point 1.2.68.
[3]   OJ C 251, 10.8.1998; Bull. 5-1998, point 1.2.89.
[4]   OJ C 284, 14.9.1998; Bull. 7/8-1998, point 1.3.115.

Section 8

Research and technology

Priority activities and objectives

279.   The main event in 1998 in the field of research and technological development (RTD) was the adoption by Parliament and the Council of the fifth framework programme covering all the Union's research activities until 2002. The new framework programme differs significantly from previous programmes both in terms of approach and in operational terms. The specific programmes through which the framework programme will be implemented were also approved. In addition, the fourth framework programme produced some significant scientific results.

Community RTD policy

Coordination and general developments

280.   On 15 July, the Commission adopted its 1998 annual report on RTD activities [1], which gives an overview of the European Union's research effort and policies. Parliament adopted a resolution [2] on the 1997 report on 17 February [3]. The Commission also published detailed reports [4] on the implementation in 1997 of several of the specific programmes of the fourth framework programme *(→ points 294 et seq.)* and the second edition of the European report on science and technology indicators [5], which places European research and innovation performance in an international context.

281.   The participation of small and medium-sized enterprises (SMEs) in the research programmes increased substantially in 1998, mainly as a result of the specially targeted technology stimulation measures [6]. Some 13 500 SMEs (more than half the firms involved in the programme)

(¹)   COM(1998) 439; Bull. 7/8-1998, point 1.3.119.
(²)   OJ C 80, 16.3.1998; Bull. 1/2-1998, point 1.3.146.
(³)   COM(97) 373; 1997 General Report, point 316.
(⁴)   Available from the Evaluation Unit of the Commission's Directorate-General for Science, Research and Development.
(⁵)   Available from the sales points of the Office for Official Publications of the European Communities.
(⁶)   1996 General Report, point 232.

took part in the fourth framework programme, which was more than double the figure for the previous framework programme. According to a study published in 1998, about two thirds of these small businesses were taking part for the first time in a public European, national or regional research programme.

282. The work of the Scientific and Technical Research Committee (CREST) ([1]) focused mainly on preparing the fifth framework programme. The Committee also collaborated with the Commission in coordinating Community and national policies. The ETAN network (European technology assessment network) ([2]), the objective of which is to promote dialogue between researchers and decision-makers, broadened its remit to the following six issues: the technological response to climate change; intellectual property rights and technology policy; indirect measures to support employment in research; research and the digital age; women in science; and assessment of the impact of scientific and technical programmes.

283. In a communication of 27 May, the Commission examined the measures needed to ensure that research, technological development and innovation contribute to economic and social cohesion and to the growth of the less favoured regions (→ point 358).

Framework programme 1994-98 ([3])

284. Information on the implementation of the framework programme through the various specific programmes ([4]) is given in the subsection 'Implementation of the fourth framework programme' of this section (→ points 294 to 318).

Framework programme 1998-2002

285. On 22 December, Parliament and the Council adopted the fifth framework programme for research and technological development (1998-2002) for the European Community (Table I). On the same day, the Council adopted this programme for Euratom (Table II). The fifth framework programme, which covers the entire Community research

---

[1]   1996 General Report, point 230.
[2]   Twenty-seventh General Report, point 210.
[3]   OJ L 126, 18.5.1994 (EC); OJ L 115, 6.5.1994 (Euratom); 1994 General Report, points 236 et seq.
[4]   1995 General Report, point 232.

effort for the next five years, marks a real departure from its predecessors, both in terms of the approach (focus on a smaller number of research programmes, integration of the Union's essential social and economic needs in the 'key actions') and in operational terms (coordination of the various activities and more efficient management). The overall budget for the programme as a whole has been set at ECU 14.96 billion.

286. On 10 June, the Commission adopted 10 proposals for specific programmes for the fifth framework programme (Table II). They include eight programmes for the European Community, comprising four thematic programmes ('Quality of life and management of living resources', 'User-friendly information society', 'Competitive and sustainable growth' and 'Preserving the ecosystem'), three horizontal programmes ('Confirming the international role of Community research', 'Promotion of innovation and encouragement of participation of SMEs' and 'Improving the human research potential and the socioeconomic knowledge base') and a programme concerning the JRC (→ *points 290 to 293)*, together with two programmes for Euratom, one entitled 'Preserving the ecosystem' and the other concerning the JRC. The Council reached agreement on these programmes on 22 December.

287. Also on 22 December, the Council adopted the decisions concerning the rules for the participation of undertakings, research centres and universities in the fifth framework programme (Table II). These decisions seek both to simplify the procedures applicable and to improve the dissemination and utilisation of research results.

288. On 13 October, the Council authorised the Commission to negotiate the arrangements for associating the prospective new members with the European Union with the fifth framework programme *(→ point 801)*.

289. As part of the preparations for implementing the key actions of the fifth framework programme, 17 expert groups were set up to assist the Commission with the content and direction of these actions [1] and 278 experts were designated. The Commission also reorganised the two research advisory bodies, the Industrial Research and Development Advisory Committee (IRDAC) [2] and the European Science and Technology

---

[1]   Decision 98/610/EC, Euratom (OJ L 290, 26.10.1998; Bull. 10-1998, point 1.2.70).
[2]   1995 General Report, point 222.

Assembly (ESTA) (¹) as a single entity, the European Research Forum (²). The Council adopted conclusions approving the Commission's approach to the implementation and management of the programme on 22 June (³).

Joint Research Centre (JRC)

290.   The Commission carried out a reorganisation of the JRC in 1998 in order to enhance its capacity to provide scientific and technical support to Community policies. One of the measures taken involved the creation of a new institute at Ispra, the Institute for Health and Consumer Protection (IHCP). The JRC continued implementing the two specific programmes (1994-98) it is carrying out on behalf of the European Community and Euratom (⁴).

Scientific and technical support for Community policies

291.   During the year the JRC redefined its role, which is to provide scientific and technical support for the formulation, implementation and monitoring of Union policies, in response to the demands of those policies. As a Commission service, the JRC acts as a science and technology and reference centre for the Union. Close to the policy formulation process, it serves the common interest of the Member States while remaining independent of vested commercial or national interests. In order to perform its tasks, it has at its disposal a unique combination of facilities and skills which transcend national frontiers. Its networks also enable it to stimulate collaborative research and enlarge its knowledge base. Among other results obtained in 1998, the JRC validated a method for the detection of genetically modified agricultural products (such as maize and soya beans). It also participated in the IDEA project on electronic identification for livestock (→ point 563).

Other activities

292.   The JRC also conducted research of a competitive nature by participating in Community programmes and shared-cost projects under the

---

(¹)   1994 General Report, point 231.
(²)   Decision 98/611/EC, Euratom (OJ L 290, 29.10.1998; Bull. 10-1998, point 1.2.68).
(³)   Bull. 6-1998, point 1.3.75.
(⁴)   OJ L 361, 31.12.1994; 1994 General Report, point 242.

framework programme and by providing research services to public or private sector clients.

293. The Commission adopted its annual report on the JRC (1997) on 29 July (¹).

Implementation of the fourth framework programme

294. It emerges from an analysis of the proposals selected in 1997 and 1998 that, on average, a shared-cost RTD project involves five partners from three Member States and a Community contribution of ECU 0.7 million. Additional information on the projects selected is available in the 1998 annual report on RTD activities *(→ point 280)*.

295. Information concerning the specific programmes on information technologies, telematics and communications technologies is provided in Section 16 ('Information society and telecommunications') of this chapter *(→ points 473 to 475)*.

Industrial and materials technologies (²)

296. In 1998, 192 projects were selected in the area of industrial research (new production technologies, new materials), eight in the field of intelligent production (IMS), five in the area of water and one in aeronautical research; 46 new thematic networks were also created. The result of a study of the economic impact of the programme, carried out on 200 projects completed five years ago, shows that, overall, the profits from these projects during this period were more than 10 times greater than the amount of the Community support they received.

Standardisation, measurement and testing (³)

297. The 89 projects selected in 1998 mainly concerned the creation of a European measurement and testing infrastructure, the development of measurements related to the needs of society, the specific needs of customs laboratories and support for Community policies. These new projects will also have spin-off effects for safety, health, the environment,

---

(¹)   COM(1998) 483; Bull. 7/8-1998, point 1.3.118.
(²)   OJ L 222, 26.8.1994; 1994 General Report, point 246.
(³)   OJ L 334, 22.12.1994; 1994 General Report, point 249.

food hygiene, justice and the protection of our cultural heritage. On 27 January, the Commission adopted a working paper on prenormative research (¹).

Environment and climate (²)

298.   Over 100 new projects were launched in 1998, mainly in the field of earth observation. A climate research project produced a model that, in certain cases, can make successful six-month forecasts. Events such as the El Niño phenomenon in 1997 or the floods in China in summer 1998 could have been predicted with the aid of this model. On 24 March, the 'Vegetation' sensor was launched on board the SPOT 4 satellite by an Ariane launch vehicle. This observation system, one of the most powerful in the world, will permit virtually daily monitoring of the earth's forests and crops.

Marine science and technology (³)

299.   The programme continued with the launch of 45 new projects, particularly in the area of operational oceanography and European management of oceanographic data. Several projects, completed or in progress, have produced remarkable results, such as: Micromare (development of marine microsensors, 12 patents filed), BROS (reduction of instrument fouling by micro-organisms), Geostar (prototype underwater observatory for abyssal research) and Proverbs (innovative method for the design of coastal breakwaters). The unifying role of the four major regional projects OMEX (Atlantic), BASYS (Baltic), MTP (Mediterranean) and Canigo (Canaries, Azores and Gibralter Strait) was confirmed, together with that of the MEDAR data management project, in which all the third countries bordering the eastern Mediterranean and the Black Sea, as well as Algeria and Morocco, are involved. Joint research efforts with oil companies operating in the north-east Atlantic were initiated in the ENAM and Corsaires projects.

(¹)   COM(1998) 31; Bull. 1/2-1998, point 1.3.145.
(²)   OJ L 361, 31.12.1994; 1994 General Report, point 252.
(³)   OJ L 334, 22.12.1994; 1994 General Report, point 257.

Biotechnology (¹)

300. Some 161 new projects were selected, covering most of the programme areas. Seven of them concern transmissible spongiform encephalopathies and focus primarily on studying the propagation and multiplication of the prion, assessing the risk of transmission to humans of bovine spongiform encephalopathy through the consumption of contaminated food, developing diagnostic methods and inactivating the infectious agent. In January, part of the complete genome sequence of a model plant, *Arabidopsis thaliana,* was decoded and presented to the international scientific community, providing a rich fund of knowledge about the plant kingdom. A new network bringing together some 400 research groups in the field of plant biotechnology was created, while the Biotechnology and Finance Forum (²) held its first conference in May.

Agriculture and fisheries (³)

301. Some 96 research projects and concerted actions have been launched in the field of nutritious foods, agriculture, sylviculture, rural development, fisheries and aquaculture. The cooperative research activities geared more specifically to SMEs have been considerably developed. A joint call for proposals on risk assessment in relation to transmissible spongiform encephalopathies was launched with the 'Biotechnology' and 'Biomedicine and health' programmes.

Biomedicine and health (⁴)

302. This programme, including the last contracts finalised in 1998, will have supported a total of 601 research projects covering the most important areas of medical research (pharmaceutical research, biomedical engineering, research on the brain, cancer, cardiovascular diseases, chronic illnesses, rare illnesses, human genome, public health and biomedical ethics). The implementation of these projects has involved more that 6 000 laboratories in Europe and a great deal of international collaboration. In addition, 10 projects were launched in 1998 in the area of transmissible spongiform encephalopathies.

(¹)   OJ L 361, 31.12.1994; 1994 General Report, point 257.
(²)   1996 General Report, point 333.
(³)   OJ L 334, 22.12.1994; 1994 General Report, point 261.
(⁴)   OJ L 361, 31.12.1994; 1994 General Report, point 265.

Non-nuclear energy [1]

303. The new activities in 1998 mainly concerned the implementation of concerted actions, accompanying measures, fellowships and measures for SMEs. Some 15 contracts have also got under way in the field of photovoltaic cells with the aim of substantially reducing the manufacturing costs, which are currently a major obstacle to the dissemination of this clean and renewable technology. Testing has begun of a new European solar collector based on the direct production of steam.

Nuclear fission safety [2]

304. Community research in 1998 contributed to a better understanding of the mechanisms and epidemiology of ionising radiation, better risk evaluation and exposure reduction. In addition, new dosimetry and environmental restoration techniques were developed. Research in the field of reactor safety led to the successful modelling of possible serious accidents and the development of efficient crisis management techniques. Scientific and technical progress was also made on the geological disposal of long-lived wastes.

Controlled thermonuclear fusion [3]

305. Operation of a Tokamak (MAST at Culham) has begun and new equipment for two other Tokamaks (ASDEX upgrade in Garching, Textor in Jülich) and a Stellarator (TJ-II in Madrid) have been approved under this programme of research on toroidal magnetic confinement. In addition, following successful experiments in operating the Joint European Torus (JET) with deuterium-tritium mixtures, the exhaust system of the torus (divertor) has been completely replaced by a remote-handling design: this technique represents a world first in fusion research.

306. On 22 June, the Council decided to extend for three years the cooperation agreement between the Community, Japan, Russia and the USA on the detailed design (EDA) of the international thermonuclear experimental reactor (ITER) [4]. It also approved, on 13 October, a new administrative and structural framework for JET's activities (Table II).

---

[1] OJ L 334, 22.12.1994; 1994 General Report, point 267.
[2] OJ L 361, 31.12.1994; 1994 General Report, point 269.
[3] OJ L 331, 21.12.1994; 1994 General Report, point 272.
[4] Bull. 6-1998, point 1.3.79.

Transport (¹)

307. Two new series of projects were selected in 1998. The 31 projects of the first series seek to consolidate the research results obtained from previous RTD projects, to support transport policy initiatives and to prepare future transport research activities. The second series of 19 projects, established on the basis of the responses to a call for proposals launched jointly with the 'Telematics applications' programme *(→ point 474),* is designed to promote intermodal transport of goods and passengers.

Targeted socioeconomic research (²)

308. In all, 52 new projects have been launched in the three programme areas: science and technology policy options; research on education and training; and research into social integration and social exclusion in Europe. An integrated approach was taken to project selection based on the following strategic goals: competition, change and dialogue; work, prosperity and employment; and innovation and institutional change. Furthermore, previous projects have begun to produce scientific results relevant to several major socioeconomic problems such as sustainable development, the transition from school to the workplace, and poverty.

Cooperation with third countries and international organisations (³)

309. In order to make the European research effort more consistent and to enhance synergies, the Commission has strengthened its links with various European scientific organisations such as the European Organisation for Nuclear Research (CERN) and the European Space Agency (ESA) (⁴). It also continued its cooperation with various countries in the framework of COST scientific and technical cooperation, which has been extended to two new areas (environmental research and nanosciences) and to which four new countries (Bulgaria, Cyprus, Latvia, Lithuania) have been admitted as observers, and of the Eureka initiative (⁵).

(¹)   OJ L 361, 31.12.1994; 1994 General Report, point 276.
(²)   OJ L 361, 31.12.1994; 1994 General Report, point 277.
(³)   OJ L 334, 22.12.1994; 1994 General Report, point 285.
(⁴)   Cooperation with the European Space Agency was the subject of a Council resolution of 22 June (Bull. 6-1998, point 1.3.76).
(⁵)   Nineteenth General Report, point 320; Twenty-sixth General Report, point 321.

310. Iceland, Liechtenstein and Norway participated in the non-nuclear specific programmes of the fourth framework programme by virtue of the Agreement on the European Economic Area (EEA). Israel was also associated with the programme in keeping with the agreement signed in 1996; on 17 July, the Commission proposed the renewal of this agreement for the fifth framework programme (Table III). Agreement was reached on Switzerland's participation in the fifth framework programme on 10 December *(→ points 792 and 793).*

311. Some 183 research projects and 29 concerted actions involving the central European countries or the independent States of the former Soviet Union were launched in 1998 in the areas of the environment, health, the information society and industrial technologies. The International Association for the Promotion of Cooperation with Scientists from the new independent States of the former Soviet Union (INTAS), mainly funded by the Community, proceeded with the launch of 339 research projects of a mainly fundamental character involving an amount of ECU 22.3 million. The Community also provided aid totalling ECU 15.3 million to scientists from Russia and other countries of the former Soviet Union through the International Science and Technology Centre (ISTC), bringing the number of scientists having benefited from this support to 22 000. On 30 July and 3 November respectively, the Council and the Commission also decided on the Community's accession to the Ukrainian Science and Technology Centre (USTC), the counterpart of the ISTC in the Ukraine (Table III).

312. In conclusions adopted on 22 December, the Council advocated strengthening Euro-Mediterranean cooperation on research and innovation ([1]).

313. The scientific and technological cooperation agreement with the United States was concluded on 13 October by the Council (Table III), which also authorised the Commission to negotiate the widening of the scope of the scientific and technological cooperation agreements with Canada (Table III) and Australia (Table III) on 22 June and 24 September respectively, and a new scientific and technological cooperation agreement with China (Table III) on 22 June. Following the completion of the negotiations, the agreement with Canada was concluded on 8 December and signed on 17 December at the Ottawa Summit *(→ point 890)*, at which a cooperation agreement in the field of nuclear research was also signed (Table III), and the agreement with China was signed on

---

([1]) Bull. 12-1998.

22 December. In addition, 76 fellowships in Japan were granted to European researchers, bringing the total number of European Union scientists sent to that country to more than 560.

314. In all, 132 projects concerning mainly nutrition, biodiversity and health were selected in the framework of cooperation with the developing countries. Accompanying measures to prepare an information system (Info-Sys) were funded under the European initiative for agricultural research for development ([1]). In addition, a European biotechnology node for interaction with China (EBNIC) was set up.

Dissemination and utilisation of research results ([2])

315. During the second phase of implementing the innovation relay centres, 25 000 bodies benefited from specific advice and assistance services and 162 transnational technology transfer agreements were concluded in 1997 (422 agreements concluded since the action began). The number of users of the CORDIS information service continued to rise, with over 1.3 million consultations per month. The Commission launched 44 technology validation and transfer projects and 42 audits of the support infrastructures for innovation and technology transfer, raising the number of participating regions of the European Union to over 90. It also established 21 European networks dedicated to stimulating and disseminating good practice in order to encourage researchers to set up businesses and to promote the use of intellectual property or the funding of innovation. In addition, a service was set up to help participants in the specific programmes with regard to intellectual property rights (IPR help desk). Finally, since its launch in 1997 ([3]), the I-TEC pilot project has led to the selection of over 25 venture capital funds representing a total investment capacity of ECU 1 billion, around one third of which will be invested at an early stage in technologically innovative SMEs.

316. In an own-initiative opinion adopted on 1 July, the Economic and Social Committee called on the Commission to develop networks providing information, back-up and exploitation services for RTD ([4]).

([1]) 1997 General Report, point 348.
([2]) OJ L 361, 31.12.1994; 1994 General Report, point 426.
([3]) 1997 General Report, point 349.
([4]) OJ C 284, 14.9.1998; Bull. 7/8-1998, point 1.3.117.

Stimulation of training and mobility of researchers (¹)

317. The implementation of the contracts in progress and the utilisation and dissemination of the results of the programme continued in 1998, and 618 new training fellowships were granted. Some of the programme activities have been evaluated by panels of independent experts, in particular the research networks, the large-scale facilities and the laboratories receiving the Marie Curie fellows, most of which were visited by the experts. A call for proposals for a study was launched with a view to the establishment of a methodology for assessing the impact of the Marie Curie fellowships.

318. The 10th European contest for young scientists (aged 15 to 20) was held in Oporto (Portugal) from 20 to 27 September. The Marie Curie Fellows Association (²), which has 1 400 members, received support from the programme to establish a secretariat, which also processed the applications for Marie Curie fellowships submitted under the other specific programmes.

Coal and steel technical research

319. Under Article 55 of the ECSC Treaty and in accordance with the guidelines for steel technical research (1996-2002) (³), 54 research projects and 15 pilot or demonstration projects were selected, the total amount involved being ECU 56 million.

(¹) OJ L 361, 31.12.1994; 1994 General Report, point 288.
(²) 1997 General Report, point 350.
(³) OJ C 294, 9.11.1995; 1995 General Report, point 265.

Section 9

Promoting innovation

320. In January, the Commission adopted the first report ([1]) on the implementation of the first action plan for innovation in Europe ([2]). The Economic and Social Committee welcomed this report in its opinion of 27 May ([3]).

321. In the context of this action plan, and with the help of a group of high-ranking national officials, the Commission drew up a trend chart on innovation in Europe as an annotated list of national policies for promoting innovation, emphasising innovation financing, the use of intellectual property and the founding of technology-based companies. It also turned its attention to the protection of intellectual property, above all as a follow-up to its Green Paper on the Community patent and the European patent system *(→ point 194)*, to innovation financing (two invitations to tender issued, one for assistance and counselling services on financing for participants in Community research programmes and the other for strengthening the links between investors in and sponsors of technology projects (I-TEC project *(→ point 315)*), and a communication on risk-capital development adopted *(→ point 263)*, to simplifying the administrative environment for businesses, with the completion of the work of the BEST task force *(→ point 260)*, and to fostering the creation of technology-based firms, on which there was a large-scale consultation exercise aimed at drawing up specific proposals for action (conferences in Luxembourg in May and in Vienna in October).

322. Further initiatives were taken in the training field, involving the launch in July of a study of the requirements for training in the innovation and technology transfer processes.

([1]) COM(97) 736; Bull. 1/2-1998, point 1.3.148.
([2]) COM(96) 589, 1996 General Report, point 265; Supplement 3/97 — Bull.
([3]) OJ C 235, 27.7.1998; Bull. 5-1998, point 1.2.92.

Section 10

Education, vocational training and youth

Priority activities and objectives

323.   The Commission adopted proposals for new Community programmes in the fields of education, vocational training and youth covering the years 2000 to 2004. Seeking to achieve greater complementarity and consistency in the spirit of the communication entitled 'Towards a Europe of knowledge', and with the aim of fostering lifelong learning, the three programmes are structured around a common framework underpinned by a range of across-the-board measures. The Commission also presented a proposal for the third phase (2000-06) of the trans-European cooperation scheme for higher education (Tempus). Further progress was made in implementing the programmes scheduled to run until 1999 with, in particular, the Parliament and Council decision to increase the overall budget for the Socrates programme, adoption of the 1998-99 Community action programme 'European voluntary service for young people' and the ongoing process of opening the programmes up to the applicant countries.

General

324.   On 27 May, the Commission adopted proposals for implementing the new generation of programmes in the fields of education (Socrates), vocational training (Leonardo da Vinci) and youth (Table I). As far as these five-year programmes (1 January 2000 to 31 December 2004) are concerned, the Commission proposes to allocate total funding of ECU 3 billion, of which ECU 1.4 billion will be earmarked for the second phase of the Socrates programme, ECU 1 billion for the second phase of the Leonardo da Vinci programme and ECU 600 million for the Community action programme targeting young people; this represents an overall increase of 60 % compared with the existing programmes. The three programmes are to be interlinked by means of a common framework encompassing six broad elements: physical mobility for people; different forms of virtual mobility (use of new information and communications technologies); development of cooperation networks; promotion of linguistic and cultural skills; development of innovation through pilot projects based on transnational partnerships; and ongoing improvement of Community references (databases, exchanges of good practice) for the systems and policies relating to education, training and youth in the Member States. In addition, each programme pursues specific objectives (→ points 332, 335 and 339). This new generation of programmes should enable a total of 2.5 million Europeans to benefit from a mobility programme: 1.2 million students and 200 000 teachers under the Socrates programme, 400 000 young people undergoing training under the Leonardo da Vinci programme and 660 000 young people under the youth-oriented programme. On 21 December, the Council adopted common positions on the proposals for programmes in the fields of education (Socrates) and vocational training (Leonardo da Vinci).

325. The Economic and Social Committee endorsed, on 28 January([1]), the Commission's 1997 review([2]) of reactions to the White Paper entitled 'Teaching and learning: towards the learning society' ([3]). The Commission communication entitled 'Towards a Europe of knowledge' ([4]) was likewise endorsed by the Economic and Social Committee on 25 March([5]), and by the Committee of the Regions on 13 March([6]). The same communication was, moreover, the subject of a Parliament resolution adopted on 13 May, calling for a substantial increase in the budgetary resources allotted to the creation of a European education area ([7]).

326. In connection with the Commission communication entitled 'Learning in the information society — action plan for a European education initiative' ([8]), the Internet-based European schools network was inaugurated on 8 September in collaboration with the Education Ministries of the Member States. In October, the Commission also organised, for the second time, an Internet-based week of activity and information (Netd@ys Europe 1998) in schools and other education and training venues. Representatives of the multimedia, audiovisual and education sectors, working to ensure the success of this initiative, together established a European federation for their particular field.

([1]) OJ C 95, 30.3.1998; Bull. 1/2-1998, point 1.3.154.
([2]) COM(97) 256; 1997 General Report, point 355.
([3]) COM(95) 590; 1995 General Report, point 266.
([4]) COM(97) 563; 1997 General Report, point 356.
([5]) OJ C 157, 25.5.1998; Bull. 3-1998, point 1.2.89.
([6]) OJ C 180, 11.6.1998; Bull. 3-1998, point 1.2.89.
([7]) OJ C 167, 1.6.1998; Bull. 5-1998, point 1.2.98.
([8]) COM(96) 471; 1996 General Report, point 271; 1997 General Report, point 358.

Education

327. With the adoption, on 23 February, of Decision No 576/98/EC (Table I), Parliament and the Council increased by ECU 70 million the overall budget (1995-99) for the Socrates programme ([1]), thus providing a total of ECU 920 million.

328. In the field of higher education (Erasmus strand of the Socrates programme), financial assistance was given, in 1998, to 1 627 higher education establishments, thereby facilitating the mobility of 200 000 students and 35 000 teachers. The academic credit transfer system was implemented in 941 establishments. In addition, 270 joint syllabus development projects (comprising 80 'Masters' programmes, 60 basic or intermediate-level curricula, 115 European modules and 15 integrated language courses) and 250 intensive programmes were selected for funding. Also, the total number of active theme-based networks rose to 50.

329. As regards school education (Comenius strand), around 2 000 new school partnerships were financed in 1998, involving almost 7 000 coordinating schools and partners. Some 10 000 teachers benefited from the mobility provided by Comenius in 1998. Moreover, since 1996, 2 500 or so teachers have spent time in another country participating in Europe-wide continuing training activities. In 1998, the Commission also gave support to 132 projects designed to upgrade European teaching aids, and helped to finance 109 projects concerned with intercultural education and the education of children of migrant or travelling workers and of other travelling tradespeople.

330. To promote the acquisition of European language skills, support was given in 1998 to 40 European cooperation programmes for the training of language teachers, involving more than 200 establishments, under the Lingua strand of the Socrates programme. The Commission also awarded 6 000 mobility grants for language teachers and more than 500 grants enabling future teachers to spend time abroad. It financed 36 cooperation projects to devise language teaching and learning instruments and tools, and some 32 000 young people took part in 1 500 joint language-learning projects entailing two-week exchange visits.

331. Under the Socrates programme, the Commission also granted aid to 63 projects concerned with the development of open and distance learning and new information technologies in the education sector, to

---

([1]) OJ L 87, 20.4.1995; 1995 General Report, point 267.

72 projects in respect of adult education, to 11 projects for exchanges of experience and information on education systems and policies, to one pilot project for assessing the quality of schooling, and to 1 750 ARION study visits for educationalists. It also continued to support the Eurydice (information on education systems) and NARIC (academic recognition of qualifications) networks. In addition, the Commission lent its support, outside the Socrates programme, to 93 projects for promoting and safe-guarding regional and minority languages and cultures, as well as to the activities of the European Bureau for Lesser-used Languages.

332.   On 27 May, the Commission adopted a proposal for a decision establishing the second phase of the Socrates programme for the period 2000-04 (→ point 324). The four primary objectives are: to strengthen the European dimension; to promote cooperation in all sectors and at all levels; to remove obstacles to such cooperation, in particular by improv-ing the recognition of diplomas and periods of study; and to encourage innovation.

333.   On 24 September, the Council adopted a recommendation on European cooperation in quality assurance in higher education (Table II), urging the Member States to establish transparent systems of quality assessment and quality assurance in higher education, with due regard for the autonomy and independence of the competent authorities.

Vocational training

334.   In the context of the Community action programme for the implementation of a vocational training policy 'Leonardo da Vinci' ([1]), for which the 1998 budget amounted to ECU 143.053 million, the call for proposals launched in December 1997 ([2]), followed for the first time by a television broadcast via the 'Europe by satellite' service (→ point 1154) in all the countries participating in the programme, resulted in the submission of 3 288 proposals. In all, in the EU Member States and the EFTA countries within the European Economic Area, 614 projects (427 pilot projects, 156 placement and exchange programmes involving 7 000 students and training providers, and 31 surveys and analyses), encom-passing some 13 000 partners, received financial support totalling ECU 81.3 million. A total of 107 projects involving more than 590 partners, with ECU 14.5 million in funding, were selected in certain applicant

---

[1]   OJ L 340, 29.12.1994; 1994 General Report, points 292 and 300.
[2]   OJ C 372, 9.12.1997.

countries (Romania, Hungary, Czech Republic and Cyprus, with the addition of Slovakia, Poland, Estonia, Latvia and Lithuania in the course of the year (→ point 809). Moreover, ECU 32.5 million (including ECU 4.7 million for the applicant countries) was granted for mobility-related measures involving some 24 000 persons, most of them young people undergoing initial training, apprentices, young workers and job-seekers. Additionally, the Commission allowed a one-year extension for carrying out 325 projects selected in 1995, at a total cost of ECU 17.025 million.

335.   On 27 May, the Commission adopted a proposal for a decision establishing the second phase of the Leonardo da Vinci programme for the period 2000-04 (→ point 324). The three objectives to be pursued are social and occupational integration of young people, development of access to high-quality continuing training, and helping those in difficult circumstances to integrate better on the labour market.

336.   The Council adopted, on 21 December, a decision on the promotion of European pathways for work-linked training, including apprenticeship (Table II). The European Parliament, on 15 January ([1]), and the Committee of the Regions, on 15 July ([2]), endorsed the Commission's report on access to continuing training in the European Union ([3]). The Economic and Social Committee meanwhile endorsed, on 28 January ([4]), the communication entitled 'Promoting apprenticeship training in Europe' ([5]).

Youth

337.   On 20 July, Parliament and the Council adopted the Community action programme 'European voluntary service for young people' (Table I). Covering a two-year period (1998-99), this programme is designed to provide young people with an educational experience which may stand them in good stead from a social and occupational point of view. With a budget totalling ECU 25 million for 1998, the programme has given more than 3 500 young people the opportunity to participate as volunteers in social, cultural or environmental activities of benefit to the local community.

([1])   OJ C 34, 2.2.1998; Bull. 1/2-1998, point 1.3.155.
([2])   OJ C 315, 13.10.1998; Bull. 7/8-1998, point 1.3.126.
([3])   COM(97) 180; 1997 General Report, point 369.
([4])   OJ C 95, 30.3.1998; Bull. 1/2-1998, point 1.3.153.
([5])   COM(97) 300; 1997 General Report, point 369.

338. New invitations to tender (¹) were issued under the 'Youth for Europe' programme (²), which seeks to help young people in their education outside the formal school system; the 1998 budget amounted to ECU 26.4 million. The number of young people able to take part in activities financed under this programme exceeds 70 000. Moreover, EU-funded assistance for 111 non-governmental youth organisations totalled ECU 1.1 million, while ECU 2 million was earmarked for the European Youth Forum.

339. On 27 May, the Commission adopted a proposal for a decision establishing a new Community action programme in the youth field for the period 2000-04 *(→ point 324).* This programme, which incorporates the existing 'Youth for Europe' *(→ point 338)* and 'European voluntary service for young people' *(→ point 337)* programmes, is intended to focus on four aspects: individual mobility within the framework of European voluntary service; group mobility entailing transnational exchanges; initiatives giving young people an opportunity to play an active role in society; and activities tying in with other areas of Community action.

340. The Council and the Ministers for Youth meeting within the Council adopted, on 26 November, a resolution on youth participation (³).

Cooperation with non-member countries

341. As part of the pre-accession strategy, the Socrates, Leonardo da Vinci and 'Youth for Europe' programmes were opened up to another five applicant countries: Poland, Slovakia, Estonia, Latvia and Lithuania. Bulgaria, though, was involved only in the 'Youth for Europe' programme *(→ point 809).*

342. On 17 July, the Commission adopted a proposal for a decision adopting the third phase (2000-06) of the trans-European cooperation scheme for higher education (Tempus III) (Table II), enabling the eligible countries (independent States of the former Soviet Union, non-associated countries of central Europe and Mongolia) to continue with the reform

---

(¹)   OJ C 86, 21.3.1998.
(²)   OJ L 87, 20.4.1995; 1995 General Report, point 259.
(³)   Bull. 11-1998, point 1.2.82.

of higher education systems set in train under the previous programme (Tempus II) (1994-2000) ([1]).

343. Under the cooperation agreements concluded in 1995 ([2]) with the United States and Canada, a third selection ([3]) of joint projects was made. In all, six cooperation projects with Canada and 11 cooperation projects with the United States were selected, involving a sum of ECU 600 000 for Canada and ECU 1.2 million for the United States.

European Training Foundation

344. On 17 July, the Council adopted Regulation (EC) No 1572/98 extending the remit of the Foundation to cover Mediterranean non-member countries and territories (Table I). The applicant countries of central Europe meanwhile took part in a seminar prior to the meeting of the Foundation's Governing Board on 20 February in Turin. The Foundation published its annual report for 1997 ([4]) on 28 July.

European Centre for the Development of Vocational Training (Cedefop)

345. Cedefop pressed ahead with its activities on the basis of the medium-term guidelines for the period 1997-2000 ([5]), encompassing research promotion and development, exchanges, debates and publications relating to vocational training. The programme of study visits for vocational training specialists involved 775 people.

European University Institute ([6])

346. The Commission contributed around ECU 5 million towards the 1998 budget of the European University Institute; the money was ear-

---

([1])   OJ L 306, 28.11.1996; Twenty-seventh General Report, point 266; 1996 General Report, point 286.
([2])   OJ L 279, 22.11.1995 (United States); OJ L 300, 13.12.1995 (Canada); 1995 General Report, point 285.
([3])   Previous selection: 1997 General Report, point 374.
([4])   COM(1998) 481.
([5])   1996 General Report, point 288.
([6])   The report by the President of the Institute and an information booklet on the Institute's activities can be obtained from its headquarters (Publications Office, via dei Roccettini 9, I-50016 San Domenico di Fiesole (Firenze)). Information about the Institute and its activities can also be found on the Internet (http://www.iue.it), including the European Foreign Policy Bulletin.

marked for scientific and research activities ([1]) and for the historical archives of the European Communities (→ *points 1166 and 1167*), which are managed by the Institute. For the 1997/98 academic year, the Institute and its four departments ([2]) had 47 professorial chairs, five of which were held jointly with the Robert Schuman Centre. There were 363 third-year research students (330 of them from the Member States) and 85 doctorates were awarded. The European Forum addressed the issue of migrations in 1997/98; the welfare state is the topic for 1998/99. The annual Jean Monnet lecture was delivered on 20 March by Mr Prodi, the Italian Prime Minister, on the subject 'European industry and finance in international competition' ([3]). In January, Mr Mandelson, a Member of the UK Government, outlined to the Institute the projects to be carried out during the United Kingdom's Presidency of the Union. In April, Mr Masterson, the President of the Institute, discussed with Mr Busek, the Polish Prime Minister, the opportunities for university cooperation between the Institute and Poland; Mr Czarnecki, the Polish Minister for European Integration, visited the Institute and took part in a research seminar. Mrs Lalumière, a Member of the European Parliament, and Mr Piris, the Director-General of the Council's Legal Service, spoke at the ninth session of the Academy of European Law. Moreover, the Academy and the Robert Schuman Centre were involved (together with Harvard University, the Max Planck Institute in Cologne and the ECSA (Austria)) in the creation of ERPA, a computerised archive providing on-line access to working papers in the field of European integration ([4]).

---

[1] 1996 General Report, point 289.
[2] History, economics, law, political and social sciences.
[3] Information on the Jean Monnet project to improve university teaching and research on European integration is contained in Section 1 ('Priority activities and objectives') of Chapter XI (→ *point 1160*).
[4] http://olymp.wu-wien.ac.at/erpa/.

Section 11

Economic and social cohesion

Priority activities and objectives

347.   As part of its work on implementing Agenda 2000, the Commission presented proposed new regulations on the Structural Funds and the Cohesion Fund. These proposals, designed to constitute the legal framework for the support measures to be financed by these Funds during the next programming period (2000-06), are based on the principles set out in Agenda 2000, i.e. concentration of funding, simplification of procedures and clarification of responsibilities [1]. The Commission also proposed a framework for action on sustainable urban development and looked at how cohesion, research and innovation influence each other.

Structural measures, regional policy

General outline

Implementation of Agenda 2000

348.   As part of its work on implementing Agenda 2000 (→ points 1 et seq.), the Commission adopted proposals for a new general regulation containing the general provisions applicable to all the Structural Funds and four 'vertical' regulations, one for each Fund (→ points 349 to 354). These proposals cover the next programming period (2000-06).

349.   The proposed general regulation containing the general provisions on the Structural Funds (Table II) set out the tasks, priority objectives (now only three, in accordance with Agenda 2000) and organisation of the four Structural Funds, the rules governing them and provisions to ensure their effectiveness and coordination both among themselves and with the other existing financial instruments. Under this proposal, the new Objective 1, financed by the ERDF, the ESF, the FIFG and the

---

[1]   An overview of these proposals and the action taken on them by the other institutions is to be found in Chapter I ('Agenda 2000') (→ points 1 et seq.). Each proposal is presented individually in this section (→ points 349 to 354, 376). In the table of legislation under the consultation and cooperation procedures (Table II at the end of this Report), they will be found under 'Agenda 2000' (at the head of the table), not under 'Economic and social cohesion.'

EAGGF Guidance Section, is to help promote the development and structural adjustment of regions whose development is lagging behind (regions whose level of development, measured on the basis of per capita GDP over the last three years available, is less than 75 % of the Community average). The most remote regions and areas qualifying under the current Objective 6 would also be eligible and those currently eligible under Objective 1 which do not satisfy the 75 % threshold would receive tapering transitional support. About two thirds of the total budget of the Structural Funds would go to the Objective 1 regions, which contain about 20 % of the population of the Union. Objective 2, financed by the ERDF, the ESF, the FIFG and the EAGGF Guarantee Section, is to help support the economic and social conversion of areas experiencing structural difficulties. Such areas, whose economies may be based on industry or services and which may be rural, urban or fisheries-dependent, should include 18 % of the Union's population (the guideline is 10 % for industrial areas and services, 5 % for rural areas, 2 % for urban areas, and 1 % for areas dependent on fisheries). A breakdown by Member State will be made on the basis of a number of criteria, with the reduction for any individual Member State limited to no more than one third of the coverage of the areas currently eligible under Objectives 2 and 5b. The areas now covered by those two objectives but not eligible under the new Objective 2 will receive transitional support phased out over four years. The new Objective 3 is intended to support the adaptation and modernisation of policies and systems relating to education, training and employment throughout the Union. It will be financed only by the ESF and will also provide a frame of reference for assistance from this Fund under Objectives 1 and 2, so ensuring a coherent approach as regards strategies and the development of human resources. The areas where Objective 3 will provide finance are those not eligible under Objectives 1 and 2. The proposal also provides for the simplification and rationalisation of the Community initiatives, which will be reduced in number from 13 to 3: cross-border, transnational and interregional cooperation, to encourage harmonious and balanced regional development planning, to be financed by the ERDF; rural development, to be financed by the EAGGF Guidance Section; and new transnational cooperation to fight all forms of discrimination and inequality which prevent access to employment, to be financed by the ESF.

350.   With regard to the implementation of structural assistance, the proposal provides for a clearer division of responsibilities and further decentralisation of programming by extending the responsibilities of the Member States, increasing transparency and the monitoring of evalua-

tions and financial control and increasing the involvement of those concerned locally, principally through global grants to intermediaries. The Commission is also proposing simplifying the financial management of these measures, mainly by making the budget commitments at the beginning of each year automatic (commitments not used within two years of the year of commitment would be cancelled) and by simplifying the rules on eligible expenditure (eligibility would be governed by national rules, except where there are common rules). The Commission is also proposing keeping back a reserve of 10 % of the total budget of the Structural Funds for allocation, in the light of intermediate assessments, to the programmes which are the most effective in achieving their targets and in terms of their management and budget implementation, subject to compliance with the principle of additionality.

351. Under the proposed regulation on the European Regional Development Fund (ERDF) (Table II), this Fund will help finance productive investment for the creation or maintenance of permanent jobs in the Objective 1 regions, investment in infrastructure in the areas eligible under Objectives 1 and 2 and measures to stimulate and support initiatives for local development and employment and small and medium-sized firms. In the Objective 1 regions, the ERDF may also help finance investment in education and health which contributes to the structural adjustment of those regions. It will also finance the Community initiative on cross-border, transnational and interregional cooperation *(→ point 349)*.

352. The proposal on the European Social Fund (Table II) makes this Fund responsible for assistance in five areas: active labour market policies to fight unemployment; encouraging social inclusion; lifelong education and training systems to promote employability; anticipating and facilitating economic and social change; and greater participation in the labour market by women.

353. The proposal on structural measures in the fisheries sector (Table II) concerns assistance from the FIFG (Financial Instrument for Fisheries Guidance) and the EAGGF Guarantee Section throughout the Union, principally to encourage modernisation of the fleet and remove excess capacity, develop aquaculture, improve port facilities, improve processing and marketing and mount promotional campaigns. Social measures for fishermen directly affected by restructuring and assistance for diversification (the present PESCA initiative) would continue to be eligible under Objectives 1 and 2.

354. Under the proposal on support for rural development from the European Agricultural Guidance and Guarantee Fund (EAGGF), the Guidance Section of this Fund will finance measures in areas eligible under Objective 1 (apart from agri-environmental measures, early-retirement schemes, woodland management and aid for agriculture in less favoured areas, which are financed from the Guarantee Section across the whole of the territory of the Union) while the Guarantee Section will finance measures in areas not eligible under Objective 1 *(→ point 554).*

Other policy measures

355. On 30 October, the Commission adopted the ninth annual report on the implementation of the Structural Funds (1997) [1] which, like previous reports [2], includes a cross-sectional theme: this time it was assistance to small and medium-sized businesses. On 27 May [3] the Economic and Social Committee and on 28 May [4] the European Parliament gave their opinions on the eighth report (covering 1996).

356. On 2 July [5] the European Parliament and on 9 September [6] the Economic and Social Committee endorsed, subject to certain comments, the main objectives of the draft European spatial development perspective (ESDP) which the Commission presented in 1997 [7]. With a view to drafting the final version of the ESDP, the Commission organised a series of transnational seminars on subjects related to development planning (the European dimension of planning, transport and telecommunications, the urban system in Europe, the integrated management of water resources). Work also began on draft preparatory studies for setting up a European Spatial Planning Observatory. On 19 November the Committee of the Regions underlined the importance of cross-border and transnational cooperation between local authorities [8].

357. Following its communication on the urban agenda, on which opinions were adopted by the Economic and Social Committee on 28

---

[1]   COM(1998) 562; Bull. 10-1998, point 1.2.81.
[2]   COM(96) 502; COM(97) 526; 1996 General Report, point 293; 1997 General Report, point 381.
[3]   OJ C 235, 27.7.1998; Bull. 5-1998, point 1.2.109.
[4]   OJ C 195, 22.6.1998; Bull. 5-1998, point 1.2.108.
[5]   OJ C 226, 20.7.1998; Bull. 7/8-1998, point 1.3.134.
[6]   OJ C 407, 28.12.1998; Bull. 9-1998, point 1.2.66.
[7]   1997 General Report, point 387.
[8]   Bull. 11-1998, point 1.2.84.

January (^{1}), and by the Committee of the Regions on 14 May (^{2}) and two resolutions were adopted by Parliament on 2 July (^{3}), the Commission presented a framework for action for sustainable urban development on 28 October (^{4}) covering both the better integration of the urban dimension into Community policies and their instruments and specific innovative measures.

358.   On 27 May, the Commission adopted a communication entitled 'Reinforcing cohesion and competitiveness through research, technological development and innovation' (^{5}) in which it picked out the promotion of innovation at regional level, improvements in industrial networking and cooperation, the development of human resources and the preparation of integrated regional strategies as ways of improving the contribution of research, technological development and innovation to the goal of cohesion and the development of the least favoured areas. On 2 December, the Economic and Social Committee welcomed the communication (^{6}). In its resolution of 15 January (^{7}), following the Commission's communication on cohesion and the information society (^{8}), Parliament stressed the need for all Union citizens to have access to the new information technologies, irrespective of their geographical or social situation.

359.   On 19 February, Parliament gave its views on the execution of Structural Fund budget appropriations (^{9}) and, on 16 July, on the priorities for the adjustment of programmes under the Structural Funds until the end of 1999 (^{10}). It also drew the attention of the Commission, on 28 May, to the problems of island regions (^{11}); on 16 July, the Committee of the Regions did likewise with regard to the most remote regions (^{12}).

(^{1})   OJ C 95, 30.3.1998; Bull. 1/2-1998, point 1.3.158.
(^{2})   OJ C 251, 10.8.1998; Bull. 5-1998, point 1.2.110.
(^{3})   OJ C 226, 20.7.1998; Bull. 7/8-1998, points 1.3.132 and 1.3.133.
(^{4})   COM(1998) 605; Bull. 10-1998, point 1.2.82.
(^{5})   COM(1998) 275; Bull. 5-1998, point 1.2.107.
(^{6})   Bull. 12-1998.
(^{7})   OJ C 34, 2.2.1998; Bull. 1/2-1998, point 1.3.157.
(^{8})   COM(97) 7; 1997 General Report, point 388.
(^{9})   OJ C 80, 16.3.1998; Bull. 1/2-1998, point 1.3.159.
(^{10})   OJ C 292, 21.9.1998; Bull. 7/8-1998, point 1.3.135.
(^{11})   OJ C 195, 22.6.1998; Bull. 5-1998, point 1.2.113.
(^{12})   OJ C 315, 13.10.1998; Bull. 7/8-1998, point 1.3.140.

Community support frameworks (CSFs) and single programming documents (SPDs)

Regions whose development is lagging behind (Objective 1)

360. The breakdown by Member State of commitments for 1998 under Objective 1 is given in Table 4.

TABLE 4

Commitments in 1998 — Objective 1

(million ECU)

Member State	ERDF	ESF	EAGGF (Guidance Section)	FIFG
Belgium	199.654	20.674	—	0.77
Germany	1 999.445	764.742	559.152	19.667
Greece	2 174.916	540.436	352.147	33.003
Spain	1 941.017	1 073.505	598.351	158.830
France	297.798	59.058	86.180	9.815
Ireland	753.873	652.794	104.457	10.445
Italy	1 856.572	304.582	367.455	68.046
Netherlands	47.797	4.457	2.432	2.358
Austria	29.760	12.276	—	—
Portugal	2 215.361	1 166.483	410.661	41.143
United Kingdom	251.090	71.174	21.973	10.148
Total	11 767.283	4 670.182	2 502.808	354.225

Declining industrial areas (Objective 2)

361. On 29 July, the Commission approved a multiregional SPD for the conversion of defence activities in France ([1]). On 27 May the Economic and Social Committee ([2]) and on 9 October the European Parliament ([3]) gave their views on the new regional programmes for 1997-99 presented by the Commission in November 1997 ([4]).

362. The breakdown by Member State of commitments for 1998 under Objective 2 is given in Table 5.

([1])   Bull. 7/8-1998, point 1.3.136.
([2])   OJ C 235, 27.7.1998; Bull. 5-1998, point 1.2.111.
([3])   OJ C 328, 26.10.1998; Bull. 10-1998, point 1.2.83.
([4])   COM(97) 524; 1997 General Report, point 393.

TABLE 5

Commitments in 1998 — Objective 2

(million ECU)

Member State	ERDF	ESF
Belgium	9.005	—
Denmark	—	—
Germany	73.886	5.540
Spain	469.408	158.656
France	396.336	83.031
Italy	11.967	15.673
Luxembourg	—	—
Netherlands	17.290	4.106
Austria	17.290	3.479
Finland	—	—
Sweden	16.060	1.070
United Kingdom	633.810	179.263
Total	1 627.762	450.818

Combating long-term unemployment and facilitating the integration into working life of women and of persons exposed to exclusion from the labour market (Objective 3)

363. The breakdown by Member State of commitments for 1998 under Objective 3 is given in Table 6.

TABLE 6

Commitments in 1998 — Objective 3

(million ECU)

Member State	ESF (outside Objective 1 regions)
Belgium	64.215
Denmark	51.782
Germany	558.285
Spain	296.805
France	602.286
Italy	227.161
Luxembourg	3.769
Netherlands	130.940
Austria	4.431
Finland	30.103
Sweden	91.499
United Kingdom	574.418
Total	2 635.693

The adaptation of workers to industrial changes and to changes in production systems (Objective 4)

364. On 11 March, the Commission approved an SPD for all the regions of the United Kingdom (other than those covered by Objective 1) (¹).

365. The breakdown by Member State of commitments for 1998 under Objective 4 is given in Table 7.

TABLE 7

Commitments in 1998 — Objective 4

(million ECU)

Member State	ESF (outside Objective 1 regions)
Belgium	7.046
Denmark	9.453
Germany	95.329
Spain	75.697
France	157.660
Italy	—
Luxembourg	0.015
Netherlands	45.066
Austria	16.317
Finland	16.166
Sweden	87
United Kingdom	111.4
Total	621.149

Adjustment of agricultural structures (Objective 5a)

366. On 20 January, the Council adopted the list of less favoured areas in Denmark (Table II). It also decided, on 22 October, to extend to 31 December 1999 the special provisions laid down for the application of compensatory allowances to small farmers in Portugal (Table II). On 24 March, the Commission amended the CSF for Italy on structural measures to improve the processing and marketing conditions for agricultural and forestry products in order to include Abruzzi, since this region has not been eligible under Objective 1 from 1997 (²).

(¹) Bull. 3-1998, point 1.2.100.
(²) Bull. 3-1998, point 1.2.101.

367. The breakdown by Member State of the commitments for 1998 under Objective 5a is shown in Table 8.

TABLE 8

Commitments in 1998 — Objective 5a

(million ECU)

Member State	EAGGF Guidance Section (areas outside Objectives 1 and 6)
Belgium	35.384
Denmark	27.442
Germany	231.188
Spain	92.606
France	307.306
Italy	139.626
Luxembourg	12.216
Netherlands	0.360
Austria	94.123
Finland	63.056
Sweden	28.337
United Kingdom	34.65
Total	1 066.294

Fisheries structures (Objective 5a 'fisheries')

368. On 3 November, the Council consolidated the regulation laying down the criteria and conditions for structural assistance in the fisheries sector (Table II). Since this regulation expires on 31 December 1999, the Commission adopted a proposal for a new regulation on 16 December which sets out the rules, terms and conditions for structural assistance in 2000-06 (Table II). On 17 December the Council adopted specific measures for fishermen affected by the ban on driftnets *(→ point 601).*

369. The breakdown by Member State of the commitments for 1998 under Objective 5a 'fishcries' is shown in Table 9.

Development of rural areas

370. The breakdown by Member State of commitments for 1998 under Objective 5b is given in Table 10.

TABLE 9

Commitments in 1998 — Objective 5a 'fisheries'

(million ECU)

Member State	FIFG (areas outside Objectives 1 and 6)
Belgium	0.826
Denmark	23.540
Germany	12.740
Spain	40.540
France	1.420
Italy	
Luxembourg	
Netherlands	
Austria	
Finland	
Sweden	
United Kingdom	14.770
Total	93.836

TABLE 10

Commitments in 1998 — Objective 5b

(million ECU)

Member State	ERDF	ESF	EAGGF Guidance Section
Belgium	6.927	0.710	3.482
Denmark	3.802	2.892	—
Germany	73.253	31.094	31.705
Spain	29.748	19.583	25.142
France	239.815	80.840	200.367
Italy	121.899	50.782	238.531
Luxembourg	1.204	0.366	—
Netherlands	6.743	2.064	5.297
Austria	29.287	21.478	32.996
Finland	21.370	—	13.310
Sweden	17.132	0.323	3.514
United Kingdom	81.553	16.222	8.456
Total	632.733	226.354	562.800

Regions with an extremely low population density (Objective 6)

371.   Following the mid-term review of implementation of the SPD for Finland, the Commission made adjustments to this document on 17 June. Commitments under Objective 6 in 1998 totalled ECU 186.3 million, of which ECU 88.4 million went to Finland and ECU 97.9 million to Sweden.

Community initiatives

372. In a report adopted on 24 February ([1]), the Commission recommended that support for the Portuguese textile industry introduced in 1995 ([2]) should continue. On 4 March, it extended the scope of the Konver initiative to further regions in the United Kingdom ([3]). It also modified, on 16 December, the indicative breakdown of funds for the Community initiatives so as to be able to finance the PEACE initiative (peace and reconciliation in Northern Ireland) in 1999 with ECU 100 million ([4]).

373. The commitments for Community initiatives in 1998 are set out in Table 11.

TABLE 11

Commitments 1998 — Community initiatives

(million ECU)

Initiative	Country	Amount per programme
ADAPT	Germany	33.390
	Greece	0.812
	Spain	80.020
	France	70.461
	Ireland	6.733
	Italy	43.920
	Netherlands	32.056
	United Kingdom	107.304

([1]) COM(1998) 91; Bull. 1/2-1998, point 1.3.162.
([2]) OJ L 86, 20.4.1995; 1995 General Report, point 319.
([3]) Bull. 3-1998, point 1.2.102.
([4]) Bull. 12-1998.

TABLE 11 (continued)

(million ECU)

Initiative	Country	Amount per programme
Employment	Belgium	7.939
	Germany	78.110
	Greece	9.656
	Spain	139.920
	France	55.315
	Ireland	22.829
	Italy	95.083
	Netherlands	16.215
	Portugal	1.420
	United Kingdom	55.106
Interreg II		572.202
Konver II	Belgium	0.940
	Germany	25.912
	Greece	9.937
	France	3.093
	Luxembourg	0.091
	Netherlands	15.325
	United Kingdom	1.673
Leader II	Belgium	2.724
	Germany	12.205
	Greece	36.547
	Spain	90.427
	France	1.881
	Ireland	53.113
	Italy	12.092
	Netherlands	2.160
	Austria	2.957
	Portugal	46.511
	Finland	0.248
	United Kingdom	2.636
PEACE		162.858
PESCA		51.020

TABLE 11 (continued)

(million ECU)

Initiative	Country	Amount per programme
SMEs	Germany	1.191
	Greece	16.862
	Spain	85.078
	France	18.095
	Ireland	0.304
	Italy	29.438
	Austria	0.760
	Portugal	8.867
	United Kingdom	7.702
	Not defined	5.234
Rechar II	Belgium	1.064
	Germany	24.594
	Greece	0.148
	France	1.579
	United Kingdom	9.684
REGIS II	Spain	41.853
	France	31.240
Resider II	Germany	15.565
	Spain	30.162
	France	3.485
	Italy	21.588
	Luxembourg	1.785
	United Kingdom	0.585
RETEX	Belgium	1.042
	Germany	14.014
	Greece	18.282
	France	3.934
	Italy	49.917
	Netherlands	0.007
	Austria	0.674
	United Kingdom	1.129
URBAN	Belgium	7.894
	Denmark	0.156
	Germany	0.513
	Spain	94.037
	France	2.988
	Ireland	8.577
	Italy	61.443
	Finland	1.632
	United Kingdom	4.697

Other structural operations

374. Following the peace agreement in Northern Ireland, the Council on 27 April (^{1}), the European Parliament on 30 April (^{2}), and the European Council in Cardiff in June (^{3}), welcomed the constructive contribution made by the Union to peace and reconciliation through its various aid programmes (^{4}). The European Council meeting in Vienna in December stressed the Union's desire to continue playing an active role in encouraging peace and lasting prosperity in Northern Ireland (^{5}).

Innovative measures and other regional operations

375. The financial assistance given in 1998 to pilot projects provided for in the basic regulation of the various Funds is set out in Table 12.

Cohesion Fund

376. As part of its work on implementing Agenda 2000 *(→ points 1 et seq.)*, the Commission adopted two proposals to amend Regulation (EC) No 1164/94 establishing a Cohesion Fund (Table II). These proposals are intended to adjust the provisions on macroeconomic conditionality with regard to the Member States participating in the single currency, increase the use made of private finance, use the rate of part-financing to encourage correct application of the 'polluter pays' principle and simplify financial management of the Fund.

377. On 7 October, the Commission adopted its annual report on the work of the Cohesion Fund in 1997 (^{6}). The report pointed out that commitment and payment appropriations were fully utilised and that the Fund has moved much closer to its goal of balanced funding for environment and transport projects, with 49.2 % of commitment appropriations going to the environment and 50.8 % to transport between 1993 and 1997. On 28 May, Parliament adopted a resolution (^{7}) on the 1996 report (^{8}).

(^{1})   Bull. 4-1998, point 1.2.73.
(^{2})   OJ C 152, 18.5.1998; Bull. 4-1998, point 1.2.74.
(^{3})   Bull. 6-1998, point I.33.
(^{4})   1994 General Report, point 474; 1995 General Report, point 321; 1996 General Report, point 313; 1997 General Report, point 405.
(^{5})   Bull. 12-1998.
(^{6})   COM(1998) 543; Bull. 10-1998, point 1.2.85.
(^{7})   OJ C 195, 22.6.1998; Bull. 5-1998, point 1.2.112.
(^{8})   COM(97) 302; 1997 General Report, point 408.

TABLE 12

Financing of pilot projects in 1998

(million ECU)

Fund/aim	Number of projects	Total amount
ERDF		
— Interregional cooperation	64	100.430
— Regional economic innovation	17	14.077
— Spatial development	33	24.625
— Urban development	3	3.382
ESF		
— Training	11	4.127
— Work organisation	1	0.315
— Job creation	17	5.174
— Employment services	3	1.177
— Social dialogue	3	9.101
EAGGF		
— Technical assistance	—	0.687
FIFG		
— Small-scale coastal fishing (fishermen and women family members)	18	1.860
— Studies, technical assistance and information	—	2.460

378. In accordance with Article 6 of Regulation (EC) No 1164/94 establishing a Cohesion Fund (^{1}), in April and November the Commission again examined the budget position of the Member States eligible under the Fund and concluded that assistance to those countries could continue.

379. Commitments for financing Cohesion Fund projects in 1998 totalled ECU 2 870.7 million. A breakdown of those commitments by country and topic is given in Table 13.

(^{1})   OJ L 130, 25.5.1994; 1994 General Report, point 434.

TABLE 13

Commitments in 1998 — Cohesion Fund

(million ECU)

Member State	Environment		Transport		Total (million ECU)	Breakdown (%)
	Million ECU	%	Million ECU	%		
Greece	209.850	13.74	306.548	22.97	516.798	17.99
Spain	871.041	57.01	704.853	52.82	1575.894	54.90
Ireland	135.358	8.86	116.352	8.72	258.482 ([1])	9.00
Portugal	311.518	20.39	206.743	15.49	518.264	18.05
Technical assistance					1.665	0.06
Total	1 527.767	100	1334.496	100	2870.700	100

([1]) Including ECU 6.772 million in other commitments than for transport and the environment.

Section 12

Measures for the most remote regions

380.   In 1998 work continued on consolidating the *acquis communautaire* in favour of the most remote regions (the French overseas departments, the Canary Islands and the Azores and Madeira). This concerned mainly agriculture and fisheries.

381.   On 8 January, the Commission adopted a supplementary plan for the restructuring and improvement of sugar cane plantations in the French overseas departments ([1]) to achieve the economic objectives laid down by the programme, i.e. an optimal replanting rate. The most remote regions which produce bananas were also affected by amendments to the regulation on the common organisation of the market in bananas following the findings of the World Trade Organisation panel *(→ point 576).*

382.   On 17 July, the Council adopted Regulation (EC) No 1587/98 introducing a scheme to compensate for the additional costs incurred in the marketing of certain fishery products from the Azores, Madeira, the Canary Islands and the French departments of Guiana and Réunion as a result of those regions' remoteness *(→ point 596).*

383.   Concerning the indirect taxation arrangements applicable in the French overseas departments, the Court of Justice gave three judgments on dock dues ([2]). The Court confirmed that these charges are compatible with Community law and authorised a system of exemptions provided these were necessary, proportionate and precisely determined.

---

[1]   OJ L 5, 9.1.1998.
[2]   Cases C-212/96 [1998] ECR I-0743, C-37/96 and C-38/96 [1998] ECR I-2039, and C-405/96 to C-408/96 [1998] ECR.

Section 13

Trans-European networks

Priority activities and objectives

384. Following the adoption of guidelines for the various trans-European networks in 1996 and 1997, 1998 was a year of consolidation. In several reports and communications, the Commission took stock of progress with the projects provided for in the guidelines, which in general was satisfactory. In the context of Agenda 2000, it also proposed a revision of the financial provisions applicable to trans-European networks.

General matters and financing

385. On 18 March, as part of the process of implementing its 'Agenda 2000' communication, the Commission proposed a revision of Regulation (EC) No 2236/95 laying down general rules for the granting of Community financial aid in the field of trans-European networks (→ *point 6*).

386. Community funding for the trans-European networks (TENs) is shown in Table 14. The TEN financial assistance committee [1] met six times in the course of the year, and endorsed the commitment of ECU 520.27 million, of which ECU 474 million for transport, ECU 27.65 million for telecommunications and ECU 18.62 million for energy.

387. On 2 October, the Commission adopted its annual report on the trans-European networks for 1997 [2].

Transport

388. On 3 June, as requested by the Luxembourg European Council on employment [3], the Commission adopted, for presentation to the Cardiff European Council, a report [4] on progress with and implementation of

[1] 1997 General Report, point 420.
[2] COM(1998) 391; Bull. 10-1998, point 1.2.87.
[3] 1997 General Report, point 418.
[4] COM(1998) 356; Bull. 6-1998, point 1.3.91.

TABLE 14

Community financing of TENs in 1998

(million ECU)

Sector	Type of aid	Instrument	1993-94	1995	1996	1997	1998	Total to date
Transport	Loans	EIB (¹) (²)	3 847	3 819	3 504	4 943	4 415	20 529
	Guarantees	EIF (²)	76	85	303	55	71	590
	Subsidies	Structural Funds (¹) (³)	884	115	2 639	527	n.a.	n.a.
		Cohesion Fund	1 887	1 108	1 221	1 251	1 337	6 805
	Subsidies, interest rebates, loan guarantees and co-financing of studies	TENs budget heading B5-70	385	240	280	352	474	1 731
		(of which 14 priority projects)	180	182	211	211	305	1 089
Energy	Loans	EIB (¹) (²)	1 077	745	1 176	854	393	4 245
	Guarantees	EIF (²)	203	12	270	4	5	498
	Co-financing of studies and subsidies	Structural Funds (¹) (³)	676	88	1 265	277	n.a.	n.a.
		TENs budget heading B5-71	0	12	9	24	19	64
Telecommuni-cations	Loans	EIB (¹) (²)	3 788	507	1 626	1 880	3 434	11 234
	Guarantees	EIF (²)	156	19	9	276	230	691
	Subsidies	Structural Funds (¹) (³)	295	0	173	n.a.	n.a.	n.a.
	Co-financing of feasibility and validation studies	TENs budget heading B5-720	22	23	16	27	28	115
Telematics networks	Subsidies	TENs budget heading B5-721	72	47	44	47	15	225

n.a. = not available.
(¹) Trans-European networks and related projects.
(²) Projects signed.
(³) Commitment of appropriations.

the 14 trans-European transport network projects identified by the Essen European Council (^{1}) as having priority. The report gives an overview as well as a timetable and a financial plan for each of the projects. Overall, significant progress has been made: three projects are near completion (the Cork-Dublin-Belfast-Larne conventional rail link, Malpensa airport and the Øresund fixed link), and most of the other projects are due for completion by around 2005. Meeting in Cardiff in June, the European Council (^{2}) recalled the importance it attaches to the implementation of the trans-European networks, including the 14 priority projects.

389.   On 28 October, the Commission adopted its first report (^{3}) on the implementation of the Community guidelines for the development of the trans-European transport network (^{4}) in 1996 and 1997. In this report it took stock, for each mode of transport, of the progress made, and put forward a number of options for the first review of the guidelines.

390.   The Commission's communication on the public-private partnership financing of trans-European transport network projects (^{5}) was endorsed by the Economic and Social Committee (^{6}), which, on 25 February, also specified the conditions which, in its opinion, govern the success of such partnerships. The Commission communication on connecting the Union's transport infrastructure network to its neighbours (^{7}) was endorsed by the Economic and Social Committee on 26 February (^{8}) and by the European Parliament on 7 October (^{9}).

391.   Activities relating to traffic and navigation management systems are dealt with in Section 15 ('Transport') of this chapter *(→ point 432).*

Telematics and telecommunications

392.   As part of the process of implementing Decision No 1336/97/EC on guidelines for trans-European telecommunications networks (^{10}), in January, the Commission adopted a work programme setting out the projects of common interest referred to in the decision. It also published

---

(^{1})   1994 General Report, point 324.
(^{2})   Bull. 6-1998, point I.16.
(^{3})   COM(1998) 614; Bull. 10-1998, point 1.2.88.
(^{4})   Decision No 1692/96/EC (OJ L 228, 9.9.1996); 1997 General Report, point 327.
(^{5})   COM(97) 453; 1997 General Report, point 421.
(^{6})   OJ C 129, 27.4.1998; Bull. 1/2-1998, point 1.3.165.
(^{7})   COM(97) 172; 1997 General Report, point 424.
(^{8})   OJ C 129, 27.4.1998; Bull. 1/2-1998, point 1.3.164.
(^{9})   OJ C 328, 26.10.1998; Bull. 10-1998, point 1.2.89.
(^{10})   OJ L 183, 11.7.1997; 1997 General Report, point 426.

three calls for proposals (¹) concerning the interoperation and development of telecommunications networks (mobile and satellite communication networks), generic telecommunications services and their applications in areas of public interest, and support and coordination schemes. On 2 February, it adopted its final report (²) concerning preparatory actions in the field of integrated broadband communications.

393.   On 21 December, the Council adopted common positions on the two proposals for decisions concerning the new IDA programme (electronic data interchange between administrations) (Tables I and II). On 28 May, the Court of Justice annulled Council Decision 95/468/EC concerning the old IDA programme, because it should have had Article 129d of the EC Treaty as the legal basis (³). The effects of the decision prior to its annulment are preserved.

Energy

394.   On 30 September, the Commission proposed to update the list of common interest projects in the energy sector provided for by Decision No 1254/96/EC, by adding 15 new projects (11 for gas and four for electricity) and amending four existing projects (three for gas and one for electricity) (Table I). On 14 December, it adopted a recommendation (⁴) concerning the improvement of the procedures for granting trans-European energy network authorisations.

Environment

395.   In a resolution adopted on 29 January (⁵), the European Parliament requested that the technological feasibility of European hydraulic networks be examined, and suggested launching a pilot project linking up the Rhône basin with the isolated hydrological networks of the Iberian peninsula.

(¹)   OJ C 10, 15.1.1998; OJ C 79, 14.3.1998.
(²)   COM(1998) 45; Bull. 1/2-1998, point 1.3.166.
(³)   Case C-22/96 *European Parliament/Council* ECR [1998] I-3231.
(⁴)   OJ L 8, 14.1.1999; Bull. 12-1998.
(⁵)   OJ C 56, 23.2.1998; Bull. 1/2-1998, point 1.3.223.

Section 14

Energy

Priority activities and objectives

396. The gradual liberalisation of the internal energy market continued in 1998 with the adoption, by the European Parliament and the Council, of the directive on the internal market in natural gas. The adoption by the Council of many of the decisions establishing the multiannual framework programme in the energy sector in turn provided a stable, multiannual budgetary and legal basis for the energy policy programmes. The Commission endeavoured to take greater account of the environmental dimension in its energy policy, paying particular attention to honouring the commitments given by the Community on climate change. The entry into force of the Energy Charter Treaty marked another milestone in cooperation on energy matters between the Union and its partners.

Community energy policy: strategic challenges

397. Acting on the Commission's proposal for a framework programme for actions in the energy sector (1998-2002) aimed at bringing together under one umbrella all the energy policy activities with a view to making them more effective and compatible with the priority objectives and ensuring closer coordination with energy measures taken under other Community policies, on 14 December the Council adopted the framework decision (Table II) and a series of related specific programmes: ETAP (studies, analyses, forecasts and other related work in the energy sector) (Table II), Synergy (international cooperation in the energy sector) *(→ point 400),* Carnot (clean and efficient use of solid fuels) *(→ point 419)* and SURE (nuclear transport safety and international cooperation) *(→ point 421).*

398. As part of the efforts to ensure transparency, the communication entitled 'An overall view of energy policy and actions' ([1]), submitted by the Commission on 22 April, gave an overview of all financial assistance from the European Communities to the energy sector between 1995 and

---

([1]) COM(97) 167; 1997 General Report, point 434.

1997 (^{1}). To allow all concerned to participate in its discussions and legislative work, the Commission also set up an Energy Consultative Committee bringing together representatives of the leading suppliers', consumers', trade union and environmental protection organisations, which held its first two plenary sessions on 28 April and 6 October.

Security of supply and international cooperation

399. The Energy Charter Treaty (^{2}) and the protocol on energy efficiency and related environmental aspects entered into force on 16 April (Table III). By 31 December, 38 countries, including 13 European Union Member States, had ratified the Treaty. On 13 July, the Council authorised provisional application of an amendment to the trade-related provisions of the Treaty (Table III). On 13 November, it welcomed initiatives for consultations on the development of an appropriate international arrangement for energy transit.

400. Under the multiannual framework programme for 1998-2002 *(→ point 397),* on 14 December the Council adopted a specific programme to promote international cooperation in the energy sector (Table II). Bearing in mind the growing energy problems in the Union (increasing dependence on external suppliers, emergence of markets with heavy demand for energy, and worldwide environmental problems), this ensures the continuity of the Synergy programme, which the Council had already extended for one year in December 1997 (^{3}).

401. With the collaboration of the pre-accession countries, the Commission started screening their energy legislation *(→ point 799).* An 'East-West' ministerial conference on energy was held in Brussels on 24 and 25 September on the initiative of the European Parliament. A task force was set up in June to implement energy cooperation projects between Europe and the Baltic countries. Cooperation with the central European countries and the independent States of the former Soviet Union continued under the PHARE *(→ points 812 et seq.),* TACIS *(→ points 862 et seq.)* and Synergy *(→ point 400)* programmes, focusing on modernisation of the electricity systems in these countries and, in particular, on reshaping the institutional arrangements for the sector and restructuring the electricity companies. The agreement regarding the modernisation of the Polish oil sector entered into force on 13 August

---

(^{1})   COM(1998) 244; Bull. 4-1998, point 1.2.81.
(^{2})   1997 General Report, point 438.
(^{3})   1997 General Report, point 439.

(Table III). On 27 April, the Council adopted conclusions stressing the importance of the Caspian region to the European Union's energy supplies ([1]).

402.   Under the Euro-Mediterranean partnership ([2]), an Energy Ministers conference held in Brussels on 11 May ([3]) adopted a statement defining the objectives of this cooperation in the energy sector and an action plan for the Euro-Mediterranean Energy Forum, covering the period 1998-2002. The Commission President, Mr Santer, attended a conference on power production in the Mediterranean area in Beirut, as part of the Synergy programme.

403.   Commissioner Papoutsis attended a G8 ministerial conference on energy in Moscow in April (→ point 881). In their final communiqué the participants stressed the need for closer international cooperation to meet the global energy challenges and, in this context, to promote an open, free environment for trade and investment in the energy sector.

404.   The second meeting of the EU-China Energy Working Group was held in Peking on 9 March to start work on a series of energy projects. An industrial round table on electricity interconnections in certain ASEAN countries was held in Singapore on 30 July (→ point 898). Mr Arriela Valera, the Venezuelan Minister for Energy, and Mr Papoutsis signed an exchange of letters in Brussels on 22 June establishing the principle of regular meetings between the two parties.

Internal energy market

Natural gas and electricity

405.   On 7 April, the Commission adopted a report on the state of liberalisation of the energy markets ([4]), which stressed the highly satisfactory progress made with implementation of Directive 96/92/EC on the internal market for electricity ([5]), which would be over 60 % liberalised by 1999, whereas a minimum target of 25 % had been set. On 16 March it had adopted the first report ([6]) on harmonisation requirements

---

([1])   Bull. 4-1998, point 1.2.89.
([2])   1996 General Report, point 366; 1997 General Report, point 443.
([3])   Bull. 5-1998, point 1.2.116.
([4])   COM(1998) 212; Bull. 4-1998, point 1.2.82.
([5])   OJ L 27, 30.1.1997; 1996 General Report, point 346.
([6])   COM(1998) 167; Bull. 3-1998, point 1.2.107.

with regard to Directive 96/92/EC. This focused on environmental aspects, particularly on electricity produced from renewable energy sources. As the aid schemes for these energy sources differed widely, the Commission stressed the need to establish common rules and to step up competition in this area. In a resolution adopted on 17 June, Parliament requested the Commission, as provided for by Article 138b of the EC Treaty, to submit a proposal for a directive to this end ([1]).

406. On 22 June, the European Parliament and the Council adopted Directive 98/30/EC on common rules for the internal market in natural gas (Table I). This directive, based on an approach striking a balance between public service obligations and the rules on competition, provides for at least 20 % of the market in each Member State to be opened up by 2000, 28 % by 2003 and 33 % by 2008. Electricity generators and large industrial consumers will be eligible as of right. Along with gas suppliers, they will have regulated or negotiated access to the transmission and distribution networks subject to certain conditions. They will be able to build direct lines between them. In principle, gas supply activities will be subject to authorisations granted on the basis of transparent, non-discriminatory criteria. Derogations will be allowed on public service grounds or to allow for certain specific situations.

Infrastructure and cohesion

407. Information on other energy-related activities under the cohesion and trans-European network policies can be found in Sections 11 ('Economic and social cohesion') (→ points 347 et seq.) and 13 ('Trans-European networks') (→ points 384 et seq.) of this chapter.

Energy and environment

General

408. At the request of the Cardiff European Council, in a communication adopted on 14 October the Commission ([2]) examined ways of strengthening environmental integration within Community energy policy. It identifies a range of priority actions in this connection, focusing on three priority areas: promotion of energy efficiency, an increase in

---

([1])   OJ C 210, 6.7.1998; Bull. 6-1998, point 1.3.96.
([2])   COM(1998) 571; Bull. 10-1998, point 1.2.95.

the market share of renewable energy sources, and a reduction in the environmental impact of conventional energy sources. The report ([1]) drawn up by the Council on the basis of this communication was favourably received by the Vienna European Council ([2]).

New and renewable energy sources

409. On 18 May the Council adopted a decision on implementation in 1998 and 1999 of the Altener II multiannual programme for the promotion of renewable energy sources (Table II).

410. The White Paper on a Community strategy and action plan on renewable sources of energy ([3]) was welcomed by the Economic and Social Committee on 29 April ([4]), by the Council on 8 June ([5]), by the European Parliament on 18 June ([6]) and by the Committee of the Regions on 16 July ([7]).

Promotion of energy efficiency and rational use of energy

411. Under the SAVE II programme concerning the promotion of energy efficiency ([8]), 96 projects received support totalling ECU 15.8 million in 1998. For the first time associated central European countries participated in some of these projects, as called for by the Economic and Social Committee in the own-initiative opinion adopted on 9 September ([9]). In addition, 33 new energy agencies were set up under the responsibility of local or regional authorities. On 17 July, the Commission adopted a report on progress on the SAVE II programme in 1996 and 1997 ([10]).

412. The Commission communication on a Community strategy to promote combined heat and power ([11]) was welcomed by the Committee

---

([1])   Bull. 11-1998, point 1.2.100.
([2])   Bull. 12-1998.
([3])   COM(97) 599; 1997 General Report, point 452.
([4])   OJ C 214, 10.7.1998; Bull. 4-1998, point 1.2.85.
([5])   OJ C 198, 24.6.1998; Bull. 6-1998, point 1.3.94.
([6])   OJ C 210, 6.7.1998; Bull. 6-1998, point 1.3.95.
([7])   OJ C 315, 13.10.1998; Bull. 7/8-1998, point 1.3.146.
([8])   OJ L 335, 24.12.1996; 1996 General Report, point 341.
([9])   OJ C 407, 28.12.1998; Bull. 9-1998, point 1.2.88.
([10]) COM(1998) 458; Bull. 7/8-1998, point 1.3.147.
([11]) COM(97) 514; 1997 General Report, point 454.

of the Regions on 13 March (¹), by the Economic and Social Committee on 25 March (²) and by the European Parliament on 15 May (³).

413. On 27 January, the Commission adopted Directive 98/11/EC concerning the energy labelling of household lamps (⁴).

Energy strategy and reduction of greenhouse gas emissions

414. On 29 April, the Commission adopted a communication (⁵) examining how far a Community strategy for the rational use of energy could contribute to meeting the commitments given, at the third conference of the parties to the United Nations Convention on Climate Change in Kyoto, on the reduction of greenhouse gas emissions and outlining an action plan to this end. This communication was endorsed by the Economic and Social Committee on 9 September (⁶) and by the Council on 7 December (⁷).

415. Information on other activities to follow up the Kyoto conference and on the preparations for and proceedings of the fourth conference of the parties to the Framework Convention on Climate Change (Buenos Aires) can be found in Section 17 ('Environment') (→ points 506 et seq.) of this chapter.

Promotion of research and technological development

416. Under the 'technological demonstration' part of the 'Non-nuclear energy' specific programme of the fourth framework programme for research and technological development (1994-98) (→ point 303), in 1998 the Commission granted ECU 14.08 million for 114 strategic and promotional actions (⁸) and ECU 103.4 million for 129 demonstration projects concerning the rational use of energy, renewable energy and fossil fuels (⁹).

(¹) OJ C 180, 11.6.1998; Bull. 3-1998, point 1.2.108.
(²) OJ C 157, 25.5.1998; Bull. 3-1998, point 1.2.108.
(³) OJ C 167, 1.6.1998; Bull. 5-1998, point 1.2.121.
(⁴) OJ L 71, 10.3.1998.
(⁵) COM(1998) 246; Bull. 4-1998, point 1.2.79.
(⁶) OJ C 407, 28.12.1998; Bull. 9-1998, point 1.2.88.
(⁷) OJ C 394, 17.12.1998; Bull. 12-1998.
(⁸) Calls for proposals: OJ C 280, 16.9.1997 and OJ C 188, 17.16.1998.
(⁹) Call for proposals: OJ C 357, 15.12.1994.

Individual sectors

Oil

417.   On 14 April, the Commission adopted a proposal for a directive to improve the arrangements introduced by Directive 68/414/EEC imposing an obligation on Member States to maintain minimum stocks of crude oil and/or petroleum products (Table II). This directive was adopted by the Council on 7 December. In addition, on 19 June the Commission adopted a proposal for a decision updating the Community procedure for information and consultation on crude-oil supply costs and the consumer prices of petroleum products (Table II). In a report ([1]) adopted on 15 July, it concluded that Directive 94/22/EC on the conditions for granting and using authorisations for the prospecting, exploration and production of hydrocarbons ([2]) was operating correctly. The Commission was also actively involved in the work on the disposal of offshore oil and gas installations (→ point 520). Parliament and the Council in turn adopted a directive on the quality of petrol and diesel fuel on 13 October (→ point 502).

Natural gas

418.   On 22 June, the European Parliament and the Council adopted Directive 98/30/EC concerning common rules for the internal market in natural gas (→ point 406).

Solid fuels

419.   Under the framework programme for 1998-2002, on 14 December the Council adopted a decision on a multiannual programme of actions promoting the clean and efficient use of solid fuels (Carnot) (Table II). On 16 December, the Commission adopted its annual report on the market in solid fuels in the Community in 1997 and the outlook for 1998 ([3]).

([1])   COM(1998) 447; Bull. 7/8-1998, point 1.3.145.
([2])   OJ L 164, 30.6.1994; 1994 General Report, point 344.
([3])   Bull. 12-1998.

Electricity

420.   Information concerning implementation of Directive 96/92/EC concerning the internal market in electricity can be found under 'Internal energy market' (→ *point 405*) of this section.

Nuclear energy

421.   To complement its proposal for a multiannual framework programme in the energy sector, on 15 July the Commission adopted a proposal for a multiannual programme (1998-2002) of actions in the nuclear sector (SURE) (Table II). This programme focuses, in particular, on the safe transport of radioactive materials in the Community, on safeguards for nuclear installations in countries currently participating in the TACIS programme (→ *points 862 et seq.*) and on international cooperation. The Council adopted this programme on 14 December.

422.   On 25 May, the Council authorised the Commission to negotiate a nuclear cooperation agreement with Japan (Table III). Following negotiations between Euratom, France and the International Atomic Energy Agency, on 11 September the Commission also proposed the conclusion of a safeguards agreement pursuant to Protocol I of the Treaty of Tlatelolco which creates a nuclear-weapons-free zone in Latin America (Table III), and, on 11 December it proposed the negotiation of a nuclear cooperation agreement with Ukraine (Table III). An agreement for cooperation on nuclear research with Canada was signed in December (→ *point 313*).

423.   Other information concerning nuclear safety and safeguards and action to combat illicit trafficking in radioactive substances can be found in Sections 18 ('Nuclear safety') (→ *points 529 et seq.*) and 19 ('Euratom safeguards') (→ *points 540 et seq.*) of this chapter.

Euratom Supply Agency

424.   A steady supply of nuclear materials and nuclear fuel cycle services was provided for users in the Community in 1998. The conclusion of multiannual contracts between users and primary producers of natural uranium, as recommended by the Euratom Supply Agency, enabled users to meet their needs at attractive prices and producers to find outlets for their products. As in previous years, the conversion, enrichment and

fabrication markets remained stable and installations in the Union covered a large proportion of users' needs.

425.   The independent States of the former Soviet Union remained the leading suppliers of natural uranium and the largest external source of enriched uranium. Their market share seems to be stabilising at a high level (around one quarter of natural uranium requirements and slightly below that level for enriched supplies). The expected sales of large quantities of natural uranium from Russia's nuclear arms to undertakings in the West failed to materialise, however, one possible reason being the announcement by the United States Enrichment Corporation (USEC) of sales of large US Government stocks of natural uranium in a few years time.

426.   The Euratom Supply Agency's annual report for 1997 was published in June (^{1}).

State aid to the coal industry

427.   State aid is covered in Section 5 ('Competition') of this chapter (→ *points 222 et seq.*).

(^{1})   Available from the Euratom Supply Agency and on the Europa server and the Internet (→ *point 1153*).

Section 15

Transport

Priority activities and objectives

428.   Integrating the environment dimension into the common transport policy and changing the modal split were again high on the list of Commission priorities. To further these aims, the Commission adopted an action programme for the period 1998-2004, a communication on transport and carbon dioxide, a White Paper on infrastructure charging, an action programme on local and regional public transport as well as proposals to amend all the legislation on the use of rail infrastructure. Substantial progress was also made on legislation in the field of safety, payment for infrastructure use, working conditions, social standards and working hours in road and sea transport in particular.

Development of the common transport policy

429.   On 1 December, the Commission adopted a communication [1] entitled 'The common transport policy — Sustainable mobility: perspectives for the future' which is intended to update the action programme adopted in 1995 [2], and outlines the prospects for the period 2000-04.

430.   The Committee of the Regions adopted an own-initiative opinion setting out the objectives of a sustainable transport strategy [3] on 12 March and another on 14 May adopting a European charter of regional and local authorities for a progressive and sustainable transport policy [4].

Infrastructures, traffic management and navigation systems

431.   As a follow-up to its Green Paper on fair and efficient pricing in transport [5], the Commission adopted a White Paper entitled 'Fair

---

[1]   COM(1998) 716; Bull. 12-1998.
[2]   COM(95) 302; 1995 General Report, point 385.
[3]   OJ C 180, 11.6.1998; Bull. 3-1998, point 1.2.110.
[4]   OJ C 251, 10.8.1998; Bull. 5-1998, point 1.2.127.
[5]   COM(95) 691; 1995 General Report, point 389; 1996 General Report, point 379.

payment for infrastructure use' on 22 July[1]. It recommends the gradual harmonisation of infrastructure charging systems based on the 'user pays' principle, according to which all users of transport infrastructure would have to pay for all the costs they generate, including environmental costs. In addition, on 21 December the Commission adopted a communication on electronic fee collection[2].

432.   On 21 January, the Commission adopted a communication defining a European strategy for global navigation satellite systems (GNSS)[3], which the Council endorsed on 17 March. The Community, the European Space Agency and Eurocontrol signed an agreement on 18 June on developing and validating the operational capacity of a European contribution to such a system (Table III). On 14 May and 7 October[4] respectively, the Committee of the Regions and the European Parliament endorsed the Commission communication on a Community strategy and framework for the deployment of road transport telematics in Europe[5].

Networks

433.   The trans-European transport networks are dealt with in Section 13 of this chapter ('Trans-European networks') (→ points 384 et seq.).

Transport and environment

434.   On 17 June, the Council, expressing its concern at the environmental impact of the increase in the provision and use of transport, confirmed that priority was to be given to integrating environmental objectives into transport policy[6]. The report[7] that it adopted on this subject on 30 November was favourably received by the Vienna European Council[8].

435.   In the context of the commitments entered into at the Kyoto conference on reducing emissions of greenhouse gases[9], the Commission

---

[1]   COM(1998) 466; Bull. 7/8-1998, point 1.3.150; Supplement 3/98 — Bull.
[2]   COM(1998) 795; Bull. 12-1998.
[3]   COM(1998) 29; Bull. 1/2-1998, point 1.3.171.
[4]   OJ C 328, 26.10.1998; Bull. 10-1998, point 1.2.98.
[5]   COM(97) 223; 1997 General Report, point 471.
[6]   Bull. 6-1998, point 1.3.103.
[7]   Bull. 11-1998, point 1.2.105.
[8]   Bull. 12-1998.
[9]   1997 General Report, point 552.

adopted a communication on 31 March entitled 'Transport and carbon dioxide — Developing a Community approach', in which it reviews the policies already implemented by the Community and presents other measures that could be adopted to reduce carbon dioxide emissions in transport (^{1}). In a working paper adopted on 14 July (^{2}), the Commission described the building blocks of a framework to deal with the environment problems of heavy goods vehicle (HGV) traffic, stressing the importance in this connection of measures to avoid unnecessary transport (diverted traffic, empty lorries), to increase the market share of environmentally friendly modes such as rail and combined transport and to minimise the environmental impact of road vehicles by raising technical standards.

436.   In the field of transport of dangerous goods the Council, on 17 July, adopted Directive 98/55/EC, which extends the scope of Directive 93/75/EEC concerning minimum requirements for vessels carrying dangerous or polluting goods to the transport of radioactive waste (Table II) and on 30 November it adopted a common position on a proposal for a directive aimed at improving the safety of transportable pressure equipment (Table II). On 19 March, the Commission proposed harmonising the examination requirements for safety advisers for the transport of dangerous goods by road, rail or inland waterway (Table II). On 15 January, it asked the Council for a mandate to open negotiations to conclude a European agreement on the international transport of dangerous goods by inland waterway (Table III).

Research and technological development

437.   Research and technological development in the transport sector is dealt with in Section 8 of this chapter ('Research and technological development') (→ point 307).

Multimodal transport

438.   In order to promote combined transport, the Commission proposed, on 10 July, that Directive 92/106/EEC on the establishment of common rules for certain types of combined transport of goods between Member States (Table II) and Directive 96/53/EC on maximum dimensions and weights of certain road vehicles (Table II) should be amended

---

(^{1})   COM(1998) 204; Bull. 3-1998, point 1.2.111.
(^{2})   COM(1998) 444; Bull. 7/8-1998, point 1.3.155.

to allow tax concessions, an exemption from certain driving restrictions and an increase in the maximum authorised weights for vehicles used in combined transport. On 1 October, the Council adopted Regulation (EC) No 2196/98 concerning the granting of Community financial assistance for actions to promote combined transport (Table II).

Inland transport

Rail transport

439.   On 31 March, in a communication ([1]) on the impact of Directive 91/440/EEC on the development of the Community's railways, the Commission suggested that the future liberalisation of this sector should focus on freight transport and should take place in stages, starting with 5 % of the market and rising to 25 % after 10 years, in order to safeguard the position of the existing companies. In addition, in order to ensure more efficient use of rail infrastructure, the Commission proposed amendments to Directives 91/440/EEC (Table II), 95/18/EC (Table II) and 95/19/EC (Table II) on 22 July. They concern, in particular, the allocation of rail infrastructure capacity, the calculation of charges for infrastructure use, the separation for accounting purposes of infrastructure management and transport operations and the licensing of railway undertakings.

440.   The Commission communication on trans-European rail-freight freeways ([2]) was endorsed by Parliament on 13 January ([3]), by the Economic and Social Committee on 28 January ([4]), and by the Committee of the Regions on 12 March ([5]).

Road transport

441.   At its meeting on 30 November and 1 December, the Council agreed a common position on a proposal for a directive on the charging of heavy goods vehicles and user charges/tolls for the use of motorway infrastructures (Table II).

---

[1]   COM(1998) 202; Bull. 3-1998, point 1.2.114.
[2]   COM(97) 242; 1997 General Report, point 477.
[3]   OJ C 34, 2.2.1998; Bull. 1/2-1998, point 1.3.175.
[4]   OJ C 95, 30.3.1998; Bull. 1/2-1998, point 1.3.176.
[5]   OJ C 180, 11.6.1998; Bull. 3-1998, point 1.2.113.

442. In a resolution of 11 March ([1]), Parliament approved the Commission's road safety programme for the period 1997-2001 ([2]). In this context, also on 11 March, the Commission proposed strengthening the provisions on roadworthiness testing of heavy goods vehicles (Table II). On 24 September, the Council adopted Regulation (EC) No 2135/98 (Table II), which provides for the obligatory installation from 1 July 2000 of new equipment to monitor the working hours of lorry drivers (tachographs). It also amended Directive 96/26/EC on admission to the occupation of road haulage operator and road passenger transport operator on 1 October (Table II), in order to tighten up the admission conditions relating to the level of professional competence required and the financial standing of the undertaking.

443. As part of the proposals relating to working hours in the excluded sectors *(→ point 138),* on 18 November the Commission adopted a proposal relating to the road haulage sector, the main aim of which is to improve drivers' health and road safety and which, to this end, provides for a maximum working week (on average 48 hours with a ceiling of 60 hours) and minimum daily and weekly rest periods; the proposal also contains rules concerning breaks, night workers and derogations.

444. On 3 November, the Council adopted Regulation (EC) No 2411/98 on the recognition in intra-Community traffic of the distinguishing sign of the Member State in which motor vehicles and their trailers are registered (Table II) and a common position on a proposal for a directive aimed at harmonising registration documents for the latter (Table II).

445. On 11 March, the Commission tabled a proposal on harmonised rules for restrictions on heavy goods vehicles involved in international transport on designated roads (Table II). In addition, it adopted the report on the system of transit through Austria ([3]) (which it proposes to keep in operation until 2001) on 16 January, the report of the impact of cabotage on the market ([4]) (which it considers small) on 4 February, and the report on the system applicable to coaches and buses no more than 15 m long ([5]) on 27 May.

([1])   OJ C 104, 6.4.1998; Bull. 3-1998, point 1.2.117.
([2])   COM(97) 131; 1997 General Report, point 478.
([3])   COM(1998) 6; Bull. 1/2-1998, point 1.3.177.
([4])   COM(1998) 47; Bull. 1/2-1998, point 1.3.179.
([5])   COM(97) 499; Bull. 5-1998, point 1.2.130.

Inland waterway transport

446. The Commission followed up its report on the impact of measures to restructure inland waterway navigation (¹), which was favourably received by the European Parliament on 3 December (²), with a proposal, on 28 September, to establish a transitional regime providing for the gradual reduction and eventual abolition of all the conditions governing the entry into service of new vessels and the setting-up of a standby mechanism which would be reactivated only in the event of a serious disturbance of the market. On 21 December, the Council adopted a common position on this proposal (Table II).

Urban transport

447. The Commission adopted a communication (³) on 10 July on the work programme it intends to implement in order to achieve the objectives identified in the Green Paper entitled 'The citizen's network' (⁴). This programme focuses on stimulating the exchange of information on local transport, developing the benchmarking of service performance, improving the legal framework of local public passenger transport and using the European Union's financial instruments effectively.

Sea transport

448. In the context of the action programme for a common policy on safe seas (⁵), the Commission proposed, on 18 February, the establishment of common safety rules for the operation of ro-ro ferry and high-speed passenger craft services in the Community (Table II), followed, on 17 July, by a proposal to improve port reception facilities for ship-generated waste and cargo residues (Table II). The Council adopted a common position on the first proposal on 21 December. As part of the proposals relating to working hours in the excluded sectors *(→ point 138)*, on 18 November the Commission adopted two proposals for directives and a recommendation aimed at applying, within the Community, for all vessels, including those flying the flag of third countries, the working hours adopted by the International Labour Organisation in October 1996. On 17 March, the Council adopted Directive 98/18/EC

(¹) COM(97) 555; 1997 General Report, point 482.
(²) OJ C 398, 21.12.1998; Bull. 12-1998.
(³) COM(1998) 431; Bull. 7/8-1998, point 1.3.158.
(⁴) COM(95) 601; 1995 General Report, point 404.
(⁵) COM(93) 66; Twenty-seventh General Report, point 322.

(Table II) in order to apply certain international safety standards for passenger vessels in the Community and, on 27 April, Directive 98/25/EC on port State control (Table II). It also adopted Directive 98/35/EC on the minimum level of training for seafarers on 25 May (Table II) and Directive 98/41/EC on the registration of persons sailing on board passenger ships on 18 June (Table II).

449.   On 29 April, in order to eliminate unfair competition due to the employment of seafarers in the Community on the terms and conditions applicable in third countries, the Commission adopted a communication ([1]), accompanied by a proposal for a regulation (Table II) and a proposal for a directive (Table II).

450.   The Commission Green Paper on ports and maritime infrastructures ([2]) was endorsed by the Economic and Social Committee on 9 September ([3]).

Air transport

451.   In a resolution of 19 February ([4]), Parliament, having examined the Commission communication on the impact of the third air transport liberalisation package ([5]), stressed the need to take account of the social repercussions of deregulation. The Commission adopted two decisions implementing Regulation (EEC) No 2408/92 on access for Community air carriers to intra-Community air routes ([6]). On 22 July, it decided that Sweden could not restrict the exercise of traffic rights on air routes between the new Karlstad airport and other Community airports by noisy aircraft, apart from operational restrictions such as the night curfew (22.00 to 7.00). On 9 September, it opposed the conditions for the compulsory transfer of most of the traffic in the Milan airport system from Linate airport to Malpensa. Following this decision, the Italian authorities decided to adopt new traffic distribution rules.

452.   The Commission also proposed improvements to the denied-boarding compensation system in air transport (Table II) on 30 January.

---

[1]   COM(1998) 251; Bull. 4-1998, point 1.2.94.
[2]   COM(97) 678; 1997 General Report, point 485.
[3]   OJ C 407, 28.12.1998; Bull. 9-1998, point 1.2.99.
[4]   OJ C 80, 16.3.1998; Bull. 1/2-1998, point 1.3.188.
[5]   COM(96) 514; 1996 General Report, point 397.
[6]   OJ L 240, 24.8.1992; Twenty-sixth General Report, point 674.

453. In the field of air transport safety, on 15 December the Commission proposed amendments to Regulation (EEC) No 3922/91 on the harmonisation of technical requirements and administrative procedures in the field of civil aviation (Table II). For its part, the Council updated Directive 92/14/EEC on the limitation of the operation of aeroplanes covered by Annex 16 to the Convention on International Civil Aviation on 30 March (Table II) and on 4 June adopted a common position on a proposal for a directive aimed at establishing a safety assessment of third countries' aircraft using Community airports, based on a common system of collecting, exchanging and processing information on such aircraft (Table II). It also authorised the Commission on 18 June to negotiate, firstly, Community membership of Eurocontrol (Table III) and, secondly, the establishment of a European Aviation Safety Authority in the legal form of an international organisation (Table III). In a resolution of 19 February, following the Mount Cermis tragedy, Parliament called on the competent aviation authorities to draw up more binding regulations for military flights ([1]).

454. On 9 March, the Commission proposed banning, from 1 April 1999, the inclusion in Member States' aircraft registers of aeroplanes which have been acoustically modified through the use of equipment to reduce aircraft noise ('hushkits') (Table II) because of the environmental impact of those aircraft. On 16 November, the Council adopted a common position on this proposal. The discussions and negotiations on environmental issues in the International Civil Aviation Organisation (ICAO) were the subject of a Commission communication of 6 May ([2]) and Council conclusions of 16 September ([3]). On 25 November, the Commission also adopted a communication ([4]) on the results of the 32nd session of the ICAO's General Assembly held in Montreal from 22 September to 2 October.

State aid

455. State aid is dealt with in Section 5 ('Competition') of this chapter (→ *points 222 et seq.*).

([1])   OJ C 80, 16.3.1998; Bull. 1/2-1998, point 1.3.189.
([2])   COM(1998) 265; Bull. 5-1998, point 1.2.133.
([3])   Bull. 9-1998, point 1.2.105.
([4])   COM(1998) 677; Bull. 11-1998, point 1.2.112.

International cooperation

456. On 16 January, the Commission adopted a communication concerning the Euro-Mediterranean partnership in the transport sector [1]. This communication seeks to define a framework for cooperation on transport within the Euro-Mediterranean partnership, with a view to establishing an integrated transport network that is efficient, ecologically sustainable and competitive in the context of a free-trade area in the Mediterranean. Following on from the Helsinki Conference [2], the Economic and Social Committee on 10 September emphasised the need to create special consultation mechanisms to involve economic and social circles in the definition of a pan-European transport policy [3].

457. Parliament adopted a resolution on 16 January supporting the Commission's position in the negotiations with Switzerland on inland transport [4]. On 10 December, the Council reached agreement on the results of these negotiations, providing in particular for a gradual increase to 40 tonnes between now and 2005 in the limit on the weight of vehicles in Switzerland, together with the introduction of a new system of user charges for the Swiss road network. These negotiations are part of a wider package of negotiations with Switzerland covering several other fields, including air transport *(→ points 792 and 793).* The Council authorised the Commission to negotiate maritime transport agreements with China (Table III) and India on 12 February [5] (Table III).

---

[1]   COM(1998) 7; Bull. 1/2-1998, point 1.3.190.
[2]   1997 General Report, point 494.
[3]   OJ C 407, 28.12.1998; Bull. 9-1998, point 1.2.108.
[4]   OJ C 34, 2.2.1998; Bull. 1/2-1998, point 1.3.178.
[5]   And not in December 1997, as erroneously stated in the 1997 General Report, point 495.

Section 16

Information society, telecommunications

Priority activities and objectives

458.   In 1998, the first year in which the telecommunications market was opened up to full competition, the Commission and the other institutions of the European Union took steps to ensure that Member States properly implemented the relevant legislation, particularly on universal service, and to complete the provisions governing such aspects as number portability, terminal equipment and mobile communications. They also took action on radio frequencies, electronic signatures, the Internet and the 'millennium bug'. The international aspects of the information society were also given special attention.

Information society

459.   On 29 July, the Commission presented a summary([1]) of the results of the public consultation on its Green Paper on the convergence of the telecommunications, media and information technology sectors and the implications for regulation([2]), on which the Economic and Social Committee had submitted an opinion on 29 April([3]). The Committee of the Regions gave its opinion on 16 September([4]) and the European Parliament adopted a resolution on this matter on 22 October([5]).

460.   In December the European Parliament and the Council reached agreement on a proposal for a decision adopting an action plan on promoting safer use of the Internet by combating illegal and harmful content on global networks (Table I). On 23 March, the Council also authorised the Commission to negotiate with the Council of Europe an agreement on the protection of privacy on the Internet (Table III). Following the publication by the US Government of a Green Paper on the technical management of Internet names and addresses, the Commission,

---

([1])   Bull. 7/8-1998, point 1.3.168.
([2])   COM(97) 623; 1997 General Report, point 500.
([3])   OJ C 214, 10.7.1998; Bull. 4-1998, point 1.2.100.
([4])   OJ C 373, 2.12.1998; Bull. 9-1998, point 1.2.110.
([5])   OJ C 341, 9.11.1998; Bull. 10-1998, point 1.2.111.

in a communication dated 20 February ([1]), stressed the need for a joint response from the European Union and its Member States, which the Council recognised in its 26 February conclusions ([2]). Next, in a new communication of 29 July ([3]), the Commission welcomed the US Government's acceptance of the observations made by the European Union. The European Parliament, in a resolution of 19 June, examined the relationships between the information society, the management of the Internet and democracy ([4]).

461.   As a follow-up to its communication entitled 'Ensuring security and trust in electronic communication: — Towards a European framework for digital signatures and encryption' ([5]), welcomed on 25 March by the Economic and Social Committee ([6]) and on 17 July by the European Parliament ([7]), on 13 May the Commission adopted a proposal for a directive on a common framework for electronic signatures (Table I), intended to lay down rules for security and responsibility in the use of electronic signatures and so provide for the legal recognition of such signatures on the basis of principles ensuring the proper functioning of the internal market. Following its communication on a European initiative in electronic commerce ([8]), on which the European Parliament adopted a resolution on 14 May ([9]), on 18 November the Commission also adopted a proposal for a directive (Table I) on certain legal aspects of electronic commerce. The proposal aims to guarantee information society service providers (electronic remote-operation services) the application of the principles of freedom to provide services and right of establishment provided they comply with the legislation of their country of origin.

462.   On 25 February, the Commission adopted a communication ([10]) on the year 2000 computer problem, or 'millennium bug' (the need to adapt computer systems whose 'date' fields contain only two digits to prevent them from interpreting the year 2000 as the year 1900). This issue was further examined in June ([11]) by the Cardiff European Council

---

([1])   COM(1998) 111; Bull. 1/2-1998, point 1.3.199.
([2])   Bull. 1/2-1998, point 1.3.199.
([3])   COM(1998) 476; Bull. 7/8-1998, point 1.3.171.
([4])   OJ C 210, 6.7.1998; Bull. 6-1998, point 1.3.117.
([5])   COM(97) 503; 1997 General Report, point 522.
([6])   OJ C 157, 25.5.1998; Bull. 3-1998, point 1.2.134.
([7])   OJ C 292, 21.9.1998; Bull. 7/8-1998, point 1.3.178.
([8])   COM(97) 157; 1997 General Report, point 499.
([9])   OJ C 167, 1.6.1998; Bull. 5-1998, point 1.2.141.
([10])   COM(1998) 102; Bull. 1/2-1998, point 1.3.196.
([11])   Bull. 6-1998, point I.13.

and gave rise to a new report from the Commission on 2 December (¹). The Vienna European Council welcomed this report and called on the Member States to implement emergency plans for protecting their infrastructures and to examine the implications of the problem of interruptions to the supply chain outside the European Union (²).

463. On 30 March, the Council adopted a multiannual Community policy to stimulate the establishment of the information society in Europe (Table II).

464. The use of the Information Society Activity Centre (ISAC) (³) services such as the Information Society Project Office (ISPO) grew in 1998. Visits to the Internet site (⁴) more than doubled to some two million per month. The ESIS (European survey of the information society in Europe) was extended to the countries of central and eastern Europe and the Mediterranean countries, and the Information Society Forum to the countries of central Europe. In March more than 550 participants from 35 countries took part in the ESIS.

465. Under the INFO 2000 programme (⁵) for developing a European multimedia content industry, 20 pilot projects for boosting the use of information held by the public sector in Europe and 10 aimed at improving the framework for negotiating intellectual property rights in the multimedia domain were selected following calls for proposals launched in December 1997 (⁶). More than 500 candidates competed for the new European Multimedia Art Prize, which was awarded to the prizewinners in Vienna in November.

466. Under the programme to promote the linguistic diversity of the Community in the information society (⁷), 19 demonstration projects and a study of the translation and interpretation markets and multilingual services were implemented in 1998.

(¹)   COM(1998) 593; Bull. 12-1998.
(²)   Bull. 12-1998.
(³)   1996 General Report, point 415; 1997 General Report, point 503.
(⁴)   http://www.ispo.cec.be/.
(⁵)   OJ L 129, 30.5.1996; 1996 General Report, point 412.
(⁶)   OJ C 381, 16.12.1997.
(⁷)   OJ L 306, 28.11.1996; 1996 General Report, point 413.

Telecommunications policy

467.   Under the terms of Commission Directive 96/19/EC ([1]), the tele-communications market was opened up to full competition on 1 January. The Commission has been monitoring the proper implementation of the regulations governing this market and the quality of the universal service which goes hand in hand with its opening. On 18 February ([2]) and 25 November ([3]), it adopted its third and fourth reports on the implementation of the telecommunications regulatory package, and, on 25 February, its first monitoring report on universal service ([4]), in which it noted a continuing improvement in the prices and quality of the services offered. On 3 September ([5]), it clarified certain aspects of its November 1996 communication on the assessment criteria for national schemes for the costing and financing of universal service ([6]). The Economic and Social Committee, giving its opinion on the Commission communication on the social and labour market dimension of the information society entitled 'People first — The next steps', had on 26 February called on the Commission to specify in more detail the field of application of the universal service concept ([7]).

468.   Under the terms of Directive 97/33/EC on interconnection, in January ([8]) and July ([9]) the Commission adopted recommendations on interconnection charges and in March ([10]) on accounting separation and cost accounting. It also specified the application of competition rules to access agreements in the telecommunications sector and to voice communications on the Internet *(→ point 202)*.

469.   The legislative framework of the telecommunications market was further strengthened when, on 26 February, the European Parliament and the Council adopted Directive 98/10/EC on the application of open network provision (ONP) to voice telephony and on universal service for telecommunications in a competitive environment (Table I), on which they had reached agreement in December 1997 ([11]), and on 24 September Directive 98/61/EC on operator number portability and carrier

---

([1])   OJ L 74, 22.3.1996; 1996 General Report, point 417.
([2])   COM(1998) 80; Bull. 1/2-1998, point 1.3.204.
([3])   COM(1998) 594; Bull. 11-1998, point 1.2.121.
([4])   COM(1998) 101; Bull. 1/2-1998, point 1.3.205.
([5])   COM(1998) 494; Bull. 9-1998, point 1.2.114.
([6])   COM(96) 608; 1996 General Report, point 419.
([7])   OJ C 129, 27.4.1998; Bull. 1/2-1998, point 1.3.14.
([8])   Recommendation 98/195/EC (OJ L 73, 12.3.1998).
([9])   Recommendation 98/511/EC (OJ L 228, 15.8.1998; Bull. 7/8-1998, point 1.3.174).
([10]) Recommendation 98/322/EC (OJ L 141, 13.5.1998).
([11]) 1997 General Report, point 508.

pre-selection (Table I), aimed at introducing these two functions in fixed networks from 1 January 2000.

470.   For the sake of transparency, on 12 February the European Parliament and the Council consolidated the legislation on telecommunications terminal equipment (Table I). On 8 June, the Council adopted a common position on a proposal for a directive on connected telecommunications equipment, aimed at updating and revising the legislation (Table I). On 20 July, it adopted a common approval procedure for modems and telephone answering machines ([1]).

471.   Concerning mobile communications, on 11 February the Commission adopted a proposal for a decision on the coordinated introduction of a third-generation mobile and wireless communications system (UMTS) in the Community, to promote the rapid and coordinated introduction of UMTS networks and services (mobile telephones, messaging, wireless Internet access, multimedia applications) which are compatible throughout the Community (Table I). The decision was adopted on 14 December by the European Parliament and the Council. On 12 October the Commission presented a communication on the implementation and functioning of the mobile communication frequency directives ([2]). The European Parliament had, on 29 January, stressed the need for a European approach to the development of mobile communications ([3]).

472.   In preparation for the 'CMR 2000' World Radio Communications Conference of the International Telecommunications Union, on 13 May the Commission adopted a communication ([4]) aimed at establishing a link between the agenda of this conference and the Community policies on radio frequencies in order to launch an early debate on the conference issues. On 9 December, the Commission adopted a Green Paper on Community radio frequency band policy ([5]) aimed at launching a debate on the need for a consolidated policy on radio frequency bands at Community level. The Green Paper examines the main issues at stake, such as planning, the allocation process, the means of allocating frequency bands and the measures to be taken concerning the use of radio equipment, and considers the optimum institutional framework for implementing radio frequency band policy.

---

[1]   Decision 98/482/EC (OJ L 216, 4.8.1998; Bull. 7/8-1998, point 1.3.173).
[2]   COM(1998) 559; Bull. 10-1998, point 1.2.114.
[3]   OJ C 56, 23.2.1998; Bull. 1/2-1998, point 1.3.208.
[4]   COM(1998) 298; Bull. 5-1998, point 1.2.138.
[5]   COM(1998) 596, Bull. 12-1998.

Technological aspects

Information technology

473. Under the specific programme for information technology research (¹), 460 new projects were financed in 1998 at a total cost of ECU 300 million. Several projects concerned efficient detection systems for antipersonnel mines. Some two thirds of the funds were granted to industrial firms; SMEs were involved in 75 % of the projects. An annual conference ('IST 98 Vienna'), bringing together for the first time the three research programmes on information and communications technology, was organised in Vienna from 30 November to 2 December in parallel with an exhibition of the results obtained by the projects and at an investment forum.

Telematics

474. Under the specific programme for telematics research (²), 255 new projects were selected following the last calls for proposals and are now under way, including 12 integrated applications on digital sites, 46 educational multimedia projects and one horizontal project which has quadrupled the transmission rate across the interconnected research networks. In February, a European conference, attended by over 2 000 participants, was held in Barcelona on the 10th anniversary of European telematics research, in parallel with an exhibition of 100 outstanding projects.

Communications technology

475. Following the last call for proposals, a series of 89 new projects were selected under the specific research programme on advanced communications technologies and services (³), strengthening Europe's role as a prime mover in digital multimedia and the management of optical communications networks and services and mobile communications. These activities served as the basis for drawing up Commission proposals for a common framework for electronic signatures (→ point 461) and the coordinated introduction of mobile and wireless telecommunications (UMTS) (→ point 471).

(¹) OJ L 334, 22.12.1994; 1994 General Report, point 237.
(²) OJ L 334, 22.12.1994; 1994 General Report, point 411.
(³) OJ L 222, 26.8.1994; 1994 General Report, point 409.

Telematic communication of administrative data, information and documents

476. The implementation of the IDA programme on data interchange between public authorities is dealt with in Section 13 ('Trans-European networks') of this chapter (→ *point 393).*

Advanced television services

477. Following the completion on 30 June 1997 of the action plan for introducing advanced television services in Europe ([1]), on 13 July the Commission adopted its final report on the implementation plan ([2]).

International cooperation

478. In a communication on globalisation and the information society, on 4 February the Commission called for strengthened international coordination on the information society and for an international tele-communications charter ([3]). The Council welcomed this approach on 19 May ([4]), and the Economic and Social Committee stressed the need for better coordination at European level ([5]). In Brussels, on 29 June, the Commission organised a round-table conference of industrialists on globalisation in communications, as a result of which a global business dialogue (GBD) was set up.

479. Following the guidelines in its communication on the information society and development ([6]), welcomed on 29 January by the Economic and Social Committee ([7]), the Commission pursued its collaboration with the World Bank, Unesco (distance learning in developing countries), the OECD (electronic commerce) and the Eureka programme (health applications for telematics).

480. As a follow-up to the third Information Society Forum between the European Union and the countries of central and eastern Europe ([8]),

---

[1]   OJ L 196, 5.8.1993; Twenty-seventh General Report, point 625; 1997 General Report, point 520.
[2]   COM(1998) 441; Bull. 7/8-1998, point 1.3.177.
[3]   COM(1998) 50; Bull. 1/2-1998, point 1.3.197.
[4]   Bull. 5-1998, point 1.2.135.
[5]   OJ C 284, 14.9.1998; Bull. 7/8-1998, point 1.3.169.
[6]   COM(97) 351; 1997 General Report, point 528.
[7]   OJ C 95, 30.3.1998; Bull. 1/2-1998, point 1.3.211.
[8]   1997 General Report, point 530.

a joint committee was set up and a round-table conference on the information society and industry organised. Joint initiatives were also
launched following the Rome Conference on the building of the Euro-
Mediterranean information society (¹). An information society working
party was also set up at the second industrial round-table conference
between the European Union and Russia.

481.   A new bilateral meeting between the Commission and representatives of the US Government was held in Brussels on 23 and 24 July, at
which subjects of mutual interest such as telecommunications regulation,
electronic commerce and protection of privacy were discussed. The European Union-Japan working party on strategy in the information domain
met in Brussels in March to examine the latest joint initiatives on industrial strategy, such as benchmarking in the information and communications technology sector, awareness programmes and initiatives in the
standardisation and electronic commerce fields. A conference to promote
cooperation between Europe and Latin America on the information society was also organised in Costa Rica from 4 to 6 March, after which a
high-level group of European industrialists was convened to specify the
strategy and objectives of cooperation between the two regions. To finalise the future joint initiatives between the European Union and
China (²), a conference on information and telecommunications technology was organised in Brussels from 29 June to 1 July, dealing with intelligent transport systems, mobile communications, satellite communications, positioning and navigation systems and multimedia healthcare
networks. Lastly, a discussion on the information society was launched
with the Republic of Korea.

(¹)   1996 General Report, point 430.
(²)   1997 General Report, point 533.

Section 17

Environment

Priority activities and objectives

482.   Substantial progress was made in 1998 with regard to greenhouse gas emissions, to meet the commitments given at the Kyoto conference on climate change, concerning air pollution from motor vehicles, with the adoption of several directives under the 'Auto-Oil' programme, and as regards acidification, as part of the strategy defined in 1997. The Commission also proposed speeding up the phasing-out of substances that deplete the ozone layer and defined a Community biodiversity strategy.

Particular attention was paid to taking environmental concerns into account in other policies. The Commission's approach was approved by the European Council which identified transport, energy and agriculture as some of the priorities in this area. The European Parliament and the Council also adopted the decision on the review of the fifth environmental action programme.

Action programme

483. On 24 September, the European Parliament and the Council adopted Decision No 2179/98/EC on the review of the fifth action programme in relation to the environment and sustainable development (Table I). This decision identified five priority areas for the programme up to the year 2000: integration of the environment into other policies, broadening the range of instruments used, better implementation and enforcement of legislation, awareness-raising, and international cooperation. It also stressed the need to step up the action taken by the Community in specific fields such as depletion of the ozone layer, climate change and combating acidification.

Taking the environment into account in other policies

484. As requested by the Luxembourg European Council ([1]), on 27 May the Commission adopted a communication, subsequently endorsed

---

([1])   Bull. 12-1997, point I.14. 56.

by the European Parliament on 15 November ([1]), outlining a strategy for integrating environment into European Union policies ([2]) in line with the provisions introduced by the Amsterdam Treaty ([3]). This strategy is based on a partnership between the European Parliament, the Council and the Commission built around guidelines and including monitoring mechanisms. In June the Cardiff European Council welcomed this approach, invited all relevant formations of the Council to establish their own strategies for giving effect to environmental integration within their respective policy areas, taking account of the Commission's suggested guidelines, and identified energy, transport and agriculture as some of the priority areas for this purpose ([4]). In December the Vienna European Council reaffirmed its commitment to integrate environment and sustainable development into all Community policies ([5]).

485.   The Commission communication on the environment and employment ([6]) was welcomed by the Economic and Social Committee on 28 May ([7]), by the European Parliament on 16 July ([8]), by the Council on 6 October ([9]) and by the Committee of the Regions on 19 November ([10]).

486.   Further information on taking the environment into account in other Community policies is given in the relevant sections, particularly Sections 14 ('Energy') (→ *points 408 et seq.*), 15 ('Transport') (→ *points 434 et seq.*) and 20 ('Agricultural policy') (→ *points 557 et seq.*) of this chapter.

Industry and environment

Emissions from industrial installations

487.   On 23 March, the Council decided to conclude the Convention on the Transboundary Effects of Industrial Accidents (Table III). On 16 June, it adopted a common position on a proposal for a directive to

---

([1])   OJ C 379, 7.12.1998; Bull. 11-1998, point 1.2.122.
([2])   COM(1998) 333; Bull. 5-1998, point 1.2.146.
([3])   Article 6 of the consolidated EC Treaty.
([4])   Bull. 6-1998, point I.11. 34.
([5])   Bull. 12-1998.
([6])   COM(97) 592; 1997 General Report, point 540.
([7])   OJ C 235, 27.7.1998; Bull. 5-1998, point 1.2.149.
([8])   OJ C 292, 21.9.1998; Bull. 7/8-1998, point 1.3.181.
([9])   Bull. 10-1998, point 1.2.116.
([10])   Bull. 11-1998, point 1.2.123.

reduce emissions of volatile organic compounds due to the use of organic solvents in certain activities and installations (Table II). The spill of toxic industrial waste in the vicinity of the Doñana National Park in Spain prompted the European Parliament to adopt a resolution on 14 May ([1]).

488.   On 30 October, the Commission adopted a proposal for a regulation allowing voluntary participation by organisations in a Community eco-management and audit scheme (EMAS) (Table II). One of the main objectives of this proposal is to extend the scope of Regulation (EEC) No 1836/93 ([2]) to include all organisations with significant environmental effects.

Chemicals and biotechnology

489.   The Convention on the Prior Informed Consent Procedure for Certain Hazardous Chemicals and Pesticides in International Trade was signed in Rotterdam on 11 September by the Community and 62 countries (Table III). This procedure had already been made mandatory for exports of hazardous chemicals from the Community to non-Community countries by Regulation (EEC) No 2455/92 ([3]). Implementation of this regulation was examined in a report adopted by the Commission on 28 April ([4]).

490.   On 30 October, the Commission proposed amending for the ninth time Council Directive 67/548/EEC relating to the classification, packaging and labelling of dangerous substances in order to extend until 31 December 2000 certain derogations granted to Austria and Sweden as regards labelling (Table I). The Council reached agreement on this proposal on 21 December. On 18 November, the Commission adopted a report on the operation of the Community legislation on chemicals ([5]) which the Council endorsed on 21 December ([6]). The European Parliament adopted a resolution on endocrine-disrupting chemicals on 20 October ([7]).

([1])   OJ C 167, 1.6.1998; Bull. 5-1998, point 1.2.152.
([2])   OJ L 168, 10.7.1993; Twenty-seventh General Report, point 470.
([3])   OJ L 251, 29.8.1992; Twenty-sixth General Report, point 604.
([4])   COM(1998) 245; Bull. 4-1998, point 1.2.106.
([5])   COM(1998) 587; Bull. 11-1998, point 1.2.126.
([6])   Bull. 12-1998.
([7])   OJ C 341, 9.11.1998; Bull. 10-1998, point 1.2.123.

491.   On 26 October, the Council amended Directive 90/219/EEC on the contained use of genetically modified micro-organisms (Table II). On 23 February, the Commission adopted a proposal amending Directive 90/220/EEC on the deliberate release of such organisms into the environment (Table I). On the basis of the same directive, it adopted four decisions authorising the placing on the market of certain varieties of maize and colza on 22 April (^{1}). On 2 June, it submitted a proposal (^{2}) to the Council calling upon Austria and Luxembourg to repeal their bans on certain varieties of genetically modified maize, after the Commission had authorised placing them on the market in 1997 (^{3}).

Waste management

492.   On 7 October, the Commission adopted a proposal for a directive on incineration of waste (Table II) aimed at broadening the scope of the existing legislation and tightening up the standards which it lays down. The Council adopted on 4 June common positions on a proposal for a directive on the landfill of waste (Table II) and on a proposal for a regulation on shipments to non-OECD countries of non-hazardous waste intended for recovery (Table II).

493.   In February, the Community participated in the fourth conference of the parties to the Basle Convention on the Control of Transboundary Movements of Hazardous Wastes and their Disposal (^{4}) in Kuching (Malaysia). On 6 November, the Commission proposed approving the amendments to the Basle Convention adopted at the same conference (Table III). Implementation of Regulation (EEC) No 259/93 (^{5}), which includes measures to give effect to certain decisions taken under the Convention, was discussed in a report adopted by the Commission on 28 July (^{6}).

494.   On 16 September, the European Parliament adopted a resolution regretting that certain Member States had not done enough to implement various Community directives on waste management (^{7}).

(^{1})   Decisions 98/291/EC to 98/294/EC (OJ L 131, 5.5.1998).
(^{2})   COM(1998) 339 and 340; Bull. 6-1998, point 1.3.129.
(^{3})   1997 General Report, point 556.
(^{4})   Bull. 1/2-1998, point 1.3.220.
(^{5})   OJ L 30, 6.2.1993; Twenty-seventh General Report, point 474; 1997 General Report, point 560.
(^{6})   COM(1998) 475; Bull. 7/8-1998, point 1.3.191.
(^{7})   OJ C 313, 12.10.1998; Bull. 9-1998, point 1.2.121.

Quality of the environment and natural resources

495.   On 2 February, the Commission adopted a report on the state of the environment in the six *Länder* of the former East Germany (¹), and on 11 December it adopted a report on stronger Community environmental standards as a result of the accession of Austria, Finland and Sweden (²) which the Council endorsed on 21 December (³).

Protection of water

496.   On 3 November, the Council adopted a directive on the quality of water intended for human consumption updating Directive 80/778/EEC to ensure that the Member States take the measures necessary to guarantee that water intended for human consumption meets the minimum requirements set (Table II).

497.   The Commission published its 15th report on the quality of bathing water in the European Union on 20 May (⁴). On 20 January (⁵), it adopted a supplement to its 1997 report (⁶) on the implementation of Directive 91/676/EEC (⁷) concerning the protection of waters against pollution caused by nitrates from agricultural sources. Parliament adopted a resolution on this subject on 20 October (⁸).

Protection of nature and biodiversity

498.   On 21 December, the Council approved an update to the list of species protected under the Berne Convention on the Conservation of European Wildlife and Natural Habitats (Table III). On 12 February, it approved the updated list of migratory species protected under the Bonn Convention (Table III) and on 23 March it concluded the European Convention for the Protection of Vertebrate Animals used for Experimental and other Scientific Purposes (Table III). On 20 July, the Council adopted a common position on the proposal for a recommendation submitted by the Commission in 1995 relating to the keeping of wild

---

(¹)   COM(1998) 33; Bull. 1/2-1998, point 1.3.212.
(²)   COM(1998) 745; Bull. 12-1998.
(³)   Bull. 12-1998.
(⁴)   Bull. 5-1998, point 1.2.153.
(⁵)   COM(1998) 16; Bull. 1/2-1998, point 1.3.222.
(⁶)   COM(97) 473; 1997 General Report, point 542.
(⁷)   OJ L 375, 31.12.1991; Twenty-fifth General Report, point 649.
(⁸)   OJ C 341, 9.11.1998; Bull. 10-1998, point 1.2.126.

animals in zoos. This common position provided for adoption of a directive instead of a recommendation (Table II).

499. To meet the Community's obligations under the Convention on Biological Diversity ([1]), a communication adopted by the Commission on 4 February ([2]) defined a Community biodiversity strategy. This communication was welcomed by the Council on 16 June ([3]) and by the European Parliament on 20 October ([4]). The Commission also participated in the fourth conference of the parties to the Convention on Biological Diversity in Bratislava from 4 to 15 May, after the Council had adopted conclusions in preparation for the conference on 23 March ([5]).

Air quality, urban environment, noise and transport

500. To implement Directive 96/62/EC on ambient air quality assessment and management ([6]), on 24 September the Council adopted a common position on a proposal for a directive relating to limit values for sulphur dioxide, oxides of nitrogen, particulate matter and lead in ambient air (Table II). The Commission adopted a proposal for a directive laying down limit values for benzene and carbon monoxide on 2 December (Table II).

501. As part of the Community strategy to combat acidification ([7]), which the Commission defined in 1997 and the European Parliament approved in a resolution adopted on 13 May ([8]), on 23 March the Council concluded a protocol to the Convention on Long-range Transboundary Air Pollution (Table III) and, on 6 October, adopted a common position on a proposal for a directive to reduce the sulphur content of certain liquid fuels (Table II). Also, on 8 July, the Commission proposed updating the directive on the limitation of emissions from large combustion plants (Table II).

502. On 13 October, the European Parliament and the Council adopted two directives under the 'Auto-Oil' programme to control air pollution caused by emissions from motor vehicles ([9]). One of these con-

([1])   OJ L 309, 13.12.1993; Twenty-seventh General Report, point 487.
([2])   COM(1998) 42; Bull. 1/2-1998, point 1.3.224.
([3])   Bull. 6-1998, point 1.3.134.
([4])   OJ C 341, 9.11.1998; Bull. 10-1998, point 1.2.128.
([5])   Bull. 3-1998, point 1.2.143.
([6])   OJ L 296, 21.11.1996; 1996 General Report, point 464.
([7])   1997 General Report, point 548.
([8])   OJ C 167, 1.6.1998; Bull. 5-1998, point 1.2.151.
([9])   1996 General Report, point 465.

cerned emissions from passenger cars and light commercial vehicles (Table I), the other petrol and diesel fuel quality (Table I). On 21 December, the Council reached agreement on a common position on a proposal for a directive relating to measures to be taken against polluting emissions from diesel-engine heavy commercial vehicles (Table I). On 3 September, the Commission adopted a proposal for a directive on action to be taken against emissions of pollutants from agricultural or forestry tractors (Table I).

503.   Conclusions adopted by the Council on 17 June called on the International Civil Aviation Organisation to introduce stricter standards on emissions of oxides of nitrogen from civil subsonic aircraft ([1]).

504.   To follow up the Commission Green Paper on future noise policy, the Danish Government and the Commission organised a conference on the subject in Copenhagen in September ([2]). On 18 February, the Commission adopted a proposal for a directive relating to the noise emission by equipment used outdoors with the dual objectives of tightening up the standards provided for by the existing directives and combining those directives in a single text (Table I).

505.   The Committee of the Regions adopted an opinion on environment policy in cities and towns on 12 March ([3]).

Global environment, climate change, geosphere, biosphere and energy

506.   To meet the binding commitments for a reduction in greenhouse gas emissions given at the third conference of the parties to the United Nations Framework Convention on Climate Change in Kyoto in December 1997 ([4]), the European Community and its Member States signed a protocol to the Convention in New York on 29 April (Table III). In a communication adopted on 3 June, the Commission defined the first steps in a strategy to enable the European Union to meet its commitments under this protocol ([5]). On 16 June, the Council agreed upon the contributions to be made by each Member State towards the European

---

[1]   Bull. 6-1998, point 1.3.139.
[2]   Bull. 9-1998, point 1.2.132.
[3]   OJ C 180, 11.6.1998; Bull. 3-1998, point 1.2.144.
[4]   1997 General Report, point 552.
[5]   COM(1998) 353; Bull. 6-1998, point 1.3.140.

Union's commitment to reduce total greenhouse gas emissions by 8 % by 2010, compared with 1990 levels ([1]).

507.   The fourth conference of the parties to the United Nations Framework Convention on Climate Change was held in Buenos Aires in November ([2]). An action plan was adopted covering development and technology transfer, the mechanisms decided at Kyoto (emissions trading, clean development mechanism and joint implementation), financing arrangements and policies and measures to attain the objective of the Convention.

508.   The follow-up to the Kyoto conference and preparations for the Buenos Aires conference were the subject of conclusions by the European Council in June ([3]), conclusions by the Council in March ([4]), May ([5]) and October ([6]), and resolutions by the European Parliament in February ([7]) and September ([8]).

509.   On 16 June, the Council adopted a common position on a proposal for a decision to extend beyond the year 2000 the mechanism established by Decision 93/389/EEC for monitoring emissions of CO_2 and other greenhouse gases in the Community (Table II). Under the Community strategy to reduce CO_2 emissions from cars ([9]), the Commission adopted a proposal for a directive establishing a scheme to monitor emissions of carbon dioxide from new passenger cars on 12 June (Table II) and a proposal for a directive to set up a system for providing consumers with information on the fuel economy of new passenger cars on 3 September (Table II). On 21 December, the Council reached agreement on common positions on these proposals. The Commission also negotiated an environmental agreement with the European Automobile Manufacturers' Association, which gave an undertaking to attain a target of reducing average CO_2 emissions by new cars sold in the European Union to 140 g/km by 2008, about 25 % below the 1995 levels. The Commission outlined this draft agreement in a communication adopted on 29 July ([10]) and welcomed on 6 October ([11]) by the

([1])   Bull. 6-1998, point 1.3.141.
([2])   Bull. 11-1998, point 1.2.130.
([3])   Bull. 6-1998, point I.11. 35.
([4])   Bull. 3-1998, point 1.2.148.
([5])   Bull. 5-1998, point 1.2.120.
([6])   Bull. 10-1998, point 1.2.123.
([7])   OJ C 80, 16.3.1998; Bull. 1/2-1998, point 1.3.233.
([8])   OJ C 313, 12.10.1998; Bull. 9-1998, point 1.2.133.
([9])   COM(95) 689; 1995 General Report, point 482.
([10]) COM(1998) 495; Bull. 7/8-1998, point 1.3.197.
([11]) Bull. 10-1998, point 1.2.134.

Council, which had previously adopted conclusions on the negotiations in progress on 23 March (¹) and 16 June (²), and then advocated, on 21 December, the conclusion of similar agreements with the Japanese and Korean manufacturers (³).

510.   On 2 April, the European Parliament approved (⁴) the strategy for reducing methane emissions submitted by the Commission (⁵) and called on the Commission to draft a specific action plan on the subject.

511.   On 14 August, the Commission proposed replacing Regulation (EC) No 3093/94 on substances that deplete the ozone layer (⁶) by a new regulation in order to meet the Community's commitments under the Montreal Protocol, as amended in 1997 (⁷), and reflect the progress made on bringing alternative substances on to the market. This proposal, on which the Council reached agreement on a common position on 21 December, is aimed at ending the use of chlorofluorocarbons and halons on Union territory, banning production and marketing by 2001 in the case of methyl bromide and gradually in the case of hydrochlorofluorocarbons and banning exports of equipment containing chlorofluorocarbons and halons (Table II). On 23 October, the Commission submitted a strategy for the phasing-out of chlorofluorocarbons in metered-dose inhalers (⁸).

Environmental instruments

512.   Following on from its 1996 communication on implementing Community environmental law (⁹), on 16 December the Commission adopted a proposal for a recommendation on minimum criteria for environmental inspections in Member States (¹⁰).

(¹)   Bull. 3-1998, point 1.2.150.
(²)   Bull. 6-1998, point 1.3.143.
(³)   Bull. 12-1998.
(⁴)   OJ C 138, 4.5.1998; Bull. 4-1998, point 1.2.115.
(⁵)   COM(96) 557; 1996 General Report, point 453.
(⁶)   OJ L 333, 22.12.1994; 1994 General Report, point 533.
(⁷)   1997 General Report, point 553.
(⁸)   COM(1998) 603; Bull. 10-1998, point 1.2.132.
(⁹)   COM(96) 500; 1996 General Report, point 440; 1997 General Report, point 536.
(¹⁰)   COM(1998) 772; Bull. 12-1998.

513. In a resolution adopted on 15 July([1]), the European Parliament welcomed the Commission communication on environmental taxes and charges in the single market([2]).

514. Based on Regulation (EEC) No 880/92([3]), the Commission adopted revised criteria for the award of the Community eco-label to soil improvers on 7 April([4]), to dishwashers on 20 July([5]) and to mattresses on 2 October([6]).

515. Under its policy on environmental agreements([7]), in July the Commission adopted a recommendation([8]) recognising the commitment by the AISE (International Association of Soaps, Detergents and Cleaning Products) to a code of good environmental practice for household laundry detergents and a communication on the commitment given by the European Automobile Manufacturers' Association to reduce CO_2 emissions from cars *(→ point 509).* Workshops on 'sustainable development — a challenge for the financial sector' and 'integrated product policy' were held in October and December respectively.

516. Under Regulation (EC) No 1404/96 establishing a financial instrument for the environment (LIFE)([9]), in 1998 the Commission financed 217 projects, 85 of which concerned nature conservation schemes, 116 other schemes to implement Community environment policy and legislation and 16 schemes to provide technical assistance to certain non-member countries in the Mediterranean or Baltic Sea regions, which were granted a total of ECU 101.3 million. On 4 December, the Commission adopted a report on the implementation of LIFE([10]) and on 9 December it adopted a proposal for a regulation aimed at continuing the action in question, subject to certain improvements, during the period 2000-04 (Table II). The Cohesion Fund *(→ points 376 et seq.)* also continued to finance environmental infrastructure in the four Member States concerned.

([1]) OJ C 292, 21.9.1998; Bull. 7/8-1998, point 1.3.180.
([2]) COM(97) 9; 1997 General Report, point 561.
([3]) OJ L 99, 11.4.1992; Twenty-sixth General Report, point 604.
([4]) OJ L 219, 7.8.1998.
([5]) OJ L 216, 4.8.1998.
([6]) OJ L 302, 17.11.1998.
([7]) 1996 General Report, point 441.
([8]) Recommendation 98/480/EC (OJ L 215, 1.8.1998).
([9]) OJ L 181, 20.7.1996; 1996 General Report, point 442.
([10]) COM(1998) 722; Bull. 12-1998.

International cooperation

517. At the sixth session of the Commission on Sustainable Development [1] in New York in April, for which the Council had prepared the ground by adopting conclusions on 23 March [2], the European Union focused, in particular, on implementation of its proposals on sustainable freshwater management and the role of industry in sustainable development and eco-efficiency, which had been included in the programme adopted in 1997 by the United Nations special session on the environment [3]. It also played an active part in the activities of the Intergovernmental Forum on Forests [4], which must report to the Commission on Sustainable Development in 2000 and which held its second meeting, in Geneva, from 24 August to 4 September. The European Union also participated in work on the United Nations Environment Programme [5], particularly in the special session of the Governing Council in Nairobi (Kenya) in May.

518. In the context of regional cooperation on environmental matters, the Commission participated in the fourth pan-European conference of Environment Ministers held in Aarhus (Denmark) from 23 to 25 June [6], for which the Council had prepared the ground by adopting conclusions on 16 June [7]. At this event the Community signed the United Nations Economic Commission for Europe (UNECE) Convention on Access to Environmental Information, Public Participation in Decision-making and Access to Justice in Environmental Matters, which aims at reinforcing the rights of citizens and non-governmental organisations and encouraging their participation in decision-making (Table III) as well as signing protocols on persistent organic pollutants (Table III) and heavy metals (Table III) under the UNECE Convention on Long-range Transboundary Air Pollution. On 6 July, the Council authorised the Commission to negotiate a further protocol under the same Convention, on nitrogen oxides and related substances (Table III), and on 21 December it authorised it to negotiate an agreement on persistent organic pollutants under the United Nations Environment Programme (Table III).

519. The Council decided, on 9 March, to conclude the United Nations Convention to Combat Desertification (Table III). The second

---

[1]   Twenty-sixth General Report, point 596.
[2]   Bull. 3-1998, point 1.2.154.
[3]   1997 General Report, point 566.
[4]   1997 General Report, point 568.
[5]   1997 General Report, point 569.
[6]   Bull. 6-1998, point 1.3.148.
[7]   Bull. 6-1998, point 1.3.147.

conference of the parties to this Convention was held in Dakar from 30 November to 11 December. The Commission also participated in the fourth meeting of the Mediterranean Commission for Sustainable Development in Monaco from 20 to 22 October. On 23 March, the Council approved Parcom Decision 96/1 (phasing-out of hexachloroethane in non-ferrous metals) under the Paris Convention for the Prevention of Marine Pollution from Land-based Sources (Table III). The Commission submitted a proposal to the Council on 16 September relating to the conclusion of the Convention on the International Commission for the Protection of the Oder (Table III).

520. Following the entry into force of the OSPAR Convention for the Protection of the Marine Environment of the North-east Atlantic on 25 March (Table III), a decision on the disposal of disused offshore installations was adopted at the first OSPAR ministerial meeting in Sintra (Portugal) in July ([1]). The European Union's position at this meeting had been prepared by a communication submitted by the Commission on 16 February ([2]), and by conclusions adopted by the Council on 16 June ([3]). Ms Bjerregaard represented the Commission at the ministerial-level meeting of the Helsinki Commission (Helcom), the executive body for the Convention for the Protection of the Baltic Sea, in March.

521. The Council decided to conclude agreements on international humane trapping standards with Canada (Table III) and Russia (Table III) on 26 January, and with the United States on 13 July (Table III). The European Parliament had rejected these agreements.

522. The Europe-Asia cooperation strategy in the field of environment submitted by the Commission in 1997 ([4]) was welcomed on 25 February by the Economic and Social Committee ([5]) and on 14 July by the European Parliament ([6]), which stressed the need to take account of poverty in the context of environmental problems. In a resolution adopted on 2 April in the wake of the fires devastating northern Brazil and south-east Asia, the European Parliament reaffirmed the importance of tropical forests for the world and the need for international cooperation in this field ([7]).

---

[1] Bull. 7/8-1998, point 1.3.193.
[2] COM(1998) 49; Bull. 1/2-1998, point 1.3.236.
[3] Bull. 6-1998, point 1.3.152.
[4] COM(97) 490; 1997 General Report, point 570.
[5] OJ C 129, 27.4.1998; Bull. 1/2-1998, point 1.3.235.
[6] OJ C 292, 21.9.1998; Bull. 7/8-1998, point 1.3.202.
[7] OJ C 138, 4.5.1998; Bull. 4-1998, point 1.2.118.

523. As part of the pre-accession strategy for the central European countries, in May the Commission adopted a communication setting out its general strategy on implementation of the Community environmental legislation in these countries *(→ point 807).*

524. Information on the European Union institutions' other international activities is given under 'Industry and environment' and 'Quality of the environment and natural resources' in this section *(→ points 487 et seq.).*

European Environment Agency

525. On 20 July, the Council adopted a common position on a proposal to amend the regulation on the establishment of the European Environment Agency designed to define the Agency's tasks more clearly. The Agency published its assessment of Europe's environment in June and its Management Board adopted a new work programme for 1999 to 2003.

Civil protection

526. On 16 December, the Commission proposed extending the Community action programme in the field of civil protection to the period from 2000 to 2004 (Table II) and setting up a Community framework for cooperation in the field of accidental marine pollution (Table II).

527. Several projects (exchanges of experts, disaster prevention, crisis management, medical assistance in the event of disasters and information for the general public) received funding totalling ECU 1 million under the Community action programme in the field of civil protection [1] in 1998.

528. The European Parliament adopted a series of resolutions in response to disasters which struck in the Community in the course of the year [2]. These generally stressed the need for closer coordination of the civil protection facilities in the Member States and to evolve a Community approach in this field.

---

[1] OJ L 8, 14.1.1998; 1997 General Report, point 576.
[2] Floods in Campania on 16 May (OJ C 167, 1.6.1998; Bull. 5-1998, point 1.2.159); earthquake in the Azores on 16 July (OJ C 292, 21.9.1998; Bull. 7/8-1998, point 1.3.199); fires in Greece on 16 July (OJ C 292, 21.9.1998; Bull. 7/8-1998, point 1.3.200); forest fires in the European Union on 17 September (OJ C 313, 12.10.1998; Bull. 9-1998, point 1.2.134).

Section 18

Nuclear safety (^{1})

Priority activities and objectives

529.   Where nuclear safety is concerned, the harmonisation of safety practices and criteria within the Union and the preparations for enlargement were the main priorities this year. The European Union also continued to develop active cooperation with the independent States of the former Soviet Union.

Radiation protection

530.   On 23 February, the Commission adopted a communication (^{2}) concerning the implementation of Council Directive 96/29/Euratom laying down basic safety standards for the protection of the health of workers and the general public against the dangers arising from ionising radiation (^{3}), which must be applied in full by May 2000. Conferences, seminars and workshops with the Member States were also organised in order to facilitate the harmonised transposition of this directive into national law.

531.   Pursuant to Article 33 of the Euratom Treaty, the Commission issued 22 recommendations on draft national measures, and under Article 35 of the Treaty, it carried out one visit to verify the operation and efficiency of facilities for monitoring the level of radioactivity in the environment.

Plant safety

532.   As part of the process of harmonising safety practices and criteria, several studies were carried out to examine the practices of the different European countries with regard to probabilistic safety analysis and safety-relevant software. These studies made it possible to adopt com-

---

(^{1})   Research activities under the specific programme 'Nuclear fission safety' are dealt with in Section 8 ('Research and technology') of this chapter (→ *point 308*). Information concerning the multiannual programme of actions in the nuclear sector are dealt with in Section 14 ('Energy') of this chapter (→ *point 421*).
(^{2})   OJ C 133, 30.4.1998; COM(1998) 87; Bull. 1/2-1998, point 1.3.234.
(^{3})   OJ L 159, 29.6.1996; 1996 General Report, point 474.

mon technical positions on key questions of safety. On 14 May, the Committee of the Regions adopted an own-initiative opinion calling for more transparency and greater participation by the regional authorities in the decision-making process on the siting, management and shutdown of nuclear facilities ([1]).

533.   In order to ensure the development of regulatory authorities able to maintain an acceptable level of nuclear safety in the central European countries and in the independent States of the former Soviet Union, cooperation with those countries continued in the context, in particular, of the Concert Group, which brings together 26 national authorities. In a resolution adopted on 14 May ([2]), the European Parliament called upon the Slovak Republic to postpone the start-up of the Mochovce nuclear power station.

Radioactive waste

534.   On 18 December, the Commission adopted its second report ([3]) (1995-96) on the application in the Member States of Directive 92/3/ Euratom on the supervision and control of shipments of radioactive waste between Member States and into and out of the Community ([4]).

Decommissioning of nuclear installations

535.   The European Union developed its cooperation with the central European countries and the independent States of the former Soviet Union with regard to the environmental and safety problems connected with the decommissioning of nuclear installations. Cooperation with the central European countries concerned in particular the management of irradiated nuclear fuel from research reactors. Cooperation with the independent States of the former Soviet Union focused on the environmental threats from irradiated nuclear fuel from submarines in the north-west region (Murmansk), large accumulations of waste around Mayak (Southern Urals) and the legacy of Chernobyl. On 5 June, the Council decided to grant a contribution of ECU 100 million, from the funds for the TACIS programme, to the Chernobyl shelter fund (Table

---

[1]   OJ C 251, 10.8.1998; Bull. 5-1998, point 1.2.161.
[2]   OJ C 167, 1.6.1998; Bull. 5-1998, point 1.2.160.
[3]   COM(1998) 778; Bull.12-1998; Previous report: COM(95) 192; 1995 General Report, point 514.
[4]   OJ L 35, 12.2.1992; Twenty-sixth General Report, point 731.

II). On 22 October, the European Parliament adopted a resolution on the decommissioning of nuclear power stations ([1]).

Transport of radioactive material

536.   On 8 April, the Commission adopted a communication presenting the fourth report of its standing working group on the safe transport of radioactive material in the European Union ([2]). On 18 June, in a resolution on the safety of transport of nuclear fuel and waste ([3]), the European Parliament, stressing that safety must have absolute priority over profitability and security of supply, called for safeguards to be stepped up in this area.

International action

537.   On 7 December, the Council adopted a decision (Table III) approving the accession of Euratom to the International Nuclear Safety Convention ([4]).

538.   In a communication adopted on 31 March, the Commission took stock of what it has done in the nuclear sector with regard to the applicant countries of central Europe and the independent States of the former Soviet Union ([5]). This matter was also the subject of conclusions by the Council on 7 December ([6]). In the context of the coordination of international assistance to those countries ([7]) with regard to nuclear safety, for which the Commission continues to provide secretariat services, the main topics addressed in 1998 were the future aid guidelines, the assessment of efforts so far and public information.

539.   Cooperation agreements in the field of nuclear safety and thermonuclear fusion were negotiated with Russia (Table III), Ukraine (Table III) and Kazakhstan (Table III). On 19 September, the agreement between Euratom and the Korean Energy Development Organisation (KEDO), one of the objectives of which is to improve nuclear safety, entered into force *(→ point 911).*

---

[1]   OJ C 341, 9.11.1998; Bull. 10-1998, point 1.2.136.
[2]   COM(1998) 155; Bull. 4-1998, point 1.2.116; Previous report: COM(96) 11; 1996 General Report, point 478.
[3]   OJ C 120, 6.7.1998; Bull. 6-1998, point 1.3.146.
[4]   1996 General Report, point 480.
[5]   COM(1998) 134, Bull. 3-1998, point 1.3.61.
[6]   Bull. 12-1998.
[7]   1997 General Report, point 585.

Section *19*

Euratom safeguards

540. In 1998, the Euratom Safeguards Directorate conducted physical and accounting checks on average stocks of 485 tonnes of plutonium, 10 tonnes of highly-enriched uranium and 303 000 tonnes of (low-enrichment, natural and depleted) uranium, thorium and heavy water. These materials were held in the 800 or so nuclear installations in the Community and gave rise to more than one and a half million operator entries concerning physical movements and stocks. As in the past, the checks also covered equipment subject to external commitments under agreements concluded with non-member countries (Australia, Canada and United States). The anomalies and irregularities detected by the Directorate were followed up rigorously by additional inspections.

541. The number of man-days of inspection throughout the Union amounted to approximately 9 000. This figure mainly reflects the inspections carried out in the major installations using plutonium, in nuclear reactors and in the major storage facilities, as well as the more technical tasks carried out in the context of the new partnership approach (→ *point 542*). The Safeguards Directorate also launched a new internal computer system for storing and processing all the accounting data from nuclear operators in the Community. This complex system, necessitated by the large quantities of data to be managed and the need to have rapid and selective access to information, has already proved to be reliable, efficient and versatile.

542. The implementation of the new partnership approach (NPA)[1] between the Commission and the International Atomic Energy Agency (IAEA) continued satisfactorily. The new inspection procedures were for the most part implemented in many installations and the new approach has also proved to be effective in the areas of logistics and the training of inspectors. Additional protocols to the three agreements with the IAEA aimed at improving its safeguard systems ('93 + 2' programme) were signed in Vienna on 22 September (Table III). The Safeguards Directorate and the Member States took the first practical steps to define the areas of responsibility and the detailed implementation of the various measures provided for in the protocols.

---

[1]   Twenty-sixth General Report, point 721.

543.   The Safeguards Directorate held a series of bilateral talks with the authorities of the Member States with a nuclear programme and various third countries, in particular Australia, Canada, Japan and the United States, and with the new Argentine-Brazil nuclear agency (ABACC). It also succeeded in stepping up cooperation with Russia which had slowed down considerably in 1997 ([1]), in order to help to develop that country's nuclear materials control and accounting system by introducing modern and more efficient procedures, but without being able to provide real on-the-spot training for Russian experts.

544.   The Safeguards Directorate installed and fine-tuned highly automated safeguards systems for the major plutonium-processing plants, in particular MELOX, UP3 and UP2-800 in France, and THORP and SMP (Sellafield Mox Plant) in the United Kingdom. In addition, after several years of operation, a full assessment was carried out of the equipment already installed, and certain systems were improved. Work also continued on the establishment of Euratom laboratories at Sellafield and La Hague, the inauguration of the Sellafield laboratory, scheduled for the end of 1997, having been delayed for technical reasons.

545.   During the year the Safeguards Directorate and the JRC's Institute for Transuranium Elements (→ *points 290 et seq.)* again took action in relation to cases of trafficking in nuclear materials, although the number of actual cases (seizures of uranium or plutonium) detected continued to fall. According to police sources in the Member States most concerned, the number of false alarms and attempted blackmail and fraud in connection with other radioactive substances is, however, still on the high side. The Safeguards Directorate is very active in numerous technical, sectoral and multidisciplinary working parties designed to develop and coordinate solutions to this problem at international level.

---

[1]   1997 General Report, point 592.

Section 20

Agricultural policy ([1])

Priority activities and objectives

546.   As part of Agenda 2000, the Commission has tabled proposals for the reform of the common agricultural policy and rural development policy which are designed to strengthen the competitiveness of European agriculture both inside and outside the Union, stressing product quality, food safety and the environment while maintaining a firm commitment to guaranteeing the farming community an equitable standard of living and promoting the economic diversification of the Union's rural areas. In advance of the introduction of a single currency, the Council adopted a new agrimonetary system. The Council has also reformed the common market organisations in olive oil, bananas and tobacco and adopted a directive to provide better welfare protection for livestock on farms.

Implementing Agenda 2000

547.   As part of Agenda 2000, the Commission adopted a set of proposals for draft legislation on agriculture on 18 March; it added a proposed regulation for the wine sector on 16 July. An overall presentation of the proposals and their treatment by the other institutions appears in Chapter I ('Agenda 2000') *(→ points 1 et seq.).* A specific presentation of each proposal appears in this section *(→ points 548 et seq.)* ([2]).

548.   The two proposals for regulations on cereals and on other arable crops (Table II) provide in particular for a single-stage cut of 20 % in the intervention price in 2000, an increase in direct payments for cereals (up from ECU 54 to 66 per tonne), oilseeds and non-fibre linseed (also raised to ECU 66 per tonne), and a continuation of compulsory set-aside but at a zero rate; voluntary set-aside would remain available.

([1])   More detail will be found in *The agricultural situation in the European Union — 1998 report* (in preparation), which is being written in parallel with this General Report. The 1997 Agriculture Report is available from the Publications Office (COM(1998) 611).

([2])   In the table showing consultation and cooperation procedures launched (Table II at the end of this Report), the proposals for agriculture as part of Agenda 2000 will be found under the heading 'Agenda 2000' at the top of the table and not under 'Common agricultural policy'.

549. The Commission is proposing recasting the common organisation of the market in beef and veal (Table II), with a cut of 30 % in support prices between 2000 and 2002 and the replacement of intervention buying by a private-storage system as from 1 July 2002, these measures being offset by an increase in premiums for livestock farmers (basic premiums to be raised in 2002 to ECU 220 for bulls, ECU 170 (in two instalments) for bullocks, ECU 180 for suckler cows and ECU 35 for dairy cows).

550. The Commission has adopted two proposals for reforming the common organisation of the market in milk and milk products (Table II). These include in particular a staged reduction in intervention prices by 15 %, a continuation of milk quotas until 2006, with an expansion of 2 % for allocation to new entrants to farming, to upland producers and to producers in sub-polar regions, and a division of direct payments to producers into a basic aid of ECU 100 per premium unit and additional aid of ECU 45 per premium unit, with the latter subject to national rules.

551. The two proposals for regulations amending the common organisation of the market in oils and fats and the general rules governing aid for olive oil (Table II) are aimed at increasing the Community-wide maximum guaranteed quantity, setting production aid at ECU 1 322.5 a tonne and abolishing aid for consumption of olive oil, for small producers and for intervention buying-in. The Council adopted these two regulations on 20 July as part of the annual farm-prices package. The changes will come in from the 1998/99 marketing year onwards and apply for three years initially.

552. The proposal for recasting the common organisation of the wine market (Table II) is designed first of all to considerably simplify the current legislation (the draft regulation will replace 23 existing ones), but is also aimed at achieving a better balance between supply and demand on the Community market and at helping the sector become more competitive in the longer run. The proposal provides in particular for the ending of intervention buying-in as an artificial outlet for surplus production, while guaranteeing supply to the potable alcohol market under a specific measure on distillation; grubbing-up schemes are to be targeted on regions with structural surpluses; the ban on planting new vines is to be loosened so as to encourage the production of wines for which demand is expanding; the role of producer groups and interbranch organisations or their equivalents is to be made more official; and the provisions on product designations and presentations are improved.

553. The proposal for a horizontal regulation setting out rules for all market organisations that involve direct payments to producers (Table II) provides in particular for a linkage between direct support and environmental requirements ('eco-conditionality'), as well as allowing Member States to modify direct aid per farm to take account of the number of farm workers and tail off aid payments above an ECU 100 000 threshold.

554. The proposal on support for rural development from the European Agricultural Guidance and Guarantee Fund (Table II) provides that schemes to improve agricultural structures and promote rural development are to be funded from the Guidance Section of the EAGGF in Objective 1 regions (except for agri-environment schemes, early-retirement schemes, woodland management schemes and aid for farming in less-favoured areas, for which funding is to come from the Guarantee Section); in areas not eligible under Objective 1, funding is to come from the Guarantee Section. This proposal amounts to the merging into a single text of all the schemes in support of rural development currently covered by nine separate regulations, that is to say: support for adjustment in agriculture (modernisation of farms, improvement of processing and marketing structures), start-up aid for new entrants, early retirement of farmers, agriculture in mountain and less-favoured areas, environmentally sound agricultural practices, woodland management and timber industry development, and specific training schemes; on top of this, it includes a broader approach to the development of rural areas by boosting their internal resources (local products, tourism, cultural heritage, diversification of the local economy), the quality of life in the countryside and the conservation of the natural environment.

555. The proposal for a new regulation on financing the CAP (Table II) is designed to recast the legislation in this field, redefining the roles of the Guidance Section (funding rural development in regions lagging behind in their development) *(→ point 554)* and the Guarantee Section (funding rural development in other areas, plus some other measures).

Agricultural structures and rural development

556. Structural measures and assistance are described in Section 11 ('Economic and social cohesion') of this chapter *(→ points 347 et seq.).*

Forests, environment and agriculture

557.   On 25 May, the Council extended Regulation (EEC) No 1615/89
establishing a European forestry information and communication system
(EFICS) (^{1}) until 31 December 2002. On the basis of a communication
from the Commission on 18 November (^{2}), the Council adopted a resolution on 14 December on a forestry strategy for the European
Union (^{3}). The Commission for its part granted a total of ECU 16 million in 1998 to projects submitted by Member States under the regulations on protecting the Community's forests against atmospheric pollution and against fire (^{4}).

558.   Reports from the Commission reviewing the implementation of
the Community aid scheme for forestry measures in agriculture (^{5}) and
the regulation (^{6}) on agricultural production methods compatible with
the requirements of the protection of the environment and the maintenance of the countryside (^{7}) were the subject of Parliament resolutions
passed on 23 October (^{8}). On the same day, Parliament also gave its
opinion on a new strategy for mountain areas, less-favoured areas and
environmentally sensitive areas (^{9}).

559.   The proposal for a regulation drawing up common rules for
direct payments under the CAP, presented by the Commission as part of
Agenda 2000, provides among other things for aid to be made conditional on compliance with environmental criteria *(→ point 553)*.

560.   The Commission's report on implementation of the regulation on
the conservation, characterisation, collection and utilisation of genetic
resources in agriculture (^{10}) was the subject of a European Parliament
resolution on 15 May (^{11}). The impact of biotechnology and the use of
genetically modified organisms in agriculture was examined by the Euro-

---

(^{1})   Regulation (EC) No 1100/98 (OJ L 157, 30.5.1998; Bull. 5-1998, point 1.2.170).
(^{2})   COM(1998) 649; Bull. 11-1998, point 1.2.137.
(^{3})   Bull. 12-1998.
(^{4})   Regulations (EC) Nos 307/97 and 308/97 (OJ L 51, 21.2.1997; 1997 General Report, point
        602).
(^{5})   COM(97) 630.
(^{6})   Regulation (EC) No 2078/92 (OJ L 215, 30.7.1992; Twenty-sixth General Report, point 516).
(^{7})   COM(97) 620; 1997 General Report, point 604.
(^{8})   OJ C 341, 9.11.1998; Bull. 10-1998, points 1.2.44 and 1.2.138.
(^{9})   OJ C 341, 9.11.1998; Bull. 10-1998, point 1.2.137.
(^{10}) 1997 General Report, point 604.
(^{11}) OJ C 167, 1.6.1998; Bull. 5-1998, point 1.2.165.

pean Parliament in a resolution of 19 February (^{1}), and by the Economic and Social Committee in an opinion of 1 July (^{2}).

Quality of agricultural products

561. As part of the implementation (^{3}) of Regulation (EEC) No 2081/92 on the protection of geographical indications and designations of origin for agricultural products and foodstuffs (^{4}), in January (^{5}), March (^{6}), June (^{7}), July (^{8}) and October (^{9}) the Commission added to the list of registered names, which now stands at 503. The Commission also introduced, on 22 July, a Community symbol (logo) to help consumers to identify the products protected by the registered names (^{10}). It also continued its publicity campaign on protected designations of origin, protected geographical indications and certificates of specific character called 'Products with a story', as well as work on the inventory of quality labels used by the Member States (^{3}). Evaluations of the campaigns to promote olive oil, fibre flax, quality beef, milk and milk products, apples, citrus fruit and grape juice showed that these campaigns had achieved their goals and had contributed to stabilising the different markets.

562. The Economic and Social Committee, in an opinion of 1 July, stated that increasing the production of quality local agricultural products could provide the key to economic progress in less-favoured rural areas (^{11}). For its part, Parliament stated on 9 October that it supported the creation of a Community quality class based on environmental criteria and the promotion of organic farming (^{12}).

(^{1})   OJ C 80, 16.3.1998; Bull. 1/2-1998, point 1.3.240.
(^{2})   OJ C 284, 14.9.1998; Bull. 7/8-1998, point 1.3.203.
(^{3})   1997 General Report, point 605.
(^{4})   OJ L 208, 24.7.1992; Twenty-sixth General Report, point 518.
(^{5})   OJ L 15, 21.1.1998; OJ L 20, 27.1.1998.
(^{6})   OJ L 87, 21.3.1998; Bull. 3-1998, point 1.2.170.
(^{7})   OJ L 175, 19.6.1998.
(^{8})   OJ L 202, 18.7.1998; OJ L 206, 23.7.1998; Bull. 7/8-1998, point 1.3.222.
(^{9})   OJ L 266, 1.10.1998; OJ L 270, 7.10.1998.
(^{10})   OJ L 224, 11.8.1998; Bull. 7/8-1998, point 1.3.223.
(^{11})   OJ C 284, 14.9.1998; Bull. 7/8-1998, point 1.3.224.
(^{12})   OJ C 328, 26.10.1998; Bull. 10-1998, point 1.2.145.

Veterinary and plant health legislation

563.   As part of the efforts to combat bovine spongiform encephalopathy (BSE)(¹) and other transmissible spongiform encephalopathies
(TSEs), the Commission introduced emergency measures on 18 November (²) to deal with the disquieting development of BSE in Portugal. It
also continued its efforts to supplement the range of protection measures
taken in 1996 and 1997; on 23 April, for instance, it took steps to
support epidemic surveillance schemes for TSEs (³), and on 18 November it adopted a proposal for a regulation (Table I) and a proposal for
a directive (Table I) aimed at consolidating and updating the existing
legislation covering all problems related to TSEs throughout the human
and animal food chains. With the same ends in view, on 22 July the
Commission defined the information required in support of applications
for the evaluation of the epidemiological status of countries with respect
to TSEs (⁴). The Commission also granted ECU 10 million in aid for the
implementation of pilot projects on the electronic identification of livestock (IDEA scheme) (⁵) on 6 March, adopted a report (⁶) on the implementation of Directive 92/102/EEC (⁷) on the identification and registration of animals on 17 April, and issued guidelines on 11 November for
detecting and estimating by microscopy the different components in animal feed, particularly those of animal origin (⁸). Finally, on 25 November, the Commission introduced a new export regime (⁹) under which,
after thorough checking of its projected operation and associated controls, a date can be set for the resumption of consignments of deboned
beef from the United Kingdom, but limited to the meat of animals born
after 1 August 1996 (when it is considered that the UK ban on the use
of meat-and-bone meal in ruminant feed actually became effective) and
aged over six months but under 30 months. The Council for its part
twice put off the entry into effect of Decision 97/534/EC on the prohibition of the use of material presenting risks as regards transmissible
spongiform encephalopathies (¹⁰); on 31 March, the entry into effect of
this decision was postponed until 1 January 1999 (¹¹) and then on 17

(¹)   1996 General Report, points 501 to 506; 1997 General Report, points 606 to 609.
(²)   Decision 98/653/EC (OJ L 311, 20.11.1998; Bull. 11-1998, point 1.2.134).
(³)   Decision 98/272/EC (OJ L 122, 24.2.1998; Bull. 4-1998, point 1.2.120).
(⁴)   Recommendation 98/477/EC (OJ L 212, 30.7.1998; Bull. 7/8-1998, point 1.3.206).
(⁵)   Bull. 3-1998, point 1.2.162.
(⁶)   COM(1998) 207; Bull. 4-1998, point 1.2.122.
(⁷)   OJ L 355, 5.12.1992; Twenty-sixth General Report, point 96.
(⁸)   Directive 98/88/EC (OJ L 318, 27.11.1998).
(⁹)   Decision 98/692/EC (OJ L 328, 4.12.1998; Bull. 11-1998, point 1.2.133).
(¹⁰) OJ L 216, 8.8.1997; 1997 General Report, point 607.
(¹¹) Decision 98/248/EC (OJ L 102, 2.4.1998; Bull. 3-1998, point 1.2.161).

December it was postponed until 31 January 1999 (^{1}). The Council further decided on 16 March to lift the ban on the dispatch to other Member States and third countries of exports of meat derived from bovine animals born and reared in Northern Ireland, originating in herds certified BSE-free, and slaughtered in Northern Ireland in slaughterhouses exclusively used for that purpose (^{2}). More information on combating TSEs appears in Sections 23 ('Public health') *(→ point 628)* and 24 'Consumer policy and health protection') *(→ points 639 and 640)* of this chapter.

564.   The Council took other important decisions on health controls. In particular it laid down, on 16 March, the methods to be used for microbiological testing for salmonella (^{3}), reinforced, on 24 June, the provisions contained in Directive 91/67/EEC to prevent the spread of diseases of animals used in aquaculture (Table II); on the same day it updated Directive 64/432/EEC on animal health problems affecting intra-Community trade in bovine animals and swine (Table II); it decided on 19 October to extend until 31 December 2000 the transitional period for the simplified approval under Decision 95/408/EC of third-country establishments permitted to export to the Community (^{4}); and on 14 December it adjusted the deadlines for transposing Directive 97/12/EC as regards combating bovine tuberculosis, bovine brucellosis and enzootic bovine leucosis (Table II). The Commission proposed, on 18 February, the implementation of the system of computerised databases provided for in Directive 64/432/EEC (Table I). In a resolution adopted on 15 May (^{5}), the European Parliament called for routine checks by the Commission on the eradication programmes part-financed by the Community budget.

565.   In the field of protecting animal welfare, the Council on 16 February, adopted Regulation (EC) No 411/98 on additional animal protection standards applicable to road vehicles used for the carriage of livestock on journeys exceeding eight hours (^{6}) and, on 20 July, Directive 98/58/EC (Table II), the purpose of which is to implement the European Convention for the Protection of Animals Kept for Farming Purposes by laying down harmonised rules for the treatment and housing of livestock

---

(^{1})   Decision 98/745/EC (OJ L 358, 31.12.1998; Bull. 12-1998).
(^{2})   Decision 98/256/EC (OJ L 113, 15.4.1998; Bull. 3-1998, point 1.2.160). As a result of Commission Decision 98/351/EC (OJ L 157, 30.5.1998; Bull. 5-1998, point 1.2.166), this measure entered into force on 1 June.
(^{3})   Decision 98/227/EC (OJ L 87, 21.3.1998; Bull. 3-1998, point 1.2.164).
(^{4})   Decision 98/603/EC (OJ L 289, 28.10.1998; Bull. 10-1998, point 1.2.142).
(^{5})   OJ C 167, 1.6.1998; Bull. 5-1998, point 1.2.180.
(^{6})   OJ L 52, 21.2.1998; Bull. 1/2-1998, point 1.3.247.

and for the care given to them. On 11 March, the Commission proposed establishing minimum standards for the protection of laying hens (Table II) and, on 22 July, revising the provisions of Directive 91/628/EEC with regard to conditions for the transport of pigs (Table II).

566. The Council adopted decisions on 16 March and 14 December respectively concluding veterinary agreements with the United States (Table III) and Canada (Table III). The agreement with Canada was signed during the EU-Canada Summit on 17 December (→ *point 890*).

567. In the field of animal feed, the Commission on 13 July proposed extending Directive 96/25/EC on the circulation of feed materials to cover feed materials directly produced and used by livestock farmers (Table I). It also adopted, on 13 July, a proposal for updating Directive 70/524/EEC on additives, Directive 95/53/EC on official inspections and Directive 95/69/EC (Table II), while on 3 November it adopted a proposal to amend Directive 95/53/EC to increase the powers it contains regarding inspections, the drafting of specific control programmes and the rapid introduction of safeguard measures concerning animal feed (Table I). On 14 December the Council adopted a directive (Table II) and a decision ([1]) to rationalise the procedures for setting the fees levied by Member States under Directive 95/69/EC.

568. On 17 December, the Council banned the use of four antibiotics in animal feedingstuffs ([2]). In a resolution adopted on 15 May, the European Parliament called for stringent scientific standards to be applied when assessing the health risk posed by antibiotics used in animal feed and for any bans resulting from this to be extended, if necessary, to imports from third countries ([3]).

569. In the plant health field, the Council on 20 July adopted the measures to be taken by the Member States to combat *Ralstonia solanacearum (Smith) Yabuuchi et al.*, the pathogen responsible for bacterial wilt in potatoes and tomatoes (Table II). It also adopted, on the same day, Directive 98/56/EC on the marketing of propagating material of ornamental plants, which is a recasting of Directive 91/682/EC proposed as part of the SLIM initiative to simplify internal market legislation (Table II) ([4]).

([1])   Decision 98/728/EC (OJ L 346, 22.12.1998; Bull. 12-1998).
([2])   Regulation (EC) No 2821/98 (OJ L 351, 29.12.1998; Bull. 12-1998).
([3])   OJ C 167, 1.6.1998; Bull. 5-1998, point 1.2.168.
([4])   1996 General Report, point 106.

Agricultural prices

570. On 26 June, the Council adopted Regulations (EC) Nos 1360/98 to 1365/98 and, on 20 July, Regulations (EC) Nos 1623/98 to 1639/98 fixing agricultural prices for the 1998/99 marketing year (Table II). These regulations are essentially a roll-over of the provisions in force for the previous marketing year, the main adjustments being the reduction of 7.5 % in the area aid for hemp and the extension to 2000 of the ban on new plantings in the wine sector, except for special authorisations limited to 10 000 ha in total. Special exemptions are laid down for the new German *Länder* in respect of arable crops and beef and veal. The Council's political agreement on the 'prices package', reached on 26 June, also included decisions on the rate of set-aside for the 1999/2000 marketing year *(→ point 571),* on protection of livestock on the farm *(→ point 565),* on the aid scheme for hemp *(→ point 578)* and on the review of the common market organisations for olive oil, bananas and tobacco *(→ points 551, 576 and 577).*

Common market organisations

Crop products

571. On 20 July, as part of the 'prices package', the Council fixed the compulsory set-aside rate at 10 % for the 1999/2000 marketing year. It also authorised the Commission, on 16 February, to negotiate a new international cereals agreement (Table III) to supersede the 1995 agreement [1]. The Court of Auditors' special report No 5/97 on restrictions on cereal exports [2] was the subject, in February, of Council conclusions [3] and a European Parliament resolution [4].

572. On 20 January, the Council adopted Regulation (EC) No 192/98 establishing a stabiliser mechanism for rice seed production (Table II). It also authorised Greece, on 24 September, to divide its national base area into two parts, rice-growing being maintained in the part where the soil is not suitable for other crops (Table II). On 16 June, the Council allocated the potato starch quota for the marketing years 1998/99, 1999/2000 and 2000/01 among the Member States (Table II).

---

[1] 1995 General Report, point 535.
[2] OJ C 159, 26.5.1997; 1997 General Report, point 1154.
[3] Bulletin. 1/2-1998, point 1.3.268.
[4] OJ C 80, 16.3.1998; Bull. 1/2-1998, point 1.3.267.

573. On 20 July, as part of the 'prices package', the Council adopted two regulations amending the common organisation of the market in oils and fats and the general rules on granting olive-oil production aid (→ *point 551*). The Commission, on 6 November, proposed a continuation of the Community contribution to funding olive-oil inspection agencies for a further three years (Table II).

574. On 20 February, the Commission proposed that Member States be allowed to make compulsory, on certain conditions, the bottling of certain quality wines produced in specified regions within their production region (Table II). On 20 January, the Council increased the number of hectares allotted to Germany under the scheme for the permanent abandonment of land under vines from 50 to 950 (Table II), while on 17 December it extended the exemptions enjoyed by the United States as regards wine imports until 2003 ([1]).

575. In the fruit and vegetables sector, the Commission continued in 1998 with its introduction of detailed rules for implementing the reform of the two common market organisations which was adopted by the Council in 1996 ([2]), especially with regard to aid for producer groups (Table II).

576. On 20 July, as part of the 'prices package', the Council amended the regulation on the common organisation of the market in bananas (Table II), so as to make it compatible with the conclusions of the World Trade Organisation panel ([3]). The main amendments involve simplification of the import-licence arrangements (licences are to be issued in future on the basis of an importer's actual imports over a reference period), increasing the size of the import quota and amending the conditions for allocating the quota among supplier countries. On 17 January, the Commission proposed a special scheme of assistance for traditional ACP banana suppliers to accompany these amendments (Table II). The Council adopted a common position on this proposal on 5 October.

577. A radical reform of the common organisation of the market in tobacco was adopted by the Council on 20 July as part of the 'prices package' (Table II). It is aimed in particular at stimulating improvements in the quality of Community production by a system of variable premiums, making the quota system more flexible, encouraging the cessation

---

[1] Regulations (EC) Nos 2838/98 and 2839/98 (OJ L 354, 30.12.1998; Bull. 12-1998).
[2] 1996 General Report, point 515.
[3] 1997 General Report, point 622.

of producers wishing to leave the sector, and taking into account public health requirements, including a doubling of the sums withheld to finance the Community fund for tobacco research and information. In this context, the Commission tabled a proposal on 6 November to set premiums and guarantee thresholds for leaf tobacco from the 1999, 2000 and 2001 harvests (Table II).

578. In view of the surpluses on the hops market, the Council adopted a regulation on 25 May introducing measures to adjust the market for a five-year period (aid for temporary resting and permanent grubbing-up) ([1]). In order to increase control of hemp production and its outlets, on 26 June it made the conclusion of contracts obligatory between producers and first processors, as well as the approval of the latter by the competent authorities of the Member States ([2]). In the seeds sector, the Council adopted two directives on 14 December to eliminate barriers to free movement by extending the scope of the existing directives (Table II) and to simplify the system of certification and inspection (Table II).

Livestock products

579. On 9 March, the Council decided to extend for a further two years the special arrangements applicable to the new German *Länder* (Table II) and, on 22 October, agreed to offer compensation to some milk producers that had suffered temporary restrictions on their farming activity (so-called SLOM III producers) (Table II).

580. In order to restore consumer confidence in beef and veal, the market for which is still depressed by the negative image created by bovine spongiform encephalopathy, the Council adopted a regulation on 28 September providing for Community financing of publicity campaigns about the new labelling scheme for beef and veal (Table II).

581. In the sheepmeat and goatmeat sector, the Commission on 10 March adopted a proposal for the consolidation of the common market organisation (Table II), and on 20 January, the Council increased the premium paid in less-favoured areas for dairy ewes and she-goats (Table II). The Commission also presented a report on 27 July on the situation in the pigmeat sector ([3]), which was also the subject of a Parliament

---

[1] Regulation (EC) No 1098/98 (OJ L 157, 30.5.1998; Bull. 5-1998, point 1.2.173).
[2] Regulation (EC) No 1420/98 (OJ L 190, 4.7.1998; Bull. 6-1998, point 1.3.171).
[3] COM(1998) 434; Bull. 7/8-1998, point 1.3.232.

resolution on 9 October (¹). On 25 May the Council amended various marketing standards applicable to poultrymeat (²).

582. On 28 September the Council amended Regulation (EC) No 1221/97 on measures to improve the production and marketing of honey (Table II), with the aim of deferring the time limit for payments effected under the initial national programmes approved in March by the Commission.

Other work

Agrimonetary measures

583. The Council adopted two regulations on 15 December (Table II). On 10 June, the Commission also adopted two proposals for regulations establishing a new agrimonetary system from 1 January 1999 which will be compatible with the introduction of the single currency and at the same time be simpler and reflect market movements more closely. In particular, special green rates are abolished; this also affects the four Member States not joining the euro area. Prior to this, the Commission authorised the United Kingdom on 3 July (³) to pay agrimonetary compensation aid as a reaction to a significant drop in the agricultural conversion rate of the pound sterling on 3 May.

Food aid for the needy in the Community

584. In 1998 the Union granted ECU 196 million under its food aid programme for the needy in the form of food products drawn from intervention stocks. Germany, the Netherlands, Austria and Sweden having withdrawn from the programme, this aid was distributed among the other 11 Member States.

Food aid for non-Community countries

585. On 17 December, the Council adopted a regulation (Table II) providing for free supplies of agricultural products to be sent to Russia, to be paid from the EAGGF Guarantee Section.

(¹) OJ C 328, 26.10.1998; Bull. 10-1998, point 1.2.149.
(²) Regulation (EC) No 1101/98 (OJ L 157, 30.5.1998; Bull. 5-1998, point 1.2.178).
(³) Regulation (EC) No 1426/98 (OJ L 190, 4.7.1998).

State aid

586. State aids are discussed in Section 5 ('Competition policy') of this chapter (→ *points 222 et seq.*).

Farm accountancy data network (FADN)

587. In 1998 the FADN published microeconomic figures for the 15 Member States, in particular on farm incomes and production costs. Some of the results are linked to simulations of the impact of the Agenda 2000 proposals. The Commission also paid close attention to improving the management and modernisation of the network (creation of a new system for consulting data, feasibility study on a new farm return).

Advisory committees and relations with farming organisations

588. At 63 meetings of advisory committees and working parties which were organised in 1998, the Commission informed the representatives of producers, processors, traders, consumers and workers about the application, development and future of the common agricultural policy.

Agricultural management and regulatory committees

589. The activities of the agricultural management and regulatory committees are set out in Table 15.

TABLE 15

Activities of the agricultural management and regulatory committees

Committee	From 1 January to 31 December 1998			
	Meetings (1)	Favourable opinion	No opinion	Unfavourable opinion
Management Committee for Cereals	48	994	59	—
Management Committee for Pigmeat	19	51	1	—
Management Committee for Poultrymeat and Eggs	11	80	—	—
Management Committee for Fruit and Vegetables	17	41	3	—
Management Committee for Wine	15	38	—	—
Management Committee for Milk and Milk Products	22	117	11	—
Management Committee for Beef and Veal	21	144	2	—
Management Committee for Sheep and Goats	9	16	—	—
Management Committee for Oils and Fats	23	50	17	—
Management Committee for Sugar	49	163	7	—
Management Committee for Live Plants and Floricultural Products	1	1	—	—
Management Committee for Products Processed from Fruit and Vegetables	14	27	3	—
Management Committee for Tobacco	8	5	—	—
Management Committee for Hops	6	6	—	—
Management Committee for Flax and Hemp	9	11	1	—
Management Committee for Seeds	6	3	1	—
Management Committee for Dried Fodder	1	1	—	—
Implementation Committee for Spirit Drinks	4	1	—	—
Implementation Committee for Aromatised Wine-based Drinks	1	—	—	—
Management Committee for Bananas	15	4	10	—
Joint Meetings of Management Committees (1)	33	39	—	—
EAGGF Committee	15	17	2	—
Standing Committee on Feedingstuffs	31	16	1	—
Standing Veterinary Committee	27	137	3	2
Standing Committee on Seeds and Propagating Material for Agriculture, Horticulture and Forestry	8	17	—	—
Committee on Agricultural Structures and Rural Development	11	141	—	—
Community Committee on the Farm Accountancy Data Network	3	1	—	—
Standing Committee on Agricultural Research	3	—	—	—

TABLE 15 (continued)

Committee	From 1 January to 31 December 1998			
	Meetings (1)	Favourable opinion	No opinion	Unfavourable opinion
Standing Committee on Plant Health	30	29	—	—
Standing Committee on Zootechnics	—	—	—	—
Standing Forestry Committee	7	8	—	—
Standing Committee on Organic Farming	5	4	—	—
Standing Committee on Propagating Material and Ornamental Plants	1	1	—	—
Standing Committee on Propagating Material and Plants of Fruit Genera and Species	1	2	—	—
Committee on Geographical Indications and Designations of Origin (2)	9	6	—	—
Committee on Certificates of Specific Character (2)	3	1	—	—
Committee on the Conservation, Characterisation, Collection and Utilisation of Genetic Resources in Agriculture	3	1	—	—
Standing Committee on Plant Variety Rights	3	1	—	—

(1) Including those relating to trade mechanisms (11 meetings), competition conditions in agriculture (0 meetings) and agrimonetary matters (6 meetings).
(2) For agricultural and food products.

Financing the common agricultural policy: the EAGGF

590.   The 1998 budget (1) allocated total appropriations of ECU 40.437 billion to the EAGGF Guarantee Section (excluding the monetary reserve of ECU 500 million, but including the appropriations allocated in reserve to Chapter B0-40), broken down as follows (in million ecus):

• crop products	26 503
• livestock products	10 742
• other measures	909
• income aids	3
• accompanying measures	2 280
Total: Guarantee Section	40 437

(1)   OJ L 44, 16.2.1998; 1997 General Report, points 640, 1062 and 1063.

591.   When the 1999 budget was adopted on 17 December *(→ points 985 to 992),* the appropriations allocated to the EAGGF Guarantee Section were fixed at EUR 40 440 million. Table 16 shows, by budget chapter, the pattern of expenditure from 1995 to 1997 and the appropriations allocated in the 1998 and 1999 budgets.

TABLE 16

EAGGF Guarantee Section expenditure, by sector ([1])

(million ECU)

Sector or type of measure	1995 expenditure	1996 expenditure	1997 expenditure	1998 ([2]) appropriations	1999 ([3]) appropriations
Arable crops ([4])	15 018.3	16 372.2	17 414.1	17 255.0	17 831.0
Sugar	1 831.0	1 711.3	1 607.9	1 674.0	1 937.0
Olive oil	807.1	1 988.1	2 196.0	2 256.0	2 251.0
Dried fodder and dry vegetables	342.0	365.2	367.4	374.0	388.0
Fibre plants	887.7	851.7	906.9	870.0	968.0
Fruit and vegetables	1 826.2	1 581.1	1 555.3	1 921.0	1 661.0
Wine	850.1	776.9	1 030.1	806.0	661.0
Tobacco	993.0	1 025.6	998.0	995.0	980.0
Other sectors	276.9	204.5	187.4	253.0	305.0
Milk and milk products	3 891.0	3 441.2	2 984.9	2 976.0	2 581.0
Beef and veal	4 090.8	6 797.0	6 580.5	5 786.0	4 916.0
Sheepmeat	2 203.9	1 681.1	1 425.0	1 413.0	1 755.0
Pigmeat, eggs and poultrymeat	343.8	262.9	557.5	415.0	365.0
Other livestock products	0.9	0.9	5.6	15.0	29.0
Fisheries	28.2	25.3	21.8	27.5	20.0
Non-Annex II products	574.3	491.1	565.9	545.0	550.0
Food programmes	371.0	265.4	328.7	429.0	348.0
Measures in favour of most remote regions and Agean Islands	241.9	213.7	187.5	208.5	231.0
Fraud control	62.9	28.9	42.8	45.0	28.0
Clearance of accounts	− 1 146.7	− 1 122.7	− 867.6	− 710.0	− 510.0
Promotion measures	48.1	49.1	54.2	95.0	77.0
Other measures ([5])	128.2	244.9	208.7	508.0	266.0
Accompanying measures	832.1	1 852.3	2 064.8	2 280.0	2 597.0
Monetary reserve	—	—	—	—	205.0
Total	34 502.8	39.107.6	40 423.4	40 437.0	40 440.0
Guideline	37 944.0	40 828.0	41 805.0	43 263.0	45 188
Margin	3 441.2	1 720.4	1 381.6	2 826.0	4 748

([1]) In accordance with the 1999 budget nomenclature.
([2]) Initial commitment appropriations entered in the 1998 budget.
([3]) Commitment appropriations entered in the 1999 budget.
([4]) Cereals, oilseeds, protein crops and set-aside.
([5]) From the 1996 budget, the chapter mainly covers agrimonetary aid.

592. The Commission cleared the Member States' accounts for EAGGF Guarantee Section expenditure on 29 April ([1]) in respect of 1997 and on

([1]) Decision 98/324/EC (OJ L 141, 13.5.1998); Bull. 4-1998, point 1.2.133.

6 May (^{1}) in respect of 1994. On 5 October it adopted the twenty-seventh financial report on the EAGGF Guarantee Section (covering 1997) (^{2}). The twenty-sixth report was the subject of a Parliament resolution on 23 October (^{3}).

593.   The EAGGF Guidance Section is dealt with in Section 11 ('Economic and social cohesion') of this chapter *(→ points 347 et seq.).*

(^{1})   Decision 98/358/EC (OJ L 163, 6.6.1998); Bull. 5-1998, point 1.2.179.
(^{2})   COM(1998) 552; Bull. 10-1998, point 1.2.153.
(^{3})   OJ C 341, 9.11.1998; Bull. 10-1998, point 1.2.152.

Section 21

Fisheries policy

Priority activities and objectives

594.   One of the main events in the fisheries sector in 1998 was the adoption of a regulation banning the use of driftnets from 1 January 2002 by all vessels in Community waters, other than the waters of the Baltic, the Belts and the Sound, and, in other waters, by all Community fishing vessels. The implementation of this regulation will be accompanied by social measures and compensation for the fishermen concerned.

Fisheries policy

595.   In a resolution([1]) on the Commission's annual report on the results of the multiannual guidance programmes for fishing fleets at the end of 1996, Parliament called on the Member States which had not yet achieved the targets set in their programmes to adopt the measures that would allow them to do so as a matter of urgency.

596.   In a communication adopted on 18 March([2]), the Commission examined the difficulties associated with single-species fisheries and suggested that the regional meetings arranged in relation to the types of fisheries and involving the participation of fishermen, administrators and scientists and held in 1997 should continue in 1998. On 24 March, the Council welcomed this initiative([3]) and underlined the need to involve fishermen and other interested parties in a dialogue which takes into account their distinctive regional features. On 17 July, it also adopted Regulation (EC) No 1587/98 (Table II) prolonging the existing arrangements([4]) compensating for the additional costs of marketing certain fishery products from the Azores, Madeira, the Canary Islands and the French department of Guiana incurred as a result of their very remote location and extending them to new products and to the French department of Réunion. On 25 February, the Economic and Social Committee said it was in favour of all existing derogations under Community leg-

---

([1])   OJ C 104, 6.4.1998; Bull. 3-1998, point 1.2.191.
([2])   COM(1998) 145; Bull. 3-1998, point 1.2.186.
([3])   Bull. 3-1998, point 1.2.186.
([4])   Council Regulation (EC) No 2337/95 (OJ L 236, 5.10.1995; 1995 General Report, point 333).

islation for the Mediterranean being removed where not scientifically justified (¹).

597.   On 19 February (²), the Commission adopted a communication on progress made in fisheries monitoring under the common fisheries policy, underlining the need to adopt an overall approach to monitoring and to improved coordination of all the services involved in the monitoring of fishing. On 5 June, it adopted a working document on 'Improving the implementation of the common fisheries policy — An action plan' (³), following on from the communication and specifying the steps to be taken in this context. On 14 May, it adopted a proposal for amending the Community inspection arrangements (Table II), which seeks to promote transparency and cooperation between Member States and the Commission and reinforce checks on third-country vessels fishing in Community waters. This regulation was adopted by the Council on 17 December. Parliament, in a resolution adopted on 18 September (⁴), said it was in favour of stepping up controls, especially on third-country vessels, and welcomed the Commission's initiatives. In a resolution (⁵) adopted on 13 March, on the Commission's report on monitoring the common fisheries policy in 1995 (⁶), Parliament had asked the Commission to examine the Member States' legislative systems, in particular in relation to penalties.

598.   On 4 June (⁷), the Council adopted Regulation (EC) No 1181/98 (Table II) amending the Community system for fisheries and aquaculture (⁸) with a view to laying down the criteria for allocating catches in Community waters to third-country vessels authorised to fish there, determining the competence of the Council to specify the fishing opportunities to be allocated to those countries and setting out the specific technical conditions on which the catches of those countries are to be taken.

599.   Parliament, in a resolution of 19 June (⁹), underlined the need for industrial fisheries to be restrained, particularly by monitoring their impact on all marine species.

(¹)   OJ C 129, 27.4.1998; Bull. 1/2-1998, point 1.3.270.
(²)   COM(1998) 92; Bull. 1/2-1998, point 1.3.269.
(³)   Bull. 6-1998, point 1.3.174.
(⁴)   OJ C 313, 12.10.1998; Bull. 9-1998, point 1.2.157.
(⁵)   OJ C 104, 6.4.1998; Bull. 3-1998, point 1.2.188.
(⁶)   COM(97) 226; 1997 General Report, point 650.
(⁷)   OJ L 164, 9.6.1998.
(⁸)   OJ L 389, 31.12.1992; Twenty-sixth General Report, point 559.
(⁹)   OJ C 210, 6.7.1998; Bull. 6-1998, point 1.3.178.

Conservation and management of resources

Internal aspects

600. On 18 December the Council adopted Regulation (EC) No 48/1999 (¹) fixing total allowable catches (TACs) and quotas for 1999. Regulation (EC) No 45/98 (²) fixing TACs and quotas for 1998 was amended three times: on 7 April by Regulation (EC) No 783/98 (³) (TACs for various species of fish in the North Sea), on 3 November by Regulation (EC) No 2386/98 (⁴) (TAC for cod) and on 14 December by Regulation (EC) No 2801/98 (⁵) (TAC for cod, Norway lobster and sprats).

601. In the area of technical measures, on 30 March (Table II) the Council adopted Regulation (EC) No 850/98, replacing Regulation (EC) No 894/97 (⁶) from 1 January 2000 on improving the selectivity of measures for taking juveniles. In October and December the Commission proposed two amendments to this regulation (Table II). On 8 June the Council adopted Regulation (EC) No 1239/98 (Table II) prohibiting the use of driftnets by all vessels in Community waters, other than the waters of the Baltic, the Belts and the Sound, and, outside those waters, by all Community fishing vessels, from 1 January 2002. Up to 31 December 2001 fishing vessels will be authorised to keep on board or use nets of up to 2.5 kilometres in length. The maximum number of fishing vessels which may be authorised by Member States to use drift-nets in 1998 may not exceed 60 % of the number which used this type of net in the period 1995-97. On 4 September (Table II) the Commission put forward social flanking measures and measures to compensate the fishermen concerned, to be met from the Financial Instrument for Fisheries Guidance (FIFG), which were adopted by the Council on 17 December.

602. On 7 April (Table II) the Council amended the regulation laying down technical measures for the conservation of fishery resources in the Mediterranean, in order to prohibit the use of purse seines and aircraft in support of fishing for bluefin tuna at certain times of the year, in accordance with ICCAT recommendations *(→ point 606).* On 29 June

---

(¹)   OJ L 13, 18.1.1999; Bull. 12-1998.
(²)   OJ L 12, 19.1.1998; 1997 General Report, point 648.
(³)   OJ L 113, 15.4.1998; Bull. 4-1998, point 1.2.135.
(⁴)   OJ L 297, 6.11.1998; Bull. 11-1998, point 1.2.142.
(⁵)   OJ L 349, 24.12.1998; Bull. 12-1998.
(⁶)   OJ L 132, 23.5.1997; 1997 General Report, point 649.

the Council also adopted a regulation (Table II) specifying conditions under which herring may be landed for industrial uses other than direct human consumption, and on 13 July a regulation (Table II) laying down certain technical measures for the conservation of fishery resources in the waters of the Baltic Sea, the Belts and the Sound, in order to give effect to the most recent recommendations of the International Baltic Sea Fishery Commission.

603. The Commission continued to monitor compliance with TACs and quotas and technical measures in Community waters and certain international waters. As a result of these controls, 40 fisheries were closed in 1998. The Commission also monitored compliance with conservation measures, agreements with third countries and international agreements, and continued monitoring fisheries in the North-West Atlantic Fisheries Organisation (NAFO) regulatory area (→ point 606).

604. The Commission was notified by the Member States of 75 national conservation measures, of which 47 were the subject of comments and 28 were still under review on 31 December 1998.

External aspects

605. On 8 June the Council adopted a decision (Table III) on the ratification by the European Community of the agreement on the application of the provisions of the United Nations Convention on the Law of the Sea as regards the conservation and management of straddling stocks and highly migratory species. The agreement promotes the conservation and sustainable exploitation of these stocks and species by strengthening the international fisheries organisations and international cooperation mechanisms ([1]).

606. The Community participated in the work of several international fisheries organisations, including the Convention on Future Multilateral Cooperation in the North-East Atlantic Fisheries, the North Atlantic Salmon Conservation Organisation, the North-West Atlantic Fisheries Organisation ([2]), the International Commission for the Conservation of Atlantic Tunas (ICCAT), the Indian Ocean Tuna Commission, the Inter-American Tropical Tuna Commission, the North-East Atlantic Fisheries Commission (NEAFC), the Commission for the Conservation of Antarc-

---

([1])   1995 General Report, point 577.
([2])   Bull. 9-1998, point 1.2.163.

tic Marine Living Resources (CCAMLR) and the General Fisheries Council for the Mediterranean (GFCM). On 16 June the Council decided that the Community would accede to the GFCM as a member (Table III), and authorised the Commission to negotiate on 20 January and 30 April respectively an international agreement on the conservation of marine living resources in certain waters in the south-west Atlantic and an agreement setting up a regional fisheries organisation in the waters of the south-west Atlantic.

607.   At the same time, on 30 March the Council adopted Regulation (EC) No 731/98 (Table II) extending to 31 December 1998 a pilot project [1] on satellite tracking in the NAFO regulatory area; on 16 June, Regulation (EC) No 1283/98 [2] introducing TACs for swordfish in the south Atlantic in accordance with ICCAT recommendations; on 29 June, Regulation (EC) No 1435/98 [3] prohibiting, at the request also of ICCAT, imports of Atlantic bluefin tuna from Belize, Honduras and Panama; on 12 November, Regulation (EC) No 2479/98 [4] putting into effect various conservation measures under the CCAMLR; on 18 December, Regulation (EC) No 49/1999 [5] fixing TACs and quotas for bluefin tuna and swordfish for 1999 and Regulations (EC) Nos 66/1999 [5] and (EC) No 67/1999 [5] laying down for 1999 conservation and management measures in the NAFO and NEAFC regulatory areas respectively. The Commission adopted proposals for regulations on the inspection of vessels flying the flag of non-contracting parties to the Convention for the Conservation of Antarctic Marine Living Resources in the area covered by the convention (Table II), the implementation of two ICCAT recommendations on a system for the statistical monitoring of trade in bluefin tuna (Table II) and the laying down of certain control measures to ensure compliance with the measures adopted by ICCAT (Table II).

608.   On 3 December (Table III) a fisheries agreement was signed with Gabon. The Council also adopted decisions and regulations renewing the protocols to the fisheries agreements with Cape Verde (Table III), the Comoros (Table III), Côte d'Ivoire (Table III), Guinea (Table III), Madagascar [6] (Table III), and Senegal (Table III), and the regulation concluding the protocol laying down the conditions for the setting up of joint enterprises as provided for in the agreement with Latvia (Table III). In

---

[1]   1995 General Report, point 579.
[2]   OJ L 178, 23.6.1998; Bull. 6-1998, point 1.3.190.
[3]   OJ L 191, 7.7.1998; Bull. 6-1998, point 1.3.191.
[4]   OJ L 209, 19.11.1998; Bull. 11-1998, point 1.2.153.
[5]   OJ L 13, 18.1.1999; Bull. 12-1998.
[6]   The Malagasy Fisheries Minister, Mr Houssene, was received at the Commission by Mrs Bonino (Bull. 6-1998, point 1.3.184).

addition the Council authorised Spain and Portugal to prolong their fisheries agreements with South Africa up to March 1999 (¹).

609.   On 18 December the Council adopted the regulations dividing up the catch quotas for 1999 for Community vessels fishing in the waters of Estonia, the Faeroes, Latvia, Lithuania, Norway, Poland and Russia, and compensating measures applying to the vessels of those countries fishing in Community waters (²). It also shared out catch quotas for Community vessels in the fishing areas of Greenland and Iceland (³). Earlier in the year it had amended the corresponding regulations for 1998, on 8 June for Lithuania (⁴) and on 16 November for Greenland (⁵).

Market organisation

610.   On 17 December the Council fixed the guide prices for fishery products for the 1999 fishing year (⁶).

611.   As a follow-up to the Commission communication on the future for the market in fishery products in the European Union (⁷), Parliament called, in a resolution of 19 June (⁸), for the market organisation to cover an information system for improved market monitoring, health control and certification of product quality, promotion of products, support measures for Community products and assistance for producer organisations. On 27 May (⁹) the Economic and Social Committee suggested expanding the market organisation by including measures to step up controls, promote fishery products to consumers and smooth the flow of supplies to the processing industry.

612.   Parliament called on the Council and the Commission, in a resolution of 19 June (¹⁰), to prepare a special plan of action to support the canning industry for fish and aquaculture products, particularly for sar-

---

(¹)   Decisions 98/557/EC and 98/558/EC (OJ L 267, 2.10.1998; Bull. 9-1998, point 1.2.159).
(²)   Regulations (EC) Nos 50/1999 to 53/1999 and 56/1999 to 65/1999 (OJ L 13, 18.1.1999; Bull. 12-1998).
(³)   Regulations (EC) Nos 54/1999 and 55/1999 (OJ L 13, 18.1.1999; Bull. 12-1998).
(⁴)   OJ L 168, 13.6.1998; Bull. 6-1998, point 1.3.182.
(⁵)   Regulation (EC) No 2480/98 (OJ L 309, 19.11.1998; Bull. 11-1998, point 1.2.146).
(⁶)   Regulations (EC) Nos 2763/98 to 2765/98 (OJ L 346, 22.12.1998; Bull. 12-1998).
(⁷)   COM(97) 719; 1997 General Report, point 657.
(⁸)   OJ C 210, 6.7.1998; Bull. 6-1998, point 1.3.176.
(⁹)   OJ C 235, 27.7.1998; Bull. 5-1998, point 1.2.182.
(¹⁰) OJ C 210, 6.7.1998; Bull. 6-1998, point 1.3.175.

dine and tuna, step up inspection of products from third countries, promote quality products and provide support for new production systems.

Fisheries and the environment

613. On 9 May the Commission and on 8 June the Council adopted respectively a report (¹) and conclusions (²) on the implementation of the conclusions from the ministerial meeting in Bergen on the integration of fisheries and environmental issues (³).

Structural action

614. Structural action is covered in Section 11 ('Economic and social cohesion') of this chapter *(→ points 347 et seq.).*

State aid schemes

615. State aid schemes are covered in Section 5 ('Competition policy') of this chapter *(→ points 222 et seq.).*

(¹)   COM(1998) 326; Bull. 5-1998, point 1.2.187.
(²)   Bull. 6-1998, point 1.3.193.
(³)   1997 General Report, point 660.

Section 22

Equal opportunities

616. In 1998, the Commission pressed on with projects geared to the exchange of information and good practice co-financed under the medium-term Community action programme on equal opportunities for women and men (1996-2000) ([1]). It also adopted, on 17 December ([2]), an interim report on the implementation of this programme, and organised, in Brussels in September, a congress on the theme 'Equality is the future', bringing together more than 500 participants, including Mr Gutiérrez Díaz, Vice-President of the European Parliament, and Mr Santer, President of the Commission, thus providing an opportunity to take stock of the programme for the first time and to identify future courses of action. Moreover, on 13 May, the Commission presented its second annual report on equal opportunities for women and men in the European Union (1997) ([3]).

617. The Commission adopted, on 4 March, a progress report ([4]) on the follow-up to its communication ([5]) entitled 'Incorporating equal opportunities for women and men into all Community policies and activities', pointing to the progress made in certain Community policy areas, with particular emphasis on external relations, education and training, employment and cohesion. The equal opportunities dimension was further cemented within the employment guidelines for 1999 (→ *point 111).*

618. On 13 July, the Council extended to the United Kingdom the directive on the burden of proof in cases of discrimination based on sex (→ *point 137).* The Commission meanwhile recommended, on 27 May, that the Member States ratify the International Labour Organisation's Convention No 177 on home work ([6]). It also adopted, on 4 February, a report ([7]) on the implementation of the Council recommendation on childcare ([8]), and published two studies on the problem of sexual harassment at the workplace in the Member States. The European Parlia-

---

([1]) OJ L 335, 30.12.1995; 1995 General Report, point 628.
([2]) COM(1998) 770; Bull. 12-1998.
([3]) COM(1998) 302; Bull. 5-1998, point 1.2.188.
([4]) COM(1998) 122; Bull. 3-1998, point 1.2.200.
([5]) COM(96) 67; 1996 General Report, point 589.
([6]) Recommendation 98/370/EC (OJ L 165, 10.6.1998; Bull. 5-1998, point 1.2.25).
([7]) COM(1998) 237.
([8]) Recommendation 92/241/EEC (OJ L 123, 8.5.1992; Twenty-sixth General Report, point 391).

ment, for its part, adopted, on 17 September, three resolutions (¹) aimed at promoting equality between women and men, focusing respectively on the particular impact of unemployment on women, the role of cooperatives in the growth of women's employment, and the situation of single mothers and single-parent families.

(¹) OJ C 313, 12.10.1998; Bull. 9-1998, points 1.2.165, 1.2.61 and 1.2.164.

Section 23

Public health

Priority activities and objectives

619. Significant progress was made in the public health field in 1998, with the setting up of a network for the surveillance and control of communicable diseases in the Community and the adoption, by Parliament and the Council, of a directive providing for a ban on all forms of advertising or sponsorship of tobacco products. Furthermore, with an eye to the entry into force of the Amsterdam Treaty, the Commission set out guidelines for future action in this field.

General

620. On 15 April, the Commission adopted a communication on the development of public health policy within the European Union [1], outlining future strategies which could be implemented in line with the Amsterdam Treaty, focusing on three strands of action: improving information for the benefit of public health; reacting swiftly to threats to health; and tackling health determinants through health promotion and disease prevention. This communication was welcomed by the Economic and Social Committee on 9 September [2], and by the Committee of the Regions on 19 November [3]. In conclusions adopted on 26 November [4], the Council proposed that future Community activities in the public health field should be set out in one overall programme. The Commission meanwhile presented, on 27 January, its third report on the integration of health protection requirements in Community policies [5], and the Council's conclusions on this subject were adopted on 30 April [6].

---

[1]   COM(1998) 230; Bull. 4-1998, point 1.2.139.
[2]   OJ C 407, 28.12.1998; Bull. 9-1998, point 1.2.167.
[3]   Bull. 11-1998, point 1.2.158.
[4]   OJ C 390, 15.12.1998; Bull. 11-1998, point 1.2.157.
[5]   COM(1998) 34; Bull. 1/2-1998, point 1.3.279.
[6]   OJ C 169, 4.6.1998; Bull. 4-1998, point 1.2.140.

Health promotion

621. Within the framework of the Community action programme on health promotion, information, education and training (1996-2000) (¹), 34 projects were financed in 1998, involving a total sum of ECU 6.623 million.

Health monitoring

622. Within the framework of the Community action programme on health monitoring (1997-2001) (²), 10 projects were launched in 1998, with funding totalling ECU 2.344 million. Moreover, the Commission proposed, on 11 June, that a common framework be established for protecting the general public against the harmful effects of exposure to electromagnetic fields (Table II).

Cancer

623. Within the framework of the action plan to combat cancer (1996-2000) (³), 59 projects were financed in 1998, with funding totalling ECU 11.732 million.

Tobacco

624. Parliament and the Council adopted, on 6 July, Directive 98/43/EC (Table I), whereby, at the end of the transposal period, all forms of advertising or sponsorship of tobacco products will be prohibited. This directive represents a milestone in the anti-smoking strategy, bearing in mind that tobacco-related deaths in the European Union are close to half a million each year.

Drugs

625. Within the framework of the Community action programme on the prevention of drug dependence (1996-2000) (⁴), the Commission financed 39 projects involving a total sum of ECU 5.1 million. Support

---

(¹)   Decision No 645/96/EC (OJ L 95, 16.4.1996; 1996 General Report, point 612).
(²)   Decision No 1400/97/EC (OJ L 193, 22.7.1997; 1997 General Report, point 670).
(³)   Decision No 646/96/EC (OJ L 95, 16.4.1996; 1996 General Report, point 606).
(⁴)   OJ L 19, 22.1.1997; 1996 General Report, point 610.

was provided in particular for organising the third European drug prevention week, which took place in November, and for a European campaign to make adults more aware of the need to prevent drug dependence, using the slogan 'Talking is the first step'. In a resolution ([1]) adopted on 16 September, Parliament welcomed the evidence of progress in combating the drug problem as shown in the 1997 annual report of the European Monitoring Centre for Drugs and Drug Addiction ([2]). Parliament also adopted, on 17 December, a resolution on doping in sport ([3]), the seriousness of which was emphasised by the Vienna European Council ([3]).

AIDS and other communicable diseases

626.   Within the framework of the Community action programme on the prevention of AIDS and certain other communicable diseases (1996-2000), the Commission financed, in 1998, some 39 projects with funding totalling ECU 9.88 million.

627.   On 24 September, Parliament and the Council adopted Decision No 2119/98/EC (Table I), setting up a network for the epidemiological surveillance and control of communicable diseases in the Community. This network will provide permanent lines of communication for the Member States' epidemiological surveillance structures and health authorities, thereby ensuring continuous surveillance of various communicable diseases and establishing an early warning and response system to deal with the appearance or recurrence of these diseases.

628.   On 29 June, the Council adopted a recommendation on the suitability of blood and plasma donors and the screening of donated blood in the Community. It also adopted, on 30 April, conclusions on transmissible spongiform encephalopathies ([4]), stressing the need for epidemiological surveillance of Creutzfeldt-Jakob disease and agreeing to keep the issue under consideration. In its half-yearly reports on bovine spongiform encephalopathy (→ point 640), the Commission took stock of the situation as regards surveillance of transmissible spongiform encephalopathies, including Creutzfeldt-Jakob disease. Additionally, an Economic

---

([1])   OJ C 313, 12.10.1998; Bull. 9-1998, point 1.2.169.
([2])   1997 General Report, point 679.
([3])   Bull. 12-1998.
([4])   OJ C 169, 4.6.1998; Bull. 4-1998, point 1.2.144.

and Social Committee opinion adopted on 9 September drew attention to the public health threat arising from resistance to antibiotics ([1]).

629. On 12 November, the Council adopted conclusions ([2]) on the activities of the joint European Union-United States task force for communicable diseases ([3]).

Pollution-related diseases

630. On 30 April, the Council adopted a common position on the proposal for a programme of Community action on pollution-related diseases (1999-2003) (Table I).

Rare diseases

631. On 30 April, the Council also adopted a common position on the proposal for a programme of Community action on rare diseases (1999-2003) (Table I).

Injury prevention

632. On 24 November, the Council adopted a common position on the proposal for a programme of Community action (1999-2003) on injury prevention (Table I). This common position was approved by Parliament on 17 December.

Alzheimer's disease

633. In March, the Commission published a specific call for proposals in respect of measures to help persons suffering from Alzheimer's disease ([4]), covered by a budget of ECU 800 000.

([1])   OJ C 407, 28.12.1998; Bull. 9-1998, point 1.2.168.
([2])   OJ C 390, 15.12.1998; Bull. 11-1998, point 1.2.160.
([3])   1996 General Report, point 613.
([4])   OJ C 75, 11.3.1998.

Section 24

Consumer policy and health protection

Priority activities and objectives

634.   With the aim of enabling Europe's consumers to play an active role in the single market, the Commission adopted a new consumer policy action plan (1999-2001). While continuing also to implement its 'Priorities for consumer policy 1996-98' action plan ([1]), the Commission advocated that a legal basis be established for financing consumer-oriented activities. Parliament and the Council for their part adopted directives on product price indication, injunctions and consumer credit. In the priority area of consumer health protection, 1998 was a year of consolidation. In the wake of the Commission's radical reorganisation of its departments in 1997, progress was made in connection with food and veterinary inspection, and scientific consultation.

General

635.   On 2 December, the Commission adopted a consumer policy action plan (1999-2001) ([2]) geared to letting consumers play an active role in the single market, the three central objectives being: to give consumers a greater say in matters; to guarantee a high level of health and safety for consumers; and to respect fully the economic interests of consumers.

636.   On 28 January, the Commission adopted a proposal aimed at establishing a general framework for Community activities in favour of consumers and, in particular, providing a legal basis for the financing of these activities (Table I). Parliament and the Council reached agreement on this proposal in December. The Commission also adopted, on 27 March, a working document ([3]) analysing the situation as regards the application and implementation in the Member States of Community

---

([1])   COM(95) 519; 1995 General Report, point 644.
([2])   COM(1998) 696; Bull. 12-1998.
([3])   Bull. 3-1998, point 1.2.213.

legislation in the consumer field. In addition, the results of a survey on the Member States' consumer policies (¹) began to appear.

Consumer representation, information and education

637. In October, the Commission launched an information campaign on food safety and consumer health protection. With the backing of national consumer organisations, this campaign entails not only the dissemination to European consumers of general information on the principles and rules governing food safety but also specific action on various themes (control systems, labelling rules, monitoring of products at source, genetically modified substances, diets, health, etc.).

638. The European young consumer competition 1998-99, for young people between the ages of 10 and 14, was launched in September on the theme of 'explaining the euro'. The network of European consumer information and advice centres was extended to the United Kingdom, where an existing consumer advisory network was selected by the Commission to join the 10 centres already operational in other Member States. The first annual assembly of European consumer associations was held on 12 and 13 November on the Commission's initiative, having been preceded, on 11 November, by a seminar for consumer associations from the applicant countries.

Consumer health protection and food safety

639. Following on from the restructuring (²), in 1997, of the Commission departments responsible for consumer health protection, the eight newly established committees and the scientific steering committee adopted a number of opinions in 1998, all of which were published on the Europa server on the Internet (³). Although focusing mainly on problems connected with bovine spongiform encephalopathy (BSE), the steering committee also addressed issues of a multidisciplinary nature, such as anti-microbial resistance, genetically modified organisms and harmonisation of the risk-assessment methods of the various scientific committees. In a communication adopted on 28 January, concerning food, vet-

---

(¹)   The summary report and the reports concerning Denmark, Germany, Spain, Italy, Austria and the United Kingdom are available from the Consumer Policy and Consumer Health Protection Directorate-General or on the Internet at http://europa.eu.int/comm/dg24.
(²)   1997 General Report, point 685.
(³)   http://europa.eu.int/comm/dg24.

erinary and plant health control and inspection ([1]), the Commission confirmed the inspection and control responsibilities of the Food and Veterinary Office, under the aegis of the Consumer Policy and Consumer Health Protection Directorate-General. This approach was endorsed by the Economic and Social Committee on 27 May ([2]). In February, moreover, the Commission adopted two decisions ([3]) concerning on-the-spot checks carried out in the veterinary field by Commission experts in the Member States and in third countries, the aim being to keep Parliament and the general public informed of the findings and recommendations for action resulting from these checks.

640. In accordance with the undertaking given in its final consolidated report to the European Parliament's temporary committee of inquiry into BSE, the Commission presented, on 6 May ([4]) and on 18 November ([5]), the first two biannual BSE follow-up reports, highlighting the efforts made to combat BSE, to protect public health and to restore consumer confidence. In October, the Commission also published the third edition of the *BSE guide — Information for consumers*, which gives a full rundown on the crisis engendered by this disease. On 30 November and 1 December, Parliament and the Commission organised a conference on the subject of the European Union and food safety and the lessons of BSE.

641. In 1998, the Commission carried out a further series of visits to the 15 Member States in order to evaluate the national systems for the official control of foodstuffs in accordance with Directive 93/99/EEC ([6]). It also adopted a report ([7]) on the previous visits. There was, in 1998, an appreciable increase in the number of notifications by Member States under the system for rapid exchange of information on foodstuffs in line with Directive 92/59/EEC ([8]) on general product safety, with most of the information having to do with products of animal origin intercepted at the borders of the European Union.

642. In the light of the conclusions of the World Trade Organisation's appellate body on the banning of growth hormones in livestock rearing (→ *point 713*), the Commission financed studies designed to boost sci-

---

([1])   COM(1998) 32; Bull. 1/2-1998, point 1.3.287.
([2])   OJ C 235, 27.7.1998; Bull. 5-1998, point 1.2.197.
([3])   Decisions 98/139/EC and 98/140/EC (OJ L 38, 12.2.1998).
([4])   COM(1998) 282; Bull. 5-1998, point 1.2.196.
([5])   COM(1998) 598; Bull. 11-1998, point 1.2.162.
([6])   OJ L 290, 24.11.1993; Twenty-seventh General Report, point 76.
([7])   COM(1998) 37; Bull. 1/2-1998, point 1.3.288.
([8])   OJ L 228, 11.8.1992; Twenty-sixth General Report, point 634.

entific information on the potential cancer risks to consumers arising from hormone residues in meat. Further risk assessment carried out on the basis of this information may help to underpin relevant Community legislation. Parliament, for its part, adopted a resolution on environmental, health and consumer protection aspects of world trade (→ point 734).

Protection of consumers' economic and legal interests

643. Parliament and the Council adopted, on 16 February, Directive 98/6/EC on consumer protection in the indication of prices of products offered to consumers (Table I), whereby, throughout the European Union, the selling price and the price per unit of measurement of products offered to consumers must be indicated; Member States may allow a transitional period exempting small retailers who would be unduly burdened by the application of these provisions. Parliament and the Council also adopted, on 19 May, Directive 98/27/EC on injunctions for the protection of consumers' interests (Table I), aimed at enabling consumer representatives (associations or other qualified entities) to bring actions for injunctions under national law, thereby ensuring effective application of Community consumer legislation throughout the European Union. Furthermore, the Council adopted, on 23 September, a common position on the proposal for a directive on the sale of consumer goods and associated guarantees (Table I) and, on 3 November, a resolution on the consumer dimension of the information society ([1]).

644. As part of the action plan on consumer access to justice ([2]), the Commission adopted, on 30 March, a communication on the out-of-court settlement of consumer disputes ([3]), the purpose of which is to ensure that out-of-court procedures afford minimum guarantees in the interests of the parties involved, such as independence, transparency, effectiveness and legality; an accompanying recommendation and European consumer complaint form ([4]) are designed to improve communication between consumers and professionals with a view to settling disputes amicably. An opinion adopted by the Economic and Social Committee on 28 January ([5]) focused on the role of middlemen in the setting of food prices.

([1])   Bull. 11-1998, point 1.2.163.
([2])   COM(96) 13; 1996 General Report, point 616.
([3])   OJ L 115, 17.4.1998; COM(1998) 198; Bull. 3-1998, point 1.2.210.
([4])   Available on the Europa server (→ point 1153) on the Internet at the following address: http://europa.eu.int/comm/dg24.
([5])   OJ C 95, 30.3.1998; Bull. 1/2-1998, point 1.3.285.

Safety of products and services

645. In line with the requirements of Directive 92/59/EEC on general product safety ([1]), the Commission adopted, on 1 July, a recommendation ([2]) calling on the Member States to adopt the measures needed to protect children's health as regards exposure to certain phthalates released by childcare articles and toys made of soft PVC. On 4 September, the Commission adopted the final report evaluating the Community system of information on home and leisure accidents (EHLASS) ([3]). The Council meanwhile adopted, on 18 December, a resolution on operating instructions for technical consumer goods ([4]).

Financial services

646. Parliament and the Council adopted, on 16 February, Directive 98/7/EC (Table I), introducing a single formula for calculating the annual percentage rate of charge (APR) for consumer credit.

([1])   OJ L 228, 11.8.1992; Twenty-sixth General Report, point 634.
([2])   OJ L 217, 5.8.1998; Bull. 7/8-1998, point 1.3.241.
([3])   COM(1998) 488; Bull. 9-1998, point 1.2.171.
([4])   Bull. 12-1998.

Section 25

Culture

647. In 1998, the Commission presented a proposal for a first Community framework programme on culture.

648.   Responding to a request by the Council ([1]), on 6 May the Commission adopted a communication on a first European Community framework programme in support of culture (2000-04), including a proposal for a decision on a single financing and programming instrument for cultural cooperation ('Culture 2000' programme) (Table I) and a policy paper ([2]). The 'Culture 2000' programme aims to treat cultural activity as a European policy in its own right, by grouping all Community action in this field together. Its main objectives are to capitalise on the existence of a common cultural area, to promote cultural diversity, to foster culture's contribution to economic development and social cohesion, and to promote dialogue with other world cultures. It provides for cultural cooperation agreements between arts professionals on projects extending over several years, major projects with a high symbolic value, such as the European City of Culture, and an arts festival in the country holding the presidency, as well as specific projects with the aim of encouraging new forms of creativity and cultural exchanges in order to promote better social integration. The funding allocated by the Commission for the duration of the programme (2000-04) is ECU 167 million. The policy paper identifies various lines of action with a view to a better integration of culture into the various Community policies.

649.   In order to prepare these proposals, the Commission launched a vast consultation process in the Member States, the countries of the European Economic Area and associated countries, and among international and non-governmental organisations and arts professionals and personalities in Europe, which was concluded by the European Union Cultural Forum, held in Brussels on 29 and 30 January. The Commission also took into consideration the evaluation of the existing programmes: Ariane, Kaleidoscope and Raphael.

650.   Under the Kaleidoscope programme for artistic and cultural activities with a European dimension ([3]), 147 initiatives were selected in 1998,

---

([1])   OJ C 305, 7.10.1997; 1997 General Report, point 698.
([2])   COM(1998) 266; Bull. 5-1998, point 1.2.200.
([3])   1997 General Report, point 700.

for a total of more than ECU 8 million. All the projects chosen involve broad transnational European cooperation (involving EFTA countries too), meet the criterion of high artistic and cultural quality, strive to promote awareness and dissemination of the culture of the peoples of Europe and training for artists and other arts professionals, and seek to facilitate access to culture for all citizens. The Commission also gave its support to the European City of Culture for 1998, Stockholm, and to the European cultural months, which took place in Linz (Austria) and Valletta (Malta). The Council, for its part, adopted a common position on 24 July on the proposal for a decision establishing a Community initiative for the 'European City of Culture' event for the years 2005 to 2019 (Table I) and, on 28 May([1]), designated the European Cities of Culture for the years 2001-04.

651. Under the Ariane programme to support books and reading([2]), 292 projects were selected in 1998, for an amount of more than ECU 3.3 million. Subsidies were provided for 224 high-quality translations, 27 literary cooperation projects were supported involving more than 200 people and professional training was encouraged by means of assistance to 20 training institutions in the book and translation sectors. On 20 November, Parliament adopted a resolution on cross-border fixed book pricing systems([3]).

652. As the Kaleidoscope and Ariane programmes will come to an end on 31 December 1998, the Commission proposed on 23 September that they be extended by one year in order to ensure the continuity of the Community's cultural activity until the framework programme for 2000-04 comes into force. The Council adopted common positions on these proposals on 20 November and Parliament approved them on 17 December (Table I).

653. The 85 projects supported in 1998 under the Raphael programme of Community action in the field of cultural heritage([4]), for a total amount of ECU 10.015 million, concerned both large-scale operations such as the 'European heritage laboratories' projects for conservation and building restoration, projects on mobility and training for professionals and cooperation between museums and events intended to raise public awareness of conservation issues.

([1]) Bull. 5-1998, point 1.2.202. The designated cities are Rotterdam and Oporto for 2001, Bruges and Salamanca for 2002, Graz for 2003, and Genoa and Lille for 2004.
([2]) 1997 General Report, point 699.
([3]) OJ C 379, 7.12.1998; Bull. 11-1998, point 1.2.168.
([4]) 1997 General Report, point 701.

654. The Commission has also launched a study of the job-creation potential of the cultural sector.

655. In the field of sport, the Commission continued to consider the direction Community action should take, with regard specifically to implementing the declaration on sport annexed to the Amsterdam Treaty. It also supported 250 projects for a total of ECU 2.7 million under the 'Eurathlon' and 'Sports for persons with disability' programmes. The Cardiff European Council asked the Council and the Member States to consider what could be done through sport to combat the exclusion of young people [1]. The European Parliament adopted resolutions on the UEFA Cup (14 January) [2] and the sale of tickets for the World Cup (12 March) [3].

[1] Bull. 6-1998, point I.10.
[2] OJ C 34, 2.2.1998; Bull. 1/2-1998, point 1.3.290.
[3] OJ C 104, 6.4.1998; Bull. 3-1998, point 1.2.48.

Section 26

Audiovisual media

656.   The year 1998 saw the start of an overall review of audiovisual policy: a third European Conference on Audiovisual Media was held, and the Commission adopted a communication entitled 'Audiovisual policy: next steps'. The Council also adopted a recommendation on the protection of minors and human dignity in audiovisual and information services.

657.   In its third report([1]), issued on 3 April, on the application of Articles 4 and 5 of the 'Television without frontiers' directive([2]), which provide that television channels should, whenever practicable, reserve a majority proportion of their transmission time for European works, and 10 % of their transmission time or their programming budget to works created by independent European producers, the Commission found that, in most Member States, the majority of channels either met or exceeded these obligations in 1995 and 1996.

658.   On 24 September, the Council adopted a recommendation (Table II) on the protection of minors and human dignity in audiovisual and information services. This recommendation, which is in line with the existing national and European rules, covers all electronic media. In the field of television, it calls on operators to experiment with new, digital methods of parental control (personal codes, filtering software); in the field of on-line services, it gives guidelines for developing self-regulation at national level.

659.   The third([3]) European Conference on Audiovisual Media was held in April in Birmingham([4]) on the theme of 'Challenges and opportunities in the digital age'. It formulated a number of concrete proposals, such as the extension of the MEDIA programme, the creation of a European film and television school, the creation of a mechanism to encourage private investment in audiovisual production and the development of focus events ('the European Oscars'). The Council adopted conclusions on 24 September, welcoming the conference's success and emphasising

---

([1])   COM(1998) 199; Bull. 4-1998, point 1.2.153; previous report: COM(96) 302; 1996 General Report, point 635.
([2])   Council Directive 89/552/EEC (OJ L 298, 17.10.1989; Twenty-third General Report, point 227) last amended by Directive 97/36/EC (OJ L 202, 30.7.1997; 1997 General Report, point 705).
([3])   Previous conference: 1994 General Report, point 712.
([4])   Bull. 4-1998, point 1.2.152.

the need to follow it up, both with support mechanisms and by reviewing the regulatory framework (¹).

660.   On the basis of the results of the Birmingham Conference, the conclusions of a high-level group on audiovisual policy (which delivered its final report in October), and the results of the consultation launched by the Green Paper on the convergence of the telecommunications, media and information technology sectors *(→ point 459)*, on 14 July the Commission adopted a communication entitled 'Audiovisual policy: next steps', (²) in which it presents its initial conclusions on the overall review of audiovisual policy. It stresses the need to strengthen mechanisms providing public support for the production and distribution of European works, to attract capital to European productions from external markets, to encourage the profession to create a European awards ceremony and to create a regulatory framework favourable to launching digital television in a competitive environment.

661.   The MEDIA II programme (1996-2000) (³), designed to encourage the development of the European audiovisual industry, reached mid-term on 30 June, at which point it was subjected to a detailed evaluation. Under the section of the programme concerned with training of professionals in the audiovisual industry, 36 projects relating in particular to production management, script writing and the use of new image technologies were selected in 1998. Under the section on encouraging development and distribution of European audiovisual works, 1 103 projects were selected, including 430 which relate to the development of film projects (pre-production), 48 to strengthening or consolidating production companies, 1 to animation (industrial platform accompanied by a medium-term sectoral plan), 430 to selective support for distribution of European films (in particular, outside their national territory), 53 to video and multimedia distribution, 89 to television, 2 to networking European cinemas and 50 to market promotion. Under the system of automatic support for film distribution (⁴), 115 film distribution companies were selected for financial support proportionate with the number of tickets sold in 1997 for non-national European films which they distributed (⁵). The agreement on Cyprus' participation in the MEDIA II programme was concluded on 3 November *(→ point 832)*.

(¹)   OJ C 306, 6.10.1998; Bull. 9-1998, point 1.2.175.
(²)   COM(1998) 446; Bull. 7/8-1998, point 1.3.244.
(³)   OJ L 321, 30.12.1995, 1995 General Report, point 677; 1996 General Report, point 637.
(⁴)   1996 General Report, point 708.
(⁵)   This potential support must be reinvested in production and/or distribution of new European films before the end of 1999. In 1998, 99.5 % of the potential support generated in 1997 on the basis of the 1996 receipts was reinvested in 128 films.

662.   On 17 November the Council adopted a resolution on public service broadcasting (¹).

663.   The technological aspects of the '16/9' action plan for the introduction of advanced television services in Europe and the follow-up work on the Green Paper on the convergence of the telecommunications, media and information technology sectors are dealt with in Section 16 ('Information society, telecommunications') of this chapter *(→ points 459 to 477)*.

(¹)   Bull. 11-1998, point 1.2.169.

Chapter V

Role of the Union in the world

Section 1

Common foreign and security policy

Priority activities and objectives

664.   *The European Union continued to develop political dialogue with individual countries or groups of countries; one focus of its efforts was an expansion of its activities to defend human rights and fundamental freedoms. It also continued to promote peace by offering its services as a mediator, by helping to relaunch dialogue between the parties to a conflict and by providing humanitarian aid for civilians [1]. As part of the common foreign and security policy (CFSP), the Council accordingly adopted 20 joint actions and defined 22 common positions under Articles J.3 and J.2 of the Treaty on European Union, plus a code of conduct on arms exports. The EU also issued a large number of statements and made a number of representations to various governments and international organisations.*

General

665.   In its annual resolution on progress in implementing the CFSP [2], adopted on 28 May, Parliament expressed the view that although the CFSP had made some headway in 1997, the criticism voiced in its previous resolution remained valid [3]. It was particularly disappointed that

---

[1]   This aspect is covered more fully in Section 5 ('Humanitarian aid') of this chapter (→ *points 776 et seq.*).
[2]   OJ C 195, 22.6.1998; Bull. 5-1998, point 1.3.1.
[3]   OJ C 200, 30.6.1997; 1997 General Report, point 712.

there had been no interinstitutional agreement regarding its right to information and consultation and that the CFSP, in its current form, was restricting Europe's ability to exercise its influence to the full. It called on the Council and the Member States to exploit and develop the instruments set up by the Maastricht and Amsterdam Treaties to achieve a genuine common policy.

666.   In December the Vienna European Council expressed the opinion that the Secretary-General of the Council and High Representative for the CFSP should be appointed as soon as possible and be a personality with a strong political profile. It invited the Council to prepare common strategies on Russia, Ukraine, the Mediterranean region and the western Balkans, on the understanding that the first would be on Russia. Welcoming the new impetus given to the debate on a common European policy on security and defence, the European Council also noted that the CFSP should be backed by credible operational capabilities ([1]).

Common foreign policy

667.   As regards common positions and joint actions ([2]), the Council:

— defined eight common positions and adopted 10 joint actions on south-eastern Europe (Common Position 98/633/CFSP concerning the process of stability and good-neighbourliness in south-east Europe *(→ point 839)*, 98/196/CFSP on Bosnia and Herzegovina *(→ point 841)*, 98/240/CFSP, 98/326/CFSP, 98/374/CFSP, 98/426/CFSP and 98/725/CFSP on the Federal Republic of Yugoslavia *(→ point 843)* and 98/498/CFSP on Slovenia *(→ point 825)*; Joint Actions 98/117/CFSP, 98/302/CFSP, 98/607/CFSP and 98/737/CFSP on Bosnia and Herzegovina *(→ point 841)*, 98/301/CFSP, 98/375/CFSP, 98/646/CFSP, 98/736/CFSP and 98/741/CFSP on the Federal Republic of Yugoslavia *(→ point 843)* and 98/547/CFSP on Albania *(→ point 840)*;

— adopted Joint Action 98/608/CFSP on the Middle East peace process *(→ point 849)*;

— defined Common Position 98/448/CFSP concerning Belarus *(→ point 876)*;

---

[1]   Bull. 12-1998.
[2]   Joint actions and common positions concerning a specific geographical area are covered more fully in the section on the area in question; this section simply lists them and gives references to the appropriate sections.

— defined five common positions on Asia (98/107/CFSP, 98/303/CFSP and 98/612/CFSP on Burma (Myanmar)(→ *point 906)*, 98/606/CFSP on south Asia *(→ point 902)* and 98/108/CFSP on Afghanistan *(→ point 903)*;

— defined six common positions and adopted three joint actions on Africa (Common Positions 98/252/CFSP on Rwanda *(→ point 952)*, 98/300/CFSP and 98/409/CFSP on Sierra Leone *(→ point 954)*, 98/425/CFSP regarding Angola *(→ point 951)*, 98/614/CFSP concerning Nigeria *(→ point 953)* and 98/350/CFSP concerning human rights, democratic principles, the rule of law and good governance *(→ point 931)*; Joint Actions 98/410/CFSP on the Democratic Republic of the Congo *(→ point 952)*, 98/452/CFSP on the Great Lakes region *(→ point 952)* and 98/735/CFSP on Nigeria *(→ point 953)*).

668. The European Union made numerous representations, approaching the governments of South Korea, the Democratic Republic of the Congo, Tunisia, Cuba, Russia, Laos and the United States regarding human rights and democracy, the authorities of Niger and Afghanistan regarding humanitarian activities, the governments of countries including India and Pakistan regarding non-proliferation, the Government of Croatia regarding UN peacekeeping missions, and the authorities of Togo, Guinea and Tanzania regarding elections. The EU's external relations action included continuing political dialogue with associated countries, non-member countries and international organisations. On 29 June the Council adopted a paper setting out the preconditions for the dispatch of EU electoral observers (¹).

Common security policy

669. In a resolution adopted on 14 May (²), Parliament called for the gradual establishment of a common EU defence policy, mainly to protect the Union's interests where diplomatic instruments were no longer sufficient, and proposed practical measures for the future integration of the Western European Union into the EU. With that aim in mind, and in accordance with the Treaty of Amsterdam, the EU and the WEU stepped up their dialogue and cooperation *(→ point 703)*. The EU requested the WEU under Article J.4(2) of the Treaty on European Union to carry out a feasibility study regarding international police operations in Albania *(→ point 840)*, to implement an EU action on assistance for mine clear-

(¹) Bull. 6-1998, point 1.4.6.
(²) OJ C 167, 1.6.1998; Bull. 5-1998, point 1.3.4.

ance in Croatia (¹) and to provide it with data from the WEU Satellite Centre on the situation in Kosovo (→ point 843). On 26 October the Council also adopted a decision regarding an initial and purely illustrative list of political situations in which the EU could approach the WEU under the provisions of the Treaty of Amsterdam to carry out humanitarian operations and rescue/evacuation missions. The EU Defence Ministers gathered for the first time at an ad hoc conference held in Vienna on 3 and 4 November.

670.   The European Union continued to work towards the goal of the total elimination of anti-personnel landmines. As one of the world's biggest contributors to the international mine-clearance effort, the EU allocated over ECU 50 million for that purpose in 1998, including ECU 15 million under the fourth framework programme for research and development (→ point 284) for advanced mine-clearance technology. The Ispra Joint Research Centre hosted an international seminar and exhibition on mine-clearance technology (²) on behalf of the European Commission from 29 September to 1 October (→ points 290 to 293). The EU also played an important role in the international anti-personnel mine conferences held in Ottawa in March, in Washington in May and in Karlsruhe and Vienna in July. Fourteen of the fifteen Member States signed the Ottawa Convention (Convention on the Use, Stockpiling, Production and Transfer of Anti-personnel Mines and on their Destruction) (³), which is due to enter into force on 1 March 1999 following the depositing of ratification instruments by the 40th signatory in September.

671.   On 23 April the Council defined Common Position 98/289/ CFSP (⁴) relating to the preparation of the second Preparatory Committee for the 2000 review conference of the parties to the Treaty on the Non-proliferation of Nuclear Weapons (NPT). This common position provides for the European Union to seek to convince States which are not yet parties to the NPT to accede to it and to take part in the conference. On 26 October, in the wake of the nuclear tests in Pakistan and India, the Council adopted a common position on the European Union's contribution to the promotion of non-proliferation and confidence-building in the south Asian region (→ point 902), followed, on 3 November,

---

(¹)   Decisions 98/627/CFSP and 98/628/CFSP (OJ L 300, 11.11.1998; Bull. 11-1998, points 1.3.4 and 1.3.5).
(²)   Bull. 10-1998, point 1.2.75.
(³)   1997 General Report, point 719.
(⁴)   OJ L 129, 30.4.1998; Bull. 4-1998, point 1.3.6.

by a decision ([1]) for the implementation of Joint Action 97/288/CFSP on the European Union's contribution to the promotion of transparency in nuclear-related export controls ([2]). On 19 February ([3]) Parliament, for its part, reaffirmed its support for the Comprehensive Test Ban Treaty and called on all governments to refrain from carrying out sub-critical tests; on 19 November ([4]) it also expressed its support for the nuclear disarmament initiative of the New Agenda Coalition.

672. In Common Position 98/197/CFSP ([5]), the Council called for progress towards a legally binding protocol to strengthen compliance with the Biological and Toxin Weapons Convention (BTWC).

673. The European code of conduct for arms exports, which Parliament had called for in January ([6]) and May ([7]) resolutions, was adopted by the Council on 8 June ([8]). While pointing out that the final decision on arms exports belongs to the national governments, the code sets out the precise terms on which such decisions should be taken and provides an operational framework for discussion of arms exports. Its implementation will be assessed annually. It establishes a system for notifying the refusal of an export licence and for consultation between Member States: if a Member State decides to grant a licence which has previously been denied for an identical transaction by another Member State, it must inform that Member State of its intention and furnish reasons for its decision. On 17 December the Council adopted a joint action on the EU's contribution to preventing the destabilising accumulation and spread of small arms and light weapons ([9]).

674. The system for the control of exports of dual-use (military and non-military) goods ([10]) was updated twice, by Decisions 98/106/CFSP (26 January) ([11]) and 98/232/CFSP (16 March) ([12]).

675. The European Union continued to contribute actively to the international effort to counter terrorism, particularly with the United Nations

---

([1]) Decision 98/623/CFSP (OJ L 297, 6.11.1998; Bull. 11-1998, point 1.3.3).
([2]) OJ L 120, 12.5.1997; 1997 General Report, point 721.
([3]) OJ C 80, 16.3.1998; Bull. 1/2-1998, point 1.4.7.
([4]) OJ C 379, 7.12.1998; Bull. 11-1998, point 1.3.7.
([5]) OJ L 75, 12.3.1998; Bull. 3-1998, point 1.3.5.
([6]) OJ C 34, 2.2.1998; Bull. 1/2-1998, point 1.4.6.
([7]) OJ C 167, 1.6.1998; Bull. 5-1998, point 1.3.5.
([8]) Bull. 5-1998, point 1.3.6; Bull. 6-1998, point 1.4.7.
([9]) Joint Action 1999/34/CFSP (OJ L 9, 15.1.1999; Bull. 12-1998).
([10]) 1997 General Report, point 723.
([11]) OJ L 32, 6.2.1998; Bull. 1/2-1998, point 1.4.5.
([12]) OJ L 92, 25.3.1998; Bull. 3-1998, point 1.3.6.

and in the G8 *(→ point 881)*. It focused on preventing the mobilisation of funds for terrorist acts, monitoring exports of weapons and explosives, ratifying international conventions to combat terrorism, putting together a draft UN convention to counter nuclear terrorism and cooperation to cope with the threat of chemical and biological terrorism. The EU-US Summit *(→ point 884)* approved a statement on combating terrorism, pinpointing areas of mutual interest. Against the background of the Middle East peace process, the EU continued its support for the Palestinian Authority's efforts to counter terrorist activities [1] and set up a joint security committee. A meeting on terrorism was also organised in November as part of the Barcelona (Euro-Mediterranean) process *(→ point 828)*.

Presidency and EU statements [2]

Central Europe

676. The European Union welcomed the abolition of the death penalty in Bulgaria [3], Estonia [4] and Lithuania [3] and the adoption by Estonia [3] and Latvia [5] of citizenship legislation allowing stateless children to acquire nationality and, in Latvia, abolishing the 'windows system' for naturalisation, and the Romanian Government's proposed amendments to the criminal code relating to homosexuality [6]. Having expressed concern in March at the amnesty order issued by Slovakia's Prime Minister Vladimir Meciar for crimes connected with the 1997 referendum [7], the EU voiced its satisfaction in September at the holding of elections in Slovakia [8].

Northern Mediterranean

677. The European Union welcomed the holding of the first political dialogue meeting within the framework of the joint declaration between the European Community and its Member States and the Former Yugo-

---

[1]   1997 General Report, points 725 and 923.
[2]   The following points are a summary of the positions set out in Presidency statements on behalf of the European Union and statements by the European Union on international political issues. The full versions are to be found in the *Bulletin of the European Union*.
[3]   Bull. 12-1998.
[4]   Bull. 3-1998, point 1.3.8.
[5]   Bull. 4-1998, point 1.3.8; Bull. 6-1998, points 1.4.20 and 1.4.21; Bull. 10-1998, point 1.3.9.
[6]   Bull. 5-1998, point 1.3.20.
[7]   Bull. 3-1998, point 1.3.15.
[8]   Bull. 9-1998, point 1.3.22.

slav Republic of Macedonia (^{1}). In January the EU praised the work of the UNTAES administration and Croatia's contribution to the peaceful reintegration of the region (^{2}); in February, however, it condemned the tone and content of President Franjo Tudjman's speech to the HDZ congress (^{3}). It welcomed the agreement allowing free transit through the territory of Croatia and of Bosnia and Herzegovina (^{4}), the formation of the new Republika Srpska Government (^{5}) and the Arbitral Tribunal's decision on Brcko (^{6}). In June the EU expressed the view that Bosnia and Herzegovina had embarked on a course of greater integration with Europe and European structures and proposed that a joint consultative task force be set up (^{7}). On 7 September it made a pre-election appeal to the population (^{8}), and on 15 September expressed its satisfaction at the way in which the election had been conducted (^{9}).

678.   With regard to the Federal Republic of Yugoslavia (FRY), the European Union expressed concern, and later alarm, at the hostilities in Kosovo (in March, June, July and October) (^{10}). When Common Position 98/240/CFSP (→ *point 843*) was adopted in March, the EU agreed to exert pressure on the government in Belgrade to find a peaceful solution to the problem (^{11}) and welcomed the signing of an agreement to implement the 1996 agreement on education in Kosovo (^{12}). The associated countries of central Europe, Cyprus (also an associated country) and the EFTA countries which are members of the European Economic Area (EEA) on several occasions backed the European Union in its action on the FRY and Kosovo (^{13}).

679.   In February the European Union expressed its deep concern at the events in Shkodër (Albania) (^{14}) and in November called on the Democratic Party not to boycott the referendum on a new constitution (^{15}).

(^{1})   Bull. 1/2-1998, point 1.4.10.
(^{2})   Bull. 1/2-1998, point 1.4.15.
(^{3})   Bull. 1/2-1998, point 1.4.16.
(^{4})   Bull. 9-1998, point 1.3.9.
(^{5})   Bull. 1/2-1998, point 1.4.13.
(^{6})   Bull. 3-1998, point 1.3.7.
(^{7})   Bull. 6-1998, point 1.4.11.
(^{8})   Bull. 9-1998, point 1.3.7.
(^{9})   Bull. 9-1998, point 1.3.8.
(^{10})   Bull. 3-1998, point 1.3.11; Bull. 6-1998, point 1.4.23; Bull. 7/8-1998, point 1.4.17; Bull. 10-1998, point 1.3.18.
(^{11})   Bull. 3-1998, point 1.3.12.
(^{12})   Bull. 3-1998, point 1.3.13.
(^{13})   Bull. 3-1998, point 1.3.14; Bull. 4-1998, point 1.3.10; Bull. 5-1998, point 1.3.18; Bull. 6-1998, points 1.4.24 and 1.4.25; Bull. 9-1998, points 1.3.18 and 1.3.19; Bull. 11-1998, point 1.3.17; Bull. 12-1998.
(^{14})   Bull. 1/2-1998, point 1.4.9.
(^{15})   Bull. 11-1998, point 1.3.9.

On Turkey, the EU voiced its regret at the banning of the Refah party (January) ([1]) and at the confirmation of the prison sentence imposed on Istanbul's mayor, Recep Tayyip Erdogan (September) ([2]). It condemned the attack on Akin Birdal, President of the Turkish Human Rights Association (May) ([3]), and expressed its full solidarity with Italy over the Öcalan affair, stressing that it rejected terrorism in any form (November) ([4]). It welcomed the agreement between Syria and Turkey on security issues (October) ([5]) and the decision by President Clerides not to install S-300 missiles on Cyprus (December) ([6]).

Maghreb, Mashreq and Middle East

680.   In July the European Union welcomed the UN Secretary-General's establishment of a panel of eminent persons to be dispatched to Algeria ([7]) and in September it expressed its approval of the panel's report ([8]). In December it gave its full backing to the UN Secretary-General's settlement plan for western Sahara ([6]). In May the EU welcomed US efforts to revive the Middle East peace process ([9]), while in August it condemned the plan to extend settlements in the Golan Heights ([10]). In October ([11]) it welcomed the signing of the Wye River Memorandum and, on 4 December ([6]), the start of its implementation. However, on 23 December it regretted its suspension ([6]). In February it expressed strong support for the UN Secretary-General's mission to Iraq ([12]); in March it welcomed the unanimous adoption of a UN Security Council resolution commending the Secretary-General's initiative to secure commitments from the Government of Iraq regarding compliance with its obligations ([13]). In November the EU condemned Iraq's decision to stop cooperating with the UN Special Commission (Unscom) ([14]). Having repeated in February that Iran's fatwa on Salman Rushdie was null and void ([15]), the Union welcomed the Iranian Government's assurances that

---

([1])   Bull. 1/2-1998, point 1.4.23.
([2])   Bull. 9-1998, point 1.3.23.
([3])   Bull. 5-1998, point 1.3.22.
([4])   Bull. 11-1998, point 1.3.19.
([5])   Bull. 10-1998, point 1.3.21.
([6])   Bull. 12-1998.
([7])   Bull. 7/8-1998, point 1.4.4.
([8])   Bull. 9-1998, point 1.3.4.
([9])   Bull. 5-1998, point 1.3.11.
([10])   Bull. 7/8-1998, point 1.4.24.
([11])   Bull. 10-1998, point 1.3.17.
([12])   Bull. 1/2-1998, point 1.4.18.
([13])   Bull. 3-1998, point 1.3.9.
([14])   Bull. 11-1998, point 1.3.15.
([15])   Bull. 1/2-1998, point 1.4.19.

the fatwa would not be carried out (September) ([1]). However, it was particularly concerned, in December ([2]), about the disappearance and killing of dissidents in Iran.

Independent States of the former Soviet Union

681.   The European Union welcomed the abolition of the death penalty in Azerbaijan ([3]) and the moratoriums on executions in Kyrgyzstan ([2]) and Turkmenistan ([2]). In February it expressed its concern at the treatment of two youths accused of painting anti-government graffiti in Belarus ([4]), and in June it protested at the Belarusian authorities' unacceptable behaviour with regard to the residences of the Member States' heads of mission ([5]). It also condemned the violence in Abkhazia (Georgia), while welcoming the signing of a ceasefire protocol ([6]). Best wishes were communicated to the chair of the Black Sea Economic Cooperation Summit held in Yalta ([7]). The EU called on Russia to implement rapidly and fully the programme it had agreed with the IMF and the economic reforms to which it had committed itself ([8]); it expressed its abhorrence at the savage killing of four engineers held hostage in Chechnya ([2]). In a statement paying tribute to Galina Starovoitova, the Union said that the outpouring of grief and sadness seen at her funeral showed that her efforts to further democracy would not be forgotten ([9]). The EU expressed its satisfaction at the readiness of the government and united opposition in Tajikistan to resume discussion of a law excluding from political life parties founded on religious principles ([10]).

Asia

682.   The European Union on more than one occasion expressed deep concern at the situation in Afghanistan: once in April, having received news of preparations for further fighting and a food blockade on central

---

([1])   Bull. 9-1998, point 1.3.14.
([2])   Bull. 12-1998.
([3])   Bull. 1/2-1998, point 1.4.11.
([4])   Bull. 1/2-1998, point 1.4.12.
([5])   Bull. 6-1998, point 1.4.10. A number of associated countries and EEA members also subscribed to Common Position 98/448/CFSP (→ point 876) regarding Belarus (Bull. 7/8-1998, point 1.4.5). The Belarusian Foreign Minister and the EU Presidency subsequently reached an arrangement on this matter (Bull. 12-1998).
([6])   Bull. 6-1998, point 1.4.16.
([7])   Bull. 6-1998, point 1.4.15.
([8])   Bull. 7/8-1998, point 1.4.18; Bull. 9-1998, point 1.3.20.
([9])   Bull. 11-1998, point 1.3.18.
([10]) Bull. 6-1998, point 1.4.26.

Afghanistan (¹), once in July, following the Taliban leaders' closure of the offices of non-governmental organisations (²), and once in September, following the death of a group of Iranian diplomats in fighting in the north and reports that civilians had been massacred (³). It condemned the attack on the Temple of the Tooth in Kandy (Sri Lanka) (⁴), the nuclear tests carried out by India (⁵) and Pakistan (⁶), the detention of political prisoners in Burma and the Burmese authorities' restriction of Aung San Suu Kyi's freedom of movement (⁷). In May, following renewed violence in Indonesia, the EU called on the government to conduct an in-depth investigation to track down the perpetrators and hold them to account (⁸). In November it welcomed the announcement that elections would be held by June 1999 (⁹). In June it expressed the hope that negotiations between Indonesia and Portugal would produce a just solution in East Timor which fully respected the rights of its inhabitants (¹⁰). In August it welcomed the results of the meeting between the UN Secretary-General and the Indonesian and Portuguese Foreign Ministers regarding East Timor (¹¹). The EU condemned the Malaysian Government's treatment of former Deputy Prime Minister, Anwar Ibrahim (¹²). In June it underlined the importance it attached to the holding of free and fair elections in Cambodia (¹³) and on 31 July it noted that the elections, held on 26 July, appeared to have been conducted satisfactorily (¹⁴); in September it noted the official results and called on all the parties to adopt a constructive attitude (¹⁵), and in November welcomed the formation of a new coalition government (¹⁶). In May the European Union expressed its support for the four-party talks and bilateral meetings between the Republic of Korea and the Democratic People's Republic of Korea (¹⁷); in September it voiced its grave concern at the latter's

---

(¹)   Bull. 4-1998, point 1.3.7.
(²)   Bull. 7/8-1998, point 1.4.3.
(³)   Bull. 9-1998, points 1.3.2 and 1.3.3. A number of associated countries and Norway also subscribed to the aims of Common Position 98/108/CFSP (→ point 903) in January (Bull. 1/2-1998, point 1.4.8).
(⁴)   Bull. 1/2-1998, point 1.4.22.
(⁵)   Bull. 5-1998, point 1.3.9; Bull. 6-1998, point 1.4.19.
(⁶)   Bull. 5-1998, point 1.3.17; Bull. 6-1998, point 1.4.19.
(⁷)   Bull. 7/8-1998, point 1.4.11; Bull. 9-1998, point 1.3.16; Bull. 10-1998, points 1.3.11 and 1.3.12. A number of associated countries and EEA members also subscribed to the extension of Common Position 96/635/CFSP (→ point 906) in May (Bull. 5-1998, point 1.3.13) and in October (Bull. 10-1998, point 1.3.13).
(⁸)   Bull. 5-1998, point 1.3.10.
(⁹)   Bull. 11-1998, point 1.3.14.
(¹⁰) Bull. 6-1998, point 1.4.27.
(¹¹) Bull. 7/8-1998, point 1.4.10.
(¹²) Bull. 10-1998, point 1.3.10; Bull. 11-1998, point 1.3.16.
(¹³) Bull. 6-1998, point 1.4.14.
(¹⁴) Bull. 7/8-1998, point 1.4.6.
(¹⁵) Bull. 9-1998, point 1.3.10.
(¹⁶) Bull. 11-1998, point 1.3.11.
(¹⁷) Bull. 5-1998, point 1.3.19.

missile test ([1]), and in October welcomed the resumption of the four-party talks ([2]).

Latin America

683. In September the European Union and the countries of Latin America and the Caribbean announced that a joint summit of Heads of State or Government would take place in June 1999 in Rio de Janeiro ([3]). The EU applauded the welcome given by Cuba to Pope John Paul II and the government's decision to free a number of prisoners ([4]). In May it urged the Guatemalan Government to carry out a thorough investigation to bring the killers of Monsignor Juan Gerardi to justice and support the work of the Truth Commission ([5]). In October it welcomed the efforts made to ensure that the Guatemalan peace accords were implemented ([6]). The Union congratulated Colombia's new president, Andrés Pastrana, on his investiture and reiterated its support for the country's peace process ([7]). In October it welcomed the conclusion of an agreement between Peru and Ecuador ([8]).

Africa

684. The European Union praised the work of South Africa's Truth and Reconciliation Commission ([9]). In June it learned with deep sadness of the death of the UN Secretary-General's special representative to Angola, Alioune Blondin Beye ([10]). In September and in December it reacted with great concern to the worsening of the situation in Angola, which it attributed primarily to UNITA ([11]). In January it condemned the massacre of civilians in the village of Rukaramu in Burundi ([12]); in June it welcomed the adoption by Burundi's National Assembly of a constitutional act and a political platform for transition ([13]), and the progress achieved at the first session of peace talks in Arusha ([14]). In

([1]) Bull. 9-1998, point 1.3.11.
([2]) Bull. 10-1998, point 1.3.15.
([3]) Bull. 9-1998, point 1.3.5.
([4]) Bull. 1/2-1998, point 1.4.17.
([5]) Bull. 5-1998, point 1.3.8.
([6]) Bull. 10-1998, point 1.3.6.
([7]) Bull. 7/8-1998, point 1.4.7.
([8]) Bull. 10-1998, point 1.3.16.
([9]) Bull. 11-1998, point 1.3.8.
([10]) Bull. 6-1998, point 1.4.9.
([11]) Bull. 9-1998, point 1.3.6; Bull. 12-1998.
([12]) Bull. 1/2-1998, point 1.4.14.
([13]) Bull. 6-1998, point 1.4.12.
([14]) Bull. 6-1998, point 1.4.13.

November and December it voiced its alarm at the renewed violence against civilians ([1]). In May the European Union expressed its concern at the reports of military clashes on the border between Eritrea and Ethiopia ([2]); in September it called on the two countries to continue to exercise restraint ([3]), and in November and December it welcomed the attempts being made to settle the conflict peacefully ([4]). It welcomed the fact that Eritrea and Yemen had accepted the International Arbitration Committee's decision on their dispute ([5]). In June it condemned the military coup in Guinea-Bissau ([6]); in June ([7]) and July ([8]) it expressed its concern at the further worsening of the situation in the wake of the coup, and in July, September, October and November ([9]) it called on all the parties involved to adhere to the memorandum of understanding signed by the government and the military junta. In October the European Union welcomed the clemency measures announced by the president of Equatorial Guinea ([10]).

685. The European Union paid tribute to the people of Kenya for the way they had exercised their right to vote and expressed its wish to see a democratic, stable and prosperous country ([11]). It expressed concern at the situation in Lesotho ([12]), urged all the parties in Mozambique to continue their dialogue ([13]), and voiced its disappointment at the upsurge of violence in Niger and the reaction of the country's authorities ([14]). In March it welcomed the Pope's visit to Nigeria, but remained worried by the lack of respect for human rights and the lack of progress towards democracy in the country ([15]); in April, it called for free and fair elections ([16]), but observed in May that the so-called transition to civilian rule was a failure and again expressed disquiet at the human rights situation ([17]). In June it expressed its hope for an early return to democracy following the death of General Sani Abacha ([18]); in July it welcomed

---

([1]) Bull. 11-1998, point 1.3.10; Bull. 12-1998.
([2]) Bull. 5-1998, point 1.3.7.
([3]) Bull. 9-1998, point 1.3.12.
([4]) Bull. 11-1998, point 1.3.12; Bull. 12-1998.
([5]) Bull. 10-1998, point 1.3.22.
([6]) Bull. 6-1998, point 1.4.17.
([7]) Bull. 6-1998, point 1.4.18.
([8]) Bull. 7/8-1998, point 1.4.8.
([9]) Bull. 7/8-1998, point 1.4.9; Bull. 9-1998, point 1.3.13; Bull. 10-1998, point 1.3.8; Bull. 11-1998, point 1.3.13.
([10]) Bull. 10-1998, point 1.3.7.
([11]) Bull. 1/2-1998, point 1.4.20.
([12]) Bull. 9-1998, point 1.3.15.
([13]) Bull. 5-1998, point 1.3.12.
([14]) Bull. 5-1998, point 1.3.14.
([15]) Bull. 3-1998, point 1.3.10.
([16]) Bull. 4-1998, point 1.3.9.
([17]) Bull. 5-1998, points 1.3.15 and 1.3.10.
([18]) Bull. 6-1998, point 1.4.22.

General Abdulsalam Abubakar's announcement of a programme of transition and of his intention to hand over power to a civilian government in 1999 (¹); in September and October it welcomed the government's commitment to begin a process of democratisation (²).

686. In July and August the European Union repeatedly expressed alarm at the situation in the Democratic Republic of the Congo (³). In February it stated its disquiet at the instability in Sierra Leone (⁴); in May it expressed its fears about rebel atrocities against the civilian population of the country (⁵), but in July welcomed the decisions reached by the presidents of Liberia and Sierra Leone to condemn and control rebel activity (⁶). In September and October, however, it expressed condemnation of the death sentences and executions carried out in Sierra Leone (⁷). The EU welcomed the continuation of discussions between the Rwandan authorities and representatives of the UN High Commissioner for Human Rights (⁸). It also welcomed the continuation of discussions between the Sudanese Government and the Sudan People's Liberation Movement (⁹), but expressed concern at the worsening of the humanitarian crisis in the south of the country (¹⁰). Another cause for concern was the way in which Togo's elections had been conducted and the lack of credibility of their results (¹¹). The EU expressed its deep concern at the Zambian National Assembly's decision to renew the state of emergency for 90 days (¹²). In June a number of associated countries and members of the EEA also subscribed to Common Position 98/350/CFSP on human rights, democratic principles, the rule of law and good governance in Africa (¹³) (→ point 931).

General

687. On the occasion of the 50th anniversary of the adoption of the Universal Declaration of Human Rights, the EU underlined the impor-

---

(¹) Bull. 7/8-1998, point 1.4.12.
(²) Bull. 9-1998, point 1.3.17; Bull. 10-1998, point 1.3.14.
(³) Bull. 7/8-1998, points 1.4.13 to 1.4.16.
(⁴) Bull. 1/2-1998, point 1.4.21.
(⁵) Bull. 5-1998, point 1.3.21.
(⁶) Bull. 7/8-1998, point 1.4.20.
(⁷) Bull. 9-1998, point 1.3.21; Bull. 10-1998, point 1.3.19.
(⁸) Bull. 7/8-1998, point 1.4.19; a number of associated countries and EEA members also subscribed to the aims of Common Position 98/252/CFSP (→ point 952) regarding Rwanda (Bull. 4-1998, point 1.3.11).
(⁹) Bull. 7/8-1998, point 1.4.21.
(¹⁰) Bull. 4-1998, point 1.3.12; Bull. 10-1998, point 1.3.20.
(¹¹) Bull. 6-1998, points 1.4.28 and 1.4.29.
(¹²) Bull. 1/2-1998, point 1.4.24.
(¹³) Bull. 6-1998, point 1.4.8.

tance it attached to the declaration *(→ point 24).* It also welcomed the successful conclusion of the conference for the establishment of the International Criminal Court [1]. It saw as positive the recent developments in the Lockerbie terrorist case [2]. It decided to step up its international campaign opposing the death penalty and work for its universal abolition [3]. It also underlined its attachment to the negotiation of a legally binding protocol to strengthen compliance with the Biological and Toxin Weapons Convention [4]. The associated countries and some members of the EEA, for their part, subscribed to the aims of Common Position 98/197/CFSP *(→ point 672)* on progress towards the conclusion of the abovementioned protocol [5], to the aims of the EU programme for preventing and combating illicit trafficking in conventional arms [6] and to the aims of the EU code of conduct for arms exports [7] *(→ point 673).*

---

[1]   Bull. 7/8-1998, point 1.4.22.
[2]   Bull. 7/8-1998, point 1.4.25.
[3]   Bull. 6-1998, point 1.4.30.
[4]   Bull. 12-1998.
[5]   Bull. 3-1998, point 1.3.16.
[6]   Bull. 6-1998, point 1.4.31.
[7]   Bull. 7/8-1998, point 1.4.23.

Section 2

International organisations and conferences

United Nations and specialised agencies (¹)

General Assembly

688. The 53rd session of the UN General Assembly opened in New York on 9 September (²). During the ministerial week of the session, the European Union was represented by Mr Wolfgang Schüssel, President of the Council, and by Sir Leon Brittan, Mr Marín and Mr Van den Broek from the Commission. Speaking on behalf of the Union, Mr Schüssel cited the euro and enlargement as part of the EU's response to the challenges of globalisation. He also underlined the Union's commitment to the United Nations and its backing for the Secretary-General's reform proposals, and the urgent need for a solution to the financial crisis facing the organisation. While in New York, Sir Leon, Mr Marín and Mr Van den Broek attended meetings at ministerial level with representatives of many countries and regional groupings, and bilateral meetings.

689. On 8 October the European Parliament adopted a resolution calling on all UN Member States in arrears, and in particular the United States, to fulfil their financial obligations (³).

690. The special session of the UN General Assembly on the fight against drugs is covered in Section 4 ('Development policy') of this chapter *(→ point 760).*

Economic and Social Council and United Nations Economic Commission for Europe (ECE)

691. The European Commission participated in several sessions of the United Nations Economic and Social Council. In particular, Sir Leon Brittan spoke at July's session on market access.

(¹) For the activities of the specialised development agencies see Section 4 ('Development policy') of this chapter *(→ points 765 to 768).*
(²) Bull. 9-1998, point 1.3.24.
(³) OJ C 328, 26.10.1998; Bull. 10-1998, point 1.3.23.

692.   The 53rd annual session of the United Nations Economic Commission for Europe took place in Geneva from 21 to 23 April ([1]). Discussion focused on the vulnerability of the economies in transition, economic globalisation, the introduction of the euro and its impact on countries not members of the European Union, and on the reform of the ECE, its role in the United Nations and its cooperation with other international organisations and institutions, including the EU and the OSCE. Mr Yves Berthelot, Executive Secretary of the ECE, visited the Commission on 10 December. On 24 March the Community acceded to the revised 1958 UN-ECE agreement on the approval of motor vehicle equipment and parts (→ point 247).

Commission on Sustainable Development and Convention on Climate Change

693.   Activities relating to the Commission on Sustainable Development and the Convention on Climate Change are covered in Section 17 ('Environment') of Chapter IV (→ points 506, 507, 508 and 517).

Convention on the Law of the Sea and the International Seabed Authority

694.   On 23 March the Council adopted a decision concerning the conclusion by the Community of the UN Convention on the Law of the Sea and the agreement on the exploitation of the seabed (Table III). The Community acceded to the Convention and the agreement on 1 May. At 31 December there were 127 parties to the Convention (including the Community and 12 of its 15 Member States).

695.   The Community also took part in the fourth session of the International Seabed Authority ([2]), which focused mainly on the 1999 budget and the authority's draft financial regulation. The draft mining code was also discussed.

---

[1]   Contrary to what was stated in the 1997 General Report (point 743), the 1997 session was not the 53rd but the 52nd.
[2]   Previous session: 1997 General Report, point 744.

International Monetary Fund (IMF) and World Bank (IBRD)

696.   In conjunction with the general assemblies of the IMF and the World Bank, the European Union, represented by Mr Rudolf Edlinger, President of the Council, and Mr de Silguy, attended a number of meetings in Washington in October. Commission representatives also took part as observers in meetings of the Group of Ten, the IMF Interim Committee (→ points 70 and 71) and the Development Committee. On 5 May Mr Santer met the President of the World Bank, Mr James D. Wolfensohn, in Washington to discuss cooperation between their respective institutions.

World Intellectual Property Organisation (WIPO)

697.   The Community, represented by the Commission, and its Member States continued to play an active role in the WIPO. In January they tabled a joint proposal for a protocol on audiovisual performances, together with a proposal for the legal protection of non-original databases, which were discussed by WIPO bodies in the course of the year.

World Trade Organisation (WTO) and World Customs Organisation (WCO)

698.   The activities of these organisations are covered in Section 3 ('Commercial policy') of this chapter (→ points 710 to 714).

Organisation for Security and Cooperation in Europe (OSCE)

699.   The main OSCE event of the year was the meeting of the Ministerial Council in Oslo on 2 and 3 December, which was attended by the Foreign Ministers of the 54 participating States (the Federal Republic of Yugoslavia (FRY) having been suspended since 1992) ([1]). Representatives of the European Union, the OSCE's Mediterranean partners (Algeria, Egypt, Israel, Jordan, Morocco and Tunisia) and the UN and other international organisations also took part in this summit. Decisions were adopted concerning the finalisation of the European Security Charter in 1999, the situation in Georgia and Moldova and OSCE activities in central Asia. A declaration on Kosovo, where an OSCE verification mission was rapidly being set up was adopted. It stressed the need, if the FRY

([1])   Bull. 12-1998.

was to resume its membership of the OSCE, to implement the recent agreement on Kosovo and achieve a lasting political settlement respecting the FRY's sovereignty and territorial integrity.

700. The sixth meeting of the OSCE Economic Forum, held in Prague in June, was devoted to security aspects of energy developments in the OSCE area. The implementation of economic commitments was also reviewed. Seminars were organised in Tashkent in September on environmental problems in central Asia, in Valetta in October on the human dimension of security and in Istanbul in November on the Black Sea region.

701. As in 1997 ([1]), the OSCE's main activities in the field of preventive diplomacy concerned the former Yugoslavia and the Caucasus, but it was also present in Estonia, Latvia, Moldova, Ukraine and Tajikistan. It continued to seek a peaceful settlement in Nagorno-Karabakh, monitor the situation in Georgia and Chechnya, and support or monitor the electoral process in Albania, Bosnia and Herzegovina, and Slovakia. It also organised a police-monitoring operation in Croatia, worked for democratisation in Belarus and decided to play a greater role in Kosovo.

702. The Commission took part in the OSCE's activities throughout the year, contributing to its work on the economic and human dimensions of the security model, the drafting of the European Security Charter, relations with the Mediterranean countries and the organisation of elections.

Western European Union (WEU)

703. At the first of the WEU's two ministerial meetings, held in Rhodes on 11 and 12 May, the ministers adopted a declaration envisaging enhanced cooperation both with the EU, via implementation of Article J.4(2) of the Treaty on European Union, exchanges of classified information, discussion of a European common defence policy and current cooperation in Albania, and with NATO, with plans to hold a joint crisis management exercise in 2000. The Rhodes Declaration also referred to the work accomplished in Albania and Kosovo by the WEU multinational police element, and to the operational development of the WEU. At the second ministerial meeting, held in Rome on 16 and 17 November, ministers adopted a declaration on developments in the latter

---

([1])   1997 General Report, point 750.

half of the year. The Rome Declaration again focused on relations with the European Union and NATO, reaffirming the WEU's desire for close cooperation and touched on the WEU's operational role and its relations with third countries. The ministers also called for the WEU to discuss a European security and defence identity in preparation for the entry into force of the Treaty of Amsterdam and the NATO Summit in Washington, stating that discussion should focus on identifying new measures aimed at strengthening European military capacities to handle crises, notably 'Petersberg'-type missions, including increased transparency and interoperability within the multinational forces.

Council of Europe

704.   The involvement of the EU institutions, in particular the Commission, in the activities of the Council of Europe continued on the basis of the arrangements of 16 June 1987 ([1]), as revised by the exchange of letters of 5 November 1996 ([2]). Accordingly, the Commission was involved in the major political events in the Council of Europe's calendar. These included the 102nd and 103rd sessions of the Committee of Ministers on 5 May and 4 November and the ministerial conferences on youth and sport, which took place in Bucharest from 27 to 29 April and Nicosia on 14 and 15 May respectively. Mr Van den Broek addressed the Parliamentary Assembly on 29 January and took part in the annual quadripartite meetings in Strasbourg on 1 April and 7 October ([3]). Meetings between the Commission and the Council of Europe continued to be held on judicial affairs, culture, mass media, sport, equal opportunities, youth, social policy, public health, environment, migration, bioethics, judicial cooperation, human rights, local and regional government, and education.

705.   The Council of Europe also stepped up its cooperation with the countries of central Europe, south-east Europe and the new independent States of the former Soviet Union. A series of priority measures and a joint programme of assistance for the reform of Albania's judicial system were signed in November. The implementation of programmes already signed with other countries continued (joint programmes with Russia, Ukraine, Moldova, the Baltic States and Bosnia and Herzegovina and joint multilateral programmes on national minorities in the central European countries and the fight against corruption and organised crime in

---

([1])   OJ L 273, 26.9.1987; Twenty-first General Report, point 902.
([2])   1996 General Report, point 692.
([3])   Bull. 4-1998, point 1.3.14; Bull. 10-1998, point 1.3.24.

the new independent States of the former Soviet Union). Other activities were carried out to encourage the creation in central and eastern Europe of independent multidisciplinary ethics committees in the field of bio-medical research.

706. On 21 December the Council adopted a decision concluding an agreement between the European Monitoring Centre on Racism and Xenophobia and the Council of Europe *(→ point 26)*.

Organisation for Economic Cooperation and Development (OECD)

707. At the annual ministerial meeting held in Paris on 27 and 28 April([1]), discussions focused on the worldwide implications of the financial crisis in Asia and its repercussions for the OECD countries, measures to increase the flexibility and adaptability of the OECD economies, and the measures needed to strengthen the multilateral system. The ministers also decided to suspend the negotiations under way for the draft multilateral agreement on investment (MAI)([2]) for six months to allow the negotiators to review progress and consult the relevant bodies of civil society in greater depth. In October the negotiations were resumed following France's decision to withdraw from them. The negotiations were also the subject of resolutions adopted by the European Parliament on 15 January([3]) and 11 March([4]).

European Bank for Reconstruction and Development (EBRD)

708. EBRD activities are described in Section 1 ('Economic and monetary policy') of Chapter IV *(→ points 94 to 96)*.

([1])   Bull. 4-1998, point 1.3.13.
([2])   1995 General Report, points 734 and 755.
([3])   OJ C 34, 2.2.1998; Bull. 1/2-1998, point 1.4.49
([4])   OJ C 104, 6.4.1998; Bull. 3-1998, point 1.3.17.

Section 3

Common commercial policy

Priority activities and objectives

709. The consolidation of progress achieved in 1996 and 1997 and preparations for the next round of trade talks were the significant events in the World Trade Organisation framework. There were important developments in Community legislation too, with the removal of China and Russia from the list of non-market-economy countries and the adoption of a directive on export credit insurance.

World Trade Organisation (WTO)

710. Two declarations were adopted at the end of the second WTO ministerial conference ([1]) held in Geneva from 18 to 20 May: ([2]) a general declaration setting out the WTO's work programme for the forthcoming round of trade talks, and another specifically concerning electronic commerce. Further to the latter, which was in response to an initiative by the Community, in September the WTO Council drew up a detailed list of items for the negotiating agenda in the field of electronic commerce. At the same time, the WTO members decided to continue their current practice of not imposing customs duties on electronic transmissions.

711. In June, Parliament ([3]) and the European Council ([4]) expressed satisfaction at the outcome of the Geneva conference, the preparations for which had previously been the subject of Council conclusions on 30 March ([5]) and 30 April ([6]). In the latter case, the Council stressed the importance it attached to transparency in WTO proceedings and the need to ensure that the general public was aware of the benefits of trade liberalisation in terms of jobs, growth and prosperity. In December the

---

([1]) First conference (Singapore): 1996 General Report, point 703.
([2]) Bull. 5-1998, point 1.3.25.
([3]) OJ C 210, 6.7.1998; Bull. 6-1998, point 1.4.35.
([4]) Bull. 6-1998, point I.22.
([5]) Bull. 3-1998, point 1.3.20.
([6]) Bull. 4-1998, point 1.3.16.

European Council expressed its support for the start of comprehensive trade negotiations in the WTO framework in 2000 (¹).

712. Following the 1997 agreement on financial services (²), a fifth protocol to the General Agreement on Trade in Services (GATS) covering this subject was opened on 27 February for acceptance by the WTO members who had taken part in the negotiations. On 14 December the Council decided to conclude the results of the talks and approve the protocol (Table III). The Community played an active role throughout the year in the ongoing proceedings of various WTO working parties and in the negotiations concerning the accession of new members to the WTO. Kyrgyzstan and Latvia joined the WTO during the year.

713. In all, 31 new cases were put to the WTO's dispute settlement body (DSB). The Appellate Body delivered conclusions on a number of cases involving the Community, finding in its favour in disputes involving the tariff classification of computing (LAN) equipment (referred by the United States), the Community's poultry import arrangements (challenged by Brazil) and the Indonesian motor industry investment scheme (referred by the Community) (→ point 741). The Appellate Body's conclusions regarding the referral by the United States and Canada of the Community ban on imports of meat produced using hormones were considerably more favourable to the Community than the earlier panel conclusions (³), but the Community was nevertheless required to back up its ban with a further assessment of the potential cancer risks associated with such meat (→ point 642).

World Customs Organisation (WCO)

714. WCO activities focused on the rules of origin, in particular the harmonisation of non-preferential origin rules and the revision of the Kyoto Convention on the Simplification and Harmonisation of Customs Procedures (⁴).

(¹) Bull. 12-1998.
(²) 1997 General Report, point 759.
(³) 1997 General Report, point 763.
(⁴) 1997 General Report, point 764.

Operation of the customs union, customs cooperation and mutual administrative assistance

715.   On 3 June the Commission proposed an amendment to Regulation (EEC) No 2913/92 establishing the Community Customs Code (Table I) with the aim of simplifying customs formalities, introducing greater flexibility on customs debt and free zones and increasing the effectiveness of measures to prevent fraud and irregularities. On 28 January it also proposed a revision to Regulation (EC) No 3295/94 on controls on counterfeit or pirated goods to extend its scope to certain intellectual property (patent) violations (Table II). On 24 July the Commission adopted a report on implementing the 'Customs 2000' programme (¹) and, on 11 November, proposed a revision designed to incorporate into the programme all Community initiatives for improving the way customs operate (Table I).

716.   On 24 September the Council adopted a common position on the proposal to amend the Community Customs Code in the field of transit (Table I) presented by the Commission under its action plan for transit in Europe (²). Progress was also made on implementing the plan's computing component (preparing the phased introduction of the new computerised transit system from January 1999) and its operational aspects (e.g. setting up a national coordinators' network).

717.   The TARIC multilingual database is used to transmit daily the information required by the national administrations to ensure consistency in the application of tariff measures. The 1998 printed version of TARIC was published on 15 April (³). Chapters 1 to 24 were updated on 11 August (⁴). The 1999 Combined Nomenclature was established on 26 October by Regulation (EC) No 2261/98 (⁵) which incorporates the initial results of the SLIM exercise (→ point 151).

718.   The agreement with Canada on customs cooperation and mutual administrative assistance in customs matters entered into force on 1 January (Table III) and a similar agreement with Hong Kong was initialled on 3 November (Table III) during Mr Santer's visit to China (→ point 909). On 17 February the Council authorised the Commission to negotiate an additional protocol to the association agreement with

---

(¹)   COM(1998) 471; Bull. 7/8-1998, point 1.4.30.
(²)   COM(97) 188; 1997 General Report, point 767.
(³)   OJ C 115, 15.4.1998.
(⁴)   OJ C 252, 11.8.1998.
(⁵)   OJ L 292, 30.10.1998.

Cyprus on mutual assistance in customs matters (Table III). In a communication on 6 May, the Commission outlined steps leading to the phased introduction of Euro-Mediterranean cumulation of origin rules ([1]).

Commercial policy instruments

Anti-dumping and anti-subsidy measures

719. On 29 July the Commission adopted its 16th annual report to Parliament on the Community's anti-dumping and anti-subsidy activities (1997) ([2]). On 3 September it also updated the basic decision on anti-subsidy measures in the ECSC sectors ([3]) principally to adapt it to WTO rules. On 27 April the Council removed Russia and China from the list of non-market-economy countries ([4]), thus allowing the Commission, in certain cases, to use the two countries' domestic price information in anti-dumping investigations.

720. The Commission published 24 notices of initiation of anti-dumping proceedings, 9 of which related to new proceedings, 12 reviews, 2 for circumvention and 1 for absorption of duties. The Council imposed definitive duties in 11 cases in the light of new proceedings; the main cases ([5]) in which measures were adopted involved stainless steel fasteners and parts ([6]), personal fax machines ([7]), synthetic fibre ropes ([8]) and magnetic disks (3.5" microdisks) ([9]). Further to reviews, the Council also confirmed or amended the definitive duties in seven proceedings and terminated two proceedings without the imposition of measures. The Commission adopted 12 provisional measures; the provisional measures involving imports of unbleached cotton fabrics ([10]) and stainless steel bars ([11]) did not become definitive. The Commission also terminated six new proceedings and seven reviews without the imposition of measures.

([1]) COM(1998) 254; Bull. 5-1998, point 1.3.26.
([2]) COM(1998) 482; Bull. 7/8-1998, point 1.4.31.
([3]) Decision 1889/98/ECSC (OJ L 245, 4.9.1998; Bull. 9-1998, point 1.3.28).
([4]) Regulation (EC) No 905/98 (OJ L 128, 30.4.1998; Bull. 4-1998, point 1.3.18).
([5]) For further information on specific cases, see the 17th annual report to Parliament of the Community's anti-dumping and anti-subsidy activities (1998) (to be published). The *Bulletin of the European Union* also provides reports, without commentary, on the various stages (notices, undertakings, duties) of ongoing proceedings.
([6]) OJ L 50, 20.2.1998.
([7]) OJ L 128, 30.4.1998.
([8]) OJ L 183, 26.6.1998.
([9]) OJ L 236, 22.8.1998.
([10]) OJ L 111, 9.4.1998.
([11]) OJ L 202, 18.7.1998.

The Court of Justice and the Court of First Instance issued nine judgments or orders relating to anti-dumping.

721.   As regards anti-subsidy measures, the Council imposed definitive countervailing duties on imports from India of broad-spectrum antibiotics ([1]) and stainless steel bright bars ([2]). New proceedings were initiated against imports of stainless steel wire from South Korea and India ([3]), polypropylene binder or baler twine from Saudi Arabia ([4]), polyester textured filament yarn from South Korea and India ([5]) and polyethylene terephthalate film from India ([6]). Three proceedings were terminated by the Commission without the imposition of measures ([7]).

722.   Many third countries initiated anti-dumping and anti-subsidy investigations against imports from EU Member States. The Commission monitored such cases to ensure that all third countries fully complied in this respect with their obligations under international agreements.

723.   The Commission arranged seminars on the trade protection instruments in Brazil (for the Mercosur Member States), Morocco and Brunei (for members of ASEAN) and in Brussels (for central and east European countries).

Barriers to trade

724.   Under the trade barriers regulation ([8]), the Commission initiated four examination procedures: Brazilian trade practices in the textile sector ([9]), imports of sorbitol ([10]), the arrangements applicable to cosmetics in the Republic of Korea ([11]) and the conditions for transhipment of swordfish in Chile ([12]). It also decided to use the WTO dispute settlement mechanism in the light of the outcome of the procedures initiated

---

([1])   OJ L 273, 9.10.1998.
([2])   OJ L 304, 14.11.1998.
([3])   OJ C 199, 25.6.1998.
([4])   OJ C 233, 25.7.1998.
([5])   OJ C 264, 21.8.1998.
([6])   OJ C 357, 21.11.1998.
([7])   OJ L 168, 13.6.1998; OJ L 203, 21.7.1998; OJ L 214, 31.7.1998.
([8])   Council Regulation (EC) No 3286/94 (OJ L 349, 31.12.1994; 1994 General Report, point
         1015), as amended by Regulation (EC) No 356/95 (OJ L 41, 23.2.1995; 1995 General Report,
         point 745).
([9])   OJ C 63, 27.2.1998.
([10])   OJ C 361, 24.11.1998.
([11])   OJ C 154, 19.5.1998.
([12])   OJ C 215, 10.7.1998.

in 1997 (¹) concerning the United States' Anti-Dumping Act of 1916 and US practices with regard to cross-border music licensing, Argentinian practices relating to exports of raw hides and skins and imports of finished leather, and Japanese trade practices in the leather sector (²). The Commission is trying to reach a 'gentleman's agreement' on the pending procedures.

Import arrangements, including safeguards

725. Regulation (EC) No 519/94 (³) on the rules applying to imports from State-trading countries was amended on 28 May by Regulation (EC) No 1138/98 (⁴) which liberalises and subjects to prior Community surveillance imports of toys originating in the People's Republic of China and increases by 5 % the level of quotas applicable to Chinese porcelain and ceramic tableware.

726. On 25 May the Council updated the arrangements applicable to certain goods resulting from the processing of agricultural products so as to take account of the results of the Uruguay Round (⁵) (Table II).

Export arrangements

727. On 15 May the Commission put forward a proposal to revise the Community regime for the control of exports of dual-use goods and technology (Table II) designed to facilitate legal trade, increase checks on exports of sensitive goods and step up action to combat fraud.

Treaties, trade agreements and agreements on mutual recognition

728. On 18 May (⁶) the Council approved the broad lines of the Commission's communication on the management of preferential tariff

---

(¹) OJ C 58, 25.2.1997 and OJ C 177, 11.6.1997 (United States); OJ C 59, 26.2.1997 (Argentina); OJ C 110, 9.4.1997 (Japan); 1997 General Report, point 776.
(²) OJ L 126, 28.4.1998 and Bull. 4-1998, point 1.3.30 (United States 1916 Act); OJ L 346, 22.12.1998 and Bull. 12-1998 (United States, music licensing); OJ L 295, 4.11.1998 and Bull. 10-1998, point 1.3.45 (Argentina); OJ L 159, 3.6.1998 and Bull. 5-1998, point 1.3.40 (Japan).
(³) OJ L 67, 10.3.1994; 1994 General Report, point 1016 (last amended: OJ L 122, 14.5.1997; 1997 General Report, point 777).
(⁴) OJ L 159, 3.6.1998.
(⁵) Twenty-sixth General Report, point 967.
(⁶) Bull. 5-1998, point 1.3.29.

arrangements (¹). Parliament also dealt with the matter in a resolution on 22 October (²).

729. Agreements on mutual recognition in the field of conformity assessment were signed with Canada on 14 May (Table III), the United States on 18 May (Table III), Australia (Table III) on 24 June and New Zealand (Table III) on 26 June. The agreement with Canada entered into force on 1 November and that with the United States on 1 December; those with Australia and New Zealand are due to enter into force on 1 January 1999. An agreement was also reached with Switzerland in December (→ *points 792 and 793*). A mutual recognition agreement with Israel on good laboratory practice was initialled on 24 November (Table III).

Export credits

730. On 7 May the Council adopted Directive 98/29/EC (³) concerning export credit insurance for transactions with medium- and long-term cover. The aim of the directive is to reduce distortion of competition caused by disparities between the various public medium- and long-term export credit insurance systems and to introduce transparency in the field.

731. On 7 May the Council also authorised the Commission to negotiate the introduction of new rules on project finance transactions in the OECD Arrangement on officially supported export credits (Table III). The aim of the resulting agreement, which the Commission on 4 November proposed transposing into Community law (Table II), is to allow flexibility in the rules regarding such transactions as the credit repayments depend on revenues generated by the projects themselves. On 15 July the Commission proposed that the Council approve the new consolidated version of the OECD Arrangement, which incorporates the amendments made since the last overall revision in 1992 (⁴) and includes in particular the new minimum premium provisions negotiated in 1997.

(¹)   COM(97) 402; 1997 General Report, point 778.
(²)   OJ C 341, 9.11.1998; Bull. 10-1998, point 1.3.26.
(³)   OJ L 148, 19.5.1998; Bull. 5-1998, point 1.3.43.
(⁴)   OJ L 44, 22.2.1993; Twenty-sixth General Report, point 985.

Market access

732.   On 8 June the Council reaffirmed its firm commitment to the market access strategy for the European Union outlined in the Commission's 1996 communication ([1]) and, on 24 September, adopted a decision providing Commission initiatives in that context with a legal basis ([2]). The number of specific barriers included in the interactive market access database ([3]) rose from 352 at its launch ([4]) to over 1 170 by the end of the year, and more than 400 others identified by businesses or by the Member States were under investigation by the Commission.

Trade and environment

733.   The Commission continued to play an active role in the work of the WTO Committee on Trade and Environment and of other international bodies, using as a basis the principles contained in its 1996 communication on trade and the environment ([5]). It also proposed that the WTO's Director-General call a high-level meeting in 1999, under the auspices of the organisation, to discuss the issue.

734.   On 30 April, Parliament adopted a resolution on the environmental, health and consumer protection aspects of world trade ([6]) in which it called for a WTO council on the environment and sustainable development to be set up.

Individual sectors

Steel

735.   On 22 December the statistical surveillance of imports originating in other countries by means of automatic licensing arrangements was extended for 1999 ([7]). On the same date the Council also agreed to extend for 1999 the dual licensing system without quantitative restric-

---

([1])   Bull. 6-1998, point 1.4.56.
([2])   Decision 98/552/EC (OJ L 265, 30.9.1998; Bull. 9-1998, point 1.3.43).
([3])   Internet address: http://mkaccdb.eu.int. Access is free and unrestricted.
([4])   1996 General Report, point 721; 1997 General Report, point 783.
([5])   COM(96) 54; 1996 General Report, point 444.
([6])   OJ C 152, 18.5.1998; Bull. 4-1998, point 1.3.17.
([7])   OJ L 354, 30.12.1998.

tions applicable to certain steel products originating in Bulgaria, the Czech Republic, Romania and Slovakia.

736. Under the agreements with Russia and Ukraine covering the period 1997-2001 ([1]), the quantitative limits were altered on 2 October in the light of the Russian and Ukrainian authorities' transfer requests ([2]); steps were taken under the TACIS programme to implement the competition, State aid and environmental protection provisions of the agreements. Autonomous quotas were set for imports of certain steel products from Kazakhstan on 17 June ([3]) and 30 November ([4]) pending the conclusion of negotiations for a similar agreement with that country.

Shipbuilding

737. Since it has not yet been ratified by the United States, the OECD agreement on shipbuilding ([5]) has still not entered into force. Pending implementation of an international agreement, the Council therefore adopted a new regulation on aid to the shipbuilding sector (→ point 226).

Textiles

738. On 1 January all quotas on imports of textiles and clothing from Bulgaria, the Czech Republic, Hungary, Poland, Romania and Slovakia were abolished. Since customs duties had already been removed on 1 January 1997, this step amounted to a total liberalisation of imports from these countries.

739. Agreements on trade in textile products with the Former Yugoslav Republic of Macedonia, Russia and Vietnam were signed on 11 March, 23 July and 10 September respectively (Table III). A similar agreement was initialled with Laos on 16 June (Table III), with the Council deciding to apply it provisionally on 9 November. The Council adopted decisions concluding textiles agreements with Egypt on 18 May (Table III) and with Azerbaijan, Georgia, Kazakhstan, Kyrgyzstan and Turkmenistan on 7 April (Table III). Additional protocols on trade in textile products with Latvia and Lithuania were also adopted on 13 July (Table III).

---

[1]   1997 General Report, point 789.
[2]   OJ L 268, 3.10.1998.
[3]   OJ L 178, 23.6.1998.
[4]   OJ L 332, 8.12.1998.
[5]   1994 General Report, point 1032.

On 24 September the Council authorised the Commission to negotiate the renewal of the 1988 agreement (¹) with China (Table III). The agreement was initialled on 20 November and the Council decided to apply it provisionally on 21 December. On 22 December the Council also introduced new autonomous arrangements for textile products originating in Taiwan (²).

740.   In the absence of denunciation by either party, the textile agreements with the Former Yugoslav Republic of Macedonia, Ukraine, Belarus, Moldova, Georgia, Armenia, Azerbaijan, Turkmenistan, Uzbekistan, Kazakhstan, Kyrgyzstan and Tajikistan were automatically extended until 31 December 1999.

Motor industry

741.   The Community twice invoked the WTO dispute settlement mechanism, requesting consultations with Canada on 17 August regarding the subsidies for car manufacturers meeting minimum local-content requirements, and consultations with India on 6 October regarding its automotive investment arrangements. The WTO's dispute settlement body found in favour of the Community in the case of the Indonesian 'national car' programme (³) and other discriminatory trading measures practised in Indonesia. In order to improve market access for EU automobile exports, the Commission started talks with a number of countries including Poland, Brazil, Colombia and the Republic of Korea.

742.   The Commission continued to ensure correct application of the EEC-Japan arrangement (⁴) for Japanese exports of cars and light commercial vehicles to the EU and the five previously restricted markets before they are fully liberalised at the end of 1999.

743.   It continued to encourage efforts to achieve further international harmonisation of automotive technical standards. On 24 March the Community acceded to the UN-ECE revised 1958 agreement on type approvals for motor vehicle equipment and parts *(→ point 247)*.

(¹)   OJ L 380, 31.12.1988; previous renewal: 1995 General Report, point 767.
(²)   Regulation (EC) No 47/99 (OJ L 12, 16.1.1999; Bull. 12-1998).
(³)   1997 General Report, point 795.
(⁴)   Twenty-fifth General Report, point 1060.

Other products

744. An agreement with Chile on controls on drug precursors was signed on 24 November (Table III).

Services

745. Developments connected with the protocols to the GATS agreements on financial services are covered in the 'World Trade Organisation' section (→ point 712).

746. The Commission has set up a European services network and a European service leaders' group to allow industry to put across its views in the light of the forthcoming round of multilateral trade talks on services. The Community continued to play an active role in the WTO working parties on rules and on professional services.

Section 4

Development policy

Priority activities and objectives

747. The European Union continued to attune its generalised scheme of preferences (GSP) more closely to the objectives of its development policy. The Council improved the conditions offered to countries that adhered to certain international social and environmental conditions, and to the least developed countries, while the Commission took initiatives in different areas of development cooperation, such as combating AIDS and promoting sustainable tourism. Cooperation with non-governmental organisations (NGOs) and decentralised cooperation were given a legal basis.

Overview

748. On 16 January([1]) Parliament underscored the need to make Community development aid more effective, particularly by improving the coordination, coherence and complementarity of operations. The Council adopted guidelines on 9 March designed to strengthen operational coordination between the Community and the Member States and with all developing countries, based on its conclusions of June 1997([2]).

749. The Council, in conclusions of 18 May([3]), examined the progress made in the fight against poverty since its 1993 resolution([4]), and stressed the need to place it at the heart of the Community and the Member States' development cooperation policy. On 30 September, in response to a 1997([5]) Council resolution, the Commission presented a communication([6]) on microfinance and poverty reduction that was endorsed by the Council on 30 November([7]). In a resolution of 1 April, Parliament welcomed the Commission communication on the follow-up to the world summit for social development([8]), calling for the debt of

---

([1]) OJ C 34, 2.2.1998; Bull. 1/2-1998, point 1.4.52.
([2]) 1997 General Report, point 804.
([3]) Bull. 5-1998, point 1.3.48.
([4]) Twenty-seventh General Report, point 807.
([5]) 1997 General Report, point 805.
([6]) COM(1998) 527; Bull. 9-1998, point 1.3.49.
([7]) Bull. 11-1998, point 1.3.40.
([8]) COM(96) 724; 1997 General Report, point 804.

the poorest countries to be reduced and an average 20 % of development aid funds to be allocated to basic social services ([1]). On 2 July it
adopted a resolution encouraging fair trade ([2]).

750. On 22 December the Council adopted a regulation on integrating
gender issues in development cooperation (Table II). In conclusions
adopted on 18 May, it emphasised the importance that it attached to
this issue ([3]).

751. On 30 November ([4]), following up a working paper presented by
the Commission on 11 May ([5]), the Council adopted a resolution on
support for indigenous peoples, putting particular emphasis on the need
to enhance their territorial rights and capacity to manage biological
resources sustainably.

752. On 14 October the Commission adopted a communication on a
strategy to support the development of sustainable tourism in the developing countries ([6]). It recommended promoting cooperation between the
tourist industry, the authorities and civil society in those countries, based
on respect for social and environmental standards. This communication
was welcomed by the Council on 30 November ([7]).

753. In its conclusions of 30 November the Council also underlined
the role of development cooperation in strengthening the peace process
and in conflict prevention and resolution ([8]).

Generalised scheme of preferences (GSP)

754. On 9 March ([9]) the Council extended the coverage of the GSP to
all least developed countries that are not party to the fourth Lomé Convention (→ point 935), thus granting them benefits equivalent to those
enjoyed by countries that are. On 25 May (Table II) it also incorporated
in the GSP special incentive arrangements concerning labour rights and
environmental protection. Countries that can demonstrate that they are
applying certain standards laid down by the International Labour

---

([1]) OJ C 138, 4.5.1998; Bull. 4-1998, point 1.3.33.
([2]) OJ C 226, 20.7.1998; Bull. 7/8-1998, point 1.4.59.
([3]) Bull. 5-1998, point 1.3.49.
([4]) Bull. 11-1998, point 1.3.41.
([5]) Bull. 5-1998, point 1.3.50.
([6]) COM(1998) 563; Bull. 10-1998, point 1.3.46.
([7]) Bull. 11-1998, point 1.3.39.
([8]) Bull. 11-1998, point 1.3.38.
([9]) Regulation (EC) No 602/98 (OJ L 80, 18.3.1998; Bull. 3-1998, point 1.3.43).

Organisation and the International Tropical Timber Organisation will enjoy an increase in preferential margins of 66 % for agricultural products and 100 % for industrial products.

755. On 21 December the Council adopted a regulation ([1]) applying a multiannual scheme of generalised tariff preferences for the period 1 January 1999 to 31 December 2001. It basically extends current provisions by merging them in a single text with a few adjustments, mainly with regard to the special 'drugs' arrangements.

International commodity agreements

756. The Council of the International Coffee Organisation met twice, in May and in September. It discussed the future of international cooperation on coffee in view of the expiry of the current agreement on 1 October 1999.

757. On 6 July the Council adopted a decision concluding the 1993 International Cocoa Agreement (Table III). The Council of the International Cocoa Organisation met in March and September, when it examined problems stemming from the winding-down of the buffer stock, which was completed at the end of the year.

758. The Commission participated in the May and November sessions of the Council of the International Agreement on Tropical Timber, which approved a range of measures and projects aimed at promoting sustainable development of tropical forests and improving the terms of trade in tropical timber.

759. In April the Commission participated in the annual meeting of the Council of the International Jute Organisation, at which the prospects for renegotiating the International Jute Agreement and the appointment of the Organisation's new executive director were discussed.

North-South cooperation on drugs and drug abuse

760. A special session of the United Nations General Assembly on drugs held in New York from 8 to 10 June concluded with the adoption

---

([1]) Regulation (EC) No 2820/98 (OJ L 357, 30.12.1998; Bull. 12-1998).

of a political declaration and specific cooperation measures (^{1}). The Commission adopted a communication on 8 January in preparation for the meeting (^{2}).

761. North-South cooperation measures against drugs and drug abuse, to which ECU 8.9 million was allocated in 1998, were implemented for the first time under Regulation (EC) No 2046/97 (^{3}). Measures covered institution building, technical aid for alternative development, and efforts to reduce both drug supply and demand and to prevent money laundering. Special initiatives were put in hand in central Asia, Latin America, the Caribbean and central Africa and a joint EU-SADC conference on the fight against drugs *(→ point 948)* was held in Gabarone, Botswana, in February.

North-South cooperation on health issues

762. On 3 July the Commission adopted a communication on increased solidarity to confront AIDS in developing countries, in which it describes the EU's current efforts to fight AIDS and examines new instruments and measures which could be implemented (^{4}).

763. Aid for the health sector in the developing countries amounted in 1998 to about ECU 265 million. Evaluations of previous years' projects confirmed that priority should go to prevention, human resources, the organisation of health systems and coordination with other donors.

Cooperation on eradicating anti-personnel mines

764. In implementing the resolution on anti-personnel mines adopted by the Council in November 1996 (^{5}), the Commission devised an action programme designed to coordinate all its operations more closely. It also continued to promote the development of new detection and clearance systems and with the Member States it set up a database for coordinating measures to eradicate anti-personnel mines.

(^{1})   Bull. 6-1998, point 1.4.59.
(^{2})   COM(97) 670; Bull. 1/2-1998, point 1.4.54.
(^{3})   OJ L 287, 21.10.1997; 1997 General Report, point 814.
(^{4})   COM(1998) 407; Bull. 7/8-1998, point 1.4.61.
(^{5})   1996 General Report, point 739.

International forms

United Nations Conference on Trade and Development (Unctad)

765.   Unctad continued to implement the institutional reforms approved at its conference in Midrand, South Africa, in 1996 (^{1}). The Commission participated fully in this work and played a particularly active role in the annual meeting of the Trade and Development Board and its committees, which discussed globalisation, competitiveness, investment, competition and the future of the least developed countries.

United Nations Food and Agriculture Organisation (FAO)

766.   A member of the FAO since 1991 (^{2}), the Community continued to take part in all the agency's activities. It presented a follow-up report on the application of the action plan adopted at the World Food Summit in 1996 (^{3}) and was also a driving force in the negotiations for international agreements under the aegis of the FAO, in particular the agreement on prior informed consent signed in September *(→ point 489)*.

World Food Programme (WFP)

767.   Products allocated to the WFP by the European Union in 1998 were worth ECU 100 million, which corresponds to over 250 000 tonnes of food products, including 217 500 tonnes of cereals.

United Nations Educational, Scientific and Cultural Organisation (Unesco)

768.   The Community financed Unesco education projects as part of rehabilitation programmes in the ACP countries, notably in the Nugal region of Somalia.

(^{1})   1996 General Report, point 742.
(^{2})   Twenty-fifth General Report, point 994.
(^{3})   1996 General Report, point 746.

EC Investment Partners (ECIP)

769.   Under Regulation (EC) No 213/96 on the implementation of the EC Investment Partners financial instrument([1]), ECU 28.4 million was allocated to schemes designed to promote investments of mutual interest, notably in the shape of joint ventures between Community and developing country operators. The Economic and Social Committee adopted an own-initiative opinion on 1 July on EC instruments for investment support in third countries, recommending that they be incorporated into a world strategy([2]).

Cooperation through non-governmental organisations (NGOs) and decentralised cooperation

770.   On 17 July the Council adopted two regulations giving a legal basis to the budget headings on cooperation with NGOs (Table II) and decentralised cooperation (Table II). Appropriations earmarked for those forms of cooperation amounted in 1998 to ECU 180 million and ECU 4 million respectively, and paid for 695 cooperation projects with NGOs (of which 538 in developing countries, 142 public awareness campaigns in Europe) and 15 decentralised cooperation projects. On 17 March the Commission adopted its 1996 annual report on cooperation with NGOs([3]).

Protecting the environment

771.   Projects worth ECU 16.2 million to protect the environment in the developing countries were implemented under Regulation (EC) No 722/97([4]), and 34 projects for the conservation of tropical forests were funded in Brazil, India, Mexico and elsewhere to a value of ECU 45.2 million.

---

[1]   OJ L 28, 6.2.1996; 1996 General Report, point 754.
[2]   OJ C 284, 14.9.1998; Bull. 7/8-1998, point 1.4.62.
[3]   COM(1998) 127; Bull. 3-1998, point 1.3.45.
[4]   OJ L 108, 25.4.1997; 1997 General Report, point 828.

Aid for population policies and programmes

772. Pilot schemes and research activities worth ECU 8 million were funded under Regulation (EC) No 1484/97 on aid for population policies and programmes in the developing countries([1]).

Rehabilitation aid

773. ECU 73.4 million was granted under Regulation (EC) No 2258/96([2]) on rehabilitation and reconstruction operations in the developing countries, of which ECU 53 million for ACP countries, ECU 5.8 million for Asian and Latin American countries and ECU 14.6 million for countries in central Asia and the Caucasus. The priorities remained health, basic infrastructure, the revival of agricultural production and economic and social reintegration. The Commission carried out an evaluation of operations in previous years which confirmed their overall effectiveness but also revealed the need to increase the participation of women and NGOs and improve coordination.

Food aid and food security

774. The appropriations available in the 1998 budget for food and food security operations in developing countries amounted to ECU 530 million, of which ECU 412 million for the purchase of products and for support schemes and the foreign currency facility, and ECU 118 million for logistics. The Commission also made a special food aid allocation of ECU 77 million for the countries affected by El Niño. The breakdown of this aid is given in Table 17.

Aid for refugees

775. Two assistance schemes for refugees, returnees and displaced persons, one in Liberia and the other in Guinea, were approved under Article 255 of the fourth Lomé Convention, for a total of ECU 2.5 million. Since the Convention entered into force, 75 schemes have been approved under Article 255 for a total of ECU 88 million.

([1]) OJ L 202, 30.7.1997; 1997 General Report, point 805.
([2]) OJ L 306, 28.11.1996; 1996 General Report, point 761.

TABLE 17

Food security and food aid programme, 1998

Region or organisation	Cereals (tonnes)	Oil (tonnes)	Sugar, milk and pulses (tonnes)	Other products (million ECU)	Cost of products (including transport) (million ECU)	Inputs and tools (million ECU)	Support action + storage + information systems (million ECU)	Exchange facilities (million ECU)	Technical assistance, follow-up (million ECU)
Direct aid									
Europe	61 150	500				9.00	30.53	5.00	0.50
Africa					16.38			23.00	7.57
Caribbean							2.00		
Latin America							6.00	27.60	0.80
Asia	170 000	3 000		1.80	32.54	8.10	8.10		2.10
Mediterranean and Middle East							2.00	10.00	2.00
Caucasus								38.00	2.00
Central Asia								8.00	0.50
Total direct aid	231 150	3 500		1.80	48.92	17.10	48.63	111.60	15.47
Indirect aid									
Various NGOs	5 000	500	1 600	1.50	5.00	0.50	54.50		
Euronaid	35 000	1 500	5 500	10.00	27.74	2.50			
WFP	217 500	12 000	1 700	10.20	100.00				
ICRC	13 500	1 500	300	2.00	8.05	1.95			
UNRWA		1 715	4 690		5.55		6.80		
Total indirect aid	271 000	17 215	13 790	23.70	146.34	4.95	61.30		
El Niño allocation	80 000			11.00	37.30	9.70	28.00		2.00
Monitoring and technical assistance									36.60
Grand total	582 150	20 715	13 790	36.50	232.56	31.75	137.93	111.60	54.07

Section 5

Humanitarian aid

776.   *Responding to crisis situations wherever they occurred, the European Union was once again the world's leading donor of humanitarian aid. In financial terms, Bosnia and Herzegovina and Africa's Great Lakes region remained the main spheres of operations. Acting through ECHO, the European Community Humanitarian Office, the Commission continued to streamline procedures to make aid more effective and its activities more consistent.*

Overall strategy

777.   In line with the approach set out in its 1996 communication ([1]), the Commission developed the linkage between emergency aid, rehabilitation and development, setting up a number of inter-departmental task forces. With the accent on coordination not only among its own departments but also with Member States, other leading donors and international and non-governmental organisations, it strengthened links with UN agencies, both in crisis situations and in overall planning, and developed its dialogue and cooperation with the Western European Union (→ *point 703*). In a resolution adopted on 16 January ([2]) on Special Report No 2/97 of the Court of Auditors ([3]), Parliament called on the Commission to make full use of its powers of initiative for coordination.

778.   Man-made disasters continued to account for the majority of situations in which the Commission took action through ECHO, which concentrated on meeting the immediate needs of victims while seeking to reduce tension between factions to prevent crises from worsening and allow short-term reconstruction. Besides cases of open warfare, ECHO operated in many situations of chronic humanitarian need or simmering unrest. Where a country's overall structures and infrastructure were shaky, Commission humanitarian aid in the form of medical programmes, rehabilitation of health-care infrastructure and mine-clearance was targeted on the most vulnerable. ECHO also stepped in with assistance in a number of neglected crises (Iraq, Afghanistan, southern Sudan, Liberia, Somalia and Sierra Leone) from which other donors had with-

---

([1])   COM(96) 153; 1996 General Report, point 769.
([2])   OJ C 34, 2.2.1998; Bull. 1/2-1998, point 1.4.58.
([3])   1997 General Report, point 840.

drawn. Ms Bonino visited Sierra Leone and southern Sudan herself. The Commission continued to fund short-term aid and rehabilitation programmes for refugees and displaced persons.

779. Following the approach laid down in 1996 ([1]), the Commission also financed the first disaster prevention and preparedness action plans (Dipecho) in south-east Asia, Bangladesh, Central America and the Caribbean, for which funding totalled ECU 6.9 million. It also financed individual projects in other parts of the world and studied the feasibility of extending Dipecho to them (ECU 1.1 million).

780. In addition to regular and ad hoc evaluations of operations, the Commission continued its overall evaluation of humanitarian aid granted in the periods 1991-96 ([2]) and from 1996 onwards under Regulation (EC) No 1257/96 ([3]), and started looking into the use of performance indicators. On 13 March it adopted a new model designed to simplify the framework partnership contract and make it more flexible while maintaining an adequate level of control ([4]). On 14 May the Commission adopted a working paper on security for relief workers and humanitarian space ([5]) and organised a seminar on the subject in Lisbon in March together with the International Committee of the Red Cross. Another seminar was held in London in April on the subject of humanitarian ethics. In the area of education and training, ECHO continued to support the humanitarian aid diploma run by NOHA (Network on Humanitarian Assistance) ([6]) under the Socrates programme (→ points 327 et seq.), for which it financed the publication of teaching modules ([7]) and various training programmes of interest to its partners. In the interests of visibility and transparency, ECHO also launched a number of publicity campaigns (e.g. 'A flower for the women of Kabul') in close cooperation with the Member States and its partners and awarded the third ECHO prize for the best television or radio report on humanitarian action. Other events sponsored by ECHO included debates in various EU capital cities, exhibitions on themes such as 'Artists at war' or anti-personnel mines, 'Children of War' day and a 'European Solidarity' festival in Barcelona. It continued publication of the *ECHO Annual Review*, *ECHO News* magazine and the *ECHO Files* reports on specific crises.

([1])   1996 General Report, point 770.
([2])   1997 General Report, point 838.
([3])   OJ L 163, 2.7.1996; 1996 General Report, point 768.
([4])   Bull. 3-1998, point 1.3.47.
([5])   SEC(1998) 797; Bull. 5-1998, point 1.3.5.
([6])   1994 General Report, point 982.
([7])   Obtainable from the Office for Official Publications of the European Communities.

781. On 15 July the Commission adopted its 1997 annual report on humanitarian aid (¹).

Humanitarian aid operations (²)

782. Over the year the Commission granted a total of ECU 517 million in humanitarian aid through ECHO. Added to aid from the Member States, this figure once again made the European Union the world's top humanitarian aid donor. Much of the aid went to refugees and displaced persons, especially in Africa's Great Lakes region.

783. The Commission gave a total of ECU 123.1 million in humanitarian aid to former Yugoslavia, most of it (ECU 88 million) to Bosnia and Herzegovina where the focus of aid has gradually shifted to rehabilitation and reconstruction so as to enable the return of refugees and displaced persons. Aid for returning refugees continued in Croatia (ECU 6.6 million), while the Red Cross took over responsibility for direct food aid. An emergency response was mounted to deal with displaced persons in Kosovo (ECU 17.5 million), which Ms Bonino visited in August (³). The remainder of the aid to the Federal Republic of Yugoslavia (ECU 7.5 million) was mainly targeted at refugees from Croatia and Bosnia and Herzegovina.

784. A total of ECU 11 million in humanitarian aid was granted to Albania (for the health system and the most vulnerable sections of the population), including ECU 1.5 million for Kosovar refugees. ECHO also provided help for the most vulnerable sections of the population in Bulgaria (ECU 1.5 million), those affected by flooding in Romania (ECU 1 million) and Slovakia (ECU 500 000) and the victims of earthquakes in Turkey (ECU 500 000).

785. In the Mediterranean and the Middle East, ECHO provided ECU 17.2 million in food aid to Sahrawi refugees in Algeria, who still depend on international aid despite the prospects for a new repatriation plan. Other operations included ECU 6 million in medical aid to Palestinians in the Occupied and Autonomous Territories, ECU 1 million for Palestinian refugees in Jordan and ECU 600 000 for those in Syria, ECU 4.3 million, mainly in medical aid, for Lebanon's poor (including Palestinian

---

(¹) COM(1998) 448; Bull. 7/8-1998, point 1.4.68.
(²) For details, see monthly tables in the *Bulletin of the European Union* (humanitarian aid section) and the 1997 annual report on humanitarian aid.
(³) Bull. 7/8-1998, point 1.4.69.

refugees) and ECU 1.57 million in aid to Yemen's health sector. Operations to provide nutritional support to children, relief to victims of anti-personnel landmines and assistance for the rehabilitation of the medical/health sector were launched under an ECU 14 million aid plan for Iraq.

786. Humanitarian aid to the independent States of the former Soviet Union totalled ECU 33.3 million. In central Asia, ECHO was mainly involved in Tajikistan (ECU 16.7 million to civil war victims) and Kyrgyzstan (ECU 1.8 million). Humanitarian aid to Armenia (ECU 1.6 million), Azerbaijan (ECU 4.5 million) and Georgia (ECU 6.5 million) was increasingly replaced by rehabilitation and development aid better suited to their needs, although ECU 500 000 was granted in emergency aid following the earthquake in Azerbaijan. ECU 900 000 went to Russia but operations were hampered by the worsening security situation in the North Caucasus, although ad hoc activities (including anti-tuberculosis campaigns) were organised elsewhere in the country. Relief for victims of the Chernobyl disaster in Ukraine (ECU 300 000) and Belarus (ECU 300 000) also continued.

787. In Asia, ECHO provided ECU 19.8 million for victims of the war and natural disasters in Afghanistan although some aid was suspended as humanitarian operations could not be carried out in Kabul. Other operations included: ECU 8.45 million for flood victims in Bangladesh; ECU 1.2 million for displaced persons and flood victims in Burma (Myanmar); ECU 10 million for victims of fighting in Cambodia; ECU 4.73 million for victims of natural disasters in China; ECU 4.66 million for victims of the humanitarian crisis in North Korea; ECU 500 000 for drought victims in India; ECU 1.4 million for flood victims in India and Nepal; ECU 2.5 million for those affected by fires and drought in the Irian Jaya region of Indonesia; ECU 890 000 for drought victims in Laos; ECU 1.7 million to victims of the drought and of typhoon Babs in the Philippines; ECU 1 million for the victims of civil war in Sri Lanka; ECU 4.6 million for Burmese refugees and displaced persons in Thailand; and ECU 1.1 million to help the victims of four typhoons in Vietnam. A further ECU 1 million went to help tackle an epidemic of dengue fever in Cambodia, Laos, the Philippines and Vietnam.

788. In Latin America, following disasters due to El Niño, ECHO granted ECU 2.104 million to Ecuador, ECU 2.94 million to Bolivia, ECU 200 000 to Venezuela, ECU 1 million to Brazil, ECU 1 million to Argentina and Paraguay, ECU 300 000 to Uruguay and ECU 4.354 million to Peru. The figure for Peru included relief for those displaced by terrorism. Aid for displaced persons also went to Colombia (ECU 6.874

million), Mexico (ECU 2.25 million) and Guatemala (ECU 1.41 million for returnees from Mexico). Humanitarian relief to Cuba continued (ECU 9 million in health and food aid), while grants of ECU 1.56 million and ECU 1.385 million were made to Nicaragua and Honduras respectively, to help prevent epidemics among vulnerable groups. A total of ECU 16.3 million was also allocated to help victims of hurricane Mitch in the Central American countries of Guatemala, Honduras, Nicaragua and El Salvador, visited by Ms Bonino in November ([1]).

789.   Humanitarian aid to the African, Caribbean and Pacific countries totalled more than ECU 162 million. The largest allocations were ECU 76 million for the Great Lakes region (Rwanda, Burundi, Tanzania, Congo-Brazzaville and the Democratic Republic of the Congo), more than ECU 18 million for Angola and ECU 36.8 million for Sudan where an acute food crisis started in June. ECHO also allocated aid to Ethiopia (ECU 2.6 million in food aid via the World Food Programme) plus a further ECU 5.64 million for the Ethiopia-Eritrea crisis, Somalia (ECU 4 million) and Guinea-Bissau (ECU 2.8 million). Guinea and Liberia received ECU 2.7 million and ECU 760 000 respectively, to aid refugees from Sierra Leone, while ECU 6.5 million went to Sierra Leone itself to help displaced persons. Chad and Liberia received ECU 1.15 million and ECU 200 000 respectively, to tackle epidemics of cholera and meningitis, while ECU 1.1 million went to Madagascar to fight locusts. A total of ECU 175 000 went to Papua New Guinea, Kenya, Somalia and Mozambique following flooding caused by El Niño. Mali received ECU 5 million and Niger ECU 2 million from ECHO for the final phase of a programme designed to resettle Tuareg and Moor returnees and local people and help them gear up to development activities. ECHO Flight kept up its airborne operations in the Horn of Africa and extended its coverage to West Africa.

([1])   Bull. 11-1998, point 1.3.44.

Section 6

European Economic Area, relations with the EFTA countries

European Economic Area (EEA)

790.   The EEA Council met on 9 June ([1]) and on 6 October ([2]) in Luxembourg. In addition to the functioning of the EEA Agreement (including the EEA financial mechanism ([3]), issues relating to European integration and EU enlargement were also discussed. The results of scrutinising the *acquis* in the applicant countries received special attention. The Joint Parliamentary Committee met in Vaduz (Liechtenstein) in May and in Luxembourg in November.

791.   Significant progress was made with incorporating the Community *acquis* into the EEA, particularly in the veterinary field (in which around 650 instruments were incorporated into the agreement). Liechtenstein continued to apply the EEA safeguard clause on the free movement of persons ([4]).

Relations with the EFTA countries

792.   The bilateral negotiations with Switzerland on the free movement of persons, research, public procurement, agriculture, transport (land and air) and mutual recognition of conformity assessment ended in 1998, and received the overall agreement of the Council on 10 December ([5]). The conclusion of these seven agreements (which was welcomed by the Vienna European Council ([5]) will add considerably to EU-Swiss cooperation and revive the process of building closer relations following Switzerland's rejection of EEA membership in 1992 ([5]).

793.   The agreement on free movement of persons (Table III) will give EU and Swiss citizens access to the labour market and non-discriminatory right of establishment. Once a transitional period has elapsed, EU

([1])   Bull. 6-1998, point 1.4.68.
([2])   Bull. 10-1998, point 1.3.56.
([3])   The Commission published its annual report on the EEA financial mechanism (COM(1998) 758) in December.
([4])   1997 General Report, point 868.
([5])   Bull. 12-1998.

citizens will have the right to work and settle in Switzerland under the same rules that apply in the EU. The agreement on research (Table III) provides for Switzerland to participate fully in the fifth framework programme (→ *points 285 et seq.*), making a financial contribution in proportion to its GNP. The two parties also agreed to reciprocal liberalisation in public procurement, with Switzerland having to set up an independent surveillance authority and introduce appeal facilities equivalent to those operating in the EU (Table III). The agreement on agriculture (Table III) provides preferential access to the Swiss market for many EU goods. The agreement on land transport provides for Switzerland to increase the current 28-tonne weight limit for trucks on Swiss roads gradually to 40 tonnes, in tandem with steps to encourage rail transit across the Alps. The agreement on air transport extends Europe's skies to Switzerland, introducing unlimited traffic rights between any EU airport and any Swiss airport. Switzerland will also apply EU competition rules (Table III). The agreement on mutual recognition of conformity assessment will make trade much easier (Table III).

794.   The Joint Committee set up by the free-trade agreement with Switzerland (¹) met in October. In July the Council authorised the Commission to negotiate the terms for the participation of Norway and Iceland in the implementation and development of the Schengen *acquis* (→ *point 975).* On 25 November the Commission adopted a communication on the northern dimension of the European Union (→ *point 877).*

(¹)   1995 General Report, point 198.

Section 7

Enlargement

795. In line with the decisions taken at the Luxembourg European Council (^{1}) to launch the enlargement process, the first meeting of the European conference was held in March. The accession process for the 10 applicant countries of central Europe and Cyprus also got under way in March, as did the negotiations with Cyprus, Hungary, Poland, Estonia, the Czech Republic and Slovenia.

796. The first meeting of the European conference, which brings together the Member States of the European Union and those European States aspiring to accede to it and sharing its values and objectives, took place in London on 12 March (^{2}). It was attended at Head of State or Government level by the 15 Member States, the Commission (represented by Mr Santer), Cyprus and the 10 applicant countries of central Europe. Turkey had been invited to participate, but had declined. It was agreed that the priority areas to be addressed by the conference would be transnational organised crime, the environment, foreign and security policy, competitive economies and regional cooperation. There was a subsequent first ministerial-level meeting in Luxembourg on 6 October (^{3}) which focused on the fight against organised crime, the environmental aspects of regional cooperation and the situation in Kosovo. Apart from the 15 Member States, the Commission, Cyprus and the other 10 applicant countries, this meeting was also attended by Switzerland. The Vienna European Council in December reiterated the invitation to Switzerland to become an associate member of the conference (^{4}).

797. The accession process for the 10 applicant countries of central Europe and Cyprus was launched in Brussels on 30 March at a meeting that brought together the foreign ministers of the 15 Member States and the 11 applicant countries. Mr Van den Broek represented the Commission (^{5}).

798. On 31 March, also in Brussels, six bilateral ministerial meetings were held to mark the start of accession negotiations with Cyprus, Hun-

---

(^{1})   1997 General Report, point 865; Bull. 12-1997, points I.3 and I.6.
(^{2})   Bull. 3-1998, point 1.3.50.
(^{3})   Bull. 10-1998, point 1.3.53.
(^{4})   Bull. 12-1998.
(^{5})   Bull. 3-1998, point 1.3.51.

gary, Poland, Estonia, the Czech Republic and Slovenia ([1]). In each meeting the EU set out the basis of the negotiations: the acceptance and effective implementation by the applicants of the *acquis communautaire* (established Community law and practice) at the time of accession — though certain technical adjustments and, in exceptional cases, transitional measures could be negotiated.

799.   On 3 April the Commission embarked on a screening of the *acquis,* which was divided up for the purpose into 31 chapters. This exercise was conducted in parallel with the six countries with which negotiations had been formally opened on 31 March, and with the five with which negotiations had not yet been started (Bulgaria, Latvia, Lithuania, Romania and Slovakia). The main aim of the multilateral approach taken with the second group is to explain the *acquis* to facilitate its incorporation into the countries' legislation in preparation for later negotiations. The screening exercise with Cyprus, Hungary, Poland, Estonia, the Czech Republic and Slovenia also involves joint briefing sessions on the content of the *acquis,* but these are followed up with bilateral sessions aimed at identifying, for each of the six, those aspects that pose difficulties in terms of acceptance or implementation. This should help with the smooth running of the actual negotiations.

800.   On the basis of a progress report on the screening presented by the Commission on 30 September ([2]), the Council decided on 5 October ([3]) to convene accession conferences at ministerial level ([4]) in order to get down to negotiations with Cyprus, Hungary, Poland, Estonia, the Czech Republic and Slovenia on those chapters that had already been covered. The meetings took place on 10 November and involved discussions on science and research, telecommunications and information technology, education and training, culture and the audiovisual media, industrial policy, small and medium-sized enterprises and the common foreign and security policy. It was agreed that for three chapters (science and research, education and training, SMEs) further negotiations with the central European countries were not necessary at this stage; the same applied to Cyprus for five chapters (the three aforementioned, plus culture and the audiovisual media and industrial policy). The applicant countries made a number of requests for transitional periods for certain aspects of the chapters on telecommunications (Cyprus, Hungary and Poland), industrial policy (Hungary) and the audiovisual media (Czech

---

([1])   Bull. 3-1998, point 1.3.52.
([2])   Bull. 9-1998, point 1.3.58.
([3])   Bull. 10-1998, point 1.3.52.
([4])   Bull. 11-1998, point 1.3.50.

Republic and Slovenia). The Vienna European Council in December welcomed the positive start to the negotiations proper (¹).

801.   Under the enhanced pre-accession strategy defined by the Luxembourg European Council (²), accession partnerships were established with the 10 central European countries *(→ point 806).* In addition, a pre-accession pact on organised crime was adopted with these 10 countries and with Cyprus *(→ point 976),* and two joint meetings between the Ministers for Justice and Home Affairs of the 11 applicant countries and the 15 Member States were held in Brussels in May (³) and September (⁴). On 13 October the Council authorised the Commission to negotiate additional protocols to the association agreements with the 11 applicants so that they could be involved in the fifth framework programme for research and technological development (Table III). For its part, the Economic and Social Committee announced on 25 March that it intended to organise annual hearings with economic and social interest groups in the applicant countries (⁵). Further information on the implementation of the pre-accession strategy with the central European countries and with Cyprus can be found later in this chapter, in Section 8 ('Countries of central Europe' and Section 9 'The Mediterranean and the Middle East') *(→   points 806 et seq. and 830 et seq.).*

802.   On 4 March the Commission outlined its initial approach for implementing a strategy to prepare Turkey for accession by bringing it closer to the EU in all spheres. It also adopted, on 21 October, proposals for regulations to deepen customs union between the Community and Turkey and to implement measures promoting the country's economic and social development *(→ point 836).*

803.   Malta reactivated its membership application on 10 September, and on 5 October the Council invited the Commission to update the opinion it had originally issued in 1993 *(→ point 835).*

804.   On 4 November the Commission approved evaluation reports plus a more general composite paper on the progress made by each of the applicant countries towards accession (⁶). In accordance with the

---

(¹)   Bull. 12-1998.
(²)   1997 General Report, point 865; Bull. 12-1997, point I.5. *11-22.*
(³)   Bull. 5-1998, point 1.3.59.
(⁴)   Bull. 9-1998, point 1.3.59.
(⁵)   OJ C 157, 25.5.1998; Bull. 3-1998, point 1.3.53.
(⁶)   COM(1998) 700 to 712; Bull. 11-1998, point 1.3.49; Bull. 12-1998; Supplements 4/98 to 16/98 — Bull.

conclusions of the Cardiff Council in June (¹), these reports cover the 10 central European countries, Cyprus and Turkey. The report on Turkey is based on Article 28 of the association agreement and on the conclusions of the Luxembourg European Council (²). The Commission noted differing degrees of progress in the applicant countries. It saw no need to make recommendations on how the negotiations should be conducted or whether they should be extended but it drew attention to the notable progress made by Latvia — with which it should be possible to propose starting negotiations before the end of 1999 if the pace of reform were maintained — and by Lithuania. The Commission also suggested that the new situation in Slovakia following the elections there meant that negotiations could probably start once it was clear that the country met the political and economic criteria. On the other hand, it detected a worrying slowdown in the rate at which the *acquis* was being transposed and applied in the Czech Republic and Slovenia. The reports were received favourably by the Council on 7 December (³), and by the Vienna European Council (³). For its part, Parliament adopted resolutions on 3 December on the membership applications of Bulgaria, Latvia, Lithuania, Romania and Slovakia, and on the situation in those countries (⁴).

(¹)   Bull. 6-1998, point I.21. 64.
(²)   Bull. 12-1997, point I.6.
(³)   Bull. 12-1998.
(⁴)   OJ C 398, 21.12.1998; Bull. 12-1998.

Section 8

Relations with central European countries

Priority activities and objectives

805. In line with the decisions taken at the Luxembourg European Council in December 1997, the process of accession of the 10 applicant countries of central Europe was launched in March and accession negotiations with Hungary, Poland, Estonia, the Czech Republic and Slovenia opened in the same month (→ points 795 et seq.). In parallel, the accession partnerships — the central element of the enhanced pre-accession strategy defined by the Council — were established, and the instruments for the reinforcement of pre-accession assistance were determined. More Community programmes were opened up to the countries of central Europe.

Pre-accession strategy ([1])

Accession partnerships

806. On 16 March the Council defined the overall framework for the accession partnerships (Table II). These partnerships, a fundamental part of the enhanced pre-accession strategy adopted at Luxembourg ([2]), aim to mobilise within a single framework all the forms of assistance to the applicant countries of central Europe. On this basis, the Council adopted on 30 March the 10 decisions ([3]) establishing the principles and priorities, intermediate objectives and conditions of each of the 10 partnerships, while the Commission presented the detailed content ([4]). Each partnership establishes specific priorities and intermediate objectives, sets out the main instruments of technical and financial assistance and programming details, and contains arrangements on conditionality (accord-

([1]) For information on the European Conference, the launch of the accession process, the opening and subsequent course of the negotiations, the screening of the *acquis communautaire* and the Commission's evaluation of the progress made by the applicant countries on the way to accession, see Section 7 ('Enlargement') of this chapter *(→ points 795 et seq.)*.
([2]) 1997 General Report, point 865; Bull. 12-1997, point I.5.
([3]) Council Decisions 98/259/EC to 98/268/EC (OJ L 121, 23.4.1998; Bull. 3-1998, point 1.3.66).
([4]) Bull. 3-1998, point 1.3.67.

ing to progress made in meeting the criteria established by the Copenhagen Council (¹), monitoring and review.

807. To back up these partnerships and support the applicant countries, on 31 March the Commission adopted a communication on measures in the nuclear sector which also applied to the new independent States *(→ point 538)*. Communications were also adopted on the restructuring of the steel industry (7 April) (²) and on environmental aspects of the accession strategies (20 May) (³). In the latter, approved in outline by the Council on 24 September (⁴), the Committee of the Regions on 19 November (⁵) and the Economic and Social Committee on 2 December (⁶), the Commission stressed that complete integration of the environmental *acquis* would be one of the biggest challenges of accession for the central European applicants. It laid down priority areas for the approximation process in this field and described the contribution that EU instruments and assistance programmes could make.

Europe Agreements

808. The Europe Agreements with Estonia, Latvia and Lithuania came into force on 1 February (Table III). The Council concluded the Europe Agreement with Slovenia on 21 December (Table III). It also concluded protocols adapting the Europe Agreements to take account of the accession of Austria, Finland and Sweden to the EU, and of the results of the Uruguay Round. The Estonia, Latvia and Lithuania protocols were concluded on 18 May (Table III), the Romania and Slovakia protocols on 5 October (Table III) and those for Hungary and the Czech Republic on 22 October (Table III). A veterinary and phytosanitary protocol to the agreement with the Czech Republic was signed in July and came into force on 20 August (Table III).

809. The Association Councils set up by these agreements took several decisions enabling the central European countries to take part in Community programmes — specifically, allowing Romania to participate in the financial instrument for the environment (LIFE); Bulgaria, Estonia, Hungary, Latvia, Lithuania, Poland, the Czech Republic and Romania in Community programmes in the field of culture; Poland, Slovakia, Esto-

(¹) Twenty-seventh General Report, point 646; Bull. 6-1993, point I.13.
(²) COM(1998) 220; Bull. 4-1998, point 1.3.39.
(³) COM(1998) 294; Bull. 5-1998, point 1.3.63.
(⁴) Bull. 9-1998, point 1.3.63.
(⁵) Bull. 11-1998, point 1.3.54.
(⁶) Bull. 12-1998.

nia, Latvia, Lithuania and the Czech Republic in education, training and youth programmes; Bulgaria in the programme for youth; Hungary in the equal opportunities programme and four programmes in the field of public health; Bulgaria and Estonia in some of these public health programmes; Bulgaria, Estonia, Hungary, Poland, the Czech Republic, Romania and Slovakia in programmes for SMEs, and Bulgaria, Poland, the Czech Republic and Slovakia in the programme promoting the efficient use of energy (SAVE II) (Table II).

810.   Meetings of the Association Councils and Committees and of the Parliamentary Association Committees also set up by the Europe Agreements are covered in the subsection 'Bilateral relations' (→ *points 816 et seq.)* in this section. The remit of these bodies was broadened to include the monitoring of the partner countries' progress in implementing the accession partnerships.

Financial and technical assistance

811.   As part of Agenda 2000, the Commission adopted three proposals on 18 March which were designed to step up pre-accession aid, in line with the recommendations of the Luxembourg European Council([1]). The proposed regulations would establish an instrument for structural policies for pre-accession (ISPA) and an agricultural pre-accession instrument and coordinate them with the PHARE programme *(→ point 7).*

812.   On 15 June the Commission laid down guidelines([2]) for the implementation of the PHARE programme([3]) in 1998 and 1999. They follow the course charted in 1997([4]) and take account of the enhanced pre-accession strategy set out in Agenda 2000 and the priorities and principles identified in the accession partnerships. All PHARE activities in the applicant countries will be harnessed to the pre-accession requirements identified in the partnerships, with 30 % of the aid going to institution-building (with a new emphasis on twinning agreements between institutions in Member States and partner countries) and 70 % to instruments for reducing sectoral, regional and structural imbalances in the applicant countries' economies. The new guidelines should also rationalise implementation and speed up the execution of PHARE operations.

([1])   1997 General Report, point 865; Bull. 12-1997, point I.5.
([2])   SEC(1998) 1012; Bull. 6-1998, point 1.4.72.
([3])   Twenty-third General Report, point 786; 1997 General Report, points 882 et seq.
([4])   COM(97) 112; 1997 General Report, point 882.

813. 1998 saw the creation of new instruments under PHARE. These included a large-scale infrastructure facility, a support mechanism for SMEs, a catch-up facility for the five countries yet to start negotiations, and a special programme to prepare the ground for EU structural policies. The Commission also agreed with the World Bank and the EBRD (→ *points 94 et seq.)* that their aid to the central European countries should henceforth focus on preparations for accession.

814. The total PHARE budget for 1998 rose to ECU 1 308.4 million. The operations financed (in million ECU) were:

— national programmes: 579.5, of which Albania 30.5; Bulgaria 68; Czech Republic 27; Estonia 21; Hungary 77; Latvia 21; Lithuania 32; Poland 125; Romania 117; Slovakia 50; Slovenia 10;

— cross-border cooperation: 180;

— multi-country programmes 349.7;

— rehabilitation of former Yugoslavia: 150;

— other 49.2.

815. On 24 March the Commission adopted its annual report on the PHARE programme for 1996 ([1]). The Technical Assistance Information Exchange Office (TAIEX) ([2]) developed its range of services to the central European countries.

Bilateral relations

816. The EC-Bulgaria Association Committee and Association Council met in Brussels on 1 and 27 October respectively ([3]). The Joint Parliamentary Committee convened in Sofia from 28 to 30 June. The Bulgarian President, Mr Petar Stoyanov, visited the Commission on 8 July ([4]), followed by the Prime Minister, Mr Ivan Kostov, on 8 October ([5]). Ms Gradin went to Bulgaria in April ([6]), and Mr Van den Broek in September ([7]).

---

[1]   COM(1998) 178; Bull. 3-1998, point 1.3.73.
[2]   1996 General Report, point 797.
[3]   Bull. 10-1998, point 1.3.67.
[4]   Bull. 7/8-1998, point 1.4.78.
[5]   Bull. 10-1998, point 1.3.68.
[6]   Bull. 4-1998, point 1.3.45.
[7]   Bull. 9-1998, point 1.3.72.

817. The first meeting of the Association Council with Estonia was held in Brussels on 23 February (¹). The Association Committee met on 11 June, also in Brussels. The Joint Parliamentary Committee met in Brussels on 27 and 28 April and in Tallinn on 3 November. Mr Flynn and Mr Fischler visited Estonia in March (²) and May (³) respectively.

818. The EC-Hungary Association Council met in Luxembourg on 10 November (⁴), the Association Committee having met earlier in Brussels, on 22 January. The Joint Parliamentary Committee met in Budapest from 25 to 27 February and in Brussels on 21 and 22 September. The new Hungarian Prime Minister, Mr Viktor Orbán, visited the Commission on 24 July (⁵) and Mr Van Miert went to Hungary in October (⁶), followed by Mr Fischler in November (⁷).

819. The first Association Council meeting with Latvia was held on 23 February (¹) in Brussels, and the Association Committee met, also in Brussels, on 28 May. The Joint Parliamentary Committee convened in Riga on 2 and 3 June. Mr Van den Broek visited Latvia in July (⁸).

820. The first meeting of the EC-Lithuania Association Council took place in Brussels on 23 February (¹). The Association Committee met in Brussels on 25 June and the Joint Parliamentary Committee in Vilnius on 21 and 22 September. Mr Yaldas Adamkus, the Lithuanian President, and Prime Minister Gediminas Vagnorius visited the Commission in April (⁹) and October (¹⁰) respectively. Ms Bjerregaard went to Lithuania in March (¹¹) and Mr Van den Broek in July (¹²).

821. The EC-Poland Association Council met in Brussels on 10 November (¹³), preceded by a meeting of the Association Committee on 4 March. The Joint Parliamentary Committee met in Brussels on 20 and 21 January and on 25 and 26 November, and in Warsaw from 22 to 24 June. Prime Minister Jerzy Buzek visited the Commission on 15 Octo-

---

(¹) Bull. 1/2-1998, point 1.4.67.
(²) Bull. 3-1998, point 1.3.74
(³) Bull. 5-1998, point 1.3.70.
(⁴) Bull. 11-1998, point 1.3.66.
(⁵) Bull. 7/8-1998, point 1.4.79.
(⁶) Bull. 10-1998, point 1.3.69.
(⁷) Bull. 11-1998, point 1.3.69.
(⁸) Bull. 7/8-1998, point 1.4.80.
(⁹) Bull. 4-1998, point 1.3.46.
(¹⁰) Bull. 10-1998, point 1.3.70.
(¹¹) Bull. 3-1998, point 1.3.75.
(¹²) Bull. 7/8-1998, point 1.4.81.
(¹³) Bull. 11-1998, point 1.3.67.

ber (¹) and Mr Monti, Mr Van den Broek, Mr Fischler and Mr Van Miert all paid visits to Poland — in January (²), February (³), June (⁴) and September (⁵) respectively.

822. The Association Committee and Association Council meetings with the Czech Republic were held, respectively, on 9 July in Prague and on 10 November in Brussels (⁶). The Joint Parliamentary Committee met in Prague on 19 and 20 March and in Brussels on 12 and 13 October. The Czech Prime Minister at the time, Mr Josef Tosovsky, visited the Commission on 28 April and his newly elected successor, Mr Milos Zeman, came on 29 September (⁷). There were visits to Prague by Mr Fischler (in April), Mrs Cresson (in June) (⁸), Mr Van Miert (in September), Mr Van den Broek (in October) (⁹) and Mr Bangemann (in November). The Economic and Social Committee adopted an own-initiative opinion on the Czech Republic on 9 September (¹⁰).

823. The EC-Romania Association Council met in Luxembourg on 28 April (¹¹) and on 15 October the Association Committee met in Brussels. There were meetings of the Joint Parliamentary Committee in Brussels on 24 and 25 February and in Bucharest on 9 and 10 November. Mr Radu Vasile, the Romanian Prime Minister, visited the Commission on 20 October (¹²). Mrs Wulf-Mathics went to Romania in February (¹³) and Mr Van den Broek in September (¹⁴).

824. The EC-Slovakia Association Council met in Luxembourg on 28 April (¹⁵). The Joint Parliamentary Committee convened in Brussels on 26 May. The Slovak Prime Minister, Mikulas Dzurinda visited the Commission on 6 November (¹⁶). Mr Bangemann, Mr Van den Broek and Ms Gradin all visited Slovakia — in March, June (¹⁷) and July respec-

---

(¹) Bull. 10-1998, point 1.3.71.
(²) Bull. 1/2-1998, point 1.4.70.
(³) Bull. 1/2-1998, point 1.4.71.
(⁴) Bull. 6-1998, point 1.4.74.
(⁵) Bull. 9-1998, point 1.3.73.
(⁶) Bull. 11-1998, point 1.3.68.
(⁷) Bull. 9-1998, point 1.3.74.
(⁸) Bull. 6-1998, point 1.4.75.
(⁹) Bull. 10-1998, point 1.3.72.
(¹⁰) OJ C 407, 28.12.1998; Bull. 9-1998, point 1.3.64.
(¹¹) Bull. 4-1998, point 1.3.42.
(¹²) Bull. 10-1998, point 1.3.73.
(¹³) Bull. 1/2-1998, point 1.4.72.
(¹⁴) Bull. 9-1998, point 1.3.75.
(¹⁵) Bull. 4-1998, point 1.3.43.
(¹⁶) Bull. 11-1998, point 1.3.70.
(¹⁷) Bull. 6-1998, point 1.4.76.

tively. Parliament adopted two resolutions on Slovakia on 12 March ([1]) and 8 October ([2]), and the Economic and Social Committee adopted an own-initiative opinion on 9 September ([3]).

825.   The Joint Cooperation Committee with Slovenia met on 12 February. Ms Gradin ([4]) and Mr Monti ([5]) (in May), Mr Flynn ([6]) (in July), Mr Fischler (in October) and Mr Bangemann (in November) all visited Slovenia. The Joint Parliamentary Committee convened in Strasbourg on 14 and 15 December. On 10 August the Council withdrew Slovenia from the scope of Common Position 96/184/CFSP, which imposes restrictive measures on arms exports to the former Yugoslavia ([7]).

Regional cooperation

826.   The Commission took part in the ministerial meeting (June) and the summit meeting (November) of the Central European Initiative ([8]), held in Brioni and Zagreb (Croatia) respectively. Mr Santer attended the meeting of Heads of State or Government of the Council of Baltic Sea States (CBSS) ([9]). Mr Van den Broek and Ms Bjerregaard represented the Commission at the annual ministerial meeting of the CBSS in Nyborg (Denmark) in June, where the ministers adopted the 'Baltic 21' agenda for sustainable development in the Baltic Sea region. On 25 November the Commission adopted a communication on the northern dimension of the EU's policies *(→ point 877)*.

([1])   OJ C 104, 6.4.1998; Bull. 3-1998, point 1.3.62.
([2])   OJ C 328, 26.10.1998; Bull. 10-1998, point 1.3.57.
([3])   OJ C 407, 28.12.1998; Bull. 9-1998, point 1.3.65.
([4])   Bull. 5-1998, point 1.3.71.
([5])   Bull. 5-1998, point 1.3.72.
([6])   Bull. 7/8-1998, point 1.4.82.
([7])   Decision 98/498/CFSP (OJ L 225, 12.8.1998; Bull. 7/8-1998, point 1.4.92).
([8])   1996 General Report, point 810.
([9])   Bull. 1/2-1998, point 1.4.73.

Section 9

Relations with the Mediterranean and the Middle East

Priority activities and objectives

827.   The European Union and its Mediterranean partners continued to develop their partnership in a variety of areas. On the basis of a communication from the Commission the EU set out the measures it intended to take in support of the Middle East peace process; it also reviewed its relations with the countries of south-eastern Europe in the light of conditionality criteria. To coincide with the start of accession negotiations it stepped up its pre-accession strategy for Cyprus and began to put into effect the strategy outlined by the Luxembourg European Council to prepare Turkey for accession by bringing it closer to the Union in every sphere. It also welcomed Malta's decision to reactivate its application for membership.

Overall strategy (including follow-up to the Barcelona conference)

828.   A Euro-Mediterranean Energy Forum was held in Brussels in May under the Euro-Mediterranean partnership established by the Barcelona conference [1], whose importance was reaffirmed by the European Council in both June and December [2] *(→ point 402).* A conference of Ministers for Culture was held in Rhodes in September and a conference of Industry Ministers took place in Klagenfurt in October. Preparations for the third Euro-Mediterranean conference of Foreign Ministers, scheduled for 1999, were discussed at an ad hoc meeting of ministers in Palermo in June, while the inaugural meeting of the Euro-Mediterranean Parliamentary Forum took place in Brussels in October. In January the Commission adopted a communication on the Euro-Mediterranean partnership in the transport sector *(→ point 456);* a similar communication on the partnership and the internal market was adopted in September *(→ point 155).* In a resolution adopted on 16 September [3], Parliament advocated stepping up cultural exchanges within the Euro-Mediterranean partnership and accordingly proposed that a European Averroës Day be

[1]   1995 General Report, point 839.
[2]   Bull. 6-1998, point I-31; Bull. 12-1998.
[3]   OJ C 313, 12.10.1998; Bull. 9-1998, point 1.3.76.

organised to celebrate the 800th anniversary of the philosopher's death. In an earlier resolution on 14 May (¹), it called on the Member States to ratify without delay the Euro-Mediterranean agreements already concluded and demonstrate greater openness, particularly on trade matters, in the conduct of the negotiations under way and in the implementation of the agreements so far ratified.

829.   Implementation of cooperation projects under the MEDA regulation (²) continued, with a total of ECU 941 million being committed. On 14 September the Commission adopted the report on implementation of the MEDA programme in 1996-97 (³), in which it was able to state that all the available commitment appropriations had been utilised. On 7 April the Council adopted Regulation (EC) No 780/98 (Table II) amending the MEDA regulation as regards the procedure for adopting the appropriate measures where an essential element for the continuation of support measures for a Mediterranean partner was lacking (i.e. where a partner violated democratic principles, the rule of law, human rights or fundamental freedoms).

Northern Mediterranean

Cyprus

830.   Following the decision of the Luxembourg European Council to start the process for Cypriot membership of the European Union (⁴), Cyprus took part in the first European Conference on 12 March, the meeting of ministers at which the accession process was launched for the 11 candidates (10 central and east European States and Cyprus). On 31 March, the inaugural ministerial meeting of the EU-Cyprus bilateral intergovernmental accession conference marked the opening of the accession negotiations proper (analysis of the Community *acquis* and compatibility of Cypriot legislation) *(→ points 798 et seq.).* At the request of the Luxembourg European Council (⁵), the President of Cyprus, Mr Glafkos Clerides, invited representatives of the Turkish/Cypriot community to join the Cypriot delegation in charge of the accession negotiations.

(¹)   OJ C 167, 1.6.1998; Bull. 5-1998, point 1.3.73.
(²)   OJ L 189, 30.7.1996; 1996 General Report, point 813.
(³)   COM(1998) 524; Bull. 9-1998, point 1.3.97.
(⁴)   1997 General Report, point 865; Bull. 12-1997, points I.3 to I.5.
(⁵)   Bull. 12-1997, point I.5. 28.

831.   On 4 November the Commission adopted an evaluation report on the progress made by Cyprus towards accession *(→ point 804).*

832.   The pre-accession strategy for Cyprus was stepped up to coincide with the start of the accession negotiations in accordance with the conclusions of the Luxembourg European Council [1] which proposed, in particular, that Cyprus should take part in a number of targeted projects to boost judicial and administrative capacity in the field of justice and home affairs, avail itself of technical assistance from TAIEX (the Technical Assistance Information Exchange Office) and participate in certain Community programmes and agencies. An agreement enabling Cyprus to participate in the MEDIA II audiovisual programme was concluded on 3 November (Table III). Cyprus has been taking part in programmes in the education field since 1997 [2].

833.   In December the European Council confirmed its support for the efforts of the UN Secretary-General to achieve a comprehensive settlement to the Cyprus problem.

Malta

834.   On 5 February the Commission adopted a communication on future relations between the EU and Malta [3], outlining ways to strengthen the political and economic ties between the parties in the light of Malta's decision in 1996 to suspend its application for EU membership [4]. The EC-Malta Association Council met on 28 April [5] and the Joint Parliamentary Committee on 1 and 2 April.

835.   Following the general election of 5 September, the new Maltese Government sent a request to the EU Presidency on 10 September for Malta's application for EU membership to be reactivated [6], a move welcomed by Parliament in a resolution adopted on 8 October [7]. The Council called on the Commission on 5 October to update its original opinion on Malta's application adopted in 1993 [8].

[1]   Bull. 12-1997, point I.5. 22.
[2]   1997 General Report, point 902.
[3]   Bull. 1/2-1998, point 1.4.88.
[4]   1996 General Report, point 815; 1997 General Report, point 903.
[5]   Bull. 4-1998, point 1.3.54.
[6]   Bull. 9-1998, point 1.3.57.
[7]   OJ C 328, 26.10.1998; Bull. 10-1998, point 1.3.51.
[8]   Twenty-seventh General Report, point 644.

Turkey

836.   In a communication adopted on 4 March (^{1}), the Commission outlined operational proposals for implementing the strategy defined by the Luxembourg European Council (^{2}) to prepare Turkey for accession by bringing it closer to the EU in all spheres. The proposals envisage development of the possibilities afforded by the association agreement (^{3}), intensification of the customs union (^{4}), and financial cooperation. In June the Cardiff European Council (^{5}) called on the Commission to implement the strategy and provide the necessary financial backing, and on 21 October the Commission accordingly adopted two proposals for regulations (Table II), one aimed at intensifying the customs union through the gradual adoption by Turkey of the Community *acquis* and the other implementing measures to promote Turkey's economic and social development. The EU strategy on Turkey was the subject of a Parliament resolution on 3 December (^{6}).

837.   On 4 March the Commission adopted its second report (^{7}) on progress in relations with Turkey since the entry into force of the customs union; it confirmed most of the conclusions of the first report (^{8}) and was welcomed by Parliament on 17 September (^{9}). Parliament also adopted a resolution on 16 July following the earthquake in Adana (^{10}).

838.   On 4 November the Commission adopted an evaluation report on Turkey's progress towards accession *(→ point 804)*.

South-eastern Europe

839.   On 27 April (^{11}), on the basis of a communication presented by the Commission on 15 April (^{12}), the Council discussed the performance of the countries of south-eastern Europe (Albania, Bosnia and Herzegovina, Croatia, the Federal Republic of Yugoslavia and the Former Yugoslav Republic of Macedonia) in meeting the criteria set out in its

---

(^{1})   COM(1998) 124; Bull. 3-1998, point 1.3.94.
(^{2})   1997 General Report, point 865.
(^{3})   OJ L 217, 29.12.1964.
(^{4})   1995 General Report, point 844.
(^{5})   Bull. 6-1998, point I.21. 68.
(^{6})   OJ C 398, 21.12.1998; Bull. 12-1998.
(^{7})   COM(1998) 147; Bull. 3-1998, point 1.3.95.
(^{8})   COM(96) 491; 1996 General Report, point 818.
(^{9})   OJ C 313, 12.10.1998; Bull. 9-1998, point 1.3.83.
(^{10})   OJ C 292, 21.9.1998; Bull. 7/8-1998, point 1.4.93.
(^{11})   COM(1998) 237; Bull. 4-1998, point 1.3.47.
(^{12})   Bull. 4-1998, points 1.3.48 and 2.2.1.

conclusions of April 1997 concerning conditionality (^{1}), and concluded that the present level of relations with the countries concerned should continue. On 9 November (^{2}), on the basis of a report adopted by the Commission on 28 October (^{3}), it returned to the subject and confirmed the conclusions it had drawn in April. Also on 9 November, the Council adopted a common position (^{4}) on EU support for the process on stability and good-neighbourliness in south-east Europe. In December the Vienna European Council reiterated the importance the EU attached to the prosperity of the region (^{5}).

840. An EU-Albania political dialogue meeting at ministerial level took place in Brussels on 27 February, focusing on the internal situation in Albania and on relations in the Balkans generally (^{6}). A meeting of the EC-Albania Joint Committee in Tirana on 23 and 24 March discussed the implementation of Community aid, including PHARE projects *(→ points 812 et seq.),* and means of improving trade cooperation. On 3 September the Commission proposed a grant of macrofinancial assistance to Albania *(→ point 78).* In view of Albania's unstable internal situation, which was the subject of Council conclusions in June and July (^{7}) and of a resolution by Parliament on 17 September (^{8}), the Council asked the Western European Union on 22 September (^{9}) to complete urgently its feasibility study on options for international police operations in order to help the Albanian authorities restore peace and order in the country. It welcomed the completion of the study in October (^{10}). On 19 February Parliament adopted a resolution on the drafting of the Albanian constitution (^{11}), the adoption of which was welcomed in December by the Vienna European Council (^{5}). On 30 October an international conference was held in Tirana at the instigation of the Albanian Government to identify the priorities for the country's stabilisation and development.

841. In Bosnia and Herzegovina the Council decided on 2 February to grant aid on an exceptional basis to the new government of Republika Srpska to help it achieve stability, after the Prime Minister undertook to

---

(^{1})   1997 General Report, point 909.
(^{2})   Bull. 11-1998, point 1.3.74.
(^{3})   COM(1998) 618; Bull. 10-1998, point 1.3.76.
(^{4})   Common Position 98/633/CFSP (OJ L 302, 12.11.1998; Bull. 11-1998, point 1.3.72).
(^{5})   Bull. 12-1998.
(^{6})   Bull. 1/2-1998, point 1.4.75.
(^{7})   Bull. 6-1998, point 1.4.78; Bull. 7/8-1998, point 1.4.83.
(^{8})   OJ C 313, 12.10.1998; Bull. 9-1998, point 1.3.79.
(^{9})   Decision 98/547/CFSP (OJ L 263, 26.9.1998; Bull. 9-1998, point 1.3.80).
(^{10})   Bull. 10-1998, points 1.3.74 and 1.3.75.
(^{11})   OJ C 80, 16.3.1998; Bull. 1/2-1998, point 1.4.76.

cooperate fully in the implementation of the Dayton peace agreements ([1]). Then on 27 February ([2]), further to a recommendation by the High Representative of the European Union in Bosnia and Herzegovina, Mr Carlos Westendorp, the Council repealed Common Position 97/625/CFSP ([3]) on restrictive measures to be taken against persons in Bosnia and Herzegovina acting against the peace agreements. On 30 April it renewed the EU's support for the supervision of elections under OSCE auspices ([4]). On 26 October it adopted a decision on additional funding for the implementing structures of the peace plan ([5]) and, on 22 December ([6]), extended Common Position 95/545/CFSP on EU participation in the structures for one year ([7]). On 2 April Parliament recommended that the Council decide on a joint action for active EU participation in a multinational force to take over from SFOR ([8]). Mr Van den Broek visited Bosnia and Herzegovina in July ([9]) in the run-up to the elections of 12 and 13 September, whose successful conduct was welcomed by the Council on 5 October ([10]). The supply of aid for rehabilitation and reconstruction in Bosnia and Herzegovina continued in 1998 (a total of ECU 203 million), focusing on programmes to assist returning refugees (ECU 108 million). Regulation (EEC) No 1628/86 governing the aid supply was amended on 20 April in order to simplify and streamline procedures (Table II), while the fourth donor conference took place in Brussels in May ([11]). On 13 November the Commission proposed granting macrofinancial aid to Bosnia and Herzegovina (→ point 78).

842. Relations between the EU and Croatia were dominated by the issue of returning refugees. A meeting took place on 23 March ([12]) between the EU troika and the Croatian Foreign Minister, Mr Mate Granic, but on 27 April ([13]) the Council expressed concern at the lack of progress on this front. On 25 May ([14]) and again on 29 June ([15]), however, it welcomed the adoption of measures by the government and parliament of Croatia to assist returning refugees. Following further

---

([1])   Joint Action 98/117/CFSP (OJ L 35, 9.2.1998; Bull. 1/2-1998, points 1.4.83 and 1.4.84).
([2])   Decision 98/196/CFSP (OJ L 75, 12.3.1998; Bull. 1/2-1998, point 1.4.82).
([3])   OJ L 259, 22.9.1997; 1997 General Report, point 906.
([4])   Joint Action 98/302/CFSP (OJ L 138, 9.5.1998; Bull. 4-1998, point 1.3.51; Bull. 6-1998, point 1.4.79).
([5])   Decision 98/607/CFSP (OJ L 290, 29.10.1998; Bull. 10-1998, point 1.3.84).
([6])   Decision 98/737/CFSP (OJ L 354, 30.12.1998; Bull. 12-1998).
([7])   OJ L 309, 12.12.1995; 1995 General Report, point 845.
([8])   OJ C 138, 4.5.1998; Bull. 4-1998, point 1.3.50.
([9])   Bull. 7/8-1998, point 1.4.84.
([10]) Bull. 10-1998, point 1.3.74.
([11]) Bull. 5-1998, point 1.3.76.
([12]) Bull. 3-1998, point 1.3.84.
([13]) Bull. 4-1998, point 1.3.53.
([14]) Bull. 5-1998, point 1.3.78.
([15]) Bull. 6-1998, point 1.4.84.

progress made in this regard by the Croatian Government, the EU took part in the conference on reconstruction and development held in Zagreb on 4 and 5 November.

843. The deteriorating situation in Kosovo and acts of repression by the Serbian authorities prompted Council conclusions([1]), statements by the European Union (→ point 678), Parliament resolutions([2]) and a declaration by the Cardiff European Council in June([3]). The EU also adopted a series of sanctions against the Federal Republic of Yugoslavia (FRY) and Serbia. Having established the framework for their implementation on 19 March([4]), the Council adopted the following restrictive measures: Regulation (EC) No 926/98 concerning the reduction of certain economic relations with the FRY (27 April)([5]); Common Position 98/326/CFSP concerning the freezing of funds held abroad by the FRY and Serbian Governments (7 May)([6]); Common Position 98/374/CFSP concerning the prohibition of new investment in Serbia (8 June)([7]); Regulation (EC) No 1295/98([8]) implementing Common Position 98/326/CFSP (22 June); Common Position 98/426/CFSP concerning a ban on flights by Yugoslav carriers between the FRY and the Community (29 June)([9]); Regulation (EC) No 1607/98([10]) implementing Common Position 98/374/CFSP (24 July); Regulation (EC) No 1901/98([11]) implementing Common Position 98/426/CFSP (7 September); Common Position 98/725/CFSP imposing a visa ban on persons identified as responsible for the repression of independent media in Serbia (14 December)([12]); and Joint Action 98/736/CFSP concerning a forensic experts' mission to sites of alleged civilian massacres in Kosovo (22 December)([13]). On 13 November the Council also adopted Joint Action 98/646/CFSP([14]) requesting the Western European Union to provide information on the Kosovo situation obtained by its Satellite Centre, while in December the

---

([1]) Bull. 1/2-1998, point 1.4.89; Bull. 3-1998, point 1.3.87; Bull. 4-1998, point 1.3.57; Bull. 5-1998, point 1.3.81; Bull. 6-1998, point 1.4.95; Bull. 7/8-1998, point 1.4.86; Bull. 10-1998, points 1.3.74 and 1.3.75; Bull. 11-1998, point 1.3.73; Bull. 12-1998.
([2]) OJ C 104, 6.4.1998; Bull. 3-1998, point 1.3.88; OJ C 167, 1.6.1998; Bull. 5-1998, point 1.3.80; OJ C 210, 6.7.1998; Bull. 6-1998, point 1.4.94; OJ C 292, 21.9.1998; Bull. 7/8-1998, point 1.4.86; OJ C 328, 26.10.1998; Bull. 10-1998, point 1.3.85.
([3]) Bull. 6-1998, point I.35.
([4]) Common Position 98/240/CFSP (OJ L 95, 27.3.1998; Bull. 3-1998, point 1.3.85).
([5]) OJ L 130, 1.5.1998; Bull. 4-1998, point 1.3.55.
([6]) OJ L 143, 14.5.1998; Bull. 5-1998, point 1.3.79.
([7]) OJ L 165, 10.6.1998; Bull. 6-1998, point 1.4.86.
([8]) OJ L 178, 23.6.1998; Bull. 6-1998, point 1.4.89.
([9]) OJ L 190, 4.7.1998; Bull. 6-1998, point 1.4.90.
([10]) OJ L 209, 25.7.1998; Bull. 7/8-1998, point 1.4.90.
([11]) OJ L 248, 8.9.1998; Bull. 9-1998, point 1.3.88.
([12]) OJ L 345, 19.12.1998; Bull. 12-1998.
([13]) OJ L 354, 30.12.1998; Bull. 12-1998.
([14]) OJ L 308, 18.11.1998; Bull. 11-1998, point 1.3.80.

Vienna European Council called on the two sides involved in the Kosovo crisis to comply with the UN resolutions (¹). On 30 April the Council adopted Joint Action 98/301/CFSP in support of the Montenegro Government (²); it continued (³) to emphasise its firm support for that government's political and economic reform effort, a stance confirmed in December by the Vienna European Council (¹). On 8 June it appointed Mr Felipe González as the EU special representative for the Federal Republic of Yugoslavia (⁴) and, on 28 December, extended his mandate until 31 January 1999 (⁵).

844. The cooperation agreement between the Community and the Former Yugoslav Republic of Macedonia (FYROM) entered into force on 1 January (Table III). At the first meeting of the Cooperation Council, which took place on 20 and 21 March in Skopje, the participants underlined the importance of full implementation of the agreement and aid under PHARE (→ points 812 et seq.). Two political dialogue meetings were held, in Skopje on 3 February and in Brussels on 8 December, on the basis of the joint declaration attached to the agreement. FYROM's Prime Minister, Mr Branko Crvenkovski, visited the Commission on 4 and 5 February (⁶). In December the Vienna European Council welcomed FYROM's contribution to stability in the region (¹).

San Marino

845. Parliament gave its assent on 9 October to the protocol to the cooperation and customs union agreement signed in 1997 (Table III).

Maghreb

846. The troika of EU ministers and a delegation from Parliament visited Algeria at the beginning of the year, and on 26 January the Council adopted conclusions (⁷) advocating extensive dialogue with Algeria at ministerial level. This dialogue was pursued in a meeting in Vienna on 21 October between the EU troika and the Algerian Minister for Foreign Affairs, Mr Ahmed Attaf. The fourth interparliamentary meeting

---

(¹) Bull. 12-1998.
(²) OJ L 138, 9.5.1998; Bull. 4-1998, point 1.3.58; Bull. 5-1998, point 1.3.82.
(³) Bull. 5-1998, point 1.3.81; Bull. 6-1998, points 1.4.92 and 1.4.93; Bull. 7/8-1998, point 1.4.85.
(⁴) Joint Action 98/375/CFSP (OJ L 165, 10.6.1998; Bull. 6-1998, point 1.4.91).
(⁵) Joint Action 98/741/CFSP (OJ L 358, 31.12.1998; Bull. 12-1998).
(⁶) Bull. 1/2-1998, point 1.4.79.
(⁷) Bull. 1/2-1998, point 1.4.91.

between the Algerian and European Parliaments was held in Strasbourg in July.

847.   A delegation from Parliament visited Morocco in May. On 10 May([1]) Parliament recommended that the Council set out a common position reaffirming the EU's full backing for every stage of the UN peace plan for Western Sahara and its intention of playing a part in organising a free and open referendum on self-determination on the scheduled date; provide the humanitarian aid needed; and draw up a programme for future long-term cooperation with a view to full and sustainable development of Western Sahara.

848.   The Council concluded a Euro-Mediterranean association agreement between the Community and Tunisia on 26 January which entered into force on 1 March (Table III). Its main features are regular political dialogue; the gradual establishment of a free-trade area; provisions on freedom of establishment, the liberalisation of services, free movement of capital and competition rules; intensified economic cooperation on the broadest possible basis; and social, cultural and financial cooperation. The Association Council held its first meeting in Brussels on 14 July([2]) and the ninth interparliamentary meeting took place in Strasbourg on 16 and 17 September.

Mashreq countries, Palestinian Territories, Israel

849.   On 16 January the Commission adopted a communication on the role of the European Union in the peace process and its future assistance to the Middle East([3]). The Commission stressed that, despite the deadlock in the peace process and, in particular, Israel's periodic closure of the Palestinian Territories, EU and Member State assistance between 1993 and 1997 (ECU 1.68 billion or 54 % of total international aid) had helped avoid the total collapse of the Palestinian economy and should therefore be maintained; but certain conditions had to be met, including an end to the closures (so that the association agreement between the Community and the PLO could be fully implemented([4]) and the introduction of genuine regional integration) if real progress were to be made. On 23 February([5]) the communication was welcomed

---

([1])   OJ C 104, 6.4.1998; Bull. 3-1998, point 1.3.96.
([2])   Bull. 7/8-1998, points 1.4.95 and 1.4.96.
([3])   COM(97) 715; Bull. 1/2-1998, point 1.4.93.
([4])   OJ L 187, 16.7.1997; 1997 General Report, point 921.
([5])   Bull. 1/2-1998, point 1.4.94.

by the Council, which later repeated (^{1}) its concern at the deadlock in the peace process and expressed its support for the steps taken by the United States to ensure a credible Israeli redeployment in the Occupied Territories. Parliament, in June and November (^{2}), and the Cardiff European Council, in June and December (^{3}), added their weight to these views with the Cardiff European Council calling on Israel to recognise the Palestinians' right to self-determination and on the Palestinians to recognise Israel's right to security. The Council also decided on 26 October to extend the mandate of the EU's special envoy for the peace process, Mr Miguel Moratinos, to 31 December 1999 (^{4}). From 6 to 13 February (^{5}) Mr Santer conducted a tour of the Middle East, taking in Egypt, Israel, the Palestinian Territories, Jordan, Lebanon and Syria, during which the main topics of discussion were the peace process, the Euro-Mediterranean partnership, the Iraq crisis and bilateral ties with the countries visited.

850.   At the same time as it adopted the communication on Euro-Mediterranean cumulation of origin (→ point 718), the Commission adopted a second communication on implementing the interim EC-Israel agreement (^{6}). It emphasised the need to ensure that the origin rules were properly applied, especially in the case of goods originating in the Occupied Territories which were being exported to the EU as if they originated in Israel. This approach received the support of Parliament on 18 June (^{7}) and the Council on 29 June (^{8}). On 26 June the Commission proposed extending technical and financial cooperation with the Occupied Territories under Regulation (EC) No 1734/94. This proposal and another on allowing interest rate subsidies on EIB operations in support of the public sector in the Occupied Territories were adopted by the Council on 21 December (Table II). On 9 November the Council authorised the Commission to negotiate the renewal of the Convention between the Community and the United Nations Relief and Works Agency for Palestine Refugees in the Near East (UNRWA) concerning the Community's contribution to the UNRWA budget (Table III). In its

---

(^{1}) Bull. 3-1998, point 1.3.97; Bull. 4-1998, point 1.3.59; Bull. 6-1998, point 1.4.100; Bull. 11-1998, point 1.3.87; Bull. 12-1998.
(^{2}) OJ C 210, 6.7.1998; Bull. 6-1998, point 1.4.99; OJ C 379, 7.12.1998; Bull. 11-1998, point 1.3.88.
(^{3}) Bull. 6-1998, point I.27; Bull. 12-1998.
(^{4}) Decision 98/608/CFSP (OJ L 290, 29.10.1998; Bull. 10-1998, point 1.3.87).
(^{5}) Bull. 1/2-1998, points 1.4.95 to 1.4.100.
(^{6}) Bull. 5-1998, point 1.3.85.
(^{7}) OJ C 210, 6.7.1998; Bull. 6-1998, point 1.4.99.
(^{8}) Bull. 6-1998, point 1.4.98.

conclusions adopted on 30 November it also outlined the EU's future assistance to the Palestinian Territories ([1]).

851. On 2 July Parliament gave its assent to the Euro-Mediterranean association agreement with Jordan (Table III).

The Middle East

852. The eighth EU-Gulf Cooperation Council Joint Council meeting held in Luxembourg on 27 October ([2]) dealt mainly with the free trade agreement negotiations and the situation in the respective regions. Prior to the Joint Council meeting, a preparatory political dialogue meeting at ministerial level took place in London on 29 April ([3]).

853. In the light of developments in Iran following the election of President Mohammad Khatami, the Council agreed on 23 February ([4]) to resume official bilateral visits and on 8 June ([5]) to start a comprehensive and substantive dialogue with the Iranians. The EU later welcomed the assurances given by the Iranian Government concerning Salman Rushdie (→ point 680).

854. In February, both Parliament ([6]) and the Council ([7]) stressed the need for Iraq to comply with UN Security Council resolutions by submitting in particular to effective inspections, and further advocated stepping up humanitarian aid to the people of Iraq, especially under the oil-for-food programme. In December the Vienna European Council again called on Iraq to comply with Security Council resolutions ([8]).

855. The EU-Yemen cooperation agreement signed in 1997 was concluded on 23 February and entered into force on 1 July (Table III). The agreement is a third generation non-preferential cooperation agreement and provides for most-favoured-nation treatment. The eighth meeting of the joint cooperation committee was held in Brussels on 4 December.

([1]) Bull. 11-1998, point 1.3.89.
([2]) Bull. 10-1998, point 1.3.89.
([3]) Bull. 4-1998, point 1.3.60.
([4]) Bull. 1/2-1998, point 1.4.101.
([5]) Bull. 6-1998, point 1.4.101.
([6]) OJ C 80, 16.3.1998; Bull. 1/2-1998, point 1.4.103.
([7]) Bull. 1/2-1998, point 1.4.104.
([8]) Bull. 12-1998.

Section 10

Relations with the independent States of the former Soviet Union and with Mongolia

Priority activities and objectives

856.   Relations between the European Union and the independent States of the former Soviet Union were further strengthened with the entry into force of partnership and cooperation agreements with Ukraine and Moldova, the signing of a similar agreement with Turkmenistan and the first meetings of the cooperation councils. The EU also lent its support to Russia in its attempts to overcome the economic and financial crisis in the summer. Relations with Belarus, on the other hand, showed no discernible improvement and remained a source of concern for the EU. The Commission also adopted a proposal for a new assistance programme for 2000-06.

Partnership and other agreements

857.   The   partnership   and   cooperation   agreement   with   Russia ([1]) entered into force on 1 December 1997 and the first meeting of the Cooperation Council was held in Brussels on 27 January ([2]). The cooperation committee met in Moscow on 15 December.

858.   The Council and the Commission adopted decisions concluding partnership and cooperation agreements with Ukraine and Moldova on 26 January (Table III) and 28 May (Table III) respectively. At the same time they decided to provisionally apply protocols (Table III) allowing Austria, Finland and Sweden to become parties to the agreements; these entered into force on 1 March (for Ukraine) and 1 July (for Moldova). The agreements will govern all political, economic and cultural relations between the parties and lay the foundations for cooperation in social, economic, financial, scientific, technological and cultural matters. The first Cooperation Council meeting with Ukraine took place in Luxembourg on 9 June ([3]) and that with Moldova in Brussels on 14 July ([4]).

([1])   1997 General Report, point 930.
([2])   Bull. 1/2-1998, point 1.4.110.
([3])   Bull. 6-1998, point 1.4.107.
([4])   Bull. 7/8-1998, point 1.4.105.

859. Another partnership and cooperation agreement — with Turkmenistan — was signed in Brussels on 25 May (Table III). Its main aim is to strengthen Turkmenistan's independence, establish democracy and develop a market economy.

860. Interim agreements on trade and trade-related matters with Uzbekistan (Table III) and Kyrgyzstan (Table III) entered into force on 1 June and 1 August respectively. The interim agreement with Azerbaijan (Table III) was concluded in December. The Commission also proposed in December concluding the interim agreement with Turkmenistan (Table III).

861. In the light of developments in Belarus (→ point 876), the Council conclusions of 15 September 1997 ([1]) continued in force. Talks and procedures for concluding a partnership and cooperation agreement and an interim agreement therefore remained in abeyance.

Assistance for the independent States of the former Soviet Union and for Mongolia

TACIS programme

862. Some ECU 507.2 million was committed from the 1998 budget under the TACIS programme, the purpose of which is to support moves to a market economy and strengthen democracy in the new independent States and Mongolia. Among the measures adopted were an ECU 50 million contribution to the special fund set up by the European Bank for Reconstruction and Development for the building of a shelter structure at Chernobyl, and funding of ECU 30 million for a cross-border cooperation programme. On 14 July Parliament adopted a resolution stressing the importance of the latter in the context of EU enlargement ([2]).

863. On 24 May the Commission addressed a communication to Parliament on the TACIS programme and the environment. A number of projects in this area are funded under the inter-State programme, the cross-border cooperation programme and action programmes for Russia and Ukraine.

---

[1]   1997 General Report, point 933.
[2]   OJ C 292, 21.9.1998; Bull. 7/8-1998, point 1.4.102.

864. Following the interim evaluation carried out in 1997 ([1]), a more comprehensive programme of evaluations was launched at national, regional and sectoral level. These confirmed that the majority of projects achieved their objectives but that their impact on the transition process depended heavily on factors such as the response of partner country governments to the need for reform and the quality of coordination between donors, both at political level and in drawing up and implementing assistance programmes. On 10 July the Commission adopted its annual report on the implementation of the TACIS programme ([2]), which was also the subject of an own-initiative opinion delivered by the Economic and Social Committee on 29 April ([3]).

865. Drawing on its experience with operating TACIS, on 22 December the Commission approved a proposal for a new programme for 2000-06 (Table II). It provides for more focused cooperation (with a maximum of three areas of cooperation in each country), the adoption of a differentiated approach in line with each country's needs and the encouragement of higher quality projects by a system of incentives, and establishes the promotion of democracy and investment as the programme's main priorities.

866. On 31 March the Commission also adopted a communication on activities to improve nuclear safety in the applicant countries of central and eastern Europe and the new independent States (→ point 538).

Other forms of assistance

867. TACIS activities in Tajikistan were suspended in 1997 and because of the situation there did not resume in 1998. Food and humanitarian aid programmes were continued, however, as in Belarus.

868. Information on macrofinancial assistance can be found in Section 1 ('Economic and monetary policy') of Chapter IV (→ points 76 et seq.).

([1])   1997 General Report, point 935.
([2])   COM(1998) 416; Bull. 7/8-1998, point 1.4.101.
([3])   OJ C 214, 10.7.1998; Bull. 4-1998, point 1.3.68.

Bilateral relations (¹)

869. Two EU-Russia summits took place, the first in Birmingham on 15 May between the Russian President, Mr Boris Yeltsin, Mr Tony Blair, President of the European Council, and Mr Santer for the Commission (²), and the second in Vienna on 27 October between Russian Prime Minister Mr Yevgeny Primakov, Council President Mr Viktor Klima and Mr Santer (³). The main issues covered at the first summit were European security, the situation in Kosovo, the Middle East peace process, the situation of Russian-speaking minorities in the Baltic States and Russia's efforts to establish a market economy. The EU representatives pointed in particular to Russia's removal from the list of State-trading countries *(→ point 719)* as recognition of the country's progress towards full integration into the global economy and membership of the World Trade Organisation. The second summit was dominated by developments linked to the economic and financial crisis in Russia in the summer, with the participants reaffirming that implementation of the partnership and cooperation agreement was a priority. The second round table for EU and Russian industrialists was held in Brussels in May *(→ point 234).*

870. Parliament adopted two resolutions on the EU's relations with Russia. On 2 April (⁴) it responded favourably to the Commission's action plan (⁵) and backed an expansion of partnership in all fields, particularly research and development, high technology, the environment and nuclear safety, whilst stressing the need to consolidate the process of democratisation in Russia. On 17 September (⁶) it stated that absolute priority must be given to resolving structural problems in the Russian economy and to embarking on a process of economic reform. The Council issued a statement on 5 June and conclusions on 5 October underlining the importance for the EU of economic stability in Russia (⁷).

871. On 17 December the Council decided to supply agricultural products free of charge to Russia *(→ point 585).* The question of food aid to

---

(¹) Information on the partnership agreements (including cooperation councils) and on the other agreements can be found in the subsection 'Partnership and other agreements' in this section *(→ points 857 et seq.).*
(²) Bull. 5-1998, point 1.3.91.
(³) Bull. 10-1998, point 1.3.98.
(⁴) OJ C 138, 4.5.1998; Bull. 4-1998, point 1.3.63.
(⁵) 1996 General Report, point 860.
(⁶) OJ C 313, 12.10.1998; Bull. 9-1998, point 1.3.102.
(⁷) Bull. 6-1998, point 1.4.105; Bull. 10-1998, point 1.3.96.

Russia had previously been the subject of a Commission working paper on 18 November ([1]), a Parliament resolution on 19 November ([2]) and Council conclusions on 9 November and 7 December ([3]). On 12 December the Vienna European Council emphasised the European Union's solidarity with Russia and its people in the economic crisis currently besetting the country ([4]).

872. An EU-Ukraine summit held in Vienna on 16 October was attended by Mr Leonid Kuchma, President of Ukraine, Mr Viktor Klima, President of the European Council, Mr Wolfgang Schüssel, President of the Council of the European Union, and Mr Santer and Mr Van den Broek for the Commission ([5]). The main areas for discussion were the impact on Ukraine of the financial crisis in Russia, the implementation of the partnership and cooperation agreement between the European Union and Ukraine, the closure of the nuclear power plant in Chernobyl and relations between Ukraine and its neighbours. At the summit the EU announced its decision to grant Ukraine further macrofinancial assistance of up to ECU 150 million (→ point 77). In December the Vienna European Council reaffirmed the fundamental importance it attached to the partnership between the European Union and Ukraine ([4]).

873. In two resolutions adopted on 12 March ([6]), the Parliament welcomed the Commission's action plan for Ukraine ([7]) and urged the Commission to speed up execution of the TACIS budget there.

874. Turkmenistan's President, Mr Sapurmurad Niyazov, visited the Commission on 24 February and saw Mr Santer and Mr Van den Broek. Talks centred on political developments in the region, the growth of democracy in Turkmenistan, and the country's energy and agricultural exports ([8]). On 6 April the Uzbek Foreign Minister, Mr Abdulaziz Komilov, met Mr Van den Broek to discuss political developments and regional cooperation in central Asia, bilateral trade and investment, and Uzbekistan's macroeconomic policies — particularly as regards exchange rates and currency convertibility. Topics raised by the President of Moldova, Mr Petru Lucinschi, during his meeting with Mr Santer on 27 January included his country's economic situation and external trade, the

---

([1]) Bull. 11-1998, point 1.3.95.
([2]) OJ C 379, 7.12.1998; Bull. 11-1998, point 1.3.96.
([3]) Bull. 11-1998, point 1.3.94; Bull. 12-1998.
([4]) Bull. 12-1998.
([5]) Bull. 10-1998, point 1.3.99.
([6]) OJ C 104, 6.4.1998; Bull. 3-1998, points 1.3.102 and 1.3.106.
([7]) COM(96) 593; 1996 General Report, point 865.
([8]) Bull. 1/2-1998, point 1.4.116.

role of EU aid in this respect, and the situation in Transdniestria (¹) which was the subject of a Parliament resolution on 17 December (²).

875. From 1 to 5 June Mr Van den Broek held talks in Armenia, Azerbaijan and Georgia with President Kocharian, President Aliyev and President Shevardnadze respectively. Among the matters discussed were prospects for resolving the conflict in the Caucasus, regional cooperation programmes, the process of democratisation, the continuation of the reform process, and the role of EU assistance, particularly under TACIS. Mr Van den Broek joined Mr Shevardnadze and the Prime Minister of Azerbaijan, Mr Artur Rasi-Zade, in officially opening the Traceca Bridge (→ point 879) on the border between Georgia and Azerbaijan.

876.   Relations with Belarus were strained further with the eviction of several EU ambassadors from their residences in Drozdy (Minsk). This violation of the Vienna Convention on diplomatic relations was the subject, in June and July, of Council conclusions (³), statements by the European Union and associated countries (→ point 681), and a Parliament resolution (⁴). The Council also adopted Common Position 98/448/ CFSP (⁵) on 9 July, ensuring that around a hundred senior representatives of the Belarus Government would be refused visas for entry to the EU.

Regional cooperation

877.   In a communication adopted on 25 November (⁶) the Commission stressed the importance of the northern dimension for the policies of the European Union. This communication was favourably received by the Vienna European Council (²).

878.   In January, Mr Van den Broek represented the Commission at the Barents Euro-Arctic Council (⁷) in Luleå (Sweden). Priorities were agreed for future regional cooperation, including the elimination of barriers to trade and investment, the processing of nuclear waste, and increased cross-border trade. The Commission also took part in the Black Sea

---

(¹) Bull. 1/2-1998, point 1.4.115.
(²) Bull. 12-1998.
(³) Bull. 6-1998, point 1.4.115; Bull. 7/8-1998, point 1.4.107.
(⁴) OJ C 292, 21.9.1998; Bull. 7/8-1998, point 1.4.109.
(⁵) OJ L 195, 11.7.1998; Bull. 7/8-1998, point 1.4.106.
(⁶) COM(1998) 589; Bull. 11-1998, point 1.3.71.
(⁷) Denmark, Finland, Iceland, Norway, Russia and Sweden.

Economic Cooperation (BSEC) Council ([1]) Summit in Yalta (Ukraine) in June, when the BSEC Charter was signed.

879. In order to help strengthen ties between central Asian and Caucasian States, two regional cooperation programmes — Inogate (oil and gas pipelines) and Traceca (land and sea transport) — were implemented with TACIS support. In September, as a sign of their shared intention to reopen the silk route between Asia and Europe, the Heads of State of the region took part in a multilateral conference on transport in Baku, which had been staged with the support of the Traceca programme ([2]).

([1]) Greece, Bulgaria, Romania, Moldova, Ukraine, Russia, Georgia, Armenia, Azerbaijan and Turkey.
([2]) Bull. 9-1998, point 1.3.103.

Section 11

Relations with the United States, Japan and other industrialised countries

Priority activities and objectives

880.   The United States and the European Union decided at their London Summit to launch a transatlantic economic partnership aiming to eliminate trade barriers and step up multilateral liberalisation. Significant progress was also made in cooperation between the European Union and its other industrialised partners. In particular, the Commission proposed redefining and intensifying relations between the EU and the Republic of Korea.

Group of Seven/Eight (G7/G8)

881.   The G8 Summit in Birmingham from 15 to 17 May was attended by the Heads of State or Government of Canada, France, Germany, Italy, Japan, Russia, the United Kingdom and the United States, with Mr Santer representing the Commission [1]. A final communiqué was adopted defining the major challenges facing the world on the threshold of the 21st century: achieving economic growth and sustainable development throughout the world in a way that protects the environment and promotes the principles of good governance, enables the developing countries to accelerate growth, restores growth in Asia and continues the liberalisation of trade in goods and services under more stable economic and financial conditions; attaining sustainable growth, creating jobs and combating unemployment and social exclusion; and fighting organised crime and drugs trafficking. The participants also addressed the issues of aid to the poorest countries, climate change, energy, non-proliferation and the computer problems associated with the millennium. (→ *point 462).* They adopted a statement on nuclear testing in India, expressing their concern at nuclear proliferation in south Asia and calling on all countries in the region to refrain from any further nuclear tests; statements were also adopted on Indonesia, the Middle East, Kosovo, Bosnia and Herzegovina and Northern Ireland.

---

[1]   Bull. 5-1998, point 1.3.92.

882. On 15 May before the start of the G8 Summit, the Heads of State or Government of the G7 (the G8 minus Russia) met to discuss the state of the world economy and how to strengthen the global financial system ([1]). In their final statement, 'Strengthening the global financial system', the participants, noting the consequences of the financial crisis in Asia, recommended that steps be taken to reduce the risks of such crises recurring in future; these steps would include increasing transparency, strengthening national financial systems, ensuring that the private sector assumes responsibility for the financial risks it takes and strengthening the role of the financial institutions and cooperation between them. They also welcomed the introduction of the single currency as a stabilising factor in the international monetary system. They reaffirmed the commitment of the G7 to cooperation with the Ukrainian Government in implementing substantial economic and financial reforms and reforms in the nuclear sector.

Quadrilateral meetings

883. A quadrilateral meeting involving the European Union, Canada, the United States and Japan was held in Versailles on 29 and 30 April ([2]). It was chiefly devoted to multilateral trade issues, in particular the preparation of the next ministerial conference of the World Trade Organisation (WTO). Participants also drew attention to the need to increase public confidence in the multilateral trade system by making the WTO more transparent and explaining the contribution it could make to growth, prosperity, employment and the protection of the environment.

United States

884. Two EU-US summits were held in 1998, the first in London on 18 May ([3]) and the second in Washington on 18 December ([4]). At the London Summit Mr Bill Clinton, Mr Tony Blair, President of the Council, Mr Santer and Sir Leon Brittan agreed, in a joint statement, to launch a transatlantic economic partnership with the aim of breaking down barriers to trade and pursuing multilateral liberalisation. They also came to an agreement on certain US extra-territorial laws, including rules on investment in illegally expropriated property and a US under-

---

[1]   Bull. 5-1998, point 1.3.92.
[2]   Bull. 4-1998, point 1.3.69.
[3]   Bull. 5-1998, point 1.3.93.
[4]   Bull. 12-1998.

taking to amend the Helms-Burton Act. They adopted statements on a number of issues, including the transatlantic partnership on political cooperation, measures to counter international terrorism and the proliferation of weapons of mass destruction, and a common approach to the development of the energy resources of the Caspian Sea basin. On the sidelines of the summit proper, the participants also signed a mutual recognition agreement on conformity assessment *(→ point 729)*. At the Washington Summit Mr Bill Clinton, Mr Viktor Klima, President of the Council, Mr Santer and Sir Leon Brittan discussed the implementation of the transatlantic economic partnership, the follow-up to the Kyoto Conference on Climate Change, the year 2000 computer problem and various bilateral trade matters (bananas, hormones and the aeronautical sector).

885.   There were two ministerial meetings between the European Union and the United States in 1998. On 15 January US Secretary of State Madeleine Albright, Mr Robin Cook, President of the Council and Sir Leon Brittan met in Washington([1]); on 3 September Mrs Albright, Mr Wolfgang Schüssel, President of the Council, and Sir Leon met in Vienna. Sir Leon and US Trade Representative, Charlene Barshevsky, also met on a number of occasions during the year. In June the 49th meeting between members of the US Congress and the European Parliament was held in Houston. Judges from the US Supreme Court also met their counterparts at the Court of Justice in Luxembourg.

886.   Both the Council, on 25 May([2]), and the Cardiff European Council, in June([3]), welcomed the results of the London Summit, in particular the launch of the new transatlantic economic partnership. On 9 November, in response to the draft submitted by the Commission on 16 September, the Council approved a plan of action to support the partnership and authorised the Commission to negotiate agreements with the United States on the elimination of technical barriers to trade in industrial products, services, public contracts and intellectual property rights (Table III). In December the Vienna European Council welcomed this plan of action([4]). On 11 March the Commission had presented a communication 'The new transatlantic market place'([5]), some aspects of which were incorporated in the transatlantic economic partnership, aiming to intensify and extend the New Transatlantic Agenda adopted in

---

([1])   Bull. 1/2-1998, point 1.4.119.
([2])   Bull. 5-1998, point 1.3.94.
([3])   Bull. 6-1998, point I.23.
([4])   Bull. 12-1998.
([5])   COM(1998) 125; Bull. 3-1998, point 1.3.107.

1995 ([1]). It was endorsed by the Economic and Social Committee on 10 September ([2]) and by Parliament on 18 November ([3]). Parliament also adopted resolutions expressing satisfaction with the development of transatlantic relations on 14 January ([4]), 15 January ([5]) and 16 September ([6]).

887.   The fourth annual conference of the Transatlantic Business Dialogue, attended by US and EU business leaders and political representatives, including Mr Bangemann and Sir Leon Brittan, was held in Charlotte (United States) from 5 to 7 November. On 27 November the Commission published its 14th annual report on barriers to trade and investment in the United States.

Japan

888.   The seventh EU-Japan Summit was held in Tokyo on 12 January, bringing together Mr Ryutaro Hashimoto, Japanese Prime Minister, Mr Tony Blair, President of the Council, Mr Santer and Sir Leon Brittan ([7]). Against the backdrop of the Asian financial crisis, which particularly affects Japan, the two sides reasserted their confidence in Asia's long-term economic prospects while stressing the need for Asian countries to continue with the reforms they had undertaken and cooperate with international financial institutions in order to get back on course for growth. At the ministerial meeting held in Tokyo on 12 October ([8]) a Japanese delegation led by Mr Masahiko Komura, Minister for Foreign Affairs, met Sir Leon Brittan, accompanied by Mr Bangemann and Ms Gradin, to discuss measures to be taken to restore growth and confidence in the Japanese economy, including reform of the banking system to eliminate bad debts, budgetary measures to stimulate demand, structural reform and deregulation. The Commission tabled a list of approximately 200 deregulation proposals. At both meetings Japan expressed the wish to see a strong and stable euro established in Europe to bring equilibrium to the international financial system. Both partners agreed to step up political dialogue, particularly under the ASEM arrangements *(→ point 897)*, and to cooperate in preparing for the next round of WTO nego-

---

([1])   1995 General Report, point 888.
([2])   OJ C 407, 28.12.1998; Bull. 9-1998, point 1.3.117.
([3])   OJ C 379, 7.12.1998; Bull. 11-1998, point 1.3.99.
([4])   OJ C 34, 2.2.1998; Bull. 1/2-1998, point 1.4.117.
([5])   OJ C 34, 2.2.1998; Bull. 1/2-1998, point 1.4.118.
([6])   OJ C 313, 12.10.1998; Bull. 9-1998, point 1.3.116.
([7])   Bull. 1/2-1998, point 1.4.121.
([8])   Bull. 10-1998, point 1.3.102.

tiations. They also discussed the integration of Russia and China into the multilateral trade system. A meeting between the EU troika and Japan was held in New York in September on the sidelines of the opening session of the UN General Assembly.

889.   Cooperation between the European Union and Japan continued in a variety of fields ([1]). The EU expressed its interest in stepping up cooperation on customs matters, checks on trade in nuclear materials and drug precursors, science and technology, higher education and humanitarian aid. The Commission launched a feasibility study on the creation of a European Institute in Japan, whose purpose would be to explain 'Europe' to Japanese politicians and decision-makers so as to raise its profile and create a better understanding. On 11 December the Commission adopted a revised proposal for a regulation on the implementation of a programme of specific measures and actions to improve access of EU goods and cross-border services to Japan (Table II). The Commission and Japan also published a full account of existing cooperation activities, to be updated periodically.

Canada

890.   Two EU-Canada summits were held, one in London on 14 May ([2]) and the other in Ottawa on 17 December ([3]). At the London Summit, Mr Jean Chrétien, the Canadian Prime Minister, Mr Lloyd Axworthy, Canadian Minister for Foreign Affairs, Mr Sergio Marchi, the Canadian Minister for International Trade, Mr Tony Blair, President of the Council, Mr Santer and Sir Leon Brittan expressed their satisfaction with the progress made in implementing the 1996 joint political declaration and associated action plan ([4]). They also discussed a number of political and trade issues such as the ratification of the Ottawa convention to ban anti-personnel landmines (→ point 670), the situation in Algeria and Cyprus, US extra-territorial legislation and Canadian fisheries legislation. A mutual recognition agreement on conformity assessment was signed at this summit. (→ point 729). At the Ottawa Summit, Mr Chrétien, Mr Viktor Klima, President of the Council, Mr Santer and Sir Leon Brittan launched a new trade initiative based on the trade chapter of the action plan and covering mutual recognition, equivalence and regulatory cooperation, services, government procurement, intellectual

---

[1]   1997 General Report, point 959.
[2]   Bull. 5-1998, point 1.3.97.
[3]   Bull. 12-1998.
[4]   1996 General Report, point 895.

property, competition, cultural cooperation and business-to-business contacts. The two parties also adopted a joint statement on small arms and
anti-personnel landmines, and signed three agreements concerning
research (→ point 313), nuclear research (→ point 313) and veterinary
matters (→ point 566).

891.   Two political dialogue meetings at ministerial level were also held,
one in Ottawa on 16 January ([1]) (and the other in Vienna on 22 October) ([2]). At the first meeting, Mr Lloyd Axworthy, Mr Robin Cook,
President of the Council, and Sir Leon Brittan discussed the situation in
Algeria, the Middle East, the former Yugoslavia and Cuba, and the
financial crisis affecting Asia. At the second meeting, Mr Axworthy, Mr
Wolfgang Schüssel, President of the Council, and Sir Leon discussed the
implementation of the joint action plan, fisheries, preparations for the
17 December summit, the situation in south-east Europe and Russia, and
issues relating to the concept of human security.

Australia

892.   At a ministerial meeting in Canberra on 24 June ([3]) organised in
the context of the 1997 joint declaration ([4]), Sir Leon Brittan met Mr
John Howard, the Prime Minister, and other members of the Australian
Government. They discussed progress in the implementation of the joint
declaration, the shared commitment to a multilateral trade system, climate change and the situation in the Asia-Pacific region, and signed a
mutual recognition agreement on conformity assessment. (→ point 729).
Political dialogue meetings between the European Union and Australia
took place in London on 29 January and Manila on 29 July. At the first
meeting, Mr Alexander Downer, Australian Foreign Minister, Mr Robin
Cook and Sir Leon Brittan discussed the enlargement of the European
Union and economic and monetary union, the most recent Asia-Europe
Summit, relations with China, the Asian economic crisis, the campaign
against anti-personnel mines and the implementation of the joint declaration. At the second meeting, Mr Downer and Mr Schüssel discussed
the impact of the Asian crisis; the agricultural aspects of Agenda 2000
and the Indian and Pakistani nuclear tests.

([1])   Bull. 1/2-1998, point 1.4.123.
([2])   Bull. 10-1998, point 1.3.103.
([3])   1997 General Report, point 963.
([4])   Bull. 6-1998, point 1.4.125.

New Zealand

893. Sir Leon Brittan was in New Zealand on 25 and 26 June. He was received by Prime Minister Jennifer Shipley and other members of the government. Discussions centred on bilateral relations and trade matters, the global environment and climate change, multilateral trade negotiations, the financial crisis in Asia and the situation in the Asia-Pacific region. A mutual recognition agreement on conformity assessment was also signed. (→ point 729). EU-New Zealand political dialogue meetings took place in London on 3 March and in Manila on 29 July. At the first meeting Mr Don McKinnon, New Zealand Foreign Minister, Mr Robin Cook and Sir Leon Brittan discussed the Asian economic crisis, the activities of the World Trade Organisation, New Zealand butter exports and the situation in Papua New Guinea. At the second meeting, Mr McKinnon and Mr Schüssel discussed the impact of the Asian economic crisis, the situation in East Timor, Asia-Pacific cooperation and the prospects for drawing up a joint declaration between the European Union and New Zealand.

Republic of Korea

894. On 9 December the Commission adopted a communication on EU policy on the Republic of Korea ([1]) presenting a new approach aimed at developing relations with that country. The economic part of the communication advocates encouraging reform, improving access to the market and stepping up cooperation within the WTO and in other contexts; the political part calls for more political dialogue, in particular as regards the situation in North Korea.

895. Sir Leon Brittan was in Seoul on 13 and 14 October ([2]) to meet Mr Kim Tae-Chung, President of the Republic of Korea, and other members of the Korean Government. The 14th ministerial meeting between the EU and the Republic of Korea was held in Brussels on 27 October between Sir Leon Brittan and Mr Hong Sun-yong, Korean Minister for Foreign Affairs and Trade. The subjects discussed at the two meetings were the Korean Government's programme of economic and structural reforms, access to the Korean market, Community participation in KEDO (→ point 911), the situation in North Korea and humanitarian aid to that country.

([1]) COM(1998) 714; Bull. 12-1998.
([2]) Bull. 10-1998, point 1.3.104.

Section 12

Relations with the countries of Asia

Priority activities and objectives

896. *The success of the second Asia-Europe Summit at a time when the EU's Asian partners were facing economic and financial problems is proof of the solidity of the partnership established at the first summit in 1996. Relations with China took an important step forward with the holding of a first summit, and the Council and Commission drew up new EU-China partnership objectives.*

Asia-Europe Summit (ASEM) and relations with regional bodies

897. The second Asia-Europe Summit was held in London on 3 and 4 April and brought together the Heads of State or Government of 10 Asian countries (the seven ASEAN member countries ([1]) plus China, Japan and Korea) and the 15 Member States of the European Union, plus Commission President, Jacques Santer ([2]). The EU and the Asian countries emphasised the importance of the partnership embarked on at the first ASEM Summit in Bangkok ([3]) (particularly in the light of Asia's current economic and financial difficulties), condemned protectionism and set up an Asia-Europe cooperation framework (AECF). The decision was made to hold the third summit in Korea in 2000 and the fourth in the EU in 2002. The London Summit approved a number of initiatives taken since the Bangkok Summit and launched several new ones, including the creation of an ASEM trust fund at the World Bank, a European network of financial experts to facilitate financial reform in Asia, action plans to promote trade and investment and a 'Vision Group' charged with examining the long-term prospects for relations between Asia and Europe. The new Bangkok-based Asia-Europe Environmental Technology Centre was officially declared open at the summit. The Asia-Europe Foundation, opened in Singapore in 1997, undertook a programme of activities in Asia and Europe during the year. The third Asia-Europe Business Forum (AEBF) was held in London in April, and an Asia-

---

([1]) Brunei, Indonesia, Malaysia, the Philippines, Singapore, Thailand and Vietnam.
([2]) Bull. 4-1998, points 1.3.71 and 2.3.1.
([3]) 1996 General Report, point 898.

Europe SME conference took place in Naples in May. The ASEM process was also the focus of a Parliament resolution of 12 March (^{1}).

898. The European Union actively pursued its cooperation with the Association of South-East Asian Nations (ASEAN), though the indefinite postponement (owing to the lack of agreement on the involvement of Myanmar (Burma)) (^{2}) of the scheduled November 1997 meeting of the Joint Committee established by the EC-ASEAN cooperation agreement (^{3}) had set back the launch of the 'new dynamic' in relations decided on by the February 1997 ministerial meeting (^{4}). The EU troika, together with Mr Marín, took part in the post-ministerial conference held in Manila in July following the annual ASEAN Foreign Ministers' meeting; following the same conference, the EU also attended the ASEAN Regional Forum.

899. On 23 September, on the sidelines of the UN General Assembly session in New York, the EU troika and the Commission took part in a meeting with the representatives of the South Asian Association for Regional Cooperation (^{5}).

Bilateral relations

South Asia

900. The annual ministerial-level meeting between the EU troika, Mr Marín (for the Commission) and India's Deputy Foreign Minister Vasundhra Raje took place in November in New Delhi (^{6}).

901. A draft cooperation agreement with Pakistan was initialled on 22 April (Table III) during Prime Minister Nawaz Sharif's visit to the Commission (^{7}). On 1 December the Commission proposed that this agreement be concluded. On 5 November (^{8}) Sri Lanka's Industrial Development Minister, Clement Gooneratne visited the Commission, while the

---

(^{1}) OJ C 104, 6.4.1998; Bull. 3-1998, point 1.3.113.
(^{2}) Burma joined ASEAN in July 1997, but not the EC-ASEAN cooperation agreement — this would require a protocol of accession to be signed.
(^{3}) OJ L 144, 10.6.1980; Fourteenth General Report, point 690.
(^{4}) 1997 General Report, point 972.
(^{5}) Bangladesh, Bhutan, India, Maldives, Nepal, Pakistan, Sri Lanka.
(^{6}) Bull. 11-1998, point 1.3.104.
(^{7}) Bull. 4-1998, point 1.3.77.
(^{8}) Bull. 11-1998, point 1.3.108.

EU-Sri Lanka Joint Committee met in December. On 17 September Parliament issued a resolution on the flooding in Bangladesh and China ([1]).

902.   In May and June, two European Union statements *(→ point 682),* the Cardiff European Council conclusions ([2]) and a Parliament resolution ([3]) condemned the nuclear tests carried out by India and Pakistan. On 26 October the Council defined a common position on the EU's contribution to the promotion of non-proliferation and confidence-building in the south Asian region ([4]).

903.   On 26 January the Council adopted a common position setting out the EU's basic objectives towards Afghanistan ([5]): to bring about a sustainable peace, promote respect for human rights and reinforce the fight against illegal drugs and terrorism. The common position included provision for continuing the embargo on shipments of arms, munitions and military hardware imposed by Common Position 96/746/CFSP ([6]). A Parliament resolution of 19 January ([7]) again condemned the Taliban regime and its systematic human rights violations and expressed solidarity with the women of Afghanistan ([8]).

South-east Asia

904.   The European Union provided logistical and financial assistance for the organisation of Cambodia's elections on 26 July and dispatched 200 observers, led by its special representative, Glenys Kinnock MEP. The conduct of the elections was satisfactory overall, a fact reflected in subsequent EU statements *(→ point 682);* before the elections, in March and June, Parliament had issued resolutions on the situation ([9]). The first meeting of the EC-Laos Joint Committee set up by the 1997 cooperation agreement ([10]) was held in Vientiane from 25 to 27 June. Vietnam's Prime Minister, Phan Van Khai visited the Commission on 8 April ([11]).

([1])   OJ C 313, 12.10.1998; Bull. 9-1998, point 1.3.122.
([2])   Bull. 6-1998, point I.28.
([3])   OJ C 210, 6.7.1998; Bull. 6-1998, point 1.4.135.
([4])   Common Position 98/606/CFSP (OJ L 290, 29.10.1998; Bull. 10-1998, point 1.3.108).
([5])   Common Position 98/108/CFSP (OJ L 32, 6.2.1998; Bull. 1/2-1998, point 1.4.124).
([6])   OJ L 342, 31.12.1996; 1996 General Report, point 904.
([7])   1997 General Report, point 974.
([8])   OJ C 80, 16.3.1998; Bull. 1/2-1998, point 1.4.125.
([9])   OJ C 104, 6.4.1998; Bull. 3-1998, point 1.3.114; OJ C 210, 6.7.1998; Bull. 6-1998, point 1.4.129.
([10]) OJ L 334, 5.12.1997; 1997 General Report, point 975.
([11]) Bull. 4-1998, point 1.3.78.

905.   Council conclusions issued in May (^{1}), June (^{2}) and July (^{3}) and European Council conclusions in June and December (^{4}) commented on the political situation in Indonesia and East Timor.

906.   As the political and human-rights situations in Myanmar (Burma) had continued to deteriorate, the Council arranged two six-month extensions (on 27 April (^{5}) and 26 October (^{6})) to Common Position 96/635/ CFSP (^{7}), which steps up sanctions against the country. Previously, on 26 January, it had amended that common position to take account of the ruling body's change of name from the State Law and Order Restoration Council (SLORC) to the State Peace and Development Council (SPDC) (^{8}). In addition, the Council confirmed on 26 October that it felt unable to agree to Burma's accession to the EC-ASEAN cooperation agreement (→ point 898) (^{9}).

The Far East

907.   On 25 March the Commission adopted a communication entitled 'Building a comprehensive partnership with China' (^{10}), which sets out five priorities for the partnership: to foster China's integration into the international community by stepping up political dialogue; to support China's transition to an open society founded on the rule of law and human rights; to make China a more integral part of the world economy; to make better use of European financing and to consolidate the image of the European Union in China. On 29 June the Council endorsed these guidelines (^{11}). Previously, in its conclusions of 23 February, it had described the results of the human-rights dialogue begun with China as encouraging (^{12}).

908.   The first EU-China Summit was held in London on 2 April (^{13}) and involved China's Prime Minister, Zhu Rongji, the President of the European Council, Mr Tony Blair, and, for the Commission, Mr Santer

---

(^{1})   Bull. 5-1998, point 1.3.101.
(^{2})   Bull. 6-1998, point 1.4.136.
(^{3})   Bull. 7/8-1998, point 1.4.118.
(^{4})   Bull. 6-1998, point I.28; Bull. 12-1998.
(^{5})   Decision 98/303/CFSP (OJ L 138, 9.5.1998; Bull. 4-1998, point 1.3.75).
(^{6})   Decision 98/612/CFSP (OJ L 291, 30.10.1998; Bull. 10-1998, point 1.3.112).
(^{7})   OJ L 287, 8.11.1996; 1996 General Report, point 903.
(^{8})   Decision 98/107/CFSP (OJ L 32, 6.2.1998; Bull. 1/2-1998, point 1.4.129).
(^{9})   Bull. 10-1998, point 1.3.111.
(^{10})   COM(1998) 181; Bull. 3-1998, point 1.3.115.
(^{11})   Bull. 6-1998, point 1.4.132.
(^{12})   Bull. 1/2-1998, point 1.4.126.
(^{13})   Bull. 4-1998, point 1.3.73.

and Sir Leon Brittan. It culminated in the adoption of a joint communiqué in which the two sides stressed the need to improve dialogue and cooperation between them and reaffirmed their commitment to China's rapid accession to the WTO. China and the EU also agreed to hold similar summits yearly. The Joint Committee set up by the trade and economic cooperation agreement ([1]) met in Brussels on 10 and 11 June ([2]).

909.　Mr Santer, Sir Leon Brittan and Mr de Silguy visited China from 29 October to 5 November where they met President Jiang Zemin and Prime Minister Zhu Rongji among others ([3]). This was the first visit by a Commission President to China since 1986. Discussion centred on China's economic reforms, the financial crisis in Asia, the human rights situation in China, the effects of the launch of the euro and EU-China trade relations and cooperation. Sir Leon had already made a trip to China in February ([4]).

910.　In the wake of the Commission communication entitled 'The European Union and Hong Kong: Beyond 1997' ([5]), Parliament adopted a resolution on 8 October ([6]) calling on the government of the Hong Kong Special Administrative Region to ensure that civil and political rights and freedom of expression were adhered to, and asking the European Union to back international autonomy for Hong Kong. In December the Vienna European Council took note of the positive development of the transition process in Macau ([7]). The EC-Macau Joint Committee met in Brussels on 28 May.

911.　The agreement on the arrangements for Euratom's accession to KEDO, the Korean Peninsula Energy Development Organisation ([8]), entered into force on 19 September (Table III). As a member of the KEDO executive board, Euratom contributed to the implementation of this important non-proliferation initiative. The food situation in the Democratic People's Republic of Korea (North Korea) remained critical, and was commented on in a Parliament resolution of 11 March ([9]).

([1])　OJ L 250, 19.9.1985; Nineteenth General Report, point 884.
([2])　Bull. 6-1998, point 1.4.131.
([3])　Bull. 11-1998, point 1.3.102.
([4])　Bull. 1/2-1998, points 1.4.127 and 1.4.128.
([5])　COM(97) 171; 1997 General Report, point 980.
([6])　OJ C 328, 26.10.1998; Bull. 10-1998, point 1.3.111.
([7])　Bull. 12-1998.
([8])　1997 General Report, point 982.
([9])　OJ C 104, 6.4.1998; Bull. 3-1998, point 1.1.8.

912.   The EU's relations with the Republic of Korea (South Korea) are covered in Section 11 ('Relations with the United States, Japan and other industrialised countries') of this chapter *(→ points 894 and 895).*

Cooperation

913.   Financial and technical cooperation amounted this year to ECU 313 million, with priority going to the overall goal of alleviating poverty and covering primary education, health care, involving women in decision-making, and rural development. The Commission also took care to involve local authorities in implementation as far as possible. Economic cooperation, which totalled ECU 83.1 million, focused on the financial sector (ASEM trust fund), intellectual property and civil aviation (programme of cooperation with India). On 29 January the Commission adopted a report on financial and technical assistance to, and economic cooperation with, the developing countries in Asia and Latin America from 1991 to 1995 ([1]).

([1])   COM(1998) 40; Bull. 1/2-1998, point 1.4.131.

Section 13

Relations with Latin American countries

Priority activities and objectives

914. Political ties between the European Union and Latin America grew closer, with an increase in trade and regional integration and better targeting of cooperation to make it more relevant, innovative and flexible. Key developments included the entry into force of the cooperation agreement with the Andean Community and the interim agreement with Mexico, the Commission's recommendation on opening negotiations for association agreements with Mercosur and Chile, and the decision by leaders of the two regions to hold a summit in 1999.

Relations with regional groupings

915. As part of the political dialogue established between the European Union and Central America in 1984 (¹), the 14th San José ministerial conference (²) was held in San José, Costa Rica, on 10 February (³). The participants adopted a joint communiqué emphasising the Central American countries' progress towards peace, democracy and modernisation, the positive impact of the special scheme of generalised agricultural preferences (⁴) and cooperation projects, and the need to step up human rights protection and the fight against drugs. The Community stated its readiness to support integration in the region, subject to agreement by the partners on sectors and methods. After several Central American countries suffered considerable damage from hurricane Mitch at the end of October, the EU and its Member States adopted a package of measures including emergency relief and debt reduction for the affected countries. In addition to rapid intervention measures *(→ point 788)*, the Commission approved a project costing ECU 8.2 million to pave the way for a regional reconstruction programme. Parliament (⁵) and the Committee of the Regions (⁶) passed resolutions on aid to countries hit by hurricane Mitch on 19 November; the hurricane also figured in

---

(¹) Eighteenth General Report, point 707.
(²) The San José group comprises Costa Rica, El Salvador, Guatemala, Honduras, Nicaragua, and Panama.
(³) Bull. 1/2-1998, point 1.4.135.
(⁴) 1996 General Report, point 740.
(⁵) OJ C 379, 7.12.1998; Bull. 11-1998, point 1.3.110.
(⁶) Bull. 11-1998, point 1.3.111.

Council conclusions of 30 November (¹) and 1 December (²), and in the conclusions of the European Council held on 15 and 16 December (²).

916. The eighth ministerial meeting between the EU and the Rio Group, part of the dialogue institutionalised by the 1990 Rome declaration (³), was held in Panama on 11 and 12 February (⁴), bringing together the Foreign Ministers of the 12 Rio Group countries (⁵) and of the EU Member States, and the Commission. The meeting culminated in the adoption of a declaration in which ministers expressed their commitment to joint responsibility and international cooperation in the fight against drugs, reaffirmed the importance they attached to political dialogue, democratic principles and the rule of law, and highlighted the results of various Community programmes in Latin America. They also welcomed the decision by EU, Latin American and Caribbean Heads of State or Government to hold their first summit in the first half of 1999, in response to the interest shown by the Amsterdam European Council (⁶). The two parties met again in September during the UN General Assembly and adopted a declaration confirming that the summit would take place (→ point 683).

917. The third EU-Mercosur ministerial meeting was held in Panama on 12 February to coincide with the EU-Rio Group ministerial meeting, continuing the political dialogue established by the interregional framework signed in December 1995 (⁷). It was attended by the Foreign Ministers of the Mercosur member countries (Argentina, Brazil, Paraguay, and Uruguay), Chile, Bolivia (as an observer) and the EU, plus the Commission. The ministers welcomed the extension of the Mercosur consultation and political coordination mechanism to Bolivia and Chile on 1 July 1997 and reiterated their interest in expanding trade, investment and cooperation ties, reaffirming their commitment to building an interregional association based on democratic principles, fundamental human rights and trade liberalisation.

918. The Commission accordingly recommended on 22 July that the Council authorise it to negotiate an interregional framework cooperation agreement with Mercosur (Table III) and a political and economic asso-

---

(¹)   Bull. 11-1998, point 1.3.112.
(²)   Bull. 12-1998.
(³)   Twenty-fourth General Report, point 750.
(⁴)   Bull. 1/2-1998, point 1.4.134.
(⁵)   Argentina, Bolivia, Brazil, Chile, Colombia, Ecuador, Mexico, Panama, Paraguay, Peru, Uruguay and Venezuela.
(⁶)   1997 General Report, point 988.
(⁷)   1995 General Report, point 26.

ciation agreement with Chile (Table III), both of them aimed at creating a political and economic association with three key components: a partnership in political and security matters, greater economic and institutional cooperation, and the establishment of a free-trade area for goods and services which would reflect the sensitive nature of some products while ensuring compliance with WTO rules. On 9 September the Economic and Social Committee welcomed the proposals for the agreements ([1]). The EU troika and the Commission met Mercosur representatives again on 24 September during the UN General Assembly.

919.   In another development coinciding with the EU-Rio Group ministerial meeting, EU representatives met the Foreign Ministers of the Andean Community (Cartagena agreement) countries ([2]). The two sides expressed satisfaction at the Andean Community's progress on integration, the completion of ratification of the framework cooperation agreement between the European Community and the Andean Community, and the signing of a financing agreement between the European Investment Bank and the Corporación Andina de Fomento (CAF); the Andean Community also highlighted the positive impact of the system of generalised preferences on the Andean countries in stimulating new economic activities and helping to combat drug production. The ministers also raised the possibility of holding a top-level meeting between the two parties in 1999 to coincide with the summit of EU, Latin American and Caribbean leaders (→ point 916).

920.   The framework agreement on cooperation between the European Community and the Cartagena agreement countries entered into force on 1 May (Table III). This wide-ranging agreement affirmed the importance of consolidating the Andean regional integration process, giving priority to social development projects.

Bilateral relations

921.   The second ministerial meeting between the EU and Chile was held in Panama on 12 February, to coincide with the EU-Rio Group ministerial meeting ([3]). On 22 July the Commission recommended that the Council authorise it to negotiate a political and economic association agreement with Chile, with the same objectives as the agreement with

([1])   OJ C 407, 28.12.1998; Bull. 9-1998, point 1.3.130.
([2])   Bolivia, Colombia, Ecuador, Peru and Venezuela.
([3])   Bull. 1/2-1998, point 1.4.138.

Mercosur *(→ point 918)*. Parliament adopted, on 22 October, a resolution on the arrest of General Pinochet([1]).

922.   The Council noted encouraging developments in Cuba, including the release of political prisoners, but concluded that it was unclear whether these were fundamental, lasting changes. It therefore decided on 8 June([2]), and again on 7 December([3]), to reaffirm its common position of 2 December 1996([4]).

923.   The interim agreement on trade and trade-related matters between the European Community and Mexico entered into force on 1 July (Table III). The first meeting of the Joint EC-Mexico Council provided for in the agreement was held in Brussels on 14 July([5]), on which occasion Mr Wolfgang Schüssel, President of the Council, stressed the importance of the agreement for the development of economic relations between the two sides. In another development, the EU Council authorised the Commission on 25 May to negotiate a trade liberalisation agreement with Mexico covering trade in goods and services, public procurement and capital movements, and the adoption of rules on competition and intellectual property (Table III). Parliament, pointing to the human rights clause in the partnership agreement with Mexico([6]), passed a resolution on 15 January on the situation in Chiapas([7]).

924.   Mr Rafael Caldera, President of Venezuela, visited the Commission on 17 March for talks with Mr Santer and Mr Marín([8]). Mr Ricardo Cabrisas Ruiz, the Cuban Minister for Foreign Trade, visited the Commission on 2 October([9]) and Mr Jorge Quiroga Ramírez, Vice-President of Bolivia, also paid a visit from 26 to 28 October([10]). Mr Marín visited Colombia's President, Mr Ernesto Samper, in February([11]), and the President of Mexico, Mr Ernesto Zedillo, in October([12]). Sir Leon Brittan visited Argentina, Brazil and Uruguay to discuss major multilateral trade issues in April.

---

[1]   OJ C 341, 9.11.1998 and Bull. 10-1998, point 1.3.117.
[2]   Bull. 6-1998, point 1.4.139.
[3]   Bull. 12-1998.
[4]   OJ L 322, 12.12.1996; 1996 General Report, point 918.
[5]   Bull. 7/8-1997, point 1.4.127.
[6]   1997 General Report, point 995.
[7]   OJ C 34, 2.2.1998; Bull. 1/2-1998, point 1.4.143.
[8]   Bull. 3-1998, point 1.3.118.
[9]   Bull. 10-1998, point 1.3.118.
[10]   Bull. 10-1998, point 1.3.116.
[11]   Bull. 1/2-1998, point 1.4.140.
[12]   Bull. 10-1998, point 1.3.120.

Development cooperation

925.   Financial and technical cooperation with the countries of Latin America totalled ECU 191 million. Thirty-three projects were financed, with the emphasis on public sector institution building, education, rural development and social issues. Some ECU 49.9 million was spent on 31 economic cooperation projects to consolidate horizontal decentralised cooperation programmes and support economic reforms, industrial co-operation, higher education and the energy sector. The Commission adopted a report in January on cooperation with developing countries in Asia and Latin America from 1991 to 1995 (→ point 913).

926.   Support for democratisation was another focus of cooperation (→ point 39). A multiannual programme to promote human rights in Central America was launched, and a total of ECU 15.3 million went to 12 projects to assist uprooted people in Latin America, with particular attention being paid to the implementation of the peace accords in Guatemala.

927.   On 22 October Parliament urged the EU to ensure that international financial support directed towards Latin America was sufficient to prevent a liquidity crisis in the region ([1]).

---

[1]   OJ C 341, 9.11.1998; Bull. 10-1998, point 1.3.114.

Section 14

Relations with the African, Caribbean and Pacific (ACP) countries and the overseas countries and territories (OCTs)

Priority activities and objectives

928. The agreement on the mid-term review of the fourth Lomé Convention and the protocol on South Africa's accession to the Convention came into force in June. September saw the official start of negotiations for a new development partnership agreement to replace the Lomé Convention after the year 2000. The Council adopted a common position on human rights, democratic principles, the rule of law and good governance in Africa. It also for the first time used the machinery in the revised Lomé IV to deal with failure by a party to respect democracy and human rights.

Relations with ACP countries

General strategy

929. On 29 June, following the Commission's recommendation of 28 January, the Council adopted negotiating directives for a new development partnership agreement with the ACP countries (Table III). This will replace the fourth Lomé Convention (→ *point 935*), which expires in February 2000. The negotiating directives are aimed at the long-term development of the partnership, closely linking political dialogue, development cooperation and economic and trade relations. In particular, they envisage enhancing the political dimension of the partnership, refocusing cooperation on poverty eradication and extending it to economic partnership. This would involve trade agreements with regional sub-groups, with the aim of helping the ACP countries to integrate gradually into the global economy. Other aims are to improve the efficiency of financial cooperation and maintain the unity of the ACP group while introducing the principle of differentiation to meet differing needs and constraints. The Council agreed with the ACP countries to give Cuba observer status at these negotiations, underlining, however, that its prospects of becoming a party to the new agreement were conditional on

significant progress being made along the lines set out in the common position on Cuba (→ point 932).

930.   Negotiations for the new development partnership agreement were officially launched in Brussels on 30 September (→ point 933). The guidelines adopted by the Commission in 1997 (¹) in preparation for the negotiations were endorsed by Parliament on 1 April (²).

931.   To clarify the EU's position on human rights, democratic principles, the rule of law and good governance in Africa with a view to the forthcoming negotiations, the Commission adopted a communication on 12 March (³) and the Council adopted Common Position 98/350/CFSP (⁴), together with conclusions, on 25 May (⁵). Fresh conclusions were adopted on 30 November (⁶). A conference on dialogue for democratisation took place in Stockholm in November (⁷) and was attended by representatives from ACP and EU governments and civil society.

Institutional relations

932.   The ACP-EC Council of Ministers held its 23rd meeting in Bridgetown (Barbados) on 7 and 8 May (⁸). On the agenda were future EU-ACP relations, EU enlargement, financial and trade cooperation and the World Trade Organisation's attitude to developing countries.

933.   An extraordinary meeting of the ACP-EC Council of Ministers was held in Brussels on 30 September to mark the official start of negotiations for a new development partnership agreement (⁹).

934.   The ACP-EC Joint Assembly held its two annual sessions in Mauritius (20 to 23 April) (¹⁰) and Brussels (21 to 24 September) (¹¹). Discussions centred on regional and intra-ACP cooperation, ACP-EU relations after the expiry of Lomé IV, the impact of climate change on small island nations, trade relations within the WTO, fisheries policy,

---

(¹)   COM(97) 537; 1997 General Report, point 1003.
(²)   OJ C 138, 4.5.1998; Bull. 4-1998, point 1.3.82.
(³)   COM(1998) 146; Bull. 3-1998, point 1.3.121.
(⁴)   OJ L 158, 2.6.1998; Bull. 5-1998, point 1.3.115.
(⁵)   Bull. 5-1998, point 1.3.115.
(⁶)   Bull. 11-1998, point 1.3.123.
(⁷)   Bull. 11-1998, point 1.3.122.
(⁸)   Bull. 5-1998, point 1.3.114.
(⁹)   Bull. 9-1998, point 1.3.132a.
(¹⁰) Bull. 4-1998, point 1.3.83.
(¹¹) Bull. 9-1998, point 1.3.132.

and the state of bilateral negotiations between the EU and South Africa. The Joint Assembly also discussed the Great Lakes region, Angola, Eritrea and Ethiopia, Guinea-Bissau, Equatorial Guinea, Haiti, Nigeria, Papua New Guinea, Sierra Leone, Somalia, Sudan, Togo and Zambia. At the Brussels meeting, South Africa took part for the first time in the Joint Assembly as a party to the Lomé Convention. On 13 March Parliament adopted a resolution on the Joint Assembly's work in 1997 ([1]).

Implementation of the Lomé Conventions

935.   The agreement on the mid-term review of the fourth Lomé Convention ([2]) entered into force on 1 June (Table III), having been concluded by the Council on 27 April.

936.   The Council adopted the financial regulation for the eighth European Development Fund (Table II) on 16 June. On 20 July it adopted Regulation (EC) No 1706/98 (Table II) granting ACP States more favourable treatment on a number of agricultural products than is normally accorded to non-member countries under the most-favoured-nation clause.

937.   On 17 June ([3]), Parliament asked to be consulted whenever the Council intended to suspend or resume cooperation with an ACP country under Article 366a of the fourth Lomé Convention ([4]). This article was used for the first time in respect of Togo (→ point 955).

Trade cooperation

938.   The Commission continued with measures introduced in 1997 to foster trade among ACP countries and make them more competitive ([5]). To improve the take-up of the new preferences, it also sought to make traders more aware of the relevant provisions of the revised Lomé IV and their incorporation into Community law.

([1])   OJ C 104, 6.4.1998; Bull. 3-1998, point 1.3.122.
([2])   1996 General Report, point 929.
([3])   OJ C 210, 6.7.1998; Bull. 6-1998, point 1.4.146.
([4])   1996 General Report, point 929.
([5])   1997 General Report, point 1010.

Stabex

939. On 17 July the Commission approved 14 Stabex transfers for 1997 ([1]). A total of ECU 64 792 822 will go to 11 ACP countries. On 23 September the Commission adopted a report on Stabex operations in 1997 ([2]).

Sysmin

940. The Commission continued to examine in 1998, Sysmin operations but no decisions were taken.

Support for ACP banana producers

941. On 14 January, in tandem with its proposed changes to the common organisation of the market for bananas, the Commission adopted a proposal for a regulation that would set up special arrangements to help traditional ACP banana producers become more competitive and adapt to the new market conditions (→ *point 576).*

Protocols

942. On 20 April the Council adopted a decision (Table III) concluding agreements on the guaranteed prices applicable for the 1997-98 delivery period for cane sugar originating in ACP countries and India. On 23 November it adopted negotiating directives for an agreement covering 1998-99 (Table III).

Industrial cooperation and development of the private sector

943. On 20 November the Commission adopted a communication on the Community's strategy for private sector development in the ACP countries ([3]). It also approved new projects in support of the private sector in a number of ACP countries. For the first time, these included commercial as well as industrial projects. To promote investment in mining, the Commission also organised a forum for central and eastern

---

([1]) Bull. 7/8-1998, point 1.4.132.
([2]) Bull. 9-1998, point 1.3.133.
([3]) COM(1998) 667; Bull. 11-1998, point 1.3.121.

Africa in Accra (Ghana) from 30 March to 2 April. Work continued on an intra-ACP business support programme.

Financial and technical cooperation

944. A total of ECU 2 288 million was granted for financial and technical cooperation under the sixth, seventh and eighth EDFs. The breakdown by sector is shown in Table 18.

TABLE 18

Annual breakdown of financing decisions for ACP countries

(million ECU)

Sector	Amount granted				
	1994	1995	1996	1997	1998 (¹)
National and regional indicative programme	(²)	(²)	(²)	(²)	1 199.06
Structural adjustment	(²)	(²)	(²)	(²)	585.56
Sysmin	(²)	(²)	(²)	(²)	0.51
Stabex	(²)	(²)	(²)	(²)	151.69
Emergency aid	(²)	(²)	(²)	(²)	35.63
Aid for refugees	(²)	(²)	(²)	(²)	0.54
Risk capital	(²)	(²)	(²)	(²)	294.55
Interest rate subsidies	(²)	(²)	(²)	(²)	19.14
Total	2 445.46	1 520.09	964.86	615.99	2 288.09

(¹) Provisional figures.
(²) Breakdown by sector not available for previous years as sectors have been redefined.

Support for structural adjustment

945. Decisions were taken to finance structural adjustment in 19 countries for a total of ECU 539 million. As required by the revised fourth Lomé Convention, priority went to the education and health sectors.

946. On 6 July the Council laid down the arrangements for the Community's participation in the World Bank/IMF initiative for the heavily indebted poor countries (¹). The Community will contribute to the debt reduction both as a donor, with increased support for structural adjustment, and as a creditor, cancelling part of the risk capital and special

(¹)   Decision 98/453/EC (OJ L 198, 15.7.1998; Bull. 7/8-1998, point 1.4.130).

loans debt. Parliament adopted a resolution on the initiative on 16 January ([1]); the Council adopted conclusions on 12 February ([2]).

947. The Commission continued to take part in the special programme of assistance for Africa ([3]), chairing a working group on the future of the programme and coordinating two missions by the donors involved in the country chosen for the pilot project on the new approach to conditionality.

Relations with regional groupings

948. The third ministerial conference ([4]) between representatives of the European Union and the Southern African Development Community (SADC) member States ([5]) was held in Vienna on 3 and 4 November ([6]).

949. The Commission continued its policy of close and active cooperation with other regional integration organisations such as the UEMOA (west African economic and monetary union), Ecowas (Economic Community of West African States), Comesa (common market of eastern and southern Africa) and the EAC (East African Community). The negotiating directives for a new development partnership agreement with the ACP countries *(→ point 929)* assign an important role to regional integration, regarded as a step towards integration into the world economy.

Bilateral relations

950. The protocol for South Africa's accession to the revised fourth Lomé Convention came into force on 1 June (Table III). The South African President, Mr Nelson Mandela, was present in Cardiff on 15 and 16 June when the European Council congratulated South Africa on its economic and social efforts and expressed the EU's determination to conclude a general agreement with it on trade, development and cooperation ([7]), a position it underlined at its meeting in Vienna in December ([8]). Parliament had also expressed support for such an agreement in

---

([1]) OJ C 34, 2.2.1998; Bull. 1/2-1998, point 1.4.147.
([2]) Bull. 1/2-1998, point 1.4.148.
([3]) 1996 General Report, point 939.
([4]) Second conference: 1996 General Report, point 940.
([5]) Angola, Botswana, Democratic Republic of the Congo, Lesotho, Malawi, Mauritius, Mozambique, Namibia, Seychelles, South Africa, Swaziland, Tanzania, Zimbabwe.
([6]) Bull. 11-1998, point 1.3.125.
([7]) Bull. 6-1998, point I.24.
([8]) Bull. 12-1998.

a resolution on 28 May (^{1}). On 3 September the Commission adopted the first annual report (^{2}) on the implementation of the European programme for reconstruction and development in South Africa (^{3}).

951.   Following new UN Security Council resolutions, the Council tightened its sanctions against UNITA in Angola, adopting Common Position 98/425/CFSP (^{4}) on 3 July, and Regulation (EC) No 1705/98 (^{5}), replacing and strengthening Regulation (EC) No 2229/97 (^{6}), on 28 July.

952.   Parliament (^{7}), the European Council (^{8}) and the Council (^{9}) continued to express concern about the situation in the Great Lakes region. On 13 July the Council extended (^{10}) Joint Action 96/250/CFSP (^{11}) appointing a special envoy for the region, and on 29 June (^{12}) it renewed Joint Action 97/875/CFSP (^{13}) in support of the democratic transition process in the Democratic Republic of the Congo. On 30 March it adopted a new common position on Rwanda (98/252/CFSP) (^{14}) to replace Common Position 94/697/CFSP (^{15}); on 29 June and 30 November it adopted conclusions on Burundi (^{16}).

953.   In June, Parliament (^{17}), the European Council (^{18}) and the Council (^{19}) expressed dismay at the hostilities between Ethiopia and Eritrea. Parliament and the Council likewise expressed concern at the humanitarian situation in Sudan (^{20}) and Guinea-Bissau (^{21}) in May and July respectively; also in July, they called on the new president of Nigeria to free all political prisoners and take initial steps towards a system of civil

---

(^{1})   OJ C 167, 1.6.1998; Bull. 5-1998, point 1.3.126.
(^{2})   COM(1998) 502; Bull. 9-1998, point 1.3.134.
(^{3})   Regulation (EC) No 2259/96 (OJ L 306, 28.11.1996; 1996 General Report, point 947).
(^{4})   OJ L 190, 4.7.1998; Bull. 7/8-1998, point 1.4.134.
(^{5})   OJ L 215, 1.8.1998; Bull. 7/8-1998, point 1.4.135.
(^{6})   OJ L 309, 12.11.1997; 1997 General Report, point 1021.
(^{7})   OJ C 313, 12.10.1998; Bull. 9-1998, point 1.3.140.
(^{8})   Bull. 12-1998.
(^{9})   Bull. 3-1998, point 1.3.128; Bull. 11-1998, point 1.3.134.
(^{10}) Decision 98/452/CFSP (OJ L 198, 15.7.1998; Bull. 7/8-1998, point 1.4.143).
(^{11}) OJ L 87, 4.4.1996; 1996 General Report, point 941.
(^{12}) Decision 98/410/CFSP (OJ L 187, 1.7.1998; Bull. 6-1998, point 1.4.161).
(^{13}) OJ L 357, 31.12.1997; 1997 General Report, point 1020.
(^{14}) OJ L 108, 7.4.1998; Bull. 3-1998, point 1.3.126.
(^{15}) OJ L 283, 29.10.1994; 1994 General Report, point 751.
(^{16}) Bull. 6-1998, point 1.4.151; Bull. 11-1998, point 1.3.128.
(^{17}) OJ C 210, 6.7.1998; Bull. 6-1998, point 1.4.156.
(^{18}) Bull. 6-1998, point I.30.
(^{19}) Bull. 6-1998, point 1.4.155.
(^{20}) OJ C 167, 1.6.1998; Bull. 5-1998, point 1.3.125 (Parliament); Bull. 5-1998, point 1.3.124 (Council).
(^{21}) OJ C 292, 21.9.1998; Bull. 7/8-1998, point 1.2.2 (Parliament); Bull. 7/8-1998, point 1.4.136 (Council).

democratic government (^{1}). Subsequently, on 30 October, the Council adopted Common Position 98/614/CFSP (^{2}) lifting the restrictive measures taken against Nigeria in Common Position 95/515/CFSP (^{3}), apart from those to do with the suspension of military cooperation and the arms embargo. On 22 December it adopted Joint Action 98/735/CFSP (^{4}), aimed at supporting the democratic process in Nigeria.

954.   In March Parliament welcomed the restoration of the elected government of Sierra Leone (^{5}). In April the Council repealed (^{6}) the sanctions that had been taken against the country in 1997 (^{7}) and then in June implemented sanctions against the forces that continued to resist the government's authority (^{8}).

955.   Alarmed by findings of irregularities during the elections in Togo, and at the Commission's initiative, the Council commenced consultations with the country in July (^{9}) under Articles 5 and 366a of the fourth Lomé Convention, which set out obligations on democracy and human rights and lay down the procedure to be followed if a party fails to fulfil those obligations, possibly resulting in the Convention being suspended (→ point 935). In September it formally asked the Togolese Government (^{10}) to tell it what measures had been taken. On 25 November the rule of law and civil peace had still not been restored and, finding the explanations given by the Togolese authorities unsatisfactory, the Council decided on 14 December to close the consultations and leave cooperation with the Togolese Government in abeyance, while seeking not to penalise civil society in the country (^{11}).

956.   Mr Pinheiro visited South Africa (^{12}), Angola (^{13}), Saint Lucia (^{14}) and Kenya (^{15}). Visitors to the Commission included Mr Edison James,

---

(^{1}) OJ C 292, 21.9.1998; Bull. 7/8-1998, point 1.4.141 (Parliament); Bull. 7/8-1998, point 1.4.140 (Council).
(^{2}) OJ L 193, 31.10.1998; Bull. 10-1998, point 1.3.131.
(^{3}) OJ L 298, 11.12.1995; 1995 General Report, point 949.
(^{4}) OJ L 354, 30.12.1998; Bull. 12-1998.
(^{5}) OJ C 104, 6.4.1998; Bull. 3-1998, point 1.3.127.
(^{6}) Common Position 98/300/CFSP and Regulation (EC) No 941/98 (OJ L 136, 8.5.1998; Bull. 4-1998, point 1.3.89).
(^{7}) 1997 General Report, point 1023.
(^{8}) Common Position 98/409/CFSP (OJ L 187, 1.7.1998; Bull. 6-1998, point 1.4.162).
(^{9}) Bull. 7/8-1998, point 1.4.150.
(^{10}) Bull. 9-1998, point 1.3.143.
(^{11}) Bull. 12-1998.
(^{12}) Bull. 1/2-1998, point 1.4.157; Bull. 10-1998, point 1.3.127; Bull. 12-1998.
(^{13}) Bull. 1/2-1998, point 1.4.152.
(^{14}) Bull. 5-1998, point 1.3.122.
(^{15}) Bull. 10-1998, point 1.3.130.

Prime Minister of Dominica (^{1}), Mr Barnabas Dlamini, Prime Minister of the Kingdom of Swaziland (^{2}), the Jamaican Finance Minister, Mr Omar Davies (^{3}) and Mr Laurent-Désiré Kabila, President of the Democratic Republic of the Congo (^{4}).

Relations with overseas countries and territories (OCTs)

957.   To implement certain trade aspects of Decision 97/803/EC (^{5}), the Commission adopted three regulations regarding arrangements for the import of rice from ACP countries and OCTs (^{6}).

(^{1})   Bull. 5-1998, point 1.3.116.
(^{2})   Bull. 6-1998, point 1.4.163.
(^{3})   Bull. 11-1998, point 1.3.131.
(^{4})   Bull. 11-1998, point 1.3.132.
(^{5})   OJ L 329, 29.11.1997; 1997 General Report, point 1027.
(^{6})   Regulations (EC) No 163/98, (EC) No 1 063/98 and (EC) No 1996/98 (OJ L 18, 23.1.1998, OJ L 152, 26.5.1998 and OJ L 257, 19.9.1998).

Section 15

Diplomatic relations

958.   Bosnia and Herzegovina's head of mission was accredited as the country's first-ever ambassador to the European Communities. The Commission and the Council approved the opening of diplomatic relations between the Community and Bosnia and Herzegovina in 1993. This leaves the number of foreign missions accredited to the European Communities unchanged at 165 ([1]).

959.   On 22 July the Commission adopted a resource allocation plan for its external representation in the period 1998-2000. It converted one delegation into an office ([2]) and reorganised three offices ([3]). It also established a list of political priorities for extension of its external representation in the future. At year's end the Commission was accredited to 128 countries and international organisations.

([1])   The *Bulletin of the European Union* contains the complete monthly list of ambassadors accredited to the European Communities.
([2])   Suriname.
([3])   Antigua and Barbuda, Tonga, Vanuatu.

Chapter VI

Cooperation in the fields of justice and home affairs

Section 1

Priority activities and objectives

960.   With a view to the entry into force of the Treaty of Amsterdam, in December the Vienna European Council approved an action plan produced by the Council and the Commission on the basic ideas and arrangements for implementing the Treaty provisions concerning the establishment of an area of freedom, security and justice (¹). *The plan was adopted by the Council on 7 December on the basis of a Commission communication of 14 July entitled 'Towards an area of freedom, security and justice'* (²), *in response to the request made by the Cardiff European Council* (³). *Emphasising the importance it attached to increasing cooperation in the fields of justice and home affairs, the European Council identified several areas calling for increased action (cross-border crime, environmental crime, drugs, the influx of migrants, racism and xenophobia* (⁴). *On 19 March the Council decided, for its part, to increase openness and transparency in its activities in the fields of justice and home affairs* (⁵). *The Vienna European Council also stressed the importance of integrating Schengen rapidly into the Union framework and agreed to hold a special meeting in October 1999 to be devoted entirely to justice and home affairs* (¹).

(¹)   Bull. 12-1998.
(²)   COM(1998) 459; Bull. 7/8-1998, points 1.5.1 and 2.2.1.
(³)   Bull. 6-1998, point I.14. 48.
(⁴)   Bull. 6-1998, point I.12.
(⁵)   Bull. 3-1998, point 1.4.1.

The year saw the entry into force of the Europol Convention and was also marked by progress on the implementation of the action programme on the fight against organised crime which had been approved in 1997, by the conclusion of a pre-accession pact on organised crime between the Member States and the applicant countries, by stronger action against trafficking in human beings (→ points 28 to 30) and by the drafting of new conventions on jurisdiction, recognition and enforcement of judgments in matrimonial matters and on driving disqualifications.

Section 2

Asylum, external borders and immigration

961. At its meeting on 3 and 4 December the Council took note of an interim report on a strategy paper produced by the presidency on immigration and asylum, which, on the basis of the Commission communications of 1991 (¹) and 1994 (²), lays the foundations for a comprehensive Union approach to these questions. In December the Council decided to establish a high-level working party to prepare integrated action plans for application in relations with the main non-member countries of origin of migrants and asylum-seekers (³).

962. On 24 June the Commission amended its proposal for a joint action (⁴) concerning the temporary protection of displaced persons (⁵), reflecting the opinions of Parliament and the results of initial discussions in the Council (⁵), adding a new proposal for a joint action concerning solidarity in the admission and residence of beneficiaries of the temporary protection of displaced persons to provide for measures to be taken to assist the Member States particularly affected (⁶). Parliament approved the proposals in November (⁷). On 16 December the Commission adopted a proposal for a joint action establishing measures to provide practical support in relation to the reception and voluntary repatriation of refugees, displaced persons and asylum-seekers (⁸), proceeding from the principle that responsibility should be shared among Member States. On 27 April the Council adopted Joint Actions 98/304/JHA and 98/305/JHA, extending for the current budget year the legal bases necessary for the financing of specific projects to support displaced persons who have found temporary protection in the Member States, and asylum-seekers and refugees. In a resolution adopted on 8 October, following the death of a young woman who had been maltreated during expulsion from a Member State, Parliament called on the Council to take steps to improve standards of conduct for the repatriation of asylum-seekers whose applications have been turned down (⁹).

(¹) Twenty-fifth General Report, points 205 and 208.
(²) 1994 General Report, point 1075.
(³) Bull. 12-1998.
(⁴) OJ C 268, 27.8.1998; COM(1998) 372; Bull. 6-1998, point 1.5.2.
(⁵) 1997 General Report, point 1032.
(⁶) OJ C 268, 27.8.1998; COM(1998) 372; Bull. 6-1998, point 1.5.3.
(⁷) OJ C 379, 7.12.1998; Bull. 11-1998, points 1.4.3 and 1.4.4.
(⁸) COM(1998) 733 final; Bull. 12-1998.
(⁹) OJ C 328, 26.10.1998; Bull. 10-1998, point 1.4.3.

963.   On 15 January Parliament approved the draft convention establishing the Eurodac system for the comparison of the fingerprints of asylum-seekers (¹), which is a key element in the implementation of the convention determining the State responsible for examining asylum applications (the Dublin Convention) (²). In the conclusions it adopted on 29 May (³) the Council confirmed its intention of extending the digital fingerprinting system to include illegal immigrants and to seek to reach agreement on the interpretation, by way of preliminary rulings by the Court of Justice, of the Eurodac Convention. In December it recorded that there was general agreement on the content of a draft convention, the text of which will stay as it is pending the entry into force of the Amsterdam Treaty; the Commission is invited to propose an instrument based on the proper legal basis at that time (⁴).

964.   In response to a request from the Luxembourg European Council (⁵), on 26 January the Council adopted conclusions on illegal immigration from Iraq and the neighbouring regions (⁶), providing for an action plan to tackle the problem of the growing influx of migrants from the area. Parliament had already passed a resolution on the matter on 15 January (⁷). In a resolution passed on 8 October Parliament called for increased cooperation with Mediterranean countries on matters of immigration (⁸).

965.   On 3 December the Council adopted a decision on common standards for the establishment of the uniform format for residence permits (⁹). In a communication adopted on 28 May (¹⁰), the Council set out details for this, the technical specifications of which had already been defined in 1997 (¹¹). On the same day, it adopted a recommendation on forgery detection equipment at ports of entry to the European Union (¹²). On 3 April the Council adopted a joint action concerning the setting up of a European image archiving system (FADO) for the computerised exchange of data held by the Member States on authentic documents and counterfeit or forged documents (¹³).

(¹)   OJ C 34, 2.2.1998; Bull. 1/2-1998, point 1.5.1.
(²)   1997 General Report, point 1033.
(³)   Bull. 5-1998, point 1.4.1.
(⁴)   Bull. 12-1998.
(⁵)   1997 General Report, point 1037.
(⁶)   Bull. 1/2-1998, point 1.5.2.
(⁷)   OJ C 34, 2.2.1998; Bull. 1/2-1998, point 1.5.3.
(⁸)   OJ C 328, 26.10.1998; Bull. 10-1998, point 1.4.2.
(⁹)   Decision 98/701/JHA (OJ L 333, 9.12.1998; Bull. 12-1998).
(¹⁰) Bull. 5-1998, point 1.4.3.
(¹¹) Bull. 12-1997, point 1.4.5.
(¹²) OJ C 189, 17.6.1998; Bull. 5-1998, point 1.4.2.
(¹³) Joint Action 98/700/JHA (OJ L 333, 9.12.1998; Bull. 12-1998).

966.   On 19 March, the Council adopted Joint Action 98/244/JHA introducing a programme of training, exchanges and cooperation in the field of asylum, immigration and crossing of external borders (Odysseus) (¹); 49 projects were financed on this basis in 1998.

(¹)   OJ L 99, 31.3.1998; Bull. 3-1998, point 1.4.2.

Section 3

Police and customs cooperation

967.   The Europol Convention, signed in July 1995 (¹), entered into force on 1 October (²). On 3 December the Council decided to extend Europol's remit to include the fight against terrorism with effect from 1 January 1999 (³). On the same day it decided to modify the concept of trafficking in human beings as used in the documents announcing the Europol Convention to include child pornography (³) and approved the principle of a joint action to combat child pornography on the Internet (³). The Council and the Commission have embarked on work to establish an effective system to protect the euro, and in particular to combat counterfeiting *(→ point 1014)*. On 28 May the Council adopted its conclusions on encryption (⁴), noting that the police authorities may need to intercept and decipher encrypted messages, but stressing the need to protect civil liberties and to present no impediment to the development of electronic commerce.

968.   As part of the process of implementing the action programme on the fight against organised crime approved by the Amsterdam European Council (⁵), on 29 March the Council adopted Joint Action 98/245/JHA establishing a programme of exchanges, training and cooperation for persons responsible for action to combat organised crime (Falcone) (⁶). The programme was endorsed by the European Parliament on 17 February (⁷), and supported some 30 European cooperation projects in 1998. On 21 December the Council adopted a resolution on the development of a European strategy to combat organised crime (⁸). Parliament passed a resolution on the same subject on 17 November (⁹).

969.   In the customs cooperation field, apart from pursuit of work on ratification of the conventions on the customs information system (CIS) (³) and on mutual assistance between customs administrations (Naples II), several joint surveillance operations were carried out in sea,

---

(¹)   1995 General Report, point 966.
(²)   Bull. 10-1998, point 1.4.4.
(³)   Bull. 12-1998.
(⁴)   Bull. 5-1998, point 1.4.12.
(⁵)   OJ C 251, 15.8.1997; 1997 General Report, point 1031.
(⁶)   OJ L 99, 31.3.1998; Bull. 3-1998, point 1.4.3.
(⁷)   OJ C 80, 16.3.1998; Bull. 1/2-1998, point 1.5.4.
(⁸)   OJ C 408, 29.12.1998; Bull. 12-1998.
(⁹)   OJ C 379, 7.12.1998; Bull. 11-1998, point 1.4.6.

road and air transport in the implementation of the third-pillar strategic action programme for customs administrations.

970. On 15 May Parliament endorsed a draft joint action concerning arrangements for the better exchange of information between Member States' law enforcement agencies and the payment-card industry on crimes involving the use of payment cards, subject to amendments relating to the protection of personal data ([1]). Parliament also adopted resolutions on the terrorist attacks in the Basque Country on 15 January ([2]), on the Commission's communication ([3]) on new synthetic drugs on 12 May ([4]) and on the annual report of the Europol Drugs Unit on 16 September ([5]).

---

[1]   OJ C 167, 1.6.1998; Bull. 5-1998, point 1.4.11.
[2]   OJ C 34, 2.2.1998; Bull. 1/2-1998, point 1.5.5.
[3]   COM(97) 249; 1997 General Report, point 1045.
[4]   OJ C 167, 1.6.1998; Bull. 5-1998, point 1.4.8.
[5]   OJ C 313, 12.10.1998; Bull. 9-1998, point 1.4.3.

Section 4

Judicial cooperation

971.   On 29 June, in a bid to improve the practical application of mutual assistance between the judicial authorities of the Member States, the Council adopted Joint Action 98/428/JHA on the creation of a European judicial network ([1]) and Joint Action 98/427/JHA on good practice in mutual legal assistance in criminal matters ([2]). On 3 April Parliament, which had delivered its opinion on the first of these joint actions in November 1997 ([3]), delivered its opinion of the second joint action as well as on a draft convention on mutual judicial assistance in criminal matters ([4]). On 13 March it called for an intensification of judicial cooperation in criminal matters in the European Union ([5]) and, on 5 October, gave its endorsement ([6]) to the communication from the Commission on a Union policy against corruption ([7]).

972.   On 17 June the Council adopted the act establishing the convention on driving disqualifications ([8]). The purpose of this convention is to ensure that individuals who have been disqualified from driving in one Member State are also disqualified in the Member State in which they reside. On 3 December the Council also adopted a joint action for the identification, tracing, freezing or seizing and confiscation of instrumentalities and the proceeds from crime ([9]), which was approved by Parliament on 17 July ([10]). The purpose of this joint action is to facilitate the implementation of the 1990 Council of Europe convention on money-laundering. On 22 December the Council adopted a joint action to combat corruption in the private sector ([11]).

973.   Pursuant to the action plan to combat organised crime approved by the European Council in Amsterdam in the criminal justice field ([12]), on 21 December the Council adopted a joint action on participation in

---

([1])   OJ L 191, 7.7.1998; Bull. 6-1998, point 1.5.4.
([2])   OJ L 191, 7.7.1998; Bull. 6-1998, point 1.5.6.
([3])   1997 General Report, point 1041.
([4])   OJ C 138, 4.5.1998; Bull. 4-1998, points 1.4.3 and 1.4.4.
([5])   OJ C 104, 6.4.1998; Bull. 3-1998, point 1.4.5.
([6])   OJ C 328, 26.10.1998; Bull. 10-1998, point 1.4.1.
([7])   COM(97) 192; 1997 General Report, point 1040.
([8])   OJ C 216, 10.7.1998; Bull. 6-1998, point 1.5.5.
([9])   Joint Action 98/699/JHA (OJ L 333, 9.12.1998; Bull. 12-1998).
([10])   OJ C 292, 21.9.1998; Bull. 7/8-1998, point 1.5.4.
([11])   Joint Action 98/742/JHA (OJ L 358, 31.12.1998; Bull. 12-1998).
([12])   OJ C 251, 15.8.1997; 1997 General Report, point 1031.

criminal organisations in the Member States of the European Union ([1]) and a resolution on the prevention of organised crime ([2]). On 1 July the Commission adopted a proposal for a joint action to combat fraud and counterfeiting of non-cash means of payment ([3]), which was approved by Parliament on 17 November ([4]).

974. As regards civil affairs, the Council established the convention on jurisdiction and the recognition and enforcement of judgments in matrimonial matters ([5]), and the protocol on the interpretation of the convention by the Court of Justice, both of which were signed on 28 May. The purpose of this convention, which had been approved by Parliament on 30 April ([6]), is to enable Member States to recognise each other's divorce and custody rulings.

---

[1] Joint Action 98/733/JHA (OJ L 351, 29.12.1998; Bull. 12-1998).
[2] Bull. 12-1998.
[3] COM(1998) 395; Bull. 7/8-1998, point 1.5.3.
[4] OJ C 379, 7.12.1998; Bull. 11-1998, points 1.4.7 and 1.4.8.
[5] OJ C 221, 16.7.1998; Bull. 5-1998, point 1.4.5.
[6] OJ C 152, 18.5.1998; Bull. 4-1998, point 1.4.6.

Section 5

External relations

975. On 25 August the Council authorised the presidency and the Commission to negotiate with Iceland and Norway the conditions for associating these countries with the implementation and development of the Schengen *acquis* (Table III).

976. As part of the preparations for enlargement, on 28 May a pre-accession pact on organised crime was concluded by the Member States of the European Union and the 11 applicant countries ([1]). It provides for a two-way flow of information, the exchange of liaison officers, as well as joint investigative activities and operations.

977. On 29 June the Council adopted Joint Action 98/429/JHA ([2]), establishing a mechanism for collective evaluation of the enactment, application and effective implementation by the applicant countries of established European Union law and practice (the *acquis)* in the fields of justice and home affairs; the mechanism consists of a group of experts who will relay to the Council the information they have received. In this context Parliament and the Council emphasised the promotion and reinforcement of the rule of law in these countries on 3 April ([3]) and 28 May ([4]) respectively. In the countries of central Europe the Commission implemented cooperation projects in the fields of justice and home affairs as part of the PHARE programme *(→ points 812 et seq.)* and organised missions, seminars, workshops and conferences to pinpoint the needs of these countries and help them to take over the *acquis.*

978. The year 1998 also saw developments with regard to cooperation with the Mediterranean countries. As part of the MEDA programme *(→ point 829)* seminars were organised on organised crime and drug-trafficking. In November a Euro-Mediterranean conference on organised crime was held in Rome. Under Article K.4 of the Treaty on European Union a meeting at coordinating committee level was also held with Turkey in June.

([1]) OJ C 220, 15.7.1998; Bull. 5-1998, point 1.3.56.
([2]) OJ L 191, 7.7.1998; Bull. 6-1998, point 1.4.66.
([3]) OJ C 138, 4.5.1998; Bull. 4-1998, point 1.4.1.
([4]) Bull. 5-1998, point 1.3.58.

979.   In accordance with the conclusions of the Dublin European Council (^{1}), missions were organised as part of the TACIS programme to identify the best ways to assist central Asian countries in combating the production and movement of drugs on their territory.

980.   The conclusions adopted by the Council on 19 March endorsed the principles adopted by the G8 group of leading industrial nations (→ *point 881)* on combating organised crime, terrorism and high-tech crime (^{2}). Cooperation with the United States was increased, leading to the implementation of a joint anti-drug initiative in the Caribbean, agreement on drug precursors (^{3}) and initiatives to combat trafficking in women in Poland and Ukraine. Several seminars on matters of common interest in the fields of justice and home affairs were also organised with Canada.

(^{1})   Bull. 12-1996, point I.9.
(^{2})   Bull. 3-1998, point 1.4.6.
(^{3})   1997 General Report, point 800.

Chapter VII

Financing Community activities, management of resources

Section 1

Priority activities and objectives

981. *The 1999 budget, the last covered by the financial perspective adopted at the Edinburgh European Council, is also one that will make the transition to Agenda 2000. Not surprisingly, the negotiations between the two arms of the budgetary authority leading to its adoption were particularly tense, although they tended to focus more on the future interinstitutional agreement and the establishment of the financial perspective for the period 2000-06 within the framework of Agenda 2000, for which the Commission presented its proposals on 18 March, than on the political priorities for 1999 and the need for budgetary rigour, on which consensus was reached fairly quickly. Parliament and the Council eventually reached a compromise involving a number of parallel procedures (the draft budget for 1999 and the subsequent letter of amendment as well as supplementary and amending budget No 1/98 and the omnibus transfer proposal), with the result that the budget was finally adopted on 17 December. The budgetary procedure was also affected when implementation of all headings in the 1998 budget not likely to have a legal base was suspended as a result of a ruling by the Court of Justice. However, this situation was soon redressed during the Council's first reading when a political agreement on the issue of legal bases and implementation of the budget was reached and embodied in the interinstitutional agreement of 13 October. The 1996 discharge and, more generally, the Commission's management of Community funds, was also the subject of lively debate. Although the matter was referred back to committee a number of times, Parliament felt that it could not*

take a decision on the discharge at the December part-session. Finally, within the framework of Agenda 2000, the Commission presented a report on the operation of the own resources system.

Section 2

Budgets

General budget

Financial perspective

982.   On 18 March, as part of the implementation of Agenda 2000, the Commission adopted a communication on the establishment of a new financial perspective for the period 2000-06 and a report on the implementation and renewal of the interinstitutional agreement on budgetary discipline and improvement of the budgetary procedure *(→ points 8 et seq.).* Tables 19 and 20 show the financial perspective up to 2006 and the financing of expenditure resulting from accession as set out in the Commission's proposals.

983.   The framework for the 1999 budget procedure was the financial perspective annexed to the interinstitutional agreement on budgetary discipline and improvement of the budgetary procedure of 29 October 1993 ([1]), as adjusted in December 1994 following the enlargement of the Union to include Austria, Finland and Sweden ([2]). In accordance with paragraphs 9 and 10 of the interinstitutional agreement, there was a technical adjustment of the financial perspective in 1998, as well as an adjustment to take account of the conditions of implementation. On 25 February the Commission made the technical adjustment of the financial perspective in line with movements in gross national product (GNP) and prices on the basis of the most recent macroeconomic forecasts available at the time ([3]). On the same date the Commission adopted a proposal for the adjustment of the financial perspective to take account of implementation, with the objective of transferring to 1999 the allocations for structural operations which were not used in 1997. Parliament and the Council reached agreement on the proposal at the trialogue meeting of 31 March and formally adjusted the financial perspective in April ([4]). As proposed by the Commission, EUR 1 433 million in appropriations for commitments for the Structural Funds that were not used in 1997 was transferred to 1999. Similarly, the EUR 101 million of the Cohesion

---

([1])   OJ C 331, 7.12.1993; Twenty-seventh General Report, points 1078 to 1080.
([2])   1995 General Report, point 1105.
([3])   Bull. 1/2-1998, point 1.6.2.
([4])   OJ C 138, 4.5.1998; Bull; 4-1998, point 1.5.2.

Fund allocation not used in 1997 was transferred to 1999. In addition to these transfers of appropriations for commitments proposed by the Commission, the two arms of the budgetary authority also raised the total appropriations for payments for 1999 by EUR 300 million. Following these operations and with the definitive agricultural guideline as set in the preliminary draft budget, the ceiling on appropriations for commitments for 1999 is EUR 103 384 million and the ceiling on appropriations for payments EUR 96 663 million. The margin available beneath the own resources ceiling (1.27 % of GNP) is 0.03 % of GNP, as shown in the updated financial perspective table (see Table 21).

TABLE 19

Financial perspective for 2000-06 proposed by the Commission

Million EUR — 1999 prices — Appropriations for commitments	1999	2000	2001	2002	2003	2004	2005	2006
1. Agriculture (¹) of which:	45 205	46 050	46 920	47 820	48 730	49 670	50 630	51 610
pre-accession aid		520	520	520	520	520	520	520
2. Structural operations	39 025	36 640	37 470	36 640	35 600	34 450	33 410	32 470
— Structural Funds	32 731	32 600	33 430	32 600	31 560	30 410	29 370	28 430
— Cohesion Fund	3 000	3 000	3 000	3 000	3 000	3 000	3 000	3 000
— Pre-accession structural instrument		1 040	1 040	1 040	1 040	1 040	1 040	1 040
— Adjustments (²)	3 294							
3. Internal policies	6 386	6 390	6 710	6 880	7 050	7 230	7 410	7 600
4. External action of which:	6 870	6 870	7 070	7 250	7 430	7 610	7 790	7 900
pre-accession aid		1 560	1 560	1 560	1 560	1 560	1 560	1 560
5. Administration	4 723	4 730	4 820	4 910	5 010	5 100	5 200	5 300
6. Reserves	1 192	850	850	600	350	350	350	350
— Monetary reserve	500	500	500	250	0	0	0	0
— Emergency aid reserve	346	200	200	200	200	200	200	200
— Guarantee reserve	346	150	150	150	150	150	150	150
Appropriations for commitments — ceiling	103 401	101 530	103 840	104 100	104 170	104 410	104 790	105 230
Appropriations for payments — ceiling	96 380	98 800	101 650	102 930	103 520	103 810	104 170	104 560
Appropriations for payments as % of GNP	1.23	1.24	1.24	1.22	1.20	1.18	1.15	1.13
Margin as % of GNP	0.04	0.03	0.03	0.03	0.03	0.03	0.03	0.03
Available for accession as % of GNP				0.02	0.04	0.06	0.09	0.11
Own resources ceiling as % of GNP	1.27	1.27	1.27	1.27	1.27	1.27	1.27	1.27

(¹) The ceiling corresponds to the agricultural guideline.
(²) Including the amount in respect of the EEA financial mechanism and the adjustment proposed by the Commission to take account of implementation of the 1997 budget.

TABLE 20

Expenditure resulting from accession; financing

Million EUR — 1999 prices	2002	2003	2004	2005	2006
Expenditure					
Heading 1 ([1])	1 600	2 030	2 450	2 930	3 400
Heading 2	3 750	5 830	7 920	10 000	12 080
Heading 3	730	760	790	820	850
Heading 5	370	410	450	450	450
Total appropriations for commitments	6 450	9 030	11 610	14 200	16 780
(1) Total appropriations for payments	4 140	6 710	8 890	11 440	14 220
Sources of financing available					
Financing of agricultural expenditure by drawing on the margin available	1 600	2 030	2 450	2 930	3 400
Amounts earmarked for accession in the financial framework of the 15-nation Community (estimate)	1 280	3 300	5 680	8 060	10 470
Increase in own resources resulting from growth in Union GNP following enlargement (estimate)	3 440	3 510	3 580	3 660	3 740
(2) Total financing available	6 320	8 840	11 710	14 650	17 610
Changes in the margins beneath the own resources ceiling					
Margin (2) − (1)	2 180	2 130	2 820	3 210	3 390
Margin in the financial framework of the 15-nation Community (0.03 % of GNP)	2 520	2 580	2 650	2 720	2 780
Total margin available in an enlarged Community (estimate)	4 700	4 710	5 470	5 930	6 170
Total margin as a percentage of the GNP of the enlarged Community	0.05	0.05	0.06	0.06	0.06

([1]) Expenditure estimated at 1999 prices for the purposes of comparison. Only estimates at current prices are relevant.

TABLE 21

Financial perspective for 1999 after technical adjustment and adjustment to take account of implementation — Appropriations for commitments

(million ECU)

	Current prices				
	1995	1996	1997	1998	1999
1. Common agricultural policy	37 944	40 828	41 805	43 263	45 188
2. Structural operations	26 329	29 131	31 477	33 461	39 025
— Structural Funds	24 069	26 579	28 620	30 482	35 902
— Cohesion Fund	2 152	2 444	2 749	2 871	3 118
— EEA financial mechanism	108	108	108	108	5
3. Internal policies	5 060	5 337	5 603	6 003	6 386
4. External action	4 895	5 264	5 622	6 201	6 870
5. Administrative expenditure	4 022	4 191	4 352	4 541	4 723
6. Reserves	1 146	1 152	1 158	1 176	1 192
— Monetary reserve	500	500	500	500	500
— Guarantee reserve	323	326	329	338	346
— Emergency aid reserve	323	326	329	338	346
7. Compensation	1 547	701	212	99	0
8. Total appropriations for commitments	80 943	86 604	90 229	94 744	103 384
9. Total appropriations for payments	77 229	82 223	85 807	90 581	96 663
Payment appropriations (as % of GNP) ([1])	1.20	1.20	1.22	1.23	1.24
Margin (as % of GNP)	0.01	0.02	0.02	0.03	0.03
Own resources ceiling (as % of GNP)	1.21	1.22	1.24	1.26	1.27

([1]) For 1995, on the basis of the GNP figure used for the adjustment of the financial perspective following enlargement. For 1996, 1997 and 1998, on the basis of the GNP figure used for the corresponding technical adjustment.

Own resources

984.   On 7 October the Commission adopted a report on the operation of the own resources system ([1]). Presentation of this report, originally scheduled for 1999 under Article 10 of Decision 94/728/EC on the own resources system ([2]), was brought forward so that the issues raised could be discussed as part of the overall debate on the proposals made under

([1])   COM(1998) 560; Bull. 10-1998, point I.1; Supplement 2/98 — Bull.
([2])   OJ L 293, 12.11.1994; 1994 General Report, point 1119; 1996 General Report, point 987.

Agenda 2000 (→ *points 1 et seq.*). The report reviews the performance of the current financing system as well as the question of budgetary balances raised by a number of Member States. The Commission notes that the current system has performed satisfactorily, but has not given the European Union real financial autonomy and also lacks transparency. It could be changed by introducing new own resources (only a modified VAT resource appears feasible) or by simplifying the system by, for example, replacing existing resources by contributions based on GNP alone. While repeating its reservations about the very concept of 'budgetary balance', the Commission notes that the circumstances leading to the correction in favour of the United Kingdom adopted at the Fontainebleau European Council[1] have changed significantly since and that several Member States record similar or greater imbalances than the United Kingdom before the correction. Pointing out that enlargement and the expected reforms of expenditure will change the situation even more, the Commission feels that, if a political consensus were to emerge on the need to address the issue of budgetary imbalances, three options could be considered: simplification of the financing system with a move to the GNP-based resource and a simultaneous reduction or even phasing-out of the correction mechanism; corrections on the expenditure side of the budget with changes in the breakdown of direct aid to farmers between the European Union and its Member States; introduction of a generalised correction mechanism. The Commission concludes by confirming the view put forward in Agenda 2000 that neither the need for an increase in the financial resources of the European Union nor the shortcomings of the financing system provide grounds for urgent modification of the own resources decision.

Budgetary procedure for 1999

985. The preliminary draft budget for 1999 adopted by the Commission on 29 April[2] after Parliament had presented its guidelines for the 1999 budgetary procedure in its resolution of 2 April[3], was the first to be expressed in euro. Proposed expenditure totalled EUR 96 902 million for commitments and EUR 86 350 million for payments. The Commission thus met the strict targets it set itself in January's debate on budget policy guidelines, with Community expenditure increasing in the same proportion as public expenditure in the Member States. The rates of increase over the 1998 budget were 3.38 % for payments and 6.47 %

---

[1]   Eighteenth General Report, point 80.
[2]   Bull. 4-1997, point 1.5.4.
[3]   OJ C 138, 4.5.1998; Bull. 4-1998, point 1.5.3.

for commitments. These increases were accounted for essentially by the substantial financing for structural operations. The appropriations earmarked for structural operations in accordance with the undertakings made at the Edinburgh European Council (^{1}) represented increases of 16.6 % for commitments and 9 % for payments. To offset this, the rates of increase for all the other headings were only 0.56 % for commitments and 0.49 % for payments. This preliminary draft thus represented 1.11 % of Member States' total GNP, well below the 1.27 % ceiling in the financial perspective. Apart from structural operations, the main priorities adopted were the employment initiative, trans-European networks, research and technological development and, in the case of external action, cooperation with central Europe and the Mediterranean countries. Agricultural expenditure remained at the 1998 level of EUR 40.4 billion, EUR 4.7 billion beneath the agricultural guideline. This stabilisation was made possible by a return to normal on the animal product markets, in particular for beef and veal, and by the favourable conditions prevailing on the international markets. The increase for structural operations was linked to the end of the 1994-99 programming period; the total appropriations for commitments for the whole period must correspond exactly to the overall amount laid down at the Edinburgh European Council and payments were therefore calculated very precisely. The appropriations for commitments for internal policies rose by an average of 3 %. The first priority was still research, with more than half the appropriations of this heading being allocated to the fifth framework programme. The Commission also proposed a substantial increase in the appropriations for the trans-European networks (up by 10 % for commitments) and an allocation of EUR 150 million for the employment initiative decided at the Luxembourg European Council on employment. The education and youth programmes were another priority under this heading and the measures for refugees were also boosted. The main priorities under the heading for external action were the PHARE and MEDA programmes; the new priority given to aid for banana producers was also taken into account. The overall increase in appropriations under this heading (in terms of commitments) was 2.67 %. Finally, with growth limited to 1.3 %, the increase in the Commission's administrative expenditure was well below that for the budget as a whole.

986.   The draft budget established by the Council at first reading on 17 July (^{2}) totalled EUR 96 520 million in appropriations for commitments and EUR 85 873 million in appropriations for payments, an increase of

---

(^{1})   Twenty-sixth General Report, point 18.
(^{2})   Bull. 7/8-1998, point 1.6.2.

6.05 and 2.81 % in relation to the 1998 budget. This left a considerable margin (a total of EUR 6 863.3 million) beneath the ceiling of all the headings except heading 2 (structural operations). As regards agricultural expenditure the Council accepted the EUR 40 440 million requested in the preliminary draft. A letter of amendment was to be presented in the autumn to update requirements. In accepting EUR 39 025 million in appropriations for commitments (16.6 % up on 1998) and EUR 30 950 million in appropriations for payments (9 % higher), the Council also took over the Commission proposals for structural operations, which use up the balance of the overall allocation in both commitments and payments for heading 2 for 1994-99 decided at the Edinburgh European Council. As regards internal policies, the Council draft contained EUR 5 449 million in appropriations for commitments and EUR 4 809 million in appropriations for payments, a reduction in relation to the Commission's preliminary draft (– 8.06 and – 5.06 %) and the 1998 budget (– 5.33 and – 1.31 %). These cuts primarily affected research, in line with the common position adopted in connection with the fifth framework research programme (→ point 285) (EUR 3 400 million in appropriations for commitments and EUR 2 975 million in appropriations for payments). The trans-European networks were also affected, with a reduction of EUR 38 million in appropriations for commitments and EUR 22 million in appropriations for payments concentrated on the transport networks (EUR 25 million and EUR 15 million down on the preliminary draft). Finally, the Council was particularly severe towards programmes in the field of education, vocational training and youth, culture, information and other social operations. The allocation for heading 4 (external action) came to EUR 5 992 million in appropriations for commitments and EUR 4 059 million in appropriations for payments, corresponding to an increase of 1.84 % over the commitments in the Commission's preliminary draft and a sharp drop of 4.89 % in payments. This surprising move was mainly due to the Council's decision to increase the PHARE programme by the EUR 150 million in appropriations for commitments transferred to the MEDA programme in 1997 in order to restore the allocation agreed at the Cannes European Council [1]. Otherwise, the Council accepted the Commission proposals concerning appropriations for commitments, except for the international fisheries agreements (down by EUR 7 million) and the external aspects of certain Community policies (down by EUR 29.5 million). On the other hand, there were more systematic cuts in appropriations for payments as all the policies under this heading, including the major regional programmes, had their appropriations reduced. Finally, the Council draft

---

[1]   1995 General Report, point 976.

was particularly severe on the administrative expenditure of the other institutions, including the Commission, as the increase in heading 5 totalled 1.6 %, while the Council allowed itself an increase of 5.14 %. The Commission budget (including pensions, 6.6 % higher than for 1998) rose by 1.63 %, limiting the increase in strictly administrative expenditure to 0.65 %.

987.   After Parliament's first reading on 22 October (¹) the amended draft budget came to EUR 98 629 million in appropriations for commitments and EUR 89 566 million in appropriations for payments, a considerable increase (of 8.37 and 7.23 %) over the 1998 budget, which was partly due to the adoption of four 'bridging amendments' setting up four special reserves totalling EUR 1 540 million in appropriations for commitments and EUR 3 750 million in appropriations for payments for headings 2 to 5 in order to establish a higher base for the future financial perspective (²). For agricultural expenditure, Parliament, like the Council, decided to wait for the letter of amendment and therefore took over the figures from the preliminary draft, with two exceptions ('Monitoring and preventative measures — Payments by the Member States' and 'Promotion measures'). In the case of structural operations, Parliament, unlike the Council, amended the preliminary draft: the appropriations for the Community support frameworks were redistributed with due allowance for past underspends, with the result that the amended draft established a reserve of EUR 1 500 million for commitments and EUR 250 million for payments, with a further cut of EUR 500 million in payments (³). The appropriations for internal policies came to EUR 6 382 million in appropriations for commitments and EUR 5 874 million in appropriations for payments, slightly more than in the preliminary draft (not including the tactical reserve). Parliament adopted the overall amount proposed for the fifth framework research programme in the preliminary draft and also restored the appropriation contained in the preliminary draft for energy networks and the IDA programme. On the other hand, it took over the Council's figures for transport and telecommunications infrastructures. Parliament also restored, or increased, the appropriations contained in the preliminary draft for various multiannual programmes (Leonardo da Vinci, Socrates, Youth for Europe, Prince, LIFE). It created a new initiative — Connect — to boost the

(¹)   OJ C 341, 9.11.1998; Bull. 10-1998, point 1.5.4.
(²)   Breakdown by heading of the financial perspective: heading 2: EUR 2 300 million for payments; heading 3: EUR 400 million for commitments and EUR 800 million for payments; heading 4: EUR 990 million for commitments and EUR 500 million for payments; heading 5: EUR 150 million for commitments and for payments.
(³)   These changes are in addition to the 'tactical' reserve of EUR 2 300 million in appropriations for payments.

integration of the various cultural programmes as part of a new framework for the 'Europe of knowledge' and a European fund for refugees and kept the heading for experimental measures in connection with culture. Some of the appropriations for the agencies were placed in reserve until their directors signed a code of conduct. Finally, in accordance with the agreement on legal bases (→ point 1033), Parliament confirmed the token entry which the Council had made for a number of headings without a legal base (tourism, social economy, drugs). The allocation for external action, not including the tactical reserve of EUR 990 million, totalled EUR 5 871 million, less than the figure in the preliminary draft. The increase in appropriations compared with the 1998 budget (again not including the tactical reserve) is thus only 2.45 % as against 2.67 % in the case of the preliminary draft. Compared with the Council's draft, Parliament made a substantial cut of EUR 290 million in appropriations for commitments and EUR 94 million in appropriations for payments in the main heading B7-500 (PHARE) to offset increases in other headings in Subsection B7, some of which also related to PHARE. As regards TACIS, it endorsed the overall appropriations in the preliminary draft and the Council draft but placed EUR 130 million in appropriations for payments and ECU 180 million in appropriations for commitments in reserve in view of the difficulties of implementation which are likely to result from the financial and government crisis affecting Russia. All the appropriations intended for Chernobyl were also placed in reserve until it was established that the other donors had paid their contribution. The appropriations in the preliminary draft and the Council draft for the reconstruction of former Yugoslavia were confirmed, with the entry of EUR 30 million in reserve until the Commission proposed a new regulation. The amounts proposed in the preliminary draft for cooperation with non-governmental organisations, tropical forests and the environment in developing countries were increased while the appropriations planned for aid to banana producers in the ACP countries were kept at the level decided by the Council. The appropriations planned for the financial protocol with Turkey, which are normally entered in the reserve, were struck out. The total allocated to administrative expenditure, not including the bridging amendment, came to around EUR 40 million more than the preliminary draft, although this increase concealed a number of tough constraints which Parliament imposed on the Commission's administrative expenditure.

988.   On 28 October the Commission adopted letter of amendment No 1/99 to the preliminary draft ([1]), the main purpose being to update

---

([1])   Bull. 10-1998, point 1.5.5.

the agricultural forecasts in the preliminary draft by increasing the EAGGF-Guarantee appropriations by EUR 513 million to take account of the downturn in a number of agricultural markets and the impact of legislation since the adoption of the preliminary draft. The Commission also proposed a slight reduction in the appropriations for the fisheries agreements and the introduction in the 1999 budget of an item B7-5320, for the time being with a token entry, for macrofinancial aid to Bosnia-Herzegovina.

989.   The Council's second reading of the draft budget for 1999 ([1]) was held at the same time as the general negotiation with Parliament on the omnibus transfer, the establishment of draft supplementary and amending budget No 1/98 and certain aspects of the future interinstitutional agreement and the financial perspective for the period 2000-06. After conciliation with Parliament, the Council decided to establish a draft budget based on the assumption that Parliament would withdraw its bridging amendments (which the Council rejected in full) and convene a further conciliation meeting on 8 December to cover the aspects related to the interinstitutional agreement, in particular the guarantee of 'flexibility' in the amounts available beneath the ceilings of the financial perspective. The draft budget for 1999 also entered all the estimated balance from 1998 on the revenue side (apart from ECU 900 million used in the supplementary and amending budget). The Council noted that Parliament's draft complied with the ceilings laid down by the interinstitutional agreement of 13 October on legal bases and implementation of the budget for the preparatory measures and pilot projects and, with the exception of general information measures, accepted the classification of the headings which the Commission could implement by virtue of its institutional prerogatives or specific powers. The appropriations entered under headings awaiting a legal base were systematically placed in reserve. The Council draft totalled EUR 96 913 million in appropriations for commitments and EUR 85 538 million in appropriations for payments, 6.5 and 2.4 % more than the 1998 budget. The appropriations for payments came to 1.10 % of GNP, as against 1.14 % in 1998. The Council's draft prompts the following comments for each heading of the financial perspective: as regards agricultural expenditure, this second reading adopted agricultural letter of amendment No 1/99 but offset the proposed increase of EUR 513 million by an equivalent volume of targeted reductions affecting arable crops. It was also decided to enter an item for food aid to Russia, to place EUR 20 million in reserve for agri-environmental measures in return for an equivalent reduction in

---

([1])   Bull. 11-1998, point 1.5.2.

item B1-1014 and transfer EUR 80 million from items B1-1501, B1-1502 and B1-2002 to the reserve. Total agricultural expenditure was thus kept at the level of the initial preliminary draft (EUR 40 440 million). As regards structural operations, the Council restored the budget it had adopted on first reading, with the notable exception of the cut of EUR 500 million confirmed for appropriations for payments for the Structural Funds; the appropriations entered in reserve (EUR 1 500 million in appropriations for commitments and EUR 250 million in appropriations for payments) were transferred to the specific heading. The total allocation for structural operations thus came to EUR 39 025 million in appropriations for commitments and EUR 30 450 million in appropriations for payments. The total allocation for internal policies came to EUR 5 830 million in appropriations for commitments and EUR 5 008 million in appropriations for payments. The reduction in relation to Parliament's first reading — apart from the rejection of the strategic reserve — comes to around EUR 140 million, most of which (EUR 120 million) is accounted for by research and reflects the political agreement on the amounts for the fifth framework programme reached at the conciliation meeting on 17 November. The Council also considered that, in the absence of a legal base, there was no need to exceed the amounts entered in reserve in its draft budget (general information measures, operations relating to energy and the internal market). It also refused to set up a refugee fund, amended the title of the heading accordingly and reduced the allocation to EUR 10 million under the specific heading and EUR 5 million in the reserve. Otherwise, the Council accepted the whole of Parliament's first reading, in particular the amounts decided for the trans-European networks and the increases for the Socrates, Youth and Raphael programmes. It also entered a higher appropriation than in the preliminary draft (EUR 14 million) to continue the Ariane and Kaleidoscope programmes. The total allocation for external action came to EUR 5 957 million in commitments and EUR 3 979 million in payments. Disregarding the fact that the 'tactical reserves' were removed, the Council thus increased the appropriations for commitments resulting from Parliament's first reading by EUR 86 million. The increase in MEDA and PHARE appropriations by EUR 50 million and EUR 48.7 million respectively was accompanied by a EUR 10 million cut for TACIS. Payments (again not including the strategic reserve) were reduced by EUR 90 million, with a cut of EUR 48 million for the MEDA programme, EUR 69 million for PHARE and EUR 10 million for TACIS. The Council also restored the appropriations from its first reading for cooperation with Turkey. Overall, the Council restored the administrative expenditure adopted on first reading. However, with Parliament's agreement, it decided to restore half the appropriations for committee procedure in

Title A-7, while the other half was kept in reserve; this showed its willingness to enter into a political dialogue with Parliament on this question and avoid paralysis of Commission operations.

990. The 1999 budget was adopted after Parliament's second reading on 17 December (¹). This budget totals EUR 96 929 million in appropriations for commitments and EUR 85 558 million in appropriations for payments, up by 6.91 % on the 1998 budget in commitments and 2.43 % in payments. Substantial margins are left beneath the financial perspective ceilings, as was the case in 1998: EUR 6 455 million for commitments and EUR 11 105 million for payments. The total appropriations for payments represent 1.10 % of GNP (compared with the 1998 figure of 1.14 % and the own resources ceiling of 1.27 % of GNP). This budget, the last covered by the Edinburgh financial perspective, testifies to the rigorous approach of the two arms of the budgetary authority. The appropriations for agricultural expenditure total EUR 40 440 million, the amount proposed by the Commission in its preliminary draft and adopted by the Council in its second reading. The margin in relation to the guideline is EUR 4 748 million. Planned expenditure on structural operations is the same adopted by the Council on second reading and comes to EUR 39 025 million for commitments and EUR 30 450 million for payments, a cut of EUR 500 million in relation to the preliminary draft. The PEACE initiative for Northern Ireland is allocated the same amount as under the redeployment decided on Parliament's first reading. Total appropriations for internal policies are EUR 5 861 for commitments, an increase of 1.68 % on the 1998 budget, and EUR 5 021 million for payments (an increase of 1.53 %). The margin beneath the heading for the ceiling is EUR 524 million in appropriations for commitments. The appropriations allocated to research stand at EUR 3 450 million, the same as in the Council's second reading. The trans-European networks are the other major item under the heading with EUR 585 million (up by 4.5 % on 1998). Among the other policies, in particular the major multiannual programmes, Parliament confirmed that it would restore the amounts adopted at first reading, in particular for general information measures, Altener and SAVE II. The allocations for external action total EUR 5 907 million, an increase of 3.27 % on the 1998 budget, leaving a margin of EUR 962 million beneath the ceiling for the heading. The total for payments is EUR 3 952 million, a very significant 9.13 % cut in relation to the 1998 budget. The PHARE programme has its allocation increased by over 28 % for commitments in relation to the 1998 budget, subject to large-scale redeployment within

---

(¹)   Bull. 12-1998.

the overall allocation. By contrast, the Commission's proposals for co-operation with Mediterranean non-member countries and with the new independent States and Mongolia were not accepted (the amounts proposed in the preliminary draft were cut by EUR 49 million and EUR 10 million respectively). The appropriations usually entered in reserve for financial cooperation with Turkey were deleted. Appropriations for payments have been cut drastically in comparison with 1998: by 12 % for cooperation with Mediterranean non-member countries, 21 % for co-operation with the countries of central and eastern Europe, 19 % for cooperation with the new independent States and Mongolia, 12 % for cooperation with former Yugoslavia and 21 % for the external aspects of certain Community policies. The appropriations for administrative expenditure total EUR 4 503 million, 0.04 % down on the 1998 budget. Of this total, EUR 2 426 million is for the Commission (excluding pensions) and EUR 1 580 million for the other institutions (down by 4.9 %), the pensions for all the institutions rising by 6.6 %.

991.   Table 23 gives a breakdown, by heading of the financial perspective, of the amounts entered at the various stages of the 1998 budget procedure.

992.   Foreseeable revenue for 1999 is shown in Table 22.

Implementation of the 1998 budget

Supplementary and amending budgets

993.   The main purpose of the preliminary draft supplementary and amending budget No 1/98, which was presented to the budgetary authority on 15 May([1]) and followed by two letters of amendment on 30 June and 30 September([2]), was to enter the 1997 budget surplus of ECU 960 million in the statement of revenue, reduce agricultural expenditure in 1998 by ECU 400 million and register the increase in the revenue forecasts for customs duties and in the VAT and GNP bases. The appropriations released as a result were used to increase the amounts available for Parliament's buildings, allocated to headings 2, 3 and 4 (in particular to the European Social Fund and the PHARE programme) or returned to the Member States. The Council delayed establishing the draft supplementary and amending budget, linking this pro-

---

([1])   Bull. 4-1998, point 1.5.5; Bull. 5-1998, point 1.5.2.
([2])   Bull. 9-1998, point 1.5.2.

cedure with the examination of the proposed omnibus transfer and the 1999 budgetary procedure. The Commission's proposal was substantially altered as part of an overall compromise accepted on 8 December. The supplementary and amending budget was finally given only one reading by Parliament and the Council and adopted on 15 December. It provided an additional ECU 150 million for Parliament's buildings, ECU 100 million for the ESF, ECU 100 million for PHARE and ECU 150 million in all for various items covered by headings 2, 3 and 4, and entered in the budget the ECU 400 million in food aid for Russia; this total of ECU 900 million was financed from the 1998 EAGGF balance and the 1997 balance entered on the revenue side.

Outturn of revenue and expenditure

994.   On 22 July the Commission presented a communication to the budgetary authority on the implementation of the 1998 budget ([1]).

995.   The implementation rates for the 1998 budget are shown in Tables 24 and 25. Non-utilised appropriations for the year were ECU 2 705 million for commitments and ECU 3 469 million for payments.

996.   On the revenue side, total own resources for 1998 came to ECU 83.3 billion, corresponding to 1.13 % of Community GNP. There was also ECU 668 million in miscellaneous revenue. Revenue for 1998 is shown in Table 22.

Discharge procedure

997.   On 9 March the Council recommended that Parliament grant a discharge to the Commission in respect of the implementation of the general budget for 1996 ([2]). According to the financial regulation, Parliament should have granted this discharge by 30 April, but, on 31 March it informed the Commission of the reasons why it was deferring its decision and listed the cases which posed particular problems in this respect ([3]). After some heated debates Parliament concluded in December that it was still unable to adopt a final position and decided to refer the matter back to the Committee on Budgetary Control at the beginning of 1999. However, it gave a discharge to the Commission on 31 March in

---

([1])   Bull. 7/8-1998, point 1.6.4.
([2])   Bull. 3-1998, point 1.5.2.
([3])   OJ C 138, 4.5.1998; Bull. 4-1998, point 1.5.6.

TABLE 22

Budget revenue

(million ECU)

	1998	1999
Agricultural duties	1 101.8	1 054.5
Sugar and isoglucose levies	1 069.8	1 080.0
Customs duties	13 504.8	13 215.4
Own resources collection costs	−1 567.6	−1 535.0
VAT own resources	32 752.8	30 374.2
GNP-based own resources	34 501.6	39 260.0
Balance of VAT and GNP own resources from previous years	988.7	p.m.
Budget balance from previous year	960.0	1 400.0
Other revenue	668.1	708.6
Total	83 967.1	85 557.7
	% of GNP	
Maximum own resources which may be assigned to the budget	1.26	1.27
Own resources actually assigned to the budget	1.13	1.09

respect of the management of the ECSC (¹) and the implementation of the sixth and seventh European Development Funds (EDF) (²) in 1996, to the administrative board of the European Foundation for the Improvement of Living and Working Conditions and the administrative board of the Centre for the Development of Vocational Training (³) also on 31 March, and to Parliament, the Ombudsman, the Court of Justice, the Court of Auditors and the Committee of the Regions on 7 October (⁴). However, again on 7 October, it postponed the discharge for the Economic and Social Committee for that year (⁵).

998.   On 31 March Parliament adopted a resolution (⁶) on the Commission report on action taken in response to the observations contained in the resolution accompanying the decision giving discharge in respect of the general budget for 1995.

(¹)   OJ C 138, 4.5.1998; OJ L 146, 16.5.1998; Bull. 4-1998, points 1.5.11 and 1.5.12.
(²)   OJ C 138, 4.5.1998; OJ L 146, 16.5.1998; Bull. 4-1998, point 1.5.7.
(³)   OJ C 138, 4.5.1998; OJ L 146, 16.5.1998; Bull. 4-1998, point 1.5.8.
(⁴)   OJ C 328, 26.10.1998; Bull. 10-1998, point 1.5.6.
(⁵)   OJ C 328, 26.10.1998; Bull. 10-1998, point 1.5.7.
(⁶)   OJ C 138, 4.5.1998; Bull. 4-1998, point 1.5.9.

ECSC operating budget

999. On 10 June the Commission adopted a draft ECSC operating budget for 1999 (¹). An exchange of views was held with the ECSC Consultative Committee on 25 June. After Parliament delivered its opinion on 22 October (²) the ECSC operating budget for 1999 was finally adopted on 9 December (³) with a levy rate of 0 %. This budget totals EUR 196 million, of which EUR 5 million is for administrative expenditure, EUR 84 million for aid for research, EUR 75 million for redeployment aid and EUR 32 million for social measures connected with the restructuring of the coal industry.

1000. The guidelines set out by the Commission in its communication of October 1997 entitled 'Future of the ECSC Treaty — Financial activities' (⁴) were welcomed by the Council on 20 July (⁵) and by Parliament on 22 October (⁶).

Financial regulations

1001. On 23 November the Council adopted the seventh series of amendments to the financial regulation of 21 December 1977 (Table II). These amendments, which form part of phase two of the SEM 2000 programme *(→ points 1141 et seq.)*, tighten up the control of commitments, lay down rules for the delegation of powers of budget execution and strengthen the position of Financial Control, which will in future be allowed to carry out spot checks. On 17 December it also adopted the eighth series of amendments to the financial regulation proposed by the Commission on 3 April to take account of the introduction of the euro and the stability and growth pact (Table II). On 22 July the Commission also adopted a working paper to launch the interinstitutional debate on the recasting of the financial regulation (⁷).

1002. In a resolution adopted on 15 July Parliament stressed the need to clarify the rules applicable to interest earned on funds from the Community budget (⁸).

(¹)   Bull. 6-1998, point 1.6.1.
(²)   OJ C 341, 9.11.1998; Bull. 10-1998, point 1.5.9.
(³)   Bull. 12-1998.
(⁴)   COM(97) 506; 1997 General Report, point 1073.
(⁵)   OJ C 247, 7.8.1998; Bull. 7/8-1998, point 1.6.8.
(⁶)   OJ C 341, 9.11.1998; Bull. 10-1998, point 1.5.11.
(⁷)   Bull. 7/8-1998, point 1.6.6.
(⁸)   OJ C 292, 21.9.1998; Bull. 7/8-1998, point 1.6.7.

1003.   As part of Agenda 2000, the Commission adopted a report and a proposal for a regulation on the Guarantee Fund for external action (→ *point 11*).

1004.   An interinstitutional agreement on legal bases and implementation of the budget was signed on 13 October (→ *point 1033*).

Section 3

Financial control

1005. In 1998 the Commission's Financial Controller continued implementing measures to foster rationalisation, simplification and transparency of procedures and also stepped up cooperation with decentralised managers.

1006. As part of the decentralisation of the management and control of Community funds in the Member States, the Financial Controller concluded cooperation protocols with Germany, Ireland, Austria and Finland and with ministerial departments in the United Kingdom not covered by the protocol signed in 1997 (¹). In contacts with bodies responsible for control at national level, the Financial Controller concentrated on the development of control methods and presented a new audit manual for the Structural Funds at a seminar on aspects of methodology attended by all the Member States and the applicant countries in June. With regard to the Structural Funds, the Financial Controller also monitored the implementation of Regulation (EC) No 2064/97 (²), on which the Member States presented their first annual reports. Coordination of on-the-spot controls continued and a study was produced on the implementation of the audit trail method in each Member State. A special planning and monitoring system for the EAGGF-Guarantee sector was developed.

1007. In accordance with the Commission decision of 7 June 1990 (³), Financial Control conducted an internal audit of six directorates-general and a performance audit of one directorate-general. It also carried out two targeted inquiries and examined the action taken in response to recommendations made to three previously audited directorates-general, bearing in mind the recommendation adopted under the SEM 2000 initiative *(→ points 1141 et seq.)* to extend and upgrade the role of internal auditing by including systems audits, management audits and performance audits as well as auditing of the accounts. As a further part of the SEM 2000 initiative, in addition to the annual report on evaluation, Financial Control also audited the performance of the evaluation function in two Commission departments and, in agreement with the depart-

---

(¹)   1997 General Report, point 1077.
(²)   OJ L 290, 23.10.1997; 1997 General Report, point 1079, as amended by Regulation (EC) No 2406/98 (OJ L 298, 7.11.1998; Bull. 11-1998, point 1.5.8).
(³)   Twenty-fourth General Report, point 1007.

ments concerned, defined quality standards for the management of this function to ensure that best practice is followed throughout the Commission. A financial audit was also conducted of the sickness insurance scheme and Assmal, its accounts system, as well as additional audits of central accounts and the ancillary accounting system for external delegations.

1008.   Under the PHARE programme *(→ points 812 et seq.)*, a sixth training seminar was held for Slovenian officials in Ljubljana in May. Fact-finding missions were carried out in the Czech Republic, Estonia, Cyprus and Poland and on-the-spot inspections were conducted in Bulgaria and Hungary, in the latter case with the national control body. A contact group consisting of European government inspection agencies, involving all the Member States and the applicant countries was also set up to help applicant countries to improve their capacity to control the financial flows from the European Union. Cooperation protocols were signed with the national control agencies of Hungary, Poland, the Czech Republic and Slovenia, and a training seminar for controllers was organised in Brussels for representatives of the national control agencies of the last three countries.

1009.   In June, to ensure the control of Community expenditure in international organisations, the Commission authorised its Financial Controller to negotiate an agreement on conditions for financing and cofinancing programmes and activities managed by the United Nations and other international organisations. The agreement with the World Health Organisation signed in 1996 was renewed until 1 March 2000 ([1]).

([1])   1996 General Report, point 1004.

Section 4

Protection of the Communities' financial interests and the fight against fraud

1010. On 6 May the Commission adopted its ninth annual report (1997) on the protection of the Communities' financial interests and the fight against fraud([1]) and its 1998-99 fraud prevention work programme ([2]).

1011. In its annual report the Commission stressed that traditional own resources (customs duties and agricultural levies) are more seriously affected by fraud and irregularities than budget expenditure. The amounts involved in cases of fraud and irregularities affecting traditional own resources in 1997 came to ECU 1 007 million (as against ECU 787 million in 1996), the goods most frequently concerned being cigarettes, alcohol and milk products; in particular, cases of cigarette smuggling detected in 1997 caused total tax losses of ECU 1.6 billion, three quarters of which to national budgets (excise duties and VAT). One particular cause of concern is the role played by international criminal organisations which are also involved in drugs trafficking, corruption and money-laundering. With regard to expenditure, however, there has been an overall reduction in the volume of fraud and irregularities, with agriculture still the prime target (export refunds, direct aid to farmers and market support measures).

1012. The 1998-99 fraud prevention work programme aims to continue the anti-fraud strategy defined in 1994([3]). It has four priority strands: the development of operational actions and strategic activities (strengthening of presence in the field, control mechanisms and cooperation in customs and tax matters, the use and analysis of intelligence and cooperation in the fight against money-laundering); strengthening of institutional structures and the legal framework (prevention, administrative sanctions, monitoring Member States' ratification of the instruments of Title VI of the Treaty on European Union); launching of targeted actions against certain types of economic crime harmful to specific Community interests, particularly the counterfeiting of the euro; protection of European finances in the framework of enlargement and cooperation

---

([1])   COM(1998) 276; Bull. 5-1998, point 1.5.7.
([2])   COM(1998) 278; Bull. 5-1998, point 1.5.8.
([3])   COM(94) 92; 1994 General Report, point 1145.

with non-member countries (Commission assistance in taking over the body of Community law in this sector).

1013. In its conclusions of 19 May (¹), the Council considered that the investigations carried out by the Commission and the Member States had produced significant results and that close cooperation between the Commission, the Member States and non-member countries was vital. It urged proper application of the regulation concerning on-the-spot checks and inspections (²) and called on the Member States to report all the information at their disposal. The Council also stressed that priority had to be given to the fight against organised crime and against fraud involving customs transit and preferential agreements and shared the Commission's objectives as regards the efforts to combat VAT fraud, protection of European finances in the framework of enlargement and the protection of monetary union and the euro.

1014. The Commission set out its strategy on a number of specific aspects involved in the protection of the Communities' financial interests. In particular, it adopted communications on efforts to tackle fraud in the field of excise duties on 29 April (³), on a framework for action on combating fraud and counterfeiting of non-cash means of payment on 1 July *(→ point 973)* and on a strategy to combat counterfeiting of euro-denominated banknotes and coins on 22 July (⁴). This strategy was also addressed in a Parliament resolution of 17 November (⁵) and the Council conclusions of 23 November (⁶). For the purposes of implementing Regulation (EC) No 515/97 (⁷), on 27 March the Commission determined the operations concerning the application of agricultural legislation for which information has to be introduced into the customs information system (CIS) (⁸). On 17 February Parliament adopted a resolution on presumed frauds and irregularities in the tourism sector (⁹).

1015. On 1 May the Commission transformed its central structure for fraud prevention (UCLAF) into a task force reporting directly to the Secretary-General. Subsequently, on 14 July (¹⁰), it defined the legal frame-

---

(¹) Bull. 5-1998, point 1.5.9.
(²) Council Regulation (EC) No 2185/96 (OJ L 292, 15.11.1996; 1996 General Report, point 1011).
(³) Bull. 4-1998, point 1.5.18.
(⁴) COM(1998) 474; Bull. 7/8-1998, point 1.6.13.
(⁵) OJ C 379, 7.12.1998; Bull. 11-1998, point 1.5.11.
(⁶) Bull. 11-1998, point 1.5.12.
(⁷) OJ L 82, 22.3.1997; 1997 General Report, point 1089.
(⁸) Regulation (EC) No 696/98 (OJ L 96, 28.3.1998).
(⁹) OJ C 80, 16.3.1998; Bull. 1/2-1998, point 1.6.10.
(¹⁰) Bull. 7/8-1998, point 1.6.12.

work of the task force's investigation responsibilities, giving it greater independence of action as requested by Parliament in its resolution of 31 March (¹). The UCLAF task force thus cooperates with the Member States in combating fraud, corruption and money-laundering and is the direct contact for the police or judicial authorities; the rules to be followed by task force inspectors when a member of the Commission's staff is involved in a case were also specified. In its conclusions of 23 November the Council then called for UCLAF to be made more effective (²). On 7 October Parliament adopted a further resolution on the independence, role and status of UCLAF (³) in which, although welcoming the measures adopted, it recommended the establishment, by a joint decision of Parliament, the Council, the Court of Justice and the Court of Auditors, of an Anti-Fraud Office (OLAF) which, in addition to taking over the UCLAF's former powers, would be responsible for combating internal corruption and fraud in all the European Union's institutions. On 1 December the Commission adopted a proposal for a regulation (Table II) establishing a European Fraud Investigation Office, which would enjoy complete independence for conducting investigations both externally (in the Member States) and internally (within the European Union institutions). The Commission would retain the responsibilities conferred on it by the Treaty (right of initiative, assisting the Member States in the coordination of their anti-fraud activities, monitoring proper application of Community law and implementation of the budget). President Santer presented this proposal to Parliament on 2 December and it was welcomed by the Vienna European Council (⁴).

(¹)   OJ C 138, 4.5.1998; Bull. 3-1998, point 1.5.17.
(²)   Bull. 11-1998, point 1.5.10.
(³)   OJ C 328, 26.10.1998; Bull. 10-1998, point 1.5.12.
(⁴)   Bull. 12-1998.

Section 5

Borrowing and lending operations

1016. Table 26 shows the loans granted each year for 1996 to 1998. In 1998 borrowing operations totalled ECU 30.5 billion (EIB included).

TABLE 26

Loans granted

(million ECU)

Instrument	1996	1997	1998
New Community instrument	—	—	—
EC — Balance of payments	—	—	—
EC — medium-term financial assistance to countries of central Europe and other non-member countries	155	195	403
EC — food aid	1	—	—
ECSC	280	541	20
Euratom	—	—	—
EIB,	23 240	26 203	29 526
of which:			
— Community	20 946	22 958	25 116
— non-member countries, of which	2 294	3 245	4 410
— ACP and overseas territories, excluding South Africa	396	60	560
— Mediterranean countries	681	1 122	966
— Central and eastern Europe	1 116	1 486	2 387
— Latin America and Asia	45	378	362
— South Africa	56	199	135
Total	23 675	26 939	29 949

Section 6

General budget guarantee for borrowing and lending operations

1017. The guarantee by the Community budget covers lenders when the Community floats an issue under one of its financial instruments: balance-of-payments facility, Euratom loans, New Community Instrument, financial assistance for various non-member countries (→ *points 76 et seq.*). The budget guarantee is also given to the European Investment Bank (EIB) for the loans it grants from its own resources to certain non-member countries([1]). At the end of 1998, the ceiling for authorised borrowing and lending operations guaranteed by the general budget was ECU 49 982 million. At 31 December, the guarantee was in operation for ECU 4 416 million of Community borrowing and for ECU 7 837 million granted by the EIB out of its own resources.

1018. The Council extended the Community guarantee granted to the EIB to cover loans in the Former Yugoslav Republic of Macedonia on 19 May (Table II) and to loans in Bosnia and Herzegovina on 14 December (Table II).

1019. The Guarantee Fund for external actions([2]), set up to reimburse the Community's creditors in the event of default by the recipient of a loan given or guaranteed by the Community in a non-member country, was again activated when certain independent States of the former Soviet Union defaulted on their payments in respect of the ECU 1.25 billion loan for food aid and medical supplies granted in 1991([3]). However, two of these States belatedly repaid a total of ECU 172.4 million for which the Guarantee Fund had already been activated. This amount was paid back to the Fund in accordance with Article 2 of Regulation (EC) No 2728/94 establishing the Fund([4]). At 31 December 1998 the aggregate amount of payments not reimbursed was ECU 63.2 million.

1020. The budget guarantee was again activated for loans granted by the EIB in certain republics of former Yugoslavia. When they failed to make repayments, the Guarantee Fund was called upon for ECU 15.4 million in all. The total amount of guarantees activated since 1992 after

---

([1])   1997 General Report, point 1092.
([2])   1994 General Report, point 1133.
([3])   OJ L 362, 31.12.1991; Twenty-fifth General Report, point 78.
([4])   OJ L 293, 12.11.1994; 1994 General Report, point 1133.

the republics of former Yugoslavia defaulted on their payments and which had not been repaid came to ECU 90.6 million at 31 December 1998.

1021.   Since the Fund's resources at 31 December 1997 were higher than the target amount of 10 % of outstanding liabilities laid down by Regulation (EC) No 2728/94, a total of ECU 66 million was repaid to the budget in the course of 1998.

1022.   Under Agenda 2000, the Commission proposed on 17 March that the regulation governing the Fund be amended *(→ point 11)*.

Chapter VIII

Institutional matters

Section 1

Amsterdam Treaty

1023. After the Treaty was signed in Amsterdam on 2 October 1997 (¹), the Member States each initiated the ratification procedures in accordance with their respective constitutional requirements. The Treaty was submitted for approval to Parliament in the 15 Member States and also had to be approved by referendum in Denmark and Ireland. At the end of 1998, 10 Member States had deposited instruments ratifying the Amsterdam Treaty. In chronological order they were Germany (²) (7 May), Sweden (³) (15 May), United Kingdom (⁴) (15 June), Denmark (⁵) (24 June), Finland (⁶) (15 July), Austria (⁶) (21 July), Italy (⁶) (24 July), Ireland (⁶) (30 July), Luxembourg (⁷) (4 September), and the Netherlands (⁸) (31 December). The Treaty will enter into force on the first day of the second month following that in which the instrument of ratification is deposited by the last signatory State to fulfil that formality (⁹).

1024. To ensure that the new provisions of the Amsterdam Treaty become operational as soon as it enters into force, the institutions have already taken steps in the following areas (¹⁰): integration of the Schengen *acquis* into the framework of the European Union (Protocol 2); establishment of the policy planning unit and early warning unit of the

---

(¹) OJ C 340, 10.11.1997; 1997 General Report, points 1 to 28.
(²) Bull. 5-1998, point 1.8.1.
(³) Bull. 5-1998, point 1.8.2.
(⁴) Bull. 6-1998, point 1.9.5.
(⁵) Bull. 6-1998, point 1.9.4.
(⁶) Bull. 7/8-1998, point 1.9.1.
(⁷) Bull. 9-1998, point 1.8.1.
(⁸) Bull. 12-1998.
(⁹) Article 14(2), Treaty of Amsterdam.
(¹⁰) The references used refer to the consolidated version in OJ C 340, 10.11.1997.

CFSP (Declaration 6) (→ *point 666);* appointment of the High Representative for the common foreign and security policy (new Article 26 of the Treaty on European Union) (→ *point 666);* relations between the European Union and the Western European Union (Protocol 1) (→ *points 669 and 703);* implementing procedures for the application of the revised co-decision procedure (Declaration 34) (→ *point 1028);* amendment of the 1987 decision relating to the exercise of implementing powers conferred on the Commission (Declaration 31) (→ *points 1030 et seq.);* common guidelines on the quality of the drafting of Community legislation (Declaration 39) (→ *point 1041);* general principles and limits on access to documents of the European Parliament, the Council and the Commission (new Article 255 of the EC Treaty) (→ *point 1039);* application of the principles of subsidiarity and proportionality (Protocol 30) (→ *points 1042 and 1043);* proposal to set up an independent supervisory body for the protection of personal data (new Article 286 of the EC Treaty); regulations governing Members of the European Parliament and uniform election procedure (new Article 190 of the EC Treaty) (→ *point 1073);* internal organisation of the Commission (Declaration 32) (→ *points 1140 et seq.).*

1025.   Protocol 11 of the Amsterdam Treaty provides for two stages in the future institutional reform: the composition of the Commission to be reduced, at the date of entry into force of the next enlargement, to one national of each of the Member States provided that, by that date, the weighting of the votes in the Council has been modified; the provisions relating to the composition and functioning of the institutions to be fully revised at least one year before the membership of the European Union exceeds 20. The conference also took note of a declaration by Belgium, France and Italy ([1]) on this protocol to the effect that they considered this exercise was linked to extending the use of qualified majority voting. In its communication 'Agenda 2000' ([2]) the Commission advocated that a new Intergovernmental Conference be convened as soon as possible after 2000. In this context, the European Council, meeting in Cardiff on 15 and 16 June ([3]), agreed that first priority should be given to the ratification of the Amsterdam Treaty and, while welcoming the progress made towards putting it into effect, called for a timetable to be set for studying the institutional issues not resolved in Amsterdam. Finally, the European Council in Vienna on 11 and 12 December ([4])

([1])   1997 General Report, points 2 to 26.
([2])   COM(97) 2000; 1997 General Report, point 30; Supplement 5/97 — Bull.
([3])   Bull. 6-1998, points I.14 and I.20.
([4])   Bull. 12-1998.

agreed to decide at its meeting in Cologne in June 1999 when and how to tackle those institutional issues left unresolved in Amsterdam that need to be settled before enlargement.

Section 2

Voting in the Council

1026.   The Council continued to adopt instruments by majority vote whenever appropriate and with the Commission's agreement. In many other cases the prospect of a qualified majority vote was sufficient to secure a unanimous decision.

Section 3

Legislative role of the European Parliament

1027.   The enhanced legislative role of the European Parliament under the decision-making procedures introduced by the Treaty on European Union has continued to affect the content of the legislation in question. On the whole, the co-decision procedure has been found to work well, with a significant increase in the proportion of matters going to conciliation (now nearly half of all cases). However, the combination of the unanimity requirement in the Council and the co-decision procedure (for example in cultural affairs) has led to additional problems at the conciliation stage. A closer examination of the procedures shows that Parliament and the Council are divided above all on institutional matters, particularly the executive powers conferred on the Commission (committee procedure) and declarations entered in the minutes, on budget questions and on a number of political problems connected for example with ethics, the environment, consumer protection, health and social policy.

1028.   On 16 July the European Parliament adopted a resolution on the new co-decision procedure due to come in with the entry into force of the Amsterdam Treaty([1]), mandating its representatives to negotiate a new interinstitutional agreement with the Council and the Commission.

([1])   OJ C 292, 21.9.1998; Bull. 7/8-1998, point 1.9.2.

Section 4

Implementing powers conferred on the Commission

1029. Although in most cases implementing powers were conferred on the Commission pursuant to Article 145 of the EC Treaty, this was not done on all occasions when the Commission so proposed nor always in the manner it proposed. In some cases the Council continued to reserve to itself the right to exercise implementing powers. As regards the use of the procedures laid down in 1987 ([1]), the advisory procedure was selected in less than a dozen cases, the management procedure in about 90 — including more than a third using variant (b) — and the regulatory procedure in more than 40 — including more than a quarter using variant (b), about which the Commission has reservations, since it offers no guarantee that a decision will be taken. The Council has continued to favour, for a single legislative instrument, the use of several procedures, depending on the matters dealt with.

1030. In response to Declaration 31 adopted by the conference of the representatives of the governments of the Member States when the Amsterdam Treaty was signed ([2]), the Commission adopted on 24 June a proposal for a decision amending the Council decision of 13 July 1987 laying down the procedures for the exercise of implementing powers conferred on the Commission (Table II). This proposal is now before the Council and Parliament.

1031. In a resolution adopted on 16 September, Parliament instructed its President to negotiate with the Council and the Commission an interinstitutional agreement which met its concerns as far as possible; it also considered the possibility of placing in reserve the appropriations in the 1999 budget for meetings of committees and groups of experts if the amendment of the Council decision failed to take due account of Parliament's positions ([3]). Following contacts between the three institutions, Parliament entered in reserve at its December part-session ([4]) just over half of the appropriations in question — rather than the whole amount, as proposed during the first reading in October — 'in order to maintain pressure on all sides to come to an equitable and effective solution on

---

([1])   Decision 87/373/EEC (OJ L 197, 18.7.1987; Twenty-first General Report, point 4).
([2])   OJ C 340, 10.11.1997; 1997 General Report, point 1098.
([3])   OJ C 313, 12.10.1998; Bull. 9-1998, point 1.8.2.
([4])   Bull. 12-1998.

the new commitology structure, before the beginning of May 1999, after real trilateral negotiations'.

1032.   In accordance with the Plumb-Delors and Klepsch-Millan agreements and the *modus vivendi* (¹), the Commission sent Parliament most of the draft implementing instruments submitted to the committees. In line with the undertakings given in 1996, it also sent the draft agendas and aggregate results of votes taken in the management and legislation committees. The total number of documents sent in 1998 was around 2 000.

(¹)   1994 General Report, point 1175; 1996 General Report, point 1036.

Section 5

Interinstitutional cooperation

1033. In the light of the judgment of the Court of Justice of 12 May (→ *point 1062)* and on the basis of the Commission communication of July 1994 on legal bases and maximum amounts ([1]), the institutions reached an agreement on legal bases on 17 July, in the conciliation procedure on the establishment of the draft budget for 1999 ([2]). The results were enshrined in an interinstitutional agreement on legal bases and implementation of the budget, approved by the Commission on 29 July, by Parliament on 16 September ([3]) and by the Council on 5 October ([4]). This agreement was signed by the representatives of the three institutions on 13 October and came into force on the same day ([5]). It was applied to the remaining stages of the 1999 budget procedure and will also be applied to the budget procedures in future years unless denounced by one of the three institutions.

In an effort to satisfy the concerns of each of the institutions, the agreement enounces the principle that 'the implementation of appropriations entered in the budget for any Community action requires the prior adoption of a basic instrument.' It then defines what constitutes a basic instrument and identifies a small number of actions that may be financed without a basic instrument.

1034. In a resolution adopted on 14 May ([6]), Parliament called for interinstitutional agreements to be concluded, pending the next Intergovernmental Conference, in areas in which it had no right of scrutiny, such as the coordination of economic policies and collective agreements between the social partners.

1035. In December, Parliament, the Council and the Commission adopted an interinstitutional agreement on the quality of the drafting of Community legislation *(→ point 1041).*

([1]) 1994 General Report, point 1103.
([2]) Bull. 7/8-1998, point 1.6.1 (this contains the full text of the agreement).
([3]) OJ C 313, 12.10.1998; Bull. 9-1998, point 1.5.1.
([4]) Bull. 10-1998, point 1.5.2.
([5]) OJ C 344, 12.11.1998; Bull. 10-1998, point 1.5.2.
([6]) OJ C 167, 1.6.1998; Bull. 5-1998, point 1.8.4.

1036. Information on the interinstitutional agreement on budgetary discipline and improvement of the budgetary procedure may be found in Sections 1 ('Priority activities and objectives') and 2 ('Budgets') of Chapter VII *(→ points 981 et seq.).*

Section 6

Openness, subsidiarity and proportionality

1037. The Cardiff European Council in June reiterated the need to bring the Union closer to the people by making it more open, more understandable and more relevant to daily life([1]).

1038. In an effort to increase the involvement of interested groups in its work, the Commission has developed channels for consultation, for example publishing its work programme on the Internet and presenting two Green Papers *(→ points 194 and 472)* and one White Paper *(→ point 431)*. It also updated its directory of interest groups, which is available in electronic form and currently contains around 800 European federations.

1039. The Commission continued to give the widest possible access to its documents, granting around 90 % of requests for access. The Council adopted its second report on the implementation of its policy on access to documents([2]), which records significant progress, with around 80 % of requests being granted and a large number of documents being requested. It also decided, on 19 March, to make a register of its unclassified documents available to the public on the Internet via the Europa server *(→ point 1153)* ([3]), thus making it easier to identify the documents available([4]). The European Monetary Institute set out the terms for public access to its documents([5]). Finally, the European Ombudsman's special report on public access to documents held by the Community institutions and bodies other than the Commission and Council was published in the Official Journal *(→ point 23)* ([6]).

1040. The Union institutions have stepped up their information activities, making increasing use of the Internet in particular. A new service 'Europe direct' was launched at the Cardiff European Council. Details of the Commission's information and communication policy can be found in Chapter XI *(→ points 1149 et seq.)*.

([1]) Bull. 6-1998, point I.10.
([2]) Bull. 6-1998, point 1.9.7.
([3]) http://register.consilium.eu.int/utfregister/frames/introfsen.htm.
([4]) Bull. 3-1998, point 1.8.1.
([5]) OJ L 90, 25.3.1998; Bull. 3-1998, point 1.8.2.
([6]) OJ C 44, 10.2.1998.

1041.   Pursuant to Declaration 39 annexed to the Treaty of Amsterdam, Parliament, the Council and the Commission worked together on drawing up guidelines to improve the quality of the drafting of Community legislation. The outcome of this cooperation was an interinstitutional agreement laying down 22 rules for the drafting of legal instruments and a number of internal organisational measures to ensure that the institutions apply these rules properly. In December this agreement was approved by all three institutions, each acting in accordance with its own internal procedures (¹).

1042.   In line with the Amsterdam Protocol on subsidiarity and proportionality, the Commission endeavoured to apply these principles rigorously without waiting for ratification of the Treaty. It took care to see that each proposal is explained in terms of subsidiarity on matters where powers are shared and in terms of proportionality in all cases. In accordance with the principle of proportionality it did its utmost to ensure that greater attention was paid to the impact of its proposals and promoted broad, open and constructive discussions with the parties concerned. Some 90 proposals were withdrawn on the grounds that they were no longer relevant.

1043.   The Commission reported on the application of these principles to the Cardiff European Council (²), the informal meetings of Heads of State or Government in Pörtschach and the Vienna European Council (³) calling on all Community institutions and Member States to act consistently in this matter without shirking their share of responsibility. The Vienna European Council reaffirmed the need for full implementation of the subsidiarity principle (¹). It also stressed that subsidiarity and proportionality were legally binding principles and that the institutions must henceforth observe the criteria and guidelines set forth in the Protocol to the Treaty of Amsterdam.

(¹)   Bull. 12-1998.
(²)   'Legislate less to act better: the facts'; COM(1998) 345; Bull. 5-1998, point 1.8.3.
(³)   'Better lawmaking 1998: a shared responsibility'; COM(1998) 715; Bull. 12-1998. In December Parliament passed a resolution on the 1997 'Better lawmaking' report; Bull. 12-1998.

Chapter IX

Community law

Section 1

Monitoring the application of Community law

1044. The Commission continued its close monitoring of the application of Community law in 1998. It commenced 1 105 infringement proceedings (1 422 in 1997), issued 674 reasoned opinions (331 in 1997), and referred 114 cases to the Court of Justice (121 in 1997). The breakdown by country of cases referred in 1997 under Articles 169 and 171 of the EC Treaty is as follows [1]: Belgium, 19; Denmark, none; Germany, 4; Greece, 17 (one of them under Article 171); Spain, 5; France, 22 (one of them under Article 171); Ireland, 10; Italy, 16; Luxembourg, 11; Netherlands, 3; Austria, 2; Portugal, 5; Finland, none; Sweden, none; United Kingdom, none.

1045. The Commission carried out an initial evaluation of the results of the reform of infringement proceedings started in 1996 [2] and, in June, drew operational conclusions intended, on the one hand, to speed up the pace at which decisions are taken and implemented, and, on the other, to improve the transparency of the infringement proceedings. Detailed information on the infringement proceedings commenced during the year and on progress in transposing directives into national law will be given in the 16th annual report on the application of Community law, to be published in 1999. On 19 May, the Commission adopted the

---

[1] These figures are provisional. The final figures will appear in the 16th annual report on the application of Community law, to be published in 1999.
[2] 1996 General Report, point 1119.

15th annual report on the application of Community law (1997)(¹). Parliament also reacted to the 14th annual report, covering 1996, in a resolution passed on 29 January (²).

(¹)   OJ C 250, 10.8.1998; COM(1998) 317; Bull. 5-1998, point 1.7.1.
(²)   OJ C 56, 23.2.1998; Bull. 1/2-1998, point 1.8.1.

Section 2

Decisions by the Court of Justice and the Court of First Instance (¹)

1046. Statistics concerning the activities of the Court of Justice and the Court of First Instance were included in the General Report until 1997 (²) but are now published by the Court itself, both on paper (³) and on the Europa server on the Internet (⁴).

General principles of Community law

1047. On 29 January the Court of First Instance ruled that the Community was not legally responsible for the consequences which the completion of the single market and the consequent abolition of customs frontiers between Member States had entailed for customs agents (⁵). Since the abolition of tax and customs frontiers was a direct result of the Single Act, the direct cause of such abolition and its impact on customs agency work was to be found in Article 13 of the Single Act (now Article 7a of the EC Treaty). The Court pointed out that only an act of the Community institutions or an act of the servants of the Community in the performance of their duties could give rise to liability on the part of the Community. The latter could not, however, be held liable for damage resulting from an instrument of primary Community law such as the Single Act, which did not constitute an act of the institutions themselves but an international treaty adopted and approved by the Member States, although the possibility could not be excluded that an obligation to provide compensation might arise under the domestic law of a Member State. The Court took the view that the Community could not be obliged to make good damage arising from a failure to adopt measures to offset the consequences which the abolition of frontiers between Member States would have for customs agents. Economic operators could not contend that they had an acquired right, under existing Community rules, to the pursuit of their trade or profession. The Court's judgment is particularly significant in view of the foresee-

---

(¹) See also the quarterly analysis of judgments in the *Bulletin of the European Union:* Bull. 4-1998, points 1.7.33 to 1.7.40; Bull. 6-1998, points 1.8.22 to 1.8.31; Bull. 9-1998, points 1.7.74 to 1.7.78; Bull. 12-1998.
(²) For example, 1997 General Report, Tables 23 to 26.
(³) In the Court's Annual Report (1998 edition forthcoming).
(⁴) http://europa.eu.int/cj/en/index.htm.
(⁵) Case T-113/96 *Edouard Dubois et Fils* v *Council and Commission* [1998] ECR II–125; Bull. 3-1998, point 1.7.49.

able consequences which the introduction of the euro will have for certain types of work in the banking and financial sector.

1048. On 17 June the Court of First Instance ruled for the first time that an individual could apply for the annulment of a directive of a general legislative nature if he could prove that he was directly and individually affected by the provisions concerned, even though that was not the case here ([1]). In doing so it ended the controversy as to whether such a directive could be contested, and asserted that an individual could apply for its annulment in the same way as for the annulment of a decision or a regulation. The Court also ruled on the question of the representativeness of the social partners who sign an agreement under the social policy. In this particular case a European association representing the interests of small and medium-sized undertakings had applied for the annulment of Council Directive 96/34/EC on the framework agreement on parental leave concluded by the Union of Industrial and Employers' Confederations of Europe, the European Centre of Enterprises with Public Participation and the European Trade Union Confederation ([2]). The said association had lodged its application for annulment on the grounds that it had not been allowed, despite several requests, to participate in the negotiations between management and labour. The Court found that the organisations which had been allowed to participate were sufficiently representative of management and labour and, having considered whether the applicant was directly and individually affected by the provisions concerned, it concluded that the applicant had failed to show that it differed from all the various management and labour organisations which the Commission had consulted and which had not concluded the framework agreement. The Court held that the applicant was not adversely affected by the directive as a result of any factual circumstances peculiar to it, and that it was not therefore individually affected by the directive. The Court of First Instance therefore declared the application inadmissible.

1049. On 16 June the Court of Justice declared itself competent to answer a question referred by a national court concerning the interpretation of a particular provision of the Agreement on Trade-related Aspects of Intellectual Property Rights (the 'TRIPS agreement'), even though questions relating to the agreement fell largely within the jurisdiction of the Member States ([3]). In this particular case a national court

---

([1]) Case T-135/96 *UEAPME* v *Council* [1998] ECR; Bull. 6-1998, point 1.8.29.
([2]) OJ L 145, 19.6.1996; 1996 General Report, point 562.
([3]) Case C-53/96 *Hermès International* v *FHT Marketing Choice* [1998] ECR I-3603; Bull. 6-1998, point 1.8.30.

had referred to the Court of Justice a question relating to the concept of 'provisional measure' within the meaning of Article 50 of the TRIPS agreement, under which the judicial authorities of the contracting parties are to be empowered to order the adoption of provisional measures to protect the interests of those holding the rights to a trade mark under the legislation of the said parties. The Court noted that the Community was a party to the TRIPS agreement and that Article 50 of the agreement had been implemented by Article 99 of Regulation (EC) No 40/94 on the Community trade mark ([1]). Where a provision was to be applied to situations covered both by national and by Community law, it was certainly in the Community interest to ensure uniform interpretation and thus avoid any future differences of interpretation, irrespective of the circumstances in which the provision was to apply. The Court drew attention to the fact that, when the courts of the Member States referred to in Article 99 of Regulation (EC) No 40/94 had occasion to order provisional measures for the protection of rights arising from a Community trade mark, they were obliged to do so, as far as possible, in the light of the content and purpose of Article 50 of the TRIPS agreement. The Court of Justice was thus competent to answer the question referred to it by the national court.

1050. On 17 December the Court of Justice rejected a plea that the excessive length of proceedings was grounds for setting aside a judgment of the Court of First Instance in its entirety ([2]). The Commission had fined companies for breaches of the competition rules, and one of the firms had asked the Court of First Instance to annul the Commission's decision. At the end of the proceedings the Court annulled part of the decision and reduced the fine to ECU 3 million. The firm appealed against the judgment of the Court of First Instance. The Court of Justice found that while the proceedings had taken six years, they had involved the examination of eleven actions, in three different languages, and concerned highly complex factual and legal issues. It ruled that the length of the proceedings had not influenced the final outcome and did not therefore constitute grounds for setting aside the entire judgment. However, it also ruled that the Court of First Instance had failed to comply with the requirements concerning reasonable length of proceedings and annulled the part of the judgment setting the fine at ECU 3 million. The Court held that that part of the judgment had to be annulled in order to guarantee an immediate and effective remedy against unduly long proceedings.

([1])   OJ L 11, 14.1.1994; Twenty-seventh General Report, point 117.
([2])   Case C-185/95 P *Baustahlgewerbe GmbH* v *Commission* [1998] ECR; Bull. 12-1998.

European citizenship

1051. On 12 May the Court held that a citizen of the European Union lawfully resident in the territory of a Member State could rely on Article 6 of the EC Treaty (which prohibits discrimination on grounds of nationality) in all situations which fell within the scope of Community law (¹). In this particular case a Spanish citizen was legally resident in Germany. The competent authorities, whilst allowing her to continue to reside in Germany, had refused to issue her a residence permit. They had also refused to grant her a child-raising allowance on the grounds that she did not possess a proper residence permit. The Court ruled that refusal by the authorities of a Member State to grant to a citizen of the European Union a benefit which was granted to all persons lawfully resident in the territory of that Member State on the grounds that the claimant was not in possession of a document which nationals of that same State were not required to have constituted discrimination directly based on nationality.

Free movement of goods

1052. On 16 July the Court gave a judgment of considerable economic importance for the proprietors of trade marks in the Community (²), interpreting Directive 89/104/EEC on the Community trade mark (³) as protecting such owners against imports into the Community, without their consent, of products bearing their trade mark which have been put on the market of a third country. This judgment considerably strengthens the means available to owners for preventing parallel imports from third countries. This particular case related to parallel imports of spectacle frames bearing a prestigious trade mark which was protected both in Austria and in most other countries of the world. The manufacturer had sold a batch of out-of-fashion spectacle frames to Bulgaria. Another Austrian company had purchased the frames delivered to Bulgaria and had offered them for sale in Austria. The owner of the trade mark took the view that the marketing of the frames in this way was harmful to the image of its product on the Austrian market and brought an action for interim relief before an Austrian court. This court had asked the Court of Justice for a preliminary ruling on whether the directive on the Community trade mark allowed Member States to apply the principle that the protection given to a trade mark was exhausted once products

---

(¹)   Case C-85/96 *Martinez Sala* v *Freistaat Bayern* [1998] ECR I-2691; Bull. 6-1998, point 1.8.27.
(²)   Case C-355/96 *Silhouette* v *Hartlauer* [1998] ECR; Bull. 9-1998, point 1.7.75.
(³)   OJ L 40, 11.2.1989; Twenty-second General Report, point 329.

had been placed on the market of a third country. The Court held that this was not so and that only an interpretation to this effect could fully achieve the purpose of the directive, which was to protect the internal market. Barriers to the free movement of goods would inevitably arise from a situation where Member States could provide for exhaustion of trade mark rights once a product was offered for sale in a third country. The owners of trade marks protected within the Community could thus ask national courts to prohibit the importation into the Community, without their consent, of products bearing their trade mark which had been marketed in a third country. The Court thus made a clear distinction between marketing in third countries, which does not entail the exhaustion of trade mark rights, and marketing within the Community and the European Economic Area, where Article 30 of the Treaty calls for the exhaustion of such rights.

Free movement of workers

1053.   On 12 March the Court found that the Treaty provisions on the free movement of workers prohibited a Member State from disregarding periods of public service in another Member State for the purposes of determining the seniority and salary grade of a worker employed in its own public service ([1]). In this particular case a Greek national who had worked for five years in the Nice municipal orchestra in France had taken up employment with the Thessaloniki orchestra, which, like that in Nice, was a public body. The Greek authorities had refused, however, to take into account his experience in France for the purposes of his grading on the salary scale and the granting of a seniority increment. The Court, to whom the matter had been referred by the Commission, noted that the national provisions and the arrangements for their implementation ruled out any possibility that account might be taken of periods of employment in the public service of a Member State other than Greece. It found, consequently, that such national provisions contravened the principle of non-discrimination enshrined in the Community rules on the free movement of workers, and in particular Article 48 of the EC Treaty and Article 7 of Regulation (EEC) No 1612/68 ([2]). The Court observed that the derogation contained in Article 48(4) of the EC Treaty, by virtue of which the provisions concerning freedom of movement for workers do not apply to employment in the public service, did not apply in this case since it merely provided that a Member State could exclude

---

([1])   Case C-187/96 *Commission* v *Greece* [1998] ECR I-1095; Bull. 4-1998, point 1.7.39.
([2])   OJ L 257, 19.10.1968; Second General Report, point 398.

nationals of other Member States from access to certain posts in its public service. The exception did not cover the factors which a Member State took into account when determining the salary arrangements for workers already admitted to its public service.

Freedom to provide services

1054.   On 28 April the Court held that the freedom to provide services precluded a Member State from requiring prior authorisation before reimbursing the cost of dental treatment by a dentist established in another Member State in accordance with the scales of the national social security scheme by which the insured person was covered ([1]). In this particular case the Luxembourg legislation stipulated that members of the national scheme would not be reimbursed for treatment received abroad unless they had first obtained authorisation from the competent social security body. The Court noted that the national legislation in question did not prevent insured persons from having medical treatment abroad. As it had consistently ruled in the past, however, the Court found that making reimbursement of the cost subject to prior authorisation discouraged insured persons from approaching providers of medical services in another Member State. The need for prior authorisation thus constituted a barrier to the freedom to provide services. In this case the member of the Luxembourg scheme was merely asking that expenses incurred in another Member State be reimbursed in accordance with the tariff of the State of insurance. The Court consequently held that the reimbursement of such expenses would have no significant effect on the financing of the social security scheme. It acknowledged, however, that in other circumstances the risk of seriously undermining the financial balance of the scheme could constitute an overriding reason in the general interest and justify a barrier to the freedom to provide services. The Court stressed that the national rules were not justified on grounds of public health. Firstly, since the conditions for taking up and pursuing the professions of doctor or dentist had been the subject of several harmonising directives, the barrier which the Luxembourg rules placed in the way of the freedom to provide services could not be justified in terms of protecting the quality of medical services provided in other Member States. Secondly, it was not contended that the rules in question were indispensable for the maintenance of an essential treatment facility or medical service on national territory. In a judgment given on the same

---

([1])   Case C-158/96 *Kohll* v *Union des caisses de maladie* [1998] ECR I-1931; Bull. 6-1998, point 1.8.22.

day the Court applied the same principles in a case relating to the free movement of goods, ruling that the principle of the free movement of goods precluded national rules under which a social security institution of a Member State could refuse to reimburse an insured person the cost of a pair of spectacles with corrective lenses purchased from an optician established in another Member State on the grounds that prior authorisation was required for the purchase of all medical products abroad ([1]).

Competition — State aids

1055. On 29 January the Court found, as it had consistently held in the past, that the only defence available to a Member State in opposing an application under Article 93(2) of the EC Treaty for a declaration that it had failed to fulfil its obligations was to plead that proper fulfilment of its obligations under Community law was absolutely impossible ([2]). In this particular case the Commission had brought an action for a declaration that Italy, by failing to recover aid to road hauliers which had been found incompatible with the common market, had failed to meet its obligations under the EC Treaty. The Member State in question had argued that recovery was technically impossible since it would involve a large number of disparate departments and could rekindle a serious industrial dispute in the road haulage sector. The Court pointed out that although insuperable difficulties might prevent a Member State from meeting its obligations under Community law, mere apprehension of such difficulties could not justify a failure to apply Community law correctly. In that connection the Court found that administrative difficulties did not exonerate a Member States from the said obligations.

1056. On 2 April the Court clarified the obligations of the Commission when it received a complaint relating to State aid ([3]). The Court held that the Commission had a duty to investigate complaints diligently and impartially, including questions which had not been explicitly raised by the applicant. Except where a diligent and impartial investigation would so require, however, the Commission was not as a rule obliged to investigate a complaint by looking into facts and points of law not raised by the complainant. If the Commission found that no State aid as alleged by a complainant existed, it had to provide the complainant with

---

([1]) Case C-120/95 *Decker* v *Caisse de maladie des employés privés* [1998] ECR I-1831.
([2]) Case C-280/95 *Commission* v *Italy* [1998] ECR I-259; Bull. 4-1998, point 1.7.33.
([3]) Case C-367/95 P *Commission* v *Sytraval and Brink's France* [1998] ECR I-1719; Bull. 6-1998, point 1.8.24.

an adequate explanation of the reasons for which the facts and points of law put forward in the complaint had failed to demonstrate the existence of aid. The Court stressed, however, that the Commission, when investigating a complaint, was not required to conduct an exchange of views and arguments with the complainant. This was at odds with the findings of the Court of First Instance, which had treated the procedure for investigating complaints concerning State aid as being the same as that for investigating complaints relating to competition. Lastly, the Court made it clear that, when the Commission adopted a decision finding that the alleged aid either did not exist or was compatible with the common market, such a decision was addressed to the Member State concerned. Although the Commission would inform the complainant of its decision in accordance with proper administrative practice, only the decision addressed to the Member State could be the subject of an application for annulment. Whereas decisions rejecting complaints constituted a category in the field of agreements, concerted practices and abuses of dominant positions, they did not constitute a category in the field of State aid.

1057. On 31 March the Court held that Council Regulation (EEC) No 4064/89 on the control of concentrations between undertakings([1]) applied to collective dominant positions([2]). It noted that neither the wording of the regulation, and in particular that of Article 2 thereof, nor the legislative history allowed any precise conclusions to be drawn as to the type of dominant position with which the regulation is concerned. Having considered the purpose and general structure of the regulation, however, the Court found that collective dominant positions fell within its scope. In particular, the Court noted that any merger which created or strengthened a dominant position enjoyed by the parties concerned with another undertaking was likely to prove incompatible with the system of undistorted competition envisaged in the Treaty. If the regulation was considered to apply only to mergers which created or strengthened the dominant position enjoyed by the parties to the merger, its purpose would be partially frustrated. The regulation would thus lose much of its impact, and unnecessarily so, given the general structure of the Community arrangements for merger control.

([1]) OJ L 395, 30.12.1989; Twenty-third General Report, point 376.
([2]) Joined Cases C-68/94 *France* v *Commission* and C-30/95 *SCPA and EMC* v *Commission* [1998] ECR I-1375; Bull. 4-1998, point 1.7.40.

Equal treatment of men and women

1058. On 17 February the Court of Justice ruled that, in the present state of the law within the Community, stable relationships between two persons of the same sex were not regarded as equivalent to marriages or stable relationships outside marriage between persons of opposite sex ([1]). In this particular case an employer, a railway company, had refused to grant travel concessions to the female partner of a woman employee. Under the company regulations these concessions were usually granted to employees and to their spouse or regular partner. The employer justified its refusal by stating that travel concessions were granted only to partners of the opposite sex, whereas the employee in question had a stable relation with a person of the same sex. The Court observed first of all that the employer refused travel concessions to any partner of the same sex as the employee. The condition laid down by the employer thus applied in the same way to both male and female workers, so that it could not be regarded as constituting discrimination directly based on sex. Having considered the relevant Community law, the past rulings of the European Commission of Human Rights and the European Court of Human Rights, and the International Covenant on Civil and Political Rights of 19 December 1966, the Court held that stable relationships between persons of the same sex could not be regarded as equivalent to marriages or stable relationships between persons of opposite sex. It was for the legislature alone to adopt, if need be, measures which might affect that position. In this connection the Court noted that the new Article 6a added by the Treaty of Amsterdam would enable the Council to take the necessary steps to eliminate various forms of discrimination, including those based on sexual orientation.

1059. On 30 June the Court, overturning an earlier ruling, extended the protection afforded to pregnant women against dismissal by their employer on grounds relating to the number of days of incapacity which their pregnancy entails ([2]). In this particular case a woman had been dismissed in the course of her pregnancy because she had exceeded the number of weeks of sick leave allowed by her contract of employment. The Court noted that, although pregnancy could not be considered an illness, it was nevertheless a period during which disorders might arise compelling a woman to undergo strict medical supervision and to refrain from any exertion for all or part of her pregnancy. Such disorders and complications, which might cause incapacity for work, were among the

---

([1])   Case C-249/96 *Grant* v *South-West Trains* [1998] ECR I-621; Bull. 4-1998, point 1.7.36.
([2])   Case C-394/96 *Brown* v *Rentokil Ltd* [1998] ECR I-4185; Bull. 6-1998, point 1.8.28.

risks inherent in the condition of pregnancy. Overturning its ruling of 29 May 1997 (^{1}), the Court therefore held that, where a woman was absent because of a pregnancy-related illness and where that illness arose during pregnancy and persisted during and after maternity leave, not only her absence during maternity leave but also that extending from the start of her pregnancy to the start of her maternity leave could not be taken into account for the purposes of calculating the period which would justify her dismissal under national law.

Institutional matters

1060.   On 3 March the president of the Court of First Instance rejected an application from individuals for access to internal documents of the Council's Legal Service (^{2}). He took the view that public access to the written opinions of the legal service of a Community institution could be refused on the grounds that disclosure of their contents could be contrary to the public interest. He pointed out that the disclosure of such legal opinions, which were described as working documents, could have the effect that the institution would see no further advantage in asking its legal staff for written opinions. This would give rise to uncertainty regarding the legality of Community instruments and would have negative consequences for the working of the institutions. Refusal to disclose the opinions of a legal service was thus covered by an exception to the public's general right of access to documents, namely that relating to the protection of the public interest, as laid down in Article 4(1) of Decision 93/731/EC (^{3}). The president of the Court of First Instance also pointed out that, in view of the special nature of the opinions delivered by legal services, the documents in question were likely to remain confidential for years to come.

1061.   On 10 February the Court of Justice annulled a Commission decision adopted after consultation of a committee on the grounds that the text of the draft decision had not been sent to one of the national delegations in the language of that delegation within the prescribed deadline and that the latter's request for postponement of the vote on the draft had not been taken into account by the Commission (^{4}). The Court pointed out that the sending of draft texts to each national delegation in its own language was an essential condition for the valid con-

---

(^{1})   Case C-400/95 *Larsson* [1997] ECR I-2757.
(^{2})   Case T-610/97 *Carlsen and Others* v *Council* [1998] ECR II-485.
(^{3})   OJ L 340, 31.12.1993.
(^{4})   Case C-263/95 *Germany* v *Commission* [1998] ECR I-441.

sultation of the committee in question and that this followed from Article 3 of Regulation No 1 determining the languages to be used by the European Economic Community (¹).

1062. On 12 May the Court annulled, for lack of legal basis, the Commission decision announcing certain grants for European projects seeking to overcome social exclusion (²). The Court found that the measures provided for in the contested decision were covered by the Council's Poverty 3 programme (³) and by the Commission's proposal for the Poverty 4 programme (⁴). It noted that the aim of the annulled decision was to continue the initiatives launched under the Poverty 3 programme, at a time when it was obvious that the Council was not going to adopt the Poverty 4 proposal, which sought to continue and extend Community action to combat social exclusion. The Court pointed out that the implementation of Community expenditure relating to any significant Community action presupposed not only the entry of the relevant appropriation in the Community budget, which was a matter for the budgetary authority, but also the prior adoption of a basic act authorising that expenditure, which was a matter for the legislative authority. The Court found that the contested decision did constitute significant action even if it entailed only limited expenditure and its effects were limited in time. It acknowledged, however, that measures designed to prepare the way for future Community action or to launch pilot projects could be considered non-significant action which did not require the prior adoption of a basic act.

1063. On 29 September the Court confirmed the validity of the procedure whereby the Commission decides on the issue of reasoned opinions and on the referral of infringement proceedings to the Court under Article 169 of the Treaty (⁵). In this particular case Germany contended that an application to the Court under the said Article was inadmissible on the grounds that the Commission had issued its reasoned opinion and brought the matter before the Court in breach of the principle that decisions must be taken collectively. Germany claimed that the text of the reasoned opinion and the referral should have been adopted by a decision of the Commission acting as a body and not by a decision taken under the delegation procedure. The Court rejected the plea that the principle in question had been breached and made it clear that it

---

(¹)   OJ No 34, 29.5.1959.
(²)   Case C-106/96 *United Kingdom* v *Commission* [1998] ECR I-2729; Bull. 6-1998, point 1.8.26.
(³)   OJ L 224, 2.8.1989; Twenty-third General Report, point 411.
(⁴)   COM(93) 435; Twenty-seventh General Report, point 436.
(⁵)   Case C-191/95 *Commission* v *Germany* [1998] ECR; Bull. 9-1998, point 1.7.77.

was not necessary for the Commission as a body to draft instruments which simply gave effect to decisions which it had already taken collectively. The Court pointed out that the issue of a reasoned opinion was a preliminary phase in the procedure which could end with a referral to the Court. A reasoned opinion was not legally binding on the addressee but was intended to define the subject of the proceedings. Similarly, a decision to refer matters to the Court did not in itself alter the legal position. Only the Court, by delivering judgment, could determine in definitive and binding terms the rights and obligations of Member States within the framework of infringement proceedings. The Court concluded that decisions to issue reasoned opinions or to refer matters to the Court had to be deliberated jointly by the Commission as a whole, given that such decisions were necessary if the Court was to rule on an application for a declaration that a Member State had failed to meet its obligations. On the other hand, it was not necessary for the Commission as a body to draft the instruments which gave effect to the said decisions.

Common agricultural policy — Veterinary inspections — Public health

1064. In two judgments given on 5 May ([1]) the Court reaffirmed the validity of the Commission decision prohibiting the export of bovine meat and derived products from the United Kingdom as a means of preventing the spread of bovine spongiform encephalopathy (BSE or 'mad cow disease') ([2]). The Court noted that, at the time when the decision was adopted, there was great uncertainty as to the risks posed by live animals, bovine meat and derived products. When there was such uncertainty regarding the risk to human health, the Community institutions were empowered to take protective measures without having to wait until the reality and seriousness of those risks became fully apparent. This view was corroborated by Article 130r(1) of the EC Treaty, which states that protecting human health is one of the objectives of Community policy on the environment. Paragraph 2 of the same Article provides that this policy is to be based on the precautionary principle and on preventive action. The Court also pointed out that, according to Article 129 of the EC Treaty, health protection requirements were to form a constituent part of the Community's other policies. The objec-

---

([1]) Case C-180/96 *United Kingdom* v *Commission* and Case C-157/96 *The Queen* v *Minister of Agriculture, Fisheries and Food,* ex parte *National Farmers' Union and Others* [1998] ECR I-2265; Bull. 6-1998, point 1.8.25.
([2]) Decision 96/239/EC (OJ L 78, 28.3.1996; 1996 General Report, point 502).

tives of the common agricultural policy could not be pursued without regard for the general interest, and in particular the need to protect consumers and human health. The Community institutions had a duty to take such needs into account when exercising their powers. Lastly, the Court set aside the argument that the contested decision had been taken on economic grounds. An analysis of the decision showed that the Commission had acted in view of the risk that BSE might be transmissible to humans, having examined the measures adopted by the United Kingdom and having consulted the Scientific Veterinary Committee and the Standing Veterinary Committee.

1065. On 30 September the Court of First Instance rejected an action for damages brought against the Commission and the Council by Italian farmers ([1]). The latter claimed that the institutions had been slow to act against the epidemic of bovine spongiform encephalopathy (BSE) and were thus responsible for the serious crisis affecting the beef sector. The Court noted that the Community institutions had adopted, from 1989 onwards, a number of measures to deal with the BSE crisis. Consumer confidence in beef had not been adversely affected until 20 March 1996, when it was announced that there might be a link between BSE and Creutzfeldt-Jakob disease in humans. Following this announcement the United Kingdom and several other Member States had rapidly taken measures to halt the spread of the disease. In the Court's view, the Council had acted in good time by adopting, on 8 July 1996, Regulation (EEC) No 1357/96 on additional measures to support the beef market ([2]). In any case, no causal link had been established between any delay on the part of the institutions and the crisis in the beef sector.

([1]) Case T-149/96 *Confederazione Nazionale Coltivatori Diretti and Others* v *Council and Commission* [1998] ECR; Bull. 9-1998, point 1.7.78.
([2]) Regulation (EC) No 1357/96 (OJ L 175, 13.7.1996; 1996 General Report, point 519).

Section 3

Simplification and consolidation

1066. As part of the better lawmaking exercise, the Commission continued the simplification work it has been engaged in for several years (¹). It adopted a proposal for a directive under the SLIM programme *(→ point 151)* to simplify the arrangements for deducting value added tax *(→ point 187)*. It also adopted a communication following up the recommendations made in the report submitted to it by BEST, the 'business environment simplification task force', which was set up at the request of the Amsterdam European Council with a view to simplifying the business environment for small and medium-sized firms *(→ point 260)*. As part of the action plan for the single market, it also launched a pilot project, the 'business test panel', the aim of which is to improve the procedures for analysing the impact on businesses of new legislative proposals *(→ point 153)*.

1067. The Commission adopted 10 consolidation proposals, involving the repeal of some 177 legislative instruments. It also undertook the informal consolidation of some 66 basic instruments, which involved the processing of around 536 instruments.

(¹) Twenty-sixth General Report, point 10; Twenty-seventh General Report, point 11.

Section 4

Computerisation of Community law

1068. During 1998 the Office for Official Publications of the European Communities *(→ points 1162 et seq.)* pursued its efforts to improve the coverage and access to CELEX (¹), the European Union's official interinstitutional database. The work was guided by the CELEX interinstitutional group (GIC) and the Council working party on the processing of legal data (GJIC). During 1998 the coverage of the Finnish and Swedish versions of the database was greatly improved. A general review of some sectors of the base was also undertaken.

1069. The new method of accessing CELEX through the Europa server *(→ point 1153)* on the Internet, which was launched in 1997 (²) and improved by the launch of a new version of the World Wide Web interface (http://europa.eu.int/celex/), has significantly increased the number of consultations (10 million documents consulted in 1998, as against 8 million in 1997 and 5 million in 1996). It has also become the most used service on the Commission's 'Europa-plus' intranet *(→ point 1132).*

1070. CELEX is also distributed through three other channels: through the Publications Office to privileged users, including the European Documentation Centres (EDC) and the Commission's Euro-Info Centres (EIC); subscriptions through the network of official agents, which act as gateways, providing on-line access to the reference version, housed in the Commission's computer centre (clients in countries where no gateway exists are administered directly by the Publications Office in Luxembourg); and 24 licence-holders disseminate derived versions of CELEX, on-line or on CD-ROM, which present CELEX data together with other relevant information.

(¹) Twenty-seventh General Report, point 1154.
(²) 1997 General Report, point 1122.

Chapter X

Institutions and organs

Section 1

Composition and functioning

European Parliament

1071. The distribution of seats among the political groups of the European Parliament at 31 December 1998 was as follows:

— Party of European Socialists (PSE), chaired by Pauline Green (UK)	214
— European People's Party (PPE), chaired by Wilfried Martens (B)	202
— European Liberal Democrat and Reform Party (ELDR), chaired by Patrick Cox (IRL)	42
— Union for Europe (UPE), chaired by Jean-Claude Pasty (F)	35
— Confederal Group of the European United Left/Nordic Green Left (GUE/NGL), chaired by Alonso José Puerta Gutiérrez (E)	34
— Green Group in the European Parliament (V), chaired by Magda Aelvoet (B)	27
— European Radical Alliance (ARE), chaired by Catherine Lalumière (F)	20

— Group of Independents for a Europe of Nations (I-EDN), chaired by Jens-Peter Bonde (DK) 15

— Non-affiliated (NI) 37

1072. At its 15-19 June part-session Parliament adopted the schedule for its part-sessions for 1999 (^{1}), with 11 plenary sessions for Strasbourg and five additional part-sessions of two half-days in Brussels.

1073. The main items of business at the plenary part-sessions were economic and monetary union, enlargement, Agenda 2000, employment, consumer health protection and the environment. On the institutional front Parliament considered the Commission's new proposal on committee procedure *(→ point 1030),* and adopted resolutions on closer co-operation (^{2}), the co-decision procedure *(→ point 1028),* interinstitutional agreements *(→ point 1034),* the procedure for electing MEPs and the draft statute for MEPs (^{3}). On economic, monetary and employment matters, Parliament approved the Council recommendation concerning the Member States fulfilling the necessary conditions for the adoption of the single currency *(→ point 49)* and the appointment of the members of the Executive Board of the European Central Bank *(→ point 57),* and adopted resolutions on various aspects of the introduction of the euro *(→ point 55),* democratic accountability in Stage III of economic and monetary union *(→ point 61),* duty-free sales *(→ point 192),* the guidelines for employment *(→ point 111),* the social dialogue *(→ point 134)* and the social action programme 1998-2000 *(→ point 106).* Parliament also gave its opinion on various aspects of Agenda 2000 (Structural Funds, reform of the common agricultural policy, pre-accession instruments *(→ points 14 and 15)).* As regards the activities of the European Council, Parliament passed resolutions on the outcome of the meeting at Cardiff (^{4}) and preparations for the informal meeting at Pörtschach on the future of Europe (^{5}).

1074. Parliament held its annual debates on racism (^{6}), the human rights situation in the European Union (^{7}), the Commission's annual economic report (^{8}), agricultural prices for 1998/99 (^{9}), petitions (^{10}), the

(^{1}) OJ Annex 511; Bull. 6-1998, point 1.10.1.
(^{2}) OJ C 292, 21.9.1998; Bull. 7/8-1998, point 1.9.3.
(^{3}) OJ C 292, 21.9.1998; Bull. 7/8-1998, point 1.10.2.
(^{4}) OJ C 210, 6.7.1998; Bull. 6-1998, point 1.9.2.
(^{5}) OJ C 341, 9.11.1998; Bull. 10-1998, point 1.8.4.
(^{6}) OJ Annex 504; Bull. 1/2-1998, point 1.10.2.
(^{7}) OJ Annex 505; Bull. 1/2-1998, point 1.10.3.
(^{8}) OJ Annex 508; Bull. 4-1998, point 1.8.2.
(^{9}) OJ Annex 511; Bull. 6-1998, point 1.10.1.
(^{10}) OJ Annex 512; Bull. 7/8-1998, point 1.10.1.

European Council report on the progress of European Union in 1997 (¹) and the state of the Union (²), and on the Cohesion Fund and the Structural Funds. On the external relations front, Parliament held debates on the first two meetings of the European Conference, guidelines for the negotiation of new cooperation agreements with the ACP countries, the gradual establishment of a common EU defence policy and implementation of the common foreign and security policy in 1997. There were also debates on the situation in the former Yugoslavia, the peace process in the Middle East, Iraq, Algeria, relations with the United States and Russia and Latin America.

1075. At the 14-18 December part-session, Jacques Santer presented the Commission's work programme for 1999. The European Ombudsman, Jacob Söderman, presented his report for 1997 at the 13-17 July part-session (³).

1076. On the budgetary front, Parliament gave the 1999 budget its two readings and the President declared it formally adopted on 17 December (→ points 987 and 990). However, Parliament failed to grant the Commission discharge in respect of the implementation of the general budget for 1996 (→ point 997) (⁴). Bernhard Friedmann, President of the Court of Auditors, presented the Court's annual report to Parliament at the 16-20 November part-session (⁵). Parliament also adopted the interinstitutional agreement on legal bases and discussed the Commission report on own resources. On the fraud prevention front, it adopted resolutions on the independence, role and status of UCLAF and on Court proceedings for the protection of the Union's financial interests (→ point 1015). Parliament also scrutinised the Commission's past management of Community aid to the tourism industry (→ point 1014) and cooperation with the Mediterranean countries (⁶).

1077. At a formal sitting in December, Parliament awarded the Sakharov prize to Mr Ibrahim Rugova (⁴).

1078. Parliament addressed 5 573 questions to the Commission and the Council — 4 114 written questions (3 737 to the Commission and 377 to the Council), 204 oral questions with debate (125 to the Commission

---

(¹) OJ Annex 516; OJ C 341, 9.11.1998; Bull. 10-1998, points 1.8.3 and 1.9.2.
(²) OJ Annex 516; Bull. 10-1998, point 1.9.2.
(³) OJ Annex 513; Bull. 7/8-1998, point 1.10.2.
(⁴) OJ Annex 519; Bull. 12-1998.
(⁵) OJ Annex 517; Bull. 11-1998, point 1.8.2.
(⁶) OJ C 379, 7.12.1998; Bull. 11-1998, point 1.5.3.

and 79 to the Council), and 1 255 during question time (788 to the Commission and 467 to the Council).

1079. A breakdown of Parliament's work in 1998 is shown in Table 27. At 31 December the establishment plan of Parliament's Secretariat comprised 3 489 permanent posts and 603 temporary posts.

Council

1080. The United Kingdom held the Council presidency in the first half of 1998 and Austria in the second half. The European Council met twice formally — in Cardiff in June and in Vienna in December — and once informally in Pörtschach in October.

1081. At its meeting in Cardiff on 15 and 16 June([1]), the European Council set out the essential components of the European Union's strategy for further economic reform to promote growth, prosperity, jobs and social inclusion and identified practical ways of bringing the Union closer to the people through greater transparency, environmental integration and more intensive efforts to combat unemployment and organised crime. It also established guidelines and a time-frame for further negotiations on Agenda 2000, reviewed other progress in developing the Union and its external relations, called for swift ratification of the Amsterdam Treaty and launched a longer-term debate on the workings of the Union, which it agreed to pursue further at an informal meeting. The European Council also adopted its report to Parliament on the Union's progress in 1997([2]) and a declaration on Kosovo *(→ point 843).* The President of South Africa, Nelson Mandela, was guest of honour of the European Council.

1082. The Vienna European Council on 11 and 12 December([3]) agreed on a 'Vienna strategy for Europe' setting out a work programme for the European Union in 1999. Stressing that Agenda 2000 forms a package on which agreement can only be reached as a whole, the European Council reiterated its determination to reach such overall agreement in 1999. It approved the 1999 guidelines for employment and agreed to step up the process of converging employment policies with a view to establishing a European employment pact. It decided to strengthen the coordination of economic and tax policies and laid down

---

([1]) Bull. 6-1998, points I.1 to I.35.
([2]) Bull. 6-1998, point 1.9.3.
([3]) Bull. 12-1998.

TABLE 27

Parliamentary proceedings from January to December 1998
Resolutions and decisions adopted

Part-session	Consultations (single reading)	Cooperation procedure		Co-decision procedure			Assent	Other opinions (1)	Budget questions	Own-initiative reports and resolutions			Miscellaneous decisions, declarations and resolutions (4)
		First reading	Second reading	First reading	Second reading	Third reading				Reports	Resolutions (2)	Urgent subjects (3)	
January I	7	1	1	1	1	1		11		5	3	11	2
January II	1	1	1	1	1	2		2		1	1	10	
February	10	5		7	5			6		4	6	10	
March I	17		2	4	3			2		5	5		1
March II	13	2	4	3				4	8	6	1	4	
April	6	1	1	2	8			3		1	2		
May I	14	4	1	1	4		1	15		3	3	12	2
May II	6	2					1	3		3	1		
June	32		2	2	2			5	1	3	6	10	1
July I	1			2			1	5	1	4			
July II	12	1	1	3	1	3		16		2	1	12	3
September	32	3	2		2	4		10		4	6	11	
October I	26	1	2	3	5		1	9	1	1	4	10	1
October II	3	4	1	1	1			10	3	5	3	1	
November I	3	1	1	4				2		1	1		
November II	12	5		4	2			7		2	5	8	
December I	2	1	3		1			8		2	1		
December II	18	5		3	7	1		7	2	5	2	8	
Total	215 (5)	38 (6)	24 (7)	41 (8)	43 (9)	11	4	135	16	55	51	107	10

(1) Mainly opinions on Commission reports or communications.
(2) Resolutions in response to statements by other institutions or following oral questions.
(3) Resolutions on topical and urgent subjects of major importance.
(4) Decisions concerning waiver of immunity, amendments to the Rules of Procedure and interinstitutional agreements.
(5) Including 138 cases in which Parliament proposed amendments to the Commission proposal.
(6) Including 37 cases in which Parliament proposed amendments to the Commission's proposal.
(7) Including 18 cases in which Parliament amended the Council's common position.
(8) Including 32 cases in which Parliament proposed amendments to the Commission's proposal.
(9) Including 22 cases in which Parliament amended the Council's common position.

the arrangements for the external representation of the euro. It also approved an action plan aimed at implementing the provisions of the Amsterdam Treaty on establishing an area of freedom, security and justice and identified the first common strategies to be developed on the foreign affairs front once the Amsterdam Treaty enters into force. The European Council awarded the former Federal German Chancellor, Helmut Kohl, the title of Honorary Citizen of Europe.

1083. On 3 May the Council, meeting at the level of Heads of State or Government, decided that 11 Member States satisfied the necessary conditions for the adoption of the single currency on 1 January 1999 (→ point 48).

1084. The Council held 94 meetings in 1998. Figures for the legislative instruments enacted this year are found in Table 28 at the end of this section.

1085. At 31 December the Council's establishment plan comprised 2 441 permanent posts and 18 temporary posts.

Commission

1086. Following President Santer's presentation of the Commission's work programme for 1998 to Parliament in October 1997 (¹) and the resolution which Parliament adopted in December 1997 (²), the Council made a declaration on the programme on 26 January in which it identified the areas of action on which it would be placing emphasis in 1998 (³). The Commission adopted its report on the implementation of this work programme on 28 October (⁴).

1087. Also on 28 October the Commission adopted its work programme for 1999 (⁵), which is aimed at consolidating recent progress in European integration and preparing for the 21st century. With these goals in mind, the programme's main strands are: modernising the Commission itself, putting into effect Agenda 2000, implementing the Amsterdam Treaty, ensuring that economic and monetary union is a success and creating the preconditions for sustainable growth and employ-

---

(¹)   OJ C 339, 10.11.1997; 1997 General Report, point 1144; Supplement 1/98 — Bull.
(²)   OJ C 14, 19.1.1998; 1997 General Report, point 1145; Supplement 1/98 — Bull.
(³)   Bull. 1/2-1998, points 1.10.12 and 2.2.1.
(⁴)   COM(1998) 610; Bull. 10-1998, point 1.9.13.
(⁵)   COM(1998) 604; Bull. 10-1998, point 1.9.12; Supplement 1/99 — Bull.

ment and promoting a strong Europe that is open to the world. The Commission considers it essential that the set of measures in Agenda 2000 on reforming structural policies and agricultural policy, defining a new financial framework for 2000-06 and preparing for enlargement are adopted in spring 1999. It believes that these measures are interdependent and form an indivisible whole and that without them it would be difficult to respond effectively to the challenges of enlargement. In implementing the Amsterdam Treaty, the Commission will concentrate its efforts on employment and the Union's social dimension, the establishment of an area of freedom, security and justice and the incorporation in Community policies of the concept of sustainable development. It will also pay special attention to health and consumer protection. The Commission feels that the question of institutional reform must be discussed further in 1999; it intends to make an active contribution to this debate and will support initiatives calling for a new Intergovernmental Conference to be convened. In an effort to ensure the success of economic and monetary union, the Commission will apply scrupulously the provisions of the Treaty and secondary legislation relating to coordination of economic policy and promotion of economic convergence, including the stability and growth pact, so as to enhance the beneficial effects of the economic reforms. It will pay particular attention to the impact of structural policies and the smooth operation of the single market and seek to improve the competitiveness of European industry through initiatives on trans-European networks, research, the information society and telecommunications. The Commission will also work towards its goal of a strong Europe open to the world by striving to enhance the Union's capacity to act as a more visible, unified and coherent — and hence stronger — entity on the international scene. It will further deepen the Union's relations with its partners, ensure that support for developing countries and countries in transition is continued and strive to promote the Union's trade interests, particularly in the next round of WTO negotiations. It will also seek to establish greater coherence in human rights policy, a vital component of the Union's relations with the outside world. The Commission attaches great importance to modernising itself and has already embarked on a wide-ranging analysis of its structures and operation with a view to gradual and thorough-going reform, with the emphasis on decentralising, assigning responsibility, tightening supervision and simplifying management (→ *points 1140 et seq.*), so that it can play a more effective role in achieving the Union's political goals by exercising its right of initiative in line with the general Community interest. In preparing 'Tomorrow's Commission', the Commission is committed to taking the first practical steps in this direction in 1999. It will also actively pursue its policy of transparency.

1088.   The 1999 work programme was accompanied by a list of 26 new legislative initiatives which the Commission plans to present in 1999 ([1]).

1089.   On 16 December Parliament passed a resolution on the implementation of the 1998 work programme and on the 1999 work programme ([2]).

1090.   The Commission held 47 meetings in the course of the year. It presented 576 proposals, recommendations or draft instruments for adoption by the Council or by Parliament and the Council together (63 directives, 230 regulations, 271 decisions and 5 recommendations). It also presented 293 communications, memorandums and reports. Apart from the new initiatives, debates, programmes and plans of action and those continued from previous years under the 1998 work programme (→ *point 1086),* these figures include proposals for routine management instruments (notably in agriculture, fisheries, customs and commercial policy) and proposals for consolidation of existing instruments. The figures for legislative instruments adopted by the Commission are set out in Table 28 at the end of this section.

1091.   The Commission's establishment plan for 1998 comprised 16 344 permanent posts (including 1 903 LA posts for the Language Service) and 750 temporary posts (including 13 LA posts) for administrative duties; 1 518 permanent posts and 114 temporary posts for research duties; 525 permanent posts for the Publications Office; 54 posts at the European Centre for the Development of Vocational Training and 83 at the European Foundation for the Improvement of Living and Working Conditions. Under the secondment and exchange arrangements between the Commission and the Member States' government departments, 19 Commission officials were seconded to national civil services and international organisations, and the number of national experts coming to work for Commission departments was equivalent to 614.4 person-years, paid from the administrative budget.

([1])   COM(1998) 609; Bull. 10-1998, point 1.9.12; Supplement 1/99 – Bull.
([2])   Bull. 12-1998; Supplement 1/99 — Bull.

Court of Justice and Court of First Instance

1092. On 14 July, the composition of the Chambers of the Court of Justice was determined as follows for the 1998/99 Court year ([1]):

— First Chamber: President: Mr Jann;
Judges: Mr Edward, Mr Sevón and Mr Wathelet;

— Second Chamber: President: Mr Hirsch;
Judges: Mr Mancini and Mr Schintgen;

— Third Chamber: President: Mr Puissochet;
Judges: Mr Moitinho de Almeida and Mr Gulmann;

— Fourth Chamber: President: Mr Kapteyn;
Judges: Mr Murray, Mr Ragnemalm and Mr Ioannou;

— Fifth Chamber: President: Mr Puissochet;
Judges: Mr Jann, Mr Moitinho de Almeida, Mr Gulmann, Mr Edward, Mr Sevón and Mr Wathelet;

— Sixth Chamber: President: Mr Kapteyn;
Judges: Mr Hirsch, Mr Mancini, Mr Murray, Mr Ragnemalm, Mr Schintgen and Mr Ioannou.

Mr Léger was appointed first advocate-general for the same period.

1093. On 27 May the representatives of the governments of the Member States appointed Mr Azizi, Mr Jaeger, Mr Lenaerts, Mr Moura Ramos, Ms Tiili, Mr Vesterdorf and Mr Vilaras members of the Court of First Instance ([2]). On 8 July they appointed Mr Meij for the period from 1 September 1998 to 31 August 2004 ([3]). On 18 February they appointed Mr Mengozzi for the period up to 31 August 2001 ([4]), to replace Mr Saggio, who had been appointed advocate-general at the Court of Justice ([5]). The judges of the Court of First Instance appointed Mr Vesterdorf President of the Court, on 4 March, for the period from 4 March to 31 August 1998 ([6]), and on 17 September for the period from 1 September 1998 to 31 August 2001 ([7]).

---

[1] OJ C 299, 26.9.1998.
[2] OJ L 171, 17.6.1998; Bull. 5-1998, point 1.9.21.
[3] OJ L 209, 25.7.1998; Bull. 7/8-1998, point 1.10.10.
[4] OJ L 63, 4.3.1998; Bull. 1/2-1998, point 1.10.18.
[5] OJ L 63, 4.3.1998; Bull. 1/2-1998, point 1.10.17.
[6] OJ C 113, 11.4.1998; Bull. 3-1998, point 1.9.15.
[7] OJ C 327, 24.10.1998.

1094.   On 21 September the composition of the Chambers of the Court of First Instance was determined as follows for the 1998/99 court year (²):

— First Chamber: President: Mr Vesterdorf;
   Judges: Mr Pirrung and Mr Vilaras;

— Second Chamber: President: Mr Potocki;
   Judges: Mr Bellamy and Mr Meij;

— Third Chamber: President: Mr Jaeger;
   Judges: Mr Lenaerts and Mr Azizi;

— Fourth Chamber: President: Mr Moura Ramos;
   Judges: Ms Tiili and Mr Mengozzi;

— Fifth Chamber: President: Mr Cooke;
   Judges: Mr García-Valdecasas and Ms Lindh;

— First Chamber (extended composition): President: Mr Vesterdorf;
   Judges: Mr Bellamy, Mr Pirrung, Mr Meij and Mr Vilaras;

— Second Chamber (extended composition): President: Mr Potocki;
   Judges: Mr Lenaerts, Mr Bellamy, Mr Azizi and Mr Meij;

— Third Chamber (extended composition): President: Mr Jaeger;
   Judges: Mr Lenaerts, Ms Tiili, Mr Azizi and Mr Mengozzi;

— Fourth Chamber (extended composition): President: Mr Moura Ramos;
   Judges: Mr García-Valdecasas, Ms Tiili, Ms Lindh and Mr Mengozzi;

— Fifth Chamber (extended composition): President: Mr Cooke;
   Judges: Mr García-Valdecasas, Ms Lindh, Mr Pirrung and Mr Vilaras.

1095.   Statistics concerning the activities of the Court of Justice are now published by the Court itself *(→ point 1046).*

1096.   On 9 June the Commission gave its opinion on the draft Council decision presented by the Court of Justice designed to enable the Court of First Instance to give decisions in cases when constituted by a single judge (¹).

(¹) Bull. 6-1998, point 1.10.16.

1097. At 31 December, the establishment plan of the Court of Justice and the Court of First Instance comprised 727 permanent posts and 226 temporary posts.

Court of Auditors

1098. In July the Court adopted the observations which it felt ought to appear in its annual report on 1997; these were transmitted to the Commission and the other institutions. The report was adopted by the Court on 14 and 15 October and published in the Official Journal together with the replies of the other institutions (¹). It covers operations under the general budget and the sixth and seventh European Development Funds (EDFs). The first part, dealing with the general budget, is in eight chapters, the first seven of them relating to the main areas of revenue and expenditure (own resources, common agricultural policy, structural measures, internal policies, external aid administrative expenditure and banking activities). For the first time they mainly consist of a summary of the special reports adopted by the Court *(→ point 1099)*. The eighth chapter contains the statement of assurance as to the reliability of the accounts and the legality and regularity of the underlying transactions. The Court gives positive global assurance on the reliability of the accounts and on the legality and regularity of revenue and commitments. However, as in previous years, it is unable to give such an assurance for payments because of the number of errors detected, particularly in the Structural Funds. Most of these errors originated in the Member States. The part relating to the sixth and seventh EDFs contains the observations concerning the activities of these Funds and a positive statement of assurance.

1099. The Court of Auditors produced 25 special reports in respect of 1997, concerning the following areas: the audit of the European Association for Cooperation (²), bilateral financial and technical cooperation with non-Member Mediterranean countries (³), the clearance of the EAGGF Guarantee Section accounts for 1993 (⁴), implementation by the Commission of EU policy and action as regards water pollution (⁵), importation at reduced rate of levy into the Community and disposal of

---

(¹) OJ C 349, 17.11.1998; Bull. 10-1998, point 1.9.18.
(²) Special report No 7/97; 1997 General Report, point 1155.
(³) Special report No 1/98 (OJ C 98, 31.3.1998; Bull. 1/2-1998, point 1.10.19).
(⁴) Special report No 2/98 (OJ C 121, 20.4.1998; Bull. 1/2-1998, point 1.10.20).
(⁵) Special report No 3/98 (OJ C 191, 18.6.1998; Bull. 3-1998, point 1.9.16).

New Zealand milk products and Swiss cheese (¹), reconstruction in former Yugoslavia (1996-97) (²), the Court's assessment of the system of resources based on VAT and GNP (³), the European Community development aid programme regarding South Africa (1986-96) (⁴), the Commission departments responsible for fighting fraud (⁵), the protection of the European Union's financial interests in the field of VAT on intra-Community trade (⁶), the expenses and allowances of the Members of the European Parliament (⁷), the development of the PHARE and TACIS private sector for the period 1991-96 (⁸), implementation of the operational programmes relating to the promotion of rural development in Objective 5(b) areas (⁹), the use of risk analysis techniques in customs control and the clearance of goods (¹⁰), the closure of forms of ERDF assistance (¹¹), the assessment of Structural Fund operations for the periods 1989-93 and 1994-99 (¹²), the implementation of appropriations for structural operations for the programming period 1994-99 (¹³), support for renewable energy sources in the shared-cost actions of the JOULE-Thermie programme and the pilot actions of the Altener programme (¹⁴), the Community measures to encourage the creation of joint enterprises in the fisheries sector (¹⁵), the Community financing of certain measures taken as a result of the BSE crisis (¹⁶), the audit of physical checks on agricultural products receiving export refunds (¹⁷), the accreditation and certification procedure applied to the clearance of EAGGF Guarantee Section accounts for 1996 (¹⁸), Commission management of equal opportunities measures (¹⁹), information and communication measures managed by the Commission (²⁰), risk-capital operations financed from European Development Fund resources (²¹) and European Union operations

---

(¹) Special report No 4/98 (OJ C 127, 24.4.1998; OJ C 191, 18.6.1998; Bull. 4-1998, point 1.8.12).
(²) Special report No 5/98 (OJ C 241, 31.7.1998; Bull. 5-1998, point 1.9.23).
(³) Special report No 6/98 (OJ C 241, 31.7.1998; Bull. 5-1998, point 1.9.24).
(⁴) Special report No 7/98 (OJ C 241, 31.7.1998; Bull. 5-1998, point 1.9.25).
(⁵) Special report No 8/98 (OJ C 230, 22.7.1998; Bull. 6-1998, point 1.10.17).
(⁶) Special report No 9/98 (OJ C 356, 20.11.1998; Bull. 7/8-1998, point 1.10.13).
(⁷) Special report No 10/98 (OJ C 243, 3.8.1998; Bull. 7/8-1998, point 1.10.14).
(⁸) Special report No 11/98 (OJ C 335, 3.11.1998; Bull. 9-1998, point 1.9.8).
(⁹) Special report No 12/98 (OJ C 356, 20.11.1998; Bull. 9-1998, point 1.9.9).
(¹⁰) Special report No 13/98 (OJ C 375, 3.12.1998; Bull. 9-1998, point 1.9.10).
(¹¹) Special report No 14/98 (OJ C 368, 27.11.1998; Bull. 9-1998, point 1.9.11).
(¹²) Special report No 15/98 (OJ C 347, 16.11.1998; Bull. 9-1998, point 1.9.12).
(¹³) Special report No 16/98 (OJ C 347, 16.11.1998; Bull. 9-1998, point 1.9.13).
(¹⁴) Special report No 17/98 (OJ C 356, 20.11.1998; Bull. 9-1998, point 1.9.14).
(¹⁵) Special report No 18/98 (Bull. 10-1998, point 1.9.22).
(¹⁶) Special report No 19/98 (OJ C 383, 9.12.1998; Bull. 10-1998, point 1.9.23).
(¹⁷) Special report No 20/98 (OJ C 375, 3.12.1998; Bull. 10-1998, point 1.9.24).
(¹⁸) Special report No 21/98 (OJ C 389, 14.12.1998; Bull. 10-1998, point 1.9.25).
(¹⁹) Special report No 22/98 (Bull. 10-1998, point 1.9.26).
(²⁰) Special report No 23/98 (Bull. 10-1998, point 1.9.27).
(²¹) Special report No 24/98 (OJ C 389, 14.12.1998; Bull. 10-1998, point 1.9.28).

in the field of nuclear safety in central Europe and in the independent States of the former Soviet Union (¹).

1100.   The Court also produced 14 specific annual reports relating to 1997 concerning the accounts of the Euratom Supply Agency (²) and the financial statements of the ECSC, JET (³), the European Schools (⁴), the European Foundation for the Improvement of Living and Working Conditions (⁵), the Centre for the Development of Vocational Training (⁶), the European Training Foundation (⁷), the European Monitoring Centre for Drugs and Drug Addiction (⁷), the Office for Harmonisation in the internal market (⁸), the European Environment Agency (⁸), the European Agency for the Evaluation of Medicinal Products (⁸), the European Agency for Health and Safety at Work (⁷), the Community Plant Variety Office (⁷) and the Translation Centre for the bodies of the Union (⁸). It also produced the annual report relating to the ECSC (⁹), including the ECSC statement of assurance.

1101.   The Court delivered a number of opinions: Opinion No 1/98 of 1-2 April concerning a proposal for a Council regulation (EC, Euratom) implementing Decision 94/728/EC, Euratom on the system of the Communities' own resources (¹⁰), Opinion No 2/98 of 13-14 May on a proposal for a Council regulation (Euratom, ECSC, EC) amending Regulation (Euratom, ECSC, EEC) No 549/69 determining the categories of officials and other servants of the European Communities to whom the provisions of Article 12, the second paragraph of Article 13 and Article 14 of the protocol on the privileges and immunities of the Communities apply (¹¹), Opinion No 3/98 of 13-14 May on the draft financial regulation applicable to the European Monitoring Centre for Racism and Xenophobia (¹²), Opinion No 4/98 of 16-17 September on a proposal to amend Regulation (EEC, Euratom, ECSC) No 259/68 laying down the Staff Regulations of Officials and the Conditions of Employment of Other Servants of the European Communities and the other regulations applicable to them with regard to the establishment of remuneration,

---

(¹)   Special report No 25/98 (Bull. 11-1998, point 1.8.24).
(²)   Bull. 5-1998, point 1.9.22.
(³)   Bull. 7/8-1998, point 1.10.12.
(⁴)   Bull. 10-1998, point 1.9.21.
(⁵)   Bull. 11-1998, point 1.8.22.
(⁶)   Bull. 11-1998, point 1.8.23.
(⁷)   Bull. 11-1998, point 1.8.21.
(⁸)   Bull. 10-1998, point 1.9.20.
(⁹)   OJ C 352, 18.11.1998; Bull. 10-1998, point 1.9.19.
(¹⁰) OJ C 145, 9.5.1998; Bull. 4-1998, point 1.8.13.
(¹¹) OJ C 191, 18.6.1998; Bull. 5-1998, point 1.9.26.
(¹²) Bull. 5-1998, point 1.9.27.

pensions and other financial entitlements in euro (^{1}), Opinions Nos 5/98 and 6/98 of 23 September on two other proposals to amend Regulation (EEC, Euratom, ECSC) No 259/68 concerning, respectively, weightings (^{2}) and Parliamentary assistants (^{3}), Opinion No 7/98 of 7 October on the effectiveness of methods of recovery applied by the Economic and Social Committee and on the new system introduced by the Committee for the administration and reimbursement of travel expenses (^{4}), Opinion No 8/98 of 14-15 October on the agrimonetary system and the euro (^{5}), Opinion No 9/98 of 22 October on proposed amendments to the financial regulation (^{6}), Opinion No 10/98 of 29 October on certain proposals for regulations within the framework of Agenda 2000 (^{7}) and Opinion No 11/98 of 26 November on a draft amendment of the financial regulation of the Office for Harmonisation in the Internal Market (^{8}).

1102. At 31 December the Court's establishment plan comprised 412 permanent posts and 91 temporary posts.

Economic and Social Committee

1103. In 1998 the Economic and Social Committee celebrated 40 years of activity as an advisory body. To mark the occasion, a new logo was created consisting of a blue rectangle bearing the European stars next to three human profiles symbolising the Committee's three groups. The Bureau of the Committee also decided to adopt the name 'European Economic and Social Committee' for everyday use and in public relations work. The Committee held nine plenary sessions during the year and adopted 192 opinions and two information reports. The Committee's opinion was requested on 71 occasions where this was compulsory and 89 times where consultation was optional, many of them relating to draft legislation. The Committee also issued 32 own-initiative opinions, including three additional opinions.

1104. At the start of the year, as in previous years, Mr Flynn, Member of the Commission, sent the Committee a list of items in the Commission's work programme on which the Committee was likely to be con-

---

(^{1})   Bull. 9-1998, point 1.9.15.
(^{2})   Bull. 9-1998, point 1.9.16.
(^{3})   Bull. 9-1998, point 1.9.17.
(^{4})   Bull. 10-1998, point 1.9.29.
(^{5})   Bull. 10-1998, point 1.9.30.
(^{6})   OJ C 7, 11.1.1999; Bull. 10-1998, point 1.9.31.
(^{7})   Bull. 10-1998, point 1.9.32.
(^{8})   Bull. 11-1998, point 1.8.25.

sulted, thus providing it with an overview of its possible advisory duties and enabling it to plan initiatives in other fields which it felt deserved particular attention from the institutions or the Member States. For example the Committee delivered own-initiative opinions on the costs of poverty and social exclusion in Europe *(→ point 141)* and the prevention of the exploitation of children and sex tourism *(→ point 278)*. It also gave special consideration to certain priority issues with major economic and social implications, taking care to ensure that its opinions accurately reflected the concerns of economic and social interest groups. This included an opinion on the Agenda 2000 proposals concerning agriculture, the Structural Funds and the Cohesion Fund *(→ point 15)*. The Committee took pains to stress the gravity of the unemployment situation at every opportunity, analysing the impact of economic and monetary union in a number of fields (employment, economic growth, social policy and the role of social and economic organisations) *(→ point 55)* and stressing the beneficial effects on employment of measures to promote research and technological development, measures to support small businesses and the development of education and vocational training *(→ point 325)*. The Committee also stepped up its role as single market observatory, holding hearings and drawing up own-initiative opinions on, for example, consumers in the insurance market *(→ point 177)*, the prevention of new barriers in the single market *(→ point 156)*, the action plan for the single market *(→ point 149)*, the freedom to set up a business *(→ point 170)* and the implications of the single currency for the internal market *(→ point 55)*. The Committee sees enlargement as one of the biggest challenges facing the Union. Accordingly, it produced several own-initiative opinions in this field, notably on reinforcing the pre-accession strategy *(→ point 801)*, on Slovakia in the context of this strategy *(→ point 824)* and on the Czech Republic in the context of enlargement *(→ point 822)*. The Committee also continued to deepen and extend its relations with social and economic interest groups in non-member countries. The Commission, for its part, kept the Committee up to date on the action taken on its opinions.

1105. Among the prominent participants in Committee meetings were Lord Whitty, Lord Simon of Highbury, Mr Farnleitner and Ms Hostasch, as Presidents-in-Office of the Council, while Mr Kinnock, Mr de Silguy, Mr Flynn and Ms Wulf-Mathies spoke at plenary sessions as Members of the Commission. The last meeting of the year was a formal sitting attended by Ms Hostasch and Mr Flynn, followed by a speech by Mr Duisenberg, President of the European Central Bank ([1]).

([1])   Bull. 12-1998.

1106. On 15 September the Council appointed the members of the Economic and Social Committee for the period from 21 September 1998 to 20 September 2002 (¹). The new Committee held its inaugural meeting on 13, 14 and 15 October (²), when it elected a new President, Ms Rangoni Machiavelli (Various Interests Group) and two new Vice-Presidents, Ms Regnell (Employers' Group) and Mr Piette (Workers' Group). At the same time certain amendments to the Committee's Rules of Procedure entered into force. The number of Bureau members was cut from 30 to 24 and the number of sections from nine to six. The new sections are: economic and monetary union and economic and social cohesion (ECO); the single market, production and consumption (INT); transport, energy, infrastructure and the information society (TEN); employment, social affairs and citizenship (SOC); agriculture, rural development and the environment (NAT); external relations (REX).

1107. At 31 December, the Committee's establishment plan comprised 135 permanent posts for the Committee itself and 516 posts in the organisational structure shared with the Committee of the Regions.

Committee of the Regions

1108. The Committee of the Regions began its second four-year term on 26 January following the Council decision appointing its members and alternate members for the period up to 25 January 2002 (³). At its inaugural session on 18 and 19 February (⁴), Mr Dammeyer (leader of the SPD group in the Parliament of North-Rhine Westphalia, PSE) was elected President and Mr Chabert (Minister for Economy and Finance in Brussels-Capital Region, PPE) First Vice-President for a two-year term. The two largest political groups (PPE and PSE) agreed to support Mr Chabert's nomination for the post of President, and Mr Dammeyer's nomination for the post of First Vice-President, for the period 2000-02, thereby ensuring that power will alternate between the parties and continuity will be preserved at the head of the Committee. The Committee also reduced the number of its commissions from eight to seven and abolished its subcommissions.

1109. The Committee continued to work closely with the Commission, which sent it a list of forthcoming items on which it was hoped the

---

(¹)   OJ L 257, 19.9.1998; Bull. 9-1998, point 1.9.19.
(²)   Bull. 10-1998, point 1.9.34.
(³)   OJ L 28, 4.2.1998; Bull. 1/2-1998, point 1.10.28.
(⁴)   Bull. 1/2-1998, point 1.10.29.

Committee would make a contribution, and kept it regularly up to date on the action taken on its opinions. Ms Wulf-Mathies (on three occasions), Mr Fischler and Mr Van Miert attended plenary sessions of the Committee to discuss some of the Union's political priorities, such as the reform of the Structural Funds and the common agricultural policy in the context of Agenda 2000 and employment policy. The Committee also extended its dialogue with the other institutions; Mr Prescott, Lord Whitty and Ms Ferrero-Waldner, Presidents-in-Office of the Council, Mr Samland, Chairman of the European Parliament's Committee on Budgets and Mr Jenkins, President of the Economic and Social Committee, all spoke at plenary sessions. The Committee's Commission on Institutional Affairs concluded a cooperation agreement with its counterpart at the European Parliament. It also published a declaration on subsidiarity shortly before the Pörtschach European Council.

1110. At its six plenary sessions in 1998, the Committee adopted four resolutions and 46 opinions, nine in cases where consultation was mandatory under the Treaty, 22 in cases where the Committee was consulted on the initiative of the Commission or the Council, eight own-initiative opinions based on Commission documents and seven other own-initiative opinions. The Committee's opinions covered a number of fields, such as structural and cohesion policy (Structural Funds, Cohesion Fund, pre-accession structural instrument) *(→ point 15)*, the link between regional policy and competition policy, urban policy *(→ point 357)*, employment guidelines for 1999 *(→ point 110)*, the framework agreement on part-time work *(→ point 137)* and financial assistance for innovative and job-creating small businesses *(→ point 262)*, culture (Culture 2000 programme *(→ point 648)*, European City of Culture) *(→ point 650)*, the environment (environment policy in cities and towns, Community action in the field of water policy *(→ point 496)*, environment and employment *(→ point 485)* and accession strategies in the environmental field) *(→ point 807)*, education and training (Socrates and Leonardo da Vinci programmes, 'Towards a Europe of knowledge') *(→ points 324 et seq.).* Other opinions concerned the broad guidelines for economic policy *(→ point 44)* and public procurement *(→ point 197).* On its own initiative, the Committee moreover gave an opinion on the peripheral regions of the Union *(→ point 359).* The Committee also adopted a resolution on nuclear safety and local and regional democracy *(→ point 532)* and a European charter of regional and local authorities for a progressive and sustainable transport policy *(→ point 430).*

1111. As in 1997 the Committee of the Regions held an essay competition on interregional cooperation. In November it hosted the awards ceremony for the European urban planning prize. Forums were held on the fringes of the plenary sessions, at which local authorities exchanged views on: regions and cities and the challenge of the euro; and education and training: the keys to employment.

1112. At 31 December the Committee of the Regions' establishment plan comprised 88 permanent posts for the Committee itself and 108 posts in the organisational structure shared with the Economic and Social Committee.

ECSC Consultative Committee

1113. At the opening meeting of its 1998-99 business year on 22 October, the ECSC Consultative Committee elected Mr Mohr Chairman and Mr Vondran and Mr Diederich Vice-Chairmen. In 1998, the Consultative Committee held four ordinary meetings.

1114. The Committee delivered opinions, after being formally consulted by the Commission, on various agreements and protocols with central and east European countries and the independent States of the former Soviet Union ([1]), on the granting of financial aid for technical steel and coal research projects ([2]) and on the forward programmes for steel ([3]). It also adopted resolutions on the increased integration of coal and steel in the fifth framework programme on research ([2]), the continuation of readaptation measures (Article 56 of the ECSC Treaty) after 2002 and the revision of the Structural Funds ([2]), the proposal to transfer ECU 60 million from the ECSC operating budget to the general budget to increase the funding for the Community initiatives Rechar II and Resider II ([3]), the need to maintain the specific nature of the Safety and Health Commission for the Mining and Other Extractive Industries ([3]) and steel imports into the European Union and the threat to the EU steel market of trade actions in the United States ([4]). It also held an exchange of views with the Commission on the monitoring of State aid to the coal industry ([1]) and the steel industry ([1]), the annual report of the Advisory Committee on Safety, Hygiene and Health Protection at Work ([2]), the expiry of the 1955 agreement on the establishment of through international railway tariffs for the carriage of coal and steel ([3]),

---

([1]) Bull. 4-1998, point 1.8.18; Bull. 6-1998, point 1.10.19.
([2]) Bull. 4-1998, point 1.8.18.
([3]) Bull. 6-1998, point 1.10.19.
([4]) Bull. 10-1998, point 1.9.37.

the draft ECSC operating budget for 1999 ([1]), the market for solid fuels ([1]), the restructuring of the steel industry in the central and east European countries ([1]), protection against imports subsidised by non-ECSC countries ([2]), the communication on adapting and promoting the social dialogue at Community level ([2]), the 1996-97 report on ECSC activities in respect of redeployment aid for workers ([2]), a proposal for a directive on large combustion plants ([3]) and the guidelines for new rules on State aid to the steel industry after expiry of the ECSC Treaty ([3]).

European Monetary Institute

1115. Information on the activities of the European Monetary Institute appears in Section 1 ('Economic and monetary policy') of Chapter IV (→ *point 60).*

European Central Bank

1116. Information on the activities of the European Central Bank appears in Section 1 ('Economic and monetary policy') of Chapter IV (→ *point 61).*

([1])   Bull. 6-1998, point 1.10.19.
([2])   Bull. 10-1998, point 1.9.37.
([3])   Bull. 12-1998.

TABLE 28

Legislative instruments enacted, repealed or expiring in 1998 (¹)

Enacting institution	Number of instruments	Regulations	Directives	Decisions	Recommen-dations
European Parliament and Council (co-decision)	enacted in 1998	0	26	7	0
	repealed or expiring in 1998	0	2	5	0
Council alone	enacted in 1998	202	27	189	10
	repealed or expiring in 1998	146	44	187	1
Commission	enacted in 1998	773	44	537	13
	repealed or expiring in 1998	551	13	260	1

(¹) Data retrieved on 20 January from CELEX, the interinstitutional computerised documentation system on Community law *(→ points 1068 to 1070)*, excluding instruments not published in the Official Journal and instruments listed in light type (routine management instruments valid for a limited period).

Section 2

Administration and management

Staff policy and Staff Regulations

Changes to the Staff Regulations

1117. On 15 May the Commission proposed extending the cover of the Conditions of Employment of Other Servants to include parliamentary assistants as auxiliary staff, subject to certain exceptions which take account of their particular function (Table II).

Equal opportunities and non-discrimination

1118. The year 1998 saw the formal recognition of equal opportunities for men and women with the adoption by the Council on 7 April of Regulation (F.C) No 781/98 (Table II) which confirms the right to equal treatment under the Staff Regulations without reference, direct or indirect, to sex and enshrines the principle of positive discrimination. As part of the third equal opportunities action plan, adopted in 1997 ([1]), the Commission directorates-general and other departments have drawn up action plans containing new practical measures.

1119. The Commission pursued its efforts to increase the number of women in category A grades by fixing recruitment targets. At 31 December 1998, 23.5 % of the recruits at grades A6, A7 and A8 were women, while 18.7 % of all A grades were women, 10.7 % at grade A2 (two women were appointed to director posts in 1998) and 12.4 % in middle management (A3, A4, A5).

1120. In accordance with the commitment given in its White Paper on European social policy ([2]), and the principle of non-discrimination as defined in the new text of Article 6a of the EC Treaty, in September the Commission adopted a code of conduct for the employment of people with disabilities, incorporating the principles of equal rights and effective

---

([1]) 1996 General Report, point 1100.
([2]) COM(94) 333; 1994 General Report, point 554.

participation of people with disabilities (particularly with regard to recruitment, career development and the layout of buildings).

Remuneration

1121.   In accordance with the salary adjustment method adopted by the Council in 1991 (¹), the Council approved a salary increase in December for staff at all the Commission's places of employment (+ 1.9 % for Brussels and Luxembourg), with effect from 1 July 1998 (²). On 12 November the Council also adopted four regulations (³) providing for the changeover to the euro for payment of remunerations, pensions and other financial entitlements of officials and other Community servants, with effect from 1 January 1999 (Table II). On 17 July the Commission proposed the adjustment of daily allowances for missions under Article 13 of Annex VII to the Staff Regulations (⁴).

Career development

1122.   Following the launch in 1997 of a new staff reports system (⁵) and the report of the group that carried out the evaluation of the 1995/97 exercise, a technical group was set up to suggest possible improvements. In terms of training, the Commission endeavoured to pinpoint needs to ensure that every official's professional potential is fully developed, they are integrated in the institution more rapidly and the individual needs of the various directorates-general are suitably addressed; special attention was paid to the development of training in management techniques at all levels, in collaboration with training institutions in the Member States.

Recruitment

1123.   On 31 March the Commission published a notice of an open competition at grade A for university graduates in six specific areas, with or without professional experience, with a view to drawing up a reserve list for the recruitment of 300 administrators and 175 assistant administrators, as dictated by the needs of the service. The procedure for

---

(¹)   Twenty-fifth General Report, point 1198; Twenty-sixth General Report, point 1134.
(²)   Regulation (EC) No 2762/98 (OJ L 346, 22.12.1998).
(³)   Regulations (EC) Nos 2458/98 to 2461/98 (OJ L 307, 17.11.1998).
(⁴)   COM(1998) 455.
(⁵)   1997 General Report, point 1185.

this competition consisted of two stages: pre-selection tests and written and oral tests. The pre-selection tests were held on 14 September, but were declared null and void. New tests will be organised early in 1999.

Integration of officials from the three new Member States

1124. In 1995, the Commission set recruitment targets of 1 050 to 1 350 officials from the three new Member States (excluding the needs of the language service), to be reached within five years (1995-99), broken down as follows: 400 to 500 Austrians, 250 to 350 Finns and 400 to 500 Swedes ([1]). Details of these recruitments at 31 December 1998 are given in Table 29.

TABLE 29

Integration of officials from the new Member States: breakdown by grade

| Grade | Officials recruited at 31 December 1998 ([1]) | | | | | | | |
| | Austrians | | Finns | | Swedes | | Total | |
	Women	Men	Women	Men	Women	Men	Women	Men
A 2	1	4	1	4	4	4	6	12
A 3 and A 4/5 ([2])	1	20	6	19	7	14	14	53
Other A 4/5	4	12	9	13	9	21	22	46
A 8 and A 7/6	30	50	29	36	41	51	100	137
B	31	25	55	43	49	29	135	97
C ([3])	46	10	101	4	92	3	239	17
D	6	3	2	7	3	5	11	15
Total	119	124	203	126	205	127	527	377
LA	13	4	95	29	69	39	177	72
Total	132	128	298	155	274	166	704	449

([1]) To these figures should be added five A 1 posts (two Austrians, two Swedes and one Finn).
([2]) Middle management.
([3]) Including secretaries (30 Finns and 17 Swedes) for the needs of the language service.

Joint sickness insurance scheme

1125. The financial figures of the joint sickness insurance scheme remained satisfactory. An interinstitutional study has been launched and

---

([1]) SEC(95) 230, 'Enlargement: objectives and practical arrangements at administrative level'.

steps have been taken in response to the remarks made by the Court of Auditors (¹).

Pensions

1126. The actuarial study launched in 1997 to check the balance of the Community pension scheme and commissioned from an outside firm was completed in December (²). The Commission is considering the applicability and relevance of the findings and will send a communication to the budgetary authority in 1999.

1127. In response to a ruling by the Court of First Instance (³), the Council adopted a regulation on 27 November amending the Staff Regulations and fixing the weighting applicable to pensions transferred outside the Community at 100 (Table II), so that only serving officials would be covered by the weightings fixed for non-member countries. Agreements have been signed with Greece and Portugal concerning the transfer of national pension rights to the Community scheme under the Staff Regulations; negotiations are continuing on this subject with Spain, Sweden, Finland and Austria.

Buildings and infrastructure

1128. The Charlemagne building is now fully operational, including its conference and catering areas. Work is continuing on the removal of asbestos from the Berlaymont building prior to renovation. The formula of long-term leases with purchase options continued to be used to make acquisitions. Ownership of buildings increased to 33 % in 1998 (10 % in 1996) without significant increases in the annual budget.

Interinstitutional cooperation

1129. The Commission took part in eight jointly organised recruitment competitions, including three in which it acted as appointing authority. This brings the number of interinstitutional competitions in which the Commission has been involved since 1994 to 49. In the field of staff training, an interinstitutional invitation to tender was launched for cer-

---

(¹) 1997 General Report, point 1188.
(²) 1997 General Report, point 1189.
(³) Case T-285/94 [1995] ECR II-3029.

tain language courses, which are themselves organised interinstitutionally. Other training measures carried out by individual institutions are accessible to staff of other institutions, depending on availability of places. Coordination meetings are regularly held between the institutions.

1130. The interinstitutional group on harmonisation of procurement procedures([1]), in which both the European Training Foundation *(→ point 344)* and the Office for Harmonisation in the Internal Market are involved, continued its work; a plan for a single office diary for 1999 has been prepared, with an introduction specific to each institution. An ad hoc interinstitutional group has also been set up to analyse the workings of the catering services and has submitted a report with a view to harmonising the services among the institutions. The Community institutions agreed to end the duty-free alcohol and tobacco package which was previously available to officials.

Data processing

1131. Continuing the modernisation of management and administrative systems, the Commission has developed several applications, such as the new accounting system (Sincom2), various programmes in the field of personnel management (concerning such areas as competitions and pay) and a new computer management system (Syslog), while taking account of the need to adapt computer systems as a result of the introduction of the euro and the new millennium. The Commission organised two symposia on these last two questions and, in response to a request from the Cardiff European Council([2]), presented a report to the Vienna European Council describing the state of preparation for the new millennium of public authority computer systems in the European Union. The Vienna European Council welcomed this report *(→ point 462).*

1132. The Commission has continued its efforts to manage all its documents in electronic form instead of using paper, by encouraging the use of e-mail for inter-departmental consultations, the electronic management of legislative documents and by introducing an electronic document register ('Greffe 2000'). The increased use of the Europa server by the general public *(→ point 1153),* the Europateam server by all the institutions and Europa-plus within the Commission serves to further this objective.

---

[1]   1996 General Report, point 1193.
[2]   Bull. 6-1998, point I.13.

1133. As regards infrastructure, the new technological platform has been set up, providing a stable base for the development of data processing systems, while modernisation of the network made it possible to cope with the rapid growth in the electronic exchange of information. Work has also started on modernising the e-mail service and widening the role of the computer centre as a central register of electronic data.

1134. The Commission has continued to simplify procedures for acquiring data-processing equipment by means of joint invitations to tender and joint management of data-processing products. Attempts at simplification and harmonisation have also led to increasingly close cooperation in relation to data processing with the agencies and other institutions.

Translation

1135. In 1998, the Translation Service translated 1 137 243 pages, (an increase of 4.3 % on the previous year), including 1 939 pages out of and 1 532 into non-Community languages. Freelance translations accounted for 16.7 % of the total.

1136. The Translation Service continued its study of the consequences of enlargement for its resources and operations. It produced a code of good practice aimed at rationalising the use of resources at all levels and continued its work on improving the quality of texts and reducing the volume of documents. Steps were taken to restore the 2/3 to 1/3 staff ratio between Brussels and Luxembourg, and the number of thematic departments was accordingly reduced from seven to six. By promoting the use of its Poetry interface [1], the Translation Service also contributed to improving electronic document transmission *(→ point 1132).*

1137. Various interinstitutional activities were continued in 1998 in connection with translation (the Interinstitutional Committee on Translation [2], joint competitions and invitations to tender for the procurement of new translation tools, preparatory work on the creation of a new terminology database). The Translation Centre for bodies of the European Union had 104 staff (including 67 translators) at the end of 1998 [3]; this year it translated 199 116 pages.

---

[1] Processing of electronic translation requests (1997 General Report, point 1200).
[2] 1995 General Report, point 1115.
[3] 1995 General report, point 1116.

Interpreting

1138. In 1998, the Joint Interpreting and Conference Service (JICS) provided 147 068 interpreter days (6.6 % up on 1997) at 11 648 meetings (6.4 % up) organised by the Commission and the other institutions and bodies of the European Union (apart from the European Parliament and the Court of Justice). Continuing the process of computerisation, the JICS created a freelance interpreters' website on the Internet ([1]) and took part in various projects involving new technologies. Training of interpreters was stepped up in 1998, with the intention of broadening the language cover and increasing the interpreters' subject knowledge, while maintaining the quality of the services provided. The JICS also stepped up its collaboration with the universities which provide training for interpreters in the Member States and third countries (renewing subsidies, providing teaching assistance and through its involvement in the European Masters in conference interpreting in eight European universities). The JICS also set up a Baltic desk to improve its collaboration with the Baltic and Nordic States.

1139. The JICS stepped up its role in organising conferences and other events held on the initiative of the Commission services in 1998, involving more than 25 000 people meeting at over 120 different events (30 in 1997), mostly organised outside traditional working places. Through this work the JICS played its part in bringing Europe closer to the people. The JICS also confirmed its consultancy role in relation to all aspects of the organisation of conferences and seminars by the Commission and the management of meeting rooms.

[1] http://europa.eu.int/scic/freelance.

Section 3

Modernisation of the role, structure and operation of the Commission: Tomorrow's Commission

1140. On 17 April (¹), the Commission combined SEM 2000 *(→ points 1141 to 1144)*, MAP 2000 *(→ points 1145 to 1147)* and the internal screening exercise *(→ point 1148)* in a single, coherent measure, 'Tomorrow's Commission', which seeks to change the Commission's management culture and prepare it for its tasks in 2000 and beyond. In June the Cardiff European Council welcomed the Commission's efforts to improve its efficiency and management in the light of the future development of the European Union (²).

Reforms in the management of resources (SEM 2000 programme)

1141. In 1998 the Commission continued implementing the SEM 2000 programme, which was launched in 1995 to promote sound and efficient management of resources (³).

1142. A report entitled 'SEM 2000: implementation by departments' (⁴), was presented to the Commission (first two stages of the SEM 2000 initiative) on 8 May. It notes that progress was made in implementing the initial SEM 2000 initiatives, but that the process needs to be continued, and contains specific recommendations on the continuing improvement of resource management. It also notes that while operational departments must assess their own performance in the light of certain indicators and fix targets for improvement, the central departments must also continue to monitor performance overall.

1143. In the framework of partnership with the Member States (stage 3 of SEM 2000), the group of personal representatives set up in 1996 (⁵) held two meetings in 1998, on 10 February and 29 September, chaired jointly by Ms Gradin and Mr Liikanen, Commission Members. In May (⁶) and November (⁷) the Commission presented two progress

---

(¹) SEC(1998) 701.
(²) Bull. 6-1998, point I.20.
(³) 1995 General Report, point 976; 1996 General Report, points 970 to 972; 1997 General Report, points 1050 to 1052.
(⁴) SEC(1998) 760.
(⁵) 1996 General Report, point 972.
(⁶) SEC(1998) 774.
(⁷) SEC(1998) 1894.

reports on the implementation of the initial recommendations (1996) of the group underlining the progress achieved, especially in the area of financial control of the Structural Funds, which was welcomed by the Council in its conclusions of 19 May [1] and 23 November [2]. The group's experience was reflected in the Commission's legislative proposals for Agenda 2000 (→ *points 1 et seq.*).

1144. An invitation to tender was published on 18 September with a view to carrying out an independent assessment of the impact of the SEM 2000 initiative [3].

Reforms in the area of staff policy and administration (MAP 2000)

1145. In 1998 the Commission implemented the first phase of the programme to modernise administration and personnel policy, MAP 2000 [4]. The first phase involves the decentralisation of certain powers from the Directorate-General for Personnel and Administration to other directorates-general and departments, devolving responsibilities to them while simplifying and rationalising procedures, with a view to ensuring that decisions are taken at the level that is best informed and closest to the user. The Commission has also started preparations for the second phase (1999), which mainly seeks to make the best use of human resources (delegation of authority, training and staff involvement). In December it took note of a progress report on the implementation of the programme as a whole [5].

1146. A group of officials representing the administration and the trade unions, chaired by Sir David Williamson, presented a report on the modernisation of personnel policy. This report will serve as the basis for a communication on the reform of the European institutions' personnel policy to be submitted to the Council and Parliament in the first half of 1999.

1147. The Commission also continued to apply the 'Green housekeeping action plan' [6], designed to incorporate the strictest standards of environmental protection throughout the Commission before the end of its term of office.

---

[1]   Bull. 5-1998, point 1.5.1.
[2]   Bull. 11-1998, point 1.5.1.
[3]   OJ S 181, 18.9.1998.
[4]   1997 General Report, point 1180.
[5]   SEC(1998) 2033; Bull. 12-1998.
[6]   1997 General Report, point 1194.

Reorganisation of the Commission on the eve of the 21st century

1148.   On 15 October 1997 ([1]) the Commission decided to launch an internal assessment of its own operation. This screening exercise known as 'Designing tomorrow's Commission' was essentially implemented in 1998; the aim is to give members of the Commission a detailed analysis of all the Commission's activities, the resources used to carry them out and the working methods applied so that they can make the necessary adjustments to the organisation of departments in coming years. It covers all directorates-general and departments of the institution, and is based on the methodological principle which entails producing an inventory of departmental tasks and activities and resources used to carry them out, followed by a comparative analysis and proposals for improvements. Thus by producing a snapshot of each department, a list of its resources (human and financial) and a breakdown of the allocation of resources by task, the exercise will produce an inventory of priorities and working methods applied. It will pinpoint best practices and the possibility of extending them, identify any duplication of tasks or any which could be done jointly, and will examine the opportunities for economising on staff and rationalising procedures. It should also help the Commission to identify the activities it should develop in the years ahead in accordance with its political priorities and needs expressed by the departments, and the activities which could be cut back.

([1])   SEC(97) 1856.

Chapter XI

Information and communication

Section 1

Information and communication activities

1149. The Commission's information and communication activities concentrated on the implementation of priority measures launched in 1996 (¹) *in partnership with the European Parliament and the Member States, the intensification of the dialogue with the general public through the development of the Europa server on the Internet and the setting-up of a new service 'Europe direct'. In a resolution on information and communication in the European Union* (²), *the European Parliament advocated closer interinstitutional cooperation in this field.*

1150. As part of the campaign 'The euro, a currency for Europe' (³), now targeting the general public, the Commission distributed various communication tools (publications, brochures and leaflets, messages, speeches, audiovisual products), continued to develop the euro site (http://europa.eu.int/euro/) on the Europa server *(→ point 1153)* by setting up a question and answer base 'Quest', published an information letter 'Infeuro', financed several projects presented by outside actors (NGOs, associations, federations), and concluded 11 partnership agreements or conventions with the Member States with a view to co-financing suitable national information programmes with a strong audiovisual bias. On 6 February the Commission adopted a communication on the information strategy for the euro *(→ point 56)*.

(¹) 1996 General Report, point 641.
(²) OJ C 167, 1.6.1998; Bull. 5-1998, point 1.2.205.
(³) 1997 General Report, point 1208.

1151. The 'Building Europe together' (¹) campaign (http://europa. eu.int/en/comm/dg10/build/) has opened the debate with the public on the current challenges facing European integration. Priority was given to informing women and young people and the use of new communication technologies made the task easier. The Commission has also financed around 125 projects in partnership with the civil society and implemented the partnership agreements with the Member States with a view to co-financing national information programmes.

1152. The 'Citizens first' (²) campaign, which aimed to inform citizens of their specific rights in the European Union, in particular in relation to the internal market, ended on 31 December 1998. On 14 June at the Cardiff European Council, the Commission launched a new and comprehensive information service, 'Europe direct', which is designed to answer the public's general information questions about Community activities and to inform citizens of their rights in the internal market by means of guides, fact sheets or practical advice (http://europa.eu.int/citi zens/).

1153. The Europa (³) server on the Internet (http://europa.eu.int/), which collects information disseminated by all the institutions of the European Union has broadened its content to include the EUR-Lex access to the legislation service *(→ point 1163),* the EURES service for job-seekers *(→ point 124),* the 'Europe direct' service *(→ point 1152),* the new site for the Commission's central library (http://europa.eu.int/ eclas/) (which offers interactive access to the ECLAS database, the Brussels and Luxembourg library services and the Eurolib group sites), and the SCADplus information dissemination service (http://europa.eu.int/ scadplus/). Its success as a special instrument for dialogue between the institutions, citizens and firms has been consolidated by the increase in the number of hits it records (over 50 million a month at the end of the year). The Europa server received the 1998 Grand Prix for the best international site at the Biarritz festival.

1154. The Commission sought to diversify its audiovisual production and to encourage dissemination (special 'European News' slot in the Eurovision exchanges) in order to improve coverage of Community topics on television. The 'Europe by satellite' (⁴) service has been stepped up in particular in the field of educational television and through pro-

---

(¹) 1997 General Report, point 1209.
(²) 1997 General Report, point 1207.
(³) 1995 General Report, point 658.
(⁴) 1996 General Report, point 642.

grammes rebroadcast at night. Following the start of enlargement negotiations, interactive conferences were organised between the delegations
of the applicant countries and Mr Van den Broek, Member of the Commission (→ points 795 et seq.).

1155. The Commission has re-edited its brochures and fact sheets for
the public and modernised the presentation (CD-ROM, Internet); a new
edition of its regional brochures came out. More than 34 000 visitors
were received by the Commission (in particular during the 'open
day')(¹) and by the European Parliament, with closer cooperation
between the two institutions. Direct contact with the public was also
achieved by means of talks by teams of speakers ('Team Europe' and
'Groupeuro') and European Union participation in conferences and ex-
ibitions. The Union pavilion at Expo 98 in Lisbon drew almost one million visitors between May and September with a wealth of lectures,
seminars and events such as Europe Day on 2 September.

1156. In parallel with these measures, the Commission followed European public opinion by means of its main opinion poll instruments,
Eurobarometer(²) and the 'European continuous tracking survey', as
well as qualitative surveys ('Focus groups').

1157. The Commission intensified its policy of decentralising information through the various relays, networks and local information structures, with the representations playing a vital part in coordination. The
extension of the networks, in particular, the Info-Points-Europe and rural
carrefours, and cooperation between the various networks and relays
were given priority in 1998 and a site giving a coherent picture of all
the relays (over 850) has been created on Europa (→ point 1153).
Cooperation with the European Parliament's decentralised offices was
also stepped up, in particular, by setting up 'European Union houses'
representing both institutions. The Commission continued to cooperate
with the European movement and the International Federation of Europe
Houses.

1158. The Commission also developed its information activities vis-à-
vis non-member countries, in particular the applicant countries, the
United States, Japan and Russia through the magazine Contact, co-pro-
duced with the Member States and distributed in over 120 countries, as
well as a series of conferences on the euro.

(¹)   1997 General Report, point 1212.
(²)   Bull. 1/2-1998, point 1.3.292.

1159. Measures targeted at specific audiences, in particular, trade unions and the business world (information measures relating to the revision of the Treaty, economic and monetary union and employment), women (publication of the *Women of Europe newsletter* and *Women of Europe supplement),* young people (information measures to alert new generations to European themes and new challenges facing the Union), and academics *(→ point 1160)* were also developed.

1160. As part of the 1998 Jean Monnet project for university teaching and research into European integration, 25 Jean Monnet European poles to develop synergy between the universities in question, 409 Jean Monnet chairs, 632 core courses and 521 European modules have been established in the European Union while 34 chairs, 122 core courses and 43 European modules have been established in the Czech Republic, Hungary and Poland. Jean Monnet professors came together in transnational and multidisciplinary working parties and study groups to discuss various topical themes. The Commission supported university seminars on these same themes. The Commission also continued to support the ECSA network (European Community Studies Association) which specialises in the study of European integration, ECSA-NET ([1]), an interactive communications network accessible on Europa *(→ point 1153).* The fourth ECSA-World conference on the euro was attended by 300 professors from 55 countries.

([1]) 1997 General Report, point 1216.

Section 2

Press and broadcasting

1161. The Commission has continued to develop a transparent and open approach towards the media. It has pursued its efforts to make the information it produces more accessible both for accredited journalists to Union institutions and for the press in the Member States and non-member countries. Thus, the daily press conferences by the Commission Spokesman are now televised on the 'Europe by satellite' programme. *Midday Express,* a summary of press releases ('IP') which is loaded at midday each day on the interinstitutional server Europa *(→ point 1153)* and the RAPID (¹) database, also accessible on Europa, are growing in popularity with journalists. The Commission has also increased the number of specialised press conferences for accredited journalists, paying special attention to Agenda 2000 and the euro. The interinstitutional pass (²) has proved a success with accredited journalists in Brussels.

(¹)   1997 General Report, point 1218.
(²)   1997 General Report, point 1219.

Section 3

Activities of the Office for Official Publications of the European Communities

1162. In 1998 the Publications Office devoted a substantial proportion of its resources to electronic publishing, not only CD-ROMs but also the Internet, which at the same time led it to reorganise its distribution network and adapt its administrative framework.

1163. The EUR-Lex service (http://europa.eu.int/eur-lex/), which was launched in April 1998 and met with immediate success, offers simple, user-friendly access free of charge to legal information produced by the institutions. EUR-Lex gives access to documents published daily in the 'L' and 'C' Official Journals, treaties currently in force or in the process of ratification, the *Directory of Community legislation in force*, consolidated versions of legislative instruments and recent Court judgments. It supplements the on-line services already on offer on the Europa server (→ *point 1153)* such as the CELEX database (http://europa.eu.int/celex/) and EUDOR, an electronic documentary delivery service (http://www.eudor.com/), aimed at a more specialised public requiring more sophisticated services.

1164. Following the decision by the budgetary authority in the interests of economy to cancel the appropriations for the paper version of the Supplement to the Official Journal (notices of public contracts), since 1 July 1998 it has been replaced by a daily multilingual CD-ROM.

1165. The Publications Office continues its day-to-day work of distribution: about 70 million brochures were sent out by the Office in 1998. It has also taken over the management of stocks and lists of addresses: over 100 administrative bodies use the Office for distributing publications.

Section 4

Historical archives

1166. The Commission released for consultation (¹), under the 30-year rule (²), the archives of the ECSC High Authority, the EEC Commission and the Euratom Commission for 1967, thereby adding 2 500 files to the 30 000 already made available to the public since 1952 in the case of the ECSC, and since 1958 in the case of the EEC and Euratom.

1167. The Commission started organisation of the second Forum on Machine-Readable Data under the title 'The European citizen and electronic information: the memory of the information society' and set up a multidisciplinary network of 'machine-readable data correspondents' in the Member States and regions, as well as upgrading its Internet site (³) for the collection and dissemination of information on electronic archives (⁴). It also continued to publish the six-monthly newsletter entitled *INSAR — Information summary on archives* (⁵), made an enlarged and more powerful version of the Archis-plus database (⁶) available on the Internet (⁷), helped to organise various conferences (⁸) and published a series of file indexes for the first volume of inventories of the ECSC High Authority files (⁹).

(¹)   The historical archive files are kept at the European University Institute in Florence.
(²)   OJ L 43, 15.2.1983; Seventeenth General Report, point 54.
(³)   1997 General Report, point 1224; Internet address: http://www2.echo.lu/dlm/en/home.html.
(⁴)   The DLM Monitoring Committee also published an experts' report on electronic archives, which is available from the Public Record Office, London/Kew.
(⁵)   1996 General Report, point 654; INSAR Nos 5 and 6 are available free of charge from the Office for Official Publications of the European Communities (in English, French and German).
(⁶)   Twenty-sixth General Report, point 1162.
(⁷)   http://europa.eu.int/comm/sg/archives/home-fr.html.
(⁸)   European conference on electronic archives and electronic access (London/Kew, 3 and 4 June); European conference of experts on electronic archives (Vienna, 15 October); transnational colloquium on the education and vocational training of archivists in Europe (Münster, 29 September); conference on archives and the history of international organisations (Rome, 29 to 31 October).
(⁹)   1997 General Report, point 1224.

The year in brief

1998

January

1   Cooperation agreement with the Former Yugoslav Republic of Macedonia enters into force *(→ point 844)*.

16   Commission adopts communication on role of European Union in Middle East peace process *(→ point 849)*.

21   Commission adopts communication on European strategy for global navigation satellite systems *(→ point 432)*.

February

1   Europe Agreements with Estonia, Latvia and Lithuania enter into force *(→ point 808)*.

4   Commission adopts communications on globalisation and the information society *(→ point 478)* and on a European Community biodiversity strategy *(→ point 499)*.

16   Parliament and Council sign directive on consumer protection in price marking *(→ point 643)* and directive on consumer credit *(→ point 646)*.

20   Commission adopts communication on management of Internet names and addresses *(→ point 460)*.

23   Parliament and Council sign decision on Community education action programme Socrates *(→ point 327)*.

25   Commission adopts communication on growth and employment in the stability-oriented framework of economic and monetary union (Annual Economic Report) *(→ point 44)*.

26   Parliament and Council sign directive on application of open network
            provision to voice telephony and on universal service for telecommuni-
            cations *(→ point 469)*.

March

1   Partnership and cooperation agreement with Ukraine *(→ point 858)* and
            Euro-Mediterranean association agreement with Tunisia *(→ point 848)*
            enter into force.

4   Commission adopts proposal for directive on common system of taxa-
            tion applicable to interest and royalty payments made between asso-
            ciated companies of different Member States *(→ point 183)*.

12   Inaugural meeting of the European conference in London *(→ point 796)*.

            Commission adopts communication entitled 'Democratisation, the rule of
            law, respect for human rights and good governance: the challenges of
            the partnership between the European Union and the ACP States'
            (→ point 931).

16   Drachma enters EMS exchange rate mechanism *(→ point 67)*.

            Council adopts regulation on assistance to applicant States as part of
            pre-accession strategy and on establishment of accession partnerships
            (→ point 806).

17 and 18 Commission adopts raft of detailed proposals translating into legislation
            the policy statements presented in Agenda 2000 *(→ points 1 et seq.)*.

25   Commission adopts convergence report and recommends that 11 Mem-
            ber States adopt the euro on 1 January 1999 *(→ point 49)*.

            Commission adopts communication on action plan against racism
            (→ point 27), proposal for directive combating late payment *(→ point
            261)* and communication entitled 'Building a comprehensive partnership
            with China' *(→ point 907)*.

30   Ministerial meeting launches accession process for the 10 central and
            east European applicant countries and Cyprus *(→ point 797)*.

            Council adopts decisions on principles, priorities, intermediate objectives
            and conditions contained in accession partnerships *(→ point 806)*.

31   Ministerial intergovernmental conferences in Brussels open accession
            negotiations (→ point 798).

            Commission adopts communications on application of competition rules
            to access agreements in telecommunications sector (→ point 202), capi-
            tal investment (→ point 263) and development of a Community
            approach as regards transport and carbon dioxide (→ point 435).

April

3 and 4   Second Europe-Asia Summit in London (→ point 897).

7   Commission adopts communication on undeclared work (→ point 117).

            Commission adopts communication entitled 'Fostering entrepreneurship
            in Europe: priorities for the future' (→ point 259).

            Council extends part-time work directive to United Kingdom (→ point
            137).

15   Commission adopts communication on development of public health
            policy in the Community (→ point 620).

16   European Energy Charter enters into force (→ point 399).

23   Commission adopts three recommendations on practical arrangements
            for introduction of the euro (→ point 55).

29   Commission adopts communications on social action programme for the
            period 1998-2002 (→ point 106) and strategy for energy efficiency in
            the Community (→ point 414).

            Commission adopts preliminary draft budget for 1999 (→ point 985).

            Kyoto Protocol on Climate Change signed in New York (→ point 506).

May

1   Framework cooperation agreement between European Community and
            members of Cartagena Agreement enters into force (→ point 920).

3	Council, meeting at level of Heads of State or Government, decides that 11 Member States satisfy conditions for adoption of the single currency on 1 January 1999; following this decision, Council adopts two regulations on technical specifications of euro coins and introduction of the euro, ministers and Central Bank governors of Member States adopting the euro as their single currency; Commission and European Monetary Institute set out conditions for determination of the irrevocable conversion rates for the euro *(→ points 48 et seq.)*.
6	Commission adopts proposal for first framework programme in support of culture *(→ point 648)*.
7	Germany deposits instruments of ratification of Treaty of Amsterdam *(→ point 1023)*.
13	Commission adopts communication on national action plans for employment *(→ point 108)*.
	Commission adopts proposal for directive on common framework for electronic signatures *(→ point 461)*.
15	Sweden deposits instruments of ratification of Treaty of Amsterdam *(→ point 1023)*.
15-17	G8 Summit in Birmingham *(→ points 881 and 882)*.
18	Transatlantic economic partnership launched at EU-US Summit *(→ point 884)*.
19	Council adopts decision on financial assistance for innovative and job-creating small and medium-sized enterprises *(→ point 262)*.
	Parliament and Council sign directive on injunctions for protection of consumers' interests *(→ point 643)*.
20	Commission adopts communication on social dialogue *(→ point 134)*.
	Commission adopts proposal for directive to ensure a minimum of effective taxation of savings income in the form of interest payments within the Community *(→ point 183)*.
21	Expo 98 opens in Lisbon; Commission has a pavilion featuring 'The builders of Europe' *(→ point 1155)*.

25   Council adopts regulation introducing into generalised preference scheme incentive arrangements concerning labour rights and environmental protection *(→ point 754)*.

            Council adopts common position on human rights, democratic principles, the rule of law and good governance in Africa *(→ point 931)*.

            Partnership and cooperation agreement signed with Turkmenistan *(→ point 859)*.

26   Governments of Member States adopting the single currency appoint by common agreement president, vice-president and other members of Executive Board of European Central Bank *(→ point 57)*.

27   Commission adopts communication on integrating the environment into European Union policies *(→ point 484)*.

            Commission adopts proposals for second phase of programmes concerning vocational training, education and youth (2000-04) *(→ point 324)*.

28   Member States sign convention on jurisdiction, recognition and execution of judgments in matrimonial matters *(→ point 974)*.

June

1   Establishment of European Central Bank *(→ point 60)*.

            Agreement amending fourth Lomé Convention following mid-term review, including new financial protocol (eighth EDF) and protocol governing accession of South Africa to Convention enter into force *(→ point 935)*.

8   Council adopts regulation banning use of driftnets *(→ point 601)* and EU code of conduct on arms exports *(→ point 673)*.

8-10   Special session of United Nations General Assembly on drugs in New York *(→ point 760)*.

15   United Kingdom deposits instruments of ratification of Treaty of Amsterdam *(→ point 1023)*.

15 and 16	European Council meeting in Cardiff sets out essential elements of European Union's strategy for further economic reform to promote growth, prosperity, jobs and social inclusion, identifies concrete ways of bringing the Union closer to the people, establishes guidelines and time frame for further negotiations on Agenda 2000 and launches longer-term debate on the Union's further development *(→ point 1081).*
16	Council sets each Member State's contribution towards reducing greenhouse gas emissions *(→ point 506).*
22	Parliament and Council sign directive on common rules for internal market in natural gas *(→ point 406).*
24	Denmark deposits instruments of ratification of Treaty of Amsterdam *(→ point 1023).*
25	United Nations Economic Commission for Europe Convention on Access to Environmental Information, Public Participation in Decision-making and Access to Justice in Environmental Matters signed in Aarhus *(→ point 518).*
29	Council adopts directive on safeguarding supplementary pension rights *(→ point 120),* regulation establishing new rules on aid to shipbuilding *(→ point 226)* and negotiating directives with a view to concluding new partnership agreement with ACP States *(→ point 929).*

July

1	Commission adopts communication on combating fraud and counterfeiting of non-cash means of payment *(→ point 973).*
	Interim agreement with Mexico on trade and trade-related matters *(→ point 923),* partnership and cooperation agreement with Moldova *(→ point 858)* and cooperation agreement with Yemen *(→ point 855)* come into force.
3	Commission adopts communication entitled 'For increased solidarity to confront AIDS in developing countries' *(→ point 762).*
6	Council adopts broad guidelines of economic policies for 1998 *(→ point 42).*
	Parliament and Council sign directive on legal protection of biotechnology inventions *(→ point 195).*

Parliament and Council sign directive banning advertising in respect of tobacco products *(→ point 624)*.

13   Council adopts directive on extension to United Kingdom of directive on the burden of proof *(→ point 137)*.

Council requests opening of negotiations with Togo (first application of Article 366a of Lomé Convention providing for partial or total suspension of cooperation in cases where human rights are violated and democratic principles not observed) *(→ point 955)*.

14   Commission adopts communication entitled 'Towards an area of freedom, security and justice' *(→ point 960)*.

Commission adopts communication entitled 'Audiovisual policy: next steps' *(→ point 660)*.

15   Finland deposits instruments of ratification of Treaty of Amsterdam *(→ point 1023)*.

16   Commission adopts proposal for regulation on common organisation of market in wine *(→ point 552)*.

20   Parliament and Council sign Community action plan 'European voluntary service for young people' *(→ point 337)*.

Council adopts regulations fixing agricultural prices for 1998/99. Following agreement on 'price package', Council also adopts regulations modifying common organisation of markets in olive oil, bananas and tobacco *(→ point 570)* and directive on protection of animals kept for farming purposes *(→ point 565)*.

21   Austria deposits instruments of ratification of Treaty of Amsterdam *(→ point 1023)*.

22   Commission adopts White Paper on Community approach to transport infrastructure charging *(→ point 431)*, communication on measures to counter counterfeiting of the euro *(→ point 1014)*, and proposals for directives amending legislation on use of rail infrastructure *(→ point 439)*.

Commission recommends to Council that negotiations begin on interregional association agreement with Mercosur and on political and economic association agreement with Chile *(→ point 918)*.

24   Italy deposits instruments of ratification of Treaty of Amsterdam
            (→ *point 1023*).

30   Ireland deposits instruments of ratification of Treaty of Amsterdam
            (→ *point 1023*).

August

14   Commission adopts proposal for regulation on substances that deplete
            the ozone layer (→ *point 511*).

September

4   Luxembourg deposits instruments of ratification of Treaty of Amsterdam
            (→ *point 1023*).

10   Malta's new government asks for application for membership of Euro-
            pean Union to be reactivated (→ *point 835*).

11   Convention on Prior Informed Consent Procedure for Certain Hazardous
            Chemicals and Pesticides in International Trade signed (→ *point 489*).

19   Agreement between Euratom and Korean Energy Development Organ-
            isation (KEDO) enters into force (→ *point 911*).

23   Commission adopts communication on Euro-Mediterranean partnership
            and single market (→ *point 155*).

24   Parliament and Council sign decision on review of fifth European Com-
            munity programme of policy and action in relation to the environment
            and sustainable development (→ *point 483*), decision setting up Euro-
            pean Centre for the Surveillance of Communicable Diseases (→ *point
            627*) and directive concerning number portability and carrier preselection
            (→ *point 469*).

            Council adopts recommendations concerning European cooperation in
            quality assurance in higher education (→ *point 333*) and concerning
            protection of minors and human dignity in audiovisual and information
            services (→ *point 658*).

30   Commission adopts communications 'The application of the European
                Union competition rules to vertical restraints' (→ point 201), 'Promoting
                entrepreneurship and competitiveness: the Commission's response to the
                BEST task force report and its recommendations' (→ point 260) and on
                microfinance and poverty reduction (→ point 749).

October

1   Europol Anti-drugs Convention enters into force (→ point 967).

7   Commission adopts report on operation of the own resources system
                (→ point 984) and proposal for directive on waste incineration (→ point
                492).

13   Parliament and Council sign two directives on measures to be adopted
                against air pollution by emissions from motor vehicles and light com-
                mercial vehicles and on quality of petrol and diesel fuels (→ point 502).

                Parliament and Council sign directive on legal protection of designs
                (→ point 195).

14   Commission adopts draft 1998 joint annual report on employment,
                together with employment guidelines for 1999 and report on employ-
                ment rates (→ points 109, 111 and 113).

15   Commission adopts Green Paper on combating counterfeiting and piracy
                in the single market (→ point 194).

21   Commission adopts two proposals for regulations implementing meas-
                ures to deepen customs union between the Community and Turkey and
                implementing measures to promote Turkey's economic and social devel-
                opment (→ point 836).

24 and 25   Informal meeting of Heads of State or Government in Pörtschach
                (→ points 1043 and 1081).

28   Commission adopts its work programme for 1999 (→ point 1087) and
                framework for action on sustainable urban development in the European
                Union (→ point 357).

November

3   Council adopts directive on quality of water for human consumption
                (→ point 496).

4   Commission adopts reports assessing progress of countries applying for accession (→ *point 804*).

9   Council approves action plan for implementing transatlantic economic partnership (→ *point 886*).

10   Ministerial-level meetings of accession conferences with Cyprus, Poland, Estonia, the Czech Republic and Slovenia (→ *point 800*).

11   Commission adopts proposal for directive laying down general framework for the information and consultation of workers (→ *point 139*).

11-13   Fourth conference of the parties to the United Nations Framework Convention on Climate Change in Buenos Aires (→ *point 507*).

13   Commission adopts communication on modernising public employment services (→ *point 115*).

18   Commission adopts communication on forestry strategy for European Union (→ *point 557*), proposal for regulation laying down rules for prevention and control of certain transmissible spongiform encephalopathies (→ *point 563*), proposals for directives on the organisation of working time in the sectors excluded by Directive 93/104/EC on working time (→ *point 138*) and proposal for directive on certain aspects of electronic commerce (→ *point 461*).

20   Parliament and Council sign directive on legal protection for services based on, or consisting of, conditional access (→ *point 179*).

25   Commission adopts communication on employment in the information society (→ *point 116*) and on modernising the organisation of work (→ *point 126*).

December

1   Commission adopts communication entitled 'The common transport policy — Sustainable mobility: perspectives for the future' (→ *point 429*).

2   Commission adopts consumer policy action plan (→ *point 635*) and communication on how year 2000 computer problem is being tackled (→ *point 462*).

9   Commission adopts Green Paper on policy concerning frequencies *(→ point 472)*, communication on measures to combat trafficking in women *(→ point 29)* and communication on policy towards Korea *(→ point 894)*.

10   Overall political agreement on negotiations for the seven draft bilateral sectoral agreements with Switzerland *(→ points 792 et seq.)*.

11 and 12   European Council meeting in Vienna adopts employment guidelines for 1999, decides to strengthen the process of convergence of employment policies with a view to a European employment pact, lays down arrangements for external representation of the euro, approves action plan for establishment of an area of freedom, security and justice and agrees on strategy for Union work in 1999 *(→ point 1082)*.

14   Council adopts first multiannual framework programme (1998-2002) for action on energy *(→ point 397)*.

15   Council adopts two regulations establishing a new agrimonetary system *(→ point 583)*.

16   Commission adopts an action programme to promote the integration of refugees *(→ point 142)*.

17   President of Parliament declares 1999 budget finally adopted *(→ point 990)*.

22   Commission adopts proposal for new programme of assistance for independent States of former Soviet Union *(→ point 865)*.

           Parliament and Council sign decision on fifth European Community framework programme for research, technological development and demonstration *(→ point 285)*.

           Council adopts decision on Community statistical programme for 1998-2002 *(→ point 97)*.

31   The Netherlands deposits instruments of ratification of Treaty of Amsterdam *(→ point 1023)*.

           Council adopts fixed and irrevocable conversion rates between national currencies of the 11 participating Member States and the euro *(→ point 53)*.

Institutions and other bodies

European Parliament

Secretariat
Centre européen
Plateau du Kirchberg
L-2929 Luxembourg
Tel. (352) 43 00-1

Council of the European Union

General Secretariat
Rue de la Loi 175
B-1048 Brussels
Tel. (32-2) 285 61 11

European Commission

Rue de la Loi 200
B-1049 Brussels
Tel. (32-2) 299 11 11

Court of Justice

Boulevard Konrad Adenauer
L-2925 Luxembourg
Tel. (352) 43 03-1

European Court of Auditors

12, rue Alcide De Gasperi
L-1615 Luxembourg
Tel. (352) 43 98-1

Economic and Social Committee

Rue Ravenstein 2
B-1000 Brussels
Tel. (32-2) 546 90 11

Committee of the Regions

Rue Belliard 79
B-1040 Brussels
Tel. (32-2) 282 22 11

European Investment Bank

100, boulevard Konrad Adenauer
L-2950 Luxembourg
Tel. (352) 43 79-1

European Central Bank

Kaiserstraße 29
D-60311 Frankfurt am Main
Tel. (49-69) 134 40

ECSC Consultative Committee

Bâtiment Jean Monnet
Rue Alcide De Gasperi
L-2920 Luxembourg
Tel. (352) 43 01-1

List of abbreviations (¹)

ABACC	Brazilian-Argentine Agency for Accounting and Control of Nuclear Materials
ACP	African, Caribbean and Pacific countries, parties to the Lomé Convention
ADAPT	Community initiative concerning the adaptation of the workforce to industrial change
Altener	specific actions to promote greater penetration for renewable energy sources
ARION	programme of study visits for decision-makers in the educational field
ASEAN	Association of South-East Asian Nations
ASEM	Asia-Europe meeting
BEST	Business Environment Simplification Task Force
BSE	bovine spongiform encephalopathy
CAF	Andean Development Corporation
CAP	common agricultural policy
CBSS	Council of the Baltic Sea States
CCAMLR	Commission for the Conservation of Antarctic Marine Living Resources
Cedefop	European Centre for the Development of Vocational Training
CELEX	interinstitutional system of computerised documentation on Community law
CEN	European Committee for Standardisation
CERN	European Organisation for Nuclear Research
CFSP	common foreign and security policy
CIS	Commonwealth of Independent States
COM	common organisation of the markets

(¹) This list is not exhaustive. It contains the more important acronyms and abbreviations which appear in several places in the Report.

CORDIS	Community Research and Development Information Service
COST	European cooperation on scientific and technical research
CREST	Scientific and Technical Research Committee
CSF	Community support framework (Structural Funds)
EACEM	European Association of Consumer Electronics Manufacturers
EAGGF	European Agricultural Guidance and Guarantee Fund
EBNIC	European Biotechnology Node for Interaction with China
EBRD	European Bank for Reconstruction and Development
ECE	Economic Commission for Europe (UN)
ECHO	European Community Humanitarian Office
ECIP	European Community Investment Partners
ECLAS	European Commission library automation system
ECSA	European Community Studies Association
EDF	European Development Fund
EEA	European Economic Area
EFTA	European Free Trade Association
EGE	European Group on Ethics in Science and New Technologies
Ehlass	European home and leisure accident surveillance system
EIB	European Investment Bank
EIC	Euro Info Centre
EIF	European Investment Fund
EMAS	eco-management and audit system
EMI	European Monetary Institute
EMU	economic and monetary union
Erasmus	European Community action scheme for the mobility of university students
ERDF	European Regional Development Fund
ESA	European Space Agency
ESA	European system of national and regional accounts
ESCB	European System of Central Banks
ESDP	European spatial development perspective

ESF	European Social Fund
ESIS	European survey of the information society in Europe
ETAN	European technology assessment network
ETAP	multiannual programme of studies, analyses, forecasts and other related work in the energy sector
EUDOR	European Union document delivery service
EURES	European employment services
EUR-Lex	interinstitutional service for on-line consultation of European Union law
Eurocontrol	European Organisation for the Safety of Air Navigation
Eurolib	European library project
EUR-OP	Office for Official Publications of the European Communities
Europol	European Police Office
Eurostat	Statistical Office of the European Communities
FAO	Food and Agriculture Organisation (UN)
FIFG	Financial Instrument for Fisheries Guidance
FISIM	financial intermediation services indirectly measured
FRY	Federal Republic of Yugoslavia
FYROM	Former Yugoslav Republic of Macedonia
G7	Group of seven major industrialised nations
G8	Group of eight major industrialised nations
GATS	General Agreement on Trade in Services
GDP	gross domestic product
GFCM	General Fisheries Council for the Mediterranean
GIC	CELEX Interinstitutional Group
GIJC	Council Working Party on Legal Data Processing
GNP	gross national product
GNSS	global navigation satellite system
Greffe 2000	electronic document register project
GSP	generalised system of preferences
IAEA	International Atomic Energy Agency (UN)
IBEX	International Buyers' Exhibition

IBRD	International Bank for Reconstruction and Development (World Bank)
ICAO	International Civil Aviation Organisation
ICCAT	International Commission for the Conservation of Atlantic Tunas
IDA	interchange of data between administrations
IDEA	electronic identification of livestock
IHCP	Institute for Health and Consumer Protection
ILO	International Labour Organisation
IMF	International Monetary Fund
IMS	intelligent manufacturing systems
Info-Sys	information system under the European initiative for agricultural research for development
INSAR	Information summary on archives
INTAS	International Association for the Promotion of Cooperation with Scientists from the New Independent States of the Former Soviet Union
Interreg	Community initiative concerning border areas
IPR	intellectual property rights
ISAC	Information Society Activity Centre
ISDN	integrated services digital network
ISPA	instrument for structural policies for pre-accession
ISPO	Information Society Project Office
ISTC	International Science and Technology Centre
ITER	international thermonuclear experimental reactor
JET	Joint European Torus
JICS	Joint Interpreting and Conference Service
JOP	joint venture programme PHARE-TACIS
JRC	Joint Research Centre
Kaleidoscope	programme to support artistic and cultural activities having a European dimension
KEDO	Korean Peninsula Energy Development Organisation
Konver	Community initiative concerning defence conversion
Leader	Community initiative concerning rural development

LIFE	financial instrument for the environment
Lingua	programme to promote foreign language competence in the European Community
MAP 2000	modernisation of administration and personnel policy
MARIE	mass transit rail initiative for Europe
MARIS	Maritime Information Society
MEDA	financial and technical measures to accompany the reform of economic and social structures in the framework of the Euro-Mediterranean partnership
MEDIA	programme to encourage the development of the audiovisual industry
Mercosur	Southern Cone Common Market
NAFO	North-West Atlantic Fisheries Organisation
NARIC	National Academic Recognition Information Centre
NATO	North Atlantic Treaty Organisation
NCI	New Community Instrument
NEAFC	North-East Atlantic Fisheries Commission
NGO	non-governmental organisation
NOHA	network on humanitarian assistance
NPT	Treaty on the Non-proliferation of Nuclear Weapons
OCTs	overseas countries and territories
OECD	Organisation for Economic Cooperation and Development
OLAF	Anti-Fraud Office
OSCE	Organisation for Security and Cooperation in Europe
OSPAR	Convention for the Protection of the Marine Environment of the North-East Atlantic
PESCA	Community initiative concerning the restructuring of the fisheries sector
PHARE	programme of Community aid for central and east European countries
PLO	Palestine Liberation Organisation
Rechar	Community initiative concerning the economic conversion of coalmining areas
REGIS	Community initiative concerning the most remote regions
Resider	Community programme to assist the conversion of steel areas

RETEX	Community initiative for regions heavily dependent on the textiles and clothing sector
RTD	research and technological development
SAVE	specific actions for vigorous energy efficiency
SEM 2000	sound and efficient management
SFOR	Multinational Stabilisation Force
Sincom2	new accounting system
SLIM	simpler legislation for the internal market
SLORC	State Law and Order Restoration Council (Myanmar)
SMEs	small and medium-sized enterprises
SPD	single programming document (Structural Funds)
SPDC	State Peace and Development Council (Myanmar)
Stabex	system for the stabilisation of export earnings
SURE	multiannual programme of actions concerning the safe transport of radio-active materials and the safety of nuclear installations in countries currently participating in the TACIS programme
Synergy	multiannual programme to promote international cooperation in the energy sector
Syslog	computer management system
Sysmin	system for the stabilisation of export earnings from mining products
TAC	total allowable catch
TACIS	programme for technical assistance to the independent States of the former Soviet Union and Mongolia
TAIEX	Technical Assistance Information Exchange Office
Tempus	trans-European cooperation scheme for higher education
TENs	trans-European networks
TRIPs	trade-related aspects of intellectual property rights
TSEs	transmissible spongiform encephalopathies
UCLAF	Unit for the Coordination of Fraud Prevention
UEMOA	West African Economic and Monetary Union
UN	United Nations
Unctad	United Nations Conference on Trade and Development

Unesco	United Nations Educational, Scientific and Cultural Organisation
UNITA	União Nacional para a Independência Total de Angola
UNRWA	United Nations Relief and Works Agency for Palestine Refugees in the Near East
URBAN	Community initiative for urban areas
USTC	Ukrainian Science and Technology Centre
VAT	value added tax
WCO	World Customs Organisation
WEU	Western European Union
WFP	World Food Programme (UN)
WIPO	World Intellectual Property Organisation (UN)
WTO	World Trade Organisation

Publications cited in this Report

General Report on the Activities of the European Union
   (abbr.: General Report), published annually by the Commission

Works published in conjunction with the General Report:

- *The Agricultural Situation in the European Union*
  (abbr.: Agricultural Report), published annually

- *Report on Competition Policy*
  (abbr.: Competition Report), published annually

- *Report on the application of Community law*
  published annually

Bulletin of the European Union
   (abbr.: Bull.), published monthly by the Commission

Supplement to the Bulletin of the European Union
   (abbr.: Supplement... — Bull.), published at irregular intervals by the Commission

   3/94   An industrial competitiveness policy for the European Union

   3/95   The European Union and human rights in the world

   3/97   First action plan for innovation in Europe

   4/97   Partnership for a new organisation of work — Green Paper

   5/97   Agenda 2000 — For a stronger and wider Union

   1/98   The Commission's programme for 1998
          The state of the Union — Address by President Jacques Santer to the European Parliament
          Resolution of the European Parliament on the programme for 1998

   2/98   Financing the European Union
          Commission report on the operation of the own resources system

   3/98   Fair payment for infrastructure use
          A phased approach to a common transport infrastructure charging framework in the EU
          White Paper

4/98   Composite Paper 1998
Progress made by the candidate countries towards accession

5/98   Regular report from the Commission on Hungary's progress towards accession

6/98   Regular report from the Commission on Poland's progress towards accession

7/98   Regular report from the Commission on Romania's progress towards accession

8/98   Regular report from the Commission on Slovakia's progress towards accession

9/98   Regular report from the Commission on Latvia's progress towards accession

10/98 Regular report from the Commission on Estonia's progress towards accession

11/98 Regular report from the Commission on Lithuania's progress towards accession

12/98 Regular report from the Commission on Bulgaria's progress towards accession

13/98 Regular report from the Commission on the Czech Republic's progress towards accession

14/98 Regular report from the Commission on Slovenia's progress towards accession

15/98 Regular report from the Commission on Cyprus' progress towards accession

16/98 Regular report from the Commission on Turkey's progress towards accession

1/99   The Commission's programme for 1999
Presentation to the European Parliament by Commission President Jacques Santer
Resolution of the European Parliament on the programme for 1999

Official Journal of the European Communities
Legislation series (abbr.: OJ L)
Information and notices series (abbr.: OJ C)
Supplement on public works and supply contracts (abbr.: OJ S)

Reports of Cases before the Court
(abbr.: ECR), published by the Court of Justice in annual series, parts appearing at irregular intervals throughout the year

Annual Report of the European Investment Bank

Annual Report of the European Investment Fund

All the above publications are printed and distributed through the Office for Official Publications of the European Communities, L-2985 Luxembourg

Annexes

Table I — Legislation under the co-decision procedure

	Commission proposal	ESC opinion/ COR opinion°	EP first reading	Amended Commission proposal	Common position Council	EP second reading a, b, c, d, e, f (¹)	

The Community economic and social area

Statistical system

Framework and guidelines

		Commission proposal	ESC opinion/ COR opinion°	EP first reading	Amended Commission proposal	Common position Council	EP second reading	
99	Proposal for a regulation amending Regulation (EEC) No 3330/91: statistics on the trading of goods between Member States	OJ C 203/3.7.97, COM(97) 252, Bull. 5-97/1.7.1	OJ C 19/21.1.98, Bull. 10-97/1.6.2	OJ C 138/4.5.98, Bull. 4-98/1.6.1	OJ C 171/5.6.98, COM(1998) 270, Bull. 4-98/1.6.1	OJ C 285/14.9.98, Bull. 7/8-98/1.7.1	Bull. 12-98 (b)	
99	Proposal for a regulation amending Regulation (EC) No 3330/91: statistics on the trading of goods between Member States (product nomenclature: Intrastat)	OJ C 245/12.8.97, COM(97) 275, Bull. 6-97/1.7.1	OJ C 19/21.1.98, Bull. 10-97/1.6.3	OJ C 138/4.5.98, Bull. 4-98/1.6.2	OJ C 164/29.5.98, COM(1998) 269, Bull. 4-98/1.6.2			

Employment and social policy

Freedom of movement for workers

		Commission proposal	ESC opinion/ COR opinion°	EP first reading	Amended Commission proposal	Common position Council	EP second reading	
123	Proposal for a regulation amending Regulation (EEC) No 1612/68: freedom of movement for workers	OJ C 344/12.11.98, COM(1998) 394, Bull. 7/8-98/1.3.13						
123	Proposal for a directive amending Directive 68/360/EEC: residence in the EC for workers of Members States and their families	OJ C 344/12.11.98, COM(1998) 394, Bull. 7/8-98/1.3.13						
123	Proposal for a decision: freedom of movement and social security for Community workers	OJ C 344/12.11.98, COM(1998) 394, Bull. 7/8-98/1.3.13						
123	Proposal for a regulation amending Regulation 1612/68/EEC on the free movement of workers	OJ C 100/21.4.89, COM(88) 815	OJ C 159/26.6.89	OJ C 68/19.3.90	OJ C 119/15.5.90, COM(90) 108			

° Opinion of the Committee of the Regions.
(¹) a = adoption (Article 189b(2)(a)); b = amendments (Article 189b(2)(c) and (d)); c = declaration of rejection (Article 189b(2)(c)); d = rejection (Article 189b(2)(c)); e = EP failure to take a decision within three months (Article 189b(2)(b)); f = amendments following a declaration of rejection; g = agreement on a common draft; h = failure to agree on a common draft.

TABLE I — CO-DECISION 473

Commission opinion (Art. 189b(2)(d))	Conciliation Committee g, h (^{1}) (Art. 189b(4))	Confirmed common position Council (Art. 189b(6))	EP rejection of confirmed common position	EP adoption of common draft (Art. 189b(5))	Adoption by Council	EP signature Council (Art. 191)	Comments	
							Regulation to be amended: OJ L 316/16.11.91, agreement on Council common position: 27.11.97	99
							Regulation to be amended: OJ L 316/16.11.91	99
								123
								123
								123
							Withdrawal by Commission: 14.10.98	123

	Commission proposal	ESC opinion/ COR opinion°	EP first reading	Amended Commission proposal	Common position Council	EP second reading a, b, c, d, e, f(¹)	
123 Proposal for a directive amending Directive 68/360/EEC	OJ C 100/21.4.89, COM(88) 815	OJ C 159/26.6.89	OJ C 68/19.3.90	OJ C 119/15.5.90, COM(90) 108			

Internal market

Implementation of the action plan for the single market

154 Decision 98/889/EC amending Decision 92/481/EEC: Karolus programme (exchange of national officials)	OJ C 274/10.9.97, COM(97) 393, Bull. 7/8-97/1.3.26	OJ C 73/9.3.98, Bull. 12-97/1.2.35	OJ C 371/8.12.97, Bull. 11-97/1.3.32	OJ C 1/3.1.98, COM(97) 635, Bull. 11-97/1.3.32	OJ C 62/26.2.98, Bull. 1/2-98/1.3.23	OJ C 104/6.4.98, Bull. 3-98/1.2.21 (a)	
154 Decision 1496/98/EC: Robert Schuman project	OJ C 378/13.12.96, COM(96) 580, Bull. 11-96/1.3.23	OJ C 206/7.7.97, Bull. 4-97/1.3.35	OJ C 339/10.11.97, Bull. 10-97/1.2.29	OJ C 368/5.12.97, COM(97) 596, Bull. 11-97/1.3.31	OJ C 135/30.4.98, Bull. 3-98/1.2.22	OJ C 152/18.5.98, Bull. 4-98/1.2.20 (a)	

Free movement of goods

158 Directive 98/34/EC: information on technical standards and regulations	OJ C 78/12.3.97, COM(96) 642, Bull. 12-96/1.3.18	OJ C 133/28.4.97, Bull. 1/2-97/1.2.23	OJ C 304/6.10.97, Bull. 9-97/1.2.8		OJ C 110/8.4.98, Bull. 1/2-98/1.3.25	OJ C 152/18.5.98, Bull. 4-98/1.2.22 (a)	
158 Directive 98/48/EC amending Directive 83/189/EEC: standards, technical regulations, regulatory transparency (the information society)	OJ C 307/16.10.96, COM(96) 392, Bull. 7/8-96/1.3.159	OJ C 158/26.5.97, Bull. 3-97/1.3.105	OJ C 167/2.6.97, Bull. 5-97/1.3.118	OJ C 65/28.2.98, COM(97) 601, Bull. 11-97/1.3.142, COM(1998) 349, Bull. 5-98/1.2.137	OJ C 62/26.2.98, Bull. 1/2-98/1.3.203	OJ C 167/1.6.98, Bull. 5-98/1.2.137(b)	
160 Directive 98/8/EC: biocidal products	OJ C 239/3.9.93, COM(93) 351, Bull. 7/8-93/1.2.5	OJ C 195/18.7.94, Bull. 4-94/1.2.22, OJ C 174/17.6.96, Bull. 3-96/1.3.11	OJ C 141/13.5.96, Bull. 4-96/1.3.9	OJ C 261/6.10.95, COM(95) 387, Bull. 7/8-95/1.3.14, OJ C 241/20.8.96, COM(96) 312, Bull. 6-96/1.3.27	OJ C 69/5.3.97, Bull. 12-96/1.3.25	OJ C 167/2.6.97, Bull. 5-97/1.3.39 (b)	
160 Directive 98/97/EC amending Directive 76/116/EEC: fertilisers containing cadmium (marketing in Austria, Finland and Sweden)	OJ C 108/7.4.98, COM(1998) 44, Bull. 1/2-98/1.3.40	OJ C 214/10.7.98, Bull. 4-98/1.2.29	OJ C 292/21.9.98, Bull. 7/8-98/1.3.23		OJ C 388/14.12.98	Bull. 12-98 (a)	

° Opinion of the Committee of the Regions.
(¹) a = adoption (Article 189b(2)(a)); b = amendments (Article 189b(2)(c) and (d)); c = declaration of rejection (Article 189b(2)(c)); d = rejection (Article 189b(2)(c)); e = EP failure to take a decision within three months (Article 189b(2)(b)); f = amendments following a declaration of rejection; g = agreement on a common draft; h = failure to agree on a common draft.

TABLE I — CO-DECISION   475

Commission opinion (Art. 189b(2)(d))	Conciliation Committee g, h (¹) (Art. 189b(4))	Confirmed common position Council (Art. 189b(6))	EP rejection of confirmed common position	EP adoption of common draft (Art. 189b(5))	Adoption by Council	EP signature Council (Art. 191)	Comments	
							Withdrawal by Commission: 14.10.98	123
				Bull. 3-98/1.2.21		OJ L 126/28.4.98, Bull. 4-98/1.2.19	Amended decision: OJ L 286/1.10.92, agreement on Council common position: Bull. 11-97/1.3.32	154
				Bull. 5-98/1.2.27		OJ L 196/14.7.98, Bull. 6-98/1.3.21	Agreement on Council common position: Bull. 11-97/1.3.31	154
					Bull. 5-98/1.2.32	OJ L 204/21.7.98, Bull. 6-98/1.3.22		158
COM(1998) 349, Bull. 5-98/1.2.137					29.6.98		Amended directive: OJ L 109/26.4.83, agreement on Council common position: Bull. 11-97/1.3.142	158
COM(97) 331, Bull. 6-97/1.3.48	Bull. 12-97/1.2.39 (g)			OJ C 34/2.2.98, Bull. 1/2-98/1.3.35	Bull. 12-97/1.2.39	OJ L 123/24.4.98, Bull. 1/2-98/1.3.35	Agreement on Council common position: Bull. 6-96/1.3.27	160
					Bull. 12-98	OJ L 18/23.1.99, Bull. 12-98	Amended directive: OJ L 24/30.1.76, agreement on Council common position: Bull. 9-98/1.2.22	160

	Commission proposal	ESC opinion/ COR opinion°	EP first reading	Amended Commission proposal	Common position Council	EP second reading a, b, c, d, e, f(^{1})	
160 Proposal for a directive amending Directive 88/379/EEC: classification, packaging and labelling of dangerous preparations	OJ C 283/26.9.96, COM(96) 347, Bull. 7/8-96/1.3.19	OJ C 158/26.5.97, Bull. 3-97/1.3.25	OJ C 222/21.7.97, Bull. 6-97/1.3.47	OJ C 337/7.11.97, COM(97) 462, Bull. 9-97/1.2.13	OJ C 360/23.11.98, Bull. 9-98/1.2.21		
160 Proposal for a directive: 18th amendment of Directive 76/769/EEC (restrictions on the marketing of dangerous substances)	OJ C 59/25.2.98, COM(97) 738, Bull. 1/2-98/1.3.36	OJ C 214/10.7.98, Bull. 4-98/1.2.63	OJ C 80/16.3.98, Bull. 1/2-98/1.3.36		Bull. 12-98		
160 Proposal for a directive amending Directive 92/109/EEC: illicit manufacture of narcotic drugs and psychotropic substances	OJ C 108/7.4.98, COM(1998) 22, Bull. 1/2-98/1.3.37	OJ C 214/10.7.98, Bull. 4-98/1.2.28	OJ C 379/7.12.98, Bull. 11-98/1.2.33				
160 Proposal for a regulation amending Regulation (EEC) No 3677/90: illicit manufacture of narcotic drugs	OJ C 108/7.4.98, COM(1998) 22, Bull. 1/2-98/1.3.37	OJ C 214/10.7.98, Bull. 4-98/1.2.28					
161 Proposal for a regulation: orphan medicinal products	OJ C 276/4.9.98, COM(1998) 450, Bull. 7/8-98/1.3.24						
161 Proposal for a directive: clinical trials of medicinal products for human use	OJ C 306/8.10.97, COM(97) 369, Bull. 9-97/1.2.15	OJ C 95/30.3.98, Bull. 1/2-98/1.3.38	OJ C 379/7.12.98, Bull. 11-98/1.2.29				
162 Directive 98/79/EC: *in vitro* diagnostic medical devices	OJ C 172/7.7.95, COM(95) 130, Bull. 4-95/1.3.10	OJ C 18/22.1.96, Bull. 10-95/1.3.29	OJ C 96/1.4.96, Bull. 3-96/1.3.10	OJ C 87/18.3.97, COM(96) 643, Bull. 12-96/1.3.33	OJ C 178/10.6.98, Bull. 3-98/1.2.32	OJ C 210/6.7.98, Bull. 6-98/1.3.25 (b)	
164 Directive 98/72/EC amending Directive 95/2/EC on additives other than colours and sweeteners	COM(96) 303, Bull. 9-96/1.3.11	OJ C 75/10.3.97, Bull. 12-96/1.3.27	OJ C 339/10.11.97, Bull. 10-97/1.2.33	OJ C 77/12.3.98, COM(97) 656, Bull. 1/2-98/1.3.32	OJ C 161/27.5.98, Bull. 3-98/1.2.28	OJ C 292/21.9.98, Bull. 7/8-98/1.3.22 (a)	
164 Proposal for a directive: foods and food ingredients treated with ionising radiation	OJ C 336/31.12.88, COM(88) 654, Bull. 11-88/2.1.27	OJ C 194/31.7.89, Bull. 5-89/2.1.28	OJ C 291/20.11.89, Bull. 10-89/2.1.25	OJ C 303/2.12.89, COM(89) 576, Bull. 11-89/2.1.16	OJ C 389/22.12.97, Bull. 10-97/1.2.31	OJ C 80/16.3.98, Bull. 1/2-98/1.3.29 (b)	
164 Proposal for a directive: coffee extracts and chicory extracts	OJ C 231/9.8.96, COM(95) 722, Bull. 4-96/1.3.8	OJ C 56/24.2.97, Bull. 10-96/1.3.31	OJ C 339/10.11.97, Bull. 10-97/1.2.34		OJ C 204/30.6.98, Bull. 4-98/1.2.26	OJ C 313/12.10.98, Bull. 9-98/1.2.20 (b)	
164 Proposal for a directive amending Directive 89/398/EEC: foodstuffs intended for particular nutritional uses	OJ C 108/16.4.94, COM(94) 97, Bull. 3-94/1.2.23	OJ C 388/31.12.94, Bull. 7/8-94/1.2.6	OJ C 287/30.10.95, Bull. 10-95/1.3.34	OJ C 35/8.2.96, COM(95) 588, Bull. 11-95/1.3.24	OJ C 297/29.9.97, Bull. 7/8-97/1.3.30	OJ C 14/19.1.98, Bull. 12-97/1.2.38 (b)	

° Opinion of the Committee of the Regions.
(^{1}) a = adoption (Article 189b(2)(a)); b = amendments (Article 189b(2)(c) and (d)); c = declaration of rejection (Article 189b(2)(c)); d = rejection (Article 189b(2)(c)); e = EP failure to take a decision within three months (Article 189b(2)(b)); f = amendments following a declaration of rejection; g = agreement on a common draft; h = failure to agree on a common draft.

TABLE I — CO-DECISION   477

Commission opinion (Art. 189b(2)(d))	Conciliation Committee g, h (¹) (Art. 189b(4))	Confirmed common position Council (Art. 189b(6))	EP rejection of confirmed common position	EP adoption of common draft (Art. 189b(5))	Adoption by Council	EP signature Council (Art. 191)	Comments	
							Directive to be amended: OJ L 187/16.7.88, agreement on Council common position: Bull. 5-98/1.2.37	160
							Directive to be amended: OJ L 262/27.9.76	160
							Directive to be amended: OJ L 370/19.12.92	160
							Regulation to be amended: OJ L 357/20.12.90	160
								161
								161
COM(1998) 548, Bull. 10-98/1.2.22				Bull. 10-98/1.2.22		OJ L 331/7.12.98,	Agreement on Council common position: Bull. 11-97/1.3.39	162
				Bull. 9-98/1.2.19		OJ L 295/4.11.98, Bull. 10-98/1.2.18	Amended directive: OJ L 61/18.3.95, agreement on Council common position: Bull. 11-97/1.3.35	164
COM(1998) 188, Bull. 3-98/1.2.30	Bull. 12-98 (g)						Agreement on Council common position: Bull. 5-97/1.3.41	164
COM(1998) 599, Bull. 11-98/1.2.28	Bull. 12-98 (g)						Agreement on Council common position: Bull. 11-97/1.3.36	164
COM(1998) 69, Bull. 1/2-98/1.3.31							Directive to be amended: OJ L186/30.6.89, agreement on Council common position: Bull. 3-97/1.3.22	164

	Commission proposal	ESC opinion/ COR opinion°	EP first reading	Amended Commission proposal	Common position Council	EP second reading a, b, c, d, e, f (^{1})	
164 Proposal for a directive: cocoa and chocolate	OJ C 231/9.8.96, COM(95) 722, Bull. 4-96/1.3.8	OJ C 56/24.2.97, Bull. 10-96/1.3.31	OJ C 339/10.11.97, Bull. 10-97/1.2.34	OJ C 118/17.4.98, COM(97) 682, Bull. 1/2-98/1.3.33			
165 Directive 98/91/EC amending Directive 70/156/EEC on motor vehicles and their trailers transporting dangerous goods	OJ C 29/30.1.97, COM(96) 555, Bull. 12-96/1.3.22	OJ C 296/29.9.97, Bull. 7/8-97/1.3.29	OJ C 80/16.3.98, Bull. 1/2-98/1.3.26	OJ C 207/3.7.98, COM(1998) 273, Bull. 6-98/1.3.23	OJ C 262/19.8.98, Bull. 6-98/1.3.23	OJ C 341/9.11.98, Bull. 10-98/1.2.17 (a)	
165 Proposal for a directive amending Directive 74/60/EEC: interior fittings of motor vehicles	OJ C 149/15.5.98, COM(1998) 159, Bull. 4-98/1.2.23	OJ C 407/28.12.98, Bull. 9-98/1.2.16					
165 Proposal for a directive amending Directive 70/221/EEC: liquid fuel tanks and rear underrun protection of vehicles	OJ C 164/29.5.98, COM(1998) 97, Bull. 4-98/1.2.24	OJ C 407/28.12.98, Bull. 9-98/1.2.17					
165 Proposal for a directive amending Directive 92/61/EEC: speedometers for motor vehicles	OJ C 212/8.7.98, COM(1998) 285, Bull. 5-98/1.2.34	Bull. 12-98					
165 Proposal for a directive amending Directive 78/548/EEC: heating systems for the passenger compartment of motor vehicles	OJ C 326/24.10.98, COM(1998) 526, Bull. 9-98/1.2.18						
165 Proposal for a directive amending Directive 92/23/EEC on tyres for motor vehicles and trailers	OJ C 30/28.1.98, COM(97) 680, Bull. 12-97/1.2.36	OJ C 235/27.7.98, Bull. 5-98/1.2.33	OJ C 80/16.3.98, Bull. 1/2-98/1.3.27				
165 Proposal for a directive amending Directive 70/156/EEC: vehicles for the carriage of passengers	OJ C 17/20.1.98, COM(97) 276, Bull. 6-97/1.3.45	OJ C 129/27.4.98, Bull. 1/2-98/1.3.28	OJ C 379/7.12.98, Bull. 11-98/1.2.27				
166 Directive 98/37/EC: approximation of the laws relating to machinery	COM(96) 667, Bull. 12-96/1.3.19	OJ C 133/28.4.97, Bull. 1/2-97/1.2.24	OJ C 304/6.10.97, Bull. 9-97/1.2.10		OJ C 161/27.5.98, Bull. 3-98/1.2.31	OJ C 152/18.5.98, Bull. 4-98/1.2.25 (a)	

Free movement of persons

	Commission proposal	ESC opinion/ COR opinion°	EP first reading	Amended Commission proposal	Common position Council	EP second reading a, b, c, d, e, f (^{1})	
170 Directive 98/5/EC: exercising the profession of lawyer	OJ C 128/24.5.95, COM(94) 572, Bull. 12-94/1.2.29	OJ C 256/2.10.95, Bull. 7/8-95/1.3.19	OJ C 198/8.7.96, Bull. 6-96/1.3.36	OJ C 355/25.11.96, COM(96) 446, Bull. 9-96/1.3.14	OJ C 297/29.9.97, Bull. 7/8-97/1.3.36	OJ C 371/8.12.97, Bull. 11-97/1.3.40 (a)	
170 Proposal for a directive: recognition of qualifications	OJ C 115/19.4.96, COM(96) 22, Bull. 1/2-96/1.3.27	OJ C 295/7.10.96, Bull. 7/8-96/1.3.21	OJ C 85/17.3.97, Bull. 1/2-97/1.2.36	OJ C 264/30.8.97, COM(97) 363, Bull. 7/8-97/1.3.37	OJ C 262/19.8.98, Bull. 6-98/1.3.26 ·	OJ C 328/26.10.98, Bull. 10-98/1.2.26 (b)	

° Opinion of the Committee of the Regions.
(^{1}) a = adoption (Article 189b(2)(a)); b = amendments (Article 189b(2)(c) and (d)); c = declaration of rejection (Article 189b(2)(c)); d = rejection (Article 189b(2)(c)); e = EP failure to take a decision within three months (Article 189b(2)(b)); f = amendments following a declaration of rejection; g = agreement on a common draft; h = failure to agree on a common draft.

TABLE I — CO-DECISION 479

Commission opinion (Art. 189b(2)(d))	Conciliation Committee g, h (¹) (Art. 189b(4))	Confirmed common position Council (Art. 189b(6))	EP rejection of confirmed common position	EP adoption of common draft (Art. 189b(5))	Adoption by Council	EP signature Council (Art. 191)	Comments	
								164
					Bull. 12-98		Amended directive: OJ L 42/23.2.70	165
							Directive to be amended: OJ L 38/11.2.74	165
							Directive to be amended: OJ L 76/6.4.70	165
							Directive to be amended: OJ L 225/10.8.92	165
							Directive to be amended: OJ L 168/26.6.78	165
							Directive to be amended: OJ L 129/14.5.92	165
							Directive to be amended: OJ L 42/23.2.70	165
					Bull. 5-98/1.2.35	OJ L 207/23.7.98, Bull. 6-98/1.3.24		166
					Bull. 12-97/1.2.40	OJ L 77/14.3.98, Bull. 1/2-98/1.3.41	Agreement on Council common position: Bull. 5-97/1.3.43	170
COM(1998) 640, Bull. 11-98/1.2.34							Agreement on Council common position: Bull. 5-98/1.2.39	170

	Commission proposal	ESC opinion/ COR opinion°	EP first reading	Amended Commission proposal	Common position Council	EP second reading a, b, c, d, e, f (^{1})	
170 Proposal for a directive amending Directives 89/48/EEC and 92/51/EEC: recognition of qualifications	OJ C 28/26.1.98, COM(97) 638, Bull. 12-97/1.2.41	OJ C 235/27.7.98, Bull. 5-98/1.2.40	OJ C 226/20.7.98, Bull. 7/8-98/1.3.25				

Freedom to provide services

	Commission proposal	ESC opinion/ COR opinion°	EP first reading	Amended Commission proposal	Common position Council	EP second reading a, b, c, d, e, f (^{1})	
173 Proposal for a directive: electronic money institutions	OJ C 317/15.10.98, COM(1998) 461, Bull. 9-98/1.2.23, Bull. 7/8-98/1.3.26						
173 Proposal for a directive amending Directive 77/780/EEC: taking-up and pursuit of the business of credit institutions	OJ C 317/15.10.98, COM(1998) 461, Bull. 9-98/1.2.23						
174 Proposal for a directive: distance marketing of consumer financial services	OJ C 385/11.12.98, COM(1998) 468, Bull. 10-98/1.2.28						
174 Proposal for a directive amending Directive 85/611/EEC: undertakings for collective investment in transferable securities	OJ C 280/9.9.98, COM(1998) 449, Bull. 7/8-98/1.3.27						
174 Proposal for a directive amending Directive 85/611/EEC: management companies and simplified prospectuses	OJ C 272/1.9.98, COM(1998) 451, Bull. 7/8-98/1.3.27						
174 Proposal for a directive amending Directive 93/6/EEC on investment in securities	OJ C 253/29.9.95, COM(95) 360, Bull. 7/8-95/1.3.21		OJ C 152/27.5.96, Bull. 5-96/1.3.26	OJ C 221/30.7.96, COM(96) 292, Bull. 6-96/1.3.39	OJ C 69/5.3.97, Bull. 12-96/1.3.38	OJ C 132/28.4.97, Bull. 4-97/1.3.46 (b)	
175 Directive 98/26/EC: payment systems and transactions in securities	OJ C 207/18.7.96, COM(96) 193, Bull. 5-96/1.3.27	OJ C 56/24.2.97, Bull. 10-96/1.3.35	OJ C 132/28.4.97, Bull. 4-97/1.3.48	OJ C 259/26.8.97, COM(97) 345, Bull. 7/8-97/1.3.41	OJ C 375/10.12.97, Bull. 10-97/1.2.39	OJ C 56/23.2.98, Bull. 1/2-98/1.3.45 (b)	
175 Directive 98/31/EC amending Directive 93/6/EEC on the capital adequacy of investment firms and credit institutions	OJ C 240/6.8.97, COM(97) 71, Bull. 4-97/1.3.45	OJ C 19/21.1.98, Bull. 10-97/1.2.40	OJ C 14/19.1.98, Bull. 12-97/1.2.43	OJ C 118/17.4.98, COM(1998) 90, Bull. 1/2-98/1.3.44	OJ C 135/30.4.98, Bull. 3-98/1.2.36	OJ C 152/18.5.98, Bull. 4-98/1.2.33 (a)	
175 Directive 98/32/EC amending Directive 89/647/EEC on the solvency ratio for credit institutions	OJ C 114/19.4.96, COM(95) 709, Bull. 1/2-96/1.3.31	OJ C 30/30.1.97, Bull. 9-96/1.3.16	OJ C 320/28.10.96, Bull. 9-96/1.3.16		OJ C 135/30.4.98, Bull. 3-98/1.2.35	OJ C 152/18.5.98, Bull. 4-98/1.2.32 (a)	

° Opinion of the Committee of the Regions.
(^{1}) a = adoption (Article 189b(2)(a)); b = amendments (Article 189b(2)(c) and (d)); c = declaration of rejection (Article 189b(2)(c)); d = rejection (Article 189b(2)(c)); e = EP failure to take a decision within three months (Article 189b(2)(b)); f = amendments following a declaration of rejection; g = agreement on a common draft; h = failure to agree on a common draft.

TABLE I — CO-DECISION   481

Commission opinion (Art. 189b(2)(d))	Conciliation Committee g, h (¹) (Art. 189b(4))	Confirmed common position Council (Art. 189b(6))	EP rejection of confirmed common position	EP adoption of common draft (Art. 189b(5))	Adoption by Council	EP signature Council (Art. 191)	Comments	
							Directives to be amended: 89/48/EEC (OJ L 19/24.1.90) and 92/51/EEC (OJ L 209/24.7.92)	170
								173
								173
								174
							Directive to be amended: OJ L 375/31.12.85	174
							Directive to be amended: OJ L 375/31.12.85	174
COM(97) 355, Bull. 7/8-97/1.3.40	31.3.98						Directive to be amended: OJ L 141/11.6.93	174
COM(1998) 151, Bull. 3-98/1.2.37					Bull. 4-98/1.2.30	OJ L 166/11.6.98, Bull. 5-98/1.2.41	Agreement on Council common position: 9.6.97	175
					Bull. 5-98/1.2.44	OJ L 204/21.7.98, Bull. 6-98/1.3.29	Amended directive: OJ L 141/11.6.93	175
					Bull. 5-98/1.2.43	OJ L 204/21.7.98, Bull. 6-98/1.3.28	Amended directive: OJ L 386/30.12.89, agreement on Council common position: Bull. 11-97/1.3.42	175

	Commission proposal	ESC opinion/ COR opinion°	EP first reading	Amended Commission proposal	Common position Council	EP second reading a, b, c, d, e, f(^{1})	
175 Directive 98/33/EC amending Directives 77/780/EEC, 89/647/EEC and 93/6/EEC on the prudential supervision of banks	OJ C 208/19.7.96, COM(96) 183, Bull. 4-96/1.3.10	OJ C 30/30.1.97, Bull. 9-96/1.3.17	OJ C 132/28.4.97, Bull. 4-97/1.3.47	OJ C 259/26.8.97, COM(97) 285, Bull. 6-97/1.3.54	OJ C 135/30.4.98, Bull. 3-98/1.2.34	OJ C 152/18.5.98, Bull. 4-98/1.2.31 (a)	
175 Proposal for a directive: taking-up and pursuit of the business of credit institutions	COM(97) 706, Bull. 12-97/1.2.42	OJ C 157/25.5.98, Bull. 3-98/1.2.38					
177 Directive 98/78/EC: monitoring of insurance companies which are part of a group	OJ C 341/19.12.95, COM(95) 406, Bull. 10-95/1.3.44	OJ C 174/17.6.96, Bull. 3-96/1.3.17	OJ C 339/10.11.97, Bull. 10-97/1.2.41	OJ C 108/7.4.98, COM(1998) 38, Bull. 1/2-98/1.3.46	OJ C 204/30.6.98, Bull. 3-98/1.2.40	OJ C 313/12.10.98, Bull. 9-98/1.2.25 (a)	
177 Proposal for a directive amending Directives 73/239/EEC and 92/49/EEC: civil responsibility and compensation of victims	OJ C 343/13.11.97, COM(97) 510, Bull. 10-97/1.2.42	OJ C 157/25.5.98, Bull. 3-98/1.2.41	OJ C 292/21.9.98, Bull. 7/8-98/1.3.29				
179 Directive 98/84/EC: legal protection for services with conditional access	OJ C 314/16.10.97, COM(97) 356, Bull. 7/8-97/1.3.166	OJ C 129/27.4.98, Bull. 1/2-98/1.3.209	OJ C 152/18.5.98, Bull. 4-98/1.2.104	OJ C 203/30.6.98, COM(1998) 332, Bull. 5-98/1.2.144	OJ C 262/19.8.98, Bull. 6-98/1.3.121	OJ C 328/26.10.98, Bull. 10-98/1.2.115 (b)	

Taxation

	Commission proposal	ESC opinion/ COR opinion°	EP first reading	Amended Commission proposal	Common position Council	EP second reading a, b, c, d, e, f(^{1})	
182 Proposal for a directive amending Directive 76/308/EEC: mutual assistance for the recovery of claims	OJ C 269/28.8.98, COM(1998) 364, Bull. 6-98/1.3.32						
186 Decision 98/888/EC: Fiscalis programme	OJ C 177/11.6.97, COM(97) 175, Bull. 4-97/1.3.50	OJ C 19/21.1.98, Bull. 10-97/1.2.48	OJ C 371/8.12.97, Bull. 11-97/1.3.51	OJ C 1/3.1.98, COM(97) 621, Bull. 11-97/1.3.51	OJ C 62/26.2.98, Bull. 1/2-98/1.3.51	OJ C 80/16.3.98, Bull. 1/2-98/1.3.51 (a)	

Intellectual and industrial property

	Commission proposal	ESC opinion/ COR opinion°	EP first reading	Amended Commission proposal	Common position Council	EP second reading a, b, c, d, e, f(^{1})	
195 Directive 98/44/EC: legal protection of biotechnological inventions	OJ C 296/8.10.96, COM(95) 661, Bull. 12-95/1.3.29	OJ C 295/7.10.96, Bull. 7/8-96/1.3.28	OJ C 286/22.9.97, Bull. 7/8-97/1.3.47	OJ C 311/11.10.97, COM(97) 446, Bull. 7/8-97/1.3.47	OJ C 110/8.4.98, Bull. 1/2-98/1.3.53	OJ C 167/1.6.98, Bull. 5-98/1.2.52 (a)	

° Opinion of the Committee of the Regions.
(^{1}) a = adoption (Article 189b(2)(a)); b = amendments (Article 189b(2)(c) and (d)); c = declaration of rejection (Article 189b(2)(c)); d = rejection (Article 189b(2)(c)); e = EP failure to take a decision within three months (Article 189b(2)(b)); f = amendments following a declaration of rejection; g = agreement on a common draft; h = failure to agree on a common draft.

TABLE I — CO-DECISION 483

Commission opinion (Art. 189b(2)(d))	Conciliation Committee g, h (¹) (Art. 189b(4))	Confirmed common position Council (Art. 189b(6))	EP rejection of confirmed common position	EP adoption of common draft (Art. 189b(5))	Adoption by Council	EP signature Council (Art. 191)	Comments	
					Bull. 5-98/1.2.42	OJ L 204/21.7.98, OJ L 270/7.10.98, Bull. 6-98/1.3.27	Amended Directives: 77/780/EEC (OJ L 322/17.2.77), 89/647/EEC (OJ L 386/30.12.89), 93/6/EEC (OJ L 141/11.6.93), agreement on Council common position: Bull. 11-97/1.3.41	175
								175
					Bull. 10-98/1.2.29	OJ L 330/5.12.98, Bull. 10-98/1.2.29	Agreement on Council common position: Bull. 11-97/1.3.43	177
							Directives to be amended: OJ L 228/16.8.73, OJ L 228/11.8.92, agreement on Council common position. Bull. 12-98	177
COM(1998) 627					Bull. 11-98/1.2.118	OJ L 320/28.11.98, Bull. 11-98/1.2.118	Agreement on Council common position: Bull. 5-98/1.2.144	179
							Directive to be amended: OJ L 73/19.3.76	182
					Bull. 3-98/1.2.44	OJ L 126/28.4.98, Bull. 3-98/1.2.44	Agreement on Council common position: Bull. 12-97/1.2.50	186
					Bull. 6-98/1.3.35	OJ L 213/30.7.98, Bull. 7/8-98/1.3.36	Agreement on Council common position: Bull. 11-97/1.3.47	195

	Commission proposal	ESC opinion/ COR opinion°	EP first reading	Amended Commission proposal	Common position Council	EP second reading a, b, c, d, e, f(¹)	
195 Directive 98/71/EC: legal protection of designs	OJ C 345/23.12.93, COM(93) 344, Bull. 12-93/1.2.39	OJ C 388/31.12.94, Bull. 7/8-94/1.2.18, OJ C 110/2.5.95, Bull. 1/2-95/1.3.19, Bull. 1/2-95/1.3.19°	OJ C 287/30.10.95, Bull. 10-95/1.3.50	COM(96) 66, Bull. 1/2-96/1.3.36	OJ C 237/4.8.97, Bull. 6-97/1.3.66	OJ C 339/10.11.97, Bull. 10-97/1.2.45 (b)	
195 Proposal for a directive: protection of inventions by means of a utility model	OJ C 36/3.2.98, COM(97) 691, Bull. 12-97/1.2.48	OJ C 235/27.7.98, Bull. 5-98/1.2.51					
195 Proposal for a directive: harmonisation of certain aspects of copyright and related rights in the information society	OJ C 108/7.4.98, COM(97) 628, Bull. 12-97/1.2.47	OJ C 407/28.12.98, Bull. 9-98/1.2.34					
195 Proposal for a directive: resale right (harmonisation of national legislations)	OJ C 178/21.6.96, COM(96) 97, Bull. 3-96/1.3.19	OJ C 75/10.3.97, Bull. 12-96/1.3.45	OJ C 132/28.4.97, Bull. 4-97/1.3.49	OJ C 125/23.4.98, COM(1998) 78, Bull. 3-98/1.2.43			

Public procurement

	Commission proposal	ESC opinion/ COR opinion°	EP first reading	Amended Commission proposal	Common position Council	EP second reading a, b, c, d, e, f(¹)	
198 Directive 98/4/EC amending Directive 93/38/EEC: public procurement	OJ C 138/3.6.95, COM(95) 107, Bull. 3-95/1.3.19	OJ C 256/2.10.95, Bull. 7/8-95/1.3.28	OJ C 347/18.11.96, Bull. 10-96/1.3.38	OJ C 28/29.1.97, COM(96) 598, Bull. 11-96/1.3.40	OJ C 111/9.4.97, Bull. 12-96/1.3.43	OJ C 167/2.6.97, Bull. 5-97/1.3.47 (b)	

Enterprise policy, distributive trades, tourism and cooperatives

Policy to assist SMEs and the craft sector

	Commission proposal	ESC opinion/ COR opinion°	EP first reading	Amended Commission proposal	Common position Council	EP second reading a, b, c, d, e, f(¹)	
261 Proposal for a directive: combating late payment	OJ C 168/3.6.98, COM(1998) 126, Bull. 3-98/1.2.78	OJ C 407/28.12.98, Bull. 9-98/1.2.60	OJ C 313/12.10.98	OJ C 374/3.12.98, COM(1998) 615, Bull. 10-98/1.2.64			

° Opinion of the Committee of the Regions.
(¹) a = adoption (Article 189b(2)(a)); b = amendments (Article 189b(2)(c) and (d)); c = declaration of rejection (Article 189b(2)(c)); d = rejection (Article 189b(2)(c)); e = EP failure to take a decision within three months (Article 189b(2)(b)); f = amendments following a declaration of rejection; g = agreement on a common draft; h = failure to agree on a common draft.

TABLE I — CO-DECISION 485

Commission opinion (Art. 189b(2)(d))	Conciliation Committee g, h ([1]) (Art. 189b(4))	Confirmed common position Council (Art. 189b(6))	EP rejection of confirmed common position	EP adoption of common draft (Art. 189b(5))	Adoption by Council	EP signature Council (Art. 191)	Comments	
COM(97) 622, Bull. 11-97/1.3.46	Bull. 6-98/1.3.36 (g)			OJ C 313/12.10.98, Bull. 9-98/1.2.33	Bull. 9-98/1.2.33	OJ L 289/28.10.98, Bull. 10-98/1.2.34	Agreement on Council common position: Bull. 3-97/1.3.30	195
								195
								195
								195
COM(97) 290, Bull. 6-97/1.3.63	Bull. 11-97/1.3.45 (g)			OJ C 14/19.1.98, Bull. 12-97/1.2.46	Bull. 12-97/1.2.46	OJ L 101/1.4.98, Bull. 1/2-98/1.3.50	Amended directive: OJ L 199/9.8.93, agreement on Council common position: Bull. 11-96/1.3.40	198
								261

	Commission proposal	ESC opinion/ COR opinion°	EP first reading	Amended Commission proposal	Common position Council	EP second reading a, b, c, d, e, f(^{1})	

Research and technology

Community RTD policy

285	Decision: fifth EC framework programme for research (1998-2002)	OJ C 173/7.6.97, COM(97) 142, Bull. 4-97/1.3.114	OJ C 355/21.11.97, Bull. 10-97/1.2.98, OJ C 73/9.3.98, Bull. 12-97/1.2.113, OJ C 379/15.12.97, Bull. 9-97/1.2.52°	OJ C 14/19.1.98, Bull. 12-97/1.2.113	OJ C 291/25.9.97, COM(97) 439, Bull. 7/8-97/1.3.123, OJ C 106/6.4.98, COM(1998) 8, Bull. 1/2-98/1.3.147	OJ C 178/10.6.98, Bull. 3-98/1.2.86	OJ C 210/6.7.98, Bull. 6-98/1.3.71 (b)

Education, vocational training, youth

General aspects

324	Proposal for a decision: second phase of the Socrates programme	COM(1998) 329, Bull. 5-98/1.2.97	OJ C 410/30.12.98, Bull. 10-98/1.2.76, Bull. 11-98/1.2.79°	OJ C 359/23.11.98, Bull. 11-98/1.2.80	COM(1998) 719, Bull. 12-98	Bull. 12-98	
324	Proposal for a decision: second phase of the Leonardo da Vinci action programme	OJ C 309/9.10.98, COM(1998) 330, Bull. 5-98/1.2.97	OJ C 410/30.12.98, Bull. 10-98/1.2.77, Bull. 11-98/1.2.80°	OJ C 359/23.11.98, Bull. 11-98/1.2.79	OJ C 14/19.1.99, COM(1998) 697, Bull. 12-98	Bull. 12-98	
324	Proposal for a decision: action programme for youth	OJ C 311/10.10.98, COM(1998) 331, Bull. 5-98/1.2.97	OJ C 410/30.12.98, Bull. 10-98/1.2.78, Bull. 11-98/1.2.81°	OJ C 359/23.11.98, Bull. 11-98/1.2.81	COM(1998) 695, Bull. 11-98/1.2.81		
327	Decision No 576/98/EC amending Decision 819/95/EC: Socrates	OJ C 113/11.4.97, COM(97) 99, Bull. 3-97/1.3.67	OJ C 287/22.9.97, Bull. 5-97/1.3.84, OJ C 379/15.12.97, Bull. 9-97/1.2.57°	OJ C 200/30.6.97, Bull. 6-97/1.3.135	OJ C 262/28.8.97, COM(97) 338, Bull. 7/8-97/1.3.135	OJ C 315/16.10.97, Bull. 9-97/1.2.57	OJ C 339/10.11.97, Bull. 10-97/1.2.101 (b)

Youth

337	Decision No 1686/98/EC: action programme 'European voluntary service for young people'	OJ C 302/3.10.97, COM(96) 610, Bull. 12-96/1.3.108	OJ C 158/26.5.97, Bull. 3-97/1.3.72, OJ C 244/11.8.97, Bull. 6-97/1.3.137°	OJ C 200/30.6.97, Bull. 6-97/1.3.137	OJ C 320/21.10.97, COM(97) 347, Bull. 7/8-97/1.3.129	OJ C 43/9.2.98, Bull. 12-97/1.2.119	OJ C 104/6.4.98, Bull. 3-98/1.2.91 (b)

° Opinion of the Committee of the Regions.
(^{1}) a = adoption (Article 189b(2)(a)); b = amendments (Article 189b(2)(c) and (d)); c = declaration of rejection (Article 189b(2)(c)); d = rejection (Article 189b(2)(c)); e = EP failure to take a decision within three months (Article 189b(2)(b)); f = amendments following a declaration of rejection; g = agreement on a common draft; h = failure to agree on a common draft.

TABLE I — CO-DECISION 487

Commission opinion (Art. 189b(2)(d))	Conciliation Committee g, h (¹) (Art. 189b(4))	Confirmed common position Council (Art. 189b(6))	EP rejection of confirmed common position	EP adoption of common draft (Art. 189b(5))	Adoption by Council	EP signature Council (Art. 191)	Comments	
COM(1998) 422, Bull. 7/8-98/1.3.120	Bull. 11-98/1.2.721 (g)			Bull. 12-98	Bull. 12-98	Bull. 12-98	Agreement on Council common position: Bull. 1/2-98/1.3.147, ECSC Consultative Committee opinion: Bull. 4-98/1.2.69	285
							Agreement on Council common position: Bull. 12-98	324
							Agreement on Council common position: Bull. 12-98	324
								324
COM(97) 636, Bull. 11-97/1.3.110	Bull. 12-97/1.2.118 (g)			OJ C 56/23.2.98, Bull. 1/2-98/1.3.151	Bull. 1/2-98/1.3.151	OJ L 77/14.3.98, Bull. 1/2-98/1.3.151	Amended decision: OJ L 87/20.4.95, agreement on Council common position: Bull. 6-97/1.3.135	327
COM(1998) 201, Bull. 3-98/1.2.91	23.6.98			OJ C 292/21.9.98, Bull. 7/8-98/1.3.127	Bull. 7/8-98/1.3.127	OJ L 214/31.7.98, Bull. 7/8-98/1.3.127	Agreement on Council common position: Bull. 10-97/1.2.102	337

	Commission proposal	ESC opinion/ COR opinion°	EP first reading	Amended Commission proposal	Common position Council	EP second reading a, b, c, d, e, f(^{1})

Trans-European networks

Telematics and telecommunications

	Commission proposal	ESC opinion/ COR opinion°	EP first reading	Amended Commission proposal	Common position Council	EP second reading
393 Proposal for a decision: guidelines and projects for trans-European networks for the electronic interchange of data between administrations (IDA)	OJ C 54/21.2.98, COM(97) 661, Bull. 12-97/1.2.133	OJ C 214/10.7.98, Bull. 4-98/1.2.78, OJ C 251/10.8.98, Bull. 5-98/1.2.114°	OJ C 379/7.12.98, Bull. 11-98/1.2.94	COM(1998) 786, Bull. 12-98	Bull. 12-98	
393 Proposal for a decision: actions and measures to ensure interoperability and access (IDA)	OJ C 54/21.2.98, COM(97) 661, Bull. 12-97/1.2.133	OJ C 214/10.7.98, Bull. 4-98/1.2.78, OJ C 251/10.8.98, Bull. 5-98/1.2.114°	OJ C 379/7.12.98, Bull. 11-98/1.2.93	OJ C 10/14.1.99, COM(1998) 785, Bull. 12-98	Bull. 12-98	

Energy

	Commission proposal	ESC opinion/ COR opinion°	EP first reading	Amended Commission proposal	Common position Council	EP second reading
394 Proposal for a decision amending Decision No 1254/96/EC: trans-European networks (energy)	OJ C 320/17.10.98, COM(1998) 542, Bull. 9-98/1.2.85					

Energy

Internal energy market

	Commission proposal	ESC opinion/ COR opinion°	EP first reading	Amended Commission proposal	Common position Council	EP second reading
406 Directive 98/30/EC: common rules for the internal market in natural gas	OJ C 65/14.3.92, COM(91) 548, Bull. 1/2-92/1.3.117	OJ C 73/15.3.93, Bull. 1/2-93/1.2.98, OJ C 195/18.7.94	OJ C 329/6.12.93, Bull. 11-93/1.2.82	OJ C 123/4.5.94, COM(93) 643, Bull. 12-93/1.2.121	OJ C 91/26.3.98, Bull. 1/2-98/1.3.168	OJ C 152/18.5.98, Bull. 4-98/1.2.83 (a)

Information society, telecommunications

Information society

	Commission proposal	ESC opinion/ COR opinion°	EP first reading	Amended Commission proposal	Common position Council	EP second reading
460 Proposal for a decision: safe use of the Internet	OJ C 48/13.2.98, COM(97) 582, Bull. 11-97/1.3.141	OJ C 214/10.7.98, Bull. 4-98/1.2.99, OJ C 251/10.8.98, Bull. 5-98/1.2.134°	OJ C 226/20.7.98, Bull. 7/8-98/1.3.170	COM(1998) 518, Bull. 9-98/1.2.113	OJ C 360/23.11.98, Bull. 9-98/1.2.113	OJ C 379/7.12.98, Bull. 11-98/1.2.115 (b)
461 Proposal for a directive: common framework for electronic signatures	OJ C 325/23.10.98, COM(1998) 297, Bull. 5-98/1.2.143	Bull. 12-98, 13.1.99°	13.1.99			

° Opinion of the Committee of the Regions.
(^{1}) a = adoption (Article 189b(2)(a)); b = amendments (Article 189b(2)(c) and (d)); c = declaration of rejection (Article 189b(2)(c)); d = rejection (Article 189b(2)(c)); e = EP failure to take a decision within three months (Article 189b(2)(b)); f = amendments following a declaration of rejection; g = agreement on a common draft; h = failure to agree on a common draft.

TABLE I — CO-DECISION 489

Commission opinion (Art. 189b(2)(d))	Conciliation Committee g, h (¹) (Art. 189b(4))	Confirmed common position Council (Art. 189b(6))	EP rejection of confirmed common position	EP adoption of common draft (Art. 189b(5))	Adoption by Council	EP signature Council (Art. 191)	Comments	
							Agreement on Council common position: Bull. 11-98/1.2.94	393
							Agreement on Council common position: Bull. 11-98/1.2.93	393
							Decision to be amended: OJ L 161/29.6.96	394
COM(1998) 299					Bull. 5-98/1.2.117	OJ L 204/21.7.98, Bull. 6-98/1.3.93	Agreement on Council common position: Bull. 12-97/1.2.137	406
COM(1998) 784, Bull. 12-98					Bull. 12-98			460
								461

	Commission proposal	ESC opinion/ COR opinion°	EP first reading	Amended Commission proposal	Common position Council	EP second reading a, b, c, d, e, f(^{1})	
461 Proposal for a directive: legal aspects of electronic commerce	COM(1998) 586, Bull. 11-98/1.2.24						

Telecommunications policy

	Commission proposal	ESC opinion/ COR opinion°	EP first reading	Amended Commission proposal	Common position Council	EP second reading a, b, c, d, e, f(^{1})	
469 Directive 98/10/EC amending Directive 95/62/EC: open network provision (ONP) and universal service for voice telephony	OJ C 371/9.12.96, COM(96) 419, Bull. 11-96/1.3.140	OJ C 133/28.4.97, Bull. 1/2-97/1.2.152	OJ C 85/17.3.97, Bull. 1/2-97/1.2.152	OJ C 248/14.8.97, COM(97) 287, Bull. 6-97/1.3.186	OJ C 234/1.8.97, Bull. 6-97/1.3.186	OJ C 304/6.10.97, Bull. 9-97/1.2.83 (b)	
469 Directive 98/61/EC: number portability and operator preselection	OJ C 330/1.11.97, COM(97) 480, Bull. 10-97/1.2.154	OJ C 73/9.3.98, Bull. 12-97/1.2.169	OJ C 371/8.12.97, Bull. 11-97/1.3.144	OJ C 13/17.1.98, COM(97) 674, Bull. 11-97/1.3.144	OJ C 91/26.3.98, Bull. 1/2-98/1.3.206	OJ C 167/1.6.98, Bull. 5-98/1.2.139 (b)	
470 Directive 98/13/EC: telecommunications equipment connected to the network	COM(95) 612, Bull. 12-95/1.3.123	OJ C 204/15.7.96, Bull. 4-96/1.3.94	OJ C 166/10.7.96, Bull. 5-96/1.3.96		OJ C 375/10.12.97, Bull. 10-97/1.2.153	OJ C 371/8.12.97, Bull. 11-97/1.3.143 (a)	
470 Proposal for a directive: connected telecommunications equipment and mutual recognition of this equipment	OJ C 248/14.8.97, COM(97) 257, Bull. 6-97/1.3.180	OJ C 73/9.3.98, Bull. 12-97/1.2.166	OJ C 56/23.2.98, Bull. 1/2-98/1.3.201	OJ C 141/6.5.98, COM(1998) 176	OJ C 227/20.7.98, Bull. 6-98/1.3.118	OJ C 328/26.10.98, Bull. 10-98/1.2.113 (b)	
471 Proposal for a decision: coordinated introduction of mobile and wireless communications (UMTS)	OJ C 131/29.4.98, COM(1998) 58, Bull. 1/2-98/1.3.207	OJ C 214/10.7.98, Bull. 4-98/1.2.102, OJ C 373/2.12.98, Bull. 9-98/1.2.115°	OJ C 210/6.7.98, Bull. 6-98/1.3.119	OJ C 276/4.9.98, COM(1998) 496, Bull. 7/8-98/1.3.175	OJ C 333/30.10.98, Bull. 9-98/1.2.115	OJ C 379/7.12.98, Bull. 11-98/1.2.120 (a)	

Environment

Action programme

	Commission proposal	ESC opinion/ COR opinion°	EP first reading	Amended Commission proposal	Common position Council	EP second reading a, b, c, d, e, f(^{1})	
483 Decision 2179/98/EC: review of the fifth action programme (sustainable development)	OJ C 140/11.5.96, COM(95) 647, Bull. 1/2-96/1.3.141	OJ C 212/22.7.96, Bull. 5-96/1.3.105, OJ C 34/3.2.97, Bull. 9-96/1.3.101°	OJ C 362/2.12.96, Bull. 11-96/1.3.145	OJ C 28/29.1.97, COM(96) 648, Bull. 12-96/1.3.153	OJ C 157/24.5.97, Bull. 4-97/1.3.166	OJ C 286/22.9.97, Bull. 7/8-97/1.3.170 (b)	

° Opinion of the Committee of the Regions.
(^{1}) a = adoption (Article 189b(2)(a)); b = amendments (Article 189b(2)(c) and (d)); c = declaration of rejection (Article 189b(2)(c)); d = rejection (Article 189b(2)(c)); e = EP failure to take a decision within three months (Article 189b(2)(b)); f = amendments following a declaration of rejection; g = agreement on a common draft; h = failure to agree on a common draft.

TABLE I — CO-DECISION 491

Commission opinion (Art. 189b(2)(d))	Conciliation Committee g, h (1) (Art. 189b(4))	Confirmed common position Council (Art. 189b(6))	EP rejection of confirmed common position	EP adoption of common draft (Art. 189b(5))	Adoption by Council	EP signature Council (Art. 191)	Comments	
								461
COM(97) 531, Bull. 10-97/1.2.149	Bull. 12-97/1.2.163 (g)			OJ C 56/23.2.98, Bull. 1/2-98/1.3.200	Bull. 1/2-98/1.3.200	OJ L 101/1.4.98, Bull. 1/2-98/1.3.200	Replaced directive: OJ L 321/30.12.95, agreement on Council common position: Bull. 3-97/1.3.107	469
COM(1998) 432, Bull. 7/8-98/1.3.176					Bull. 7/8-98/1.3.176	OJ L 268/3.10.98, Bull. 9-98/1.2.111	Amended directive: OJ L 199/26.7.97, agreement on Council common position: Bull. 12-97/1.2.169	469
					Bull. 12-97/1.2.167	OJ L 74/12.3.98, Bull. 1/2-98/1.3.202	Consolidated Directives: 91/263/EEC (OJ L 128/23.5.91) and 93/97/EC (OJ L 290/24.11.93)	470
COM(1998) 692, Bull. 12-98	Bull. 12-98 (g)						Agreement on Council common position: Bull. 1/2-98/1.3.201	470
					Bull. 11-98/1.2.120	Bull. 12-98		471
COM(97) 471, Bull. 10-97/1.2.163	Bull. 6-98/1.3.125 (g)			OJ C 292/21.9.98, Bull. 7/8-98/1.3.182	Bull. 7/8-98/1.3.182	OJ L 275/10.10.98, Bull. 9-98/1.2.116	Agreement on Council common position: Bull. 12-96/1.3.153	483

	Commission proposal	ESC opinion/ COR opinion°	EP first reading	Amended Commission proposal	Common position Council	EP second reading a, b, c, d, e, f (^{1})	

Industry and the environment

| 490 | Proposal for a directive amending Directive 67/548/EEC: packaging and labelling of dangerous substances | OJ C 374/3.12.98, COM(1998) 561, Bull. 10-98/1.2.119 | Bull. 12-98 | Bull. 12-98 | | | | |
| 491 | Proposal for a directive amending Directive 90/220/EEC: deliberate release into the environment of genetically modified organisms | OJ C 139/4.5.98, COM(1998) 85, Bull. 1/2-98/1.3.216 | OJ C 407/28.12.98, Bull. 9-98/1.2.119 | | | | | |

Quality of the environment and natural resources

502	Directive 98/69/EC amending Directive 70/156/EEC on pollution by emissions from motor vehicles	OJ C 77/11.3.97, COM(96) 248, Bull. 6-96/1.3.140	OJ C 206/7.7.97, Bull. 4-97/1.3.172	OJ C 132/28.4.97, Bull. 4-97/1.3.172, OJ C 80/16.3.98, Bull. 1/2-98/1.3.229	OJ C 106/4.4.97, COM(97) 61, Bull. 1/2-97/1.2.170, OJ C 106/4.4.97, COM(97) 77, Bull. 1/2-97/1.2.170, OJ C 257/22.8.97, COM(97) 255, Bull. 6-97/1.3.205	OJ C 351/19.11.97, Bull. 10-97/1.2.179, OJ C 161/27.5.98, Bull. 3-98/1.2.145	OJ C 80/16.3.98, Bull. 1/2-98/1.3.229 (b), OJ C 152/18.5.98, Bull. 4-98/1.2.111 (b)	
502	Directive 70/98/EC amending Directive 93/12/EEC on the quality of petrol and diesel fuels	OJ C 77/11.3.97, COM(96) 248, Bull. 6-96/1.3.140	OJ C 206/7.7.97, Bull. 4-97/1.3.173	OJ C 132/28.4.97, Bull. 4-97/1.3.173	OJ C 209/10.7.97, COM(97) 271, Bull. 6-97/1.3.206	OJ C 351/19.11.97, Bull. 10-97/1.2.180	OJ C 80/16.3.98, Bull. 1/2-98/1.3.230 (b)	
502	Proposal for a directive: emission of gaseous pollutants from diesel engines	OJ C 173/8.6.98, COM(97) 627, Bull. 12-97/1.2.190	OJ C 407/28.12.98, Bull. 9-98/1.2.126	OJ C 341/9.11.98, Bull. 10-98/1.2.131	COM(1998) 776, Bull. 12-98			
502	Proposal for a directive amending Directive 74/150/EEC: air pollution from road traffic	OJ C 303/2.10.98, COM(1998) 472, Bull. 9-98/1.2.124						

° Opinion of the Committee of the Regions.

(^{1}) a = adoption (Article 189b(2)(a)); b = amendments (Article 189b(2)(c) and (d)); c = declaration of rejection (Article 189b(2)(c)); d = rejection (Article 189b(2)(c)); e = EP failure to take a decision within three months (Article 189b(2)(h)); f = amendments following a declaration of rejection; g = agreement on a common draft; h = failure to agree on a common draft.

TABLE I — CO-DECISION 493

Commission opinion (Art. 189b(2)(d))	Conciliation Committee g, h ([1]) (Art. 189b(4))	Confirmed common position Council (Art. 189b(6))	EP rejection of confirmed common position	EP adoption of common draft (Art. 189b(5))	Adoption by Council	EP signature Council (Art. 191)	Comments	
							Directive to be amended: OJ L 196/16.8.67, agreement on Council common position: Bull. 12-98	490
							Directive to be amended: OJ L 117/8.5.90	491
COM(1998) 211, Bull. 4-98/1.2.110, COM(1998) 397, Bull. 6-98/1.3.137	Bull. 6-98/1.3.136 and 1.3.137			OJ C 313/12.10.98 Bull. 9-98/1.2.127 and 1.2.128	Bull. 9-98/1.2.127	OJ L 350/28.12.98, Bull. 10-98/1.2.129	Amended directive: 70/156/EEC (OJ L 42/23.2.70), EP opinion of 18.2.98 on the part covered by amended proposal COM(97) 61, agreement on Council common position: Bull. 6-97/1.3.205	502
COM(1998) 241, Bull. 5-98/1.2.156	Bull. 6-98/1.3.138			OJ C 313/12.10.98 Bull. 9-98/1.2.129	Bull. 9-98/1.2.129	OJ L 350/28.12.98, Bull. 10-98/1.2.130	Amended directive: OJ L 74/27.3.93, agreement on Council common position: Bull. 6-97/1.3.206	502
							Directive to be amended: OJ L 36/9.2.88, agreement on Council common position: Bull. 12-98	502
							Directive to be amended: OJ L 24/28.3.74	502

	Commission proposal	ESC opinion/ COR opinion°	EP first reading	Amended Commission proposal	Common position Council	EP second reading a, b, c, d, e, f(^{1})	
504 Proposal for a directive: noise emission by equipment used outdoors	OJ C 124/22.4.98, COM(1998) 46, Bull. 1/2-98/1.3.231	OJ C 407/28.12.98, Bull. 9-98/1.2.131	OJ C 138/4.5.98, Bull. 4-98/1.2.113				

Agricultural policy

Veterinary and plant-health legislation

	Commission proposal	ESC opinion/ COR opinion°	EP first reading	Amended Commission proposal	Common position Council	EP second reading a, b, c, d, e, f(^{1})	
563 Proposal for a regulation: prevention and control of certain transmissible spongiform encephalopathies	COM(1998) 623, Bull. 11-98/1.2.131						
563 Proposal for a directive with a view to amending Directive No 91/68/EEC	COM(1998) 623, Bull. 11-98/1.2.131						
564 Proposal for a directive amending Directive 64/432/EEC: health problems affecting intra-Community trade in bovine animals and swine	OJ C 100/2.4.98, COM(1998) 81, Bull. 1/2-98/1.3.244	OJ C 235/27.7.98, Bull. 5-98/1.2.167	OJ C 210/6.7.98, Bull. 6-98/1.3.156				
564 Proposal for a directive amending Directive 89/662/EEC: veterinary checks	OJ C 13/17.1.98, COM(97) 643, Bull. 12-97/1.2.204	OJ C 157/25.5.98, Bull. 3-98/1.2.163	OJ C 80/16.3.98, Bull. 1/2-98/1.3.246				
565 Proposal for a directive: vehicles for the transport of animals	OJ C 290/24.9.97, COM(97) 336, Bull. 7/8-97/1.3.190	OJ C 73/9.3.98, Bull. 12-97/1.2.208	OJ C 292/21.9.98, Bull. 7/8-98/1.3.209				
567 Proposal for a directive amending Directives 79/373/EEC and 96/25/EC: feedingstuffs	OJ C 261/19.8.98, COM(1998) 435, Bull. 7/8-98/1.3.214		Bull. 12-98				
567 Proposal for a directive amending Directive 95/53/EC: official inspections regarding animal nutrition	OJ C 346/14.11.98, COM(1998) 602, Bull. 11-98/1.2.135		Bull. 12-98				
568 Proposal for a directive: feedingstuffs	OJ C 298/30.9.97, COM(97) 408, Bull. 7/8-97/1.3.188	OJ C 129/27.4.98, Bull. 1/2-98/1.3.248	OJ C 80/16.3.98, Bull. 1/2-98/1.3.248	OJ C 273/2.9.98, COM(1998) 484, Bull. 7/8-98/1.3.210			

° Opinion of the Committee of the Regions.
(^{1}) a = adoption (Article 189b(2)(a)); b = amendments (Article 189b(2)(c) and (d)); c = declaration of rejection (Article 189b(2)(c)); d = rejection (Article 189b(2)(c)); e = EP failure to take a decision within three months (Article 189b(2)(b)); f = amendments following a declaration of rejection; g = agreement on a common draft; h = failure to agree on a common draft.

TABLE I — CO-DECISION   495

Commission opinion (Art. 189b(2)(d))	Conciliation Committee g, h (¹) (Art. 189b(4))	Confirmed common position Council (Art. 189b(6))	EP rejection of confirmed common position	EP adoption of common draft (Art. 189b(5))	Adoption by Council	EP signature Council (Art. 191)	Comments
							Directives to be repealed: 79/113/EEC (OJ L 33/8.2.79), 84/532/EEC (OJ L 300/19.11.84), 84/533/EEC and 84/538/EEC (OJ L 300/19.11.84) 504
							563
							Directive to be amended: OJ L 46/19.2.91 563
							Directive to be amended: OJ L 121/29.7.64 564
							Directive to be amended: OJ L 395/30.12.89 564
							Directive to be amended: OJ L 42/23.2.70 565
							Directives to be amended: 79/373/EEC (OJ L 86/6.4.79) and 96/25/EC (OJ L 125/23.5.96) 567
							Directive to be amended: OJ L 265/8.11.95 567
							Directives to be amended: 74/63/EEC (OJ L 38/11.2.74), 79/373/EEC (OJ L 86/6.4.79), 82/471/EEC (OJ L 213/21.7.82) 568

	Commission proposal	ESC opinion/ COR opinion°	EP first reading	Amended Commission proposal	Common position Council	EP second reading a, b, c, d, e, f(^{1})	
568	Proposal for a directive amending Directive 95/69/EC: approving and registering establishments operating in the animal feed sector	OJ C 300/1.10.97, COM(97) 409, Bull. 7/8-97/1.3.189	OJ C 129/27.4.98, Bull. 1/2-98/1.3.249	OJ C 80/16.3.98, Bull. 1/2-98/1.3.249	OJ C 270/29.8.98, COM(1998) 485, Bull. 7/8-98/1.3.211			

Public health

Tobacco

	Commission proposal	ESC opinion/ COR opinion°	EP first reading	Amended Commission proposal	Common position Council	EP second reading a, b, c, d, e, f(^{1})	
624	Directive 98/43/EC: advertising of tobacco products	OJ C 124/19.5.89, COM(89) 163, Bull. 3-89/2.1.85	OJ C 62/12.3.90, Bull. 12-89/2.1.116, OJ C 313/30.11.92, Bull. 9-92/1.2.151	OJ C 67/16.3.92, Bull. 1/2-92/1.3.257, OJ C 96/17.4.90, Bull. 4-90/1.3.193	OJ C 116/11.5.90, COM(90) 147, Bull. 4-90/1.2.162, OJ C 167/27.6.91, COM(91) 111, Bull. 5-91/1.2.165, OJ C 129/21.5.92, COM(92) 196, Bull. 4-92/1.3.181	OJ C 91/26.3.98, Bull. 1/2-98/1.3.280	OJ C 167/1.6.98, Bull. 5-98/1.2.192 (a)	

AIDS and other communicable diseases

	Commission proposal	ESC opinion/ COR opinion°	EP first reading	Amended Commission proposal	Common position Council	EP second reading a, b, c, d, e, f(^{1})	
627	Decision No 2119/98/EC: network for the surveillance of communicable diseases	OJ C 123/26.4.96, COM(96) 78, Bull. 3-96/1.3.167	OJ C 30/30.1.97, Bull. 9-96/1.3.163, OJ C 337/11.11.96°	OJ C 362/2.12.96, Bull. 11-96/1.3.212	OJ C 103/2.4.97, COM(97) 31, Bull. 1/2-97/1.2.222	OJ C 284/19.9.97, Bull. 7/8-97/1.3.229	OJ C 34/2.2.98, Bull. 1/2-98/1.3.281 (b)	

Pollution-related diseases

	Commission proposal	ESC opinion/ COR opinion°	EP first reading	Amended Commission proposal	Common position Council	EP second reading a, b, c, d, e, f(^{1})	
630	Proposal for a decision: action programme on pollution-related diseases	OJ C 214/16.7.97, COM(97) 266, Bull. 6-97/1.3.266	OJ C 19/21.1.98, Bull. 10-97/1.2.238, OJ C 64/27.2.98, Bull. 11-97/1.3.212°	OJ C 104/6.4.98, Bull. 3-98/1.2.205	OJ C 156/21.5.98, COM(1998) 231, Bull. 4-98/1.2.141	OJ C 227/20.7.98, Bull. 4-98/1.2.141	OJ C 328/26.10.98, Bull. 10-98/1.2.160 (b)	

Rare diseases

	Commission proposal	ESC opinion/ COR opinion°	EP first reading	Amended Commission proposal	Common position Council	EP second reading a, b, c, d, e, f(^{1})	
631	Proposal for a decision: action programme 1999-2003 on rare diseases	OJ C 203/3.7.97, COM(97) 225, Bull. 5-97/1.3.176	OJ C 19/21.1.98, Bull. 10-97/1.2.237, OJ C 64/27.2.98, Bull. 11-97/1.3.211°	OJ C 104/6.4.98, Bull. 3-98/1.2.203	OJ C 160/27.5.98, COM(1998) 232, Bull. 4-98/1.2.142	OJ C 227/20.7.98, Bull. 6-98/1.3.196	OJ C 328/26.10.98, Bull. 10-98/1.2.161 (b)	

° Opinion of the Committee of the Regions.

(^{1}) a = adoption (Article 189b(2)(a)); b = amendments (Article 189b(2)(c) and (d)); c = declaration of rejection (Article 189b(2)(c)); d = rejection (Article 189b(2)(c)); e = EP failure to take a decision within three months (Article 189b(2)(b)); f = amendments following a declaration of rejection; g = agreement on a common draft; h = failure to agree on a common draft.

TABLE I — CO-DECISION 497

Commission opinion (Art. 189b(2)(d))	Conciliation Committee g, h (^{1}) (Art. 189b(4))	Confirmed common position Council (Art. 189b(6))	EP rejection of confirmed common position	EP adoption of common draft (Art. 189b(5))	Adoption by Council	EP signature Council (Art. 191)	Comments	
							Directive to be amended: OJ L 332/30.12.95	568
					Bull. 6-98/1.3.198	OJ L 213/30.7.98, Bull. 7/8-98/1.3.239	Agreement on Council common position: Bull. 12-97/1.2.273	624
COM(1998) 79, Bull. 1/2-98/1.3.281	Bull. 5-98/1.2.193 (g)			OJ C 292/21.9.98, Bull. 7/8-98/1.3.238	Bull. 7/8-98/1.3.238	OJ L 268/3.10.98, Bull. 9-98/1.2.166	Agreement on Council common position: Bull. 6-97/1.3.269	627
								630
COM(1998) 643							Agreement on Council common position: Bull. 4-98/1.2.142	631

	Commission proposal	ESC opinion/ COR opinion°	EP first reading	Amended Commission proposal	Common position Council	EP second reading a, b, c, d, e, f(¹)	

Injury prevention

| 632 | Proposal for a decision: action programme on injury prevention | OJ C 202/2.7.97, COM(97) 178, Bull. 5-97/1.3.175 | OJ C 19/21.1.98, Bull. 10-97/1.2.236, OJ C 379/15.12.97, Bull. 9-97/1.2.122° | OJ C 104/6.4.98, Bull. 3-98/1.2.204 | OJ C 154/19.5.98, COM(1998) 229, Bull. 4-98/1.2.143 | OJ C 404/23.12.98, Bull. 11-98/1.2.159 | Bull. 12-98 (a) | |

Consumer policy and health protection

General aspects

| 636 | Decision: general framework for Community activities in favour of consumers | OJ C 108/7.4.98, COM(97) 684, Bull. 1/2-98/1.3.282 | OJ C 235/27.7.98, Bull. 5-98/1.2.195 | OJ C 328/26.10.98, Bull. 10-98/1.2.164 | OJ C 390/15.12.98, COM(1998) 642, Bull. 10-98/1.2.164 | OJ C 404/23.12.98, Bull. 11-98/1.2.161 | Bull. 12-98 (a) | |

Protection of consumers' economic and legal interests

643	Directive 98/6/EC: indication of prices for consumers	OJ C 260/5.10.95, COM(95) 276, Bull. 7/8-95/1.3.196	OJ C 82/19.3.96, Bull. 12-95/1.3.215	OJ C 141/13.5.96, Bull. 4-96/1.3.155	OJ C 249/27.8.96, COM(96) 264, Bull. 6-96/1.3.221, COM(97) 136	OJ C 333/7.11.96, Bull. 9-96/1.3.164	OJ C 85/17.3.97, Bull. 1/2-97/1.2.224 (b)	
643	Directive 98/27/EC: injunctions for the protection of consumers' interests	OJ C 107/13.4.96, COM(95) 712, Bull. 1/2-96/1.3.217	OJ C 30/30.1.97, Bull. 9-96/1.3.166	OJ C 362/2.12.96, Bull. 11-96/1.3.218	OJ C 80/13.3.97, COM(96) 725, Bull. 12-96/1.3.230	OJ C 389/22.12.97, Bull. 10-97/1.2.244	OJ C 104/6.4.98, Bull. 3-98/1.2.212 (a)	
643	Proposal for a directive: sale of consumer goods, guarantees and after-sales service	OJ C 307/16.10.96, COM(95) 520, Bull. 6-96/1.3.222	OJ C 66/3.3.97, Bull. 11-96/1.3.219	OJ C 104/6.4.98, Bull. 3-98/1.2.211	OJ C 148/14.5.98, COM(1998) 217, Bull. 3-98/1.2.211	OJ C 333/30.10.98, Bull. 9-98/1.2.172	Bull. 12-98 (b)	

Financial services

| 646 | Directive 98/7/EC amending Directive 87/102/EEC on approximation of the laws on consumer credit | OJ C 235/13.8.96, COM(96) 79, Bull. 4-96/1.3.156 | OJ C 30/30.1.97, Bull. 9-96/1.3.165 | OJ C 85/17.3.97, Bull. 1/2-97/1.2.228 | OJ C 137/3.5.97, COM(97) 127, Bull. 3-97/1.3.161 | OJ C 284/19.9.97, Bull. 7/8-97/1.3.233 | OJ C 371/8.12.97, Bull. 11-97/1.3.216 (a) | |

° Opinion of the Committee of the Regions.
(¹) a = adoption (Article 189b(2)(a)); b = amendments (Article 189b(2)(c) and (d)); c = declaration of rejection (Article 189b(2)(c)); d = rejection (Article 189b(2)(c)); e = EP failure to take a decision within three months (Article 189b(2)(h)); f = amendments following a declaration of rejection; g = agreement on a common draft; h = failure to agree on a common draft.

TABLE I — CO-DECISION 499

Commission opinion (Art. 189b(2)(d))	Conciliation Committee g, h ([1]) (Art. 189b(4))	Confirmed common position Council (Art. 189b(6))	EP rejection of confirmed common position	EP adoption of common draft (Art. 189b(5))	Adoption by Council	EP signature Council (Art. 191)	Comments	
							Agreement on Council common position: Bull. 11-98/1.2.159	632
					Bull. 12-98			636
COM(97) 136, Bull. 4-97/1.3.216	Bull. 11-97/1.3.214 (g)			OJ C 14/19.1.98, Bull. 12-97/1.2.275	Bull. 12-97/1.2.275	OJ L 80/18.3.98, Bull. 1/2-98/1.3.284	Agreement on Council common position: Bull. 4-96/1.3.155	643
					Bull. 4-98/1.2.149	OJ L 166/11.6.98, Bull. 5-98/1.2.199	Agreement on Council common position: Bull. 4-97/1.3.220	643
							Agreement on Council common position: Bull. 4-98/1.2.148	643
					Bull. 12-97/1.2.277	OJ L 101/1.4.98, Bull. 1/2-98/1.3.289	Amended directive: OJ L 42/12.2.87, agreement on Council common position: Bull. 4-97/1.3.219	646

	Commission proposal	ESC opinion/ COR opinion°	EP first reading	Amended Commission proposal	Common position Council	EP second reading a, b, c, d, e, f(^{1})

Culture

	Commission proposal	ESC opinion/ COR opinion°	EP first reading	Amended Commission proposal	Common position Council	EP second reading a, b, c, d, e, f(^{1})
648 Proposal for a decision: cultural cooperation (Culture 2000)	OJ C 211/7.7.98, COM(1998) 266, Bull. 5-98/1.2.200	Bull. 11-98/1.2.165°	OJ C 359/23.11.98, Bull. 11-98/1.2.165	COM(1998) 673, Bull. 11-98/1.2.165		
650 Proposal for a decision: Community initiative for the European City of Culture	OJ C 362/28.11.97, COM(97) 549, Bull. 10-97/1.2.246	OJ C 180/11.6.98, Bull. 3 98/1.2.215°	OJ C 152/18.5.98, Bull. 4-98/1.2.150	OJ C 208/4.7.98, COM(1998) 350, Bull. 5-98/1.2.201	OJ C 285/14.9.98, Bull. 7/8-98/1.3.243	13.1.99
652 Proposal for a decision extending the Ariane cultural programme for a year	OJ C 319/16.10.98, COM(1998) 539, Bull. 9-98/1.2.173	Bull. 11-98/1.2.166°	OJ C 328/26.10.98, Bull. 10-98/1.2.169	OJ C 372/2.12.98, COM(1998) 608, Bull. 10-98/1.2.169	OJ C 404/23.12.98, Bull. 11-98/1.2.166	Bull. 12-98 (a)
652 Proposal for a decision extending the Kaleidoscope cultural programme for a year	OJ C 319/16.10.98, COM(1998) 539, Bull. 9-98/1.2.173	Bull. 11-98/1.2.167°	OJ C 328/26.10.98, Bull. 10-98/1.2.170	OJ C 372/2.12.98, COM(1998) 608, Bull. 10-98/1.2.170	OJ C 404/23.12.98, Bull. 11-98/1.2.167	Bull. 12-98 (a)

The European Union's role in the world

Common commercial policy

Operation of the customs union, customs cooperation and mutual administrative assistance

	Commission proposal	ESC opinion/ COR opinion°	EP first reading	Amended Commission proposal	Common position Council	EP second reading a, b, c, d, e, f(^{1})
715 Proposal for a regulation amending Regulation (EEC) No 2913/92: Community Customs Code	OJ C 228/21.7.98, COM(1998) 226, Bull. 6-98/1.4.36					
715 Proposal for a decision amending Decision No 210/97/EC: Customs 2000	OJ C 396/19.12.98, COM(1998) 644, Bull. 11-98/1.3.22					
716 Proposal for a regulation amending Regulation (EEC) No 2913/92 establishing the Community Customs Code (transit)	OJ C 337/7.11.97, COM(97) 472, Bull. 9-97/1.3.18	OJ C 73/9.3.98, Bull. 12-97/1.3.28	OJ C 167/1.6.98, Bull. 5-98/1.3.27	OJ C 261/19.8.98, COM(1998) 428, Bull. 7/8-98/1.4.29	OJ C 333/30.10.98, Bull. 9-98/1.3.27	Bull. 12-98 (b)

° Opinion of the Committee of the Regions.
(^{1}) a = adoption (Article 189b(2)(a)); b = amendments (Article 189b(2)(c) and (d)); c = declaration of rejection (Article 189b(2)(c)); d = rejection (Article 189b(2)(c)); e = EP failure to take a decision within three months (Article 189b(2)(b)); f = amendments following a declaration of rejection; g = agreement on a common draft; h = failure to agree on a common draft.

TABLE I — CO-DECISION   501

Commission opinion (Art. 189b(2)(d))	Conciliation Committee g, h (¹) (Art. 189b(4))	Confirmed common position Council (Art. 189b(6))	EP rejection of confirmed common position	EP adoption of common draft (Art. 189b(5))	Adoption by Council	EP signature Council (Art. 191)	Comments
							Agreement on Council common position: Bull. 11-98/1.2.165 **648**
							Agreement on Council common position: Bull. 5-98/1.2.201 **650**
							Agreement on Council common position: OJ C 404/23.12.98, Bull. 11-98/1.2.166 **652**
							Agreement on Council common position: OJ C 404/23.12.98, Bull. 11-98/1.2.167 **652**
							Regulation to be amended: OJ L 302/19.10.92 **715**
							Decision to be amended: OJ L 33/4.2.97 **715**
							Regulation to be amended: OJ L 302/19.10.92 **716**

TABLE II — CONSULTATION, COOPERATION   503

Table II — Legislation under the consultation and cooperation procedures

Agenda 2000

	Commission proposal	ESC opinion/ COR opinion°	EP first*/ sole reading	Amended Commission proposal	Council common position	EP second reading	Re-examined Commission proposal	Adoption by Council	Comments
2	Proposal for a regulation: standard qualities for common wheat, rye, barley, maize and durum wheat	OJ C 170/4.6.98, COM(1998) 158, Bull. 3-98/I.10	OJ C 284/14.9.98, Bull. 7/8-98/I.3.224, 13.1.99°						Regulation to be repealed: OJ L 281/1.11.75
2	Proposal for a regulation: support system for producers of certain arable crops	OJ C 170/4.6.98, COM(1998) 158, Bull. 3-98/I.10	OJ C 284/14.9.98, Bull. 7/8-98/I.1, 13.1.99°						
2	Proposal for a regulation: COM in beef and veal	OJ C 170/4.6.98, COM(1998) 158, Bull. 3-98/I.11	OJ C 407/28.12.98, Bull. 9-98/I.4, 13.1.99°						Regs to be repealed: 805/68 (OJ L 148/28.6.68) and 1892/87 (OJ L 182/3.7.87)
2	Proposal for a regulation: COM in milk and milk products	OJ C 170/4.6.98, COM(1998) 158, Bull. 3-98/I.12	OJ C 407/28.12.98, Bull. 9-98/I.5, 13.1.99°						
2	Proposal for a regulation: additional levy in the milk and milk products sector	OJ C 170/4.6.98, COM(1998) 158, Bull. 3-98/I.13	OJ C 407/28.12.98, Bull. 9-98/I.5, 13.1.99°						Regulation to be amended: OJ L 405/31.12.92
2	Regulation (EC) No 1638/98 amending Regulation (EEC) No 136/66: COM in oils and fats	OJ C 136/1.5.98, COM(1998) 171, Bull. 3-98/I.16	OJ C 235/27.7.98, Bull. 5-98/I.2	OJ C 210/6.7.98, Bull. 6-98/II.4				OJ L 210/28.7.98, Bull. 7/8-98/I.3.221	Amended regulation: OJ L 172/30.9.66, Council agreement: Bull. 6-98/II.4

° = Opinion of the Committee of the Regions.

* = Cooperation procedure used.

	Commission proposal	ESC opinion/ COR opinion°	EP first*/ sole opinion°	Amended Commission proposal	Council common position	EP second reading	Re-examined Commission proposal	Adoption by Council	Comments
2	Regulation (EC) No 163/98 amending Regulation (EEC) No 2261/84: aid for the production of olive oil and aid to producer organisations	OJ C 136/1.5.98, COM(1998) 171, Bull. 3-98/I.17							OJ L 210/28.7.98, OJ L 288/27.10.98, Bull. 7/8-98/1.3.221	Amended regulation: OJ L 208/3.8.84, Council agreement: Bull. 6-98/II.4
2	Proposal for a regulation: direct support schemes under the common agricultural policy	OJ C 170/4.6.98, COM(1998) 158, Bull. 3-98/I.14	OJ C 407/28.12.98, Bull. 9-98/I.6, 13.1.99°							
2	Proposal for a regulation: financing of the common agricultural policy	OJ C 170/4.6.98, COM(1998) 158, Bull. 3-98/I.15	OJ C 407/28.12.98, Bull. 9-98/I.7, 13.1.99°							
2	Proposal for a regulation: support for rural development	OJ C 170/4.6.98, COM(1998) 158, Bull. 3-98/I.7	OJ C 407/28.12.98, Bull. 9-98/I.6, 13.1.99°							Regulation to be repealed: OJ L 94/28.4.70
2	Proposal for a regulation: COM in wine	OJ C 271/31.8.98, COM(1998) 370, Bull. 7/8-98/1.3.231	13.1.99°							
4	Proposal for a regulation laying down general provisions on the Structural Funds	OJ C 176/9.6.98, COM(1998) 131, Bull. 3-98/I.3	OJ C 407/28.12.98, Bull. 9-98/I.1, OJ C 373/2.12.98, Bull. 9-98/I.1°							Procedure for EP assent (Art. 130 D), Regulations to be repealed: 2052/88 (OJ L 185/15.7.88) and 4253/88 (OJ L 374/31.12.88)
4	Proposal for a regulation: European Regional Development Fund	OJ C 176/9.6.98, COM(1998) 131, Bull. 3-98/I.4	OJ C 407/28.12.98, Bull. 9-98/I.1, Bull. 11-98/I.4°	OJ C 379/7.12.98, Bull. 11-98/I.4*						
4	Proposal for a regulation: European Social Fund	OJ C 176/9.6.98, COM(1998) 131, Bull. 3-98/I.5	OJ C 407/28.12.98, Bull. 9-98/I.1, Bull. 11-98/I.5°	OJ C 379/7.12.98, Bull. 11-98/I.5*						
4	Proposal for a regulation: structural measures in the fisheries sector	OJ C 176/9.6.98, COM(1998) 131, Bull. 3-98/I.6	OJ C 407/28.12.98, Bull. 9-98/I.1, 13.1.99°							

TABLE II — CONSULTATION, COOPERATION 505

	Commission proposal	ESC opinion/ COR opinion°	EP first*/ sole reading	Amended Commission proposal	Council common position	EP second reading	Re-examined Commission proposal	Adoption by Council	Comments
4	Proposal for a regulation amending Regulation (EC) No 1164/94: Cohesion Fund	OJ C 159/26.5.98, COM(1998) 130, Bull. 3-98/I.8	OJ C 407/28.12.98, Bull. 9-98/I.1, Bull. 11-98/I.6°						Procedure for EP assent (Art. 130 D), regulation to be amended: OJ L 130/25.5.94
4	Proposal for a regulation amending Annex II of Regulation (EC) No 1164/94: Cohesion Fund	OJ C 159/26.5.98, COM(1998) 130, Bull. 3-98/I.8	OJ C 407/28.12.98, Bull. 9-98/I.1						Regulation to be amended: OJ L 130/25.5.94
6	Proposal for a regulation amending Regulation (EC) No 2236/95: general rules for the granting of financial aid in the field of trans-European networks	OJ C 175/9.6.98, COM(1998) 172, Bull. 3-98/I.9	OJ C 407/28.12.98, 13.1.99°	OJ C 379/7.12.98, Bull. 11-98/I.8*	COM(1998) 723, Bull. 12-98	Bull. 12-98			Regulation to be amended: OJ L 228/23.9.95, agreement on Council common position: Bull. 12-98
7	Proposal for a regulation: instrument for structural policies for pre-accession	OJ C 164/29.5.98, COM(1998) 138, Bull. 3-98/I.20	OJ C 407/28.12.98, Bull. 9-98/I.8, Bull. 11-98/I.9°						
7	Proposal for a regulation: Community support for agriculture and rural development in the applicant countries of central and eastern Europe	OJ C 150/16.5.98, COM(1998) 153, Bull. 3-98/I.21	13.1.99°						
7	Proposal for a regulation: coordination of aid to the applicant countries in the framework of the pre-accession strategy	OJ C 140/5.5.98, COM(1998) 150, Bull. 3-98/I.22			OJ C 329/27.10.98, COM(1998) 551, Bull. 9-98/I.9				
8	Proposal for a regulation: Guarantee Fund for external actions	COM(1998) 168, Bull. 3-98/I.25							

° = Opinion of the Committee of the Regions.
* = Cooperation procedure used.

Human rights and fundamental freedoms

Trafficking in human beings

	Commission proposal	ESC opinion/ COR opinion°	EP first*/ sole reading	Amended Commission proposal	Council common position	EP second reading	Re-examined Commission proposal	Adoption by Council	Comments
28	Proposal for a decision: action relating to violence against children, young persons and women (Daphne programme)	OJ C 259/18.8.98, COM(1998) 335, Bull. 5-98/1.1.1	OJ C 407/28.12.98, Bull. 9-98/1.1.2						

The Community economic and social area

Economic and monetary policy

Preparations for the third stage of EMU

	Commission proposal	ESC opinion/ COR opinion°	EP first*/ sole reading	Amended Commission proposal	Council common position	EP second reading	Re-examined Commission proposal	Adoption by Council	Comments
52	Regulation (EC) 974/98: introduction of the euro	OJ C 369/7.12.96, COM(96) 499, Bull. 10-96/1.3.11		OJ C 380/16.12.96, Bull. 11-96/1.3.15					OJ L 139/11.5.98, Bull. 5-98/1.2.8	Conclusions of the Dublin European Council: Bull. 12-96/I.3, conclusions of the Amsterdam European Council: Bull. 6-97/I.5, Council resolution: Bull. 7/8-97/1.3.18, Council agreement: Bull. 12-96/1.3.12, Bull. 6-97/1.3.33

TABLE II — CONSULTATION, COOPERATION   507

	Commission proposal	ESC opinion/ COR opinion°	EP first*/ sole reading	Amended Commission proposal	Council common position	EP second reading	Re-examined Commission proposal	Adoption by Council	Comments
54	Regulation (EC) No 975/98: denominations and technical specifications of the euro	OJ C 208/9.7.97, COM(97) 247, Bull. 5-97/1.3.27		OJ C 358/24.11.97, Bull. 11-97/1.3.25*	OJ C 386/20.12.97, COM(97) 615, Bull. 11-97/1.3.25	OJ C 23/23.1.98, Bull. 11-97/1.3.25	OJ C 14/19.1.98, Bull. 12-97/1.2 29	COM(1998) 17, Bull. 1/2-98/1.3.5	OJ L 139/11.5.98, Bull. 5-98/1.2.9	Conclusions of the European Council: Bull. 6-97/I.5, Council resolution: Bull. 1/2-98/1.3.5, Agreement on Council common position: Bull. 11-97/1.3.25
54	Proposal for a regulation amending Regulation (EC) No 975/98: denominations and technical specifications of euro coins	OJ C 296/24.9.98, COM(1998) 492, Bull. 7/8-98/1.3.7		OJ C 379/7.12.98, Bull. 11-98/1.2.7*		Bull. 12-98				Regulation to be amended: OJ L 139/11.5.98
58	Decision 98/382/EC: determination of the key for subscription of the capital of the ECB (statistical data)	OJ C 118/17.4.98, COM(97) 725, Bull. 1/2-98/1.3.3		OJ C 195/22.6.98, Bull. 5-98/1.2.13					OJ L 171/17.6.98, Bull. 6-98/1.3.7	
58	Decision 98/415/EC: ECB consultation (draft legislative provisions)	OJ C 118/17.4.98, COM(97) 725, Bull. 1/2-98/1.3.3		OJ C 195/22.6.98, Bull. 5-98/1.2.13					OJ L 189/3.7.98, Bull. 6-98/1.3.9	
58	Regulation (EC) No 1197/98 amending Regulation (EEC, Euratom, ECSC) No 260/68: laying down the conditions and procedure for applying the tax for the benefit of the EC	OJ C 118/17.4.98, COM(97) 725, Bull. 1/2-98/1.3.3		OJ C 195/22.6.98, Bull. 5-98/1.2.13					OJ L 166/11.6.98, Bull. 6-98/1.3.8	Amended regulation: OJ L 56/4.3.68
58	Regulation (EC) No 1198/98 amending Regulation (EEC, Euratom, ECSC) No 549/69: categories of EC officials and other servants/application of Articles 12, 13 and 14 of the protocol on the privileges and immunities of the EC	OJ C 118/17.4.98, COM(97) 725, Bull. 1/2-98/1.3.3		OJ C 195/22.6.98, Bull. 5-98/1.2.13					OJ L 166/11.6.98	Amended regulation: OJ L 74/27.3.69

° = Opinion of the Committee of the Regions.
* = Cooperation procedure used.

		Commission proposal	ESC opinion/ COR opinion°	EP first*/ sole reading	Amended Commission proposal	Council common position	EP second reading	Re-examined Commission proposal	Adoption by Council	Comments
59	Regulation (EC) No 2531/98: application of minimum reserves by the ECB	COM(1998) 556, Bull. 10-98/1.2.3		OJ C 328/26.10.98					OJ L 318/27.11.98, Bull. 11-98/1.2.8	Recommendation of the ECB: OJ C 246/6.8.98 and Bull. 7/8-98/1.3.4
59	Regulation (EC) No 2532/98: powers of the ECB to impose sanctions	COM(1998) 556, Bull. 10-98/1.2.3		OJ C 328/26.10.98, Bull. 10-98/1.2.3					OJ L 318/27.11.98, Bull. 11-98/1.2.8	Recommendation of the ECB: OJ C 246/6.8.98 and Bull. 7/8-98/1.3.4
59	Regulation (EC) No 2533/98: collection of statistical information by the ECB	COM(1998) 556, Bull. 10-98/1.2.3		OJ C 328/26.10.98, Bull. 10-98/1.2.3					OJ L 318/27.11.98, Bull. 11-98/1.2.8	Recommendation of the ECB: OJ C 246/6.8.98 and Bull. 7/8-98/1.3.4

Financial activities

		Commission proposal	ESC opinion/ COR opinion°	EP first*/ sole reading	Amended Commission proposal	Council common position	EP second reading	Re-examined Commission proposal	Adoption by Council	Comments
77	Decision 98/592/EC: supplementary macro-financial assistance for Ukraine	OJ C 386/20.12.97, COM(97) 588, Bull. 11-97/1.4.80		OJ C 80/16.3.98, Bull. 1/2-98/1.4.114					OJ L 284/22.10.98, Bull. 10-98/1.3.95	
78	Proposal for a decision: exceptional financial assistance to Azerbaijan	OJ C 150/16.5.98, COM(1998) 205, Bull. 4-98/1.3.67		OJ C 341/9.11.98, Bull. 10-98/1.3.94						
78	Proposal for a decision: macro-financial assistance to Albania	OJ C 302/1.10.98, COM(1998) 507, Bull. 9-98/1.3.78								
78	Proposal for a decision: macro-financial assistance to Bosnia-Herzegovina	OJ C 396/19.12.98, COM(1998) 652, Bull. 11-98/1.3.76								

TABLE II — CONSULTATION, COOPERATION 509

Statistical system

Priority activities and objectives

	Commission proposal	ESC opinion/ COR opinion°	EP first*/ sole reading	Amended Commission proposal	Council common position	EP second reading	Re-examined Commission proposal	Adoption by Council	Comments
97	Decision: Community statistical programme (1998-2002)	COM(97) 735, Bull. 1/2-98/1.7.1	OJ C 235/27.7.98, Bull. 5-98/1.6.11	OJ C 328/26.10.98, Bull. 10-98/1.6.1					Bull. 12-98	

Framework and guidelines

	Commission proposal	ESC opinion/ COR opinion°	EP first*/ sole reading	Amended Commission proposal	Council common position	EP second reading	Re-examined Commission proposal	Adoption by Council	Comments
98	Regulation (EC) No 448/98: financial intermediation services indirectly measured (FISIM)	OJ C 124/21.4.97, COM(97) 50, Bull. 1/2-97/1.6.4		OJ C 339/10.11.97, Bull. 10-97/1.6.4					OJ L 58/27.2.98, Bull. 1/2-98/1.7.3	Amended regulation: OJ L 310/30.11.96, Council agreement: Bull. 1/2-98/1.7.3
98	Regulation (EC) No 1165/98: short-term statistics	OJ C 267/3.9.97, COM(97) 313, Bull. 6-97/1.7.2	OJ C 19/21.1.98, Bull. 10-97/1.6.5	OJ C 80/16.3.98, Bull. 1/2-98/1.7.5					OJ L 162/5.6.98, Bull. 5-98/1.6.2	
98	Regulation (EC, Euratom) No 410/98 amending Regulation No 58/97: structural business statistics	OJ C 310/10.10.97, COM(97) 411, Bull. 9-97/1.6.1	OJ C 95/30.3.98, Bull. 1/2-98/1.7.2	OJ C 14/19.1.98, Bull. 12-97/1.6.1					OJ L 52/21.2.98, Bull. 1/2-98/1.7.2	Amended regulation: OJ L 14/17.1.97
101	Regulation (EC) No 2329/98 amending Regulation (EEC) No 357/79: statistical surveys of areas under vines	OJ C 257/15.8.98, COM(1998) 420, Bull. 7/8-98/1.7.5		OJ C 328/26.10.98, Bull. 10-98/1.6.3					OJ L 291/30.10.98, Bull. 10-98/1.6.3	Amended regulation: OJ L 54/5.3.79
101	Proposal for a decision: aerial survey and remote-sensing techniques for agricultural statistics (1999-2003)	OJ C 372/2.12.98, OJ C 396/19.12.98, COM(1998) 601, Bull. 11-98/1.6.1								

° = Opinion of the Committee of the Regions.
* = Cooperation procedure used.

	Commission proposal	ESC opinion/ COR opinion°	EP first*/ sole reading	Amended Commission proposal	Council common position	EP second reading	Re-examined Commission proposal	Adoption by Council	Comments
102	Regulation (EC) No 1172/98: statistical returns for the carriage of goods by road	OJ C 341/11.11.97, COM(97) 443, Bull. 9-97/1.6.2	OJ C 95/30.3.98, Bull. 1/2-98/1.7.7	OJ C 104/6.4.98, Bull. 3-98/1.6.1					OJ L 163/6.6.98, Bull. 5-98/1.6.3	Repealed Dir: 78/546/EEC (OJ L 168/26.6.78), Council agreement: Bull. 3-98/1.6.1

Employment and social policy

Employment

	Commission proposal	ESC opinion/ COR opinion°	EP first*/ sole reading	Amended Commission proposal	Council common position	EP second reading	Re-examined Commission proposal	Adoption by Council	Comments
118	Decision 98/171/EC on the Commission's activities of analysis, research, cooperation and action in the field of employment	OJ C 235/9.9.95, COM(95) 250, Bull. 6-95/1.3.199	OJ C 18/22.1.96, Bull. 10-95/1.3.212, OJ C 126/29.4.96, Bull. 11-95/1.3.184°	OJ C 166/10.7.96, Bull. 5-96/1.3.161	OJ C 342/14.11.96, COM(96) 449, Bull. 9-96/1.3.149				OJ L 63/4.3.98, Bull. 1/2-98/1.3.13	Council agreement: Bull. 12-97/1.2.259

Social protection and social security

	Commission proposal	ESC opinion/ COR opinion°	EP first*/ sole reading	Amended Commission proposal	Council common position	EP second reading	Re-examined Commission proposal	Adoption by Council	Comments
120	Dir. 98/49/EC: safeguarding the supplementary pension rights of workers moving within the EU	OJ C 5/9.1.98, COM(97) 486, Bull. 10-97/1.2.227	OJ C 157/25.5.98, Bull. 3-98/1.2.14	OJ C 152/18.5.98, Bull. 4-98/1.2.13	OJ C 205/1.7.98, COM(1998) 325, Bull. 5-98/1.2.20				OJ L 209/25.7.98, Bull. 6-98/1.3.17	Council agreement: Bull. 6-98/1.3.17
121	Regulation (EC) No 1223/98 amending Regulation (EEC) No 1408/71 on the application of social security schemes to employed persons, to self-employed persons and to members of their families moving within the Community	OJ C 290/24.9.97, COM(97) 378, Bull. 7/8-97/1.3.219	OJ C 73/9.3.98, Bull. 12-97/1.2.263	OJ C 152/18.5.98, Bull. 4-98/1.2.12					OJ L 168/13.6.98, Bull. 6-98/1.3.15	Amended Regs.: 1408/71 (OJ L 149/5.7.71) and 574/72 (OJ L 74/27.3.72)

TABLE II — CONSULTATION, COOPERATION   511

	Commission proposal	ESC opinion/ COR opinion°	EP first*/ sole reading	Amended Commission proposal	Council common position	EP second reading	Re-examined Commission proposal	Adoption by Council	Comments
121	Regulation (EC) No 1606/98 amending Regs (EEC) Nos 1408/71 and 574/72: application of social security schemes to workers moving within the Community	OJ C 46/20.2.92, COM(91) 528, Bull. 12-91/1.2.138	OJ C 98/21.4.92, Bull. 1/2-92/1.3.124	OJ C 94/13.4.92, Bull. 3-92/1.2.94					OJ L 209/25.7.98, Bull. 6-98/1.3.16	Amended Regs: 1408/71 (OJ L 149/5.7.71) and 574/72 (OJ L 74/27.3.72), Council agreement: Bull. 6-98/1.3.16
121	Proposal for a regulation amending Regs (EEC) Nos 1408/71 and 574/72: procedure for the application of the social security scheme	OJ C 325/23.10.98, COM(1998) 547, Bull. 9-98/1.2.11								Regs to be amended: 1408/71 (OJ L 149/5.7.71) and 574/72 (OJ L 74/27.3.72)
121	Proposal for a regulation on co-ordination of social security systems	COM(1998) 779, Bull. 12-98								
121	Proposal for a regulation: extension of Regulation (EEC) No 1408/71 to nationals of third countries	OJ C 6/10.1.98, COM(97) 561, Bull. 11-97/1.3.201	OJ C 157/25.5.98, Bull. 3-98/1.2.13	OJ C 328/26.10.98, Bull. 10-98/1.2.13						Regulation to be amended: OJ L 149/5.7.71

Labour law and industrial relations

	Commission proposal	ESC opinion/ COR opinion°	EP first*/ sole reading	Amended Commission proposal	Council common position	EP second reading	Re-examined Commission proposal	Adoption by Council	Comments
127	Dir. 98/50/EC: safeguarding of employees' rights in the event of transfers of undertakings	COM(94) 300, Bull. 9-94/1.2.182	OJ C 133/31.5.95, Bull. 3-95/1.3.145, Bull. 4-95/1.3.127°	OJ C 33/3.2.97, Bull. 1/2-97/1.2.217	OJ C 124/21.4.97, COM(97) 60, Bull. 1/2-97/1.2.217				OJ L 201/17.7.98, Bull. 6-98/1.3.18	Council agreement: Bull. 6-98/1.3.18
127	Dir. 98/59/EC: collective redundancies (consolidated version)	COM(96) 620, Bull. 11-96/1.3.199	OJ C 158/26.5.97, Bull. 3-97/1.3.153	OJ C 167/2.6.97, Bull. 5-97/1.3.171, OJ C 210/6.7.98, Bull. 6-98/1.3.14	COM(97) 653, Bull. 12-97/1.2.260				OJ L 225/12.8.98, Bull. 7/8-98/1.3.10	
127	Proposal for a dir: informing and consulting the employees of undertakings with complex structures	OJ C 297/15.11.80, COM(80) 423	OJ C 77/29.3.82	OJ C 13/17.1.83	COM(83) 292					Withdrawal by Commission: OJ C 40/7.2.98, Bull. 1/2-98/1.3.19

° = Opinion of the Committee of the Regions.
* = Cooperation procedure used.

Health and safety at work

	Commission proposal	ESC opinion/ COR opinion°	EP first*/ sole reading	Amended Commission proposal	Council common position	EP second reading	Re-examined Commission proposal	Adoption by Council	Comments
127	Proposal for a dir. on employment relationships with regard to distortions of competition	OJ C 224/8.9.90, COM(90) 228, Bull. 1/2-98/1.3.18	OJ C 332/31.12.90, Bull. 9-90/1.2.56	OJ C 295/26.11.90, Bull. 10-90/1.3.48	OJ C 305/5.12.90, COM(90) 533, Bull. 10-90/1.3.48				Change of legal basis by Commission: COM(93) 570, withdrawal by Commission: OJ C 40/7.2.98
127	Proposal for a dir. on a European works council for informing employees	OJ C 39/15.2.91, COM(90) 581, Bull. 12-90/1.3.93	OJ C 120/6.5.91, Bull. 3-91/1.2.79	OJ C 240/16.9.91, Bull. 7/8-91/1.2.143	OJ C 336/31.12.91, COM(91) 345				Withdrawal by Commission: OJ C 40/7.2.98, Bull. 1/2-98/1.3.17
130	Dir. 98/24/EC: protection of workers from exposure to chemical agents	OJ C 165/16.6.93, COM(93) 155, Bull. 5-93/1.2.94	OJ C 34/2.2.94, Bull. 11-93/1.2.128	OJ C 128/9.5.94, Bull. 4-94/1.2.161*	OJ C 191/14.4.94, COM(94) 230, Bull. 6-94/1.2.193	OJ C 375/10.12.97, Bull. 10-97/1.2.231	OJ C 80/16.3.98, Bull. 1/2-98/1.3.20	COM(1998) 162, Bull. 3-98/1.2.16	OJ L 131/5.5.98, Bull. 4-98/1.2.14	Agreement on Council common position: Bull. 6-97/1.3.261
130	Proposal for a dir.: minimum health and safety requirements for workers at risk from explosive atmospheres	OJ C 332/9.12.95, COM(95) 310, Bull. 9-95/1.3.120	OJ C 153/28.5.96, Bull. 1/2-96/1.3.199	OJ C 198/8.7.96, Bull. 6-96/1.3.213*	OJ C 184/17.6.97, COM(97) 123, Bull. 4-97/1.3.211	Bull. 12-98				Agreement on Council common position: Bull. 12-98
131	Proposal for a dir. amending for the second time Dir. 90/394/EEC: protection of workers from the risks related to exposure to carcinogens	OJ C 123/22.4.98, COM(1998) 170, Bull. 3-98/1.2.15	OJ C 284/14.9.98, Bull. 7/8-98/1.3.18	OJ C 341/9.11.98, Bull. 10-98/1.2.15*	COM(1998) 665, Bull. 11-98/1.2.18	Bull. 12-98				Dir. to be amended: OJ L 196/26.7.90, agreement on Council common position: Bull. 12-98
131	Proposal for a dir. amending Dir. 89/655/EEC: safety and health of workers	COM(1998) 678, Bull. 11-98/1.2.20								Dir. to be amended: OJ L 393/30.12.89

TABLE II — CONSULTATION, COOPERATION 513

Social dialogue

	Commission proposal	ESC opinion/ COR opinion°	EP first*/ sole reading	Amended Commission proposal	Council common position	EP second reading	Re-examined Commission proposal	Adoption by Council	Comments
134	Proposal for a decision amending decision 70/352/EEC: setting up the Standing Committee on Employment	COM(1998) 322, Bull. 5-98/1.2.23	13.1.99°						

Implementation of the protocol on social policy

	Commission proposal	ESC opinion/ COR opinion°	EP first*/ sole reading	Amended Commission proposal	Council common position	EP second reading	Re-examined Commission proposal	Adoption by Council	Comments
137	Dir. 98/23/EC: extension of Dir. 97/81/EC on the framework agreement on part-time work to the United Kingdom	OJ C 123/22.4.98, COM(1998) 84, Bull. 3-98/1.2.17	OJ C 157/25.5.98, Bull. 3-98/1.2.17	OJ C 138/4.5.98, Bull. 4-98/1.2.17				OJ L 131/5.5.98, Bull. 4-98/1.2.17	Amended dir.: OJ L 14/20.1.98
137	Dir. 98/52/EC: extension of Dir. 97/80/EC on the burden of proof to the United Kingdom	OJ C 123/22.4.98, COM(1998) 84, Bull. 3-98/1.2.17	OJ C 157/25.5.98, Bull. 3-98/1.2.17	OJ C 167/1.6.98, Bull. 5-98/1.2.24				OJ L 205/22.7.98, Bull. 7/8-98/1.3.19	
138	Proposal for a dir. amending Dir. 93/104/EC: organisation of working time	COM(1998) 662, Bull. 11-98/1.2.19								Dir. to be amended: OJ L 307/13.12.93
138	Proposal for a dir.: organisation of working time for mobile workers	COM(1998) 662, Bull. 11-98/1.2.19								
138	Proposal for a dir.: working time of seafarers	COM(1998) 662, Bull. 11-98/1.2.19								
138	Proposal for a dir.: seafarers' hours of work on board ships using Community ports	COM(1998) 662, Bull. 11-98/1.2.19								
139	Proposal for a dir.: informing and consulting employees	OJ C 2/5.1.99, COM(1998) 612, Bull. 11-98/1.2.22								

° = Opinion of the Committee of the Regions.
* = Cooperation procedure used.

	Commission proposal	ESC opinion/ COR opinion°	EP first*/ sole reading	Amended Commission proposal	Council common position	EP second reading	Re-examined Commission proposal	Adoption by Council	Comments
142	Proposal for a decision: Community action plan for the integration of refugees	COM(1998) 731, Bull. 12-98							

Measures to promote social integration

Internal market

Free movement of goods

	Commission proposal	ESC opinion/ COR opinion°	EP first*/ sole reading	Amended Commission proposal	Council common position	EP second reading	Re-examined Commission proposal	Adoption by Council	Comments
156	Regulation (EC) No 2679/98: free movement of goods	OJ C 10/15.1.98, COM(97) 619, Bull. 11-97/1.3.33	OJ C 214/10.7.98, Bull. 4-98/1.2.21	OJ C 359/23.11.98, Bull. 11-98/1.2.26				OJ L 337/12.12.98, Bull. 12-98	
161	Regulation (EC) No 2743/98 amending Regulation (EC) No 297/95: fees payable to the European Agency for the Evaluation of Medicinal Products	COM(1998) 21, Bull. 1/2-98/1.3.39		OJ C 328/26.10.98, Bull. 10-98/1.2.23	COM(1998) 648, Bull. 11-98/1.2.32				OJ L 345/19.12.98, Bull. 12-98	Regulation to be amended: OJ L 35/15.2.95, Council agreement: Bull. 11-98/1.2.32
164	Regulation (EC) No 1139/98: labeling of foodstuffs produced from genetically modified organisms	COM(1998) 99, Bull. 1/2-98/1.3.34		OJ C 167/1.6.98, Bull. 5-98/1.2.36		Bull. 12-98			OJ L 159/3.6.98, Bull. 5-98/1.2.36	
164	Proposal for a dir. amending Dir. 85/374/EEC on liability for defective products	OJ C 337/7.11.97, COM(97) 478, Bull. 10-97/1.2.28	OJ C 95/30.3.98, Bull. 1/2-98/1.3.24	OJ C 359/23.11.98, Bull. 11-98/1.2.25						Dir. to be amended: OJ L 210/7.8.85, Agreement on Council common position: Bull. 12-98

TABLE II — CONSULTATION, COOPERATION   515

Taxation

	Commission proposal	ESC opinion/ COR opinion°	EP first*/ sole reading	Amended Commission proposal	Council common position	EP second reading	Re-examined Commission proposal	Adoption by Council	Comments
183	Proposal for a dir: common system of taxation applicable to interest and royalty payments made between companies	OJ C 123/22.4.98, COM(1998) 67, Bull. 3-98/1.2.45	OJ C 284/14.9.98, Bull. 7/8-98/1.3.31	OJ C 313/12.10.98, Bull. 9-98/1.2.27					
183	Proposal for a dir: guarantee of a minimum of effective taxation of income in the form of interest payments within the Community	OJ C 212/8.7.98, COM(1998) 295, Bull. 5-98/1.2.48							
187	Proposal for a dir: amending Dir. 77/388/EEC: rules governing the right to deduct VAT	OJ C 219/15.7.98, COM(1998) 377, Bull. 6-98/1.3.33							Dir. to be amended: OJ L 145/13.6.77
187	Proposal for a regulation: measures necessary for the application of VAT Directive 77/388/EEC	OJ C 219/15.7.98, COM(1998) 377, Bull. 6-98/1.3.33		14.1.99					
188	Proposal for a dir: amending Dir. 77/388/EEC: determination of the person liable for payment of VAT	OJ C 409/30.12.98, COM(1998) 660, Bull. 11-98/1.2.38							Dir. to be amended: OJ L 145/13.6.77
189	Dir. 98/80/EC on a VAT scheme for gold	OJ C 302/19.11.92, COM(92) 441, Bull. 10-92/1.3.47	OJ C 161/14.6.93, Bull. 4-93/1.2.23	OJ C 91/28.3.94, Bull. 3-94/1.2.31				OJ L 281/17.10.98, Bull. 10-98/1.2.31	Amended dir: OJ L 145/13.6.77
189	Proposal for a dir: amending Dir. 77/388/EEC: standard rate of VAT	OJ C 409/30.12.98, COM(1998) 693, Bull. 11-98/1.2.37							Dir. to be amended: OJ L 145/13.6.77
189	Proposal for a dir: amending Dir. 77/388/EEC: common system of VAT	OJ C 278/13.9.97, COM(97) 325, Bull. 6-97/1.3.60	OJ C 19/21.1.98, Bull. 10-97/1.2.50	OJ C 313/12.10.98, Bull. 9-98/1.2.29					Dir. to be amended: OJ L 145/13.6.77
191	Proposal for a dir: tax treatment of private motor vehicles	OJ C 108/7.4.98, COM(1998) 30, Bull. 1/2-98/1.3.52	OJ C 235/27.7.98, Bull. 5-98/1.2.50	OJ C 210/6.7.98, Bull. 6-98/1.3.34					

° = Opinion of the Committee of the Regions.
* = Cooperation procedure used.

		Commission proposal	ESC opinion/ COR opinion°	EP first*/ sole reading	Amended Commission proposal	Council common position	EP second reading	Re-examined Commission proposal	Adoption by Council	Comments
191	Proposal for a dir. amending Dirs. 92/79/EEC, 92/80/EEC and 95/59/EC: approximation of taxes (tobacco)	OJ C 203/30.6.98, COM(1998) 320, Bull. 5-98/1.2.49	OJ C 410/30.12.98, Bull. 10-98/1.2.33							Dirs to be amended: 92/79/EEC and 92/80/EEC (OJ L 316/31.10.92), 95/59/EC (OJ L 291/6.12.95)
191	Proposal for a decision: reduced rates of excise duty or exemptions from excise duty derogating from Article 8, paragraph 4 of Directive 92/81/EEC	COM(1998) 793, Bull. 12-98								
191	Proposal for a dir. amending Dir. 92/12/EEC: general arrangements, holding, movement and monitoring of products subject to excise duty	OJ C 267/3.9.97, COM(97) 326, Bull. 6-97/1.3.59	OJ C 19/21.1.98, Bull. 10-97/1.2.49	OJ C 313/12.10.98, Bull. 9-98/1.2.30						Dir. to be amended: OJ L 76/23.3.92
192	Dir. 98/94/EC amending Dir. 94/4/EC: derogation applicable to Germany and Austria	OJ C 273/2.9.98, COM(1998) 473, Bull. 7/8-98/1.3.34		Bull. 12-98					OJ L 358/31.12.98, Bull. 12-98	Amended dir.: OJ L 60/3.3.94
192	Regulation (EC) No 2744/98 amending Regulation (EC) No 355/94: derogation applicable to Germany and Austria	OJ C 273/2.9.98, COM(1998) 473, Bull. 7/8-98/1.3.34	OJ C 410/30.12.98, Bull. 10-98/1.2.32	Bull. 12-98					OJ L 345/19.12.98, Bull. 12-98	Amended regulation: OJ L 46/18.2.94

TABLE II — CONSULTATION, COOPERATION 517

Competition policy

Competition rules applying to businesses

		Commission proposal	ESC opinion/ COR opinion°	EP first*/ sole reading	Amended Commission proposal	Council common position	EP¹ second reading	Re-examined Commission proposal	Adoption by Council	Comments
201	Proposal for a regulation amending Regulation (EEC) No 19/65: application of Article 85 (3) of the Treaty to certain categories of agreements and concerted practices	OJ C 365/26.11.98, COM(1998) 546, Bull. 9-98/1.2.36								
201	Proposal for a regulation amending Regulation No 17: implementation of Articles 85 and 86 of the Treaty	OJ C 365/26.11.98, COM(1998) 546, Bull. 9-98/1.2.36								
202	Proposal for a regulation on the application of Article 85, paragraph 3 of the Treaty to certain categories of agreements and practices in the air transport sector	OJ C 165/31.5.97, COM(97) 218, Bull. 5-97/1.3.55	OJ C 95/30.3.98, Bull. 1/2-98/1.3.56	OJ C 167/1.6.98, Bull. 5-98/1.2.53						Regulation to be amended: OJ L 374/31.12.87
202	Proposal for a regulation on the application of Article 85, paragraph 3 to certain categories of agreements and concerted practices in the air transport sector	OJ C 165/31.5.97, COM(97) 218, Bull. 5-97/1.3.55	OJ C 95/30.3.98, Bull. 1/2-98/1.3.56	OJ C 167/1.6.98, Bull. 5-98/1.2.53						
215	Regulation (EC) No 1310/97 amending Regulation (EEC) No 4064/89: control of concentrations	OJ C 350/21.11.96, COM(96) 313, Bull. 7/8-96/1.3.30, Bull. 9-96/1.3.24	OJ C 56/24.2.97, Bull. 10-96/1.3.40	OJ C 362/2.12.96, Bull. 11-96/1.3.46					OJ L 180/9.7.97, OJ L 40/13.2.98, Bull. 6-97/1.3.68	Amended regulation: OJ L 395/30.12.89, Council agreement: Bull. 4-97/1.3.53

° = Opinion of the Committee of the Regions.
* = Cooperation procedure used.

	Commission proposal	ESC opinion/ COR opinion°	EP first*/ sole reading	Amended Commission proposal	Council common position	EP second reading	Re-examined Commission proposal	Adoption by Council	Comments

State aid

223	Proposal for a regulation: detailed rules for the application of Article 93 of the EC Treaty	OJ C 116/16.4.98, COM(1998) 73, Bull. 1/2-98/1.3.109	OJ C 284/14.9.98, Bull. 7/8-98/1.3.69, 13.1.99°						
223	Regulation (EC) No 994/98: application of Articles 92 and 93 of the Treaty to certain categories of horizontal State aid	OJ C 262/28.8.97, COM(97) 396, Bull. 7/8-97/1.3.77	OJ C 129/27.4.98, Bull. 1/2-98/1.3.110	OJ C 138/4.5.98, Bull. 4-98/1.2.47				OJ L 142/14.5.98, Bull. 5-98/1.2.66	
226	Regulation (EC) No 1540/98 establishing new rules on aid to shipbuilding	OJ C 114/15.4.98, COM(97) 469, Bull. 10-97/1.2.72	OJ C 129/27.4.98, Bull. 1/2-98/1.3.111	OJ C 138/4.5.98, Bull. 4-98/1.2.48				OJ L 202/18.7.98, Bull. 6-98/1.3.52	Council agreement: Bull. 5-98/1.2.67

Enterprise policy, distributive trades, tourism and cooperatives

Policy to assist SMEs and the craft sector

262	Decision 98/347/EC: financial assistance for SMEs	OJ C 108/7.4.98, COM(1998) 26, Bull. 1/2-98/1.3.141	OJ C 157/25.5.98, Bull. 3-98/1.2.81, OJ C 251/10.8.98, Bull. 5-98/1.2.86°	OJ C 138/4.5.98, Bull. 4-98/1.2.67				OJ L 155/29.5.98, Bull. 5-98/1.2.86	Council agreement: Bull. 4-98/1.2.67
262	Proposal for a decision: investments by SMEs creating employment	OJ C 146/21.5.96, COM(96) 155, Bull. 4-96/1.3.45		OJ C 362/2.12.96, Bull. 11-96/1.3.76					Withdrawal by Commission: OJ C 40/7.2.98

TABLE II — CONSULTATION, COOPERATION   519

Research and technology

Community RTD policy

	Commission proposal	ESC opinion/ COR opinion°	EP first*/ sole reading	Amended Commission proposal	Council common position	EP second reading	Re-examined Commission proposal	Adoption by Council	Comments
285	Decision: Euratom research framework programme (1998-2002)	OJ C 173/7.6.97, COM(97) 142, Bull. 4-97/1.3.114	OJ C 355/21.11.97, Bull. 10-97/1.2.98, OJ C 73/9.3.98, Bull. 12-97/1.2.113, OJ C 379/15.12.97, Bull. 9-97/1.2.52°	OJ C 14/19.1.98, Bull. 12-97/1.2.113	OJ C 291/25.9.97, COM(97) 439, Bull. 7/8-97/1.3.123, OJ C 106/6.4.98, COM(1998) 8, Bull. 1/2-98/1.3.147				Bull. 12-98	Council agreement: Bull. 1/2-98/1.3.147
286	Proposal for a decision: implementation of the fifth framework programme for research (1998-2000) (quality of life and management of living resources)	OJ C 260/18.8.98, COM(1998) 305, Bull. 6-98/1.3.72, Bull. 5-98/1.2.90	OJ C 407/28.12.98, Bull. 9-98/1.2.63	Bull. 12-98						Council agreement: Bull. 12-98
286	Proposal for a decision: implementation of the fifth framework programme for research (1998-2002) (user-friendly information society)	OJ C 260/18.8.98, COM(1998) 305, Bull. 5-98/1.2.90, Bull. 6-98/1.3.72	OJ C 407/28.12.98, Bull. 9-98/1.2.63	Bull. 12-98						Council agreement: Bull. 12-98
286	Proposal for a decision: implementation of the fifth framework programme for research (1998-2002) (competitive and sustainable growth)	OJ C 260/18.8.98, COM(1998) 305, Bull. 6-98/1.3.72, Bull. 5-98/1.2.90	OJ C 407/28.12.98, Bull. 9-98/1.2.63	Bull. 12-98						Council agreement: Bull. 12-98
286	Proposal for a decision: implementation of the fifth framework programme for research (1998-2002) (preserving the ecosystem)	OJ C 260/18.8.98, COM(1998) 305, Bull. 6-98/1.3.72, Bull. 5-98/1.2.90	OJ C 407/28.12.98, Bull. 9-98/1.2.63	Bull. 12-98						Council agreement: Bull. 12-98

° = Opinion of the Committee of the Regions.
* = Cooperation procedure used.

	Commission proposal	ESC opinion°/ COR opinion°	EP first*/ sole reading	Amended Commission proposal	Council common position	EP second reading	Re-examined Commission proposal	Adoption by Council	Comments
286	Proposal for a decision: implementation of the fifth framework programme for research (1998-2002) (international role of Community research)	OJ C 260/18.8.98, COM(1998) 305, Bull. 6-98/1.3.72, Bull. 5-98/1.2.90	OJ C 407/28.12.98, Bull. 9-98/1.2.63	Bull. 12-98						Council agreement: Bull. 12-98
286	Proposal for a decision: implementation of the fifth framework programme for research (1998-2002) (promotion of innovation and encouragement of participation of SMEs)	OJ C 260/18.8.98, COM(1998) 305, Bull. 6-98/1.3.72, Bull. 5-98/1.2.90	OJ C 407/28.12.98, Bull. 9-98/1.2.63	Bull. 12-98						Council agreement: Bull. 12-98
286	Proposal for a decision: implementation of the fifth framework programme for research (1998-2002) (improving the human research potential and the socio-economic knowledge base)	OJ C 260/18.8.98, COM(1998) 305, Bull. 6-98/1.3.72, Bull. 5-98/1.2.90	OJ C 407/28.12.98, Bull. 9-98/1.2.63	Bull. 12-98						Council agreement: Bull. 12-98
286	Proposal for a decision: implementation of the fifth framework programme for research by the JRC (1998-2002)	OJ C 260/18.8.98, COM(1998) 305, Bull. 6-98/1.3.72, Bull. 5-98/1.2.90	OJ C 407/28.12.98, Bull. 9-98/1.2.63	Bull. 12-98						Council agreement: Bull. 12-98
286	Proposal for a decision: specific programme on the preservation of the ecosystem (Euratom)	OJ C 236/28.7.98, COM(1998) 306, Bull. 6-98/1.3.72, Bull. 5-98/1.2.90	OJ C 407/28.12.98, Bull. 9-98/1.2.63	Bull. 12-98						Council agreement: Bull. 12-98
286	Proposal for a decision: specific programme for the implementation of the fifth framework programme by the JRC (1998-2002)	OJ C 236/28.7.98, COM(1998) 306, Bull. 6-98/1.3.72, Bull. 5-98/1.2.90	OJ C 407/28.12.98, Bull. 9-98/1.2.63	Bull. 12-98						Council agreement: Bull. 12-98
287	Decision: rules for the participation of companies, research centres and universities (EC)	OJ C 3/7.1.98, OJ C 40/7.2.98, COM(97) 587, Bull. 11-97/1.3.97	OJ C 214/10.7.98, Bull. 4-98/1.2.70	OJ C 195/22.6.98, Bull. 5-98/1.2.91*		OJ C 262/19.8.98, Bull. 7/8-98/1.3.121	OJ C 328/26.10.98, Bull. 10-98/1.2.66	COM(1998) 654, Bull. 11-98/1.2.73	Bull. 12-98	Agreement on Council common position: Bull. 6-98/1.3.73
287	Decision: rules for the participation of companies, research centres and universities (EAEC)	OJ C 3/7.1.98, OJ C 40/7.2.98, COM(97) 587, Bull. 11-97/1.3.97	OJ C 214/10.7.98, Bull. 4-98/1.2.70	OJ C 195/22.6.98, Bull. 5-98/1.2.91					Bull. 12-98	Council agreement: Bull. 6-98/1.3.73

TABLE II — CONSULTATION, COOPERATION   521

Implementation of the fourth framework programme

	Commission proposal	ESC opinion/ COR opinion°	EP first*/ sole reading	Amended Commission proposal	Council common position	EP second reading	Re-examined Commission proposal	Adoption by Council	Comments
306 Decision 98/585/EC: amendments to the Statutes of the Joint European Torus	OJ C 108/7.4.98, COM(1998) 13, Bull. 1/2-98/1.3.149	OJ C 214/10.7.98, Bull. 4-98/1.2.71	OJ C 313/12.10.98, OJ C 328/26.10.98, Bull. 10-98/1.2.69					OJ L 282/20.10.98, Bull. 10-98/1.2.69	

Education, vocational training, youth

General aspects

	Commission proposal	ESC opinion/ COR opinion°	EP first*/ sole reading	Amended Commission proposal	Council common position	EP second reading	Re-examined Commission proposal	Adoption by Council	Comments
333 Recommendation 98/561/EC on quality assurance in higher education	COM(97) 159, Bull. 5-97/1.3.82	OJ C 19/21.1.98, Bull. 10-97/1.2.100, OJ C 64/27.2.98, Bull. 11-97/1.3.107°	OJ C 371/8.12.97, Bull. 11-97/1.3.107*	COM(97) 707, Bull. 1/2-98/1.3.152	O° C 178/10.6.98, Bull. 1/2-98/1.3.152	OJ C 195/22.5.98, Bull. 5-98/1.2.99	COM(1998) 405, Bull. 7/8-98/1.3.125	OJ L 270/7.10.98, Bull. 9-98/1.2.65	Agreement on Council common position: Bull. 11-97/1.3.107

Vocational training

	Commission proposal	ESC opinion/ COR opinion°	EP first*/ sole reading	Amended Commission proposal	Council common position	EP second reading	Re-examined Commission proposal	Adoption by Council	Comments
336 Decision: European pathways for work-linked training, including apprenticeship	OJ C 67/3.3.98, COM(97) 572, Bull. 11-97/1.3.111	OJ C 214/10.7.98, Bull. 4-98/1.2.72, OJ C 180/11.6.98, Bull. 3-98/1.2.90°	OJ C 152/18.5.98, Bull. 4-98/1.2.72*	OJ C 218/14.7.98, COM(1998) 342, Bull. 5-98/1.2.101	OJ C 262/19.8.98, Bull. 6-98/1.3.81	OJ C 359/23.11.98, Bull. 11-98/1.2.78	COM(1998) 675, Bull. 12-98	Bull. 12-98	Council agreement: Bull. 12-98, Agreement on Council common position: Bull. 6-98/1.3.81

° = Opinion of the Committee of the Regions.
* = Cooperation procedure used.

	Commission proposal	ESC opinion/ COR opinion°	EP first*/ sole reading	Amended Commission proposal	Council common position	EP second reading	Re-examined Commission proposal	Adoption by Council	Comments

Cooperation with non-member countries

342	Proposal for a decision: third phase of the Tempus programme (2000-06)	OJ C 270/29.8.98, COM(1998) 454, Bull. 7/8-98/1.3.129	Bull. 12-98, Bull. 11-1998/1.2.83°	Bull. 12-98					

European Training Foundation

344	Proposal for a regulation: establishment of the European Training Foundation	OJ C 156/24.5.97, COM(97) 177, Bull. 4-97/1.3.118	OJ C 19/21.1.98, Bull. 10-97/1.2.105	OJ C 104/6.4.98, Bull. 3-98/1.2.92	OJ C 213/9.7.98, COM(1998) 337, Bull. 5-98/1.2.104					Regulation to be amended: OJ L 131/23.5.90, Council agreement: Bull. 10-97/1.2.105

Economic and social cohesion

Structural measures, regional policy

366	Dir. 98/9/EC: less-favoured farming areas (Denmark)	OJ C 372/9.12.97, COM(97) 575, Bull. 11-97/1.3.119		OJ C 34/2.2.98, Bull. 1/2-98/1.3.161					OJ L 22/29.1.98, Bull. 1/2-98/1.3.161	
366	Regulation (EC) No 2331/98 amending Regulation (EC) No 950/97: agricultural structures in Portugal	OJ C 281/10.9.98, COM(1998) 462		OJ C 328/26.10.98, Bull. 10-98/1.2.84					OJ L 291/30.10.98, Bull. 10-98/1.2.84	Amended regulation: OJ L 142/2.6.97

TABLE II — CONSULTATION, COOPERATION 523

		Commission proposal	ESC opinion/ COR opinion°	EP first*/ sole reading	Amended Commission proposal	Council common position	EP second reading	Re-examined Commission proposal	Adoption by Council	Comments
368	Regulation (EC) No 2468/98: criteria and arrangements regarding Community structural assistance in the fisheries and aquaculture sector (consolidated version)	COM(97) 723, Bull. 1/2-98/1.3.160	OJ C 129/27.4.98, Bull. 1/2-98/1.3.160	OJ C 313/12.10.98, Bull. 9-98/1.2.77					OJ L 312/20.11.98, Bull. 11-98/1.2.90	Regulation to be consolidated: OJ L 346/31.12.93
368	Proposal for a regulation: rules and arrangements regarding structural assistance in the fisheries sector	COM(1998) 728, Bull. 12-98								

Energy

Community energy policy: strategic challenges

		Commission proposal	ESC opinion/ COR opinion°	EP first*/ sole reading	Amended Commission proposal	Council common position	EP second reading	Re-examined Commission proposal	Adoption by Council	Comments
397	Decision: framework programme in the energy sector (1998-2002)	OJ C 46/11.2.98, COM(97) 550, Bull. 11-97/1.3.127	OJ C 214/10.7.98, Bull. 4-98/1.2.80, OJ C 315/13.10.98, Bull. 7/8-98/1.3.143°	OJ C 328/26.10.98, Bull. 10-98/1.2.90	OJ C 382/9.12.98, COM(1998) 607, Bull. 10-98/1.2.90				OJ L 7/13.1.99, Bull. 12-98	Council agreement: Bull. 11-98/1.2.96
397	Decision: multiannual programme in the energy sector (ETAP) (1998-2002)	OJ C 261/19.8.98, COM(1998) 423, Bull. 7/8-98/1.3.142		OJ C 328/26.10.98, Bull. 10-98/1.2.91	OJ C 382/9.12.98, COM(1998) 607, Bull. 10-98/1.2.91				OJ L 7/13.1.99, Bull. 12-98	Council agreement: Bull. 11-98/1.2.97

Security of supply and international cooperation

		Commission proposal	ESC opinion/ COR opinion°	EP first*/ sole reading	Amended Commission proposal	Council common position	EP second reading	Re-examined Commission proposal	Adoption by Council	Comments
400	Regulation: international cooperation in the energy sector (Synergy)	COM(97) 550	OJ C 214/10.7.98, OJ C 315, 13.10.98	OJ C 328/26.10.98, Bull. 10-98/1.2.93	OJ C 382/9.12.98, COM(1998) 607, Bull. 10-98/1.2.93				OJ L 7/13.1.99, Bull. 12-98	Council agreement: Bull. 11-98/1.2.99

° = Opinion of the Committee of the Regions.
* = Cooperation procedure used.

Energy and environment

	Commission proposal	ESC opinion/ COR opinion°	EP first*/ sole reading	Amended Commission proposal	Council common position	EP second reading	Re-examined Commission proposal	Adoption by Council	Comments
409	Decision 98/352/EC: renewable energy (Altener II)	OJ C 192/24.6.97, COM(97) 87, Bull. 3-97/1.3.94	OJ C 19/21.1.98, Bull. 10-97/1.2.127, OJ C 379/15.12.97, Bull. 9-97/1.2.71°	OJ C 358/24.11.97, Bull. 11-97/1.3.130*	OJ C 29/27.1.98, COM(97) 646, Bull. 12-97/1.2.139	OJ C 62/26.2.98, Bull. 1/2-98/1.3.169	OJ C 152/18.5.98, Bull. 4-98/1.2.84	COM(1998) 301, Bull. 5-98/1.2.118	OJ L 159/3.6.98, Bull. 5-98/1.2.118	Council agreement: Bull. 5-98/1.2.118, agreement on Council common position: Bull. 12-97/1.2.139
409	Proposal for a decision: promotion of renewable energy sources (Altener II)	COM(97) 550	OJ C 214/10.7.98, Bull. 4-98/1.2.85, OJ C 315/13.10.98, Bull. 7/8-98/1.3.146°							
411	Proposal for a decision: promotion of energy efficiency (1998-2002) (SAVE)	COM(97) 550	OJ C 214/10.7.98, Bull. 4-98/1.2.85, OJ C 315/13.10.98, Bull. 7/8-98/1.3.143°							

Individual sectors

	Commission proposal	ESC opinion/ COR opinion°	EP first*/ sole reading	Amended Commission proposal	Council common position	EP second reading	Re-examined Commission proposal	Adoption by Council	Comments
417	Dir. 98/93/EC amending Dir. 68/414/EEC: maintaining minimum stocks of petroleum products	OJ C 160/27.5.98, COM(1998) 221, Bull. 4-98/1.2.86	OJ C 407/28.12.98, Bull. 9-98/1.2.90	OJ C 359/23.11.98, Bull. 11-98/1.2.101					OJ L 358/31.12.98, Bull. 12-98	Amended dir.: OJ L 308/23.12.68, Council agreement: Bull. 11-98/1.2.101
417	Proposal for a decision: procedure for information on petroleum products	OJ C 232/24.7.98, COM(1998) 363, Bull. 6-98/1.3.97	OJ C 407/28.12.98, Bull. 9-98/1.2.89	OJ C 313/12.10.98, Bull. 9-98/1.2.89						
419	Decision: clean and efficient use of solid fuels (1998-2002) (Carnot)	COM(97) 550	OJ C 214/10.7.98, OJ C 315/13.10.98°	OJ C 328/26.10.98, Bull. 10-98/1.2.96	OJ C 382/9.12.98, COM(1998) 607, Bull. 10-98/1.2.96				OJ L 7/13.1.99, Bull. 12-98	Council agreement: Bull. 11-98/1.2.102
421	Decision: multiannual programe in the nuclear sector (SURE) (1998-2002)	OJ C 261/19.8.98, COM(1998) 423, Bull. 7/8-98/1.3.142		OJ C 328/26.10.98, Bull. 10-98/1.2.92	OJ C 382/9.12.98, COM(1998) 607, Bull. 10-98/1.2.92				OJ L 7/13.1.99, bull. 12-98	Council agreement: Bull. 11-98/1.2.98

TABLE II — CONSULTATION, COOPERATION   525

Transport

Infrastructures, traffic management and navigation systems

	Commission proposal	ESC opinion/ COR opinion°	EP first*/ sole reading	Amended Commission proposal	Council common position	EP second reading	Re-examined Commission proposal	Adoption by Council	Comments
432	Proposal for a regulation: code of conduct for the use of computer-ised reservation systems	OJ C 267/3.9.97, COM(97) 246, Bull. 7/8-97/1.3.148	OJ C 95/30.3.98, Bull. 1/2-98/1.3.172	OJ C 167/1.6.98, Bull. 5-98/1.2.126*	OJ C 240/31.7.98, COM(1998) 381, Bull. 6-98/1.3.112	OJ C 360/23.11.98, Bull. 9-98/1.2.104	Bull. 12-98			Agreement on Council common position: Bull. 6-98/1.3.112

Transport and the environment

	Commission proposal	ESC opinion/ COR opinion°	EP first*/ sole reading	Amended Commission proposal	Council common position	EP second reading	Re-examined Commission proposal	Adoption by Council	Comments
436	Dir. 98/55/EC amending Dir. 93/75/EEC: ships transporting dangerous or polluting goods	OJ C 334/8.11.96, COM(96) 455, Bull. 9-96/1.3.84	OJ C 133/28.4.97, Bull. 1/2-97/1.2.137	OJ C 150/19.5.97, Bull. 4-97/1.3.155*	OJ C 264/30.8.97, COM(97) 344, Bull. 7/8-97/1.3.157	OJ C 23/23.1.98, Bull. 12-97/1.2.152	OJ C 104/6.4.98, Bull. 3-98/1.2.123	COM(1998) 319, Bull. 5-98/1.2.131	OJ L 215/1.8.98, Bull. 7/8-98/1.3.160	Amended dir.: OJ L 247/5.10.93
436	Proposal for a dir.: transportable pressure equipment	OJ C 95/24.3.97, COM(96) 674, Bull. 1/2-97/1.2.130	OJ C 296/29.9.97, Bull. 7/8-97/1.3.147	OJ C 80/16.3.98, Bull. 1/2-98/1.3.173*	OJ C 186/16.6.98, COM(1998) 286, Bull. 5-98/1.2.125	Bull. 11-98/1.2.104				Agreement on Council common position: Bull. 10-98/1.2.97
436	Proposal for a dir.: safety advisers for the transport of dangerous goods	OJ C 148/14.5.98, COM(1998) 174, Bull. 3-98/1.2.112	OJ C 407/28.12.98, Bull. 9-98/1.2.94	OJ C 341/9.11.98, Bull. 10-98/1.2.100*	COM(1998) 803					

Multimodal transport

	Commission proposal	ESC opinion/ COR opinion°	EP first*/ sole reading	Amended Commission proposal	Council common position	EP second reading	Re-examined Commission proposal	Adoption by Council	Comments
438	Proposal for a dir. amending Dir. 92/106/EEC: common rules for combined transport of goods	OJ C 261/19.8.98, COM(1998) 414, Bull. 7/8-98/1.3.164	OJ C 410/30.12.98, Bull. 10-98/1.2.109							Dir. to be amended: OJ L 368/17.12.92

° = Opinion of the Committee of the Regions.

* = Cooperation procedure used.

	Commission proposal	ESC opinion/ COR opinion°	EP first*/ sole reading	Amended Commission proposal	Council common position	EP second reading	Re-examined Commission proposal	Adoption by Council	Comments
438	Proposal for a dir. amending Dir. 96/53/EC: maximum dimensions and weights of road vehicles	OJ C 261/19.8.98, COM(1998) 414, Bull. 7/8-98/1.3.164	OJ C 410/30.12.98, Bull. 10-98/1.2.109						Dir. to be amended: OJ L 235/17.9.96
438	Regulation (EC) No 2196/98: combined goods transport (financial assistance)	OJ C 343/15.11.96, COM(96) 335, Bull. 7/8-96/1.3.143	OJ C 89/19.3.97, Bull. 1/2-97/1.2.136, OJ C 379/15.12.97, Bull. 9-97/1.2.79°	OJ C 200/30.6.97, Bull. 6-97/1.3.171*	OJ C 364/2.12.97, COM(97) 507, Bull. 10-97/1.2.139	OJ C 161/27.5.98, Bull. 3-98/1.2.128	OJ C 226/20.7.98, Bull. 7/8-98/1.3.163	COM(1998) 519, Bull. 9-98/1.2.107	OJ L 277/14.10.98, Bull. 10-98/1.2.108

Inland transport

	Commission proposal	ESC opinion/ COR opinion°	EP first*/ sole reading	Amended Commission proposal	Council common position	EP second reading	Re-examined Commission proposal	Adoption by Council	Comments
439	Proposal for a dir. amending Dir. 91/440/EEC on the development of the Community's railways	OJ C 321/20.10.98, COM(1998) 480, Bull. 7/8-98/1.3.152							Dir. to be amended: OJ L 10/16.1.92
439	Proposal for a dir. amending Dir. 95/18/EC on the licensing of railway undertakings	OJ C 321/20.10.98, COM(1998) 480, Bull. 7/8-98/1.3.152							Dir. to be amended: OJ L 143/27.6.95
439	Proposal for a dir.: railway infrastructure, charges and safety certification	OJ C 321/20.10.98, COM(1998) 480, Bull. 7/8-98/1.3.152							Dir. to be amended: OJ L 143/27.6.95
441	Proposal for a dir. amending Dir. 93/89/EEC: charges for heavy goods vehicles	OJ C 59/26.2.97, COM(96) 331, Bull. 7/8-96/1.3.144	OJ C 206/7.7.97, Bull. 4-97/1.3.152, OJ C 116/14.4.97, Bull. 1/2-97/1.2.133°	OJ C 286/22.9.97, Bull. 7/8-97/1.3.153*	OJ C 261/19.8.98, COM(1998) 427, Bull. 7/8-98/1.3.156	18.1.99				Dir. to be amended: OJ L 279/12.11.93, agreement on Council common position: Bull. 11-98/1.2.108
442	Proposal for a dir.: roadside inspection of commercial vehicles circulating in the Community	OJ C 190/18.6.98, COM(1998) 117, Bull. 3-98/1.2.116	OJ C 407/28.12.98, Bull. 9-98/1.2.96							

TABLE II — CONSULTATION, COOPERATION 527

	Commission proposal	ESC opinion/ COR opinion°	EP first*/ sole reading	Amended Commission proposal	Council common position	EP second reading	Re-examined Commission proposal	Adoption by Council	Comments
442 Regulation (EC) No 2135/98 amending Regulation (EEC) No 3821/85: tachograph	OJ C 243/31.8.94, COM(94) 323, Bull. 7/8-94/1.2.89	OJ C 110/2.5.95, Bull. 1/2-95/1.3.90	OJ C 249/25.9.95, Bull. 7/8-95/1.3.114*	OJ C 25/31.1.96, COM(95) 550, Bull. 11-95/1.3.113	OJ C 43/9.2.98, Bull. 12-97/1.2.146	OJ C 138/4.5.98, Bull. 4-98/1.2.92	COM(1998) 355, Bull. 7/8-98/1.3.153	OJ L 274/9.10.98, Bull. 9-98/1.2.97	Amended regulation: OJ L 370/31.12.85, agreement on Council common position: Bull. 6-97/1.3.162
442 Dir. 98/76/EC amending Dir. 96/26/EC: admission to the occupation of road haulage operator and road passenger transport operator	OJ C 95/24.3.97, COM(97) 25, Bull. 1/2-97/1.2.132	OJ C 287/22.9.97, Bull. 5-97/1.3.112	OJ C 286/22.9.97, Bull. 7/8-97/1.3.150*	OJ C 324/25.10.97, COM(97) 501, Bull. 10-97/1.2.132	OJ C 161/27.5.98, Bull. 3-98/1.2.119	OJ C 210/6.7.98, Bull. 6-98/1.3.106	COM(1998) 501, Bull. 7/8-98/1.3.154	OJ L 277/14.10.98, Bull. 10-98/1.2.101	Amended dir: OJ L 124/23.5.96, agreement on Council common position: Bull. 10-97/1.2.132
444 Regulation (EC) No 2411/98: registration of vehicles	OJ C 290/24.9.97, COM(97) 366, Bull. 7/8-97/1.3.149	OJ C 95/30.3.98, Bull. 1/2-98/1.3.180	OJ C 80/16.3.98, Bull. 1/2-98/1.3.180*	OJ C 159/26.5.98, COM(1998) 227, Bull. 4-98/1.2.93	OJ C 227/20.7.98, Bull. 6-98/1.3.105	OJ C 328/26.10.98, Bull. 10-98/1.2.102		OJ L 299/10.11.98, Bull. 11-98/1.2.106	Agreement on Council common position: Bull. 3-98/1.2.118
444 Proposal for a dir: registration documents for motor vehicles	OJ C 202/2.7.97, COM(97) 248, Bull. 5-97/1.3.113	OJ C 19/21.1.98, Bull. 10-97/1.2.133	OJ C 195/22.6.98, Bull. 5-98/1.2.129*	OJ C 301/30.9.98, COM(1998) 508, Bull. 7/8-98/1.3.157	OJ C 388/14.12.98, Bull. 11-98/1.2.107				
445 Proposal for a dir: transparent system of rules for restrictions on heavy goods vehicles	OJ C 198/24.6.98, COM(1998) 115, Bull. 3-98/1.2.115	OJ C 407/28.12.98, Bull. 9-98/1.2.95	Bull. 12-98*	COM(1998) 792, Bull. 12-98					
446 Proposal for a regulation: Community fleet capacity (inland waterway transport)	OJ C 320/17.10.98, COM(1998) 541, Bull. 9-98/1.2.98	Bull. 12-98	Bull. 12-98*	COM(1998) 792, Bull. 12-98	Bull. 12-98				
446 Proposal for a dir: transport of dangerous goods by inland waterway	OJ C 267/3.9.97, COM(97) 367, Bull. 7/8-97/1.3.154	OJ C 157/25.5.98, Bull. 3-98/1.2.121	Bull. 12-98*						
446 Proposal for a dir amending Dir. 82/714/EEC: technical requirements for inland waterway vessels	OJ C 105/6.4.98, COM(97) 644, Bull. 12-97/1.2.148	OJ C 157/25.5.98, Bull. 3-98/1.2.120	OJ C 341/9.11.98, Bull. 10-98/1.2.103*						Dir. to be amended: OJ L 301/28.10.82

° = Opinion of the Committee of the Regions.

* = Cooperation procedure used.

Sea transport

	Commission proposal	ESC opinion/ COR opinion°	EP first*/ sole reading	Amended Commission proposal	Council common position	EP second reading	Re-examined Commission proposal	Adoption by Council	Comments
448 Proposal for a dir.: regular ro-ro ferry and high-speed passenger craft services	OJ C 108/7.4.98, COM(1998) 71, Bull. 1/2-98/1.3.182	OJ C 407/28.12.98, Bull. 9-98/1.2.100	OJ C 328/26.10.98, Bull. 10-98/1.2.104*	COM(1998) 636, Bull. 11-98/1.2.109	Bull. 12-98				
448 Proposal for a dir.: port reception facilities for ship-generated waste and cargo residues	OJ C 271/31.8.98, COM(1998) 452, Bull. 7/8-98/1.3.159								
448 Dir. 98/18/EC: safety of passenger ships	OJ C 238/16.8.96, COM(96) 61, Bull. 1/2-96/1.3.128	OJ C 212/22.7.96, Bull. 5-96/1.3.92	OJ C 277/23.9.96, Bull. 9-96/1.3.85*	OJ C 68/5.3.97, COM(96) 536, Bull. 11-96/1.3.123	OJ C 293/26.9.97, Bull. 6-97/1.3.164	OJ C 358/24.11.97, Bull. 11-97/1.3.135	COM(97) 716, Bull. 12-97/1.2.155	OJ L 144/15.5.98, Bull. 3-98/1.2.124	
448 Dir. 98/25/EC amending Dir. 95/21/EC: ship safety standards, pollution prevention and shipboard living and working conditions (port State control)	OJ C 264/30.8.97, COM(97) 416, Bull. 7/8-97/1.3.155	OJ C 73/9.3.98, Bull. 12-97/1.2.154	OJ C 388/22.12.97, Bull. 12-97/1.2.154*		OJ C 91/26.3.98, Bull. 1/2-98/1.3.184	OJ C 138/4.5.98		OJ L 133/7.5.98, Bull. 4-98/1.2.1995	Amended dir: OJ L 157/7.7.95, agreement on Council common position: Bull. 12-97/1.2.154
448 Dir. 98/35/EC amending Dir. 94/58/EC: training of seafarers	OJ C 367/5.12.96, COM(96) 470, Bull. 10-96/1.3.99	OJ C 206/7.7.97, Bull. 4-97/1.3.157	OJ C 182/16.6.97, Bull. 5-97/1.3.114*	OJ C 337/7.11.97, COM(97) 375, Bull. 9-97/1.2.77	OJ C 389/22.12.97, Bull. 10-97/1.2.135	OJ C 56/23.2.98, Bull. 1/2-98/1.3.181		OJ L 172/17.6.98, Bull. 5-98/1.2.131	Amended dir: OJ L 319/12.12.94, agreement on Council common position: Bull. 6-97/1.3.166
448 Dir. 98/41/EC: registration of persons on passenger ships	OJ C 31/31.1.97, COM(96) 574, Bull. 11-96/1.3.124	OJ C 206/7.7.97, Bull. 4-97/1.3.156	OJ C 182/16.6.97, Bull. 5-97/1.3.115*	OJ C 275/11.9.97, COM(97) 340, Bull. 7/8-97/1.3.156	OJ C 23/23.1.98, Bull. 12-97/1.2.151	OJ C 104/6.4.98, Bull. 3-98/1.2.122		OJ L 188/2.7.98, Bull. 6-98/1.3.107	Agreement on Council common position: Bull. 6-97/1.3.165
449 Proposal for a regulation amending Regulation (EEC) No 3577/92: maritime cabotage	OJ C 213/9.7.98, COM(1998) 251, Bull. 4-98/1.2.94	Bull. 12-98							Regulation to be amended: OJ L 364/12.12.92
449 Proposal for a dir. on manning conditions for regular passenger and ferry services	OJ C 213/9.7.98, COM(1998) 251, Bull. 4-98/1.2.94								

TABLE II — CONSULTATION, COOPERATION 529

Air transport

		Commission proposal	ESC opinion/ COR opinion°	EP first*/ sole reading	Amended Commission proposal	Council common position	EP second reading	Re-examined Commission proposal	Adoption by Council	Comments
452	Proposal for a regulation amending Regulation (EEC) No 295/91: denied-boarding compensation system in scheduled air transport	OJ C 120/18.4.98, COM(1998) 41, Bull. 1/2-98/1.3.186	OJ C 284/14.9.98, Bull. 7/8-98/1.3.161	OJ C 292/21.9.98, Bull. 7/8-98/1.3.161*	OJ C 351/18.11.98, COM(1998) 580, Bull. 10-98/1.2.107					Regulation to be amended: OJ L 36/8.2.91
452	Proposal for a dir.: airport charges	OJ C 257/22.8.97, COM(97) 154, Bull. 4-97/1.3.158	OJ C 73/9.3.98, Bull. 12-97/1.2.157, OJ C 64/27.2.98, Bull. 11-97/1.3.137°	OJ C 138/4.5.98, Bull. 4-98/1.2.96*	OJ C 319/16.10.98, COM(1998) 509, Bull. 9-98/1.2.101					
453	Proposal for a regulation amending Regulation (EEC) No 3922/91: harmonisation of technical requirements and administrative procedures in civil aviation	COM(1998) 759, Bull. 12-98								Regulation to be amended: OJ L 373/31.12.91
453	Dir. 98/20/EC amending Dir. 92/14/EEC: limitation of the operation of aircraft	OJ C 309/18.10.96, COM(96) 413, Bull. 9-96/1.3.86	OJ C 66/3.3.97, Bull. 11-96/1.3.127	OJ C 115/14.4.97, Bull. 3-97/1.3.100*	OJ C 253/19.8.97, COM(97) 253, Bull. 6-97/1.3.170	OJ C 375/10.12.97, Bull. 10-97/1.2.137	OJ C 34/2.2.98, Bull. 1/2-98/1.3.185	COM(1998) 70, Bull. 1/2-98/1.3.185	OJ L 107/7.4.98, Bull. 3-98/1.2.127	Amended Dir.: OJ L 76/23.3.92, agreement on Council common position: Bull. 3-97/1.3.100
453	Proposal for a dir.: safety assessment of third countries' aircraft using Community airports	OJ C 124/21.4.97, COM(97) 55, Bull. 1/2-97/1.2.138	OJ C 19/21.1.98, Bull. 10-97/1.2.138	OJ C 371/8.12.97, Bull. 11-97/1.3.136*	OJ C 122/21.4.98, COM(1998) 123, Bull. 3-98/1.2.125	OJ C 227/20.7.98, Bull. 6-98/1.3.109	OJ C 313/12.10.98, Bull. 9-98/1.2.103	COM(1998) 597, Bull. 10-98/1.2.106		
453	Proposal for a dir.: civil aviation cabin crews	OJ C 263/29.8.97, COM(97) 382, Bull. 7/8-97/1.3.160	OJ C 214/10.7.98, Bull. 4-98/1.2.97	OJ C 80/16.3.98, Bull. 1/2-98/1.3.187*						
454	Proposal for a dir.: registration and use of certain types of civil subsonic jet aircraft	OJ C 118/17.4.98, COM(1998) 98, Bull. 3-98/1.2.126	OJ C 284/14.9.98, Bull. 7/8-98/1.3.162	OJ C 313/12.10.98, Bull. 9-98/1.2.102*	OJ C 329/27.10.98, COM(1998) 549, Bull. 9-98/1.2.102	OJ C 404/23.12.98, Bull. 11-98/1.2.111				Agreement on Council common position: Bull. 10-98/1.2.105

° = Opinion of the Committee of the Regions.
* = Cooperation procedure used.

	Commission proposal	ESC opinion/ COR opinion°	EP first*/ sole reading	Amended Commission proposal	Council common position	EP second reading	Re-examined Commission proposal	Adoption by Council	Comments

Information society, telecommunications

Information society

	Commission proposal	ESC opinion/ COR opinion°	EP first*/ sole reading	Amended Commission proposal	Council common position	EP second reading	Re-examined Commission proposal	Adoption by Council	Comments
463	Decision 253/98/EC: multiannual programme to stimulate the establishment of the information society	OJ C 51/21.2.97, COM(96) 592, Bull. 12-96/1.3.144		OJ C 222/21.7.97, Bull. 6-97/1.3.176	OJ C 344/14.11.97, COM(97) 460, Bull. 10-97/1.2.144				OJ L 107/7.4.98, Bull. 3-98/1.2.131	Council agreement: Bull. 12-97/1.2.160

Environment

Industry and the environment

	Commission proposal	ESC opinion/ COR opinion°	EP first*/ sole reading	Amended Commission proposal	Council common position	EP second reading	Re-examined Commission proposal	Adoption by Council	Comments
487	Proposal for a dir.: limitation of volatile organic compound emissions	OJ C 99/26.3.97, COM(96) 538, Bull. 11-96/1.3.153	OJ C 287/22.9.97, Bull. 5-97/1.3.133	OJ C 34/2.2.98, Bull. 1/2-98/1.3.215*	OJ C 126/24.4.98, COM(1998) 190, Bull. 3-98/1.2.137	OJ C 248/7.8.98, Bull. 6-98/1.3.127	OJ C 341/9.11.98, Bull. 10-98/1.2.122	COM(1998) 681, Bull. 12-98		Agreement on Council common position: Bull. 3-98/1.2.137
488	Proposal for a regulation: eco-management and audit scheme (EMAS)	OJ C 400/22.12.98, COM(1998) 622, Bull. 10-98/1.2.120								
491	Dir. 98/81/EC amending Dir. 90/219/EEC on genetically modified micro-organisms	OJ C 356/22.11.97, COM(95) 640, Bull. 12-95/1.3.131	OJ C 295/7.10.96, Bull. 7/8-96/1.3.168	OJ C 115/14.4.97, Bull. 3-97/1.3.119*	OJ C 369/6.12.97, COM(97) 640, Bull. 6-97/1.3.195	OJ C 62/26.2.98, Bull. 12-97/1.2.179	OJ C 210/6.7.98, Bull. 6-98/1.3.128	COM(1998) 479, Bull. 7/8-98/1.3.203	OJ L 330/5.12.98, Bull. 10-98/1.2.124	Amended dir: OJ L 117/8.5.90
492	Proposal for a dir.: incineration of waste	OJ C 372/2.12.98, COM(1998) 558, Bull. 10-98/1.2.125								
492	Proposal for a dir.: landfill of waste	OJ C 156/24.5.97, COM(97) 105, Bull. 3-97/1.3.123	OJ C 355/21.11.97, Bull. 10-97/1.2.169, OJ C 244/11.8.97, Bull. 6-97/1.3.197°	OJ C 80/16.3.98, Bull. 1/2-98/1.3.218*	OJ C 126/24.4.98, COM(1998) 189, Bull. 3-98/1.2.140	OJ C 333/30.10.98, Bull. 6-98/1.3.130				Agreement on Council common position: Bull. 3-98/1.2.140

TABLE II — CONSULTATION, COOPERATION   531

	Commission proposal	ESC opinion/COR opinion°	EP first*/sole reading	Amended Commission proposal	Council common position	EP second reading	Re-examined Commission proposal	Adoption by Council	Comments
492	Proposal for a regulation: shipments of waste to certain non-OECD countries	COM(94) 678, Bull. 1/2-95/1.3.106	OJ C 214/10.7.98, OJ C 338/6.11.98, Bull. 4-98/1.2.107	OJ C 286/22.9.97, Bull. 7/8-97/1.3.176	COM(97) 685, Bull. 1/2-98/1.3.217	OJ C 333/30.10.98, Bull. 6-98/1.3.131			Agreement on Council common position: Bull. 12-97/1.2.183
492	Proposal for a dir.: disused vehicles	OJ C 337/7.11.97, COM(97) 358, Bull. 7/8-97/1.3.175	OJ C 129/27.4.98, Bull. 1/2-98/1.3.219						
492	Proposal for a dir. amending Dir. 94/67/EC: incineration of hazardous waste	OJ C 13/17.1.98, COM(97) 604, Bull. 11-97/1.3.155	OJ C 214/10.7.98, Bull. 4-98/1.2.108						Dir. to be amended: OJ L 365/31.12.94

Quality of the environment and natural resources

	Commission proposal	ESC opinion/COR opinion°	EP first*/sole reading	Amended Commission proposal	Council common position	EP second reading	Re-examined Commission proposal	Adoption by Council	Comments
496	Dir. 98/83/EC: quality of water intended for human consumption	OJ C 131/30.5.95, COM(94) 612, Bull. 1/2-95/1.3.107	OJ C 82/19.3.96, Bull. 12-95/1.3.134, OJ C 100/2.4.96, Bull. 9-95/1.3.89°	OJ C 20/20.1.97, Bull. 12-96/1.3.161*	OJ C 213/15.7.97, COM(97) 228, Bull. 6-97/1.3.198	OJ C 91/26.3.98, Bull. 12-97/1.2.187	OJ C 167/1.6.98, Bull. 5-98/1.2.154	COM(1998) 388, Bull. 7/8-98/1.3.192	OJ L 330/5.12.98, Bull. 11-98/1.2.129	Amended dir.: OJ L 229/30.8.80, agreement on Council common position: Bull. 10-97/1.2.170
497	Proposal for a dir.: water policy	OJ C 184/17.6.97, COM(97) 49, Bull. 1/2-97/1.2.165	OJ C 355/21.11.97, Bull. 10-97/1.2.171, OJ C 180/11.6.98, Bull. 3-98/1.2.141°		OJ C 16/20.1.98, COM(97) 614, Bull. 11-97/1.3.158, OJ C 108/7.4.98, Bull. (1998) 76, Bull. 1/2-98/1.3.221					
498	Proposal for a recommendation: the keeping of wild animals in zoos	COM(95) 619, Bull. 12-95/1.3.133	OJ C 204/15.7.96, Bull. 4-96/1.3.100	OJ C 56/23.2.98, Bull. 1/2-98/1.3.225*		OJ C 364/25.11.98, Bull. 7/8-98/1.3.194				Agreement on Council common position: Bull. 6-98/1.3.132
500	Proposal for a dir.: limit values for sulphur dioxide, oxides of nitrogen, particulate matter and lead in ambient air	OJ C 9/14.1.98, COM(97) 500, Bull. 10-97/1.2.178	OJ C 214/10.7.98, Bull. 4-98/1.2.109	OJ C 167/1.6.98, Bull. 5-98/1.2.155*	OJ C 259/18.8.98, COM(1998) 386, Bull. 7/8-98/1.3.196	OJ C 360/23.11.98, Bull. 9-98/1.2.130	14.1.99			Agreement on Council common position: Bull. 6-98/1.3.135

° = Opinion of the Committee of the Regions.

* = Cooperation procedure used.

		Commission proposal	ESC opinion/ COR opinion°	EP first*/ sole reading	Amended Commission proposal	Council common position	EP second reading	Re-examined Commission proposal	Adoption by Council	Comments
500	Proposal for a dir.: limit values for benzene and carbon monoxide in ambient air	Bull. 12-98								
501	Proposal for a dir.: sulphur content of certain liquid fuels and amendment of Dir. 93/12/EEC	OJ C 190/21.6.97, COM(97) 88, Bull. 3-97/1.3.121	OJ C 355/21.11.97, Bull. 10-97/1.2.167, OJ C 64/27.2.98, Bull. 11-97/1.3.154°	OJ C 167/1.6.98, Bull. 5-98/1.2.150*	OJ C 259/18.8.98, COM(1998) 385, Bull. 7/8-98/1.3.186	OJ C 364/25.11.98, Bull. 10-98/1.2.121				Dir. to be amended: OJ L 74/27.3.93, agreement on Council common position: Bull. 6-98/1.3.126
501	Proposal for a dir. amending Dir. 88/609/EEC: emissions of pollutants from large combustion plants	OJ C 300/29.9.98, COM(1998) 415, Bull. 7/8-98/1.3.185								Dir. to be amended: OJ L 336/7.12.88
509	Proposal for a decision amending decision 93/389/EEC: monitoring of CO_2 emissions	OJ C 314/24.10.96, COM(96) 369, Bull. 9-96/1.3.112	OJ C 89/19.3.97, Bull. 1/2-97/1.2.172	OJ C 304/6.10.97, Bull. 9-97/1.2.91*	OJ C 120/18.4.98, COM(1998) 108, Bull. 3-98/1.2.149	OJ C 333/30.10.98, Bull. 6-98/1.3.144				Decision to be amended: OJ L 167/9.7.93, agreement on Council common position: Bull. 3-98/1.2.149
509	Proposal for a decision: scheme to monitor CO_2 emissions from vehicles	OJ C 231/23.7.98, COM(1998) 348, Bull. 6-98/1.3.142	Bull. 12-98	Bull. 12-98*						Agreement on Council common position: Bull. 12-98
509	Proposal for a dir.: information on fuel economy	OJ C 305/3.10.98, COM(1998) 489, Bull. 9-98/1.2.125	Bull. 12-98	Bull. 12-98*						Agreement on Council common position: Bull. 12-98
511	Proposal for a regulation: substances that deplete the ozone layer	OJ C 286/15.9.98, COM(1998) 398, Bull. 7/8-98/1.3.198	Bull. 12-98	Bull. 12-98*						Regulation to be replaced: OJ L 333/22.12.94, agreement on Council common position: Bull. 12-98

TABLE II — CONSULTATION, COOPERATION   533

	Commission proposal	ESC opinion/ COR opinion°	EP first*/ sole reading	Amended Commission proposal	Council common position	EP second reading	Re-examined Commission proposal	Adoption by Council	Comments

Environmental instruments

	Commission proposal	ESC opinion/ COR opinion°	EP first*/ sole reading	Amended Commission proposal	Council common position	EP second reading	Re-examined Commission proposal	Adoption by Council	Comments
514	Proposal for a regulation: eco-label award scheme	OJ C 114/12.4.97, COM(96) 603, Bull. 12-96/1.3.155	OJ C 296/29.9.97, Bull. 7/8-97/1.3.172	OJ C 167/1.6.98, Bull. 5-98/1.2.158*					
516	Proposal for a regulation: financial instrument for the environment (LIFE)	COM(1998) 720, Bull. 12-98							

Civil protection

	Commission proposal	ESC opinion/ COR opinion°	EP first*/ sole reading	Amended Commission proposal	Council common position	EP second reading	Re-examined Commission proposal	Adoption by Council	Comments
526	Proposal for a decision: Comunity action programme for civil protection in relation to the environment	COM(1998) 768, Bull. 12-98							
526	Proposal for a decision: Community framework for cooperation in the field of accidental marine pollution	COM(1998) 769, Bull. 12-98							

Nuclear safety

Decommissioning of nuclear installations

	Commission proposal	ESC opinion/ COR opinion°	EP first*/ sole reading	Amended Commission proposal	Council common position	EP second reading	Re-examined Commission proposal	Adoption by Council	Comments
535	Decision 98/381/EC: construction of a shelter at Chernobyl	OJ C 364/2.12.97, COM(97) 448, Bull. 9-97/1.2.94	OJ C 138/4.5.98, Bull. 4-98/1.2.117					OJ L 171/17.6.98, Bull. 6-98/1.3.145	

° = Opinion of the Committee of the Regions.
* = Cooperation procedure used.

Agricultural policy

Quality of agricultural products

	Commission proposal	ESC opinion/ COR opinion°	EP first*/ sole reading	Amended Commission proposal	Council common position	EP second reading	Re-examined Commission proposal	Adoption by Council	Comments
562 Proposal for a regulation supplementing Regulation (EEC) No 2092/91: method of organic production and indication on agricultural products	OJ C 293/5.10.96, COM(96) 366, Bull. 7/8-96/1.3.187	OJ C 133/28.4.97, Bull. 1/2-97/1.2.187	OJ C 167/2.6.97, Bull. 5-97/1.3.147,	OJ C 61/26.2.98, COM(97) 747, Bull. 1/2-98/1.3.252					Regulation to be supplemented: OJ L 198/22.7.91

Veterinary and plant health legislation

	Commission proposal	ESC opinion/ COR opinion°	EP first*/ sole reading	Amended Commission proposal	Council common position	EP second reading	Re-examined Commission proposal	Adoption by Council	Comments
564 Dir. 98/45/EC amending Dir. 91/67/EEC on animal health conditions (aquaculture)	COM(96) 279, Bull. 6-96/1.3.161	OJ C 56/24.2.97, Bull. 10-96/1.3.133	OJ C 362/12.12.96, Bull. 11-96/1.3.170					OJ L 189/3.7.98, Bull. 6-98/1.3.160	Amended dir.: OJ L 46/19.12.91
564 Dir. 98/46/EC amending Annexes A, D and F of Dir. 64/432/EEC: intra-Community trade in bovine animals and swine	OJ C 266/3.9.97, COM(97) 404, Bull. 7/8-97/1.3.187		OJ C 14/19.1.98, Bull. 12-97/1.2.205					OJ L 198/15.7.98, Bull. 6-98/1.3.155	Dir. to be amended: OJ L 121/29.7.64
564 Dir. 98/99/EC amending Dir. 97/12/EC: health problems affecting intra-Community trade in bovine animals and swine	OJ C 217/11.7.98, COM(1998) 338, Bull. 6-98/1.3.157	OJ C 407/28.12.98, Bull. 9-98/1.2.140	OJ C 313/12.10.98, Bull. 9-98/1.2.140					OJ L 358/31.12.98, Bull. 12-98	Amended dir.: OJ L 109/25.4.97
564 Proposal for a dir. consolidating Dir. 80/217/EEC: control of swine fever	COM(95) 598, Bull. 12-95/1.3.20	OJ C 153/28.5.96, Bull. 1/2-96/1.3.23	OJ C 166/10.7.96, Bull. 5-96/1.3.125, OJ C 210/6.7.98, Bull. 6-98/1.3.158	COM(97) 724, Bull. 1/2-98/1.3.245					Dir. to be consolidated: OJ L 47/21.2.80
564 Proposal for a dir. consolidating Dir. 74/63/EEC: animal nutrition	COM(95) 598, Bull. 12-95/1.3.23	OJ C 153/28.5.96		COM(1998) 453, Bull. 7/8-98/1.3.210					Dir. to be consolidated: OJ L 38/11.2.74

TABLE II — CONSULTATION, COOPERATION 535

No.		Commission proposal	ESC opinion°/ COR opinion°	EP first*/ sole reading	Amended Commission proposal	Council common position	EP second reading	Re-examined Commission proposal	Adoption by Council	Comments
565	Dir. 98/58/EC: protection of animals kept for farming purposes	OJ C 156/23.6.92, COM(92) 192, Bull. 5-92/1.1.150	OJ C 332/16.12.92, Bull. 10-92/1.3.113	OJ C 337/21.12.92, Bull. 11-92/1.3.169					OJ L 221/8.8.98, Bull. 7/8-98/1.3.207	Council agreement: Bull. 6-98/1.3.161
565	Proposal for a dir: protection of laying hens kept in various systems of rearing	OJ C 123/22.4.98, COM(1998) 135, Bull. 3-98/1.2.165	OJ C 407/28.12.98, Bull. 9-98/1.2.141							Dir. to be repealed: OJ L 74/19.3.88
565	Proposal for a decision amending the Annex to Directive 91/628/EEC: pigs passing through staging points	OJ C 269/28.8.98, COM(1998) 478, Bull. 7/8-98/1.3.208								Dir. to be amended: OJ L 340/11.12.91
567	Proposal for a dir. amending Dirs 70/524/EEC, 95/53/EC and 95/69/EC: animal nutrition	OJ C 266/25.8.98, COM(1998) 438, Bull. 7/8-98/1.3.213	Bull. 12-98	OJ C 328/26.10.98, Bull. 10-98/1.2.143						Dirs to be amended: 70/524/EEC (OJ L 270/14.12.70), 95/53/EC (OJ L 265/8.11.95) and 95/69/EC (OJ L 332/30.12.95)
567	Dir. amending Dirs 70/524/EEC and 95/69/EC: additives in feedingstuffs	OJ C 155/20.5.98, COM(1998) 216, Bull. 4-98/1.2.123	OJ C 284/14.9.98, Bull. 7/8-98/1.3.212	OJ C 292/21.9.98, Bull. 7/8-98/1.3.212					Bull. 12-98	Dirs to be amended: 70/524/EEC (OJ L 270/24.12.70) and 95/69/EC (OJ L 332/30.12.95)
568	Proposal for a dir. consolidating Dir. 74/63/EEC: animal nutrition	COM(95) 598, Bull. 12-95/1.3.23	OJ C 153/28.5.96		COM(1998) 453, Bull. 7/8-98/1.3.210					Dir. to be consolidated: OJ L 38/11.2.74
569	Dir. 98/57/EC: control of Ralstonia solanacearum (Smith) (previously Pseudomonas)	OJ C 124/21.4.97, COM(97) 15, Bull. 1/2-97/1.2.186	OJ C 206/7.7.97, Bull. 4-97/1.3.182	OJ C 14/19.1.98, Bull. 12-97/1.2.209	OJ C 108/7.4.98, COM(1998) 57, Bull. 1/2-98/1.3.250				OJ L 235/21.8.98, Bull. 7/8-98/1.3.217	
569	Dir. 98/56/EC: marketing of ornamental plant propagating material	OJ C 50/17.2.98, COM(97) 708, Bull. 12-97/1.2.211	OJ C 157/25.5.98, Bull. 3-98/1.2.166	OJ C 104/6.4.98, Bull. 3-98/1.2.166					OJ L 226/13.8.98, Bull. 7/8-98/1.3.216	

° = Opinion of the Committee of the Regions.
* = Cooperation procedure used.

	Commission proposal	ESC opinion/ COR opinion°	EP first*/ sole reading	Amended Commission proposal	Council common position	EP second reading	Re-examined Commission proposal	Adoption by Council	Comments
569 Proposal for a dir. consolidating Dir. 66/403/EEC: marketing of seed potatoes	COM(95) 622, Bull. 12-95/1.3.24	OJ C 153/28.5.96, Bull. 1/2-96/1.3.25	OJ C 347/18.11.96, Bull. 10-96/1.3.134	COM(1998) 506, Bull. 9-98/1.2.142					Dir. to be consolidated: OJ L 125/11.7.66
569 Proposal for a dir. consolidating Dir. 66/400/EEC: marketing of beet seed	COM(95) 622, Bull. 12-95/1.3.24	OJ C 153/28.5.96, Bull. 1/2-96/1.3.25	OJ C 347/18.11.96, Bull. 10-96/1.3.134	COM(1998) 504, Bull. 9-98/1.2.142					Dir. to be consolidated: OJ L 125/11.7.66
569 Proposal for a dir. consolidating Dir. 69/208/EEC on the marketing of seed of oil and fibre plants	COM(95) 622, Bull. 12-95/1.3.24	OJ C 153/28.5.96, Bull. 1/2-96/1.3.25	OJ C 347/18.11.96, Bull. 10-96/1.3.134	COM(1998) 533, Bull. 9-98/1.2.142					Dir. to be consolidated: OJ L 169/10.7.69
569 Proposal for a dir. consolidating Dir. 70/458/EEC on the marketing of vegetable seed	COM(95) 628, Bull. 12-95/1.3.25	OJ C 153/28.5.96, Bull. 1/2-96/1.3.26	OJ C 261/9.9.96, Bull. 7/8-96/1.3.186	COM(1998) 505, Bull. 9-98/1.2.143					Dir. to be consolidated: OJ L 225/12.10.70
569 Proposal for a dir. consolidating Dir. 70/457/EEC: common catalogue of varieties of agricultural plant species	COM(95) 628, Bull. 12-95/1.3.25	OJ C 153/28.5.96, Bull. 1/2-96/1.3.26	OJ C 320/28.10.96, Bull. 9-96/1.3.121	COM(1998) 470, Bull. 7/8-98/1.3.219					Dir. to be consolidated: OJ L 225/12.10.70
569 Proposal for a dir.: introduction into the Community of organisms harmful to plants (consolidated version)	COM(97) 651, Bull. 12-97/1.2.210	OJ C 129/27.4.98, Bull. 1/2-98/1.3.251	OJ C 210/6.7.98, Bull. 6-98/1.3.162						Dir. to be consolidated: OJ L 26/31.1.77

Agricultural prices

	Commission proposal	ESC opinion/ COR opinion°	EP first*/ sole reading	Amended Commission proposal	Council common position	EP second reading	Re-examined Commission proposal	Adoption by Council	Comments
570 Regulation (EC) No 1623/98: monthly increases in the intervention price for cereals for the 1988/99 marketing year	OJ C 87/23.3.98, COM(1998) 51, Bull. 1/2-98/1.3.253	OJ C 214/10.7.98, Bull. 4-98/1.2.126	OJ C 210/6.7.98, Bull. 6-98/1.3.163					OJ L 210/28.7.98, Bull. 7/8-98/1.3.221	Council agreement: Bull. 6-98/1.3.163
570 Regulation (EC) No 1624/98 amending Regulation (EEC) No 1765/92: support for producers of certain arable crops	OJ C 87/23.3.98, COM(1998) 51, Bull. 1/2-98/1.3.253	OJ C 214/10.7.98, Bull. 4-98/1.2.126	OJ C 210/6.7.98, Bull. 6-98/1.3.163					OJ L 210/28.7.98, Bull. 7/8-98/1.1	Amended regulation: OJ L 90/14.4.93, Council agreement: Bull. 6-98/1.3.163

TABLE II — CONSULTATION, COOPERATION 537

		Commission proposal	ESC opinion/ COR opinion°	EP first*/ sole reading	Amended Commission proposal	Council common position	EP second reading	Re-examined Commission proposal	Adoption by Council	Comments
570	Regulation (EC) No 1625/98: monthly price increases for paddy rice for the 1998/99 marketing year	OJ C 87/23.3.98, COM(1998) 51, Bull. 1/2-98/1.3.253	OJ C 214/10.7.98, Bull. 4-98/1.2.126	OJ C 210/6.7.98, Bull. 6-98/1.3.163					OJ L 210/28.7.98, Bull. 7/8-98/1.3.221	Council agreement: Bull. 6-98/1.3.163
570	Regulation (EC) No 1360/98: sugar prices and the standard quality of beet for the 1998/99 marketing year	OJ C 87/23.3.98, COM(1998) 51, Bull. 1/2-98/1.3.253	OJ C 214/10.7.98, Bull. 4-98/1.2.126	OJ C 210/6.7.98, Bull. 6-98/1.3.164					OJ L 185/30.6.98, Bull. 6-98/1.3.164	
570	Regulation (EC) No 1361/98: intervention prices for white sugar, raw sugar, minimum prices for A and B beet for the 1998/99 marketing year	OJ C 87/23.3.98, COM(1998) 51, Bull. 1/2-98/1.3.253	OJ C 214/10.7.98, Bull. 4-98/1.2.126	OJ C 210/6.7.98, Bull. 6-98/1.3.164					OJ L 185/30.6.98, Bull. 6-98/1.3.164	
570	Regulation (EC) No 1626/98: amount of aid for fibre flax and hemp; finance measures to promote the use of flax fibre for the 1998/99 marketing year	OJ C 87/23.3.98, COM(1998) 51, Bull. 1/2-98/1.3.253	OJ C 214/10.7.98, Bull. 4-98/1.2.126	OJ C 210/6.7.98, Bull. 6-98/1.3.163					OJ L 210/28.7.98, Bull. 7/8-98/1.3.221	Council agreement: Bull. 6-98/1.3.163
570	Regulation (EC) No 1362/98: amount of aid for silkworms for the 1998/99 rearing year	OJ C 87/23.3.98, COM(1998) 51, Bull. 1/2-98/1.3.253	OJ C 214/10.7.98, Bull. 4-98/1.2.126	OJ C 210/6.7.98, Bull. 6-98/1.3.164					OJ L 185/30.6.98, Bull. 6-98/1.3.164	
570	Regulation (EC) No 1628/98 fixing guide prices for wine for the 1998/99 wine year	OJ C 87/23.3.98, COM(1998) 51, Bull. 1/2-98/1.3.253	OJ C 214/10.7.98, Bull. 4-98/1.2.126	OJ C 210/6.7.98, Bull. 6-98/1.3.163					OJ L 210/28.7.98, Bull. 7/8-98/1.3.221	Council agreement: Bull. 6-98/1.3.163
570	Regulation (EC) No 1627/98 amending Regulation (EEC) No 822/87: COM in wine	OJ C 87/23.3.98, COM(1998) 51, Bull. 1/2-98/1.3.253	OJ C 214/10.7.98, Bull. 4-98/1.2.126	OJ C 210/6.7.98, Bull. 6-98/1.3.163					OJ L 210/28.7.98, Bull. 7/8-98/1.3.221	Amended regulation: OJ L 84/27.3.87, Council agreement: Bull. 6-98/1.3.163
570	Regulation (EC) No 1629/98 amending Regulation (EEC) No 2322/92 (sparkling wines) and Regulation (EEC) No 4252/88 (liqueur wines)	OJ C 87/23.3.98, COM(1998) 51, Bull. 1/2-98/1.3.253	OJ C 214/10.7.98, Bull. 4-98/1.2.126	OJ C 210/6.7.98, Bull. 6-98/1.3.163					OJ L 210/28.7.98, Bull. 7/8-98/1.3.221	Amended regs: OJ L 231/13.8.92 and OJ L 373/31.12.88, Council agreement: Bull. 6-98/1.3.163

° = Opinion of the Committee of the Regions.

* = Cooperation procedure used.

	Commission proposal	ESC opinion/ COR opinion°	EP first*/ sole reading	Amended Commission proposal	Council common position	EP second reading	Re-examined Commission proposal	Adoption by Council	Comments
570 Regulation (EC) No 1630/98 amending Regulation (EEC) No 1442/88: granting of permanent abandonment premiums in respect of wine-growing areas	OJ C 87/23.3.98, COM(1998) 51, Bull. 1/2-98/1.3.253	OJ C 214/10.7.98, Bull. 4-98/1.2.126	OJ C 210/6.7.98, Bull. 6-98/1.3.163					OJ L 210/28.7.98, Bull. 7/8-98/1.3.221	Amended regulation: OJ L 132/28.5.88, Council agreement: Bull. 6-98/1.3.163
570 Regulation (EC) No 1631/98 amending Regulation (EEC) No 2392/86 establishing a vineyard register	OJ C 87/23.3.98, COM(1998) 51, Bull. 1/2-98/1.3.253	OJ C 214/10.7.98, Bull. 4-98/1.2.126	OJ C 210/6.7.98, Bull. 6-98/1.3.163					OJ L 210/28.7.98, Bull. 7/8-98/1.3.221	Amended regulation: OJ L 326/17.12.96, Council agreement: Bull. 6-98/1.3.163
570 Regulation (EC) No 1632/98: premiums for leaf tobacco by group of tobacco varieties for the 1998 harvest	OJ C 87/23.3.98, COM(1998) 51, Bull. 1/2-98/1.3.253	OJ C 214/10.7.98, Bull. 4-98/1.2.126	OJ C 210/6.7.98, Bull. 6-98/1.3.163					OJ L 210/28.7.98, Bull. 7/8-98/1.3.221	Council agreement: Bull. 6-98/1.3.163
570 Regulation (EC) No 1363/98: target price for milk and intervention prices for butter and skimmed-milk powder for the 1998/99 milk year	OJ C 87/23.3.98, COM(1998) 51, Bull. 1/2-98/1.3.253	OJ C 214/10.7.98, Bull. 4-98/1.2.126	OJ C 210/6.7.98, Bull. 6-98/1.3.164					OJ L 185/30.6.98, Bull. 6-98/1.3.164	
570 Regulation (EC) No 1364/98: intervention price for adult bovine animals for the 1998/99 marketing year	OJ C 87/23.3.98, COM(1998) 51, Bull. 1/2-98/1.3.253	OJ C 214/10.7.98, Bull. 4-98/1.2.126	OJ C 210/6.7.98, Bull. 6-98/1.3.164					OJ L 185/30.6.98, Bull. 6-98/1.3.164	
570 Regulation (EC) No 1633/98 amending Regulation (EEC) No 805/68: beef and veal	OJ C 87/23.3.98, COM(1998) 51, Bull. 1/2-98/1.3.253	OJ C 214/10.7.98, Bull. 4-98/1.2.126	OJ C 210/6.7.98, Bull. 6-98/1.3.163					OJ L 210/28.7.98, Bull. 7/8-98/1.3.221	Amended regulation: OJ L 148/28.6.68, Council agreement: Bull. 6-98/1.3.163
570 Regulation (EC) No 1634/98: basic price and seasonal adjustments to the basic price for sheepmeat for the 1998/99 marketing year	OJ C 87/23.3.98, COM(1998) 51, Bull. 1/2-98/1.3.253	OJ C 214/10.7.98, Bull. 4-98/1.2.126	OJ C 210/6.7.98, Bull. 6-98/1.3.163					OJ L 210/28.7.98, **Bull.** 7/8-98/1.3.221	
570 Regulation (EC) No 1365/98: basic price and standard quality for pig carcasses for the period 1 July 1998 to 30 June 1999	OJ C 87/23.3.98, COM(1998) 51, Bull. 1/2-98/1.3.253	OJ C 214/10.7.98, Bull. 4-98/1.2.126	OJ C 210/6.7.98, Bull. 6-98/1.3.164					OJ L 185/30.6.98, Bull. 6-98/1.3.164	

TABLE II — CONSULTATION, COOPERATION 539

Common market organisations

	Commission proposal	ESC opinion/ COR opinion°	EP first*/ sole reading	Amended Commission proposal	Council common position	EP second reading	Re-examined Commission proposal	Adoption by Council	Comments
572	Regulation (EC) No 192/98 amending Regulations 3072/95 and 2358/71: COM in rice and seeds OJ C 312/14.10.97, COM(97) 421, Bull. 9-97/1.2.101	OJ C 73/9.3.98, Bull. 12-97/1.2.214	OJ C 34/2.2.98, Bull. 1/2-98/1.3.256					OJ L 20/27.1.98, Bull. 1/2-98/1.3.256	Amended Regs.: 3072/95 (OJ L 329/30.12.95), 2358/71 (OJ L 246/5.11.71)
572	Regulation (EC) No 2072/98 amending Regulation (EC) No 3072/95: COM in rice (compensatory payment) OJ C 159/26.5.98, COM(1998) 247, Bull. 4-98/1.2.128		OJ C 292/21.9.98, Bull. 7/8-98/1.3.230					OJ L 265/30.9.98, Bull. 9-98/1.2.145	Amended regulation: OJ L 329/30.12.95
572	Regulation (EC) No 1284/98 amending Regulation (EC) No 1868/94: quota system in relation to the production of potato starch OJ C 369/6.12.97, COM(97) 576, Bull. 11-97/1.3.170	OJ C 129/27.4.98, Bull. 1/2-98/1.3.255	OJ C 195/22.6.98, Bull. 5-98/1.2.171					OJ L 178/23.6.98, Bull. 6-98/1.3.167	Amended regulation: OJ L 197/30.7.94
572	Proposal for a regulation amending Regulation (EEC) No 3508/92: applications for aid for rice producers OJ C 160/27.5.98, COM(1998) 228, Bull. 4-98/1.2.129		OJ C 313/12.10.98, Bull. 9-98/1.2.146						Regulation to be amended: OJ L 355/5.12.92
573	Proposal for a regulation amending Regulation (EEC) No 2262/84: special measures in respect of olive oil COM(1998) 631, Bull. 11-98/1.2.138							18.1.99	Regulation to be amended: OJ L 208/3.8.84
574	Proposal for a regulation amending Regulation (EEC) No 823/87: quality wines OJ C 108/7.4.98, COM(1998) 86, Bull. 1/2-98/1.3.261	OJ C 214/10.7.98, Bull. 4-98/1.2.131							Regulation to be amended: OJ L 84/27.3.87
574	Regulation (EC) No 191/98 amending Regulation (EEC) No 1142/88: permanent abandonment premiums in respect of winegrowing areas, 1988/89 to 1997/98 OJ C 312/14.10.97, COM(97) 423, Bull. 9-97/1.2.104	OJ C 73/9.3.98, Bull. 12-97/1.2.217	OJ C 34/2.2.98, Bull. 1/2-98/1.3.260					OJ L 20/27.1.98, Bull. 1/2-98/1.3.260	Amended regulation: OJ L 132/28.5.88

° = Opinion of the Committee of the Regions.
* = Cooperation procedure used.

	Commission proposal	ESC opinion/ COR opinion°	EP first*/ sole reading	Amended Commission proposal	Council common position	EP second reading	Re-examined Commission proposal	Adoption by Council	Comments
575 Proposal for a regulation amending and correcting Regulation (EC) No 2200/96: COM in fruit and vegetables	OJ C 381/8.12.98, COM(1998) 647, Bull. 11-98/1.2.140								Regulation to be amended: OJ L 297/21.11.96
575 Proposal for a regulation amending Regulation (EC) No 2202/96: aid scheme for citrus fruits producers	OJ C 381/8.12.98, COM(1998) 647, Bull. 11-98/1.2.140								Regulation to be amended: OJ L 297/21.11.96
575 Proposal for a regulation amending Regulation (EEC) No 42686 on the COM in processed products and amending Regulation (EEC) No 2658/87 on the tariff and statistical nomenclature and the common customs tariff	OJ C 272/17.10.91, COM(91) 332		22.11.91						Withdrawal by Commission: OJ C 40/7.2.98
576 Regulation (EEC) No 1637/98 amending Regulation (EEC) No 404/93: COM in bananas	OJ C 75/11.3.98, COM(1998) 4, Bull. 1/2-98/1.3.257	OJ C 235/27.7.98, Bull. 5-98/1.2.176	OJ C 210/6.7.98, Bull. 6-98/1.3.169					OJ L 210/28.7.98	Amended regulation: OJ L 47/25.2.93, Council agreement: Bull. 6-98/1.3.169
576 Proposal for a regulation: assistance for ACP suppliers of bananas	OJ C 108/7.4.98, COM(1998) 5, Bull. 1/2-98/1.3.258		OJ C 210/6.7.98, Bull. 6-98/1.3.170*		OJ C 364/25.11.98, Bull. 10-98/1.2.150				
577 Regulation (EC) No 1636/98 amending Regulation (EEC) No 2075/92: COM in tobacco	OJ C 108/7.4.98, COM(1998) 19, Bull. 1/2-98/1.3.262		OJ C 218/14.7.98, OJ C 210/6.7.98, Bull. 6-98/1.3.172					OJ L 210/28.7.98	Amended regulation: OJ L 215/30.7.92, Council agreement: Bull. 6-98/1.3.172
577 Proposal for a regulation: premiums and guarantee thresholds for leaf tobacco (1999, 2000 and 2001 harvests)	OJ C 361/24.11.98, COM(1998) 633, Bull. 11-98/1.2.139								Regulation to be amended: OJ L 215/30.7.92
578 Dir: marketing of seed	OJ C 29/31.1.94, COM(93) 598, Bull. 11-93/1.2.153	OJ C 195/18.7.94, Bull. 4-94/1.2.119	OJ C 286/22.9.97, Bull. 7/8-97/1.3.199	OJ C 53/20.2.98, COM(97) 690, Bull. 12-97/1.2.216				Bull. 12-98	Council agreement: Bull. 11-98/1.2.136

TABLE II — CONSULTATION, COOPERATION   541

	Commission proposal	ESC opinion/ COR opinion°	EP first*/ sole reading	Amended Commission proposal	Council common position	EP second reading	Re-examined Commission proposal	Adoption by Council	Comments
578	Dir.: marketing of beet seed, fodder plant seed, cereal seed, seed of oil and fibre plants and vegetable seed	OJ C 289/24.9.97, COM(97) 403, Bull. 7/8-97/1.3.200	OJ C 73/9.3.98, Bull. 12-97/1.2.215	OJ C 167/1.6.98, Bull. 5-98/1.2.172	OJ C 305/3.10.98, COM(1998) 499, Bull. 7/8-98/1.3.220				Bull. 12-98	Amended dirs: OJ L 125/11.7.66, OJ L 169/10.7.69 and OJ L 225/12.10.70
579	Regulation (EC) No 551/98 amending Regulation (EEC) No 3950/92: additional levy in the milk and milk products sector	OJ C 1/3.1.98, COM(97) 606, Bull. 11-97/1.3.173		OJ C 80/16.3.98, Bull. 1/2-98/1.3.265					OJ L 73/12.3.98, Bull. 3-98/1.2.177	Amended regulation: OJ L 405/31.12.92
579	Regulation (EC) No 2330/98: compensation to producers of milk and milk products	OJ C 273/2.9.98, COM(1998) 464, Bull. 7/8-98/1.3.233	OJ C 410/30.12.98, Bull. 10-98/1.2.148	OJ C 328/26.10.98, Bull. 10-98/1.2.148					OJ L 291/30.10.98, Bull. 10-98/1.2.148	
580	Regulation (EC) No 2071/98: measures to promote and market beef and veal and measures on labelling	OJ C 149/17.5.97, COM(97) 70, Bull. 3-97/1.3.141		OJ C 304/6.10.97, Bull. 9-97/1.2.205	OJ C 364/2.12.97, COM(97) 518, Bull. 10-97/1.2.202				OJ L 265/30.9.98, Bull. 9-98/1.2.151	
581	Regulation (EC) No 2467/98: COM in sheepmeat and goatmeat (consolidated version)	COM(1998) 88, Bull. 3-98/1.2.181	OJ C 214/10.7.98, Bull. 4-98/1.2.132	OJ C 313/12.10.98, Bull. 9-98/1.2.153					OJ L 312/20.11.98, Bull. 11-98/1.2.141	
581	Regulation (EC) No 193/98 amending Regulation (EEC) No 1323/90: specific aid for sheep and goat farming	OJ C 264/30.8.97, COM(97) 407, Bull. 7/8-97/1.3.201		OJ C 34/2.2.98, Bull. 1/2-98/1.3.264					OJ L 20/27.1.98, Bull. 1/2-98/1.3.264	Amended regulation: OJ L 132/23.5.90
582	Regulation (EC) No 2070/98 amending Regulation (EC) No 1221/97: production and marketing of honey	OJ C 222/16.7.98, COM(1998) 313, Bull. 5-98/1.2.177	OJ C 407/28.12.98, Bull. 9-98/1.2.149	OJ C 313/12.10.98, Bull. 9-98/1.2.149					OJ L 265/30.9.98, Bull. 9-98/1.2.149	Amended regulation: OJ L 173/1.7.97

° = Opinion of the Committee of the Regions.
* = Cooperation procedure used.

Other work

	Commission proposal	ESC opinion/ COR opinion°	EP first*/ sole reading	Amended Commission proposal	Council common position	EP second reading	Re-examined Commission proposal	Adoption by Council	Comments
583	Regulation (EC) No 2799/98: agrimonetary arrangements for the euro	OJ C 224/17.7.98, COM(1998) 367, Bull. 6-98/1.3.165	OJ C 407/28.12.98, Bull. 9-98/1.2.144	OJ C 328/26.10.98, Bull. 10-98/1.2.146					OJ L 349/24.12.98, Bull. 12-98	
583	Regulation (EC) No 2800/98: introduction of the euro in the CAP	OJ C 224/17.7.98, COM(1998) 367, Bull. 6-98/1.3.165	OJ C 407/28.12.98, Bull. 9-98/1.2.144	OJ C 328/26.10.98, Bull. 10-98/1.2.147					OJ L 349/24.12.98, Bull. 12-98	
585	Regulation (EC) No 2802/98: programme to supply agricultural products to the Russian Federation	OJ C 408/29.12.98, OJ C 10/14.1.99, COM(1998) 725, Bull. 12-98		Bull. 12-98					OJ L 349/24.12.98, Bull. 12-98	

Financing the common agricultural policy: the EAGGF

	Commission proposal	ESC opinion/ COR opinion°	EP first*/ sole reading	Amended Commission proposal	Council common position	EP second reading	Re-examined Commission proposal	Adoption by Council	Comments
592	Proposal for a regulation: financing of the CAP	COM(97) 607, Bull. 12-97/1.2.198	OJ C 95/30.3.98, Bull. 1/2-98/1.3.239	OJ C 138/4.5.98, Bull. 4-98/1.2.119						Regulation to be consolidated: OJ L 94/28.4.70, Withdrawal by Commission: 17.12.98

Fisheries policy

Fisheries policy

	Commission proposal	ESC opinion/ COR opinion°	EP first*/ sole reading	Amended Commission proposal	Council common position	EP second reading	Re-examined Commission proposal	Adoption by Council	Comments
596	Regulation (EC) No 1587/98: compensation for the fishing industry in very remote locations	OJ C 292/26.9.97, COM(97) 389, Bull. 7/8-97/1.3.215	OJ C 73/9.3.98, Bull. 12-97/1.2.256	OJ C 34/2.2.98, Bull. 1/2-98/1.3.276	OJ C 125/23.4.98, COM(1998) 141, Bull. 3-98/1.2.199				OJ L 208/24.7.92, Bull. 7/8-98/1.3.237	

TABLE II — CONSULTATION, COOPERATION   543

	Commission proposal	ESC opinion/ COR opinion°	EP first*/ sole reading	Amended Commission proposal	Council common position	EP second reading	Re-examined Commission proposal	Adoption by Council	Comments
597	Regulation (EC) No 2846/98 amending Regulation (EEC) No 2847/93: control system applicable to the common fisheries policy	OJ C 201/27.6.98, COM(1998) 303, Bull. 5-98/1.2.181	OJ C 407/28.12.98, Bull. 9-98/1.2.156	OJ C 328/26.10.98, Bull. 10-98/1.2.154					OJ L 358/31.12.98, Bull. 12-98	Regulation to be amended: OJ L 261/20.10.93, Council agreement: Bull. 10-98/1.2.154
598	Regulation (EC) No 1181/98 amending Regulation (EEC) 376/92: Community system for fisheries and aquaculture	OJ C 316/25.10.96, COM(96) 350, Bull. 9-96/1.3.132	OJ C 89/19.3.97, Bull. 1/2-97/1.2.202	OJ C 286/22.9.97, Bull. 7/8-97/1.3.206					OJ L 164/9.6.98, Bull. 6-98/1.3.173	Amended regulation: OJ L 389/31.12.92

Conservation and management of resources

	Commission proposal	ESC opinion/ COR opinion°	EP first*/ sole reading	Amended Commission proposal	Council common position	EP second reading	Re-examined Commission proposal	Adoption by Council	Comments
601	Regulation (EC) No 850/98 on the conservation of fishery resources (juveniles of marine organisms)	OJ C 292/4.10.96, COM(96) 296, Bull. 6-96/1.3.189	OJ C 30/30.1.97, Bull. 9-96/1.3.135	OJ C 132/28.4.97, Bull. 4-97/1.3.198	OJ C 245/12.8.97, COM(97) 258, Bull. 6-97/1.3.240				OJ L 125/27.4.98, OJ L 318/27.11.98, Bull. 3-98/1.2.190	Repealed regulation: OJ L 288/11.10.86, Council agreement: Bull. 10-97/1.2.209
601	Proposal for a regulation amending Regulation (EC) No 850/98: protection of juveniles of marine organisms	OJ C 337/5.11.98, COM(1998) 570, Bull. 10-98/1.2.156	Bull. 12-98							Regulation to be amended: OJ L 125/27.4.98
601	Proposal for a regulation amending Regulation (EC) No 850/98: protection of juveniles of marine organisms	OJ C 11/15.1.99, COM(1998) 788, Bull. 12-98								Regulation to be amended: OJ L 125/27.4.98
601	Regulation (EC) No 1239/98 amending Regulation (EC) No 894/97: technical measures for conservation of fishery resources	OJ C 118/29.4.94, COM(94) 131, Bull. 4-94/1.2.129	OJ C 393/31.12.94, Bull. 9-94/1.2.152	OJ C 305/31.10.94, Bull. 9-94/1.2.152					OJ L 171/17.6.98, Bull. 6-98/1.3.177	Amended regulation: OJ L 132/23.5.97
601	Decision: diversification out of certain fishing activities and amendment of decision 97/292/EC	COM(1998) 515, Bull. 9-98/1.2.155		Bull. 12-98					OJ L 8/14.1.99, Bull. 12-98	

° = Opinion of the Committee of the Regions.
* = Cooperation procedure used.

	Commission proposal	ESC opinion/ COR opinion°	EP first*/ sole reading	Amended Commission proposal	Council common position	EP second reading	Re-examined Commission proposal	Adoption by Council	Comments
602	Regulation (EC) No 782/98 amending Regulation (EC) No 1626/94: technical measures for the conservation of fishery resources in the Mediterranean	OJ C 337/7.11.97, COM(97) 459, Bull. 9-97/1.2.109	OJ C 73/9.3.98, Bull. 12-97/1.2.232	OJ C 104/6.4.98, Bull. 3-98/1.2.189				OJ L 113/15.4.98, Bull. 4-98/1.2.137	Amended regulation: OJ L 171/6.7.94
602	Regulation (EC) No 1434/98: herring for industrial purposes other than human consumption	OJ C 25/24.1.98, COM(97) 694, Bull. 12-97/1.2.233		OJ C 210/6.7.98, Bull. 6-98/1.3.179				OJ L 191/7.7.98, Bull. 6-98/1.3.179	
602	Regulation (EC) No 1520/98: conservation of fishery resources in the waters of the Baltic Sea, the Belts and the Sound	OJ C 4/8.1.98, COM(97) 675, Bull. 12-97/1.2.250		OJ C 210/6.7.98, Bull. 6-98/1.3.186				OJ L 201/17.7.98, Bull. 7/8-98/1.3.236	Amended regulation: OJ L 9/15.1.98
607	Regulation (EC) No 731/98 amending Regulation (EC) No 3070/95 on fishing in the north-west Atlantic	OJ C 6/10.1.98, COM(97) 671		OJ C 104/6.4.98, Bull. 3-98/1.2.197				OJ L 102/2.4.98, Bull. 3-98/1.2.197	Amended regulation: OJ L 329/30.12.95
607	Proposal for a regulation: control measures in respect of vessels of non-contracting parties to the CCAMLR (Antarctic)	OJ C 218/14.7.98, COM(1998) 362, Bull. 6-98/1.3.189		Bull. 12-98					
607	Proposal for a regulation amending Regulation (EC) No 858/94: statistical monitoring of trade in bluefin tuna	OJ C 264/21.8.98, COM(1998) 400, Bull. 6-98/1.3.192		Bull. 12-98					
607	Proposal for a regulation: ICCAT control measures	OJ C 371/1.12.98, COM(1998) 620, Bull. 10-98/1.2.159							

TABLE II — CONSULTATION, COOPERATION   545

Public health

Health monitoring

	Commission proposal	ESC opinion/ COR opinion°	EP first*/ sole reading	Amended Commission proposal	Council common position	EP second reading	Re-examined Commission proposal	Adoption by Council	Comments
622	Proposal for a recommendation: limitation of exposure of the general public to electromagnetic fields	COM(1998) 268, Bull. 6-98/1.3.197								

Audiovisual media

	Commission proposal	ESC opinion/ COR opinion°	EP first*/ sole reading	Amended Commission proposal	Council common position	EP second reading	Re-examined Commission proposal	Adoption by Council	Comments
658	Recommendation: protection of minors and human dignity in audiovisual and information services	COM(97) 570, Bull. 11-97/1.3.218	OJ C 214/10.7.98, Bull. 4-98/1.2.154, OJ C 251/10.8.98, Bull. 5-98/1.2.204°	OJ C 167/1.6.98, Bull. 5-98/1.2.204					OJ L 270/7.10.98, Bull. 9-98/1.2.176	Council agreement: Bull. 5-98/1.2.204

° = Opinion of the Committee of the Regions.
* = Cooperation procedure used.

The European Union's role in the world

Common commercial policy

Operation of the customs union, customs cooperation and mutual administrative assistance

	Commission proposal	ESC opinion/ COR opinion°	EP first*/ sole reading	Amended Commission proposal	Council common position	EP second reading	Re-examined Commission proposal	Adoption by Council	Comments
715	Proposal for a regulation: amending Regulation (EC) No 3295/94: prohibition of the release for free circulation, export, re-export or entry for a suspensive procedure of counterfeit and pirated goods	OJ C 108/7.4.98, COM(1998) 25, Bull. 1/2-98/1.4.30	OJ C 284/14.9.98, Bull. 7/8-98/1.4.28	OJ C 210/6.7.98, Bull. 6-98/1.4.37	OJ C 377/5.12.98, COM(1998) 639, Bull. 11-98/1.3.23					Regulation to be amended: OJ L 341/30.12.94

Commercial policy instruments

	Commission proposal	ESC opinion/ COR opinion°	EP first*/ sole reading	Amended Commission proposal	Council common position	EP second reading	Re-examined Commission proposal	Adoption by Council	Comments
726	Regulation (EC) No 1097/98 amending Regulation (EC) No 3448/93 on trade arrangements resulting from the processing of agricultural products	OJ C 105/11.4.96, COM(96) 49, Bull. 1/2-96/1.4.29		OJ C 347/18.11.96, Bull. 10-96/1.4.27	OJ C 123/22.4.98, COM(1998) 139, Bull. 3-98/1.3.21				OJ L 157/30.5.98, Bull. 5-98/1.3.30	Amended regulation: OJ L 318/20.12.93
727	Proposal for a regulation: Community procedure for the control of exports of dual-use goods and technology	OJ C 399/21.12.98, COM(1998) 257, Bull. 5-98/1.3.28								

Export credits

	Commission proposal	ESC opinion/ COR opinion°	EP first*/ sole reading	Amended Commission proposal	Council common position	EP second reading	Re-examined Commission proposal	Adoption by Council	Comments
731	Proposal for a decision: framework agreement (export credits)	COM(1998) 583, Bull. 11-98/1.3.34								

TABLE II — CONSULTATION, COOPERATION   547

Development policy

Overview

	Commission proposal	ESC opinion/COR opinion°	EP first*/sole reading	Amended Commission proposal	Council common position	EP second reading	Re-examined Commission proposal	Adoption by Council	Comments
750	Regulation (EC) No 2836/98: sexual equality in development co-operation	COM(97) 265, Bull. 6-97/1.4.54		OJ C 371/8.12.97, Bull. 11-97/1.4.37*	COM(1998) 82, Bull. 1/2-98/1.4.53	OJ C 204/30.6.98, Bull. 3-98/1.3.42	OJ C 313/12.10.98, Bull. 9-98/1.3.48	COM(1998) 694, Bull. 12-98	OJ L 354/30.12.98, Bull. 12-98

Generalised scheme of preferences (GSP)

	Commission proposal	ESC opinion/COR opinion°	EP first*/sole reading	Amended Commission proposal	Council common position	EP second reading	Re-examined Commission proposal	Adoption by Council	Comments
754	Regulation (EC) No 1154/98: implementation of Articles 7 and 8 of Regs (EC) Nos 3281/94 and 1256/96	OJ C 360/26.11.97, COM(97) 534, Bull. 10-97/1.3.37	OJ C 73/9.3.98, Bull. 12-97/1.3.51	OJ C 14/19.1.98, Bull. 12-97/1.3.51					OJ L 160/4.6.98, Bull. 5-98/1.3.51

Cooperation through non-governmental organisations (NGOs) and decentralised cooperation

	Commission proposal	ESC opinion/COR opinion°	EP first*/sole reading	Amended Commission proposal	Council common position	EP second reading	Re-examined Commission proposal	Adoption by Council	Comments
770	Regulation (EC) No 1658/98: co-financing operations with NGOs in the developing countries	OJ C 251/27.9.95, COM(95) 292, Bull. 7/8-95/1.4.53		OJ C 17/22.1.96, Bull. 12-95/1.4.49*		OJ C 307/8.10.97, Bull. 7/8-97/1.4.65	OJ C 14/19.1.98, Bull. 12-97/1.3.55	COM(1998) 404, Bull. 7/8-98/1.4.65	OJ L 213/30.7.98, Bull. 7/8-98/1.4.65	Agreement on Council common position: Bull. 6-97/1.4.57
770	Regulation (EC) No 1659/98: decentralised cooperation	OJ C 250/26.9.95, COM(95) 290, Bull. 7/8-95/1.4.49		OJ C 17/22.1.96, Bull. 12-95/1.4.44*		OJ C 43/9.2.98, Bull. 11-97/1.4.41	OJ C 138/4.5.98, Bull. 4-98/1.3.34	COM(1998) 408, Bull. 7/8-98/1.4.64	OJ L 213/30.7.98, Bull. 7/8-98/1.4.64	

° = Opinion of the Committee of the Regions.
* = Cooperation procedure used.

Relations with central European countries

Pre-accession strategy

	Commission proposal	ESC opinion/ COR opinion°	EP first*/ sole reading	Amended Commission proposal	Council common position	EP second reading	Re-examined Commission proposal	Adoption by Council	Comments
806	Regulation (EC) No 622/98: aid to central and east European countries which are applicants for accession	OJ C 48/13.2.98, COM(97) 634, Bull. 12-97/I.5		OJ C 104/6.4.98, Bull. 3-98/1.3.65					OJ L 85/20.3.98, Bull. 3-98/1.3.65	
809	Decision: position of the EC within the Association Council on the participation of Romania in LIFE	OJ C 122/21.4.98, COM(1998) 112, Bull. 3-98/1.3.72		OJ C 167/1.6.98, Bull. 5-98/1.3.66					Bull. 7/8-98/1.4.74	Association Council decision: 15.9.98
809	Decision: position of the EC within the Association Council on the participation of Bulgaria in cultural programmes	OJ C 182/12.6.98, COM(1998) 239, Bull. 4-98/1.3.44		OJ C 313/12.10.98, Bull. 9-98/1.2.68					Bull. 11-98/1.3.55	Association Council decision: OJ L 343/18.12.98
809	Decision of the EC-Czech Republic Association Council on participation in the Raphaël cultural programme	OJ C 182/12.6.98, COM(1998) 239, Bull. 4-98/1.3.44		OJ C 313/12.10.98, Bull. 9-98/1.2.68					Bull. 11-98/1.3.55	Association Council decision: OJ L 313/21.11.98
809	Decision 4/98 of the Association Council on the participation of Estonia in cultural programmes	OJ C 182/12.6.98, COM(1998) 239, Bull. 4-98/1.3.44		OJ C 313/12.10.98, Bull. 9-98/1.2.68					Bull. 11-98/1.3.55	Association Council decision: OJ L 307/17.11.98
809	Decision 3/98 of the Association Council on the participation of Hungary in cultural programmes	OJ C 182/12.6.98, COM(1998) 239, Bull. 4-98/1.3.44		OJ C 313/12.10.98, Bull. 9-98/1.2.68					Bull. 11-98/1.3.57	Association Council decision: OJ L 343/18.12.98
809	Decision: position of the EC within the Association Council on the participation of Lithuania in cultural programmes	OJ C 182/12.6.98, COM(1998) 239, Bull. 4-98/1.3.44		OJ C 313/12.10.98, Bull. 9-98/1.2.68					Bull. 11-98/1.3.57	Association Council decision: 22.12.98

TABLE II — CONSULTATION, COOPERATION 549

	Commission proposal	ESC opinion/ COR opinion°	EP first*/ sole reading	Amended Commission proposal	Council common position	EP second reading	Re-examined Commission proposal	Adoption by Council	Comments
809	Decision 3/98: position of the EC within the Association Council on the participation of Poland in cultural programmes OJ C 182/12.6.98, COM(1998) 239, Bull. 4-98/1.3.44		OJ C 313/12.10.98, Bull. 9-98/1.2.68					Bull. 11-98/1.3.55	Association Council decision: OJ L 315/25.11.98
809	Decision: position of the EC within the Association Council on the participation of Romania in cultural programmes OJ C 182/12.6.98, COM(1998) 239, Bull. 4-98/1.3.44		OJ C 313/12.10.98, Bull. 9-98/1.2.68					Bull. 11-98/1.3.55	Association Council decision: 14.12.98
809	Decision 3/98 of the Association Council on the participation of Latvia in the Raphael programme OJ C 215/10.7.98, COM(1998) 358, Bull. 6-98/1.4.70		OJ C 313/12.10.98, Bull. 9-98/1.3.67					Bull. 11-98/1.3.56	Association Council decision: OJ L 6/12.1.99
809	Proposal for a decision: position of the EC within the Association Council on the participation of the Slovak Republic in cultural programmes OJ C 182/12.6.98, COM(1998) 239, Bull. 4-98/1.3.44		OJ C 313/12.10.98, Bull. 9-98/1.2.68						
809	Decision 1/98: position of the EC within the Association Council on the participation of Poland in training, youth and education programmes OJ C 337/7.11.97, COM(97) 422, Bull. 9-97/1.3.39		OJ C 80/16.3.98, Bull. 1/2-98/1.4.68					Bull. 1/2-98/1.4.68	Association Council decision: OJ L 76/13.3.98
809	Decision 1/98: position of the EC within the Association Council on the participation of Slovakia in programmes in the fields of training, youth and education OJ C 337/7.11.97, COM(97) 422, Bull. 9-97/1.3.39		OJ C 80/16.3.98, Bull. 1/2-98/1.4.69					Bull. 1/2-98/1.4.69	Association Council decision: OJ L 88/24.3.98
809	Decision 3/98 of the Association Council on the participation of Estonia in Community programmes (training, youth, education) OJ C 205/1.7.98, COM(1998) 308, Bull. 5-98/1.3.69		OJ C 328/26.10.98, Bull. 10-98/1.3.59					Bull. 10-98/1.3.59	Association Council decision: OJ L 307/17.11.98
809	Decision: position of the EC within the Association Council on the participation of Latvia in Community programmes (training, youth, education) OJ C 197/23.6.98, COM(1998) 309, Bull. 5-98/1.3.69		OJ C 328/26.10.98, Bull. 10-98/1.3.59					Bull. 10-98/1.3.59	Association Council decision: OJ L 313/21.11.98

° = Opinion of the Committee of the Regions.
* = Cooperation procedure used.

		Commission proposal	ESC opinion/ COR opinion°	EP first*/ sole reading	Amended Commission proposal	Council common position	EP second reading	Re-examined Commission proposal	Adoption by Council	Comments
809	Decision 2/98 of the Association Council on the participation of Lithuania in Community programmes (training, youth, education)	OJ C 188/17.6.98, COM(1998) 310, Bull. 5-98/1.3.69		OJ C 328/26.10.98, Bull. 10-98/1.3.59					Bull. 10-98/1.3.59	Association Council decision: OJ L 307/17.11.98
809	Decision: position of the EC within the Association Council on the participation of the Czech Republic in Community programmes (training, youth, education)	OJ C 116/16.4.98, COM(1998) 93, Bull. 1/2-98/1.4.69		OJ C 292/21.9.98, Bull. 7/8-98/1.4.75						Association Council decision: 12.12.98
809	Decision: position of the EC within the Association Council on the participation of Bulgaria in youth programmes	OJ C 181/12.6.98, COM(1998) 281, Bull. 5-98/1.3.67		OJ C 328/26.10.98, Bull. 10-98/1.3.60					Bull. 10-98/1.3.60	Association Council decision: OJ L 340/16.12.98
809	Decision: position of the EC within the Association Council on the participation of Hungary in programmes connected with health and social policy	OJ C 185/15.6.98, COM(1998) 263, Bull. 5-98/1.3.68		OJ C 292/21.9.98, Bull. 7/8-98/1.4.76					Bull. 9-98/1.3.70	Association Council decision: OJ L 295/4.11.98
809	Decision: position of the EC within the Association Council on the participation of Bulgaria in programmes connected with health and social policy	OJ C 185/15.6.98, COM(1998) 263, Bull. 5-98/1.3.68		OJ C 292/21.9.98, Bull. 7/8-98/1.4.76					Bull. 11-98/1.3.60	Association Council decision: 23.11.98
809	Decision 6/98 of the Association Council on the participation of Estonia in programmes connected with health and social policy	OJ C 185/15.6.98, COM(1998) 263, Bull. 5-98/1.3.68		OJ C 292/21.9.98, Bull. 7/8-98/1.4.76					Bull. 11-98/1.3.61	Association Council decision: OJ L 343/18.12.98
809	Decision: position of the EC within the Association Council on the participation of Lithuania in programmes connected with health and social policy	OJ C 185/15.6.98, COM(1998) 263, Bull. 5-98/1.3.68		OJ C 292/21.9.98, Bull. 7/8-98/1.4.76					Bull. 11-98/1.3.60	

TABLE II — CONSULTATION, COOPERATION   551

		Commission proposal	ESC opinion/ COR opinion°	EP first*/ sole reading	Amended Commission proposal	Council common position	EP second reading	Re-examined Commission proposal	Adoption by Council	Comments
809	Decision: position of the EC within the Association Council on the participation of Romania in programmes connected with health and social policy	OJ C 185/15.6.98, COM(1998) 263, Bull. 5-98/1.3.68		OJ C 292/21.9.98, Bull. 7/8-98/1.4.76					Bull. 10-98/1.3.62	
809	Decision: conditions and procedures for the participation of Bulgaria in the third multiannual programme for SMEs	OJ C 119/17.4.98, COM(1998) 113, Bull. 3-98/1.3.70		OJ C 313/12.10.98, Bull. 9-98/1.3.69					Bull. 11-98/1.3.58	Association Council decision: 23.11.98
809	Decision 3/98 of the Association Council on the participation of the Czech Republic in the third multiannual programme for SMEs	OJ C 119/17.4.98, COM(1998) 113, Bull. 3-98/1.3.70		OJ C 313/12.10.98, Bull. 9-98/1.3.69					Bull. 11-98/1.3.58	Association Council decision: OJ L 6/12.1.99
809	Decision 5/98 of the Association Council on conditions and procedures for the participation of Estonia in the third multiannual programme for SMEs	OJ C 119/17.4.98, COM(1998) 113, Bull. 3-98/1.3.70		OJ C 313/12.10.98, Bull. 9-98/1.3.69					Bull. 11-98/1.3.59	Association Council decision: OJ L 307/17.11.98
809	Decision: conditions and procedures for the participation of Hungary in the third multiannual programme for SMEs	OJ C 119/17.4.98, COM(1998) 113, Bull. 3-98/1.3.70		OJ C 313/12.10.98, Bull. 9-98/1.3.69					Bull. 11-98/1.3.58	Association Council decision: OJ L 343/18.12.98
809	Decision: conditions and procedures for the participation of Poland in the third multiannual programme for SMEs	OJ C 119/17.4.98, COM(1998) 113, Bull. 3-98/1.3.70		OJ C 313/12.10.98, Bull. 9-98/1.3.69					Bull. 11-98/1.3.59	Association Council decision: OJ L 315/25.11.98
809	Decision: conditions and procedures for the participation of Romania in the third multiannual programme for SMEs	OJ C 119/17.4.98, COM(1998) 113, Bull. 3-98/1.3.70		OJ C 313/12.10.98, Bull. 9-98/1.3.69					Bull. 11-98/1.3.59	Association Council decision: 14.12.98
809	Decision: conditions and procedures for the participation of Slovakia in the third multiannual programme for SMEs	OJ C 119/17.4.98, COM(1998) 113, Bull. 3-98/1.3.70		OJ C 313/12.10.98, Bull. 9-98/1.3.69					Bull. 11-98/1.3.59	Association Council decision: 4.11.98

° = Opinion of the Committee of the Regions.
* = Cooperation procedure used.

	Commission proposal	ESC opinion/ COR opinion°	EP first*/ sole reading	Amended Commission proposal	Council common position	EP second reading	Re-examined Commission proposal	Adoption by Council	Comments
809	Decision: position of the EC within the Association Council on the participation of Bulgaria in SAVE II	OJ C 163/28.5.98, COM(1998) 152, Bull. 3-98/1.3.71		OJ C 167/1.6.98, Bull. 5-98/1.3.65					Bull. 12-98	Association Council decision: 11.12.98
809	Decision No 4/98 of the Association Council on the participation of Poland in SAVE II	OJ C 163/28.5.98, COM(1998) 152, Bull. 3-98/1.3.71		OJ C 167/1.6.98, Bull. 5-98/1.3.65					Bull. 9-98/1.3.71	Association Council decision: OJ L 6/12.1.99
809	Decision 4/98 of the Association Council on the participation of the Czech Republic in SAVE II	OJ C 163/28.5.98, COM(1998) 152, Bull. 3-98/1.3.71		OJ C 167/1.6.98, Bull. 5-98/1.3.65					Bull. 11-98/1.3.62	Association Council decision: OJ L 6/12.1.99
809	Decision 98/593EC: position of the EC within the Association Council on the participation of the Slovak Republic in SAVE II	OJ C 163/28.5.98, COM(1998) 152, Bull. 3-98/1.3.71		OJ C 167/1.6.98, Bull. 5-98/1.3.65					Bull. 10-98/1.3.63	Association Council decision: OJ L 284/22.10.98
809	Decision: position of the EC within the Association Council on the participation of Lithuania in SAVE II	OJ C 163/28.5.98, COM(1998) 152, Bull. 3-98/1.3.71		OJ C 167/1.6.98, Bull. 5-98/1.3.65					Bull. 9-98/1.3.71	
809	Decision: position of the EC within the Association Council on the participation of Romania in SAVE II	OJ C 163/28.5.98, COM(1998) 152, Bull. 3-98/1.3.71		OJ C 167/1.6.98, Bull. 5-98/1.3.65					Bull. 10-98/1.3.61	

Relations with Mediterranean and Middle East countries

General strategy (including follow-up to the Barcelona conference)

	Commission proposal	ESC opinion/ COR opinion°	EP first*/ sole reading	Amended Commission proposal	Council common position	EP second reading	Re-examined Commission proposal	Adoption by Council	Comments
829	Regulation (EC) No 780/98 amending Regulation (EC) No 1488/96: adoption of measures to be taken under the MEDA programme	OJ C 386/20.12.97, COM(97) 516, Bull. 11-97/1.4.75		OJ C 104/6.4.98, Bull. 3-98/1.3.99					OJ L 113/15.4.98, Bull. 4-98/1.3.61	Amended regulation: OJ L 189/30.7.96

TABLE II — CONSULTATION, COOPERATION   553

Northern Mediterranean

	Commission proposal	ESC opinion/ COR opinion°	EP first*/ sole reading	Amended Commission proposal	Council common position	EP second reading	Re-examined Commission proposal	Adoption by Council	Comments
836	Proposal for a regulation: implementation of the European strategy for the EC-Turkey customs union	OJ C 408/29.12.98, COM(1998) 600, Bull. 10-98/1.3.77							
836	Proposal for a regulation: implementation of the European strategy for economic and social development in Turkey	OJ C 408/29.12.98, COM(1998) 600, Bull. 10-98/1.3.77							
841	Council Regulation (EC) No 851/98 amending Regulation (EC) No 1628/96: aid for Bosnia-Herzegovina, Croatia, Federal Republic of Yugoslavia and the FYROM	OJ C 100/2.4.98, COM(1998) 18, Bull. 1/2-98/1.4.81		OJ C 138/4.5.98					OJ L 122/24.4.98, OJ L 152/26.5.98, Bull. 4-98/1.3.49	Amended regulation: OJ L 204/14.8.96

Mashreq countries, Palestinian Territories, Israel

	Commission proposal	ESC opinion/ COR opinion°	EP first*/ sole reading	Amended Commission proposal	Council common position	EP second reading	Re-examined Commission proposal	Adoption by Council	Comments
850	Regulation (EC) No 2824/98 amending Regulation (EC) No 1734/94 on financial and technical cooperation with the Occupied Territories	COM(97) 552, Bull. 12-97/1.3.88		OJ C 313/12.10.98, Bull. 9-98/1.3.96*		CJ C 388/14.12.98, Bull. 10-98/1.3.91	Bull. 12-98		OJ L 351/29.12.98, Bull. 12-98	Regulation to be amended: OJ L 182/16.7.94
850	Regulation (EC) No 2840/98 amending Regulation (EC) No 1734/94: financial and technical cooperation with the Occupied Territories	OJ C 253/12.8.98, COM(1998) 392, Bull. 6-98/1.4.102		OJ C 313/12.10.98, Bull. 9-98/1.3.96*		OJ C 388/14.12.98, Bull. 10-98/1.3.91	Bull. 12-98		OJ L 354/30.12.98, Bull. 12-98	Regulation to be amended: OJ L 182/16.7.94

° = Opinion of the Committee of the Regions.
* = Cooperation procedure used.

	Commission proposal	ESC opinion/ COR opinion°	EP first*/ sole reading	Amended Commission proposal	Council common position	EP second reading	Re-examined Commission proposal	Adoption by Council	Comments

Relations with the independent States of the former Soviet Union and with Mongolia

Assistance for the independent States of the former Soviet Union and for Mongolia

| 865 | Proposal for a regulation: aid to the new independent States and Mongolia | COM(1998) 753, Bull. 12-98 | | | | | | | |

Relations with the United States, Japan and the other industrialised countries

Japan

| 889 | Proposal for a regulation: promotion of exports to Japan | COM(95) 188, Bull. 5-95/1.4.93 | | | COM(1998) 722, Bull. 12-98 | | | | |

Relations with the African, Caribbean and Pacific (ACP) countries and the overseas countries and territories (OCTs)

Relations with the ACP countries

| 936 | Financial regulation applicable to financing development cooperation/fourth ACP-EEC Convention | OJ C 63/28.2.97, COM(96) 676, Bull. 12-96/1.4.101 | OJ C 80/16.3.98, Bull. 1/2-98/1.4.150 | | | | | OJ L 191/7.7.98, Bull. 6-98/1.4.147 | |
| 936 | Regulation (EC) No 1706/98: arrangements applicable to agricultural products from the ACP | OJ C 108/7.4.98, COM(1998) 11, Bull. 1/2-98/1.4.149 | OJ C 292/21.9.98, Bull. 7/8-98/1.4.131 | | | | | OJ L 215/1.8.98, OJ L 261/24.9.98, Bull. 7/8-98/1.4.131 | Repealed regulation: OJ L 84/30.3.90 |

TABLE II — CONSULTATION, COOPERATION   555

Financing Community activities, management of resources

Budget

General budget

	Commission proposal	ESC opinion/ COR opinion°	EP first*/ sole reading	Amended Commission proposal	Council common position	EP second reading	Re-examined Commission proposal	Adoption by Council	Comments
984	Proposal for a regulation: the Communities' own resources	OJ C 267/3.9.97, COM(97) 343, Bull. 7/8-97/1.6.1		OJ C 80/16.3.98, Bull. 12-98/1.6.1	OJ C 150/16.5.98, COM(1998) 209, Bull. 4-98/1.5.1					Regulation to be amended: OJ L 155/7.6.89

Financial regulations

	Commission proposal	ESC opinion/ COR opinion°	EP first*/ sole reading	Amended Commission proposal	Council common position	EP second reading	Re-examined Commission proposal	Adoption by Council	Comments
1 001	Regulation (EC) No 2458/98 amending the regulation of 21.12.77 (general budget): amendment of the financial regulation	OJ C 296/8.10.96, COM(96) 351, Bull. 7/8-96/1.6.6		OJ C 286/22.9.97, Bull. 7/8-97/1.6.7,	OJ C 359/25.11.97, COM(97) 542, Bull. 10-97/1.5.6				OJ L 320/28.11.98, Bull. 11-98/1.5.5	Amended regulation: OJ L 356/31.12.77
1 001	Regulation (EC) No 2779/98 amending the financial regulation of 21.12.77 (eighth version)	OJ C 149/15.5.98, COM(1998) 206, Bull. 4-98/1.5.10	OJ C 284/14.9.98, Bull. 7/8-98/1.6.5	OJ C 313/12.10.98, Bull. 9-98/1.5.3, Bull. 12-98	OJ C 396/19.12.98, COM(1998) 676, Bull. 11-98/1.5.6				OJ L 347/23.12.98, Bull. 12-98	
1 001	Proposal for a regulation amending the financial regulation of 21.12.77 applicable to the general budget of the EC	OJ C 89/26.3.94, COM(93) 683, Bull. 12-93/1.6.4		OJ C 128/9.5.94, Bull. 4-94/1.5.14						Withdrawal by Commission: OJ C 40/7.2.98
1 001	Proposal for a regulation amending Regulation (EC) No 40/94: Community trade mark	OJ C 335/6.11.97, COM(97) 489, Bull. 10-97/1.5.11		OJ C 104/6.4.98, Bull. 3-98/1.5.11	OJ C 194/20.6.98, COM(1998) 289, Bull. 4-98/1.5.16					Regulation to be amended: OJ L 11/14.1.94

° = Opinion of the Committee of the Regions.
* = Cooperation procedure used.

		Commission proposal	ESC opinion/ COR opinion°	EP first*/ sole reading	Amended Commission proposal	Council common position	EP second reading	Re-examined Commission proposal	Adoption by Council	Comments
1 001	Proposal for a regulation amending Regulation (EC), No 2100/94: plant variety rights	OJ C 335/6.11.97, COM(97) 489, Bull. 10-97/1.5.11		OJ C 104/6.4.98, Bull. 3-98/1.5.11	OJ C 194/20.6.98, COM(1998) 289, Bull. 4-98/1.5.16					Regulation to be amended: OJ L 277/1.9.94
1 001	Proposal for a regulation amending Regulation (EEC) No 2309/93: authorisation and supervision of medicinal products and the European Agency for the Evaluation of Medicinal Products	OJ C 335/6.11.97, COM(97) 489, Bull. 10-97/1.5.11		OJ C 104/6.4.98, Bull. 3-98/1.5.11	OJ C 194/20.6.98, COM(1998) 289, Bull. 4-98/1.5.16					Regulation to be amended: OJ L 214/24.8.93
1 001	Proposal for a regulation amending Regulation (EEC) No 1210/90 setting up a European Environment Agency and information network	OJ C 335/6.11.97, COM(97) 489, Bull. 10-97/1.5.11	OJ C 95/30.3.98, Bull. 1/2-98/1.6.9	OJ C 104/6.4.98, Bull. 3-98/1.5.11	OJ C 194/20.6.98, COM(1998) 289, Bull. 4-98/1.5.16					Regulation to be amended: OJ L 120/11.5.90
1 001	Proposal for a regulation amending Regulation (EC) No 2062/94 setting up a European Agency for Safety and Health at Work	OJ C 335/6.11.97, COM(97) 489, Bull. 10-97/1.5.11		OJ C 104/6.4.98, Bull. 3-98/1.5.11	OJ C 194/20.6.98, COM(1998) 289, Bull. 4-98/1.5.16					Regulation to be amended: OJ L 216/20.8.94
1 001	Proposal for a regulation amending Regulation (EEC) No 302/93 setting up a European Monitoring Centre on Drugs and Drug Addiction	OJ C 335/6.11.97, COM(97) 489, Bull. 10-97/1.5.11		OJ C 104/6.4.98, Bull. 3-98/1.5.11	OJ C 194/20.6.58, COM(1998) 289, Bull. 4-98/1.5.16					Regulation to be amended: OJ L 36/12.2.93
1 001	Regulation (EC) No 1572/98 amending Regulation (EEC) No 1360/90 setting up a European Training Foundation	OJ C 335/6.11.97, COM(97) 489, Bull. 10-97/1.5.11		OJ C 104/6.4.98, Bull. 3-98/1.5.11	OJ C 194/20.6.98, COM(1998) 289, Bull. 4-98/1.5.16				OJ L 206/23.7.98, Bull. 7/8-98/1.3.128	Amended regulation: OJ L 131/23.5.90
1 001	Proposal for a regulation amending Regulation (EC) No 2965/94 setting up a Translation Centre for the bodies of the Union	OJ C 335/6.11.97, COM(97) 489, Bull. 10-97/1.5.11		OJ C 104/6.4.98, Bull. 3-98/1.5.11	OJ C 194/20.6.98, COM(1998) 289, Bull. 4-98/1.5.16					Regulation to be amended: OJ L 314/7.12.94
1 001	Proposal for a regulation amending Regulation (EC) No 1035/97 setting up a European Monitoring Centre on Racism and Xenophobia	OJ C 335/6.11.97, COM(97) 489, Bull. 10-97/1.5.11		OJ C 104/6.4.98, Bull. 3-98/1.5.11	OJ C 194/20.6.98, COM(1998) 289, Bull. 4-98/1.5.16					Regulation to be amended: OJ L 151/10.6.97

TABLE II — CONSULTATION, COOPERATION 557

Protection of financial interests and the fight against fraud

General budget guarantee for borrowing and lending operations

Institutional matters

Implementing powers conferred on the Commission

	Commission proposal	ESC opinion/ COR opinion°	EP first*/ sole reading	Amended Commission proposal	Council common position	EP second reading	Re-examined Commission proposal	Adoption by Council	Comments
1 005 Proposal for a regulation: European Fraud Investigation Office	COM(1998) 717, Bull. 12-98								
1 018 Decision 98/348/EC: granting a guarantee to the EIB against losses under loans for projects in the FYROM and other countries outside the EC	COM(1998) 2, Bull. 1/2-98/1.6.6		OJ C 108/7.4.98, Bull. 4-98/1.5.14					OJ L 155/29.5.98, Bull. 5-98/1.5.4	Decision to be amended: OJ L 102/19.4.97
1 018 Decision amending Decision 97/256/EC: loans for projects in Bosnia-Herzegovina	COM(1998) 315, Bull. 5-98/1.5.5		OJ C 192/19.6.98, Bull. 10-98/1.5.10					Bull. 12-98	Decision to be amended: OJ L 102/19.4.97
1 030 Proposal for a decision: implementing powers conferred on the Commission	OJ C 279/8.9.98, COM(1998) 380, Bull. 6-98/1.9.6								

° = Opinion of the Committee of the Regions.
* = Cooperation procedure used.

Institutions

Administration and management

Staff policy and Staff Regulations

	Commission proposal	ESC opinion/ COR opinion°	EP first*/ sole reading	Amended Commission proposal	Council common position	EP second reading	Re-examined Commission proposal	Adoption by Council	Comments
1117 Proposal for a regulation amending Regulation (EEC) No 259/68: Staff Regulations of parliamentary assistants	OJ C 179/11.6.98, COM(1998) 312								Regulation to be amended: OJ L 56/4.3.68
1118 Regulation (EC) No 781/98 amending the Staff Regulations of officials: equal treatment of men and women	OJ C 104/15.4.93, COM(93) 106		OJ C 329/6.12.93, OJ C 85/17.3.97	OJ C 144/16.5.96, COM(96) 77				OJ L 113/15.4.98	
1121 Regulation (EC) No 2458/98 amending Regulation (EEC, Euratom, ECSC) No 259/68: Staff Regulations of Officials and Conditions of Employment of Other Servants with regard to the establishment of remuneration and other financial entitlements in euro	OJ C 192/19.6.98, COM(1998) 324		OJ C 313/12.10.98					OJ L 307/17.11.98	Regulation to be amended: OJ L 56/4.3.68
1127 Regulation (EC, ECSC, Euratom) No 2594/98 amending the Staff Regulations of Officials and Other Servants (weightings for third countries)	OJ C 266/25.8.98, COM(1998) 421		OJ C 313/12.10.98					OJ L 325/3.12.98	

TABLE III — INTERNATIONAL AGREEMENTS   559

Table III — International agreements procedure

	Commission recommendation	Council decision/ negotiating directives	Initials	Signature	Commission proposal/ conclusion	ESC opinion/ COR opinion°	EP opinion/ EP assent*	Council regulation (or decision) conclusion	Comments

Human rights and fundamental freedoms

Fight against racism and xenophobia

	Commission recommendation	Council decision/ negotiating directives	Initials	Signature	Commission proposal/ conclusion	ESC opinion/ COR opinion°	EP opinion/ EP assent*	Council regulation (or decision) conclusion	Comments
26 Draft EC-Council of Europe agreement on arrangements for cooperation with the European Monitoring Centre on Racism and Xenophobia		Bull. 6-97/1.2.4			OJ C 171/5.6.98, COM(1998) 255, Bull. 5-98/1.1.2		OJ C 359/23.11.98, Bull. 11-98/1.1.1	Bull. 12-98	

The Community economic and social area

Internal market

Intellectual and industrial property

	Commission recommendation	Council decision/ negotiating directives	Initials	Signature	Commission proposal/ conclusion	ESC opinion/ COR opinion°	EP opinion/ EP assent*	Council regulation (or decision) conclusion	Comments
195 Prop. for a dec.: WIPO Treaty		Bull. 3-93/1.2.33			COM(1998) 249, Bull. 4-98/1.2.39				Proposal signature: COM(97) 193, Bull. 5-97/1.3.53, Council decision concerning the signature: Bull. 7/8-97/1.3.48

° Opinion of the Committee of the Regions.
* Agreements requiring Parliament's assent.
NB: Agreements that do not require consultation of Parliament are not followed by an asterisk.

	Commission recommendation	Council decision/ negotiating directives	Initials	Signature	Commission proposal/ conclusion	ESC opinion/ COR opinion°	EP opinion/ EP assent*	Council regulation (or decision) conclusion	Comments

Data protection

	Commission recommendation	Council decision/ negotiating directives	Initials	Signature	Commission proposal/ conclusion	ESC opinion/ COR opinion°	EP opinion/ EP assent*	Council regulation (or decision) conclusion	Comments
196	Draft Council of Europe recommendation on the protection of personal data (insurance)	Bull. 7/8-98/1.3.38							
196	Draft agreement on the collection and processing of personal data on the information highway	16.1.98	23.3.98						

Competition policy

International cooperation

	Commission recommendation	Council decision/ negotiating directives	Initials	Signature	Commission proposal/ conclusion	ESC opinion/ COR opinion°	EP opinion/ EP assent*	Council regulation (or decision) conclusion	Comments
230	Dec. 98/386/EC: agreement with the United States on the application of the rules of competition	Bull. 10-96/1.3.55		Bull. 6-98/1.3.67	COM(97) 233, Bull. 6-97/1.3.116		OJ C 138/4.5.98, Bull. 4-98/1.2.60*	OJ L 173/18.6.98, Bull. 5-98/1.2.81	Entry into force: Bull. 6-98/1.3.67
230	Draft agreement with Canada on competition	Bull. 1/2-95/1.3.59			COM(1998) 352, Bull. 6-98/1.3.68				Recommendation for signature: Bull. 10-94/1.2.48

TABLE III — INTERNATIONAL AGREEMENTS 561

Industrial policy

Individual sectors

	Commission recommendation	Council decision/ negotiating directives	Initials	Signature	Commission proposal/ conclusion	ESC opinion/ COR opinion°	EP opinion/ EP assent*	Council regulation (or decision) conclusion	Comments
247					OJ C 69/7.3.96, COM(95) 723, Bull. 1/2-96/1.3.9		OJ C 371/8.12.97, Bull. 11-97/1.3.52*	OJ L 346/17.12.97, Bull. 11-97/1.3.52	Entry into force: OJ L 53/24.2.98, Bull. 3-98/1.2.47

Prop. for a dec.: accession of the EC to the 1958 revised agreement on the approval of motor vehicle equipment and parts

Research and technology

Implementation of the fourth framework programme

	Commission recommendation	Council decision/ negotiating directives	Initials	Signature	Commission proposal/ conclusion	ESC opinion/ COR opinion°	EP opinion/ EP assent*	Council regulation (or decision) conclusion	Comments
310		Bull. 5-98/1.2.95	19.6.98		OJ C 283/12.9.98, COM(1998) 457, Bull. 7/8-98/1.3.124				
311		Bull. 5-97/1.3.81			COM(97) 718, Bull. 1/2-98/1.3.150		OJ C 226/20.7.98, Bull. 7/8-98/1.3.122	OJ L 225/12.8.98, Bull. 7/8-98/1.3.122, OJ L 297/6.11.98, Bull. 11-98/1.2.75	
313	Bull. 11-97/1.3.102	Bull. 6-96/1.3.80		Bull. 12-97/1.2.114	OJ C 162/28.5.98, COM(1998) 137, Bull. 3-98/1.2.88		OJ C 328/26.10.98, Bull. 10-98/1.2.73	OJ L 284/22.10.98, Bull. 10-98/1.2.73	

310 Draft new agreement between the EC and Israel on scientific and technical cooperation

311 Reg. (EC) No.1766/98, Reg. (Euratom) No 2387/98: accession of the EC and Euratom to the Centre for Science and Technology in Ukraine

313 Agreement with the United States on scientific and technical cooperation

° Opinion of the Committee of the Regions.
* Agreements requiring Parliament's assent.
NB: Agreements that do not require consultation of Parliament are not followed by an asterisk.

	Commission recommendation	Council decision/ negotiating directives	Initials	Signature	Commission proposal/ conclusion	ESC opinion/ COR opinion°	EP opinion/ EP assent*	Council regulation (or decision) conclusion	Comments
313 Draft EC-Canada agreement on scientific and technological cooperation	Bull. 3-98/1.3.110	Bull. 6-98/1.3.77		Bull. 12-98	COM(1998) 664, Bull. 11-98/1.2.76				Commission decision on the signature: Bull. 12-98, Council decision concerning the signature: Bull. 12-1998
313 Draft amendment to the EC-Australia agreement on scientific and technical cooperation	Bull. 5-98/1.2.94	Bull. 9-98/1.2.64							
313 Draft EC-China agreement on scientific and technological cooperation	25.3.98	Bull. 6-98/1.3.78		Bull. 12-98					Recommendation for signature: Bull. 10-98/1.2.74, Council decision concerning the signature: Bull. 12-98
313 Euratom-Canada cooperation agreement on nuclear research		Bull. 7/8-97/1.3.143		Bull. 12-98	OJ C 400/22.12.98, COM(1998) 575, Bull. 10-98/1.2.94			Bull. 12-98	
313 Draft EC-Argentina agreement: scientific and technological cooperation	Bull. 10-98/1.2.72								

TABLE III — INTERNATIONAL AGREEMENTS 563

Energy

Security of supply and international cooperation

	Commission recommendation	Council decision/ negotiating directives	Initials	Signature	Commission proposal/ conclusion	ESC opinion/ COR opinion°	EP opinion/ EP assent*	Council regulation (or decision) conclusion	Comments
399 Dec. 98/181/EC, ECSC, Euratom: European Energy Charter Treaty	COM(94) 531, Bull. 11-94/1.2.94			Bull. 12-94/1.2.110	OJ C 344/6.12.94, COM(94) 405, Bull. 9-94/1.2.108, OJ C 372/28.12.94, COM(94) 557, Bull. 11-94/1.2.93, COM(95) 440, Bull. 9-95/1.3.68		OJ C 85/17.3.97, Bull. 1/2-97/1.2.124*, OJ C 18/23.1.95, Bull. 12-94/1.2.110	Bull. 5-97/1.3.104, OJ L 69/9.3.98, Bull. 9.97/1.2.72	Decision concerning the provisional application: OJ L 380/31.12.94, Bull. 12-94/1.2.110, Council decision concerning the signature: Bull. 11-94/12.93, Entry into force: Bull. 4-98/1.2.88
399 Dec. 98/537/EC on the Energy Charter (trade provisions)					COM(1998) 267, Bull. 5-98/1.2.115			OJ L 252/12.9.98, Bull. 7/8-98/1.3.144	
401 Dec. 98/367/EC: EC-Poland agreement on the oil sector					COM(97) 391, Bull. 7/8-97/1.3.144			OJ L 165/10.6.98, Bull. 11-97/1.3.131	Entry into force:; OJ L 265/30.9.98

Individual sectors

	Commission recommendation	Council decision/ negotiating directives	Initials	Signature	Commission proposal/ conclusion	ESC opinion/ COR opinion°	EP opinion/ EP assent*	Council regulation (or decision) conclusion	Comments
422 Draft EC-Japan agreement on nuclear cooperation		25.5.98							
422 Draft safeguards agreement between the EC and the IAEA (Tlatelolco):		15.9.97			COM(1998) 525, Bull. 9-98/1.2.92				
422 Draft EAEC-Ukraine agreement on nuclear energy	COM(1998) 746, Bull. 12-98								

° Opinion of the Committee of the Regions.
* Agreements requiring Parliament's assent.
NB: Agreements that do not require consultation of Parliament are not followed by an asterisk.

Transport

Infrastructures, traffic management and navigation systems

	Commission recommendation	Council decision/ negotiating directives	Initials	Signature	Commission proposal/ conclusion	ESC opinion/ COR opinion°	EP opinion/ EP assent:*	Council regulation (or decision) conclusion	Comments
432 Agreement with the ESA and the European Organisation for the Safety of Air Navigation (global navigation satellite system)		Bull. 6-96/1.3.118		Bull. 6-98/1.3.102	OJ C 337/7.11.97, COM(97) 442, Bull. 9-97/1.2.74		OJ C 138/4.5.98, Bull. 4-98/1.2.90*	Bull. 6-98/1.3.102	Recommendation for signature: Bull. 6-96/1.3.118, Council decision concerning the signature: Bull. 12-97/1.2.141

Transport and the environment

	Commission recommendation	Council decision/ negotiating directives	Initials	Signature	Commission proposal/ conclusion	ESC opinion/ COR opinion°	EP opinion/ EP assent:*	Council regulation (or decision) conclusion	Comments
436 Draft Europe Agreement on the international carriage of dangerous goods by inland waterway	COM(1998) 23, Bull. 1/2-98/1.3.191								

Air transport

	Commission recommendation	Council decision/ negotiating directives	Initials	Signature	Commission proposal/ conclusion	ESC opinion/ COR opinion°	EP opinion/ EP assent:*	Council regulation (or decision) conclusion	Comments
453 Draft accession of the Community to Eurocontrol		Bull. 6-98/1.3.113							Recommendation for signature: Bull. 11-96/1.3.126
453 Plan for setting up a European organisation for civil aviation safety		Bull. 6-98/1.3.114							Recommendation for signature: Bull. 12-96/1.3.141

TABLE III — INTERNATIONAL AGREEMENTS 565

	Commission recommendation	Council decision/ negotiating directives	Initials	Signature	Commission proposal/ conclusion	ESC opinion/ COR opinion°	EP opinion/ EP assent*	Council regulation (or decision) conclusion	Comments
International cooperation									
457 Draft EC-China agreement on maritime transport	Bull. 1/2-97/1.2.144	Bull. 1/2-98/1.3.192							
457 Draft EC-India agreement on maritime transport	Bull. 1/2-97/1.2.143	Bull. 1/2-98/1.3.193							
457 Dec. 97/863/EC: additional protocol to the transport agreement with Slovenia	22.2.95	29.6.95	9.7.96	Bull. 12-97/1.2.158	OJ C 369/7.12.96, COM(96) 544, Bull. 10-96/1.3.110		OJ C 339/10.11.97, Bull. 10-97/1.2.142*	OJ L 351/23.12.97, Bull. 12-97/1.2.158	Entry into force: OJ L 282/20.10.98, Bull. 9-98/12.109
Information society, telecommunications									
Information society									
460 Draft EC-Council of Europe cooperation agreement on the protection of privacy on the Internet	Bull. 1/2-98/1.3.210	Bull. 3-98/1.2.135							

° Opinion of the Committee of the Regions.
* Agreements requiring Parliament's assent.
NB: Agreements that do not require consultation of Parliament are not followed by an asterisk.

Environment

Industry and the environment

	Commission recommendation	Council decision/ negotiating directives	Initials	Signature	Commission proposal/ conclusion	ESC opinion/ COR opinion°	EP opinion/ EP assent*	Council regulation (or decision) conclusion	Comments
487 Dec. 98/685/EC: Convention on the Transboundary Effects of Industrial Accidents		Bull. 7/8-91/1.2.264		Bull. 3-92/1.2.130	OJ C 267/3.9.97, COM(97) 330, Bull. 6-97/1.3.194		OJ C 339/10.11.97, Bull. 10-97/1.2.168*	OJ L 326/3.12.98, Bull. 3-98/1.2.139	Proposal signature: Bull. 1/2-92/1.3.160, Council decision concerning the signature: Bull. 3-92/1.2.130
489 Draft convention: internationally traded dangerous chemicals		Bull. 3-96/1.3.119		Bull. 9-98/1.2.120	COM(1998) 437, Bull. 7/8-98/1.3.188				Recommendation for signature: Bull. 1/2-96/1.3.145, Council decision concerning the signature: Bull. 7/8-98/1.3.188
493 Draft amendment to the Basle Convention (hazardous wastes)					COM(1998) 634, Bull. 11-98/1.2.127				

Quality of the environment and natural resources

	Commission recommendation	Council decision/ negotiating directives	Initials	Signature	Commission proposal/ conclusion	ESC opinion/ COR opinion°	EP opinion/ EP assent*	Council regulation (or decision) conclusion	Comments
498 Berne Convention on the Conservation of European Wildlife and Natural Habitats	Bull. 11-97/1.3.161	Bull. 12-97/1.2.186			COM(1998) 100, Bull. 1/2-98/1.3.227		OJ C 328/25.10.98, Bull. 10-98/1.2.127	Bull. 12-98	
498 Dec. 98/145/EC on the Bonn Convention on Migratory Species					OJ C 267/3.9.97, COM(97) 349, Bull. 7/8-97/1.3.180		OJ C 339/10 11.97, Bull. 10-97/1.2.176	OJ L 46/17.2.98, Bull. 1/2-98/1.3.228	

TABLE III — INTERNATIONAL AGREEMENTS   567

	Commission recommendation	Council decision/ negotiating directives	Initials	Signature	Commission proposal/ conclusion	ESC opinion/ COR opinion³	EP opinion/ EP assent*	Council regulation (or decision) conclusion	Comments
498 Convention on the Protection of Vertebrate Animals				Bull. 2-87/2.1.94	OJ C 200/5.8.89, OJ C 266/13.9.96, COM(89) 302, COM(94) 366, COM(96) 293, Bull. 7/8-89/2.1.135, Bull. 9-94/1.2.173, Bull. 7/8-96/1.3.174	OJ C 329/30.12.89, Bull. 10-89/2.1.116	OJ C 291/20.11.89, OJ C 269/16.10.95, Bull. 10-89/2.1.116, Bull. 9-95/1.3.92	Bull. 3-98/1.2.142	
501 Dec. 98/686/EC: second protocol to the 1979 Convention on Air Pollution (reduction of sulphur emissions)	Bull. 12-92/1.3.196	Bull. 11-93/1.2.132		Bull. 6-94/1.2.175	OJ C 190/21.6.97, COM(97) 88, Bull. 3-97/1.3.122		OJ C 14/19.1.98, Bull. 12-97/1.2.182	OJ L 326/3.12.98, Bull. 3-98/1.2.138	Proposal signature: OJ C 190/21.6.97, COM(94) 177, Bull. 5-94/1.2.123, Council decision concerning the signature: Bull. 6-94/1.2.175
506 Protocol to the United Nations Framework Convention on Climate Change				Bull. 4-98/1.2.114				Bull. 3-98/1.2.147	Proposal signature: COM(1998) 96, Bull. 1/2-98/1.3.232

International cooperation

	Commission recommendation	Council decision/ negotiating directives	Initials	Signature	Commission proposal/ conclusion	ESC opinion/ COR opinion³	EP opinion/ EP assent*	Council regulation (or decision) conclusion	Comments
518 Draft convention: information from and participation by the public in environmental matters		Bull. 12-97/1.2.196		Bull. 6-98/1.3.149					Conclusions of the Council: OJ L 159/3.6.98, Bull. 6-98/1.3.149, Recommendation for signature: Bull. 11-96/1.3.147, Proposal signature: COM(1998) 344, Bull. 6-98/1.3.149

³ Opinion of the Committee of the Regions.
* Agreements requiring Parliament's assent.
NB: Agreements that do not require consultation of Parliament are not followed by an asterisk.

	Commission recommendation	Council decision/ negotiating directives	Initials	Signature	Commission proposal/ conclusion	ESC opinion/ COR opinion°	EP opinion/ EP ass:nt*	Council regulation (or decision) conclusion	Comments
518 Draft protocol to the UN-EEC Convention on Transboundary Air Pollution (persistent organic pollutants)		Bull. 10-97/1.2.181		Bull. 6-98/1.3.151					Proposal signature: Bull. 5-98/1.2.163, Council decision concerning the signature: Bull. 6-98/1.3.151
518 Draft protocol to the Convention on Long-range Transboundary Air Pollution (heavy metals)	Bull. 1/2-98/1.3.238								Proposal signature: Bull. 5-98/1.2.162, Council decision concerning the signature: Bull. 6-98/1.3.150
518 Draft protocol to the Convention on Long-range Transboundary Air Pollution (nitrogen oxides and related substances)									
518 Recommendation for a decision: persistent organic pollutants in the framework of UNEP	Bull. 9-98/1.2.118	Bull. 12-98							
519 Dec. 98/216/EC: United Nations Convention to Combat Desertification	COM(94) 373, Bull. 9-94/1.2.166	Bull. 6-94/1.2.171		Bull. 10-94/1.2.100	OJ C 299/30.9.97, COM(97) 410, Bull. 7/8-97/1.3.184		OJ C 339/10.11.97, Bull. 10-97/1.2.186*	OJ L 83/19.3.98, Bull. 3-98/1.2.155	Council decision concerning the signature: Bull. 10-94/1.2.100
519 Dec. 98/241/EC: amendment to Parcom decisions on marine pollution from land-based sources	Bull. 3-96/1.3.122	Bull. 3-96/1.3.122			OJ C 364/2.12.97, COM(97) 540, Bull. 11-97/1.3.160		OJ C 80/16.3.98, Bull.1/2-98/1.3.237	OJ L 96/28.3.98, Bull. 3-98/1.2.156	
519 Prop. for a dec.: protection of the Oder	Bull. 5-91/1.2.157	Bull. 7/8-91/1.2.278		11.4.96	COM(1998) 528, Bull. 9-98/1.2.122				Council decision concerning the signature: Bull. 7/8-92/1.3.150
520 Dec. 98/149/EC: Convention for the Protection of the Marine Environment of the North-East Atlantic	Bull. 7/8-92/1.3.153	Bull. 7/8-92/1.3.153		Bull. 9-92/1.2.102	OJ C 172/7.7.95, COM(94) 660, Bull.1/2-95/1.3.110		OJ C 89/10.4.95, Bull. 3-95/1.3.107	OJ L 104/3.4.98, Bull. 10-97/1.2.172	Proposal signature: COM(92) 322, Bull. 7/8-92/1.3.153, Council decision concerning the signature: Bull. 9-92/1.2.102, Entry into force: 25.3.98

TABLE III — INTERNATIONAL AGREEMENTS 569

	Commission recommendation	Council decision/ negotiating directives	Initials	Signature	Commission proposal/ conclusion	ESC opinion/ COR opinion°	EP opinion/ EP assent*	Council regulation (or decision) conclusion	Comments
521 Dec. 98/142/EC: EC-Canada agreement on humane animal trapping standards		Bull. 6-96/1.3.139	6.12.96, Bull. 5-97/1.3.138	Bull. 12-97/1.2.188	OJ C 95/24.3.97, COM(97) 17, Bull.1/2-97/1.2.167 OJ C 207/8.7.97, COM(97) 251, Bull. 5-97/1.3.138		OJ C 200/30.6.97, Bull. 6-97/1.3.202, OJ C 14/19.1.98, Bull. 12-97/1.2.188	OJ L 42/14.2.98, Bull.1/2-98/1.3.226	Conclusions of the Council on the draft agreement: Bull. 1/2-97/1.2.167, Council decision concerning the signature: Bull. 7/8-97/1.3.177
521 Dec. 98/142/EC: EC-Russia agreement on humane animal trapping standards		Bull. 6-96/1.3.139	17.12.96, Bull. 5-97/1.3.138	22.4.98	OJ C 95/24.3.97, COM(97) 17, Bull.1/2-97/1.2.167		OJ C 200/30.6.97, Bull. 6-97/1.3.202, OJ C 85/17.3.97, Bull.1/2-97/1.2.167	OJ L 42/14.2.98, Bull.1/2-98/1.3.226	Proposal signature: OJ C 95/24.3.97, COM(97) 17, Bull. 1/2-97/1.2.167, Council decision concerning the signature: Bull. 7/8-97/1.3.177, Adoption by Commission of amended proposal: OJ C 207/8.7.97, COM(97) 251, Bull. 5-97/1.3.138
521 Dec. 98/487/EC: EC-USA agreement on humane animal trapping standards		Bull. 6-96/1.3.139		Bull. 12-97/1.2.189	OJ C 32/30.1.98, COM(97) 726, Bull. 12-97/1.2.189		OJ C 210/6.7.98, Bull. 6-98/1.3.133	OJ L 219/7.8.98, Bull. 7/8-98/1.3.195	Signature of an agreed minute: 7.7.98

° Opinion of the Committee of the Regions.
* Agreements requiring Parliament's assent.
NB: Agreements that do not require consultation of Parliament are not followed by an asterisk.

Nuclear safety

International action

	Commission recommendation	Council decision/ negotiating directives	Initials	Signature	Commission proposal/ conclusion	ESC opinion/ COR opinion°	EP opinion/ EP assent*	Council regulation (or decision) conclusion	Comments
537	Convention on Nuclear Safety			Bull. 9-94/1.2.177	COM(94) 362, Bull. 9-94/1.2.177			Bull. 12-98	Recommendation for signature: Bull. 9-93/1.2.112
539	Draft agreement on cooperation between the EAEC and the Russian Federation (nuclear fusion)	Bull. 6-91/1.2.99			Bull. 9-92/1.2.74				Recommendation for signature: Bull. 7/8-90/1.3.302
539	Draft agreement with Ukraine on nuclear cooperation	Bull. 6-95/1.3.119							Recommendation for signature: Bull. 7/8-94/1.2.85
539	Draft agreement with Kazakhstan on nuclear cooperation	Bull. 6-95/1.3.119			COM(96) 572, Bull. 11-96/1.3.113			26.10.98	Recommendation for signature: Bull. 7/8-94/1.2.85

Euratom safeguards

	Commission recommendation	Council decision/ negotiating directives	Initials	Signature	Commission proposal/ conclusion	ESC opinion/ COR opinion°	EP opinion/ EP assent*	Council regulation (or decision) conclusion	Comments
542	Protocols on international nuclear guarantees (IAEC '93-2')	15.7.97			Bull. 9-98/1.2.91	COM(1998) 314, Bull. 5-98/1.2.122			Bull. 6-98/1.3.99	

TABLE III — INTERNATIONAL AGREEMENTS 571

Agricultural policy

Veterinary and plant-health legislation

	Commission recommendation	Council decision/ negotiating directives	Initials	Signature	Commission proposal/ conclusion	ESC opinion/ COR opinion°	EP opinion/ EP assent*	Council regulation (or decision) conclusion	Comments
566 Draft EC-United States agreement on sanitary measures for trade in live animals and animal products		Bull. 1/2-95/1.3.10			COM(97) 566, Bull. 11-97/1.3.166			OJ L 118/21.4.98, Bull. 3-98/1.2.167	Declaration of the Council: OJ C 122/21.4.98 and OJ C 136/1.5.98
566 Draft EC-Canada agreement on sanitary measures for trade in live animals		Bull. 1/2-95/1.3.10			COM(1998) 293, Bull. 5-98/1.2.169			Bull. 12-98	Entry into force: Bull. 12-98

Common market organisations

	Commission recommendation	Council decision/ negotiating directives	Initials	Signature	Commission proposal/ conclusion	ESC opinion/ COR opinion°	EP opinion/ EP assent*	Council regulation (or decision) conclusion	Comments
571 Draft international cereals agreement	COM(97) 717, Bull. 12-97/1.2.225	Bull. 1/2-98/1.3.266							
574 Draft EC-FYROM agreement on the description of wines and spirits	Bull. 11-97/1.3.177	Bull. 3-98/1.2.185							

° Opinion of the Committee of the Regions.
* Agreements requiring Parliament's assent.
NB: Agreements that do not require consultation of Parliament are not followed by an asterisk.

Fisheries policy

Conservation and management of resources

	Commission recommendation	Council decision/ negotiating directives	Initials	Signature	Commission proposal/ conclusion	ESC opinion/ COR opinion°	EP opinion/ EP assert*	Council regulation (or decision) conclusion	Comments
605	Agreement on the Convention regarding the Law of the Sea: management of straddling stocks and highly migratory species	Bull. 4-96/1.3.140		27.6.96	OJ C 367/5.12.96, COM(96) 472, Bull. 10-96/1.3.163		OJ C 167/2.6.97, Bull. 5-97/1.3.68*	OJ L 189/3.7.98, Bull. 6-98/1.3.185	Recommendation for signature: COM(95) 591, Bull. 11-95/1.3.181, Council decision concerning the signature: Bull. 6-96/1.3.199
606	Draft accession to the General Fisheries Council for the Mediterranean		1.4.98		OJ C 124/21.4.97, COM(97) 67, Bull.12-97/1.2.206		OJ C 195/22.6.98, Bull. 5-98/1.2.185*	OJ L 190/4.7.98, Bull. 6-98/1.3.187	
608	Reg. (EC) No 2469/98: fisheries agreement with Gabon		10.7.97		OJ C 240/31.7.98, COM(1998) 376, Bull. 6-98/1.3.180		OJ C 313/12.10.98, Bull. 9-98/1.2.160	OJ L 308/18.11.98, Bull. 11-98/1.2.145	Entry into force: Bull. 12-98
608	Reg. (EC) No 20/98 on the EC-Cape Verde fisheries protocol (1997-2000) and financial contribution		10.7.97		COM(97) 521, Bull. 10-97/1.2.213		OJ C 371/8.12.97, Bull. 11-97/1.3.180	OJ L 21/28.1.98, Bull. 1/2-98/1.3.271	
608	Reg. (EC) No 2127/98: fisheries protocol with the Comores (1998-2001)		27.2.98		OJ C 245/5.8.98, COM(1998) 264, Bull. 5-98/1.2.184		OJ C 292/21.9.98, Bull. 7/8-98/1.3.234	OJ L 269/6.10.98, Bull. 10-98/1.2.157	
608	Reg. (EC) No 238/98 on the draft EC-Ivory Coast fisheries protocol (1997-2000) and financial contribution		Bull. 6-97/1.3.245		OJ C 361/27.11.97, COM(97) 520, Bull. 10-97/1.2.214		OJ C 371/8.12.97, Bull. 11-97/1.3.181	OJ L 25/31.1.98, Bull. 1/2-98/1.3.272	
608	Reg. (EC) No 1660/98 or the EC-Guinea fisheries protocol and financial contribution (1998-99)		Bull. 12-97/1.2.239		COM(1998) 129, Bull. 3-98/1.2.192		OJ C 210/6.7.98, Bull. 6-98/1.3.83	OJ L 211/29.7.98, Bull. 7/8-98/1.3.235	

TABLE III — INTERNATIONAL AGREEMENTS 573

	Commission recommendation	Council decision/ negotiating directives	Initials	Signature	Commission proposal/ conclusion	ESC opinion/ COR opinion°	EP opinion/ EP assent*	Council regulation (or decision) conclusion	Comments
608	Reg. (EC) No 2585/98: protocol to the fisheries agreement between the EC and Madagascar (1998-2001)		Bull. 3-98/1.2.194		COM(1998) 390, Bull. 6-98/1.3.183		OJ C 313/12.10.98, Bull. 9-98/1.2.162	OJ L 324/2.12.98, Bull. 11-98/1.2.150	
608	Reg. (EC) No 542/98: EC-Senegal fisheries protocol and financial contribution (1997-2001)		26.3.97		OJ C 267/3.9.97, COM(97) 324, Bull. 6-97/1.3.253		OJ C 286/22.9.97, Bull. 7/8-97/1.3.212	OJ L 72/11.3.98, Bull. 3-98/1.2.195	
608	Reg. (EC) No 373/98: protocol to the EC-Latvia fisheries agreement on conditions relating to joint enterprises		14.2.97		OJ C 248/14.8.97, COM(97) 323, Bull. 6-97/1.3.249		OJ C 34/2.2.98, Bull. 1/2-98/1.3.273	OJ L 48/19.2.98, Bull. 1/2-98/1.3.273	Entry into force: 25.5.98

The European Union's role in the world

International organisations and conferences

United Nations and specialised agencies

	Commission recommendation	Council decision/ negotiating directives	Initials	Signature	Commission proposal/ conclusion	ESC opinion/ COR opinion°	EP opinion/ EP assent*	Council regulation (or decision) conclusion	Comments
694	Dec. 98/392/EC: United Nations Convention on the Law of the Sea dated 10.12.82			7.12.84	OJ C 155/23.5.97, COM(97) 37, Bull. 1/2-97/1.3.20		OJ C 325/27.10.97, Bull. 10-97/1.3.11*	OJ L 179/23.6.98, Bull. 3-98/1.3.18	

° Opinion of the Committee of the Regions.
* Agreements requiring Parliament's assent.
NB: Agreements that do not require consultation of Parliament are not followed by an asterisk.

Common commercial policy

World Trade Organisation (WTO)

	Commission recommendation	Council decision/ negotiating directives	Initials	Signature	Commission proposal/ conclusion	ESC opinion/ COR opinion°	EP opinion/ EP assent^a	Council regulation (or decision) conclusion	Comments
712 Fifth protocol to the WTO Agreement: results of negotiations (financial services)					OJ C 271/31.8.98, COM(1998) 440, Bull. 7/8-98/1.4.27	OJ C 407/28.12.98, Bull. 9-98/1.3.26	OJ C 379/7.12.98, Bull. 11-98/1.3.21	Bull. 12-98	Adoption by Commission of amended proposal: OJ C 400/22.12.98, COM(1998) 659
712 Fourth protocol to the general agreement on basic telecommunications services in the context of the WTO	Bull. 3-95/1.4.14	Bull. 3-95/1.4.14			OJ C 267/3.9.97, COM(97) 368, Bull. 7/8-97/1.4.30		OJ C 339/10.11.97, Bull. 10-97/1.3.14	OJ L 347/18.12.97, Bull. 11-97/1.4.17	Conclusions of the Council on the state of negotiations: Bull. 3-96/1.4.13, Bull. 4-96/1.4.19, Bull. 1/2-97/1.3.24, Drawing up a list of undertakings: Bull. 1/2-97/1.3.24, Entry into force: Bull. 1/2-98/1.4.27

Operation of the customs union, customs cooperation and mutual administrative assistance

	Commission recommendation	Council decision/ negotiating directives	Initials	Signature	Commission proposal/ conclusion	ESC opinion/ COR opinion°	EP opinion/ EP assent^a	Council regulation (or decision) conclusion	Comments
718 Dec. 98/18/EC: EU-Canada customs cooperation agreement	Bull. 10-92/1.3.21	Bull. 4-93/1.3.60	Bull. 1/2-97/1.3.27	Bull. 12-97/1.3.29	OJ C 20/7.7.97, COM(97) 206, Bull. 5-97/1.4.24			OJ L 7/13.1.97, Bull. 11-97/1.4.21	Entry into force: OJ L 7/13.1.98, Bull. 1/2-98/1.4.28
718 Draft EC-Hong Kong agreement on customs cooperation and mutual administrative assistance			Bull. 11-98/1.3.24						

TABLE III — INTERNATIONAL AGREEMENTS 575

	Commission recommendation	Council decision/ negotiating directives	Initials	Signature	Commission proposal/ conclusion	ESC opinion/ COR opinion°	EP opinion/ EP assent*	Council regulation (or decision) conclusion	Comments
718 Draft additional protocol to the agreement between the EC and Cyprus on administrative assistance in customs matters	Bull. 1/2-98/1.4.29	Bull. 1/2-98/1.4.29							

Treaties, trade agreements and agreements on mutual recognition

	Commission recommendation	Council decision/ negotiating directives	Initials	Signature	Commission proposal/ conclusion	ESC opinion/ COR opinion°	EP opinion/ EP assent*	Council regulation (or decision) conclusion	Comments
729 Dec. 98/566/EC: EC-Canada agreement on conformity assessment	Bull. 4-92/1.3.10	Bull. 9-92/1.3.62	Bull. 6-97/1.4.44	Bull. 5-98/1.3.41	COM(1998) 271, Bull. 5-98/1.3.41			OJ L 280/16.10.98, Bull. 7/8-98/1.4.54	Council decision concerning the signature: Bull. 5-98/1.3.41, Entry into force: OJ L 280/16.10.98, Bull. 11-98/1.3.35
729 EC-United States agreement on conformity assessment	Bull. 4-92/1.3.10	Bull. 9-92/1.3.62	Bull. 6-97/1.4.44	Bull. 5-98/1.3.42	COM(1998) 180, Bull. 3-98/1.3.34			Bull. 6-98/1.4.55	Council decision concerning the signature: Bull. 5-98/1.3.42
729 Dec. 98/508/EC: EC-Australia agreement on conformity assessment, certificates and markings	Bull. 4-92/1.3.10	Bull. 9-92/1.3.62	Bull. 7/8-96/1.4.57	Bull. 6-98/1.4.53	COM(1998) 179, Bull. 3-98/1.3.35			OJ L 229/17.8.98, Bull. 6-98/1.4.53	Entry into force: OJ L 5/9.1.99
729 Dec. 98/509/EC: agreement with New Zealand on conformity assessment		Bull. 9-92/1.3.62	Bull. 7/8-96/1.4.57	Bull. 6-98/1.4.54	COM(1998) 179, Bull. 3-98/1.3.36			OJ L 229/17.8.98, Bull. 6-98/1.4.54	Recommendation for signature: Bull. 4-92/1.3.10, Entry into force: OJ L 5/9.1.99
729 Draft EC-Israel agreement on the mutual recognition of good laboratory practices			24.11.98						

° Opinion of the Committee of the Regions.
* Agreements requiring Parliament's assent.
NB: Agreements that do not require consultation of Parliament are not followed by an asterisk.

Export credits

	Commission recommendation	Council decision/ negotiating directives	Initials	Signature	Commission proposal/ conclusion	ESC opinion/ COR opinion°	EP opinion/ EP assent*	Council regulation (or decision) conclusion	Comments
731	Draft amendment to the OECD arrangement (export credits) on financing operations	Bull. 5-98/1.3.44							

Individual sectors

	Commission recommendation	Council decision/ negotiating directives	Initials	Signature	Commission proposal/ conclusion	ESC opinion/ COR opinion°	EP opinion/ EP assent*	Council regulation (or decision) conclusion	Comments
739	Dec. 98/333/EC: agreement with the FYROM on textile products	19.2.97	16.4.97	Bull. 3-98/1.3.39	COM(97) 505, Bull. 10-97/1.3.35			OJ L 147/18.5.98, Bull. 12-97/1.3.45	Entry into force: OJ L 241/29.8.98, Bull. 9-98/1.3.44
739	Dec. 98/669/EC: EC-Vietnam agreement on textile and clothing products	Bull. 9-97/1.3.34	17.11.97	Bull. 9-98/1.3.46	COM(1998) 156, Bull. 3-98/1.3.38			OJ L 319/27.11.98, Bull. 6-98/1.4.58	
739	Dec. 98/491/EC: EC-Russia agreement on trade in textile products	Bull. 10-95/1.4.40	28.3.98	Bull. 7/8-98/1.4.58	Bull. 5-97/1.4.42			OJ L 222/10.8.98, Bull. 7/8-98/1.4.58	
739	Draft agreements with Cambodia, Laos and Nepal on trade in textile products	Bull. 11-97/1.4.36	16.6.98						
739	Dec. 98/355/EC: memorandum of understanding between the EC and Egypt on textile products	Bull. 9-97/1.3.35	6.11.97		COM(1998) 120, Bull. 3-98/1.3.37			OJ L 162/5.6.98, Bull. 5-98/1.3.47	
739	Dec. 98/447/EC: agreements with Azerbaijan, Georgia, Kazakhstan, Kyrgyzstan and Turkmenistan on trade in textile products	Bull. 3-93/1.3.68	28.9.93,		OJ C 110/20.4.93, COM(93) 101, Bull. 3-93/1.3.68			OJ L 199/15.7.98, Bull. 4-98/1.3.31	
739	Draft additional protocol to the free-trade agreement and the Europe Agreement between the EC and Latvia on textile products	10.11.97	13.11.97		2.12.97			Bull. 7/8-98/1.4.57	

Note: In the row for Dec. 98/491/EC, the Commission recommendation column shows Bull. 10-95/1.4.40; in the row for Dec. 98/447/EC, the Commission recommendation column shows Bull. 1/2-93/1.3.75.

TABLE III — INTERNATIONAL AGREEMENTS   577

	Commission recommendation	Council decision/ negotiating directives	Initials	Signature	Commission proposal/ conclusion	ESC opinion/ COR opinion*	EP opinion/ EP assent*	Council regulation (or decision) conclusion	Comments
739 Draft additional protocol to the free-trade agreement and the Europe Agreement between the EC and Lithuania on textile products		10.11.97	19.11.97		Bull. 12-97/1.3.46			Bull. 7/8-98/1.4.57	
739 Draft new agreement between the EC and China on textile products (1998)	Bull. 7/8-98/1.4.56	Bull. 9-98/1.3.47	Bull. 11-98/1.3.37						
744 Dec. 98/708/EC: EC-Chile agreement on drugs		25.9.95	3.12.97	Bull. 11-98/1.3.114	COM(1998) 359, Bull. 9-98/1.3.129			OJ L 336/11.12.98, Bull. 11-98/1.3.114	

Development policy

International commodity agreements

	Commission recommendation	Council decision/ negotiating directives	Initials	Signature	Commission proposal/ conclusion	ESC opinion/ COR opinion*	EP opinion/ EP assent*	Council regulation (or decision) conclusion	Comments
757 Dec. 98/489/EC: International Cocoa Agreement				1.2.94	COM(93) 513, Bull. 10-93/1.3.61, COM(94) 8, Bull. 1/2-94/1.3.143			OJ L 220/7.8.98, Bull. 7/8-98/1.4.60	Council decision concerning the signature: OJ L 52/23.2.94, Bull. 1/2-94/1.4.143

° Opinion of the Committee of the Regions.
* Agreements requiring Parliament's assent.
NB: Agreements that do not require consultation of Parliament are not followed by an asterisk.

European Economic Area, relations with the EFTA countries

Relations with the EFTA countries

	Commission recommendation	Council decision/ negotiating directives	Initials	Signature	Commission proposal/ conclusion	ESC opinion/ COR opinion°	EP opinion/ EP assent^a	Council regulation (or decision) conclusion	Comments
793	Draft agreement with Switzerland on the free movement of persons	Bull. 10-94/1.3.17							Recommendation for signature: Bull. 12-93/1.2.32, Council agreement: Bull. 12-98
793	Draft agreement with Switzerland on participation in the Community's research programmes	Bull. 10-94/1.3.17							Recommendation for signature: Bull. 6-94/1.2.102, Council agreement: Bull. 12-98
793	Draft EC-Switzerland agreement on liberalisation of government procurement	Bull. 10-94/1.3.17							Council agreement: Bull. 12-98
793	Draft bilateral agreement with Switzerland on agriculture	Bull. 10-94/1.3.17							Recommendation for signature: Bull. 7/8-94/1.2.150, Council agreement: Bull. 12-98
793	Draft agreement with Switzerland on road and air transport	Bull. 1/2-94/1.2.97, Bull. 9-93/1.2.80	Bull. 3-95/1.3.102					OJ C 77/14.3.94, Bull. 1/2-94/1.2.98	Recommendation for signature: Bull. 3-95/1.3.102 Council agreement Bull. 12-98

TABLE III — INTERNATIONAL AGREEMENTS 579

	Commission recommendation	Council decision/ negotiating directives	Initials	Signature	Commission proposal/ conclusion	ESC opinion/ COR opinion°	EP opinion/ EP assent*	Council regulation (or decision) conclusion	Comments

Enlargement

	Commission recommendation	Council decision/ negotiating directives	Initials	Signature	Commission proposal/ conclusion	ESC opinion/ COR opinion°	EP opinion/ EP assent*	Council regulation (or decision) conclusion	Comments
801 Draft additional protocols to the association agreements on research, technological development and demonstration projects		Bull. 10-98/1.3.54							
801 Draft additional protocols to the association agreements on research and training (Euratom)		Bull. 10-98/1.3.54							

Relations with central European countries

Pre-accession strategy

	Commission recommendation	Council decision/ negotiating directives	Initials	Signature	Commission proposal/ conclusion	ESC opinion/ COR opinion°	EP opinion/ EP assent*	Council regulation (or decision) conclusion	Comments
808 Dec. 98/180/EC: Europe Agreement on association with Estonia	Bull. 10-94/1.3.22	Bull. 11-94/1.3.25	Bull. 4-95/1.4.64	Bull. 6-95/1.4.63	COM(95) 207, Bull. 6-95/1.4.63		OJ C 323/4.12.95, Bull. 11-95/1.4.52*	OJ L 68/9.3.98, Bull. 12-97/1.3.71	Council decision concerning the signature: Bull. 6-95/1.4.63, Consultation of ECSC Cons. Committee by Council: Bull. 12-97/1.3.71, Entry into force: OJ L 68/9.3.98, Bull. 1/2-98/1.4.65

° Opinion of the Committee of the Regions.
* Agreements requiring Parliament's assent.
NB: Agreements that do not require consultation of Parliament are not followed by an asterisk.

		Commission recommendation	Council decision/ negotiating directives	Initials	Signature	Commission proposal/ conclusion	ESC opinion/ COR opinion°	EP opinion/ EP assent*	Council regulation (or decision) conclusion	Comments
808	Europe Agreement on association with Latvia		Bull. 11-94/1.3.25	Bull. 4-95/1.4.64	Bull. 6-95/1.4.63	COM(95) 207, Bull. 6-95/1.4.63		OJ C 323/4-12.95, Bull. 11-95/1.4.52*	OJ L 26/2.2.98, Bull. 12-97/1.3.71	Recommendation for signature: Bull. 10-94/1.3.22, Council decision concerning the signature: Bull. 6-95/1.4.63, Consultation of ECSC Cons. Committee by Council: Bull. 12-97/1.3.71, Entry into force: OJ L 26/2.2.98, Bull. 1/2-98/1.4.65
808	Europe Agreement on association with Lithuania	Bull. 10-94/1.3.22	Bull. 11-94/1.3.25	Bull. 4-95/1.4.64	Bull. 6-95/1.4.63	COM(95) 207, Bull. 6-95/1.4.63		OJ C 323/-12.95, Bull. 11-95/1.4.52*	OJ L 51/20.2.98, Bull. 12-97/1.3.71	Council decision concerning the signature: Bull. 6-95/1.4.63, Consultation of ECSC Cons. Committee by Council: Bull. 12-97/1.3.71, Entry into force: OJ L 51/20.2.98, Bull. 1/2-98/1.4.65
808	Dec. 96/752/Euratom, ECSC, EC: Europe Agreement with Slovenia		Bull. 3-95/1.4.64	Bull. 6-95/1.4.62	Bull. 6-96/1.4.52	COM(95) 341, Bull. 7/8-95/1.4.64		OJ C 347/18.11.96, Bull. 10-96/1.4.52*	Bull. 12-98	Amended prop.: C(98) 4333, Bull. 12-98, Recommendation for signature: Bull. 4-94/1.3.33, Consultation of ECSC Cons. Committee by Council: Bull. 10-95/1.4.64, Bull. 10-98/1.3.64
808	Protocol for the adaptation of the trade aspects of the EC-Estonia Europe Agreement					COM(1998) 9, Bull. 1/2-98/1.4.66			Bull. 5-98/1.3.64	
808	Protocol to the agreement adapting the trade aspects of the EC-Latvia Europe Agreement					COM(97) 720, Bull. 1/2-98/1.4.66			Bull. 5-98/1.3.64	

TABLE III — INTERNATIONAL AGREEMENTS 581

		Commission recommendation	Council decision/ negotiating directives	Initials	Signature	Commission proposal/ conclusion	ESC opinion/ COR opinion°	EP opinion/ EP assent*	Council regulation (or decision) conclusion	Comments
808	Protocol for the adaptation of the trade aspects of the EC-Lithuania Europe Agreement					COM(1998) 23, Bull. 1/2-98/1.4.66			Bull. 5-98/1.3.64	
808	Draft protocol for the adaptation of the trade aspects of the EC-Romania Europe Agreement	Bull. 11-94/1.3.21	Bull. 3-95/1.4.53, Bull. 11-95/1.4.50, Bull. 12-95/1.4.63			COM(97) 297, Bull. 10-97/1.3.50			OJ L 301/11.11.98, Bull. 10-98/1.3.65	
808	Dec. 98/638/EC: protocol for the adaptation of the trade aspects of the EC-Slovakia Europe Agreement	Bull. 11-94/1.3.21	Bull. 3-95/1.4.53, Bull. 11-95/1.4.50, Bull. 12-95/1.4.63			COM(97) 297, Bull. 10-97/1.3.50			OJ L 306/16.11.98, Bull. 10-98/1.3.65	Entry into force: OJ L 324/2.12.98, Bull. 11-98/1.3.64
808	Draft protocol for the adaptation of the trade aspects of the EC-Hungary Europe Agreement	Bull. 11-94/1.3.21	Bull. 3-95/1.4.53, Bull. 11-95/1.4.50, Bull. 12-95/1.4.63			Bull. 10-97/1.3.50			Bull. 10-98/1.3.66	
808	Dec. 98/707/EC: protocol for the adaptation of the trade aspects of the EC-Czech Republic Europe Agreement	Bull. 11-94/1.3.21	Bull. 3-95/1.4.53, Bull. 11-95/1.4.50, Bull. 12-95/1.4.63			COM(97) 297, Bull. 10-97/1.3.50			OJ L 341/16.12.98, Bull. 10-98/1.3.66	
808	Protocol to the Europe Agreement between the EC and the Czech Republic: veterinary and phytosanitary matters		Bull. 1/2-95/1.3.10		Bull. 7/8-98/1.4.77	OJ C 229/28.7.97, COM(97) 173, Bull. 5-97/1.4.59			Bull. 10-97/1.3.51	Entry into force: OJ L 219/7.8.98, Bull. 7/8-98/1.4.77

Relations with Mediterranean and Middle East countries

Northern Mediterranean

		Commission recommendation	Council decision/ negotiating directives	Initials	Signature	Commission proposal/ conclusion	ESC opinion/ COR opinion°	EP opinion/ EP assent*	Council regulation (or decision) conclusion	Comments
832	Agreement on the participation of Cyprus in audiovisual policy (particularly MEDIA II)	Bull. 10-96/1.3.184				OJ C 162/28.5.98, COM(1998) 242, Bull. 4-98/1.3.52		OJ C 313/12.10.98, Bull. 9-98/1.3.81	Bull. 11-98/1.3.84	Recommendation for signature: Bull. 4-96/1.3.159

° Opinion of the Committee of the Regions.
* Agreements requiring Parliament's assent.
NB: Agreements that do not require consultation of Parliament are not followed by an asterisk.

	Commission recommendation	Council decision/ negotiating directives	Initials	Signature	Commission proposal/ conclusion	ESC opinion/ COR opinion°	EP opinion/ EP assent*	Council regulation (or decision) conclusion	Comments
844	Dec. 97/831/EC: agreement with the FYROM on trade and cooperation		Bull. 12-95/1.4.84	Bull. 6-96/1.4.73	Bull. 4-97/1.4.73	OJ C 79/12.3.97, COM(96) 533, Bull. 11-96/1.4.82		OJ C 325/27.10.97, Bull. 10-97/1.3.72*	OJ L 348/18.12.97, Bull. 11-97/1.4.69	Recommendation for signature: Bull. 11-95/1.4.64, Council decision concerning the signature: Bull. 4-97/1.4.73, Entry into force: OJ L 348/18.12.97, Bull. 1/2-98/1.4.78
845	Protocol to the EC-San Marino agreement on customs union and cooperation				Bull. 10-97/1.3.63	OJ C 124/21.4.97, COM(97) 8, Bull. 1/2-97/1.3.95		OJ C 328/26.10.98, Bull. 10-98/1.3.82*		Council decision concerning the signature: Bull. 9-97/1.3.44

Maghreb

	Commission recommendation	Council decision/ negotiating directives	Initials	Signature	Commission proposal/ conclusion	ESC opinion/ COR opinion°	EP opinion/ EP assent*	Council regulation (or decision) conclusion	Comments
848	Dec. 98/238/EC, ECSC: Euro-Mediterranean association agreement with Tunisia		Bull. 12-93/1.3.38	Bull. 4-95/1.4.80	Bull. 7/8-95/1.4.84	COM(95) 235, Bull. 5-95/1.4.74		OJ C 17/22.1.96, Bull. 12-95/1.4.90*	OJ L 97/30.3.98, Bull. 1/2-98/1.4.92	Recommendation for signature: Bull. 11-93/1.3.26, Entry into force: OJ L 132/6.5.98

Mashreq countries, Palestinian Territories, Israel

	Commission recommendation	Council decision/ negotiating directives	Initials	Signature	Commission proposal/ conclusion	ESC opinion/ COR opinion°	EP opinion/ EP assent*	Council regulation (or decision) conclusion	Comments
850	Draft EC-UNWRA Convention: contribution to the UNWRA budget (1999-2001)	4.9.98	Bull. 11-98/1.3.90							

TABLE III — INTERNATIONAL AGREEMENTS   583

	Commission recommendation	Council decision/ negotiating directives	Initials	Signature	Commission proposal/ conclusion	ESC opinion/ COR opinion°	EP opinion/ EP assent*	Council regulation (or decision) conclusion	Comments
851 Euro-Mediterranean agreement with Jordan		Bull. 6-95/1.4.82	Bull. 4-97/1.4.75	Bull. 11-97/1.4.72			OJ C 226/20.7.98, Bull. 7/8-98/1.4.99*		Recommendation for signature: Bull. 5-95/1.4.75, Proposal signature: COM(97) 554, Bull. 10-97/1.3.73, Council decision concerning the signature: Bull. 11-97/1.4.72, Consultation of ECSC Cons. Committee by Council: Bull. 12-97/1.3.86

The Middle East

	Commission recommendation	Council decision/ negotiating directives	Initials	Signature	Commission proposal/ conclusion	ESC opinion/ COR opinion°	EP opinion/ EP assent*	Council regulation (or decision) conclusion	Comments
855 Dec. 98/189/EC: EC-Yemen cooperation agreement		Bull. 1/2-97/1.3.100	Bull. 4-97/1.4.81	Bull. 11-97/1.4.74	OJ C 317/18.10.97, COM(97) 435, Bull. 9-97/1.3.51		OJ C 56/23.2.98, Bull. 1/2-98/1.4.108	OJ L 72/11.3.98, Bull. 1/2-98/1.4.108	Recommendation for signature: Bull. 1/2-97/1.3.100, Council decision concerning the signature: Bull. 11-97/1.4.74, Entry into force: Bull. 7/8-98/1.4.97

° Opinion of the Committee of the Regions.
* Agreements requiring Parliament's assent.
NB: Agreements that do not require consultation of Parliament are not followed by an asterisk.

Relations with the independent States of the former Soviet Union and with Mongolia

Partnership and other agreements

	Commission recommendation	Council decision/ negotiating directives	Initials	Signature	Commission proposal/ conclusion	ESC opinion/ COR opinion°	EP opinion/ EP assent^a	Council regulation (or decision) conclusion	Comments
858 Dec. 98/149/EC, ECSC, Euratom: draft partnership and cooperation agreement with Ukraine		Bull. 10-92/1.4.19, Bull. 3-94/1.3.51	Bull. 3-94/1.3.51	Bull. 6-94/1.3.34	COM(94) 226, Bull. 6-94/1.3.34, COM(95) 137, Bull. 5-95/1.4.87		OJ C 339/18.12.95, Bull. 11-95/1.4.83*	OJ L 49/19.2.98, Bull. 1/2-98/1.4.112	Recommendation for signature: Bull. 7/8-92/1.4.3, Bull. 1/2-94/1.3.52, Council decision concerning the signature: Bull. 6-94/1.3.34, Entry into force: Bull. 3-98/1.3.101
858 Dec. 98/401/EC, ECSC: partnership and cooperation agreement with Moldova		Bull. 10-92/1.4.19, Bull. 7/8-94/1.3.43	Bull. 7/8-94/1.3.43	Bull. 11-94/1.3.35	COM(94) 477, Bull. 11-94/1.3.35, COM(95) 137, Bull. 5-95/1.4.86, COM(1998) 307, Bull. 5-98/1.3.88			OJ L 181/24.6.98, Bull. 5-98/1.3.88	Recommendation for signature: Bull. 7/8-92/1.4.3, Council decision concerning the signature: Bull. 11-94/1.3.35, Consultation of ECSC Cons. Committee by Council: Bull. 12-94/1.3.52, Entry into force: Bull. 7/8-98/1.4.104
858 Protocol to the partnership agreement with Ukraine				Bull. 4-97/1.4.89	COM(96) 133, Bull. 3-96/1.4.69, COM(1998) 28, Bull. 1/2-98/1.4.113		OJ C 286/22.9.97, Bull. 7/8-97/1.4.123*		Council decision concerning the signature: Bull. 7/8-96/1.4.110, Consultation of ECSC Cons. Committee by Council: Bull. 4-96/1.4.75, Bull. 4-98/1.3.66

TABLE III — INTERNATIONAL AGREEMENTS   585

		Commission recommendation	Council decision/ negotiating directives	Initials	Signature	Commission proposal/ conclusion	ESC opinion/ COR opinion°	EP opinion/ EP assent*	Council regulation (or decision) conclusion	Comments
858	Protocol to the EC-Moldova partnership agreement: provisional application					COM(1998) 307, Bull. 5-98/1.3.89			Bull. 5-98/1.3.89	
859	Partnership and cooperation agreement with Turkmenistan		5.10.92	24.5.97	Bull. 5-98/1.3.90	COM(97) 693, Bull. 1/2-98/1.4.111				Council decision concerning the signature: Bull. 4-98/1.3.65; Consultation of ECSC Cons. Committee by Council: Bull. 4-98/1.3.65
860	Dec. 98/138/EC and 98/343/ECSC: interim agreement with Uzbekistan on trade and trade-related matters				Bull. 11-96/1.4.91	COM(96) 466, Bull. 9-96/1.4.48		OJ C 14/19.1.98, Bull. 12-97/1.3.92	OJ L 43/14.2.98, Bull. 1/2-98/1.4.109, OJ L 153/27.5.98, Bull. 4-98/1.3.64	Council decision concerning the signature: Bull. 11-96/1.4.91, Consultation of ECSC Cons. Committee by Council: Bull. 10-96/1.4.78, Entry into force: OJ L 151/21.5.98, Bull. 6-98/1.4.106
860	Interim agreement with Kyrgyzstan	Bull. 7/8-94/1.3.42	Bull. 7/8-94/1.3.42			COM(95) 49, Bull. 3-95/1.4.72		OJ C 222/21.7.97, Bull. 6-97/1.4.95*	OJ L 235/26.8.97, Bull.7/8-97/1.4.121, Bull. 11-97/1.4.78	Council decision concerning the signature: Bull. 7/8-96/1.4.108, Consultation of ECSC Cons. Committee by Council: Bull. 3-95/1.4.72, Entry into force: OJ L 189/3.7.98, Bull. 7/8-98/1.4.103
860	Draft interim agreement with Turkmenistan			24.2.98		COM(1998) 617, Bull. 12-98				
860	Dec. 98/588/EC: interim agreement with Azerbaijan on trade and trade-related matters				Bull. 10-97/1.3.78	COM(96) 613, Bull. 11-96/1.4.89		OJ C 313/12.10.98, Bull. 9-98/1.3.100	OJ L 285/22.10.98, Bull. 10-98/1.3.93	Council decision concerning the signature: Bull. 3-97/1.4.78

° Opinion of the Committee of the Regions.
* Agreements requiring Parliament's assent.
NB: Agreements that do not require consultation of Parliament are not followed by an asterisk.

Relations with the United States, Japan and the other industrialised countries

United States

	Commission recommendation	Council decision/ negotiating directives	Initials	Signature	Commission proposal/ conclusion	ESC opinion/ COR opinion°	EP opinion/ EP assent:*	Council regulation (or decision) conclusion	Comments
886 Draft agreement between the EC and the United States on technical barriers to trade in industrial goods, services, public procurement and intellectual property	Bull. 9-98/1.3.115	Bull. 11-98/1.3.98							

Relations with the countries of Asia

Bilateral relations

	Commission recommendation	Council decision/ negotiating directives	Initials	Signature	Commission proposal/ conclusion	ESC opinion/ COR opinion°	EP opinion/ EP assent:*	Council regulation (or decision) conclusion	Comments
901 Draft cooperation agreement with Pakistan		Bull. 7/8-96/1.4.129	Bull. 4-98/1.3.76		COM(1998) 357, Bull. 12-98				
911 Accession of Euratom to KEDO	Bull. 4-96/1.4.85	Bull. 10-96/1.4.87	Bull. 12-96/1.4.82, Bull. 5-97/1.4.83	Bull. 9-97/1.3.66	Bull. 6-97/1.4.107			Bull. 6-97/1.4.107, OJ L 70/10.3.98, Bull. 7/8-97/1.4.129	Recommendation for signature: Bull. 5-96/1.4.86 Entry into force: Bull. 9-98/1.3.120

TABLE III — INTERNATIONAL AGREEMENTS   587

Relations with Latin American countries

Relations with regional groupings

	Commission recommendation	Council decision/ negotiating directives	Initials	Signature	Commission proposal/ conclusion	ESC opinion/ COR opinion^c	EP opinion/ EP assent^a	Council regulation (or decision) conclusion	Comments
918 Draft interregional association agreement between the EC and Mercosur	Bull. 7/8-98/1.4.123								
918 Draft political and economic association agreement between the EC and Chile	Bull. 7/8-98/1.4.123								
920 Dec. 98/278/EC: framework co-operation agreement between the EC and the Cartagena Agreement (Andean Pact)	Bull. 3-92/1.3.33	Bull. 5-92/1.2.31	Bull. 6-92/1.4.31	Bull. 4-93/1.3.39	OJ C 25/28.1.93, COM(92) 463, Bull. 11-92/1.4.42		OJ C 255/20.9.93, Bull. 7/8-93/1.3.50, OJ C 80/16.3.98, Bull. 1/2-98/1.4.137	OJ L 127/29.4.98, Bull. 4-98/1.3.80	Entry into force: Bull. 5-98/1.3.107

Bilateral relations

	Commission recommendation	Council decision/ negotiating directives	Initials	Signature	Commission proposal/ conclusion	ESC opinion/ COR opinion^c	EP opinion/ EP assent^a	Council regulation (or decision) conclusion	Comments
923 Dec. 98/504/EC: interim trade agreement with Mexico	Bull. 10-95/1.4.109	Bull. 6-96/1.4.106	Bull. 7/8-97/1.4.140	Bull. 12-97/1.3.108	OJ C 356/22.11.97, COM(97) 525, Bull. 10-97/1.3.100		OJ C 167/1.6.98, Bull. 5-98/1.3.110*	OJ L 226/13.8.98, Bull. 6-98/1.4.140	Council decision concerning the signature: Bull. 12-97/1.3.108, Entry into force: OJ L 226/13.8.98, Bull. 7/8-98/1.4.126
923 Draft EC-Mexico agreement on trade liberalisation	Bull. 3-98/1.3.117	Bull. 5-98/1.3.111							

° Opinion of the Committee of the Regions.
* Agreements requiring Parliament's assent.
NB: Agreements that do not require consultation of Parliament are not followed by an asterisk.

Relations with the African, Caribbean and Pacific (ACP) countries and the overseas countries and territories (OCTs)

Relations with the ACP countries

	Commission recommendation	Council decision/ negotiating directives	Initials	Signature	Commission proposal/ conclusion	ESC opinion/ COR opinion°	EP opinion/ EP assent*	Council regulation (or decision) conclusion	Comments
929 Draft EC-ACP partnership agreement	Bull. 1/2-98/1.4.146	Bull. 6-98/1.4.144							
935 Dec. 98/344/EC: amendment to the fourth Lomé Convention		Bull. 1/2-94/1.3.80		Bull. 11-95/1.4.102	COM(95) 707, Bull. 1/2-96/1.4.153		OJ C 20/20.1.97, Bull. 12-96/1.4.99*	Bull. 4-96/1.4.93, OJ L 156/29.5.98, Bull. 4-98/1.3.85	Recommendation for signature: Bull. 9-93/1.3.44, Council decision concerning the signature: Bull. 10-95/1.4.112, Entry into force: OJ L 156/29.5.98, Bull. 6-98/1.4.145
942 Draft agreement on the prices for cane sugar for the ACP States referred to in Protocol 8 (1997-98)		Bull. 9-97/1.3.76			COM(1998) 187, Bull. 3-98/1.3.124				
942 Draft agreement on cane sugar prices for the ACP countries (1998-99)	Bull. 10-98/1.3.125	Bull. 11-98/1.3.124							
950 Protocol: accession of South Africa to the fourth ACP-EC Lomé Convention				Bull. 11-95/1.4.104				OJ L 220/11.8.97, Bull. 4-97/1.4.121	Entry into force: OJ L 156/29.5.98, Bull. 6-98/1.4.168

TABLE III — INTERNATIONAL AGREEMENTS   589

Cooperation in the fields of justice and home affairs

External relations

	Commission recommendation	Council decision/ negotiating directives	Initials	Signature	Commission proposal/ conclusion	ESC opinion/ COR opinion°	EP opinion/ EP assent*	Council regulation (or decision) conclusion	Comments
975	Draft EC-Iceland agreement on the Schengen *acquis*	Bull. 7/8-98/1.5.2							
975	Draft EC-Norway agreement on the Schengen *acquis*	Bull. 7/8-98/1.5.2							

° Opinion of the Committee of the Regions.
* Agreements requiring Parliament's assent.
NB: Agreements that do not require consultation of Parliament are not followed by an asterisk.

Index (¹)

A

Accession
— negotiations: 798, 830
— partnerships: 73, 288, 806, 807
— process: 797, 830
— applications: 803, 834, 835
Accounting system: see Sincom2
Acidification: 501
ACP banana producers: 941
ACP Convention: 775, 928, 929, 937
ACP States: 89, 768, 773, 789, 928 to 956
ACP-EC Council of Ministers: 932, 933
ACP-EC Joint Assembly: 934
Acquis communautaire: 791, 799, 800
ADAPT: 373
Adaptation of workers to industrial changes: 364, 365
Adjustment of agricultural structures: 366, 367
Administrative expenditure: 985 to 987, 990
Advanced communications technologies and services: 475
Advanced television services: 663
Afghanistan: 35, 667, 682, 778, 787, 903
Africa: 34, 684 to 686, 789, 928 to 956
Agenda 2000: 1 to 15
— CAP: 2, 3, 13
— economic and social cohesion: 14, 348 to 354
— enlargement: 811, 812
— financial perspective: 8 to 12
— pre-accession instruments: 7
— prior informed consent: 489, 766
— rural development: 5
— Structural Funds and Cohesion Fund: 4, 5

— trans-European networks: 6, 81, 385 to 387
Agreements
— cooperation: 26, 718, 845, 856 to 861
— Europe: 808 to 810
— interinstitutional: 1033 to 1036
— mutual recognition: 729
— research: 306, 310, 313, 314, 793
— trade: 728, 729
Agricultural conversion rates: 583
Agricultural expenditure: 986, 987, 989, 990
Agricultural management committees: 589
Agricultural pre-accession instrument: 7
Agricultural prices and related measures: 570
Agrimonetary system: 583
Aid for refugees: 775, 778, 913
AIDS: 626 to 629, 762
Air quality: 500
Airports: 211, 212, 451
Albania: 78, 667, 669, 679, 701, 703, 705, 784, 814, 839, 840
Algeria: 35, 680, 699, 846
Altener II: 409
Alzheimer's disease: 633
Amsterdam Treaty: 669, 1023 to 1025
Andean Community: 919
Angola: 667, 684, 789, 934, 951, 956
Animal health: 564
Antarctic: 606, 607
Anti-dumping and anti-subsidy measures: 719 to 723
Anti-fraud measures: 1015
Anti-Fraud Office: see OLAF
Anti-fraud programme: 1012
Anti-personnel landmines: 670, 764
Appropriations available: 774

(¹) The figures refer to point numbers in the Report.

European Commission

General Report on the Activities of the European Union — 1998

Luxembourg: Office for Official Publications of the European Communities

1999 — XVII, 607 pp. — 16.2 × 22.9 cm

ISBN 92-828-4924-4

Price (excluding VAT) in Luxembourg: EUR 35

The General Report on the Activities of the European Union is published annually by the Commission as required by Article 156 of the EC Treaty, Article 17 of the ECSC Treaty and Article 125 of the EAEC Treaty.

The Report is presented to the European Parliament and provides a general picture of Community activities over the past year.